Wisdom of Communities

Cohousing - private ownership of homes
& collective ownership of common space

cluster concept - All units possible in a zoning area
clustered together, leaving maximum common area

Wisdom of Communities

Volume 1
Starting a Community

Published by
The Fellowship for Intentional Community
Rutledge, Missouri

The Fellowship for Intentional Community, Rutledge, MO 63563

ISBN: 978-0-9995885-8-1
Printed by CreateSpace.

Cover design: Megan Cranford, www.megancranforddesign.com

Layout design: Marty Klaif

Project managers: Chris Roth, Christopher Kindig

[handwritten top margin:] Ross Chapin — pocket neighborhood in Langley — first of its kind.
City of 1100 created CAP zoning code — ground floor less than 700 sq.'

STARTING A COMMUNITY
(Wisdom of Communities, Volume 1)

CONTENTS

II. CREATING INTENTIONAL COMMUNITY

Handwritten annotations:
- (next to FEC) Shared resources — land, labor, + income: loan $$ to start-up communities
- (next to Legal Structures) basic, comprehensive
- Creating the ideal Intentional Comm. Sahmat, free workshops + book (63) the community guy, org.
- (next to Buying Your Community Property) practical — have to know your people first — purpose, personal finances.
- (next to Exit Dynamics) So practical! 12 reasons why people leave. + what to ask in an exit interview. Facilitation trainers + consultant. Exemplars. (66) World Creating sustainable community w/ a progressive mayor — Bernie Sanders!
- (next to II. CREATING) Tries for years to start communities + finally goes back to Dancing Rabbit, Mo.
- (next to Establishing Community Swedish) Swedish govt supported cohousing pre-empts grassroots efforts. Creating clear profile of what we're about so those who share our idea will be able to + find us
- (next to Somerville Culture) After 5 years, haven't built but have community. Everyone participates + contributes to Somerville Way ✓
- (next to Somerville Statutory) Celebrate the milestones, big + small, w/ events involving food, wine, + music!
- (next to Moon Valley) See Wm. Noël, p. 249 Turning a trailer park into a community by buying it cooperatively. ✓
- (next to Affording) AMMA — our Mother who dwells in Earth — Dreamed big, got real, + brought to scale by 4 families! Maine good writing!
- (next to Going from Vision) find your vision, make it clear, + start living it ✓

12

Handwritten annotations:
- Squatters — no plan, no process, no ... ✓
- Large, strong city neighborhood ✓
- Guelph, Ontario
- Working together activates energy ✓ in Canada
- Looking for new members ✓
- Key is land — plans are particular to each parcel + land "grounds" the project.
- 28 flats + townhouses, common house + garden on 2.3 acres along Willamette Riv (438)
- how begin
- "We are defined not just by self, but by who we are in community." Authentic access to other human beings is sorely lacking in society today
- Completely off-grid ✓
- free Common-Unity Skills Workshop 146
- Creating the Ideal — Nevada City Cohousing ✓
- NW California ✓
- In Vanuatu debt ensure ongoing relationships ✓
- 22 farm members own + work the land. 2 egg clubs + "3 flocks of meat birds." ✓
- Passion for living off the land. in Midcoast Maine

i9

General Circle - leaders + delegates from all cmtes - meets 2 X monthly
Diana Leafe Christian - Creating a Life Together - getting acquainted

12

Janelle is Exec. dir. of SELC — Sustainable Economies Law Center, a holding co. for land that will take it out of competitive market + limit on profit

12

III. CULTIVATING NON-RESIDENTIAL COMMUNITY

(p. 301 Alliance For Global Community + free book: Skill Building For
Global Common unity – Sahmat, thecommunityguy.org)

Introduction

In *Creating a Life Together*, Diana Leafe Christian estimates that 90 percent of attempts to start an intentional community do not survive past the initial stages.

Similarly, many personal searches for intentional community fizzle out due to lack of adequate information, guidance, or exposure to fellow travelers' stories.

In both cases, ignorance of the wide array of options possible, and of the breadth of resources and support available through the Fellowship for Intentional Community and allied groups, undoubtedly contributes to the "failure" rate.

This volume on "Starting a Community" and the next volume in this series, on "Finding a Community," address the need for one-stop collections of stories to help founders and seekers. They are meant to complement the *Communities Directory* (available in print and online: ic.org/directory), COMMUNITIES magazine, a quarterly publication focused on Life in Cooperative Culture, and educational resources available through Community Bookstore (ic.org/bookstore).

These books should broaden anyone's outlook on what is possible and how to pursue their dreams of community. Within each section we hear from a range of voices spanning a great diversity of perspectives and experiences. In this volume, following more general "overview" articles, we dive into on-the-ground stories from founders, arranged roughly chronologically, followed by a separate roughly chronological flow about experiences of community that don't fit the classic intentional community definition but are nonetheless powerful for their creators and participants.

Most articles are drawn from the past decade of COMMUNITIES magazine, with several excerpted from the *Communities Directory* and a few from older issues of COMMUNITIES that were also excerpted in our *Best of* collections, Volumes I and II. Every issue of COMMUNITIES contains further treatments of these same themes, so we hope that you'll not only learn from these past stories, but also keep up with new ones by subscribing to the magazine (ic.org/subscribe).

Thanks for making use of these resources, and good luck on your community journey!

Chris Roth
Editor, COMMUNITIES
March 2018

I

INTENTIONAL COMMUNITY ESSENTIALS

Six Ingredients
for Forming Communities
(That Help Reduce Conflict Down the Road)

by Diana Leafe Christian

*I*found the land!" Jack exclaimed over the phone. As the originator of Skydance Farm, a small forming community in northern Colorado, he had been searching for just the right community land for years, long before he and a circle of acquaintances had begun meeting weekly to create community. He was so sure it was the land, he said, that he'd plunked down $10,000 of his own savings as an option fee to take it off the market long enough for us to decide.

I had joined the group several weeks earlier. I knew nothing about intentional communities at the time. However, it had seemed in their meetings that something was missing.

"What's the purpose of your community?" I had finally asked. "What's your vision for it?" No one could really answer.

That Saturday we all drove out to the land to check it out.

And promptly fell apart. Confronting the reality of buying land, no one wanted to commit. Frankly, there was nothing to commit to. No common purpose or vision, no organizational structure, no budget, no agreements. In fact we hadn't made decisions at all, but had simply talked about how wonderful community life would be. Although Jack tried mightily to persuade us to go in with him on the land, there were no takers, and he barely got his money out before the option deadline.

I became intensely curious about what it would take for a newly forming community to succeed. So over the next seven years, first as publisher of a newsletter about forming communities and then as editor of Communities magazine, I interviewed dozens of people involved in communities forming in the '90s as well as founders of long-established ones. I wanted to know what worked, what didn't work, how not to reinvent the wheel.

I learned that no matter how inspired and visionary the community founders, only about one out of 10 new communities actually seemed to get built. The other 90 percent seemed to go nowhere, occasionally because of lack of money or the right land, but mostly because of . . . conflict.

And usually, conflict accompanied by heartbreak, and often, lawsuits. Many of these community break-ups resulted from what I call "structural conflict"—problems that arose when founders didn't explicitly take care of certain important issues at the outset, creating one or more flaws in their organizational structure. Several weeks, months, or even years later, the group ran into major problems that could have been largely prevented if they had handled these issues early on. Naturally, a great deal of interpersonal conflict arose at the same time, making the initial conflict much worse. I've seen forming communities founder and sink on such issues as:

- *"But our main purpose is not to run a retreat center; that's just a business. We can't spend money on that until we take care of our needs first!"*
- *"What? I have to cough up $10,000 more for 'land development'?"*
- *"My brother can't live here? But he's my brother. I didn't*

Diana Leafe Christian has studied intentional communities since 1992, and edited *Communities* magazine since 1993. She is author of *Forming an Intentional Community: What Works, What Doesn't Work, How Not to Reinvent the Wheel*, and offers introductory and weekend workshops on this topic. She is cofounder of a small community in North Carolina. Email: diana@ic.org.

agree to this!"

- *"What do you mean I can't get my money out again when I leave?!"*
- *"Maybe you think it's important to stay in the room and 'resolve the conflict' but I'm outta here! Have your 'conflict resolution' session without me!"*
- *"Ever since Carl joined we've been dealing with his hurt feelings. It's exhausting. How did we let this happen?"*

You get the picture. While interpersonal conflict is normal and expected, I believe that much of the structural conflict in these communities could have been prevented, or at least greatly reduced, if the founders had paid attention to six "ingredients":

1. Choosing a fair, participatory decision-making process that is appropriate for the group. And if it's consensus, getting trained in it.
2. Identifying their vision and creating a vision statement.
3. Learning what resources, information, skills, and tasks they would need, and then either learning or hiring them.
4. Drawing up clear agreements, in writing.
5. Learning good communication skills, and making clear communication a priority, including ways of reducing conflict.
6. Selecting cofounders and new members for emotional well-being.'

To be fair, a number of well-established North American communities never included many of these structural ingredients at their origin. In the '60s, '70s, or '80s, people usually just bought land and moved on. Some of these communities are with us today, and proud of it.

Nonetheless, I recommend these "ingredients" for communities forming now. Why? Because establishing a new community is not easy. Since the mid '80s through the early '90s, the cost of land and housing has skyrocketed, relative to people's assets and earning power. Zoning regulations and building codes are considerably more restrictive than in earlier decades. And because of the media coverage that highlights any violent or extreme practices of a group, the "cult" stereotype is still in public consciousness, and may affect how potential neighbors feel about your group moving into their neighborhood.

The challenges facing new communities today have convinced me that nowadays community founders must be more organized and purposeful—not to mention better capitalized—than their counterparts of earlier years.

1. Fair, Participatory Decision Making

It's probably pretty obvious that a great deal of conflict would arise if people didn't feel that they had enough say in community decisions, unless the community has explicitly created a structure in which members are not expecting to participate in decisions, such as one where a leader or small group of members make decisions, as is sometimes the case in spiritual communities. So, one of the first things I believe a forming community not structured this way should do is to choose a fair, participatory form of decision making.

Most communities I've observed use consensus. However, herein also lies a source of potential conflict. First, the group needs to know that consensus is right for them, which presumes that everyone has equal access to power. It may not work out if one person is the landowner and the rest tenants, for example.

Second, the group needs to get trained, and, ideally, have a consensus facilitator for meetings. Consensus does not mean, as many mistakenly assume, "We'll just keep talking about a proposal for hours and hours until we all agree." It's far more complex and subtle than that. (See the article that immediately follows, called "Consensus Basics.") Unlike majority-rule voting, in which people argue for or against a proposal and it either passes or not, in consensus the proposal itself is modified as people express their concerns about it. If everyone can support a final revision of the proposal, it passes; if even one person blocks the proposal, it doesn't. Consensus therefore only allows decisions that the whole group can live with and implement without resentment. The process should not take hours and hours. If it does, it means the group is not well-facilitated. A good facilitator schedules breaks, suggests issues be tabled for later discussion, or suggests certain items be sent to committee. Blocking is used rarely, and only when someone, after long and heartfelt soul-searching, feels that the proposal would harm the group in the long run—morally, ethically, financially, legally, or in some other way.

Unfortunately, many well-meaning but untrained groups fall into using what I call "pseudo-consensus":

- *"Everything we decide on must be decided by consensus! It 'betrays' consensus to use any other method."*
- *"Everyone in the group must be involved in every decision, no matter how small."*
- *"We'll stay in this room until we make a decision—no matter how long it takes!"*
- *"I block! This proposal just won't work for me."*

- *"I plan to block the proposal we're going to discuss today. So, since I'm already against it and plan to stop it, there's no need to even bring it up!"*

Consensus is like a chain saw. Consensus can chop a lot of wood; "pseudo-consensus" can chop your leg. While majority-rule voting can trigger conflict because up to 49 percent of the people can be unhappy with a decision, poorly understood and improperly practiced consensus can generate every bit as much conflict.

In the consensus process, deciding on a proposal usually takes more time than with majority rule voting. However, implementing a proposal once it's agreed upon usually takes far less time, since everybody is behind it. Nevertheless, because of the time factor, some community veterans recommend having two, or more, participatory decision-making methods, for example, consensus and one other "agreement-seeking" method, such as 70 percent voting, 80 percent voting, 90 percent voting, consensus-minus-two, or consensus-minus-one, etc. Some cohousing groups have an alternative method in place for when they need to make exceptionally fast decisions, such as when they have a narrow window of opportunity to tie up a parcel of sought-after land, or when they make decisions involving some but not all the members. And some communities may split up the kind of decisions made, for example using consensus for most decisions and an alternate method such as 90 percent voting for decisions affecting property value and only among members with equity in the land.

On the other hand, other experienced communitarians caution against using two methods. They assert that consensus is not a method but a philosophy of inclusion, and when people are less able to influence decisions while using a faster method it breaks down the trust and the cohesion of the group.

I believe that the decision-making method best for you depends on whether your group is together primarily to build the physical infrastructure of a community (regardless of what members you may lose due to a faster decision-making process), or for your connection and friendship (regardless of the great land deals you may lose due to a slower, more inclusive process).

Whatever method or methods your forming com

> I learned that no matter how inspired and visionary the community founders, only about one out of 10 new communities actually seemed to get built.

munity chooses, if one of them involves consensus, please get good training in it first!

2. Vision and Vision Statement: "What We Are About"

Your vision is a compelling idea or image that inspires and motivates your members to keep on creating community, to persevere through the rough times, to remember why you're there, and to help guide your decisions. This is not necessarily verbal, but can be a feeling, or an energy presence. It gives voice to your group's deeply held values and intuitions. It is your picture or "feel" of the kind of life you'd like to lead together.

The vision is often described or otherwise implied in your collection of written expressions—your agreements, flyer, brochure, and/or Web site. These documents often include a paragraph or two describing what your community will be like, a list of shared values, a list of goals, often a "how we'll do it" mission statement, and . . . the vision statement.

The vision statement is a condensed version of your vision. The vision statement is a clear, compelling expression of your group's overall purpose and goals. Each of you can identify with it. It helps to unify your effort; it helps focus everyone's energy like a lens. Because it reveals and announces your group's core values, it gives you a reference point to return to in decisions or during confusion or disagreement. It keeps you all inspired, as it is a shorthand reminder of why you're forming community When times get tough, the vision statement helps awaken your vision as an energetic presence. Ideally it is memorized, and everyone can state it.

The vision statement also communicates your group's core purpose to others and to potential new members quickly: "This is what we're about; this is what we hope to accomplish." It allows you to be specific about what you are—and are not. Some recommend that the vision statement express the "who," the "what," and the "why" of your forming community (and leave the "where," "when," and "how" for the mission statement or strategic plan). I think it's more potent if it's short, about 20⊕40 words.

We have joined together to create a center for renewal, education, and service, dedicated to the positive transformation of our world.

—*Shenoa Retreat and Learning Center, Philo, California*

We are creating a cooperative neighborhood of diverse individuals sharing human resources within an ecologically responsible community setting.

—*Harmony Village Cohousing, Golden, Colorado*

We are a neotribal permaculture village, actively engaged in building sacred community, supporting personal empowerment, and catalyzing cultural transformation. We share a commitment to a vital, diversified spirituality; healthy social relations; sustainable ecological systems; and a low-maintenance/high-satisfaction lifestyle.

—*Earthaven Community,*
Black Mountain, North Carolina

While these vision statements leave plenty of room for interpretation, they are considerably more concrete and grounded than many I've seen. Some newly forming communities represent themselves with flowery, overly vague, or just plain pretentious vision statements, and . . . these are often the first to go bust. It seems that communities with vision statements that are more focused, specific, and grounded are often the ones that actually get built.

It is quite possible that people in a forming group have more than one vision among them—which means that the individuals present may represent more than one potential community. It's crucial to find this out early—before the group buys land together.

Imagine founders of a community with no common vision who buy land, move on, put up a few buildings—and begin to run out of money. Now they must decide how they'll spend their remaining funds. But they can't agree on priorities. Some want to finish the community building because they believe that creating a sense of community is the primary reason they're together, and know that having a community building will help focus their community spirit. Others want to finish the garden and irrigation system because they see their primary purpose as becoming self-reliant homesteaders. Different members have different visions, which they incorrectly assume everyone shares. By this time the members are arguing mightily most of the time, but the core of their problem is structural; it's built into the system. This is a "time-bomb" kind of conflict, with members unable to see it's not that "John's being unreasonable" or "Sue's irresponsible," but that each member is operating from a different assumption about why they're there in the first

place. So what now? Which members get to stay on the land and which ones must either live with a vision that doesn't fit them or move out?

Identifying a vision and crafting a vision statement is an enormous task, often requiring plenty of discussion, meditation, spiritual guidance, and "sleeping on it," through a series of meetings over many weeks.

Many community veterans believe that consensus is the appropriate process for this critical decision. As Betty Didcoct of TIES consulting says, "the consensus process itself fosters an attitude that can help forge a bond and build trust in your group. When the input of everyone is honored, who knows what might surface—a strong single vision that draws everyone, or multiple visions that suggest the presence of more than one potential forming community."

Other community activists, such as Rob Sandelin of Northwest Intentional Communities Association, suggest not using consensus to determine your vision and vision statement. It's a catch-22: for consensus to work well your group must have a common purpose, and at this point, it doesn't. A group needs a method, he says, (such as 90 percent voting, for example) in which some people can diverge radically from others about what they want in the community without bringing the whole process to a crushing halt. I personally agree with this view, although there are groups out there who employed consensus for the vision statement process and it worked just fine.

It is best if a strong, mutually reinforcing relationship exists between your community's values, goals, and vision and the legal structure or structures with which it will one day own or manage its land and assets. (See the article on legal structures, later in this section.) Identify your forming community's values, goals, and vision early in the formation process, and let these determine your legal structures—not the other way around!

3. Know What You Need to Know

Forming a new community, like simultaneously starting up a new business and beginning a marriage, can be a complex, time-consuming process requiring both business skills and interpersonal communication skills. Founders of successful new communities seem to know this. And those that get mired in severe problems have usually leapt in without a clue. These well-meaning folks didn't know what they didn't know.

This seems particularly true of spiritual communities.

I've often seen founders with spiritual ideals and compelling visions flounder and sink because they had no idea how to conduct a land search or negotiate a bank loan. I've also seen people with plenty of technical or business savvy—folks able to build a nifty composting toilet or craft a solid strategic plan—who didn't know the first thing about how to communicate with people. And I've seen sensitive spiritual folks as well as get-the-job-done types crash and burn the first time they encountered any real conflict.

Consider the story of Sharon, who bought and attempted to develop land for a spiritual community. At first it looked promising. Sharon had received zoning approval for an innovative clustered-housing site plan. She met regularly with a group of friends and supporters to envision and meditate. But over the next 18 months this and a subsequent forming community group fell apart, disappointed and often bitter. Sharon struggled with money issues, land-development issues, interpersonal issues. After two years she said she was no longer attempting community, in fact loathed the idea of community, and didn't even want to hear the "C" word.

What had Sharon not known?

- How much money it would take to complete the land development process before she could legally transfer title to a buyer.
- How much each lot would eventually cost.
- That she shouldn't foster hope in those who could never afford to buy in.
- That she'd need adequate legal documents and financial data to secure private financing.
- That she should make it clear to everyone at the outset that as well as having a vision she was also serving as land developer.
- That she needed to explain that she fully intended to reimburse her land-purchase and development costs and make a profit to compensate her time and entrepreneurial risk.
- That she needed to tell people that, as the developer, she would make all land-development decisions.
- That a process was needed for who was in the group and who wasn't, and for what kinds of decisions the group would make and which Sharon alone would make.
- That consensus was the wrong decision-making op-

tion for a group with one landowner and others with no financial risk.
- That they weren't in fact practicing consensus at all, but some vaguely conceived idea of it.

I believe that community founders would experience much less conflict if they understood the need for both "heart" and "head" skills. The latter include drafting clear written agreements; creating budgets, a timeline, a strategic plan; choosing legal structure(s) for land ownership or any planned business or educational activities; learning local zoning or land-use laws; and understanding finance and real estate, site planning, and the land development process (roads, power, water, sewage, etc.).

Not everyone in your forming group needs to have all these skills—that's one reason you're a group! Nor must you possess all this skill and expertise among yourselves. Many successful groups have hired an accountant, lawyer, project manager, meeting facilitator, and so on.

Nowadays community founders must anticipate challenges not faced by communities formed in earlier times. First, "ideal" land isn't ideal if zoning regulations and building codes prevent your developing it the way you want to. Second, if your group wants rural land, a lack of decent-paying local jobs will affect your attractiveness to future members. Difficulty attracting members will affect your ability to recoup early land investment costs, so think about the site relative to available jobs before you buy the land. And third, keep in mind that the initial impression you make on potential neighbors will affect whether or not they will support you in getting a needed zoning variance. If you call your endeavor a community or an intentional community, people may only hear "hippie commie cult." Perhaps call it a center, a project, or even a household, but be cautious with the loaded term "community" until they have a chance to learn, over time, that you're in fact fine, upstanding neighbors.

Forming communities need enough time, money, and "community glue" to pull off a project of this magnitude. To start with, it takes a great deal of committed time and hard work. Even if you meet weekly, you'll often need people on various committees—gathering information, drafting proposals, and so on—in between regular meetings. In my experience, this amount of work is equivalent to one or more group members working

> [C]ommunities with vision statements that are more focused, specific, and grounded are often the ones that actually get built.

part-time or even full time.

It also takes adequate capitalization, often several hundred thousand dollars—for land purchase, land development if needed, new construction or renovation, and myriad lesser costs. As soon as it's feasible, you'll need to know roughly how much money your project will cost. Some people raise the money from others; some fund the whole thing themselves. And please don't put every last cent down on the land. Keep enough available for land development, construction, etc., even if that means buying a more modest parcel.

Elana Kann and Bill Fleming of Neighborhood Design Build, former project managers of Westwood Cohousing in Asheville, North Carolina, recommend that forming community groups understand and accept the difference between what is and what is not in their control. They've observed that probably 95 percent of the major variables involving a forming community are not in a group's control. (Land criteria is in a group's control; land use may not be if local zoning requirements are in place.) The group would ideally have a mechanism for building on each decision and moving forward, rather than meandering or even backtracking, as many groups unfortunately do. They would learn what questions to ask, how to research answers, how to present information to the group, and how to base decisions on the best information available. And, recommend Elana and Bill, they would talk frankly about the required financial and work commitments, as well as other real-world constraints, from the start.

It takes a sense of connection, a shared sense of "us"—the community "glue." This is usually born of group experiences: potluck dinners, preparing meals together, weekend camping trips, solving problems together. Work parties are one of the best ways for people to get to know each other, and not incidentally, great ways to learn each other's approaches to responsibility and accountability. Storytelling evenings are great ways to get to know each other on deeper levels, especially if the topics are self-revealing and personal, such as family attitudes about religion, child raising, or money and social class. Such sharing sessions also reveal issues relevant to community living and shared resources later on.

Gathering this range of skills and information in order to reduce future conflict is complex, time-consuming, and often overwhelming.

Can your forming community afford to do without it? I don't think so.

4. Clear Agreements, in Writing

Many forming communities flounder because they haven't written down their agreements, and when people try to conjure up what they thought they had agreed on months or years before, they remember things differently. Unfortunately even people with the greatest good will can recall a conversation or an agreement in such divergent ways that each may wonder if the other is trying to cheat or abuse or manipulate them! This is one of the greatest stumbling blocks in newly forming communities—and it's so easily prevented.

Many agreements are of course embedded in legal documents such as corporation bylaws, lease agreements, or private contracts. Others are simple agreements with no legal "teeth," but which help the participants stay on track with each other nevertheless. Write out your agreements, read them, and for good measure, sign what you've agreed to, whether or not they're formal legal documents. Keep your agreements in a safe place and refer to them as needed.

What do you need to agree on?

- Who your members are.
- Your qualifications to become a member and the process to do so.
- Whether new people need to attend a minimum number of meetings and be approved by others.
- How new members are brought up to speed.
- How decisions are made, and who gets to make them.
- How meetings are run.
- How records are kept.
- Who takes notes, how are they distributed, and to whom.
- Your group's record of decisions to show new members.
- How tasks are assigned to members, and how people are held accountable for them.
- Expected expenses, how they are to be paid, and what happens in case of cost overruns.
- Any dues structure. (Many groups have found that a nonrefundable investment of some minimal amount such as $100 differentiates those "just looking" from those willing to commit time and energy to the project.)
- Who keeps records of what has been paid.
- Whether such monies are refundable, and from what source.
- Your criteria for whether, and how, people may be asked to leave the group.

Learn skills before conflict comes.

Having these and other issues in writing, along with proper legal documents for financial matters such as land purchase, can prevent some of the most heart-rending misunderstandings in the months ahead.

5. Good Communication Skills

dealing w/ conflict

Every community experiences conflict—including those which include all the above ingredients at their origin! Interpersonal conflict is a given; it will arise. I believe a community is healthy when it deals openly with conflict and doesn't pretend it isn't there. Healthy communities recognize that community offers living "mirrors" for each other, and an opportunity for faster-than-normal spiritual and emotional growth. Dealing with conflict is an opportunity, not a problem.

Some people are naturally skillful and effective communicators. Most of us, however, probably need to unlearn many of our habitual ways of communicating. Unfortunately, Western culture tends to systematically train people away from any tendencies toward cooperation and empathy. We're taught to be competitive and win at all costs, to see conflict in terms of what's wrong with someone else, and to decide things in terms of "us versus them."

I've usually seen conflicts arise because of a misunderstanding, or when someone wants something he or she is not getting, or wants something to stop, and there's emotional charge on the issue. Conflict is exacerbated when someone refuses to speak up about what they want or need, or asks for it in a way that alienates others. Unfortunately, most people's unskilled ways of communicating about the conflict generates even more conflict than was there in the first place.

Fortunately there are plenty of books, courses, and workshops on communication methods that reduce conflict rather than amplify it.

NVC

My personal favorite is Marshall Rosenberg's Nonviolent Communication model. He suggests that most of us respond to something we don't like with an attitude and language that subtly blames, threatens, judges, or criticizes others, even if that's not our intention. His process involves a perceptual shift and a four-step process that defuses the level of conflict. Many other good methods exist as well. (See the "Conflict" issue of Communities magazine, No. 104, Fall 1999.)

> Forming communities need enough time, money, and "community glue" to pull off a project of this magnitude.

I believe that the higher the degree of communication skill a forming community has, the greater its chances of success. So I urge your group to develop such skills, including some form of conflict resolution—ideally learned with a trainer. And learn these skills early on, when there's little or no conflict, for the same reason schools practice fire drills when there's no fire. Learning such skills at the outset can help reduce the potential destructiveness of poorly handled interpersonal conflict later on.

6. Select for Emotional Well-Being

Some people believe it's not really "community" unless it's inclusive and open and anyone can join. Others believe a community should have membership criteria and a multi-step process for assessing potential new members.

Some veteran communitarians point out that people will naturally mature in community because of the (hopefully) constructive feedback they'll receive and the natural tendency to learn from the (hopefully) good communication skills modeled by more experienced members. This happens naturally in community; I call it the "rocks in the rock polisher" effect—everyone's rough edges can be worn smoother by contact with everyone else. Many communitarians know people who were really tough to be around when they first arrived, but who were so motivated that they learned fast and became model community members.

My observation of "the successful 10 percent" taught me that it's all in the willingness of the potential new member or cofounder. If he or she has what I call "high woundedness" *or low awareness* (hey, don't we all?), it seems to only work if the person simultaneously has "high willingness"—to grow and learn and change. I have seen several forming communities in recent years—even those with powerful vision statements, fine communication skills, and good consensus training—break apart in conflict and sometimes lawsuits because even just one member didn't have enough self-esteem to function well in a group. The person's "stuff came up"—as everyone's does in community—but theirs was too destructive for the community to absorb. When a person is wounded and having a difficult time in life, he or she can certainly benefit from living in community, and, ideally, can heal and grow because of the support and feedback offered by others. But a certain level of woundedness—without "high *[awareness]* willingness"—appears to be too deep for many new communities to handle. I believe one deeply wounded person can affect a group far more than 10 healthy people, because of that person's potential destructiveness to the group. Such a person can repeatedly derail the community's agenda and drain its energy.

This seems especially true of a potential new member or cofounder who has been abused as a child and hasn't had much healing before walking into your meeting. The person may unconsciously be desperately seeking community as a safe haven that will finally make things right. Such a person usually feels needy, and tends to interpret other people's refusal to or inability to meet his or her needs as further abuse. The person usually (subconsciously) expects to be victimized, and tends to seek out, provoke, or project onto others annoyance or anger and then conclude, "See, I knew you'd abuse me." *all of us, to some extent.*

Where should this person go, besides those communities that are explicitly set up as therapeutic settings? A large, old, and well-established community can often take on difficult and wounded people without damage to itself. A mature oak tree, after all, can handle being hit by a truck. But I don't recommend taking on this challenge if your group is small, or brand new. It's just a sapling, not an oak tree, and still too vulnerable.

How can you determine the level of emotional health and well-being in prospective members and cofounders? One way is through questionnaires and interviews. Let's say you're seeking someone who is fairly financially stable and emotionally secure, who has some experience living cooperatively and a willingness to persevere through the rough spots. Irwin Wolfe Zucker, a psychiatric social worker and former Findhorn member, suggested asking: "How have you supported yourself financially until now? Can you describe some of your long-term relationships? What was your experience in high school or college? If you chose to leave school, why was that? Have you pursued alternative educational or career paths such as internships, apprenticeships, or on-the-job trainings? Where, and for how long? Did you complete them?" ("Admissions Standards for Communities?" Communities magazine, No. 96, Fall 1997.)

You can also ask for references, from former partners, employers, landlords, housemates, and former traveling companions. *Lama Foundation in N.M. did this.*

I suggest "long engagements"—extended guest visits or provisional memberships of six months to a year, so the group and the prospective member can continue to get to know each other. Sometimes it takes a year to find out what someone is really like when the stress gets high.

"If your community front door is difficult to enter," writes Zucker, "healthy people will strive to get in. If it's wide open, you'll tend to attract unhealthy people, well-versed in resentful silences, subterfuge, manipulation, and guilt trips." Once these people become members, he warns, the energy of the group may be tied up in getting them to leave again.

So the last ingredient is to choose people who've already demonstrated they can get along well with others.

Creating healthy, viable communities is one of the finest projects we can undertake. And we can learn to set systems in place—right from the beginning—that give us the best chance of success.

I know of a new community dedicated to teaching ecological living via a community demonstration model. Its founders mastered consensus and good group process skills and created a new-member outreach process through a newsletter and Web site. They set up telecommuting jobs so they could live anywhere. They conducted a national rural county search, and when they found the right county with no zoning regulations, they took a pro-active approach to finding their ideal land. They raised the necessary land-purchase funds in loans from supporters, and drew up effective agreements, covenants, and nonprofit and lease documents. They set up an impressive internship program to help them build their physical infrastructure. Right now they're living in their new straw bale cabins, eating from their organic garden, and making their own biodiesel fuel. Their new community is thriving. And so can yours. *Wow!*

> [T]he higher the degree of communication skill a forming community has, the greater its chances of success.

interview prospective members

Tracking the Communities Movement:
70 YEARS OF HISTORY AND THE MODERN FIC

By Sky Blue and Betsy Morris

Since 1987 The Fellowship for Intentional Community (FIC; ic.org) has been a primary resource for documentation, support, and networking among secular and religiously based intentional communities. While several associations and networks exist for some of the specific types of intentional community (which include communes, housing cooperatives, student cooperatives, ecovillages, and cohousing), FIC has the largest reach and history. New experiments in shared living continue to pop up, under new names, such as coliving or cohouseholding.

FIC began as the Fellowship of Intentional Communities, formed in 1948/49 as a mutual aid network among 20 communities mostly in the eastern US. Pacifism, simple living, equality, and agrarian self-sufficiency on land held in common were common values. A majority were religiously affiliated, but not in mainstream traditions. Secular influences included Robert Owen, the Rochdale Pioneers, Bolton Hall, writings of Henry George, and Ralph Borsodi's *Flight from the City*, which spoke of the value of returning to agrarian lifestyles and attracted educated professionals and artisans.

One of the early FIC's founders was Arthur Morgan, later president of Antioch College. Morgan, among other things is credited with conceiving of the land trust (based on the principles of Henry George). In 1937, Morgan cofounded Celo Community, Inc., a land trust community of 40 homesteaders in rural North Carolina that continues to govern itself by consensus. Celo residents also started a private "organic school" based on child-centered education methods, developed by Mildred Loomis, an influential educator, and later cofounder of the Heathcote community in Freehold, Maryland. Morgan's children continue his legacy through several intentional communities and the nonprofit Community Solutions, Inc. (www.communitysolution.org). Celo and Heathcote still operate and are among the oldest ICs in the *Communities Directory.* Although FIC's members and ICs in general remain predominantly European American, several other of the founding communities started by Quakers were among the first places in the United States where whites and blacks could choose to live as equals. Early founders also helped create the first Black community land trust (CLT) in the US.[1]

Pre-FIC communitarians had already split with other US cooperativists who favored urban programs with government financing to build housing cooperatives and publicly managed housing projects for the poor and working class. By 1961, another split by members primarily seeking expression of their religious way of life left FIC in a near dormant state for many years. The rapid increase in ICs from the 1960s, '70s, and '80s prompted another round of outreach and organizing. Leadership transferred to another generation of younger, mostly rural communitarians.

The change in name to Fellowship for Intentional Community in 1987 was subtle but important. Rather than an informal mutual aid association, the new Fellowship for Intentional Community restructured its gover-

---

1. Antioch College was a pioneer in educating both women and African Americans. Robert and Marjorie Swann—an Antioch graduate and a Quaker, respectively—were students of Morgan and classmates of Coretta Scott King. They helped King relatives create the first large-scale land trust/farmer's cooperative with African American farmers (the Federation of Southern Cooperatives), as well as the National Community Land Trust Network and important land trust initiatives in Massachusetts. In 1972, Bob Swann with Ralph Borsodi also founded the E.F. Schumacher Society and the local currency movement.

nance and administration, incorporated as a 501(c)(3) nonprofit governed by a board of directors, and developed ongoing projects managed by staff, most of whom live in intentional communities around the country. The board expanded its mission to promoting the principles of intentional community to the larger world. Its activities include publishing COMMUNITIES magazine (starting in 1992, when it revived then-20-year-old magazine after a very brief hiatus) and the *Communities Directory*, in print since 1994 and online since 2004 (ic.org/directory).

Definitions

The mission statement of the FIC is *to support and promote the development of intentional communities and the evolution of cooperative culture.*

FIC defines cooperative culture as encompassing both ICs and a broad array of other practices, found in other organizations and in movements. It offers the following definition.

Cooperative Culture: *The sum of attitudes, customs, and beliefs among people that are characterized by sharing, empathy, self-responsibility, understanding and celebration of differences, peaceful conflict resolution, high regard for connection and relationship, interdependence, and care for how things are done as much as what gets done.*

> An intentional community can be thought of as a set of social and economic relationships, the physical place where these relationships intersect, and explicit common values.

Examples of movements and organizations that current FIC leadership sees as representing cooperative culture include worker cooperatives (usworker.coop) and other kinds of cooperative business (www.ncba.coop), Transition Towns (transitionus.org), permaculture networks (www.permaculture.org), time banks (www.timebanks.org), community gardens (www.communitygarden.org), car sharing (carsharing.org), and the wide range of groups represented by the New Economy Coalition (www.neweconomy.net) and the US Solidarity Economy Network (www.ussen.org).

The FIC's definition of *community* is not meant to contradict or replace other definitions of community. It is simply the definition the organization uses to help give context to its definition of *intentional community.*

Community: *A group of people who identify with each other. The association could be based on any combination of geography, history, language, religion, vision, purpose, philosophy, or common social, economic, or political interests.*

The FIC's definition of intentional community is meant to be as broadly encompassing as possible while clearly delineating a specific set of groups:

Intentional Community: *A group of people who live together or share common facilities and who regularly associate with each other on the basis of explicit common values.*

No one owns the term intentional community. Anyone who wants to identify as an intentional community is free to do so, and some groups that the FIC would identify as intentional communities do not choose to use that label. FIC communities, board, and staff have personal and business ties with many other secular IC networks, as well as research groups such as the Communal Studies Association (www.communalstudies.org), Cohousing Research Network (www.cohousingresearchnetwork.org), and Commonomics USA (www.commonomicsusa.org).

An intentional community can be thought of as a set of social and economic relationships, the physical (as opposed to online, or virtual) place or places where these relationships intersect and are carried out, and the explicit common values that provide the basis for members to decide how these relationships and places are organized.

In more illustrative terms, conjure up an image of an extended family compound or a traditional village and you will have an idea of what many people are attempting to emulate or replicate. In our modern world, and especially in urban centers, life is necessarily more complicated than in a traditional village, but, in rural or urban settings, the aim is to have an integrated, interconnected, interdependent life with others that provides both social and economic benefit, as well as providing a place to live out other values, such as sustainability, social justice, or spiritual/religious tenets.

The *Directory*

There are 1442 public listings in 65 countries in the online *Communities Directory* as of July 2017, including ICs in various phases of development (forming, reforming, established, or disbanded).

Listing in the *Communities Directory* is voluntary, by answering a lengthy online questionnaire. FIC does reserve the right to request more information or edits and, if necessary, exclude listings that appear to:
• Advocate violence;
• Restrict the ability of their members to leave or to contact people outside the community;
• Substantively misrepresent themselves in their listing.

In 1990, the first published Directory reported: "More than 8,000 people, including over 2,000 children, live in 186 of the more established North American intentional communities and extended family groups listing in the first edition of the Directory of Intentional Communities (1990). Of course, these 186 communities represent just a small fraction of the North American communities movement.

"Over 700 more intentional communities in FIC address files have declined to provide public listings for the Directory. There are thousands more residing in traditional monastic enclaves or service groups, tens of thousands living in Hutterite colonies, and millions of indigenous Americans living communally. So the information in this Directory describes just a small portion of the cooperative lifestyles practiced in North America."

As of July 2017, of the 1442 public listings, 747 were "established" (at least four adults living together on a site for at least two years), and 79% of the Directory's "established" listings are in North America (US, Canada, Mexico). The 544 established communities in the US identify themselves with the following community types (multiple responses are frequent):

Established Communities in US by Selected Types		
Total Respondents	544	100.00%
Communes (income sharing)	87	15.99%
Ecovillages (focus on sustainability)	139	25.55%
Cohousing (private homes with common facilities)	214	39.34%
Shared House/Cohousehold/Coliving	170	31.25%
Student Coops	40	7.35%
Transition Town	2	0.36%
Religious/Spiritual	13	2.39%
School/Educational/Experience	3	0.55%
Other (including economic enterprises)	77	14.15%

These numbers need further clarifying. These are voluntary categories not legal structures or screened in any way. Newer communities are frequently small and aspirational, and use models of existing communities as a touchstone for future development. A few entries are multi-site networks or include multiple neighborhoods. Also, many communities identify with multiple types. And, as mentioned before, many communities (including many religious/spiritual communities with their own pre-existing networks, most indigenous groups, and groups which wish to remain more private) choose not to list themselves at all.

Community Types and Organizing Principles

Housing Cooperatives and Student Co-op Houses: The Cooperatives movement began in 17th century England and France as a concerted resistance to the loss of cultural and economic resources under rapid industrialization fueled by capitalism. Housing cooperatives, built and financed by unions and socialist/communist parties for their members, were a source of urban housing, endorsed by federal policies through the 1980s. Federal policies and programs encouraged and helped finance thousands of cooperatives, both in business and housing, from the 1930s to the 1980s.

The Rochdale Principles of Cooperation (established in England in 1844 and with minor additions; see en.wikipedia.org/wiki/Rochdale_Principles) remain as values espoused by the National Association of Housing Cooperatives established in 1958 and the North American Students of Cooperation founded in 1960s. Both groups offer some combination of training, communications, financing, and political lobbying for members along with annual conferences open to the public. They are:
• Open, voluntary membership *without discrimination to those who wish to join.*
• Democratic governance; one member–one vote.
• Economic participation of members (shared or limited return on equity).
• Surplus belongs to members.
• Education of members and public in cooperative principles.
• Cooperation among cooperatives.
• Concern for the community (in which they are located).

Communes: ICs that identify as communes typically involve higher levels of economic involvement, social engagement, accountability, and participation. Historically, religion combined with ethnic ties and/or political ideologies brought people into communal living groups, each with their own internal economies. The Hutterites and Bruderhof were communal income-sharing societies present in the 1940s founding of FIC. The Federation of Egalitarian Communities (FEC), whose purpose is similar to the original FIC, was founded in December 1976 for secular purposes. The organization was originally inspired by the networks of mutual support observed among Israeli kibbutzim by Kat Kinkade, cofounder of Twin Oaks, East Wind, and Acorn Communities.

Cooperation amongst FEC communities ranges from loans and labor exchange to sharing community-building skills and shared outreach. FEC also administers PEACH (www.thefec.org/about/projects/peach), a cooperatively financed "self-insurance" health care fund, which also acts as a revolving loan fund. The FEC currently has six full member groups and 11 other allied Communities in Dialogue. (See www.thefec.org.)

Each member community of the FEC agrees to these commitments:
• Holds its land, labor, income, and other resources in common.
• Assumes responsibility for the needs of its members, receiving the products of their labor and distributing these and all other goods equally, or according to need.
• Practices nonviolence.
• Uses a form of decision making in which members have an equal opportunity to participate, either through consensus, direct vote, or right of appeal or overrule.
• Actively works to establish the equality of all people and does not permit discrimination on the basis of race, class, creed, ethnic origin, age, sex, sexual orientation, or gender identity.
• Acts to conserve natural resources for present and future generations while striving to continually improve ecological awareness and practice.
• Creates processes for group communication and participation and provides an environment which supports people's development.

> Historically, religion combined with ethnic ties and/or political ideologies brought people into communal living groups, each with their own internal economies.

Cohousing: The term cohousing was coined by architects Katherine McCamant and Charles Durrett in their highly influential book, *Cohousing: A Contemporary Model for Housing Ourselves*, published in 1987. The term and the first edition were based on a type of intentional community that had become widespread in Denmark by the 1980s (and that has continued to grow and evolve). For many years, the Cohousing Association of the US and cohousing communities identified with these six characteristics of cohousing McCamant and Durett summarized from their extensive study of Danish cohousing:
• Participatory Design Process
• Neighborhood Design balancing privacy and spaces for spontaneous socializing
• Extensive Common Facilities
• Resident Management
• Non-Hierarchical Leadership
• Independent Incomes

The Cohousing Association of the US website (cohousing.org) currently characterizes cohousing communities by:

Relationships
• Neighbors commit to being part of a community for everyone's mutual benefit.
• Cohousing cultivates a culture of sharing and caring.
• Design features and neighborhood size (typically 20-40 homes) promote frequent interaction and close relationships.

Balancing Privacy and Community
• Cohousing neighborhoods are designed for privacy as well as community.
• Residents balance privacy and community by choosing their own level of engagement.

Participation
• Decision making is participatory and often based on consensus.
• Self-management empowers residents, builds community, and saves money.

Shared Values
• Cohousing communities support residents in actualizing shared values.
• Cohousing communities typically adopt green approaches to living.

Ecovillages: The Global Ecovillage Network (GEN) emerged through American and European communitarian environmentalists, in response to the Club of Rome's *Limits to Growth* Report. The definition that first became widely used was Robert Gilman's: "a human scale, full-featured settlement, in which human activities are harmlessly integrated into the natural world, in a way that is supportive of healthy human development, and can be continued into the indefinite future."

16

Today, the Global Ecovillage Network "embraces a holistic approach to sustainability encompassing the Social, Cultural, Ecological and Economic dimensions of human existence." "Ecovillages are communities in which people feel supported by and responsible to those around them. They provide a deep sense of belonging to a group. They are small enough that everyone feels safe, empowered, seen and heard. People are then able to participate in making decisions that affect their own lives and that of the community on a transparent basis."

(See ecovillage.org/en/article/dimensions-sustainability.)

One-hundred-fifty-nine ICs in the Directory identify GEN and 46 identify the Ecovillage Network of the Americas as networks with which they affiliate.

Religious Communities: Thirty-seven Directory entries define themselves as primarily religious or spiritual organizations—while many others reported religious affiliations as a group or among their members, and only 228 checked the box for "Not a particularly religious or spiritual community." Many communities are unaffiliated with any particular tradition, or consider themselves religiously ecumenical while still having a dominant spiritual practice, such as the Zen Center or the Maharishi University Fellowship in Iowa (transcendental meditators). Christian and Jewish communes or student coops may be listed in both of their categories, or just one. Other ICs, however, are clearly associated by religious affiliation, such as the Catholic Order of Benedictine Fathers, the Catholic Worker House network, Camphill communities (associated with Rudolf Steiner), and the Twelve Tribes.

Implications

The ICs that we know are not isolated utopias, romantic idylls, or scientific experiments. They consist of living, breathing people who know what the world has to offer, and are doing their best to bring their desires for peace, sociability, cooperative autonomy, economic justice, and environmental responsibility to life pro-actively. These values are ones many people around the world share, but cannot realize alone or within institutions dominated by people seeking profit or power above concern for people and the planet. Intentional communities are broadly characterized by an emphasis on

- **Cooperative/participatory democracy**
- **Cooperative economics**
- **Gender equality**
- **Satisfying interpersonal relationships and conflict resolution**
- **Living well while decreasing waste and increasing renewable resource consumption and waste**

The *Communities Directory* provides multiple snapshots into a parallel world, where people are dreaming and then becoming empowered agents, able to take collective and personal actions in creating and then sustaining a nexus of institutions, relationships, and activities made real by their choice to continue participating in them over time.

Most forming groups and young ICs fail, and many established communities grow, decline, and learn by trial and error on their own what works and does not. Nevertheless, we observe convergences, groups learning from experience and observation of other ICs to find core values and practices that work best over time. ICs may start as unique to their own time and place, but become examples for managing and incorporating key features, such as shared governance, use of consensus, or shared ownership of land.

Secular ICs can become quite sophisticated and multidimensional over time, within the context of transparent vision and purpose and consent-based governance. The communities are not simply engineering solutions; they function because of the willingness of members to put collective attention and creativity to sustaining and supporting high quality communication and personal relationships—foundational to any material or technological success they reach.

The articulation of cooperative culture—*in practice*—is one of the contributions of ICs to

a world seemingly dominated by competitive global capitalism and exploitive relationships of people and planet. IC pioneers have also written and trained thousands, offering a unique depth of experience gained in practices of team-building, trust-building, and getting the work done cooperatively. A number of communitarians have gone professional and influenced the larger field of organizational development. One example is the GroupWorks Card Deck (groupworksdeck.org), instigated by a former member of Twin Oaks and Acorn, and promoted widely in the National Coalition for Dialog and Deliberation. Fifty people contributed to the final product, which is available as a free download. Another example

> # The articulation of cooperative culture—*in practice*—is one of the contributions of ICs to a world seemingly dominated by competitive global capitalism and exploitive relationships of people and planet.

is the Network For a New Culture (www.nfnc.org) which offers workshops in human awareness and intimacy, but specifically designed to help people live more cooperatively with each other in everyday circumstances.

We invite researchers to look more deeply at ICs, beyond the typical one-off case study. FIC would be happy to collaborate with efforts to do high quality independent research to test the findings presented here that can be shared within the communities movement and with the rest of the world. ✍

Sky Blue is Executive Director of the Fellowship for Intentional Community. Betsy Morris, Ph.D. is co-organizer of Cohousing California. This article is adapted and updated from a paper first presented at the mini-conference "Re-embedding the Social: New Modes of Production, Critical Consumption and Alternative Lifestyles" hosted by the Society for the Advancement of Socio-Economics, June 24-26, 2016 at the University of California, Berkeley.

REFERENCES AND RESOURCES

FIC Identity Statement: docs.google.com/document/d/1mVMJmpEDh4xN6LSKC76ww53mS4JsyWrcC4O4EET5LHo/edit?usp=sharing.

Curl, John. 2008. *For All the People: Uncovering the hidden history of cooperation, cooperative movements, and communalism in America*: library.uniteddiversity.coop/Cooperatives/For_All_The_People-History_of_Cooperation_in_America.pdf.

Miller, Timothy (1998). *The Quest for Utopia in Twentieth-century America: 1900-1960*. Syracuse University Press. ISBN 0-8156-2775-0.

Christian, Diana Leafe, 2003, *Creating a Life Together: Practical Tools to Grow Ecovillages and Intentional Communities*, New Society Publishers; New Edition, ISBN 0-86571-471-1, foreword by Patch Adams.

Christian, Diana Leafe, 2007, *Finding Community: How to Join an Ecovillage or Intentional Community*, New Society Publishers, ISBN 0-86571-578-5.

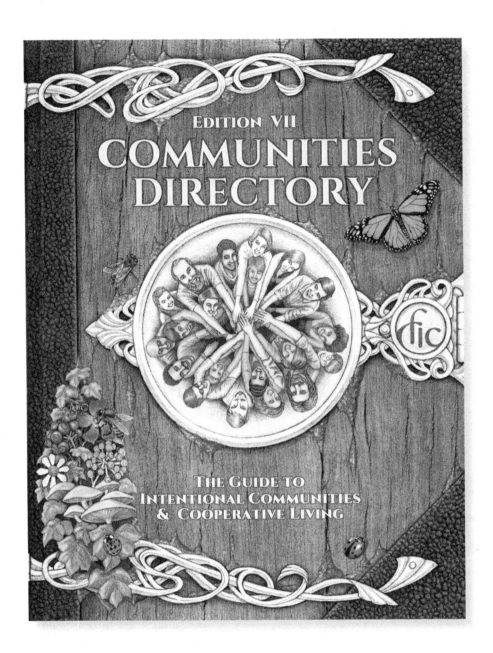

Communities Directory book!

In addition to profiling more than 1,000 communities, this new book includes full-page maps showing where communities are located, charts that compare communities by more than 30 qualities, and an easy index to find communities interested in specific pursuits. Also included are articles on how to start or join a community, the basics of group dynamics and decision-making, and countless additional resources and links to help your community thrive!

Order your book today: www.ic.org/New-Directory

HAPPY, HEALTHY, FUNCTIONAL, FIT:
What Works Best in Present-Day Intentional Communities

By Zach Rubin, Ma'ikwe Ludwig, and Don Willis

The *Communities Directory* is best known as an invaluable resource for community seekers: many a dog-eared copy has traveled the country on road trips in search of cooperative culture, and many a community enthusiast has the online Directory bookmarked. But the Directory is also an invaluable resource for a growing number of researchers. Yet, because cataloging can be a tedious process both for the FIC and member communities, the Directory's data is in some ways a superficial snapshot of the state of communities today.

We wanted to delve more deeply into the social systems of communities. Have you ever wondered what actually works? What leads to greater satisfaction, and what traits are common among communities that have survived the test of time? We wondered too, and this article is our first public presentation of the results of an 80-question survey we conducted of communities in the Directory in early 2017, created out of those curiosities. Almost 300 communities responded to this survey, though not every community answered every question, so not every chart in this article adds up to 300.

We are grateful to both the FIC and all of the communities that participated in this study, which paints a much deeper picture of the intentional community (IC) movement as it exists today. There is no way we could cover the full breadth of new knowledge created in just one magazine article, so here we focus on several key and salient themes that we think communities will find the most interest in: decision making, age of community, community satisfaction, and conflict resolution.

The topic that perhaps interested us the most was how communities make decisions, because that is linked to almost every other aspect of the community experience. There were two questions on the survey about community governance types: one that asked for the "Decision-Making Types" as formally outlined by the community (reported here in Chart 1), and one that asked for the "Decision-Making Structures" in how decision making actually happens in the community (reported here in Chart 2). These may seem like very similar categories, yet when the results are presented side-by-side the differences are palpable. The first question reveals that most communities use some form of consensus as their formal means of decision making, with a smattering of communities relying on majority votes, community councils, or sole leaderships.

For the second question, based on the prevalence of consensus, we might expect that most people would describe their community as having functional equality in decision making. Yet that number is less than half—only 60 report functional equality compared to the 139 consensus communities, and nine of those 60 that reported it also reported some other decision-making type than consensus. That, combined with the large number of respondents who said their community has a group of informal leaders, means many communities have a consensus-based structure that is not living up to its name. This overlaps to some extent with the response in Chart 2 that the community has a small group of leaders making the decisions, which is about 30 percent higher than the number of communities that reported being run by council, which also suggests that there are a number of communities whose consensus process is dominated by a few rather than being fully egalitarian.

Veterans of consensus decision making know that it doesn't necessarily eliminate power dynamics right away, nor promise to be the perfect end of community squabbles and struggles. Rather, consensus can help equalize power and create more equality even if they don't reach the "leaderless" idealized arrangement.

We know from previous research and personal experiences that these problems are not new to purportedly "leaderless" organizations—indeed it is often a pitfall when trying to run an organization with egalitarian decision-making structures that those who are either more outspoken, know how to manipulate group feelings better, or are simply more stubborn about group discussions will see that *their* consensus often wins out. Such groups tend to benefit from training on decision making and conflict resolution, which is discussed later.

Regardless of leadership type or structure, some ICs are happier than others when it comes to their group's ability to reach a decision. The use of consensus, or the presence of a sole leader who manages the community through charismatic authority, or informal leaders that rise to the top may influence how satisfied a group is with their leadership, though those should be considered alongside several other factors.

To capture community satisfaction with decision making, we built a *satisfaction scale* through combining the survey questions about each community's decision-making process, which are found in Box 1. Each question poses a ranking of 1 to 10, and with 13 questions that made for a maximum possible score on the scale of 130. Not a single community scored themselves as perfect, though a handful (five) were above 120. Only 12 percent of communities were below the halfway point on the scale, and the overall distribution skewed towards higher satisfaction. The average score on this scale was an 87, which implies that the average community is happier than not with their decision-making processes yet sees room for improvement.

Chart 3 breaks down average satisfaction and population across community age groups. Age, for this chart, was broken down into roughly equal cohorts of 20 percent of the respondent sample. What this means is that roughly 20 percent of the communities that responded to the survey were between zero and six years old (zero meaning that the community has not yet officially been established), with the oldest community reporting in the survey an age of 80 years. In parallel are the community populations, which show a predictable trend of increasing, on average, as the community gets older, though with a leveling off somewhere between 12 and 27 years old.

Age, though, seems to have little effect on a community's satisfaction with their decision-making processes. This tells us a few possible things: 1) communities will always struggle with their decision making, and getting it right is more of a journey than a destination, 2) population size doesn't seem to have a distinguishable effect on satisfaction, since communities do tend to grow as they age if they make that a part of their model, and 3) there are a healthy number of young groups buoyant with optimism about the community they are working to create. The only cohort that reports a notably higher score on the satisfaction scale is the youngest one, which is likely due to the presence of newly established or not fully established communities that have yet to run into their first major conflicts or roadblocks in decision making. While we might expect that as those communities age (if they survive) their satisfaction level will go down after encountering inevitable conflict, they also represent a rather notable cohort of new communities being formed. If the youngest cohort contained a wider set of ages than it does, that would mean few communities being formed, and if it were a narrower set of ages that would mean either explosive growth or a wave of utopian experiments forming much like we saw in the 1960s and 70s—and being similarly unlikely to survive long-term as many of them from that era didn't.

It would seem that leadership structure has more to do with satisfaction with community governance processes than age. It doesn't matter how long your community has been around, getting governance right is what predicts whether a community will be happy with their decision making. In Charts 4 and 5 there are the same questions about community decision-making types and structures—except that instead of measuring the number of communities that practice each type those have been replaced with the average satisfaction level for that type. Chart 4 shows that the most satisfied communities are those with a community council. That smaller group of respondents shown in Chart 1 seem to have figured out something that other communities haven't, a right combination of egalitarian decision-making that gives everyone the feeling of an equal stake while also reducing the amount of work each individual needs to commit to by vesting some degree of it in a council. Often, community councils can rotate among community membership, so no one leader or group of leaders can ever claim too much power for too long, so it is also possible that the community council form helps to bypass the frustrations mentioned above with consensus decision making and the possibility of informal leadership.

The least satisfied communities were those with a sole leader at the helm. Those communities were also the least common type among communities surveyed, and this is a leadership style with a couple of caveats worth noting in the context of this survey. First, many communities that have a sole leader are often organized around a charismatic religious leader. Our data shows that communities with a sole leader are slightly more likely than others to report being based on a specific religious background or ideology. These may sometimes be better characterized as apocalyptic or millenarian, unconcerned with communities as a movement. It's not surprising then that fewer communities with sole leaders would be registered with the FIC Directory, or respond to our survey, as they would see themselves as part of some movement or tradition that is very different from the mission of building a sustainable and cooperative world. (At the same time, while this is FIC's mission, it is hardly universal among communities listed in the Directory.) Second is that sole leadership seems to be waning in popularity in communal experiments, though we can't make such conclusion from this survey alone. Compared to historical data on ICs, there are far fewer sole leaderships represented in this survey than in past snapshots of the movement (like Rosabeth Moss Kanter's book *Commitment and Community*, or Foster Stockwell's *Encyclopedia of American Communes*).

We know, though, from the survey responses that the most popular decision-making structure among communities is consensus or modified consensus. This is by no means a surprising revelation, and something we fully anticipated by adding an extra section of questions for consensus communities. Several of these pertain to the use of blocking, which is a key feature that distinguishes consensus as an egalitarian decision-making strategy. Typically, blocking is something that happens when an individual or small group exercises a form of veto power over finalizing a group decision because they see it as inherently damaging to the group or as contravening the group's values. So we assumed as part of the survey that the more a community permits or uses blocking, the more difficulty they would encounter in making decisions and smoothly governing the community. Box 2 shows the criteria we tested, as well as how they were assigned values in creating a blocking scale. For most of the statements, answering in a way that we expected to make blocking a bigger barrier to finalizing decisions in a smooth and easy manner were coded positively, and for a few we assigned a negative value because we expected them to demonstrate blocking was less of a barrier to smooth and easy decision making in the community. For example, if a community answered affirmatively to "we have never had a block," that was considered an indicator that blocking did not hold up decision making in the community, whereas if they answered "anyone can block a decision for any reason," we considered that as an indicator that blocking was more likely to hold up decision making either more regularly or for longer (or both).

The scale is presented in Chart 6, where we have designated communities on a scale from "Low Blocking" (those with blocking criteria that didn't interfere with decision making) to "High Blocking" (those with blocking criteria that more often interfered with decision making). Based on the answers to the questions in Box 2, we would expect blocking to happen a lot

---

Box 1 – Decision Making Satisfaction Scale

Rate the following statement from strongly disagree (1) to strongly agree (10). My community's decision making process...

1. is functional
2. is complicated
3. has served us well so far
4. is fair to all involved
5. reflects our common values
6. needs to change for the community to be successful
7. excludes some voices*
8. is perfect
9. has more flaws than the decision-making processes of other communities*
10. involves everyone
11. has been the source of a lot of struggle in my community*
12. is easy to understand
13. generally has a high satisfaction rating from members

*these question scores were inverted in building the satisfaction scale.

Box 2 – Blocking Use Scale

How does blocking in your consensus system operate? Check all that apply.

1. Anyone can block a decision for any reason
2. We only allow blocks for reasons tied to group held values
3. We have a specific process in place for validating a block
4. We use a modified form of consensus that allows some number of blocks
5. Blockers must work with the group (or a subgroup) to create alternate proposal
6. People have to explain why they are blocking a decision*
7. People do not have to explain why they are blocking
8. Blocks happen regularly--more than once a year
9. Blocks happen very rarely*
10. We have never had a block*

*these options were encoded with a negative value on the scale, since they indicate lower barriers in blocking decisions.

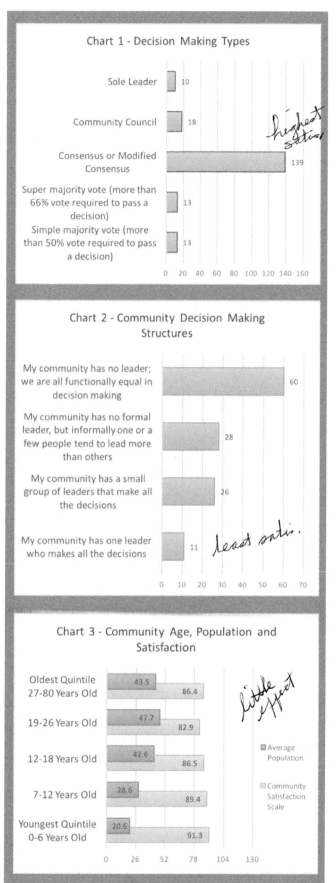

Chart 1 - Decision Making Types

Sole Leader — 10
Community Council — 18
Consensus or Modified Consensus — 139
Super majority vote (more than 66% vote required to pass a decision) — 13
Simple majority vote (more than 50% vote required to pass a decision) — 13

highest satis.

Chart 2 - Community Decision Making Structures

My community has no leader; we are all functionally equal in decision making — 60
My community has no formal leader, but informally one or a few people tend to lead more than others — 28
My community has a small group of leaders that make all the decisions — 26
My community has one leader who makes all the decisions — 11 *least satis.*

Chart 3 - Community Age, Population and Satisfaction

Oldest Quintile 27-80 Years Old — 43.5 / 86.4
19-26 Years Old — 47.7 / 82.9
12-18 Years Old — 42.6 / 86.5
7-12 Years Old — 28.6 / 89.4
Youngest Quintile 0-6 Years Old — 20.6 / 91.3

little effect

■ Average Population
▨ Community Satisfaction Scale

more often in High Blocking communities, and less often in Low Blocking ones. Another way to think about this would be that blocking interferes with a group's ability to make decisions more regularly in High Blocking communities than in Low Blocking ones. Therefore, we compared this to the Satisfaction scale (seen in Chart 6) and found that the more towards Low Blocking the community was, the greater level of satisfaction reported in their decision-making process.

To some extent, this is unsurprising: communities whose decisions are not obstructed with the use of blocks probably have a smoother decision-making process in general. We can't really say that blocks are a key cause of lower satisfaction, but rather that they are likely a symptom of some other type of discord in the community or a less well-functioning consensus system.

Rather than there being a causal connection between the use of blocking and dissatisfaction, it makes more sense to think of some other factor(s) that would have an effect on both satisfaction and the use of blocking. We can't really separate cause and effect from each other, though, as it is probably more of a feedback loop between community members holding up decisions through blocking and other reasons for community dissatisfaction.

A couple of other factors included in the survey may also have an effect on satisfaction. The first is the extent to which a community practices income sharing, which usually means that all income (from community businesses or other sources) is combined into one pool, from which everyone's needs are met. The data arranged in Chart 7 shows us that communities with full income sharing tend to report a higher degree of satisfaction with community decision making, and that communities without full income sharing tend to report similar but lower levels of satisfaction regardless of how sharing they were. (This conclusion comes with a caution, though: very few communities reported as full income sharing, so margins of error are higher; furthermore, deeper statistical analysis suggests that confounding factors that affect both income sharing and satisfaction may be yielding these results, rather than the two affecting each other directly.) Note that most communities reported no income sharing (177 of them), and only a few reported each for partial <50 percent on average (18), partial >50 percent of income on average (4), and full income sharing (16). None of the other variables considered here manifested such lopsided distributions. In order to say something more definitive about income sharing and satisfaction, a deeper study is warranted. At the very least, we can say that there is a weak but positive correlation between income sharing and decision-making satisfaction level, though nothing firmer than that.

A second factor was how communities handled conflict between community members, which we broke down into two categories: "minor" conflicts, which included interpersonal disputes on issues not critical to the community as a whole, and "major" conflicts, which included acts of violence, threats, or disputes that threaten the integrity of the community. These are reported in Chart 8, which shows that there is little difference in satisfaction reported between how communities handle major and minor conflicts, but a large degree of difference in satisfaction between communities that have formal requirements for members to go through community-mediated conflict resolution and those that make it optional to some degree or have no formal conflict-resolution process.

Those that have mandatory requirements for conflict resolution are strongly related to those that report a high level of satisfaction with decision-making processes. While the two measures are distinct, they are nonetheless related. Decision making often uses the same skill set as conflict resolution: careful listening, a willingness to take into account what is important to others, and ability to shift perspectives in light of new information. Therefore, the work a community and its members do towards maintenance of relationships also transfers to decision making, as individual conflicts either erupt in a group setting over group issues or well-maintained rapports support each other in resolving points of controversy.

A third factor we examined was how much a community spent on training for conflict-resolution processes. Communities were prompted with a series of questions on whether they deployed common conflict-resolution techniques like restorative circles, co-counseling, a public airing of grievances, and mediation, then asked how much their community spent in a typical year for training on the use of those tools. In Chart 9, we see that communities with the highest level of satisfaction are those that actually spend nothing on conflict-resolution trainings. It is likely that many of those communities are either very new, and therefore have not yet encountered conflicts that have spurred them to seek outside help; are very homogeneous, and that helps them avoid conflict; or they have developed their own tools without the aid of outside help. Those that do spend money on trainings seem to benefit most from a high level of commitment to it—those that spent a little ($1-$500 per year) reported a low level of satisfaction in decision making, while those that reported a higher level of spending ($500+ per year) were almost as satisfied as those that expended nothing on training. The lesson here is that communities that wish to commit to getting outside trainings on conflict resolution should not skimp, as a small investment doesn't seems to yield the same outcomes as a larger investment.

A final factor we examined is whether communities are particularly selective in bringing in new members. Unlike income sharing, membership selectivity did not seem to track in any particular way with community satisfaction. This is shown in Chart 10, which displays a fairly even level of satisfaction across a range of possible selectiveness, from being very selective to just letting in pretty much anybody who wants to join the community. Therefore, it would seem that community decision-making satisfaction is more closely tied to how members integrate into decision-making structures once they enter the community, rather than whether they are a good fit upon entry.

The aggregate of these results tells us a couple of very compelling things. First and foremost is that, on average, the more an IC works towards *community*—that is, the sharing of life's activities and necessities—the greater satisfaction level they report with their communal experiments. A lot of factors can be mixed into this (somewhat vague) notion of community feeling: how homogeneous a population they are, how radically different they are from the mainstream culture, and just how communal they start out. But determining whether they will be happy with it is much more a product of the mutual energies they expend toward their experiment.

There seem to be two sides to the coin for community. On the one, those individuals who are likely to find happiness in a fully communal lifestyle can more easily integrate into communities that place more communal requirements on them while those communities that try to strike a middle ground and are communal only in some ways will attract a membership with more varied orientations to communalism. On the other, communities that have a better sense of community in the first place are probably more likely to develop more communal mechanisms over time.

The second conclusion is that commitment mechanisms are a key part of generating satisfaction with community decision making. The more people are required to give of themselves—economically, behaviorally, emotionally—the more likely they are to have higher satisfaction in community decision making. This reaffirms what many studies of historical ICs have already told us, so we know the lessons of the past still hold true in some form to today. For example, Rosabeth Moss Kanter's 1972 book *Commitment and Community* (also mentioned above) was a historical survey of ICs from the 19th century and the 1960s. She found that communities that had a greater number of commitment mechanisms persisted for longer, and were therefore in her estimation considered more successful.

More recently, Richard Sosis and Eric Bressler elaborated on this hypothesis in the academic journal *Cross-Cultural Research* by re-examining many of the same communities and describing the key commitment mechanisms as those that were "costly to fake." Commitments such as belief structures are easy to say that one adheres to, but commitments like abstention from alcohol or daily prayer are difficult to avoid doing, and therefore communities with commitments members would have difficulty faking were more successful in building a long-lasting community through quickly and easily weeding out the uncommitted. Likewise, some of the commitment mechanisms we've covered here like income sharing and mandatory conflict resolution are very costly, if not impossible, commitments to fake. A community's initial selectiveness in finding new members didn't have anything to do with this, either. Our survey reconfirms the centrality of commitment mechanisms to community success.

Of course, success should not only be measured in longevity as those previous

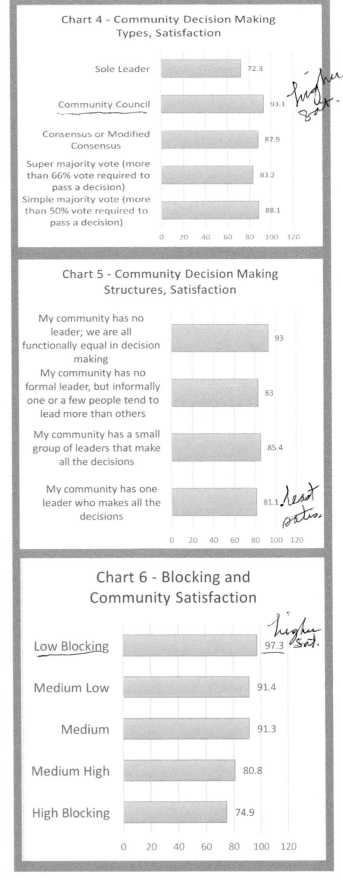

Chart 4 - Community Decision Making Types, Satisfaction

Sole Leader — 72.3
Community Council — 93.1
Consensus or Modified Consensus — 87.9
Super majority vote (more than 66% vote required to pass a decision) — 83.2
Simple majority vote (more than 50% vote required to pass a decision) — 88.1

Chart 5 - Community Decision Making Structures, Satisfaction

My community has no leader; we are all functionally equal in decision making — 93
My community has no formal leader, but informally one or a few people tend to lead more than others — 83
My community has a small group of leaders that make all the decisions — 85.4
My community has one leader who makes all the decisions — 81.1

Chart 6 - Blocking and Community Satisfaction

Low Blocking — 97.3
Medium Low — 91.4
Medium — 91.3
Medium High — 80.8
High Blocking — 74.9

studies have used, so we think that this survey adds some nuance to their conclusions by introducing the importance of satisfaction in community decision making. That may or may not predict longevity, but given that our data is about the present we have no way of predicting such things. Besides, people move to communities for reasons rooted in the present: self-actualization, a feeling of connection with others, reducing consumption, etc. Perhaps the historians of the future will use a different metric of success for the ICs of today.

We caution the reader to not take our results as gospel for what works to make a successful community. It's worth pointing out that using survey data comes with some key limitations, most notably that we are forced to talk in terms of averages and aggregates instead of individuals. Whether you are in a community presently and thinking of ways to improve your decision-making processes, or are thinking of founding one and deliberating what those processes could look like, this should only be a suggestion point for understanding what sort of practices will work best in your situation, and perhaps encouragement to discuss options you may not have otherwise considered.

Nonetheless, these data represent what we think are significant indicators of what makes for a happier, more cohesive and functional community. Should your community take steps to increase the level of egalitarian practice, create stronger commitment mechanisms, and seek outside assistance in conflict resolution, we would expect that community to become more

satisfied with the outcomes in decision making.

If this seems like common sense, then all we've done is put some empirical weight behind your view of communities. If it seems extraordinary, then perhaps it will open you up to thinking about new arrangements and possibilities. Either way, we hope to have contributed in some small way to a healthier, more functional communities movement. ⌁

Zach Rubin is a Ph.D. candidate in sociology at the University of Missouri, where he also earned a M.A. in Geography, and an adjunct professor of Geography at State Fair Community College. His dissertation research is focused on present-day intentional communities known as "ecovillages" and their connections to social movement theory. In particular, his research site is Dancing Rabbit Ecovillage, where he spent eight months collecting ethnographic and interview data.

Ma'ikwe Ludwig works with intentional communities as a consultant and trainer, has lived in community for 20 years, and is working on starting an income-sharing ecovillage in Laramie, Wyoming. She is the executive director of Commonomics USA, which works at the intersection of economic and ecological justice, and is on the FIC's Board. Her most recent book is Together Resilient: Building Community in the Age of Climate Disruption.

Don Willis is a Huggins Fellow and doctoral candidate in sociology at the University of Missouri-Columbia. He earned a B.A. in sociology from the University of Central Arkansas and a M.A. in sociology from the University of Arkansas-Fayetteville, where he completed a thesis entitled "Resources and Relationships: Food Insecurity and Social Capital among Middle School Children." Broadly, his interests are in social inequality, health disparities, food insecurity, youth, and the life course.

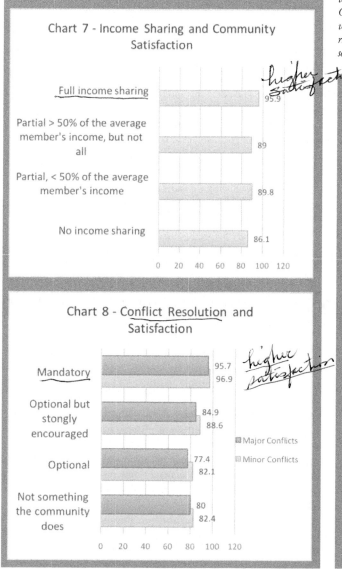

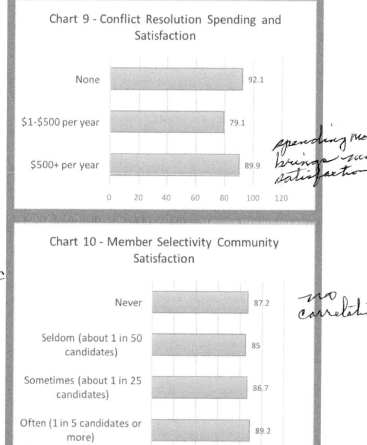

A Useful Tool for Founders and Seekers: SPECTRUMS

By Ma'ikwe Ludwig

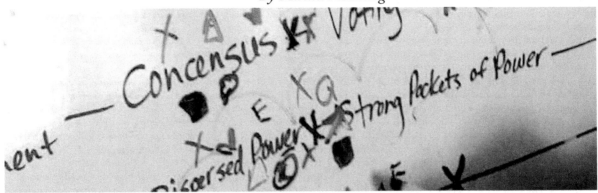

I'm a little obsessed with spectrums. The world is pretty much one big grey area as near as I can tell. Anyone who has ever spent any time with me as a facilitator or a facilitation teacher knows that spectrums are one of my go-to tools.

In workshops I teach about starting an Intentional Community as well as finding a community home, I use this particular set of spectrums (see worksheets). These are things that every community lands on somewhere, either deliberately or by default.

Here's how I suggest people use them.

For Founders

It is very important that you get clear about what things are essential to you in your community vision and what things you don't really care about. I recommend going through these spectrums and marking on each one the perfect spot in your mind of how your community will be set up. (I do this with an X or some other simple symbol.) Then I would also mark (perhaps using a highlighter marker or brackets) your range of tolerance. In other words, you might have a preference, but for most of these you also will likely have some flexibility about how close to the ideal it needs to be in order for you to feel excited about all the work of creating a community.

As an example, you might ideally want to be very rural, but could live with being in a small town. So in that case, you'd mark an X all the way over on the far side above rural, and then place a bracket or highlighter mark from the rural side to, say, one-third of the way across the spectrum.

You may find that you have no opinion or preference for some of them. That's great! That means that your vision has some flexibility and will allow other people's preferences to come into play. However, it is very important to be as honest as you can be about your answers. If you really want to live in a community that is income-sharing or has a strong spiritual orientation, it is fine to place an X and then have no brackets at all. This will help people who are considering joining you know exactly what they are joining.

Many founders make the mistake of thinking that they can answer all these questions after they have five or six or 10 people they really like who have decided to join. The pitfall in waiting to get clear about that is that you run the risk of not having enough alignment among that group and wasting a lot of everyone's time.

Get clear about your must-haves, articulate those clearly, and recruit from that place. Then drag this spectrum worksheet out and let folks know that the group is welcome to answer the rest of those questions or just let yourselves default to something. Doing this well will create a much stronger, aligned, and clear core group to build from.

For People Seeking a Community

I recommend following the same procedure as above for seekers: mark on each of these spectrums your ideal and your range of tolerance. Then step back and do a little soul searching. You may have a preference, but how strong is it? Which ones of these are your make or break criteria? The same advice about honesty applies here. Be as real with yourself about these answers as you can be.

Hint: If each of your answers is just an X or has a very narrow range to it, you are likely to be very disappointed when you get out there and start searching. One of the first lessons of community is to be able to articulate your preferences and then widen back into flexibility for the sake of being able to connect and work with others. Filling this worksheet out is a first chance at seeing just how flexible or rigid you currently are. Having a strong preference on four to six of these is probably healthy and will help your search be productive.

Seekers should take this with them when they visit places. I'd recommend sitting down with someone who has been in the community you are visiting for a while (at least three years if the group is established) and asking them for their realistic take on their community and how well it matches your preferences. This can be an invaluable guide for sorting out the communities that might really work well for you.

Once you've narrowed your search in this more logical way, I'd recommend setting this aside and considering communities from a more intuitive or felt place. Regardless of what the spectrums say, which one feels right or the most like home? Is there a community that didn't quite match your answers, but your attention keeps getting drawn back to it? Can you flex and grow into that community? Is there something the spectrums didn't cover that you have found through your process really is more important than these criteria?

By the same token, if a place looks great on paper but feels wrong, trust your gut. Preferences can (and very likely will) change, but a good intuitive hit is almost always worth listening to.

Choosing an intentional community home is really all about being intentional. And generally, that will be a healthy mix of logic and love, criteria and intuition. Let me know if these spectrums help you on your journey! ✍

Ma'ikwe Ludwig lives at Dancing Rabbit Ecovillage, where she serves as the Executive Director of the ecovillage's nonprofit. She teaches workshops on group process, sustainability, and starting intentional communities. Her latest project is the Materialized Empathy project, a model policy development organization dedicated to economic and ecological justice, including helping reduce legal barriers to sustainable community formation. She can be reached at maikwe.ludwig@gmail.com.

Spectrums for Individuals within Groups

The following are common scales that describe basic approaches to life. In a healthy group, there are people spread out throughout these scales. All traits have a valuable aspect to them and all have pitfalls. Ideally, the membership of an organization takes into account these sorts of things when trying to find a good roles for someone to play, e.g., quick decision-making is valuable in a work-party leader, but not so much for budget team members, where you want more measured thinking; good facilitators see meetings as being both for decisions and connection; if everyone has a strong sense of aesthetics, you need great alignment or you're in trouble.
Suggested uses: Perspective. Create an exercise to get to know each other better.
Use to reduce judgment.

Interprets Negatively ⟶ Interprets Positively
Slow to Decide ⟶ Quick to Decide
Slow to Change ⟶ Quick to Change
Fact-Based ⟶ Non-Rational-Based
Meetings Are to Decide ⟶ Meetings Are to Connect
Manifest by Actions ⟶ Manifest by Intention
Follower ⟶ Leader
Planner ⟶ Doer
Holds a Grudge ⟶ Lets Things Go
Works on Stuff Privately ⟶ Enrolls Others in Process
Sticks to First Take ⟶ Changes Mind Easily
Gives Mostly Work ⟶ Gives Mostly Thinking
Strong Aesthetic Sense ⟶ Not Strong on Aesthetics
Prefers Noisy Bustle ⟶ Prefers Solitude
Comfortable in Groups ⟶ Nervous in Groups

Copyright 2007/2013 Sol Space Consulting www.maikwe.net maikwe.ludwig@gmail.com

Spectrums for Intentional Communities

ICs come in lots of flavors. Every group falls somewhere on these spectrums, which affect the feel, culture, and experience of being in the group (though be aware that the answers to these can change over time, and changes are not necessarily about how healthy or vibrant the group is). Misalignment in any one of these spectrums makes it a tough fit.

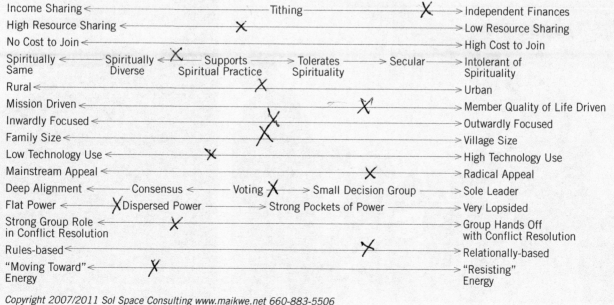

Income Sharing ⟵ Tithing ✗ ⟶ Independent Finances
High Resource Sharing ⟵ ✗ ⟶ Low Resource Sharing
No Cost to Join ⟵ ⟶ High Cost to Join
Spiritually Same ⟵ Spiritually Diverse ⟵ ✗ Supports Spiritual Practice ⟶ Tolerates Spirituality ⟶ Secular ⟶ Intolerant of Spirituality
Rural ⟵ ✗ ⟶ Urban
Mission Driven ⟵ ✗ ⟶ Member Quality of Life Driven
Inwardly Focused ⟵ ✗ ⟶ Outwardly Focused
Family Size ⟵ ✗ ⟶ Village Size
Low Technology Use ⟵ ✗ ⟶ High Technology Use
Mainstream Appeal ⟵ ✗ ⟶ Radical Appeal
Deep Alignment ⟵ Consensus ⟵ Voting ✗ ⟶ Small Decision Group ⟶ Sole Leader
Flat Power ⟵ ✗ Dispersed Power ⟶ Strong Pockets of Power ⟶ Very Lopsided
Strong Group Role in Conflict Resolution ⟵ ✗ ⟶ Group Hands Off with Conflict Resolution
Rules-based ⟵ ✗ ⟶ Relationally-based
"Moving Toward" Energy ⟵ ✗ ⟶ "Resisting" Energy

Copyright 2007/2011 Sol Space Consulting www.maikwe.net 660-883-5506

Common Fire's Top Ten Hard-Earned
TIPS FOR COMMUNITY SUCCESS

By Jeff Golden

The Common Fire Foundation was established in the early 2000s to support the development of intentional communities strongly committed to social justice and environmental sustainability. It was involved in the establishment of a housing co-op in Tivoli, New York (shuttered in 2013) and a cohousing community in Beacon, New York, and it was involved with a group of people in the Bay Area in California that did extensive foundational work over several years but never turned the corner of acquiring property or moving in together.

Common Fire is no longer actively working with groups, but some of the resources they created, including their original vision document and video, are available at www.commonfire.org.

The author cofounded Common Fire, worked with each of the three groups to some degree, and played a central role and lived in the two communities in New York.

Anybody striving to create an intentional community couldn't do better than to read Diana Leafe Christian's book, *Creating a Life Together*. The depth and breadth of information she offers is staggering and invaluable. The following tips are humbly intended to add to or tweak some of what she and others offer, or to highlight some of what she offers that we think is just so important (or that might be taken for granted or misinterpreted, etc.) that we urge everyone to really take the time to appreciate them.

They come from our own sometimes triumphant, sometimes traumatic experiences in community. Some represent things we did really well and are grateful for. More often they are things we didn't do well and we paid a heavy price for. Our prayer is that they may help you tip the scale towards ever more triumph and ever less trauma in your own journey with intentional community.

A number of people collaborated with me on this article, and these are ideas that have been voiced in different ways by many people in the three Common Fire communities. So I offer them as "our" collective learnings. However, this article still very much reflects my own perspective, and the way I have come to understand our experiences and prioritize the lessons learned. So in that sense, I want to be clear that I am not writing this as representative of anyone else who has been

The author Jeff Golden giving a tour of the Tivoli Housing Co-op while under construction.

Photo courtesy of Jeff Golden

The Tivoli Housing Co-op was a new construction project.

Residents at the Tivoli Housing Co-op cooked for each other six nights a week and all sat down together to eat once or twice a week.

Preparing a meal at the Tivoli Co-op.

involved in those communities or the Common Fire Foundation.

1. Set a High Bar for Selecting People Who Fit Your Vision, and Stick With It

Diana Leafe Christian's chapter on "Selecting People to Join You" is fabulous and you should take her advice very seriously. If you have misgivings about anyone joining your founding group or community, or just have a gut concern, no matter how wonderful they may seem in other ways, you should simply say no, or at least hold off on accepting them. And if you think you're already setting a high bar, set it just a little higher. Really. And that includes being sure that you're selecting people who will themselves help to maintain that high bar for other people joining.

Think especially about how people seem to handle conflict, and explore how successful they have been in long-term relationships including friends, family, and partners, as well as their history in past communities and group living situations. Talk with some of these people or involve them in the process in some way.

People have compared joining a community to marrying someone. The comparison has its limitations, but it can be a very helpful idea. The interweaving of lives on such an intimate scale, and the interplay of such complex and often triggering elements as money, family, home and place, power, decision making, and legal structures—all of these mean that we become very interdependent and have a huge impact on each others' lives exactly as we are dancing with very profound personal questions and issues. This can be a good thing—it is exactly why many of us are drawn to community—but it amplifies the challenge and gravity of grappling with these issues, and can be deeply draining and traumatic. We need to be very thoughtful in who we bind to our lives in this way.

As hard as it may feel to say no to someone, take any feelings of regret, shame, sadness, resentment, distrust, etc., that come up and imagine them being blown up a hundred times over, and imagine being tied to that person. That and more is what you are quite possibly inviting into your life and the lives of everyone else in the community, including this person, by dealing with someone who is not right for your community *after* they've been accepted rather than before.

(One person with extensive experience in community who gave feedback on this document suggested that we offer a tip entirely on the topic of "We Live in a Violent, Disassociated World and Everyone Is Screwed Up and You Are Screwed Up Too." I didn't manage to make this its own tip, but I think the title alone says worlds about tips 1, 2 and 3.)

Depending on how we approach it, conflict can be a path to self-discovery and stronger connections or it can make people want to run for the hills.

2. Deal with Conflict and Conflictual People Immediately

Conflict is inevitable. Depending on how we approach it, it can be a path to self-discovery and stronger connections within the community or it can block all forward movement in the community and make people want to run for the hills. Part of addressing conflict in a positive way is dealing with it *as quickly as possible*, when it comes to both small and big things. The small things add up to big things fast, and they set the tone for how easily and effectively people deal with the big things. A seemingly minor conflict that is not addressed can become toxic.

The same thing goes with someone who is very conflictual or doesn't deal with conflict in a healthy, proactive way. Set some clear boundaries for them and stick with them, including requiring them to leave if necessary, or you will pay a *much* higher cost down the road.

Most people are conflict-averse. Many are VERY conflict-averse. One thing we did in the Tivoli community that was *very* helpful: at our one night a week together, we had a specific time for "Elephants in the Room." People were expected to use that time to name anything large or small that was bothering them, and we made it clear that it was unacceptable for people to let anything bothering them sit beyond that weekly gathering. In that way we helped normalize discussing concerns and problems, people got more comfortable and skilled at it, and people didn't have to take the initiative or find the time during the rest of the busy week.

(Sometimes we didn't need much time at all for this. However, we capped Elephants in the Room time to 30 minutes unless the whole group agreed that extending was more important than moving on to the other things on the agenda. I should also note that we tried to introduce this practice at the Beacon community at a point where there was already some serious conflict and it was too late to be effective or welcome.)

3. Adopt Some Clear Norms around Good Communication, Deep Connection, and Conflict Resolution

We were very successful in creating spaces that invited people to share deeply with each other, to invite the fullness of who we each are and what we are experiencing in our lives into our communities, and to really go deep when problems arose to try to get at the fundamental issues within ourselves that were being triggered or stimulated. This was primarily thanks to our use of the Be Present Empowerment Model and trainings from Be Present, Inc., which are incredible resources. (See www.bepresent.org.)

This allowed our communities to be very rich and connected, and it promoted a huge degree of personal growth. This level of seeing and knowing each other went a long way to helping prevent conflict in the first place, and to easing moving through conflict when it did come up. More than once this was named as essential to the Beacon community sur-

Tivoli residents enjoyng breakfast outside.

Most of the electricity for the Tivoli Co-op was provided by on-site solar panels.

viving some challenging times, and it was cited by many people in all three communities as the glue that held them together and the most precious part of their community experience.

At the same time, what we did not do so well was have a more immediate and solution-oriented process for our groups to use when conflict came up. People are not always able to rise to the occasion of trying to process things at a deeper level, of being that vulnerable and introspective or compassionate, and in that case a complex and demanding tool like the one we used is vulnerable to being undermined or abused. That kind of processing can also require a good amount of time. When people are pressed for time or when a number of different issues start to come up at the same time, it can overwhelm even a group that has a strong commitment and practice of doing deep work with each other.

There needs to be something in place to provide some immediate relief and clarity, to help the group get through those times, and to provide some accountability and clear next steps around particular issues or individuals. Having these norms and processes in place early on is critical, because trying to introduce them when something really big has already come up can be very tricky, and you miss the opportunity of practicing and getting everyone more comfortable with the

process by working on smaller issues.

[We created a draft document on the topic of "Empowered Relationships and Conflict Transformation," that is available on the Common Fire website that goes into all of this in more detail.]

4. Hold a Balance of Connection Time and Logistics Time (or "Don't Rush! But Don't Be Too Slow Either")

In California the time for checking in, connecting with each other, and learning more about each other often took up most or all of the monthly meeting time, leaving little room for any forward movement on the logistics front. The group did powerful work creating a rich human community, but after several years they had not been able to move forward much in terms of a physical site. For some in the group who had long been dissatisfied with the group spending so much time on connecting, this was demoralizing, and it undermined some people's faith in the group's ability to move forward.

In Beacon, there came a point where the emphasis shifted so significantly to the logistics side of things that almost no time was given to the connection time for a number of months. Most people felt a strong need to take a step back from the emotional processing of the group for a while because things had been so emotionally taxing leading up to and during people's move-in, and there were so many logistical things to take care of. But it meant that issues lingered for months, people became disconnected from each other, and some of the tensions in the group deepened and contributed to the eventual fracturing of the group.

Both pieces are necessary for the group to not only thrive but even survive as a human community and as a group of people striving to accomplish some very real logistical goals as well.

5. Sequence the Big Things So They Come at You One at a Time and Stagger When and How They Affect People

The Beacon community purchased a small apartment building one October. The months leading up to October were very stressful, dealing with money and legalities, deciding who would live in which apartment, and so on. There were some important renovations to do before we moved in as well. While those were going on, people were paying the monthly costs on their new apartment while also paying for the place they were still really living. Then we all had to move, which involves time and money and support from friends, and also affects us deeply in terms of our connection with

may not be able to identify up front some of the topics that will be central to the community experience further along. For example, in one situation someone felt deeply betrayed by the community when some of us had hesitations about loaning her $300 a month for six months while she transitioned to a new job. ("I thought we were a community.") In another situation someone was disappointed and scornful that the rest of the community didn't hang out more outside of our scheduled time together. ("Where is our community spirit?") In another situation, we experienced a conflict in which someone was deeply hurt and angry that the community didn't agree to add a training on race issues to our schedule. This person felt that a training on race should be a top priority; others felt it was not so important as to bump the other trainings scheduled or to add onto the existing schedule. ("What kind of community won't add a training around something one of the members is really struggling with?")

> ## Taking the time to go a level or two deeper with your visions will help you identify potentially serious differences.

place and people and things familiar to us. All of this means that there was no time for us to process people's issues and triggers right at the very time when lots of issues and triggers were inclined to come up.

By January most of us had moved in, but not before some of our relationships were damaged and we were deeply wounded as a group.

What if we had bought the building and then filled much of it with short-term tenants from outside our community, perhaps with a mix of six-month and 12-month leases? We could have spread out the stress and been more available to support each other.

6. Be Detailed in Your Visioning

Diana Leafe Christian's chapters on "Community Vision" and "Creating Vision Documents" are invaluable: yes, start with a very small group; yes, make the visioning one of the very first things you do; yes, write it all down; etc. The idea of community can be deeply seductive, and it can indeed be very rewarding and purposeful. But a bunch of people banding together to pursue the seduction without getting really clear about just what that means for each of them is a recipe for potentially serious conflict down the line.

That was true with our Beacon community. What we did not have the insight to do well was to make our visions sufficiently detailed. Make sure you have someone with experience living in community providing support around what kinds of guiding questions to use. Folks who don't have experience in community

I don't think there is a right answer to how a "community" should respond to each of these situations. Yes, you want to support each other in times of need, but are there limits to what seems fair or healthy in terms of time or money and how it balances with other commitments? Yes, you want to live sustainably, but are there limits to what you should expect of each other in your daily lives? Yes, you want to be kid-friendly, but what should be expected in terms of community members being available to look after other people's kids? And so on.

You aren't going to be able to figure everything out ahead of time, and you are going to have disagreements about what is right for the community for as long as the community exists. But taking the time to go a level or two deeper with your visions will help you identify potentially serious differences that will help people make the best decisions for themselves and the group about how to move forward.

(Another tip that was suggested to me for this article was "Developing Appropriate Boundaries in a Counterculture." I think that is relevant to thinking about conflict resolution as well as to clearly articulating expectations of each other in community.)

[Common Fire has a guide for groups to use in discussing this topic entitled "Why Community?" It is very rough but it is on our website in case it is helpful.]

7. Establish a Clear and Relatively Easy Process for Removing Someone from the Community

We used consensus decision-making in all three of our communities and were generally happy with it. The Beacon group had an important exception to consensus, requiring only a simple majority vote to remove someone from the community. The idea was that most people will set a very high bar for themselves around this kind of decision already, so if more than 50 percent of the community believes that someone really needs to go without any more processing or trying to work things out, then the community—and probably that person as well—will be much better off just getting on with it than investing the vast amount of time and energy it would take to get to consensus-minus-one or somehow keep that person in the community in a way that doesn't leave other people feeling completely exasperated and exhausted, and quite likely to just leave themselves.

Also, our experience is that there are some people who are so uncomfortable with the idea of kicking someone out that they cannot ever bring themselves to do it, short of that person perhaps being a physical threat to other community members. It was difficult to actually exercise this 50 percent option when the question of removing someone from the group came up because we had developed such a strong norm around consensus. So we spent a huge amount of time trying to get to consensus because one person continually rejected the idea of kicking someone out, and this was immensely damaging to the group. So when we did finally use the 50 percent rule we were deeply grateful we had it to turn to, and most of us wished we had used it *much* sooner.

Don't try to "do it all" together — be focused, clear, & selective. eg CSA? birthing center?
Err on the side of autonomy!

Intentional Community Essentials

8. Strive to Balance Autonomy and Community, and When in Doubt Go With Autonomy

In seeking to create a community, we are all seeking a greater degree of closeness and inter-relation than we already have with each other and with most other people. And yet, the more we weave our lives together:

• the more opportunity for conflict to emerge, which requires additional time and energy to process;

• the more each of our lives can be disrupted by what's going on in other people's lives, as well as by each other's baggage;

• the more decisions that have to be made collectively rather than individually or as families, requiring more time and more shared vision.

This means that the more we weave our lives together, the more time and the more aligning of visions and values that will be needed from each person. Think about what it takes to launch even a single project or nonprofit or business. Between 50 and 80 percent of businesses fail within the first few years. Diana Leafe Christian has estimated that 90 percent of communities "never get off the ground."

We want to give ourselves the best shot at success by keeping things as simple as possible. Through the visioning process we want to establish some real confidence about the things we definitely *do* want to do together and the ways we *do* definitely want to be in each other's lives more, and anything that does not feel essential is best left to be done separate from the community—either as individuals, collectives, businesses, or workshops, either within the community or with people and groups outside the community.

For example, is a birthing center, a CSA, or homes for immigrants, etc., an essential part of the community this group wants to create? Or is it instead an important dream of some or many of the people present, but distinct from the essence of what people want in community? We want any ventures that are not essential to the community to experience their own challenges, slow-downs, speed-ups, shifts in members, conflicts, etc. without having too significant an impact on the success of the community and the "essential" aspects of the community.

[That same guide, "Why Community?" can be helpful with this.]

9. Some Brief Offerings on Decision-Making

All three groups came away with appreciation for the benefits of modified consensus but many people in the Beacon community also had serious concerns about it, feeling that the benefits simply were not worth the vast amounts of time it required. We did not ever get to the point of exploring other options, but the idea of supermajority voting was named as attractive to some because of the idea of "most people getting most of what they want most of the time" while spending so much less time on decision-making. Also attractive to some was the idea of sociocracy.

The Tivoli co-op very happily used a modified form of Formal Consensus as described by C.T. Butler and Amy Rothstein in *On Conflict and Consensus* (www.consensus.net/oc-

accontents.html). Our most significant departure was that we allowed more time for processing emotions than that process generally allows because we were a small enough group and we saw that as a key part of how we learned and grew as a community, even though it compromised some efficiency.

10. It Takes a Lot of Time to Create Community

It's just that simple. It takes a lot of time. So people need to be ready and able to commit to carving out a good chunk of their lives to make this real. Some people can't do that, and that's fine. Have them be consultants. Invite them to join later. But make sure you have a critical mass of three to 10 people who are committed and can make the time. Otherwise you'll spend all your time trying to just corral people to meetings and there will be little forward progress—a disappointment to you and to the people who were gung ho and only later realized they can't really make the commitment.

At some point in all the communities that we know of, one or more people made the switch to working for the community at least part-time if not full-time. This is especially critical at certain junctures (like when you're purchasing property). There will be certain tensions around power and vision as the people with more time move things forward for the group, but you just have to work with that as best you can.

Creating community is important and potentially deeply-nourishing work. We wish you all the best in your journey! 🖎

Jeff Golden cofounded Common Fire and worked with each of the three intentional community groups that it nurtured.

The kitchen at the Tivoli Housing Co-op, featuring extensive salvaged wood.

A gathering of residents and friends at the Tivoli Co-op.

Thanks to Our Supporters!

Special Acknowledgements are due to these supporters of our Kickstarter Campaign who made this book series possible.

$150 Series Supporters

Cohousing Coaches
Betsy Morris and Raines Cohen

Ken Schaal
Autumm Sun Community

Chong Kee Tan

Alexis Spradling

Cynthia Fisher

Liam Higgins

Susan Forkush

Laurie McMillan

Jason Ryer

Carl McDaniel

2 anonymous

$250 Series Supporter

Shabir S

$500 and up Series Supporters

Stephen Quinto

Michael Watson

Fund for Democratic Communities

Community Essentials

By Arty Kopecky

Sometimes, when explaining intentional communities (ICs) to people, I say "we" are living in the future: communitarians are developing the ethics of a more sharing, cooperative economy and lifestyle that will be more prevalent in the future. And this I very much believe. But the two communities that I was devoted to, New Buffalo (NB—near Taos, New Mexico) in the 1970s, and Green Valley Village (GVV—north of San Francisco, California) in recent years, both foundered on some very basic principles, though the visions had such high hopes. So believing ICs are still in the formative stage, I want to share my experience, in the firm hope that more of you pioneers will get it right and make ICs a bigger part of our culture.

I was not an initiator of either of these "on a farm" communities, but instead, found them and then spent hundreds of hours working to help them. New Buffalo and Green Valley Village shared a number of common features though they came from different eras. They both involved a lot of people, hundreds anyhow. They were what I call "welcoming communities"—they had a lot of flow, many guests, friends, visitors, and new members, as well as a hard core who lived there for years. And they were accepting of all. They weren't intentionally Buddhist or Christian or centered around a leader either; they were very democratic. They did circle at meals, were thankful, and had a home-made spiritual life with chants and prayers. And they were both on what was a former farm with fabulous vistas and with the possibility to be a very productive farm.

Now to the crux of the matter. New Buffalo was started with a gift of money to purchase the land, and a corporation was formed to own the land. This is essential: to create an LLC or some organization to own, or be purchasing, the property. Green Valley Village was started by Chris and Kai and friends, with the funds supplied by Chris' dad. Sadly they never got beyond this personal ownership of the land, which is one of the prime no-nos of community formation. It was hoped that, in time, this would be rectified, but there never was a "land fund" and not until the last year or so was a serious effort made to transfer title to an LLC. But by then the property had been put on the open market, the owner never having become infatuated with the group that had

Family moment from Art Kopecky's book **Leaving New Buffalo Commune.** *Front row: Sandy, Art, Emil, Heaven.*

gathered. I never could transfer to him my love of the group, though I tried.

But Green Valley Village did become a marvelous example of democratic governance through a village council that met frequently, an elected board of directors called the "nitty gritty," and some very skilled moderators and mediators. I would marvel at the love and commitment of the people as they continually refined the tiers of membership and dealt with all issues. They would be gathered around on old couches and stuffed chairs or on carpets on the barn floor, or the Vic floor, or the school room. Often a projection screen was used with a laptop. To reconvene they sometimes sang a song: "We are circling, we are community, we are sacred."

They were doing what New Buffalo failed to do. In the anarchistic ethic of the day, similar to the fabled Morningstar Ranch (circa 1968), the NB group was all-embracing, had the idea of including "everyone," thus they failed to seriously establish a defined group with membership rules. We used what Diana Christian called "a kind of amorphous vibe grok among folks there at the time." This is another of the prime no-nos of the communities movement.

GVV had an eight-year run, NB a 15-year run. But NB is still there! It's in a toned-down version and is actually up for a new governance and ownership. Hundreds of people used these places, made them work, pioneered this essential cause and gave thousands of hours of volunteer service. I thank you, thank you, thank you. And thousands of people will follow in service to each other in community, in love of the land, and in turning greed to non-greed, a most revolutionary endeavor.

New Buffalo got the ownership right. GVV got the membership right. If they had each gotten both things right, perhaps they'd still be contributing to this revolution today.

Since we are discussing essentials of ICs let me add a few more, now that I am reaching elder status and heading for the end of my road. Pepe, I, and friends had a communal scene in Bolinas, California starting in 1969. Woody Ransom of Rock Bottom, a community in Vermont, donated use of a charming West Coast house. I've had a lot of experience since then, some of which is

(continued on p. 76)

COMMUNITY ESSENTIALS
(continued from p. 44)

recorded in my two books about the New Buffalo Commune published by UNM Press. Now I am 71 years old, just as enthusiastic about communities as when I was 23. I thank COMMUNITIES for this opportunity to share some of my thoughts.

To ownership by a democratically run entity and a membership process add, 3) need for one or more community businesses, 4) a friendly, open-to-society, nonparanoid attitude and 5) love, caring, and commitment.

The communitarians for the most part are a loving people and want society to calm down and stop chasing the almighty buck all the time. I am sympathetic with this view, but nevertheless I have always been keenly aware that ICs need to pay their way and establish successful businesses, not an easy thing to do. Occidental Arts and Ecology Center (OAEC), in Sonoma County, California has a thriving plant and seed sale business. In the last few years they have added two very professional propagation greenhouses and a charming nursery display area convenient to the upper parking lot. They have a series of display notice boards that they put up on some of the major thoroughfares, which gets the word to almost everyone. At New Buffalo we were establishing a cow dairy and so was a group at GVV running a dairy. I want to see a network of IC-run farms, with the Amish-style love of farming. At the Farm in Tennessee is the organization called Plenty, and plenty should be one of our goals. Get good at this: Food production. Of course those who are not farmers find other ways to contribute.

This is a peaceful revolution. But it is still a vital cause. It has to do with generosity, sharing wealth—not through laws, but through a change of heart. Make it shine, friends; make it work. It is not easy, this getting along, but it can be done. 🌿

Arty AnSwei Kopecky lives in Sebastopol, California and works as a finish carpenter. He also has a small bonsai nursery and, with his ex-wife Sandy, maintains a beautiful property. Art is hoping yet to find further ways to contribute to the IC movement.

Learning from Our Past

By Bill Metcalf

The theme of this edition of COMMUNITIES invites us to learn from the past of the intentional community in which we live, and to learn from our own, personal past—including whenever we have lived within or without community. This has led me to reflect on 45 years of researching, writing and teaching about, and living within intentional communities around the globe.

My first foray into this movement came as a young graduate student: four friends and I formed an urban commune in 1972. In hindsight, given our ignorance about what we were trying to do, it is a miracle that we lasted almost two years and parted as friends.

Since then I have lived communally for much of my life, have almost continuously been researching intentional communities past and present, and have written seven books, my doctoral thesis, and several dozen academic and popular articles about this movement. As COMMUNITIES' "International Correspondent" I have written about intentional communities from around the globe and from the past two centuries.

I want to share some of what I have learned.

Global/Eternal Patterns: First, I have learned that intentional communities have existed throughout, and probably before recorded history. Homakoeion, established by Pythagorus in about 625 in what is now Italy, some think to be the earliest known group, while others think one or more of the early Indian Ashrams predated it. But there might well have been even earlier ones that left no record. There have certainly been peaks and troughs in the formation of intentional communities but it seems to be a natural human urge to try to create a better society through enhanced cooperation. While some of these social experiments have been intensely communal, others have limited the daily social interaction. For example, some have had forms of open sexual relationships while others have segregated the sexes.

One observation, from looking at this millennia-long pattern, is that most groups become less communal across time. And we can see the same pattern today with intentional communities—the shift within any group is usually away from communalism and towards individualism. If not checked, this will obviously lead to the end of the intentional community. Most intentional communities end "not with a bang, but a whimper" (with acknowledgements to T.S. Elliot) because unchecked individualism has sapped the communal drive to the point when the intentional community does not collapse so much as simply cease to exist.

Forming: Whenever people ask for advice on forming an intentional community, of any sort, I have learned to respond "Don't!" I then clarify with "at least not until you have lived long enough in several intentional communities to know what you really want/love, what is available, and what drives you nuts." I follow: "Are you sure that intentional community living is for you?" "Are you sure there are no intentional communities out there looking for someone like you?" "Have you the emotional, social, and financial resources and background to give this project a good chance of success?" Money and energy are wasted by people without appropriate skills trying to create an intentional community which has almost no chance of being born, let alone surviving.

Joining: I have learned that when anyone wants to join an intentional community, it is important to have enough personal and social awareness to see a good fit. I have known non-Christians upset after joining a Christian group, prudish people upset after joining a clothing-optional group, and other such absurdities. Joining an intentional community is a bit like finding a life partner(s); one must first know oneself very, very well.

Recruitment: I have learned that whenever members of an intentional community are looking for new members, the same rule applies—members must be open and clear about what they are doing, what they want in a new member, and what they have to offer. It is unfair, almost fraudulent, to entice someone to join a group under false pretences. It is vital that a prospective member understands and accepts the group's *raison d'être*, why they do what they do, how they operate, etc. Of course all of this can change but to allow in anyone whose goal is to change the group is downright stupid. *—just as w/ a marriage partner!*

Socialising: I have learned that the most important social interactions within intentional community do not take place during meetings but over meals, chats, working bees, etc. Social interaction, at some level, is an almost constant feature in successful intentional community—even if it is as simple as making warm eye contact. We all need "time-out" but too much means the end of community life. It is important for people wanting to join to know what will be expected and assess whether they are up for this.

Governance: Many people assume that intentional communities must operate under consensus, and that such consensus means a loss of individuality, and aiming for the lowest common denominator. I have learned that this is all wrong. Consensus can work only when people are close enough to have a "we-consciousness," that is to think of "us" as being more important than "me." This happens often in normal families as well as with life-partners. It can also happen within intentional communities but only after a great deal of interpersonal work. Group decisions can then be made on the basis of "what is best for us" rather than "what is best for me." Until a group has achieved this level of interpersonal intimacy then it is better to follow a form of democracy, needing supermajorities for certain issues, or perhaps sociocracy. Good governance, using other formats, can lead to interpersonal confidence and shared trust—then consensus can, like a flower in spring, emerge.

Conflict: I have learned that conflict can arise whenever humans interact—and much of that is healthy and productive. Whenever we have different goals, perspectives, opinions, or passions, we shall have conflict. The issue is not how to avoid conflict but how to deal constructively with it. In conflict we must listen extra-well, try to get into the head/heart-space of the other, try to understand his/her position—and try to calmly and clearly share our own perspective. Only then can people look for common ground. And, in intentional community as in every other aspect of life, there are sometimes winners and losers and that is just life.

Children/Elderly: Many people assume that children are good in intentional communities and that too many elderly members are a problem. When challenged, rarely can anyone cite evidence. I have learned that the evidence is clear that intentional community is good for children—but the opposite is problematic. Children, like pets, take energy and resources, and can be points of conflict around noise, messiness, etc. A large number of children within an intentional community can mean that there is little spare energy and time for adults to devote to communal functions such as sound governance, interpersonal growth, and conflict resolution. For these reasons, many mature intentional communities are wary of accepting too many children. Another observation is that parents of young children are often incredibly conservative and can stymie needed changes in

35

an intentional community. Perhaps counter-intuitively, elderly members are often the most willing to make dramatic changes, try new processes, etc. They usually have more free time to devote to communal activities, generally have more social maturity, usually have better interpersonal insight and skills, etc., hence they are often observed to be core people in an intentional community.

Impermanence and Non-attachment: One of Buddhism's many lessons is impermanence, that everything is changing all the time. I have learned that within intentional community this means that the rules members established last year and which have worked well might no longer be germane. Because we did something last time, shall we do it again? Because you and I have clashed in the past are we likely to clash again? Intentional community, like every other social construct and every human, is always changing. Change is neither good nor bad—it simply is. Non-attachment does not mean indifference. So while members must not be indifferent to change, they must not be so attached to one way of doing things that they will suffer if this changes. Intentional community is about growth on all levels.

What Goes Wrong: I am astonished at the energy people within intentional communities devote to strawbale construction, solar power, and organic gardening, while ignoring the human dimensions. As Karen Litfin wrote, on page 147 of *Ecovillages: Lessons for Sustainable Community,* "no community has ever collapsed for want of solar panels or composting toilets, but many have been torn asunder when trust wore thin." I have learned that failure can be a great teacher, and most people in thriving intentional communities are there because they have learned from previous errors. Everyone makes mistakes but only idiots keep repeating—without learning. Focus on interpersonal relations, and the solar panels, strawbale construction, and organic veggies will all happen.

Future: Intentional communities seem to be on the increase everywhere I look. The two best-known forms are ecovillages and cohousing groups. I am sure that new rural ecovillages will be formed around the globe but expect the rate of growth will decrease. On the other hand, cohousing, particularly elder-cohousing, I predict will grow rapidly as baby-boomers age. It is such an obvious form of intentional community, aimed at a demographic often with the financial resources, social maturity, and life experiences to make this work. The second form of intentional community that I predict will grow rapidly is urban communes, either in apartment/unit blocks or large houses. Escalating house prices, falling rates of marriage, increasing single-person households, and environmental concerns in most western countries, all converge to point out the logic of urban communal living—probably in groups of 10 or less. I wrote about one such group, Mish'ol, in COMMUNITIES #149, 2010, pp. 57-9. A subset of this communal form that seems to be dramati-

cally increasing throughout modern society is "multiple-generations plus" where urban communes are formed by at least three generations of a core family, with others joining them. Their financial capacity to buy up large urban homes, and their extensive age range mean that many operate very well. This form will surely increase.

Summary and Conclusion: I have learned that intentional communities, of whatever size and with whatever orientation, answer so many human needs that they can only increase. That said, there is still much ignorance about this form of social life, where many people try and fail, then foolishly conclude there is something fundamentally wrong with communal living. To live in intentional community is to be in a collective experiment, and a lifelong personal growth workshop. Communal living, like any form of human social interaction such as being a friend, parent, or life-partner, needs to be learned and techniques honed. For those who seriously engage, the payoff is fantastic. ❧

Dr. Bill Metcalf, of Griffith University, Australia, is the author of numerous scholarly and popular articles, plus seven books, about intentional communities, the most recent being The Findhorn Book of Community Living. *He is Past President of the International Communal Studies Association and has been* COMMUNITIES *magazine's International Correspondent for many years.*

Life Lessons for Community Longevity

By Graham Ellis

The life which is unexamined is not worth living.
—Plato

My advice for creating longevity for intentional communities comes from my own experience living for over 27 years in a community I founded. It was a super fun but often bumpy ride and now my personal dream of living there for the rest of my life has gone.

If I knew what I know now would I have done things differently? YES! Do I regret my commitment to this experiment? No! My life is so abundantly rich with memorable experiences and great friends that I know it was all totally worth it.

Bellyacres Artistic Ecovillage was founded in 1987 and is located in the Big Island's lower Puna District. It sits between the Pacific Ocean and Kilauea Volcano, which has been erupting ash and oozing or spurting lava for all of our community existence.

My motivation for living in community came after two residencies at Israeli kibbutzim and from cofounding a workers' collective in Canada. I saw the opportunity to manifest an innovative community based on principles such as living cooperatively with a convivial and fair way of life, causing minimal ecological impact, and striving to become more socially, economically, and ecologically sustainable.

I made the huge assumption that my international busker friends whom I invited to participate also supported this as our vision but later realized that our common bond was a love for performing, partying, and independent living and not for intentional community. My belief that a group of anarchist jugglers could learn to live harmoniously in a Hawaiian jungle has been seriously compromised in many ways in recent years, leaving me with many lessons learned from this experiment.

Here are a few of those lessons:

Having a shared vision is crucial for any community.

We originally described ourselves as a jugglers "collective" without thinking much about the meaning of the word. We entered a state that author Scott Peck describes as "community chaos" and so I focused on creating some structure within our anarchist gang. Slowly and painfully, we started having more engaging meetings, improving our communication skills, and even adopting bylaws, articles of incorporation, and the legal name "Village Green Society." I strongly believed in the old adage that "it takes a village to raise a child" and, as a teacher, I was always focused on providing for kids.

Other members were not so enthusiastic; in fact, a majority at an early meeting voted to keep kids excluded from our land as much as possible because "they made too much noise." I

Photos courtesy of Graham Ellis

laughed knowing that it was impossible and predicted that these same troubadours would have kids of their own when they grew up; but, this proved only partly true.

> # I erroneously held the belief that embracing diversity meant adopting the principle of total inclusivity.

Recruiting community members needs to be done very consciously and carefully.

We all have challenges learning to live communally. With very few exceptions, we have been raised outside of intentional communities and bring our deep-rooted conditioning based upon competition, scarcity, individualism, and personal ownership. Human nature itself has a predisposition to reject many of the compromises required for community and to underappreciate the value of all that communities can

provide. This was definitely the case with our group.

I erroneously held the belief that embracing diversity meant adopting the principle of total inclusivity and so our original membership was open to any of my juggling friends who wanted to join. The only financial commitment they had to make was a lifetime, non-refundable membership fee of $2,000. This entitled them to set up a campsite and maybe a jungalow. For an additional $4,000, they could build a full-sized house. I realize now how seriously naïve and flawed this model was.

We really should have adopted a carefully thought-out recruitment process including a detailed interview procedure; a contract outlining responsibilities, rights, and values; and a well monitored probationary system.

In 1990, after we already had 21 members, we established a new member recruitment procedure. It definitely reflects how alternative and inexperienced we were at the time by inclusion of questions like "What is your favorite Beatles song?" We increased our membership fee to a whopping $3,000 and house sites to $5,000. All new members were put on a 12-month probationary trial; however, this was flawed because most of them did not stay living on the land during this time. New members were accepted by consensus at our AGM, even though most had never lived with existing members for more than a couple of weeks.

Every member needs to fully embrace the decision-making process.

I introduced our group to the concept of consensus decision making, as I had two years' personal experience using the method with a workers' collective in Victoria, Canada. With our Bellyacres experiment, I learned for consensus to work it is imperative that everyone is committed to learning the process and be willing to donate the time and energy to practice it. No one in our group disputed our decision to have a consensus-minus-two process (until 2014); however, we never had

any study sessions, training, or workshops on how to effectively utilize it in our meetings. Looking back, this was a mistake.

Two regular weekly meetings is a basic minimum requirement.

Our early meetings were hilarious with more of a party scene than community organizing—people would drink, smoke, and share jokes, so keeping conversations on track was crazy. I introduced the concept of rotating facilitators, agendas, minute keeping, and motions. We were on a steep learning curve and two members expressed their distaste for meetings by heckling randomly from the outside.

I would have liked to have had three weekly meetings: one for business, one for personal communication and check ins, and one potluck for food and fun, but this never happened. We functioned best when we had two weekly meetings and regressed when these connections lapsed.

I created the tradition—and even made it a serious request—for all residents on the land to attend a Sunday potluck and a weekly campfire on Tuesdays. Despite our busy schedules and other events, many of us acknowledged the value and importance of getting together, with the work-exchange folks and guests, to talk story and deal with issues. Ironically, when more of our members arrived in the wintertime, weekly meetings often got superseded by party or vacation plans.

Expect and accept unequal participation.

Structure is important in any organization but participation is what determines effectiveness. Even though our original membership of 12 eventually increased to 35, we have never had more than six members living full-time on our land at any one time, for various reasons, and sometimes I was the only resident member.

While major decisions are made at our annual general meetings and attendance has varied from 12 to 22 members, we have had severe limitations on the possibilities for full participation in ongoing decision making. As technology has improved, we have used newsletters, telephone conference calls, and emails. However, without a clearly approved process and with a membership geographically dispersed across several countries and half a dozen time zones, it has worked only marginally for improving communication, but not much for decision making or for involvement.

The Bellyacres experiment has taught me to not expect everyone to be equally involved or to contribute the same amount of work. This fact of community life is not easy to accept but is necessary. It is also cruelly ironic that members who are only peripherally involved and contributing very little in work still often demand a full role in decision making.

From my two stays on kibbutzim in 1969 and 1973, I was introduced to the socialist concept "to everyone according to their needs and from everyone according to their abilities" and it fit my humanitarian ideals. As I brought together our collective, I tried to factor in the wisdom of a kibbutz founding member who told me that despite their egalitarian principles, when the annual elections of officers happened, the same 20 people always volunteered. This seems to be the situation in almost every community and inevitably results in power being concentrated within a small group.

Be honest and realistic about leadership.

Our transient membership and lack of resident members often resulted in decisions being made by me or just a few individuals out of necessity. As the founder, I was always the public face of the organization and originally accepted

responsibility for the legal, financial, and physical-reality development of Bellyacres.

Personally, I have never desired to amass power and control, yet I found myself constantly playing the role of leader by necessity. I only ever wanted this to be temporary until other members began to take on more responsibility and become more involved in activities that moved us along. Unfortunately, this was not our reality and what I discovered instead was a serious case of Founders' Syndrome, which came to a head in 2014 and contributed to me deciding to leave.

My studies of sustainable community development show that most have a hierarchical organization with a spiritual guru, a charismatic leader, or a group of "elders." Secular egalitarian communities seem to have the greatest difficulty in staying together after the initial idealistic euphoria wears off. I know of a very few (Twin Oaks, Sandhill, East Wind, The Farm) that have survived more than 25 years, outlasting their founders and developing identities not dependent on particular personalities. The development of an egalitarian structure of governance is a huge challenge facing communities and one that requires commitment, training, and consultation with experts if it is to succeed smoothly. Regretfully, while our ecovillage still exists after 30 years, it did none of these and is now paying the price.

Share a common vision regarding children.

From our beginning, we were very divided about the desire to include children in our community and this has plagued us still today. During my two kibbutz visits and my workers' collective experience, I was impressed that children were always a big part of the ideology and it led to my belief that children are an essential part of any sustainable community.

Unfortunately, when I gathered the founding members of Bellyacres, we never discussed this until after we'd started our settlement. A major factor I had seriously overlooked was that all my new partners were bohemians. They were in a phase in their lives where they believed kids would severely threaten their freedom to party hearty and to travel to the streets of busking cities worldwide.

My naiveté on this subject was clearly expressed one evening over dinner at our first encampment. A friend was visiting us with his girlfriend and a newborn baby. This little addition to our party was prone to get a little restless in the night and her sweet shrill cries cut through the jungle air. We had some late-night party people who expected to get a deep and undisturbed sleep when they eventually crashed. When we went around the circle, one by one everyone said how kids didn't belong here and that was not what they signed up for.

How different this perspective was to mine—I looked around and reckoned that many of these same people would have their own kids in a few years and attitudes would change. I was only partly right on this and never expected that it would be the childless partners who'd end up living at Bellyacres while members with families would choose the better education and work opportunities of the mainland US or Europe.

I thought we failed really badly by never having an official policy regarding children. Over the years, I offered single-family accommodations, counseling, transport, and free circus classes for loads of kids. But when parents had expectations of finding a community with compassion that embraced their kids by providing supportive aunties and uncles and surrogate parents, they were generally very disappointed by many members' responses. In most cases, there was a "clear hands-off approach," coupled with the feeling that they were just "not a kids person," or having worked entertaining kids

for many years had an attitude of "I need to take a break while I'm on holiday." I felt very differently, I was not on holiday, this was my permanent home and I wanted to have loads of happy, thriving kids around.

In all my years at Bellyacres, this issue alone caused me the most grief. My own daughter lived there from birth but never established anything close to the connection that occurs in blood families with grandparents, aunts, uncles, and cousins sending birthday cards, Christmas presents, and checking in regularly about school grades, favorite hobbies, and bad colds. There are very few long-lasting bonding relationships between the different generations at Bellyacres, and sadly when the opportunity has existed the general membership has not embraced it.

Establish a clear pet policy.

Pet ownership has been another reoccurring issue for us, with the understanding that owners are responsible for pets' behavior and some do a better job than others. Because of repeated bad experiences with neighbors' unruly dogs roaming our land, pooping, killing our chickens, and even a goat, we adopted a "no dogs policy." There have been controversial exceptions and some very heated debates regarding members who had dogs or renters who wanted to bring dogs. Not all dogs are alike and our decisions about which dogs and owners are acceptable have been erratic and often not rational and have had some severe negative effects on residents' relationships.

Cats tend to be more benign, at least as far as humans go (impacts on wildlife are a different matter); however, they can be unbearable at times with wild cat fights and raids on neighbors' homes for food, usually at night. Sometimes, with a cat population close to exceeding the number of residents, we've had to place household limits and insist on neutering. Not every owner willingly ac-

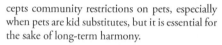

cepts community restrictions on pets, especially when pets are kid substitutes, but it is essential for the sake of long-term harmony.

Establish a clear drugs policy.

Drug policy is often a defining issue in the membership of a community and my understanding is that the longest-lasting spiritual communities are very restrictive. Being renowned for our amazing parties, we have had no rules and a very liberal attitude to drug use and our members have indulged, mostly very responsibly and without adverse consequences.

Drug use, both legal and illegal, is generally considered a personal and private issue; but, where communities do not create clear standards and boundaries, major problems can arise. We had to impose strict rules regarding the cultivation of illegal cannabis on our land until medical marijuana permits became an option. After a particularly bad experience, we insisted that illegal drugs are not stored in our communal spaces.

We have attempted to establish a culture of responsible drug use and have mostly succeeded given that Bellyacres is located in one of the marijuana capitals of the country and our modern society accepts tobacco addiction and alcoholism as socially acceptable. We adopted no-smoking zones and have taken car keys away from inebriated residents and guests wanting to drive. Apart from this, we have been extremely tolerant of drug use and some abuse. This could have been an issue we dealt with better when recruiting members, but people's habits change over time so having a clear policy could really help reduce later issues.

Late in our development, I learned to ask work-exchange folks and interns if they were on or had been on any medications for mental health issues. Having lived for three years with one of our founding members going through severe manic depressive episodes due to a bipolar condition, I learned how crucial medication can be for stabilizing health. If answered honestly, this question enabled us to be more supportive and understanding when living with anyone mentally challenged. It's very hard to enforce responsible medication practices but since we all are impacted, it is a respectful request to make.

Be prepared to deal with mental illness, depression, and withdrawal.

These problems affect many in our society at some point in their lives and will inevitably impact your community. After years attempting to support our bipolar member, we made one of the hardest of our group decisions and revoked his membership because we believed he would get better treatment and support if he moved back to North Carolina. It was a huge lesson in tough love but we were right because he regained control of his life and now appreciates that we were caring for him the best way we could.

Choose a location that suits your lifestyle.

Where your community is located will seriously affect your healthy development so think ahead and get a good picture of how your neighborhood will look 30 years into the future. You will need to have neighbors who accept you.

We bought 11 acres of Hawaiian jungle for $55,000 in an area where unpermitted structures and squatting were common practices. Our land was close to a beach, warm ponds, and lava adventures. It had lots of useful trees, a great climate, and adequate rainfall to fill catchment water tanks. It was also adjacent to an undeveloped subdivision with 933 lots selling for less than $5,000 and we envisioned our friends buying many of them and expanding our community.

We chose to live with the predictable mosquitoes and jungle critters, droughts, tropical storms, rocky terrain, etc. What we did not anticipate were new issues like climate change, fire ants, rat lung worm disease, invasive tree overwhelm, discretionary permitting enforcement by County and State agencies, and the build-out of three neighborhood subdivisions which brought a huge influx of people, including many supporters of our community development programs, but also a few opponents who managed to successfully impose a tyranny of the minority.

In our idealistic early days at Bellyacres, we studied and dreamt of living off the land. We put a great deal of energy, money, and other resources into a variety of agricultural projects that, for one reason or another, were incompatible with our membership, other projects, or the suitability of our environment and land. We had to constantly make compromises and adjust our perception of what was possible given our resources and location. Trial and error has its price.

I discovered over time that a subtropical jungle and climate was not the most conducive place to live as we grew older. Perceiving ourselves as eco-warriors, we originally removed a minimum of trees to accommodate our basic needs. Eventually we realized that air and light and distance from bugs and creeping foliage was essential for our healthy living. Removing more trees around houses also became a safety issue and a necessity to prevent leaves contaminating catchment water systems. If we had originally made a lot more clearings and cut down more trees we would have saved ourselves the huge amounts of work required later. The jungle never sleeps or takes a vacation!

In striving for a high level of sustainable living, we also committed ourselves to lots more hard work with off-grid power, catchment water, and organic farming, and are only now realizing how challenging this is for our aging membership.

Learn to love the food that loves to grow where you live.

While our group officially committed to increasing our level of sustainability, I'm not sure if members understood the implications of this. In terms of food, my view was that we should be growing locally appropriate foods that were suited to our subtropical climate. Having lived in the tropics for over 40 years, I found it easy and preferable for my staple foods to be breadfruit, avocados, bananas, citrus, and exotic fruits, etc. I estimated that 70-80 percent of my food was grown on the island.

By comparison, my partners preferred to maintain their temperate-climate diet and struggled to grow lettuce, spinach, tomatoes, and cucumbers, etc. in our greenhouse. While the crops I was eating were drought-resistant and required virtually no maintenance, the greenhouse crops need watering twice daily by hand. This practice placed a huge burden on our labor pool when other work needed to be done and could have been more efficiently resolved by members' eating the food that grew easily on our land and/or purchasing temperate crops from our weekly farmers' market.

Define what sustainable living means to your community.

In my view, sustainable living goes far beyond permaculture systems, organic gardens, fruit trees, and animal husbandry. It has to include membership, community service, buildings, transport, recycling, energy, and more.

Wherever you live, raise worms and rebuild your soil, for continuum.

Living on lava rock, I was very motivated to experiment with soil production and eventually learned the importance of earthworms. Aristotle called them "the intestines of the earth," Charles Darwin wrote a whole book about them, and for the organic gardener, they are the single most important element in the program of building a rich, healthy soil. Using manure from our two horses to feed the worms, I was able to produce enough worm castings and worm tea to feed all our crops without needing to purchase any imported fertilizers for the last seven years I lived there.

Have a clear exit strategy.

This is most critical for community members who invest large amounts of time and energy. Our original exit strategy did not take this into account and I now realize it needed to be clearer and more detailed to allow for the changes in people's relationships, values, and beliefs that inevitably happen over time. Many communities fold because they cannot survive the impact of founding members' pulling out and needing to get repaid. I ensured the future for Bellyacres by buying the land outright and putting it into a land trust. However, my own future has now been compromised due to complications in selling the two houses I own on the land.

Stay legal if you want an easy ride.

If you want to challenge laws and bring changes, be prepared. Recruit a good lawyer as a member. For details on this issue, see my article in Communities #168 (Fall 2015), "My Struggle to Legalize Sustainable Living."

I'm presently working on a book entitled *My Sustainable Community Experience: 27 Years Living with Jugglers in the Jungle*. It's an autobiography with lots of juicy personal stories that I hope will serve to make the community experience relevant, important, and more successful for present and future communitarians.

Here's a sampling of a few additional lessons from the book:

Be prepared to deal with disasters by keeping your whole group committed to staying united.

Start by building an amazing communal kitchen–it's your most important structure.

Do not try to live out of sight of your community members.

Do not build anything temporary.

Don't share cars, houses, or partners.

Celebrate the financial successes of other members.

Don't let the bookkeeper run your organization.

Be open to different spiritual practices and beliefs.

Develop rituals for meals, meetings, and celebrations.

Have group projects.

Be patient with those who work slower or work less than you.

Don't permit passivity and non-participation.

Review your group vision every three to five years and get 100 percent buy-in.

Post bylaws, rules, minutes of meetings, vision, and community events prominently.

Recruit a community archivist.

Have a clear enforcement policy.

Celebrate weddings, births, birthdays, etc. together.

Give priority to your community members over other outside friends.

Be hospitable–invite guests.

Identify the talents and weaknesses of your fellow members.

Don't assume smart people have learned basic life skills.

Have flexibility, compassion, and forgiveness. Be human.

Do not expect people to be perfect all the time.

If you want community longevity, build a cemetery.

Have a sense of humor and always remember this old English saying: "There's nought as queer as folks."

In 1987 Graham Ellis founded Bellyacres Artistic Ecovillage on a 10 acre jungle lot with a vision to experiment with sustainable community living practices. By 2007 Graham had raised $500,000 to build the Seaview Performance Arts Center for Education (S.P.A.C.E.), which in 2010 was described as "perhaps the most sustainable community center in the USA." His article "My Struggle to Legalize Sustainable Living" appeared in Communities #168, Fall 2015, and he is currently writing a book, My Sustainable Community Experience: 27 Years Living with Jugglers in the Jungle. *As we prepared this issue for press, we learned that Graham was deported from the US on July 19, 2017 for an expired visa under the stricter immigration enforcement protocols put in place by the Trump administration. He, his wife, and their five children had already been planning to relocate later this year to the UK, where he hopes to serve as a community consultant—but uncertainty remains about when or if the rest of his family will be granted the visas necessary to join him. See www.civilbeat.org/2017/06/a-big-island-juggler-with-leukemia-faces-deportation.*

My Advice to Others
Planning to Start an Ecovillage, Revisited

By Lois Arkin

*T*his advice was originally prepared for the book Eco-Villages and Sustainable Communities: A Report for Gaia Trust *by the Context Institute (1991), Robert and Diane Gilman. The 1991 version was written when I had been engaged in Los Angeles Eco-Village (LAEV) planning processes for about four years, but had not yet begun LAEV on-the-ground in our current location, nor was there an intentional community at that point. Now, after almost 25 years of living in the fully functioning, intensely urban LAEV intentional community, at times up to 40 persons, here are the original 10 pieces of advice from 1991 and how I refined the advice in 2005, again in 2011, and most recently in 2017.*

1. Start with people. Ultimately, land and buildings are always accessible to a group of people who have a common vision and commitment.

2005 Refinement: A strong vision, good planning, groundedness, and perseverance are the four qualities that will generally get you what you need and want, eventually.

2011 Refinement: It takes some of us longer than others.

2017 Refinement: Be clear at the front end about the personal qualities and habits you want your initial members to have. They will be the foundation for the emerging culture of your community. If you choose carelessly, be prepared for lots of drama and delays, if your community survives at all.

2. Develop a core group of people who have some kind of existing track record. If you don't have one, find those who do and sell them on your vision.

2005 Refinement: Make sure you get a congenial core group of folks with complementary skills and knowledge who can make a five-year commitment to one another. Then learn to care deeply for one another in relation to the land where you want to work, in relation to the problems with the life support systems in your chosen bioregion, and in relation to the issues in your local political jurisdiction..

2011 Refinement: Learn early how to pick and choose your battles with one another, and do not tolerate unresolved negative conflicts; agree to disagree and love each other anyway.

2017 Refinement: People and their priorities change. Much as those initial members may have contributed in the start-up phase, most of them will leave before the ecovillage is significantly manifested. Make sure succeeding members in those early years share your start-up group's vision and core values and have needed knowledge and skills to contribute or passion for learning them.

3. Don't be in a hurry, but do be persistent and persevering. We have been very fortunate in focusing on a site that has not been immediately available to us. It's given us the time to develop the culture of the Design Team, develop political and community support, enhance our track record, and attract resources for moving forward. Of course, for a group that already has all that together, this advice is not applicable.

2005 Refinement: It's about process as much as place. So get your team geographically contiguous as quickly as practical, but don't worry about it being your final location. The experience of interactive processes working on making the connections between and among the ecological, economic, and social systems of your community can go with you wherever you ultimately settle.

2011 Refinement: In the world we live in today, it is critical not to be too attached to place, but to be fully engaged with place wherever we are. The world-changing work we are engaged in and the pace at which the earth herself is changing may require us to relocate from time to time.

2017 Refinement: Many neighborhoods today are advancing in their sustainable practices through their growing associations with the Transition Town Movement, the Cool Blocks Movement, TimeBanking, or a few neighborhood leaders doing local outreach and just tagging themselves as a "Sustainable" or "Resilient" community project. So, don't be attached to the word "ecovillage." Congratulations if a neighborhood becomes sustainable or an ecovillage through the accident of residential choices and doing the work where you're at!

4. Do not compromise your vision to acquire funding.

2005 Refinement: Look for creative ways to solve potential funding problems that advance your vision.

2011 Refinement: Often, the less money you have the more creative you are. Our movement is about doing more with less. Brag about it a lot.

2017 Refinement: Develop your constituency before, during, and after your project has been manifested. Communicate with them often. Lots of people want to support your project even if they have no need or interest in living in your community.

5. Keep educating all members of the group on the overview. Provide opportunities for members to learn in informal and exciting ways about all the major systems and sub-systems of an ecovillage: social, economic, ecological.

2005 Refinement: Make the time to do it. Everyone won't have the same understanding, no matter what you do, but they'll bring fresh energy and help the founding core group to see things in new ways too.

2011 Refinement: Institute story-telling as early as possible. You don't have to wait 10 years to share memories. Begin your own rituals as early as possible. Let them flourish.

2017 Refinement: A lot of story-telling will happen informally in the social context of living together. But don't depend on that. Incorporate

Kids on LAEV tour hug our 106-year-old sycamore tree.

43

Goal is facilitating widespread sustainability consciousness.

story-telling into your celebrations: birthdays, anniversaries, solstices, equinoxes. These more formal occasions are an opportunity to correct inaccuracies too.

6. Let your integrity combined with your pragmatism be your guide. Don't be immobilized by ideology.

2005 Refinement: Those who don't agree with the founding vision or have not taken the time to understand it, but enjoy the fruits of the labor of the founders, may try to convince others that you are inflexible, a control freak, attached, stuck in your ways, crazy, evil, and worse. Stay strong, focused, loving, and forgiving in the path of these attacks. But at any point that the shoe really fits, be willing to recognize it, and change your ways. Work on improving your selection process to secure diversity with emotional maturity.

2011 Refinement: Learn to let go when the time is right. What it develops into may be very different than what you originally imagined, but you'll have changed too.

2017 Refinement: Yes, now it's been 25 years. At 80, I've grown old and have less energy too. I'm ready to simply admit that I've done the best I could in the time and place that this L.A. Eco-Village has happened, and it's doing just fine. Now my organization has just acquired an adjacent property that will probably take another 10 years to develop. So, that could extend my life and add fresh excitement and energy to the existing L.A. Eco-Village community. Footnote: an ecovillage is never finished; like an eco-system, it's fluid and ever changing.

7. Don't be attached to the project or being number 1. Facilitating widespread sustainability consciousness is the goal; "ecovillage" is a method of helping people get there.

2005 Refinement: Form coalitions with groups as they come on-line advocating for, teaching, demonstrating what you have been working on for years. Or once the ecovillage ideas "catch on" in your bioregion, go to the next phase of sustainability, e.g., developing curriculum for local schools, creating your own school, engaging in more public advocacy, writing the zoning codes, giving public talks, civic engagement, running for public office, etc.

2011 Refinement: ...unless you just want to retire to the garden. You've earned it!

2017: Refinement: If you stick with it long enough, all those "e.g.,"s will come to fruition and more!

8. Do not use or exploit guilt to motivate people, but recognize that many people depend on guilt for their own self-motivation. Help people transcend guilt by keeping focused on the vision. Keep your doors open to fresh and exciting energy. Generate excitement through art, parties, issues-oriented dialogue, etc.

2005 Refinement: Show a lot of appreciation for what others do to generate excitement.

2011 Refinement: Help others to overcome this tendency as well. Learn, teach, use an effective feedback method such as nonviolent communication.

2017 Refinement: In the intensely urban area we function in, and the growing disaster on the planet, everyone is over-extended, doing too much, not always stopping to smell the roses or engage in self-care. Become a hugger! Thirteen hugs a day may be the answer to a healthier you, and, thus, a healthier planet.

9. Keep borrowing from others; always credit when you can, but if there is not space or time or memory, trust our sustainability networks to know that you are trying to act on behalf of all of us.

2005 Refinement: Recognize others at every opportunity.

2011 Refinement: ...even when they don't really deserve it. Hopefully, they'll be inspired to rise to their publicity.

2017 Refinement: Generally, you can accomplish anything you want to in life, if you don't care who gets the credit!

10. Be gracious, maintain your sense of humor, keep people on track, forgive people from your heart; we're all doing the best we can; keep the air cleared; work at manifesting the values in the processes that you want to live with.

2005 Refinement: Attend to your own health first.

2011 Refinement: Attend to your own health first.

2017 Refinement: Attend to your own health first. We need each other to live as long and productively as we can. ❧

Contact Los Angeles Eco-Village cofounder Lois Arkin at crsp@igc.org; www.laecovillage.org.

Lois meets with Los Angeles Mayor Eric Garcetti to share sustainable urban living ideas.

Group photo of L.A. Eco-Village community.

Photos courtesy of Helene Raisin

Shares resources - land, labor, income

Creating Cooperative Culture BY MATTHEW CULLEN

ESTABLISHING A COMMUNITY:
Perspectives from the FEC

The Federation of Egalitarian Communities is an organization that exists to help communities who want to create a lifestyle based on equality, cooperation, and harmony with the earth. At our most recent annual Assembly, delegates from the seven FEC communities and three newer communities in dialog with the FEC found ourselves discussing a question we're happy to be faced with: how do we as an organization give more help to forming groups that want to become new communities?

In recent years, the number of new groups who want to form an intentional income-sharing community (and of older groups who want to reorganize into something more in line with the FEC model) has exploded. The established FEC communities couldn't be more pleased by this, and have offered energetic and widespread support to several new communities.

We brainstormed about ways in which new groups can make themselves into established, functioning communities. We identified three basic categories of processes that need to happen simultaneously: planning, building power, and establishing credibility. As often happens in community, all of the recommendations that follow should be understood to be happening all at once. These sections don't represent a sequential roadmap, but an amalgam of what needs to be going on in a coalescing community. In fact, doing just about any of these things should make doing almost all of the other things easier.

The FEC can be thought of as the "orthodox" communities within the wider movement: our ideals regarding sharing are much more strict than most other types of groups in the communities movement. The assembled delegates created this framework for FEC-type communities (see sidebar) who want to share power and income as equally as is practicable. However, almost all of what follows could be applied to any group that wants to form a successful community.

Planning

Not surprisingly, a good plan is an essential early step to starting a community. Any number of individuals involved can have any number of different ideas about exactly what they want the new community to be. In order for a group of individuals to come together and form a cohesive whole, it is first (and perhaps most) critical that they identify common purposes. I have never met the group in which all individuals want exactly the same thing in their community. Keeping that in mind, the importance of identifying goals, visions, and values that are important to all or most of the participants is hard to overstate.

Numerous and specific conversations about vision should happen before a group embarks on its journey toward a functioning community. One way this prefiguration process might best be approached is to ask each group member to "imagine what the life you want to *Vision* have is going to be." Try to focus on accentuating commonalities in your respective dreams that you can build on together, but don't just skip over major differences. If members have vastly different conceptions of what ideals and practices are important to the community, this will be a constant source of conflict later on.

Building Power

The next kind of process that is critical in a new community is finding a way to get building power: the hands, money, and infrastructure creation necessary to make the community a physical reality.

Hopefully, if you have a group that is interested in forming a community, then you already have some willing hands prepared to get themselves dirty. Hands are also often the easiest help for a new community to get. If you can spread your name and your mission ideas out into the wider world, you may be surprised at the good will prepared to manifest itself in the form of a hard day's work, from a recent stranger, for free. It is also much easier to make this happen if you're farther along in the establishing credibility processes discussed below.

Having land (or a house) and places for people to live is the next area of building power necessary, and it goes arm in arm with money. Many new communities are faced with the conundrum that you can't get land without money, and it's hard to get people to

(continued on p. 78)

45

ESTABLISHING A COMMUNITY: PERSPECTIVES FROM THE FEC

(continued from p. 80)

invest in a forming community that doesn't provide members with a place to live, and hence the community can't get enough income-generating hands on deck to establish critical mass. Almost all new communities make it past this hurdle only through the generosity of others or the sweat and sacrifice of true believers who are willing to work for years in order to make their ideal community a physical reality.

Building power is one of the areas in which the FEC has done its best work to help establish new communities. Members of established FEC communities are often willing to expend large chunks of their time and expertise to help the movement grow. The FEC's expansion fund has also been able to provide loans to thoroughly vetted groups that are in line with the FEC's values. These loans have allowed that first critical beginning in a physical space to happen for more than one community.

Establishing Credibility

This brings us to perhaps the trickiest field of community establishment: how to create credibility, both internally and with the outside world. This aspect is twofold: members (and especially new members) have to believe in the integrity of what they're bending their efforts toward, and the community must be sufficiently established, legally and on paper, to enable itself to do business and relate to the greater society of laws that it must necessarily be surrounded by.

Member security is largely a practical assurance of ideological consistency. If the community is to attract more members (and retain current ones), then it must create some sort of structure that ensures members that the community will live up to its stated principles. Having clearly written agreements of what those principles are is a great first step.

Who will own common property? How will income be shared? What does the community provide for its members? What are members expected to contribute to community, in terms of both labor and income/property? How will decisions be made? How will records of decisions and finances be kept? If a community is expecting an in-

coming member to jump out of the mainstream and into communal life, then the community needs to provide clear answers to these questions, and assure incoming members that all the agreements discussed or hinted at above are on the level.

One great way to do this, especially if your group is income- and property-sharing, is to establish a corporate framework. Creating a corporation that holds the community's property and describes the community's decision-making process is a great way to safeguard principles and interests of both the members and the community itself. Bylaws can clearly spell out what kind of community the group intends to create; at the same time they give potential recruits a clear idea of what they're getting into and allow the security afforded by the expectation that written agreements are likely to be followed.

For new and old members to feel comfortable throwing their lives into their new home, two things need to be abundantly clear: how decisions are made, and how money is handled. It is also important to clearly spell out any specific agreements if you intend them to be integral characteristics of your community. If your group is "fossil fuel free," create a document that spells out precisely what that means in practical terms, and maybe even an explanation of how such a rule's integrity will be guaranteed (meaning how you intend to ensure it doesn't just fall by the wayside).

Establishing some sort of legal identity also creates a context for the community to relate to the outside world. Who pays your utility bills? What's the common bank account held as? How do you present your organization to the "locals"? Having a ready-made answer of "Your Community, Inc." is easily more comprehensible to middle Americans than a long explanation that always seems to have to include the word "commune." The phrase "cooperatively owned" comes in handy when trying to wrap the head of, say, a truck driver around exactly what it is he's delivering stuff to. And, most especially if your community has a common business, it often transforms the new community in the area from potentially dangerous hippie radicals into that nice group of people with a farm and a cottage industry (at least in the eyes of most Americans). Most community-minded people are generally anti-corporation, but by incorporating, a community is able to take advantage of the public respectability that it lends and use it to gain the acceptance it needs to relate to its neighbors.

Another advantage to establishing credibility through clear agreements and legal frame-

work is that it helps to prevent blowback and radical change from new members. If a community is to actually become something like the community it initially sets out to be, it has to find a way to create some sort of "cultural buy-in" among new members. If you're looking to create a certain type of culture, you need to find a way to communicate that subtly, and to adapt people into that culture in a way that allows them to feel included and not controlled. It helps to accept that not everyone who wants (or thinks they want) to come to community will share the community's values. Some people just aren't going to fit.

For the people who do fit, it's also important to create a dynamic whereby they believe they can take on responsibility and have a positive impact on the community. This inevitably means accepting new and different opinions. Doing so is important in keeping the community a vital organization, but it's also important to create a culture that maintains its core values, and can assimilate new members without over-constraining their energy and new ideas.

At the same time, a community isn't really a community if it doesn't have a collective sense of togetherness, a real belief that the community is a whole which will take care of its individuals and vice versa. This is probably the most important sense in which a community is a community, and is (for me, anyway) the result toward which all the legal, monetary, and communicative processes bend themselves. A community becomes a Community when it can credibly establish a sense of whole togetherness, when members can buy into an "all for one and one for all" mindset without having to try too hard.

• • •

Let's face it: starting a new intentional community is hard. It's also one of the most worthwhile things you can do with your life in this modern mess we're in. Hopefully some of the ideas presented here were helpful to anyone reading this who might try their hand at community building (even if they're useful only because they help you to realize that you reject them entirely). And don't forget that there are organizations out there like the Federation of Egalitarian Communities whose purpose it is to try to make this difficult process easier.

Matthew Cullen has lived in FEC communities for seven years. He currently lives at Sapling Community in Louisa, Virginia.

Principles of the FEC

The Federation of Egalitarian Communities is a network of communal groups spread across North America. We range in size and emphasis from small agricultural homesteads to village-like communities to urban group houses.

Each of the FEC communities:
1. Holds its land, labor, income, and other resources in common.

2. Assumes responsibility for the needs of its members, receiving the products of their labor and distributing these and all other goods equally, or according to need.

3. Practices nonviolence.

4. Uses a form of decision making in which members have an equal opportunity to participate, either through consensus, direct vote, or right of appeal or overrule.

5. Actively works to establish the equality of all people and does not permit discrimination on the basis of race, class, creed, ethnic origin, age, sex, sexual orientation, or gender identity.

6. Acts to conserve natural resources for present and future generations while striving to continually improve ecological awareness and practice.

7. Creates processes for group communication and participation and provides an environment which supports people's development.
—thefec.org

Consider the 501(d)

If your group intends to be an FEC-type community, or at least will share income and have a common treasury, then I always recommend incorporating as a 501(d) according to IRS categorization. This is a category created by good ol' Uncle Sam to suit the Shakers and similar religious groups. It fits more income-sharing communities than one might immediately assume. Is your group formally committed to nonviolence or providing for all the needs of its members? In the eyes of the law, you've got a religious precept. It often helps to adopt a "statement of faith" with your bylaws if you're going this route, but most communal statements of faith I've seen don't mention deities and really only restate the more ethereal of the group's principles (nonviolence, sharing, harmony with the earth, creating togetherness, the veneration of a Bob Marley tapestry, whatever it is you're into).
—M.C.

Photos courtesy of Matthew Cullen

LEGAL STRUCTURES FOR
Intentional Communities in
the United States

By Diana Leafe Christian, Dave Henson, Allen Butcher, and Albert Bates

*E*very forming community makes crucial decisions about whether and how it may comply with various local, state, and federal laws and regulations, and which legal entity, or several entities, it will use to co-own land, run educational programs, and/or manage any community-owned businesses—all of which affects the group's relation to the wider public. This article, excerpted from the new 7th edition of the Communities Directory, explores this issue. It was substantially revised and updated by Diana Leafe Christian from previous versions of this Directory article, and shortened slightly for this issue of COMMUNITIES.

"Thank you very much, but your advice really doesn't apply to us," wrote a community I'll call Buckeye Farm to their lawyer. He had just reviewed their proposed legal plan for co-owning their 98 acres of farmland and their new-member joining document.

The lawyer cautioned against their proposed plan, saying it wasn't legally sound and could be considered fraudulent if anyone took them to court. But the community considered this advice irrelevant because, for them, Buckeye's spiritual and ecological intentions, values, and mission morally superseded any laws of mainstream culture. They executed their legal-financial plan.

A decade later an incoming member's questions triggered a second look at these issues, and they hired another lawyer. He concluded members were seriously vulnerable legally and financially, and to protect their community from potential disaster they should change their legal arrangements significantly. They learned, for example, that with their current legal arrangement, if a member were sued for any reason, lost the suit, and couldn't pay damages or legal costs, the court could compel the sale of the person's assets. And because they all owned all of the property, this could include the forced sale of all or part of the property to pay the money owed. Their financial-legal structure also made them subject to local subdivision regulations—which, if enforced, would require two to three million dollars of road-paving costs, which they couldn't possibly afford. Lastly, and even worse, their financial document for new members promised rights in the land that, it turns out, were not true, and so if taken to court, the document would most likely be declared as fraudulent. Once they absorbed this news—with members in various states of shock, incredulity, confusion—they stopped accepting new members until they could decide what to do. That was their first problem.

Their second problem was the fierce conflict and years of heartbreak arising when various community members couldn't agree on what to do, and some of their older, more countercultural members still didn't believe there was actually a problem. A new lawyer advised that all three problems could be resolved by re-apportioning land ownership among various smaller groups of members and creating several new legal entities to do this. But six years later things still weren't resolved. No members had been sued, the group hadn't been cited by local authorities for subdivision violation, and they hadn't been taken to court for fraud, yet they were still vulnerable to any of these potentially occurring at any time. While members had agreed on some aspects of implementing the lawyer's recommended legal changes, with no new members for six years—and some departing in frustration—Buckeye had no new capital and far less annual income from remaining members with which to pay mounting legal expenses.

The Seven Steps Every Community Needs to Follow

Buckeye could have avoided its legal-financial vulnerabilities and years of conflict if they'd taken seven simple steps at the beginning. For example, what if the founders and early members had done what newly forming communities *need* to do—and what your community should do:

(1) Clearly understand the community is embedded within and subject to local, state, and federal laws and regulations.

(2) Know what these laws and regulations are, how they will affect your community over time, and what the risks may be if you don't comply with them. These include federal tax requirements; federal laws regarding illegal substance use, firearms, and other issues; federal and state laws regarding the rights and responsibilities of your chosen legal entities; annual legal-entity reporting

requirements with the state, and state health department and environmental quality regulations; county subdivision regulations, zoning regulations, building codes, and property tax requirements.

(3) Orient all members, especially new ones, to these laws and regulations.

(4) Make a well-informed, conscious decision to either comply or not comply with the laws and regulations, or comply with some but not others.

(5) If you decide not to comply with some laws, you are willing to take the risks. You *fully inform all potential members of these risks*. New people get full disclosure.

(6) Orient all members, especially new ones, to the legal entity(ies) your community uses and the benefits, responsibilities, and challenges of these entities.

(7) Orient people especially to liability issues, so everyone understands the degree of liability protection the community does and does not offer its members.

Fortunately, many community founders do understand the need to understand the law and design their projects to be legally sustainable. See, for example, the combined multiple legal entities of Occidental Arts and Ecology Center (OAEC), Los Angeles Eco-Village, Mariposa Grove, and EcoVillage at Ithaca, below.

What's a "Legal Entity"?

A legal entity is a recognized set of rights, protections, and requirements created and regulated by each state for activities such as owning property, conducting a for-profit business or providing a nonprofit service, or investing money in stocks and securities. A legal entity confers the same rights that an individual person has and can function as an individual person functions. A legal entity is able to buy and sell assets—for example, it can buy your community's property—and enter into business contracts, such as hiring contractors and other building professionals, Permaculture designers, workshop trainers for your community, and so on.

In the US, legal entities have been created for businesses and nonprofit organizations, for securities and stock ventures, and for co-owning real estate. Most intentional communities use business and nonprofit legal entities even though none of these exactly fits how most intentional communities function. The five most commonly used legal entities used by intentional communities in the US are homeowners associations, condominium associations, housing cooperatives (which can be used for land as well as buildings and housing), limited liability companies (LLCs), and 501(c)3 nonprofits. Three others used occasionally (and examined more fully in the longer version of this article in the *Communities Directory*) are non-exempt nonprofits, 501(c)2 title-holding nonprofits, and, for income-sharing communities, 501(d) nonprofits.

HOA
Condo Assoc.
coops
LLC
501c-3
501(c)2
501(d)

Two real estate legal entities, Joint Tenancy and Tenants in Common, can be used to own shared property, but they have serious limitations and are not ideal for communities. (See "The Disadvantages of Joint Tenancy and Tenants in Common," p. 55.) 57

How a Legal Entity Benefits Your Community

(1) Limited liability protection. In addition to allowing your community to function like a person re buying and selling assets and entering into contracts, a legal entity also confers limited liability protection for community members. That is, community members (and any board members, officers, employees, or shareholders, if applicable) are not held *personally* responsible for any criminal wrongdoing or debts incurred by the community. No one's personal bank accounts or other assets are vulnerable to court-ordered fines. (It's called "limited" liability because in some cases when a court can show that a specific board member, officer, or employee knowingly caused their organization to break the law or take out a loan knowing there was no possibility of repayment, that person *is* held personally responsible—that is, liable. The person can be subject to criminal charges or court-ordered fines or punishment.

(2) Buying your community's property is easier. Having a legal entity will make the process of buying land easier. A seller, bank, or other lending institution will take a legal entity with tens of thousands in the bank and a brief credit history more seriously than it would take a collection of individuals trying to buy property together.

(3) Higher credibility. In doing business with others—buying liability insurance, pay-

Members of Rocky Corner Cohousing in Bethany, Connecticut set up an irrigation system during a work party on their 33 acres.

ing property taxes, getting a loan, hiring people for various services, and entering into business contracts with building contractors and other professionals—having a legal entity offers more credibility than if you were just a collection of individuals with no recognized business or nonprofit entity.

(4) Your community's intentions, values, mission, and major agreements are backed by law. Any agreements the group states in the documents of its legal entity (such as bylaws, articles of incorporation, an LLC's operating agreements, etc.), will be compatible with federal and state law, and thus legally enforceable. If a member violates one of these agreements and if the issue goes to court, your community will have the force of law behind it to induce the errant member to comply.

The same is true if your community is sued or cited for violating a law by a government authority. If a court has to consider your community's intentions, mission, and shared values in light of the lawsuit's claims or the government authorities' claims, having them written clearly in your legal documents will have far more credibility with a court or judge than if the only way you convey them is by your members testifying simply verbally.

(5) Land ownership is easier. Some legal entities are more compatible than others for the various ways you can own property together, such as: (a) everyone owns the property in common; (b) each household owns its own individual plot; or (c) each household owns its own individual plot and everyone owns the rest. Whichever entity you use, it allows your group to co-own property in a more secure and sustainable way than if just one member owned it, or if multiple members' names were on the deed, which unfortunately requires officially revising and re-registering the deed when anyone joins or leaves.

(6) Reduced taxes. If you use any legal entity other than a 501(c)3 nonprofit, the federal and state governments will tax your community's income (and the county will require property taxes). Thus you can choose a legal entity that saves the most taxes relative to your community's particular circumstances.

For-Profit and Nonprofit Corporations

The word "corporation" is a term for a legal entity which, as noted, confers some of the same rights and functions on an organization as an individual person has. More importantly, a legal entity offers limited liability protection for community members as well as for board members, officers, and employees and/or shareholders, if you have them. (When a community uses a corporation legal entity either all community members function as board members or they annually elect people to serve on the board. In either case, everyone has limited liability protection.)

Before limited liability companies (LLCs) were available, some intentional communities used the for-profit Subchapter S corporation to own shared property, because it was specifically designed for small companies without shareholders. But nowadays most intentional communities use LLCs instead, because they offer much better benefits and none of the disadvantages of a Subchapter S corporation. (LLCs are not corporations, but offer the same advantages; please see below.)

Communities also use nonprofit corporations. These are designed for organizations that intend to benefit people but not earn a profit for owners or shareholders, and they offer exactly the same liability protection. Like for-profit corporations, nonprofits can earn income by selling products or offering services (as long as that income and how it's earned is connected to its purpose) and can hire employees.

Nonprofits offer various kinds of tax-exempt corporations. The 501(c)3 nonprofit, created for educational, charitable, scientific, literary, or religious reasons, can receive tax-deductible donations, as noted above, and is used by many communities. Other nonprofit corporations include 501(c)2 title-holding nonprofits and 501(d) religious and apostolic corporations (used by most income-sharing communities).

Homeowners associations and condominium associations use nonprofit legal entities.

Housing co-ops are nonprofits (though in some states housing co-ops have their own legal entity). Private land trusts and community land trusts which are created using nonprofit legal entities are not themselves specific nonprofit entities.

Corporations are created by registering with the state—filing a list of corporate officers and

Rocky Corner Cohousing members celebrate Winter Solstice on their land.

articles of incorporation, and receiving state approval. Nonprofit corporations are also created by registering with the state; after receiving state approval the organization may apply with the IRS for a specific federal tax exemption like those noted above.

Let's look at five of the most common kinds of legal entities used by intentional communities.

Limited Liability Companies (LLCs)

Limited liability companies (LLCs), which were created for small businesses, are not corporations but have many of the same advantages, including limited liability protection. They are created by filing an "operating agreement" with the state, and participants are called "members." A group qualifies to use an LLC if it intends to continue through time, has centralized management, and ownership in the LLC can be transferred easily. The LLC law in most states makes it pretty easy to comply with these qualifications.

An LLC's operating agreement can allocate different decision-making rights to different kinds of members (for example, if there are outside investors, community members can decide most day-to-day decisions but only investors can make decisions about expenditures over a certain dollar amount). In addition to individuals, members of an LLC can also be other legal entities, including partnerships, corporations, other LLCs, and/or trusts. Unlike a corporation, LLCs are not required to keep minutes, hold meetings, or make resolutions.

LLCs must distribute their earnings the same year the earnings are made. An LLC's income taxes are not paid by the LLC itself, but passed through to each member to pay in their individual income taxes (called "pass through" taxation).

Benefits: Limited liability protection; ease of setting up, using, and changing; banks and lending institutions are familiar with LLCs.

Challenges: None that we know of.

Examples: Sowing Circle Community in California, known as Occidental Arts and Ecology Center (OAEC), uses an LLC to own their land. Many forming cohousing communities start off owning their land and bank accounts with an LLC, and then switch to a homeowners association or condominium association after construction is finished.

> **A legal entity offers limited liability protection for community members, board members, officers, and employees and/or shareholders.**

Homeowners Associations and Condominium Associations

These are property ownership arrangements which allow people to own their own individual housing unit (or lot, house, or apartment) and, through the association, share ownership in the rest of the property.

A homeowners association (HOA) owns the common elements of the property—roads and footpaths, bridges, community buildings, common green areas (lawns, gardens, fields, woods), parking lots, children's playgrounds, ponds, etc.—and is obligated to manage and maintain everything. People own their own individual units, including the structural components (roof, walls, floor, foundation, etc.).

In a condominium association, everyone shares an undivided interest in all the common elements named above, as well as in the structural components of each individual dwelling (roof, walls, etc.). People own the air space inside their individual dwellings. A condominium association is obligated to maintain all the common elements.

While HOAs are most often used for planned housing developments with houses and lots, and condo associations are most often used for apartment buildings, this is not always the case. Sharingwood Cohousing in Washington State, for example, uses a condo association for its individual lots and houses.

Homeowners and condominium associations are not legal entities themselves, and are usually organized as nonprofits under IRS Section 528 tax designation. The 528 tax designation means that any funds collected for buying, developing, building, repairing, maintaining, and/or managing the property are not taxable if the association meets two tests. First, it must receive at least 60 percent of its gross income in a given tax year specifically to pay the above-named expenses (such as collecting membership fees, dues, assessments, etc.). Second, it must spend at least 90 percent of its gross income on these same expenses. If the association doesn't meet the 60 percent and 90 percent tax-exemption requirements in a given year, all their income that year is taxed at the corporate rate of 30 percent.

This tax-exemption may even include property owned privately by an individual community member on their own lot, such as a greenhouse, meeting space, retreat cabin, etc. But to qualify for this tax exemption, the greenhouse, etc. needs to meet these criteria: (1) it must affect the overall appearance of the community, (2) the owner must maintain it to community standards, (3) there must be an annual pro-rata assessment of all members to maintain it, and (4) it must be used only by association members and not rented out.

When intentional communities use HOAs or condo associations, they are either all members of the board of directors or they choose board members from among their members.

A downside is that homeowners associations and condominium associations cannot choose their members because of Federal Fair Housing laws. This means they must say "Yes" to any interested new people who can pay the purchase price and meet the terms of the sale _if property is offered on the open market_. They cannot say "No, thanks" to people who seem not to understand and support the community's purpose, values, and lifestyle, or who seem to offer red flags to the group, such as having substance addictions, a history of financial irresponsibility, or undesirable behaviors or attitudes. They can choose people for a waiting list, however, and use the list to draw from when a lot, house, apartment, or housing unit may be for sale, if the property is offered privately, not publicly.

> **Federal Fair Housing laws require HOAs and condo associations to say "Yes" to any interested new people who can pay the purchase price and meet the terms of sale.**
>
> *If property is offered on the open market.*

Or they can choose from a list + sell privately

Not all states have HOAs (e.g., Massachusetts doesn't) and condo associations.

Benefits: Limited liability protection; credibility with banks and lending institutions who will loan money and create mortgages for individual members; and tax breaks.

Challenges: The community can't choose their own members (unless they have a waiting list); not all states have both of these.

Examples: Most cohousing communities, including Sharingwood, as noted above, use either a homeowners association or condominium association to co-own their property after their initial development and construction phases.

Housing Cooperatives (Housing Co-ops)

A housing co-op owns the land and buildings. Its members don't own any part of the property, but own shares in the co-op and have a lease to a specific house, lot, apartment, or housing unit.

Housing cooperative law varies slightly from state to state. In general, however, members own shares in the housing cooperative, which, with a lease, gives them the right to live in a particular dwelling. And again, depending on the state, in general the number of shares the members buy is based on the current market value of the dwelling in which they intend to live. People pay a monthly fee—usually a prorated share of the co-op's monthly mortgage payment, if there is one, and property taxes, combined with a general fee for maintenance and repairs. The monthly fee is generally based on the number of shares each of the members holds, which is equivalent to the dollar value given to the member's individual dwelling.

While housing co-ops are legal in all states, some states have clear laws for housing co-ops and other states don't. Housing co-ops are usually organized as nonprofit corporations; however, some states have a special "cooperative corporation" category that is neither nonprofit or for-profit.

Most banks and lending institutions won't loan to a co-op or to co-op members because they don't want to own shares. This is because if the bank had to foreclose on the loan they would rather own tangible, sellable assets like a title to a house or housing unit. The National Co-op Bank was created to loan to housing co-ops and other kinds of co-ops, though it usually charges a higher rate of interest for loans than other banks do. There are several kinds of housing co-ops including student housing co-ops, senior housing co-ops, and limited equity housing co-ops.

Benefits: Limited liability protection; the community can choose its members.

Challenges: It can be difficult to get a bank loan and loans have higher interest rates than loans for HOAs and condo associations.

Examples: Walnut Street Co-op, a shared house in Oregon; Los Angeles Eco-Village; Miccosukee Land Co-op, which uses a housing co-op to own their 344 acres in rural Florida.

501(c)3 Nonprofits

Communities primarily use 501(c)3s to own land in order to preserve and protect the land from future real-estate speculation and development. This entity can also be used to receive tax-deductible donations and grants, which can come from corporations, individuals, government agencies, and/or private foundations.

Some communities use the same 501(c)3 or a different 501(c)3 to own and manage their educational programs as well.

A 501(c)3 nonprofit is created by registering as a nonprofit corporation with the state and applying to the IRS for the specific 501(c)3 tax designation. In order to qualify for receiving this tax status the group needs to either provide educational services to the public, offer charitable services to an indefinite class of people (rather than to specific individuals), combat negative social conditions, or provide a religious service to its members and/or the public. (This nonprofit is designed for charitable, religious, educational, scientific, or literary organizations. The IRS interprets "religious" liberally; this can include self-described spiritual beliefs or practices.)

As well as receiving tax-deductible donations, 501(c)3 nonprofits pay no income taxes, and are exempt from most forms of property tax. They are eligible for lower bulk mailing rates, and for some government loans and benefits. Communities that are also religious orders may also be exempt from Social Security, unemployment, and withholding taxes in some cases, if they qualify.

In order to receive a 501(c)3 nonprofit tax status, an intentional community must meet two IRS tests. It must be organized, as well as operated, exclusively for one or more of the above tax-exempt purposes. To determine the "organizational test," the IRS reviews the nonprofit's articles of incorporation and bylaws.

To determine the "operational test," the IRS conducts an audit of the nonprofit's activities in its first years of operation. Many communities have difficulty passing the operational test because of the requirement that no part of the net earnings may benefit any individual (except as compensation for labor or as a *bona fide* beneficiary of the charitable purpose). If the primary activity of the organization is to own land and operate businesses for the mutual benefit of its own community members, it fails the operational test.

Even if the community passes the operational test by virtue of other, more charitable, public benefits—running an educational center, providing an ambulance service, or making toys for handicapped children, for instance—it can still be taxed on the profits it makes apart from its strictly charitable activities.

These profits, called "unrelated business taxable income" (UBTI), have been a source of disaster and dissolution for some nonprofits because of the requirement to pay all back taxes and penalties arising from unrelated business taxable income, which can assume massive proportions in just a few years of unreported earnings. The IRS has the rule about unrelated business taxes in order to prevent tax-exempt nonprofits from unfairly competing with taxable entities, such as for-profit businesses, which may offer the same kinds of services or sell the same kinds of products. The IRS determines a nonprofit's unrelated business income in two ways: the destination of the income and the source of the income. If a community uses profits from bake sales to build a community fire station (presumably a one-time project related to the community's purpose), the IRS may consider that income "related" to its educational or charitable purpose and not tax it. If, however, the bake sales expand the general operations of the community, or pay the electric bill, the IRS may consider that "unrelated" income, and tax it.

A 501(c)3 nonprofit may not receive more than 20 percent of its annual income from passive sources, such as rents or investments. If the community has an educational purpose, it may not discriminate on the basis of race and must state this in its organizing documents. 501(c)3s are not allowed to participate in politics—they can't back a political campaign, attempt to influence legislation (other than on issues related to the 501(c)3 category), or publish political advocacies.

A serious downside is that if a 501(c)3 community disbands, it may not distribute any residual assets to community members. Rather, after payment of debts, all remaining assets must pass intact to another tax-exempt beneficiary such as another 501(c)3. In the early 2000s a relatively new community in South Carolina disbanded and gave its land to a church. Various members who'd spent their life savings paying the community's joining fee and building their house lost everything. This financial aspect of 501(c)3 nonprofits may dissuade some potential new members from joining a community that owns its land this way—those with significant assets or those who have children and who want to build a house and sink deep roots in the community. Some communities protect against this outcome by owning their land with a different legal entity (and protecting it from future speculation by other means), and creating a separate 501(c)3 nonprofit to run their community's educational

Chickens can be both alarming and engaging for children. Rocky Corner Cohousing will raise chickens on their farm.

53

programs. Occidental Arts and Ecology Center (OAEC) did this. (See below.)

Benefits: Limited liability protection; can protect land from later speculation and development; can receive tax-deductible donations and grants; exempt from income taxes and property taxes.

Challenges: Elaborate and time-consuming to set up and maintain; the 501(c)3 cannot engage in political activity; if the community disbands it must donate the organization's property and assets to another 501(c)3. For this last reason, sometimes people with equity and families with children tend to not join, seeking instead a community where they can have equity and financial sustainability even if the 501(c)3 later disbands. Also for this reason, communities owning their land this way tend to attract many nomadic young people interested in community adventures but uninterested in establishing equity and sinking roots into any one place, so the community can have higher than normal turnover as its young people move on to their next adventure.

Examples: Lost Valley Educational Center in Oregon owns its land through a 501(c)3; EcoVillage at Ithaca in New York owns some but not all of its land with this nonprofit. Occidental Arts and Ecology Center in California uses a 501(c)3 for its educational programs.

Please note, a "Land Trust" is not a legal entity per se, but a way of preserving land for a specific use, and land trust nonprofits or individual communities that organize themselves as land trusts generally use a 501(c)3 nonprofit, sometimes in combination with a 501(c)2 (title-holding) nonprofit.

Non-exempt Nonprofits

This is a legal structure created by setting up a nonprofit corporation with one's state but not seeking any tax-exemption status with the IRS, hence it is a "non-exempt" nonprofit. It can be used to own or manage assets with limited liability protection but with no intention to either make a profit or seek tax exemptions. EcoVillage at Ithaca (EVI) in New York uses a non-exempt nonprofit, the "EVI Village Association," as a kind of member-owned co-op. All community members are automatically also members of the EVI Village Association, which owns the two roads into the property, the water and sewer lines, the three neighborhood parking lots, the swimming pond, and the land around each housing co-op.

Benefits: Limited liability protection.

Challenges: Income is taxed at the corporate rate.

Examples: Abundant Dawn Community, Virginia owns its land this way. A non-exempt nonprofit is one of six legal entities used by EcoVillage at Ithaca in New York.

How Four Communities Use Multiple Legal Entities Together

1. Occidental Arts and Ecology Center (OAEC) in California uses an LLC, a 501(c)3 nonprofit, and a lease. They own and manage their 80 rural acres through an LLC, called the Sowing Circle LLC, and own and manage their educational programs through a 501(c)3 nonprofit, the Occidental Arts and Ecology Center 501(c)3, which itself owns nothing. Sowing Circle LLC leases most of its community land to the OAEC nonprofit. Their permanent community members (rather than their two-year temporary residents) are members of the Sowing Circle LLC as well as members of the board of the nonprofit OAEC. This arrangement works very well, for three reasons. First, the commercial lease mandates that the lessee, OAEC 501(c)3 nonprofit, maintains and repairs all the property they lease. This means that some money earned by the 501(c)3 nonprofit through classes, workshops, tours, and donations, can be used to keep the community's property well-maintained. Second, OAEC's landlords are wholly supportive of the nonprofit's activities, as they are the same community members. And third, if for any reason the OAEC nonprofit couldn't pay the full amount of their annual lease fee to Sowing Circle LLC, the LLC could claim a loss on their income taxes.

2. Los Angeles Eco-Village (LAEV) uses a housing co-op and a 501(c)3 nonprofit and many leases. About half of LAEV's members created Urban Soil/Terra Urbana (USTU), a 501(c)3 nonprofit used as a limited equity housing co-op, which owns two adjacent two-story apartment buildings and a four-plex unit across the street, but not the ground beneath these buildings.

The ground underneath the three buildings, as well as other parcels in the Beverly-Vermont area, are owned by the Beverly-Vermont Community Land Trust, a 501(c)3 nonprofit cre-

Hart's Mill members use machetes to cut brush on their land.

ated by several LAEV members and other local affordable eco-housing activists.

UrbanSoil/Terra Urbana is considered a limited equity co-op because shares in the co-op apartments are much more affordable to purchase than other, similar apartments in the area because the owners don't own the ground underneath their building. Also the purchase price is not based on the exorbitantly expensive land values in the Los Angeles area. Some LAEV members couldn't afford to become owners, however, so they remained renters. All the residents of all three buildings, owners and renters, as well as a few people living in other nearby buildings on the street, are members of LAEV, and have full decision-making rights. Each renter has a lease for their apartment with USTU, and each owner has their certificate of shares and a lease allowing them to live in their apartment.

3. Mariposa Grove Community in Oakland, California uses a condominium association and a local 501(c)3 nonprofit. Mariposa Grove Condominium Association owns six apartments and shared community building space renovated from three small single-family houses on two adjacent city lots. The ground underneath these buildings is owned by the Northern California Community Land Trust (NCLT), a local 501(c)3 nonprofit devoted to limited equity housing in the northern California region.

> ## Because the owners don't own the ground underneath their building, the purchase price is not based on Los Angeles' exorbitantly expensive land values.

Each of the six owner households in the condo association has a ground lease with the community land trust. In addition the community founder owns a large house with rental units—two small apartments and seven bedrooms—directly behind one of the community land trust lots. He owns the property with a deed, and each of the tenants has a lease. The four buildings share a big yard with all fences removed, and all residents are Mariposa Grove members and share the amenities of the community building.

4. EcoVillage at Ithaca (EVI), a rural community in New York State with three separate cohousing neighborhoods, has six legal entities, 100 co-op leases, and two ground leases.

(1) EcoVillage at Ithaca, Inc., a 501(c)3 nonprofit, owns all the community's 175 acres not owned by one of the community's other legal entities.

(2) FROG Housing Co-op, the legal entity of the community's first 30-unit cohousing neighborhood with two-story townhouses, owns the duplex buildings and the land directly under each unit; it purchased the land from EcoVillage at Ithaca's 501(c)3 nonprofit. Each FROG neighborhood household owns shares in the co-op and has a lease for their individual townhouse unit.

(3) SONG Housing Co-op, the legal entity of the second 30-unit cohousing neighborhood with two-story townhouses, owns the duplex buildings. The SONG Housing Co-op owns only the buildings; it leases the land underneath with the SONG Neighborhood Ground Lease, a 99-year lease from the EcoVillage at Ithaca, Inc. 501(c)3 nonprofit. This was done in order to create more affordable housing, and was required by Equity Trust, the organization that gave the SONG neighborhood a construction loan. Each SONG household owns shares in the SONG Housing Co-op and has a lease for their individual housing unit. (SONG also created two temporary legal entities—joint venture partnerships of 21 and 14 future residents respectively—in order to raise money for construction. When construction was finished the joint venture partnerships were dissolved.)

(4) TREE Housing Co-op, the legal entity of the third cohousing neighborhood, owns 40 units in several buildings and the land under each unit. TREE Housing Co-op purchased the land from EcoVillage at Ithaca's 501(c)3 nonprofit, and each TREE household owns shares in the TREE Housing Co-op and has a lease for their individual townhouse unit.

(5) EcoVillage at Ithaca Village Association (EVIVA), a non-exempt nonprofit, functions like a member co-op (although it's not legally a co-op), through which all community members co-own the two roads into the property, the water and sewer lines, the three neighborhood parking lots, the swimming pond, and the land around each of the three housing co-ops.

(6) The Center for Transformative Consciousness is a 501(c)3 nonprofit that promotes EcoVillage at Ithaca, develops each neighborhood, and runs EVI's onsite educational programs. Like OAEC's educational 501(c)3 nonprofit, it doesn't own anything.

The community, through its EcoVillage at Ithaca, Inc. nonprofit, leases 10 acres to West Haven Farm, a CSA farm owned by two community members, and leases 5 acres to Kestrel Perch Berry Farm, another CSA farm owned by another community member. The community also created a Conservation Easement for 35 acres of the property to remain wetlands and woodlands in perpetuity, and this is on the deed to EcoVillage at Ithaca, Inc. If the community ever disbanded and gave the land and assets of the EcoVillage at Ithaca, Inc. nonprofit to another 501(c)3 nonprofit, the new nonprofit owner would have to honor this conservation easement.

"One of the reasons for creating so many different entities," writes Bill Goodman, an EVI resident and lawyer, "is our need to satisfy the requirements of other parties, including the town of Ithaca, the New York Attorney General's Office, banks, and insurance companies.... Because this project is so unusual, we have had to create a complex framework to fit both our needs and the expectations of the legal and financial worlds."

Eleven Issues to Consider When Choosing Your Legal Entity(ies)

 (1) Does the entity resonate with your community's values, intentions, and mission? Intentional communities generally arise from a specific set of values and intentions, often stated as its mission or purpose. The founders may want to create an economically equitable lifestyle, a self-reliant and ecologically sustainable lifestyle, or a contemplative or spiritual lifestyle. They may want to educate or serve others, provide a nice place to live, or several of these. Given your community's values, intentions, and specific mission, what kind of formal, legal organization best suits your group?

(2) To what degree would the legal entity confer limited liability protection?

(3) Would the community pay federal income taxes, and at what rate? Would a different legal entity confer better tax benefits?

(4) If you'll need to borrow money, for example for a development loan or construction loan, how would your entity influence banks and other lending institutions? Are they familiar with this legal entity? Does it have credibility with them?

(5) How would the entity affect people's joining or leaving your community?

(6) Does the entity allow your group to assign its own criteria for governance and decision-making authority, or does it mandate specific rules for decision making within the group?

(7) Does the entity allow your group to choose its members?

(8) Does the entity set requirements or restrictions for how your community must divide any annual profits or losses among community members? Would it mandate how you must divide any assets if the community disbanded?

(9) How easy would the entity be to set up and manage over time? How vulnerable would it be to changes in the law or to changes in the Internal Revenue Service (IRS), or to other governmental scrutiny? How much are annual filing fees?

(10) How easy would it be to make changes in the bylaws, articles of incorporation, or operating agreements?

(11) Would the entity limit your community's political activity? If so, is that important to your group?

> **Does the legal entity you're considering allow your group to assign its own criteria for governance and decision-making authority, or does it mandate specific rules?**

Legal Resources

Please get advice from a lawyer and a CPA about the legal entity(ies) your community is considering. You'll need a real estate lawyer for buying your community property. Not all lawyers know about all legal entities, so in addition to your real estate lawyer, choose one who specializes in the kind of legal entity(ies) you're considering. Get advice from other intentional communities in your state who use the same kind(s) of legal entity you're considering. What lawyer did they use? Do they recommend that lawyer?

It can save you money to draft your articles of incorporation and bylaws or operating agreements (for an LLC) ahead of time and ask your lawyer to alter them to fit the specific requirements for that entity in your state.

The internet is an excellent place to find free legal advice: you can find many sites with very clear and lengthy legal notes about the options discussed here.

Legal clinics at law schools often offer legal advice inexpensively or for free, and may be able to connect community members up with law students looking for a research project.

Nolo Press offers excellent self-help legal forms and online documents, books, and software for almost every kind of legal entity and legal issue: www.nolo.com.

The Community Associations Institute (CAI) offers information, education, and resources about homeowners associations, condominium associations, and housing cooperatives: www.caionline.org.

The National Association of Housing Cooperatives (NAHC) offers the same services for housing cooperatives: coophousing.org.

The Institute for Community Economics (ICE) is a federally certified Community Development Financial Institution that makes loans for permanently affordable housing across the US: www.enterprisecommunity.com. 🐦

Diana Leafe Christian, author of Creating a Life Together *and* Finding Community, *has also contributed chapters to the books* Beyond You and Me, Gaian Economics, *and* Ecovillage: 1001 Ways to Heal the Planet. *She speaks at conferences, offers consultations to communities, and leads workshops internationally on creating successful new intentional communities—including legal issues, what helps existing communities thrive, and governance and decision-making. She lives at Earthaven Ecovillage. See www.dianaleafechristian.org.*

Dave Henson is a founding member of the Sowing Circle Community in Sonoma County, California and founder and Director of its affiliated Occidental Arts and Ecology Center (OAEC), an educational and rural retreat center. Dave leads many workshops at OAEC, including "Creating and Sustaining Intentional Communities," and is available for phone or in-person consultation about legal entities and organizational structures, group process and facilitation, and setting up nonprofit educational centers. See www.oaec.org.

Allen Butcher was a founder of the Fellowship for Intentional Community (FIC), and was a board member of the FIC and many other organizations. Allen lived at East Wind (1975-83) and at Twin Oaks (1985-89) communities. He now lives collectively in Denver, Colorado. His most recent book is The Intentioneer's Bible: Interwoven Stories of the Parallel Cultures of Plenty and Scarcity. *His book on the theory, design, and history of intentional community is available free at culturemagic.org.*

Albert Bates, a resident of The Farm Community in Tennessee since 1972, is a former environmental attorney and author of books on law, energy, and environment, including The Biochar Solution: Carbon Farming and Climate Change *(2010);* The Post-Petroleum Survival Guide and Cookbook: Recipes for Changing Times *(2006);* The Paris Agreement *with Rex Weyler (2015);* Communities that Abide *with Dmitry Orlov (2014); and* Climate in Crisis *(1990). Albert has been Director of the Ecovillage Training Center at The Farm in Summertown, Tennessee since 1994. See peaksurfer.blogspot.com.*

The Disadvantages of Joint Tenancy and Tenants in Common

These are two legal entities from the realm of real estate entities, not business entities, which allow two or more people to co-own a piece of property. While there are advantages to each, the disadvantages are especially onerous for intentional communities.

In *Joint Tenancy* all of the joint tenants have an equal interest in and rights in the property and all share equally in liabilities and profits. This most often includes sharing all necessary maintenance costs, taxes, and work responsibilities. However, a tenant is solely responsible for the costs of improvements made without the consent of the other tenants.

A Joint Tenancy has the "right of survivorship." which means that a joint tenant cannot will their interest in the property to heirs, but rather upon that joint tenant's death, the title is automatically passed to the surviving joint tenants.

The disadvantages of Joint Tenancy are significant for most communities. For example, a joint tenant may sell or give their interest to another person without the approval of the other tenants. This means a community could end up with a resident they don't know and don't want. Another big disadvantage is that if one joint tenant goes into debt, the creditor seeking collection could force the sale of the community's property to get the cash value of the person's share in the property.

Tenancy in Common is when two or more people have undivided interest in a property. If not otherwise specified, all the tenants in common share interests in the property equally. They can, however, distribute interest in the ownership of the property in whatever fractions they wish. Taxes and maintenance expenses, profits, and the value of improvements on the property must be distributed in the same proportion as the fractional distribution of their shares of ownership. There is no right of survivorship—the ownership interest of a deceased tenant in common passes to their heirs.

A tenant in common may sell, mortgage, or give their interest in the community's property as they wish, and the new owner becomes a tenant in common with the other co-tenants, again, whether or not the community members know the person or want them as a community member. Even worse, if a tenant in common in the property wants to sell their interest and get out but the community can't afford it right then, that person **can force a sale of the property** in order to recover the value of their interest in the property.

—DLC

Starting a Community

Just as in a prism we can see the different colors of the spectrum, so a fellowship will have a diversity of individuals. When starting a community, rejoice in each of these, and reject all attempts to make people uniform. The more originality there is, the more vibrant a fellowship will be. At the same time, it's important to distinguish between healthy self-determination and the self-centered individualism that sees everything from its own perspective and seeks its own advantage. While the former is vital in a living community, the latter will destroy it.

Can this work in real life? We don't always get it right, but have been trying almost 100 years! Schedule a visit today at **bruderhof.com**

Buying Your Community Property

by Frances Forster and Byron Sandford

Frances Forster and Byron Sandford offer an upbeat primer on criteria for evaluating property, with special emphasis on the how-tos and how-comes of financing, insurance, and legal considerations.

Buying your community property will be a lot like buying a home. If you've ever done that you know it can be a roller coaster ride, but eventually it does end! The process itself will provide many good opportunities to practice your group decision-making procedures, and test your abilities to trust that your decision to pursue this venture is right.

So where do you start? By answering three simple questions:

(1) Where do you want to be (geographically)?

(2) What do you need?

(3) How much can you afford?

After you've addressed these questions, the next steps are a little more mechanical—after all, there are only so many ways of identifying property and paying for it. Just trust that your decision makers will stay focused on the big picture and not get distracted by the zillion and one (sometimes insignificant) details.

Where Do You Want to Be?

Consider what your members are going to be doing for work and recreation. What are your needs for land, water, transportation, proximity to towns? What are your needs for an audience or market, for schools and con-tinuing education? What about climate, rainfall, or soil types?

Make your lists and consult some maps. Chambers of commerce, local governments, newspapers, and libraries can be good sources of information about places you're considering.

What Do You Need?

A number of things need to fit together, or be developed hand in hand, so you need to have a rough idea of the number and types of people, animals, buildings, cars, and land uses that are going to be a part of the planned picture. For example, your county health department may require a certain type or size of septic system based on the number of people, and the septic fields need to be a certain distance from wells, waterways, and swimming areas.

Operations that require special permits, like the use of chemicals or machinery, merit special consideration, as do services or activities that will bring traffic or require animal management. Check out local ordinances or restrictions related to such special issues now, before you start the property search.

Sketch out a couple of rough site plans showing the desired relationships between buildings or functions. Having these will help in the site-selection process.

How Much Can You Afford?

Unless someone is giving you all the funds (or the land) with no strings attached, you will most likely need

---

Frances Forster and Byron Sandford are part of a new community, Quakerland, west of San Marcos, Texas, to be based on land currently used as a retreat by Quaker meetings in the area. They have traveled to Friends' Meetings throughout the region, building consensus for intentional community use of the retreat land, and recruiting folks to join the Quakerland community. Frances is a licensed real estate broker and Byron, a former mortgage banker, renovates dwellings and apartment buildings for rent or resale.

150

a loan from a mortgage company, bank, savings and loan, the actual seller, or other lender. This will apply whether you need funds for land alone, improvements (buildings), or both.

The lender will assess your borrowing power based on the collective income, assets, and debts of the persons who will be responsible for the note. These persons will sign the mortgage and deed documents for your community, based on whatever internal agree ment you have. It may be to your advantage to have as many people as possible for cosigners, because it will boost your assets— the lender will like having lots of responsible parties.

To determine where you are financially, gather all your financial records and add up four sets of figures: (1) gross monthly incomes, interest, dividends, child support received, and other predictable income; (2) bank accounts, IRAs, trusts, whole life va lues, stocks, bonds, and other as sets; (3) total of all debts (credit cards, loans, child support owed, etc.), and (4) the monthly obligation for these debts.

Once you have your totals, a lender can give you an estimate of how much you can borrow. While the figures will vary from lender to lender, you can get a ballpark estimate of what the lenders are thinking by doubling your cosigners' total annual gross inc ome—this approximates the loan amount; one percent of that amount is your monthly payment. For another approximation, if your cosigners already have a debt load, multiply your cosigners' total monthly gross income by 29 percent—this is your maxi mum monthly payment (PITI: principal, interest, taxes, and insurance); unless your group already owes monthly debts of more than ten percent of the total monthly income. If your debts are higher, the amount available for the monthly land payments is reduced p roportionately. If you put these calculations on paper you'll see how easy they are to figure. *debt to income ratio*

Points of caution about your cosigners: (1) get cred it reports for each cosigner early on and take a good hard look at them—you don't want surprises later; and (2) if cosigners are self-employed, make sure the lender considers their income eligible; if you do include future business income in your financial picture, be sure to pro vide profit and loss statements reflecting past experience.

> After visiting with a few real estate brokers, you'll have to decide whether your group has the time, experience, and contacts to manage the land purchase without professional assistance.

Visit with Lenders

At this point you have a fairly good idea of where you want to be, what you need, and how much money you have to work with. Now it's time to make intro ductory visits to senior officers of some lenders in your area. Ask for information on rates, loan alter natives, what other things you need to look at, and if they would con sider loaning money to your group (not all lenders make all types of loans). Provide possible lenders with an over view sheet. Remember, you're just gathering informa tion, not making a fo rmal loan application.

Visit with Appraisers and Real Estate Brokers

Make brief visits with some ap praisers and brokers who specialize in farm and ranch properties, or com mercial or multi-family properties if your community will be in an urban location. Again, your goal is to gather information about the vicinity, the mark et, the possibilities. You should be able to learn about good areas to consider, what the average cost per acre or per square foot is in those ar eas, and which factors are most sig nificant in determining price in your vicinity. Significant factors include size, location, view, water, type of soil, trees, and proximity to major roads.

Broker Commissions, Inspections, and Appraisals

You may not be responsible for the broker commis sion—in some places it is customary for the seller to pay the commission to the listing broker, who shares it with the buyer's broker. So payment may not be an is sue. Yet, many folks will consider trying to save money by avoiding the use of brokers, or even inspectors and appraisers. On the other hand, professionals can save you money, and a lot of time and energy. Their experience and specialized training can help you to avoid making mistakes. Only if yo u feel you have enough expertise and time should you shepherd a real estate transaction by yourselves.

Another word about brokers. There is some debate in the realty world at this time about whether the buy er's broker will actually represent the buyer or the seller. There's no need to get caught up in that concern if you

10 people X $10K each = $100,000.
1% X 100,000 = $1000.

• 10 people X $30,000 ann. income X 2 = $600,000
60 loan amt. Mo. pmt. = $6000.
• 10 people X $2500 mo. = $25,000 X 30% = $7500/mo. pmt.

are honest, fair, shop in the price range you can afford, and don't play games. Then, you'll do fine.

Inspections are usually performed soon after you enter into a contract. The private inspection is a very thorough inspection of structures and systems (electrical, plumbing, heating, and air conditioning, etc.). The inspector is hired and paid by the buye r, and costs in the vicinity of $200. The purpose of the inspection is to acquaint the buyer with the workings of the property and the condition of the dwelling systems.

Appraisals are also sometimes called inspections, but their role is different. Appraisers provide an independent estimate of the dollar value of a property for the lender, usually, or the buyer or seller. The general rule for pricing a property is to lear n what comparable properties (comps) have sold for in the last six months. If the market is rapidly changing, and there are enough comps, the time limit may be shortened to three months, or appropriate adjustments can be factored in for market price changes.

Finding Your Property

After visiting with a few real estate brokers, you'll have to decide whether your group has the time, experience, and contacts to manage the land purchase without professional assistance. If you decide to contract with a broker instead, select one that un derstands your needs, has appropriate expertise, and is willing to put in the time that you'll need, because you'll need plenty of time. Everything about an intentional community buying property is unusual, so you'll need a strong, creative advocate who c an help with the other professionals who are part of the purchase process.

The obvious places to look for properties are the local newspapers and free real estate brochures. Another way of locating property, especially in the country, is to drive around the area you're considering. There may be properties for sale by owners, or listed by licensed agents who are not members of the local board. A broker will also have other resources, which will vary in format from place to place, but will include new listings and properties that are for sale but may not have signs.

For-sale-by-owner is simply that—the owners themselves are handling the sale without the involvement of a listing agent. Sometimes owners have enough expertise to do the job right, sometimes not; they may not realize what is involved other than saving the cost of a commission. Be sure to find out what the picture really is. And if you decide to pursue a transaction with no agents involved, for sure get an appraisal, survey, inspection,

and especially title insurance, even if you must pay for it yoursel f. (Please note: For-sale-by-owner is different from owner financing, which is discussed later.)

Properties on the market should have an owner's disclosure statement, or a list showing any problems with appliances and systems, structural items, environmental factors, and any legal issues that may affect the property. These statements are now required in some states for the protection of both the sellers and the buyers. If the property you want doesn't have a disclosure statement, insist on one!

Also check on deed restrictions and zoning regulations for your selected property to make sure you can operate the kind of business you want, or build the kind of buildings you need. Review your rough sketches and needs lists—don't overlook something i mportant!

You've Found the Property, Now What?

Submit an offer. If you've done your homework you know everything you need to know to make a realistic offer. Your offer, generally on standard contract forms, will propose your sales price, method of financing, closing date, and other details. Keep it as simple as possible, and don't ask for insignificant concessions. It's OK to make your price a little below where you want to end up, but you don't want to make it so low you insult the seller. You may be buying a family home, not just some corporate tax shelter. The seller may sign (accept) your offer or make a counter, in which case the house is still on the market. Hopefully you will come to terms quickly and move into the closing period—the evaluation period between contract signing and the closing , or actual property title transfer.

You've Signed, So You're Ready to Move In? Whoa!

Give yourself enough time in the closing period to work up a good case of the jitters—if not this whole process is no fun! Actually, from this point a lot depends on the property and the financing method.

In a nutshell, during the next two weeks you'll do the inspection (if there are any structures), the appraisal, and start the loan process, if you haven't already. The loan is usually the part that takes time—anywhere between two weeks and two months, depending on how much information on how many people the lender wants. After the loan is approved, the boundary survey is ordered and any other contingencies are resolved—which can take a while, too. Then you can close, and that just takes an hour or s o. Then you can move.

While the lender is doing its thing, the title company is researching the property records to make sure, for one thing, that the person selling the property has the right to do so, and that the title will be clear when it is transferred to you. That means that no back taxes, liens, judgments, or other claims will be transferred to you, and that any easements, encroachments, rights of way, mineral rights, or anything else that will affect your usage and enjoyment of the property will be made known to you p rior to closing. Your insurance on the title is forever, so they like to be sure about these things!

The title insurance is usually paid by the seller, with a second document going to the lender. The cost to the seller is usually around one percent of the sales price, and to the lender about $200. A copy to the buyer costs a little less. A copy for yours elves would be a good idea—and if you order it up front the cost is a lot less than if you do it later.

Let's Talk Attorneys

Attorneys have a place in the transaction if you want them, and they can be invisible if you prefer. They can prepare and review contracts prior to submittal, during negotiations, and after; they can prepare loan and deed documents; they can order title w ork from a title company; and attorneys can be helpful at closings. If you and the seller prefer to close with the title company, the title company and the lender will simply have their usual attorneys draw up the papers and send them to the title company for closing. Also, in some states, attorneys can still act as brokers. A broker can tell you about local regulations.

Let's Talk Owner Financing

In owner financing, the owner is willing to forego receiving his full equity all at once, and instead will earn interest on his equity from you. Normally the seller will want 25 to 30 percent down payment, and monthly payments at or above market rates, al though he may be flex-

> [C]heck on deed restrictions and zoning regulations for your selected property to make sure you can operate the kind of business you want, or build the kind of buildings you need. Review your rough sketches and needs lists—don't overlook something i mportant!

ible on this point. It is very common for rural properties to be financed this way.

Sometimes the owner agrees to carry the note for only a few years until it's a good time (for you or him) to refinance, or sell the note. Don't let the idea that your note might be sold scare you—the note is a commodity, like stocks, that can be bought and sold, but your terms remain the same.

In setting up this note, the seller most likely will want to see your financial documents just as a banker would. The difference is that a private seller may be a little more flexible than regular lenders, which are highly regulated and in most cases must meet required guidelines.

By the same token, you should also ask to see the seller's documents to ascertain either that the note has been paid off, or that the seller has the right to sell the property without paying the note off. If the note has a ¼due on sale¼ clause, then the o wner cannot sell the property this way, at least not without written authorization from the lender. And that should be reviewed by an attorney.

Also, with owner financing you need to be clear, in your documentation, about who will be responsible for paying the taxes and insurance, and when the title will transfer. Even if you don't use a lawyer or a broker, you should still close with a title com pany to make sure everything is done correctly and recorded with the county clerk. A flawed title can be a long-term cause for insecurity and legal expenses, dragging on for years to a very uncertain outcome.

With owner financing you may be tempted to forego the appraisal, boundaries survey, title search, and title insurance to save money. Think again. And if you decide you can do without one of them, think yet again! Honest mistakes are made every day, and yo ur community's future is at stake.

Aren't you chomping at the bit to get started on this community adventure? Just think of all the things you'll learn, and think of all the opportunities you'll have to practice your group-decision-making skills! It will all be worth it in the end. And you 'll know it!

CREATING THE IDEAL INTENTIONAL COMMUNITY
(OR REVITALIZING AN EXISTING ONE)

I, Sahmat, grew up in intentional communities and have lived in 10 of them. I have been so dedicated to Community with both humans and Nature that I've been called "The Community Guy". The communities I grew up in shared a fairly strong "sense of community". I call this deep and sustained sense of community "Common-unity" because it's a state of unity we share in common, with the unique individuality of each human and each species still honored. It's this state of Common-unity that I've found most valuable in life and to me it's the main reason for living in an intentional community. When a group is deep in Common-unity together, there's a shared sense of love, joy, and peace that tops any other group experience.

However, I've found that in all the communities I've lived in, the sense of community is not nearly as deep and sustained as it could be. It's precisely this lack of Common-unity that is the root cause of the catastrophic global suffering of racism, wars, child abuse, abuse of women, environmental and species destruction, etc. So the ultimate goal is ending global suffering through "Global Common-unity": the spreading of Common-unity throughout the world by forming a global network of Common-unity-dedicated Communities.

So I've spent my life learning how to create Common-unity-dedicated communities that share true Common-unity: a deeper and more sustained sense of community. There are two keys to starting a Common-unity community (or moving an existing community into deeper Common-unity):

1. The first key to Common-unity is for everyone to be "Common-unity-dedicated" as their top common priority. This doesn't seem to be the case in any existing community, which results in focus and energies being bled off into other priorities. So maintenance of Common-unity doesn't get enough time and energy.

2. The second key to Common-unity is to learn "Common-unity Skills", skills that must be practiced to maintain Common-unity: Speaking from the Heart, Empathetic Listening, Emptying of Ego-attachments, Conflict Resolution, Consensus, Heart Wound Healing, Cooperative Housing, and Cooperative Economics. Modern culture does not teach us these skills.

We at the Alliance for Global Community have developed free workshops that train you in these Common-unity Skills. The workshops contain the Sharing Circle process developed by M. Scott Peck, a Nature connection exercise developed by John Seed and Joanna Macy, healing exercises developed by Byron Katie and Richard Moss, and exercises in creating Cooperative Housing and Cooperative Econom-

ics. We've tested various versions of these Common-unity Skill Building workshops over the past 25 years, and we've found them to be quite effective in teaching Common-unity skills that can help maintain Common-unity. If you'd like to start a Common-unity-dedicated community, or if you'd like to bring more Common-unity into an existing community (perhaps through a Common-unity sub community or "pod"), you need to learn or improve these Common-unity skills as soon as possible.

To find out how to sign up for a free public Common-unity Skills workshop or schedule a free workshop for an existing group or community, please go to my website thecommunityguy.org There you can also find out how to get a free copy of the book "Skill Building for Global Common-unity". You can contact Sahmat directly at info@thecommunityguy.org or at 434-305-4770.

COMMON-UNITY WITH HUMANITY AND NATURE

Creating Cooperative Culture BY LAIRD SCHAUB

EXIT DYNAMICS IN COMMUNITY

Although it's not what folks generally have their attention on when they start or join communities, the other side of the coin is that people leave. To be sure, this can happen for a wide variety of reasons. Let me give you a hypothetical dozen—all of which I've witnessed:

1. Maybe the bread winner in your household just had their job transferred to Kalamazoo or Timbuktu, and they *really* want to keep that job.

2. Maybe your 15-year-old got busted for smoking pot in the bathroom of the public library (there's a reason that "sophomoric" is an adjective that refers to poor judgment) and you're heart sick over the possibility that the negative publicity will give the community a black eye and lead to your family being ostracized in the community.

3. Maybe your mother is getting to the point where she needs one of her adult children to live nearby, and none of your siblings has enough flexibility in their life to answer the bell. You do what you gotta do and it's time to give back to Mom.

4. Maybe your daughter's asthma has worsened to where you have to move to a climate with lower humidity.

5. Maybe you love all the coffee shops, liberal politics, and Powell's bookstore, but if you spend one more winter in Portland's gray drizzle your SAD (which is bad) will make your partner mad and it's time to move to a sunnier pad where you can both be glad.

6. Maybe you're sick unto death of your neighbor's barking dog and, after years of struggle, you're willing to move so you can finally count on getting a decent night's sleep.

7. Maybe you can no longer tolerate the interminable meetings. Making decisions together sounded OK in theory, but OMG.

8. Maybe your youngest child just left for college and the nest is empty. You don't want to be rattling around in all that house but there is nothing smaller available in the community, so downsizing means moving.

9. Maybe your marriage has just dissolved and you cannot bear the thought of continuing to live in the same community as your ex. (Maybe 10 years from now, but not next week.)

10. Maybe your mildly hyperactive daughter has been accused of bullying the neighbor kids and is no longer welcome in community play groups with her peers. Though the kids still want to be together, the other parents won't allow it. You feel your kid is being scapegoated, and don't want to live in a community where other parents seem unwilling to look at how *their* child is contributing to challenging dynamics.

11. Maybe you came to community expressly to learn natural building techniques and how to incorporate energy saving technology into everyday life. Now that you've learned all that, you're ready to head off to your mountaintop property in Colorado to build your dream home and retire next to a trout stream.

12. Maybe you can no longer tolerate hearing youngsters scream at community dinners (ruining adult conversation) and you're bone weary of tripping over scooters and Big Wheels strewn about the pathways at night—right where the kids left them.

I could go on, but you get the picture. There are many reasons why people leave. Sometimes it's because there's a problem in the community that's not resolving; sometimes there are personal reasons that have nothing to do with the community; sometimes it's a bit of both.

From the community's perspective there are three particular possibilities that I want to highlight. These are important both because there may be chances to turn things around even at the 11th hour, and because it's an opportunity for the community to learn what it might do differently in the future.

Possibility A: Where the member is facing a personal challenge that suggests leaving and may not have explored how much the community could be an ally in finding a response that wouldn't require moving

In this dynamic there is probably no expectation that the community has anything to offer, and it's quite possible that the member has not even made an attempt to seek help from the community. But that doesn't mean there are no options!

For this to have room to fully bloom I think it makes sense for

(continued on p. 79)

EXIT DYNAMICS IN COMMUNITY

(continued from p. 80)

representatives of the community (Membership Committee?) to pro-actively, yet discreetly, approach the person or couple to see if they're open to exploring how the community might be able to provide some outside-of-the-box support.

If the openness is there (no arm twisting, please) the support team can find out details of the situation beyond what is known publicly and perhaps help with spade work to follow through on promising suggestions, either on the private side (directly with individuals) or the public side (using community resources). Even if no appreciable help is realized through this effort, it will land well that the attempt was made and the community will feel better that it went the extra mile.

Possibility B: Where there are challenges in the community that have been named, but attempts at resolution have been unsatisfactory and the person is ready to leave in frustration

In this dynamic there is likely to be some hurt feelings, perhaps in many directions. It is a delicate thing knowing when you've tried enough, and when it's time to let go and move on. Not all problems are solvable and not all people are meant to live together. Exit can be the right choice.

Yet there can be considerable gold in panning through the dross of failed attempts at conflict resolution—if you approach it with an open, what-can-we-learn attitude, rather than with a how-can-we-assign-blame perspective. While it may not be easy to get the protagonists to engage in a post-mortem analysis (who wants to pick the scab off?), you might have success if a neutral team (Membership, I'm thinking of you again) approaches with a promise to simply listen, to make sure there's clarity about that person's side of events and how it landed for them.

It's possible that this kind of listening will lead to an insight about how things could get unstuck if approached differently, and—if it's not too late—those may still be tried. But I wouldn't hold my breath. Mostly the point of this kind of examination is to learn how to do things better next time; how to not dig the hole so deep that no one can get out.

Possibility C: Where there are challenges in the community that have not been named publicly, yet the person is willing to leave over them

This dynamic is a particularly interesting one because you may not know it's even in play unless you're privy to inside information or someone tips you off. The public presentation is that the person (or couple) has announced that they're leaving for personal reasons that have nothing to do with community dynamics (after all, they have to say *something* about why they're leaving), but that's not the case, or at least not the whole story. How will you know to ask about this if you don't know it's happening?

Why would people do this? Perhaps it's too embarrassing to disclose their reactions in group. Maybe they're conflict averse and would rather leave than try to work it out. Possibly they're intimidated by the particular folks they're conflicted with and don't have the gumption to face bully dynamics. Maybe there are a bunch of small things, no one of which is fatal, but the accumulation is overwhelming.

The beauty of this possibility is that if you're following my advice about being pro-active in Possibility A, the interviewing group might discover that it's really Possibility C (where the "personal reasons" were trumped up to deflect inquiries about community dynamics), or a combination of the two (where there are both personal reasons and community reasons). If you uncover this dynamic, you may have a chance to still work the conflict (by whatever means your group has in place for that purpose). But even if it's too late for that, you get more accurate information about the ways in which the community has fallen short, which gives you a leg up on dealing with whatever broke down.

Exit Interviews

With all of the above in mind, let's drill down on what you might ask if you're interviewing someone who has announced they intend to leave. Here are some questions you might pose:

• How well did life in the community work for you and your family? What were the highlights; what was hard?

• Did you find the community to be as advertised? If not, please describe the ways in which there was a misunderstanding about what you'd find, and give us any suggestions you have about how to correct those.

• What suggestions do you have for how we could more accurately describe what life in our community is like? Please be specific.

• What would you say to a prospective or incoming new member that you wished had been said to you?

• Did you get the interpersonal support you were looking for as a member of the community? If not, what can you tell us about how we fell short?

• Are there ways that you wish the community could be doing more for its members? If so, please describe the ways.

• What, if any, aspects of community agreements did you really appreciate, and which do you wish were different?

• What, if any, aspects of community culture did you really appreciate, and which do you wish were different?

• Are there any unresolved issues related to community life that were a factor in your decision to leave? If so, please tell us what they are.

• To the extent that there are personal reasons (unrelated to community life) influencing your decision to leave, have you tried to get help from the community in resolving those issues such that you could stay? If not, or you are willing to try more, we invite you to tell us in detail what those personal factors are. (While we cannot promise to pull a rabbit out of the hat, we're willing to give it a try.)

• If you had sufficient support from the community, would you be willing to try further to work things out so that you could stay in the community? If so, what would that support look like? ☙

Laird Schaub is former Executive Secretary of the Fellowship for Intentional Community (FIC), publisher of this magazine, and co-founder of Sandhill Farm, an egalitarian community in Missouri. He currently lives in Chapel Hill, North Carolina where he is exploring community building with two close friends. He is also a facilitation trainer and process consultant, and authors a blog that can be read at communityandconsensus.blogspot.com. This article is adapted from his blog entry of July 25, 2014.

Wisdom begins with recognizing we are not alone...

www.exemplars.world – a resource for creating community

Building a sustainable, more collaborative and community-oriented future often means rephrasing past virtues that had been swept aside, but with a little tweaking become relevant again. Every town or city worthy of being called a community has people both out front and working behind the scenes. They are the glue that keeps things together.

Exemplars.world is a portal to help us understand and organize; a searchable, on-line library of the possible. There is a narrative that ties it all together, and for each organization or community, there is a brief description and a link to their web page. To add Exemplars, or comment, contact pfreundlich@comast.net

EXAMPLE: BURLINGTON, VT

Starting Point: An elected mayor providing leadership. **Organizing Strategy:** Appeal to the pride and capacity of local population and institutions. **Tools:** The convening and budgetary power of local government. **Outcomes:** Success, both in achieving a sustainable community, and in proving to often divided interests that collaboration and compromise work. **Prime Sources: https://www.burlingtonvt.gov/ and "Sustainable Communities",** available from Amazon. In "Sustainable Communities," Bruce Seifer and his co-authors lay out how Burlington solved vexing problems and created a productive and livable town. An activist municipal government, led by Mayor Bernie Sanders, working in partnership with the private sector and a network of municipally supported nonprofit organizations, pursued a sustainable development strategy by generating new sources of public revenue; creating and retaining jobs; encouraging and regulating growth; ensuring a publicly controlled waterfront; producing permanently affordable housing; stabilizing residential neighborhoods; reducing energy consumption; requiring the recycling of solid waste; and removing barriers preventing women from enjoying the fruits of economic growth.

II

CREATING INTENTIONAL COMMUNITY

Throwing in the Founder's Towel

By Ma'ikwe Schaub Ludwig

The following article is adapted from a blog entry originally written in mid-2008; because it encapsulates so well the challenges and "hard times" often involved in starting a new community, we reprint it here.

I've just thrown in the towel.

It's not like me, and I'm a bit embarrassed to admit it. But the truth is that I've spent the past seven years working on the rather intimidating goal of starting a residential intentional community, and I've finally admitted that I might not be up to the task. Conventional wisdom says that every new community needs a burning soul, and I've burned brightly, burned joyfully, and finally, burned out.

The first year and a half, I lived with my mother, stepfather, and son, and the three of us adults worked diligently on visioning a community that we could be happy with. But it turned out that our visions were too different, and my relationship with my stepfather deteriorated to the point that it wasn't worth the effort anymore. I had one of my worst-ever human behavior moments about a month before we called it quits, and actually threw a plate during a meeting. (You can't tell me that people can't behave badly and intend well in the same breath!) Garden-variety conflict, combined with a lack of a basic values match, killed the first project.

I spent that next summer at Dancing Rabbit Ecovillage in Missouri. It was a great summer: inspirational, reinvigorating, and just plain fun. But there weren't other kids for my incredibly social son, and I couldn't figure out how to make a living in rural Missouri. I left with some real regret, but the confidence and hope that I, too, could make something like this project happen in the world. So I moved to Albuquerque with a promise from my son's father that we'd start a community together.

The next year and a half was a time of concentrated growth and learning. We rented two houses next to each other in a residential neighborhood, painted the porches a wild turquoise and lavender combination that just screamed "cultural creatives here!," hosted weekly neighborhood dinners until all hours, and supported each other in following our dreams. In a classic example of too-clunky process without much training, it took months to arrive at a name: Sol Space was christened months after we moved in. (Sing it to the tune of "Soul Train," bob your head a little, and you can capture a little of the giddiness when we finally arrived at that one!)

This was the group that supported me in writing a book, having a baby for close friends, and learning about just how important good facilitation is. We shared expenses (and therefore all of our various neuroses around money) and tight quarters (which meant sharing lost its charm fairly quickly and became instead a platform for growth and clarifying what was really important to each of us). Sol Space was a truly amazing social scene…a little wild at times, but characterized by a lot of care and grounding.

Things came apart for two main reasons. The bad news was that we weren't savvy enough about our conflicts, in spite of being creative and dedicated to our friendships with each other. On the good side of the ledger, half of us were chasing bigger dreams: we combined efforts with another cooperative group and began

Photos courtesy of Ma'ikwe Schaub Ludwig

From the left: Welcoming sign to the Dancing Rabbit Ecovillage. Road to the Ecovillage. The old swimming pond is a place of tranquility. The courtyard as you come in: Skyhouse and the Common House. As in traditional villages, courtyards are a big feature for design here, literally holding space for social interaction.

work on a full-fledged ecovillage, wanting to be a model project for urban revitalization. Sol Space was a limited success, short-term but with high impact on a lot of lives, and the initial testing ground for a lot of our ideas and relationships.

So Sol Space morphed into a project that eventually became known as Zialua Ecovillage (or ZEV) and had a much wider draw than the dozen or so folks who lived together in our small co-op. For four years, a typically urban mix of dreamers, teachers, activists, artists, and business people shared a dream of cooperative living. We did our best to correct for past weak points: we committed to consensus training, spent a lot of time working on our vision, and made efforts to get real about money, diversity, and space issues early in the process. It felt, most days, like we were just keeping our heads above the water, but ZEV was powered by inspiration and honesty, and most days that was enough.

I made some huge mistakes as a leader. I confess to pushing the group too fast, being unable to separate my personal needs from the group's agenda, and doing my share of simple whining when things didn't go my way. I also did a lot of things right: got that facilitation training I had been missing, insisted that we learn consensus, connected individually with everyone who showed the slightest interest, and preserved all the friendships I ever made in the process. And yes, I got good at confession, and slightly better at humility.

Things almost fell apart in mid-2006.

It was the first period where we started to understand that the three women who had been most central in the leadership of the group had different enough priorities that things were not moving easily ahead. I think, in retrospect, that we loved each other too much and just couldn't bring ourselves to let go of the particular individuals in order to get to the point of having an ecovillage. The wisest of the three of us stepped back into a support role. The other two of us apparently couldn't

take a hint: we barreled ahead, convinced we could hold everyone's dreams in one container, if we just tried hard enough.

In the fall of 2006, the group landed on a city block with a vibrant, member-owned business, and a development model similar to N-Street Cohousing. This move was an interesting one, and for me, a compromise. We lost people, some of whom were really close friends of mine, and the people who shared the more communal and radical parts of the social vision. I think we lost me, too, though that wasn't immediately clear.

Somehow, I had missed the sweet spot between flexibility and sticking with a vision that inspires me. While the less structured model of community building, in which you let it unfold organical-

ly, has huge advantages financially, and also keeps open space for a spontaneity that fed a lot of my companions, it left me feeling flat and unmet in my heart's deeper needs.

I wanted people in my life who were excited to commit to showing up for a shared adventure, not just sharing our tales of the individual ones we were each pursuing. I wanted meals together and a shared vision that we could each contribute to in a meaningful way. I wanted to know that

---

The wisest of the three of us stepped back into a support role. The other two of us apparently couldn't take a hint: we barreled ahead.

---

the people I see every day have made a commitment to something bigger than ourselves and that we can lean into each other when we need it. At the bottom of it all, my ecologist's daughter's roots were too strong to ignore, and the chance to really experiment with sustainability outweighed the stubbornness that had kept me at it in New Mexico for five years.

In the fall of 2007, just a year after my group migrated to a city block in Albuquerque, I found myself at the 10-year reunion for Dancing Rabbit. I looked around and realized that the village dream I had found so compelling (and really, had been trying to re-create in the five interim years) was progressing along quite nicely while I was off somewhere

(continued on p. 78)

THROWING IN THE FOUNDER'S TOWEL

(continued from p. 41)

else. And suddenly, being "somewhere else" was untenable. After years of being the "starter," I found myself wanting to join in. And my practical side could finally see it too: enough kids to satisfy even my rambunctious 11-year-old, while the progressed finances of both my life and Dancing Rabbit's suddenly opened a door I had shut, with regrets, five years earlier.

Something else got triggered that weekend, too: in a way I never anticipated, I found myself longing to return to the country. Urban living had worn me thin, and I wanted to wake up to the sound of crickets instead of jet engines, look out at gardens instead of streets.

And so now, almost a year later, I am happily settling back in as the latest resident at Dancing Rabbit, humbled and a bit battered by the lessons and hurts and stretches of the past seven years. I find myself both relieved and inspired to serve a vision that someone else crafted, with a group that happens to hit that sweet spot for me between flexibility and a strong vision. Now when someone wants to know

what the hell the founders were thinking, or why we do things like that, people's eyes train on my friend Tony and not me. I feel a little guilty that I am finding it far easier to support him than to be him.

But only a little. I feel like I did my time in that particular hot seat, and am enjoying a well-deserved break and a chance to develop other parts of myself that were put on hold while trying to hold it all together.

What I left in Albuquerque was another qualified success. While the ecovillage never fully manifested, our work over those years spawned a dozen or so meaningful projects that are a legacy of sorts for the Southwest. We still love each other, but now, it isn't "too much" because we aren't trying to make each other fit into a box that doesn't work. The block we claimed is a vibrant neighborhood, in part because we claimed it, and may yet be an exemplary example of what the Fellowship for Intentional Community calls "creating community where you are." In the sense that community means having

people who see each other, care about each other, and are genuinely interested in each other's lives, ZEV was (and is) spectacularly successful.

And I've walked away with a profound respect for founders and their unique struggles: feeling responsible for everything, the exhaustion of constantly re-explaining why we are here, and the flashes of joy and pardonable pride when your dream suddenly manifests as a real, meaningful thing (flashes that no one else seems to really grok). Your work has made it possible for me to take the next steps in my own life and, perhaps, finally find my best way to serve and create community. Thank you. ✿

Ma'ikwe Schaub Ludwig lives at Dancing Rabbit Ecovillage in northeastern Missouri, just down the road from Sandhill Farm where her husband, Laird, resides. She teaches workshops on starting communities, consensus-inspired facilitation, and various ecovillage-related topics. She is the author of Passion as Big as a Planet: Evolving Eco-activism in America. *Ma'ikwe is currently involved in something more mundane than starting a new group: building a strawbale house.*

William Hederman

Establishing Community in Hard Times: A Swedish Case

By Robert Hall

Looking across the half-excavated fields of our ecovillage site in late spring, I wonder what we got ourselves into some nine months ago, just before the financial crisis hit Wall Street. Our attempt to build up an intentional community in Sweden could not have been more closely timed with the global financial crisis, which quickly spread through the banking system from the US to the Baltic states and into Sweden.

We launched our embryonic community in September 2008, just as the global economy was beginning to falter. In some ways this situation has both helped and hurt our community-building process, but we have not allowed it to shake us from our admittedly ambitious intentions. Luckily those of us who pay monthly rent to the cooperative—crucial for making loan repayments—have more stable incomes not affected by the growing number of layoffs especially in the auto industry. The global economic slowdown, on top of the broader environmental and climate crises, has perhaps been helpful in convincing people of the need to find other, more sustainable ways of living.

That my wife Ingrid and I wanted to live in a community was obvious, but just three years ago it was not even clear in which country we should make it happen. Having stayed more than four years in Albania, we knew it was high time to move on, and finally to start living more in line with "the talk" and the books on the coffee table. In fact, we were in a relatively good position to make the transition to a sustainable lifestyle, but just like most people we have attachments to "modern decadence" that take a considerable amount of self-discipline to control or if possible rid oneself of. After various considerations, we chose to return to my wife's native Sweden, where we were best able to utilize the advantages of a progressive, well-functioning welfare state to create the ecovillage intentional community we had been seeking elusively for two decades.

So how does one go about establishing an ecovillage community? Thanks to the progressive state, many visibly similar, often

Gabe and Robert on barn roof, September 2008.

> *The seller of the 80-acre forest six miles from town wanted double what we could pay—so our hopes were again crushed and we had to look elsewhere.*

top-down substitutes for community living are already on offer, quelling the demand for grassroots-initiated alternative communities. Squeaky clean cohousing associations, modern housing cooperative estates, agricultural cooperatives, often initiated by government-supported national federations, are commonplace, and the critical mass to create alternative communities that one finds in the US, Germany, or the UK just never is sufficient in Sweden. And creating a community anywhere is often a lengthy ordeal that we really wanted to short-circuit.

I managed to get a job in Stockholm while the rest of the family decided they wanted to live on our home island of Gotland, a picturesque historic and insular province in the middle of the Baltic Sea. Immediately on moving to the island—from which I started weekly five-hour commutes by ferry—we decided to found the Gotland Ecovillage Association, based solely on a membership of my own nuclear family. However, we realized that this step was perhaps not the right way to build community, so we shelved the unregistered association and started to network with others in the local community who might be interested in the same goal of an ecovillage community. The municipality helped with names of other people who had asked about ecovillages. The local health food shop became a key contact point in finding others. While all my energy was being used to commute to Stockholm, and later to Kyiv, Ukraine, my wife was able to network with other associations and people on the island. After six months, we had a core of four families and another five-ten families and individuals on the periphery. We decided then to establish Gotland Eco-village Network. One of the core individuals, Peter, worked with Markus to establish a web portal for ecologic living, www.ekobogotland.se, documenting examples that already existed on the island financed by European Union rural development LEADER funds. Ingrid and Liselotte worked to organize excursions to these existing examples. However, the main work was to find land for a village and at the same time get to know each other more to see if we really had the same vision. We felt that it was entirely OK if we should realize in the process that we were in fact striving after different community visions and separate into two or more sub-groups, established at different sites—for we would still then have the network of ecovillages I hoped for. We all agreed upon a list of criteria, and then searched, asked around, got land maps, and called owners from the phone book. The network grew to 30 interested, even if only about nine people paid membership dues.

After a year and a half, I was able to get a job transfer to the island, and soon afterwards, Ingrid got a good job locally. This enabled us to intensify the search for land, and I felt urgency in finding a place to live out all the ideas we had always talked about. At the same time, others in the network had new problems with employment or personal life that caused them to pull back from the main search effort of what my biologist son labeled the "alpha group." When "alpha group" finally found a perfect property, we were down to just two families. But the seller of the 80-acre forest six miles from town wanted double what we could pay—so our hopes were again crushed and we had to look elsewhere. Then a small farm without the desired forest but just four miles from town, much closer to the coast, came up on the internet, to be auctioned off by the estate of the deceased owner. We finally had a fair chance! With our vision of a community we should be able to compete with others interested in the dilapidated farm. Then the other family left "alpha group" on the eve of the internet auction, leaving just our family. After nearly two years of networking, in the end we were alone when we had to make the critical decisions. We did not know that some businesses would be bidding against us, and the price soon surpassed what we thought we were willing to pay. Should we drop out or dare raise our bid? We did continue, but each bid was a crisis decision. Finally the real estate agent called and said the owners had stopped the bidding and wished to

While we wanted to roll up our sleeves and jump into the practical work, we knew that communication and networking were actually more crucial.

offer the property to us. They knew their mother would have wanted it kept as a family farm rather than become a golf course or tire warehouse.

Within a few hours of receiving the offer to buy, we founded Suderbyn Cooperative Society, consisting of just our family, on May 8, 2008. Our friends in the network offered their names so we could have enough adults to legally register the society. This was not the way we wanted

it to develop, but the cooperative society would facilitate taking in new members that we felt would come once the dust settled and they could calmly decide on buying into the cooperative-owned ecovillage property. Our first event inviting in the network to the property brought only one couple that wished us the best of luck.

We had plenty to do registering the cooperative, finding eco- and ethical financ-

ing, and organizing all the due diligence work to take over the beautiful property with its very run-down buildings. While we wanted to roll up our sleeves and jump into the practical work, we knew that communication and networking were actually more crucial in getting a community going than laboring alone. We had bought a similar farm on the island 12 years previously and in the end sold it due to the social isolation it created.

Utilizing the network's web portal, we were able to create invaluable web pages for the new ecovillage project to be seen. This was complemented by getting listed with ic.org, GEN, Eurotopia, and the Swedish site www.alternativ.nu. Just weeks after my family and one university student, Disa, moved in at the beginning of September 2008, we received an international work camp of 10 volunteers from Service Civil International for a two-week work-stay. The work camp not only gave us practical help, but created the atmosphere of the international intentional community I had longed for. While it lasted only the two weeks, news of our ecovillage project had been advertised around the world in several dozen languages. The work camp also gave us good local press, which led to growing curiosity by the islanders. The municipality asked if we could receive a twin city energy-interested group from the Netherlands. We had somehow become recognized by the local authorities as a grassroots project worth visiting, even if it all was still mostly on paper.

In November we organized a permaculture introductory course for local and mainland Swedes interested in the ecovillage project. We brought in qualified trainers from Denmark and southern Sweden. We succeeded in gathering 20 participants. While we had hoped the course would be an injection of new members and project activists, it gave us one new member and a few activists. This was the second major effort to build up a broader group behind the initiative, and it seemed to not really succeed. A third of the participants requested to pay in our alternative currency, Kufic grivna, which we created on-the-spot to accommodate all those interested but who could not pay in national currency. Several of these interested had become or were becoming unemployed during autumn 2008, but saw ecovillage living as a possible way out of looming private financial hard times. Financially and physically, the course took resources from other investments, but we felt it was a necessary statement about what type of community we were trying to establish and thus which type of individuals we were seeking. All the sweat and long hours spent creating the training room in the dilapidated barn also resulted in a permanent exhibition to show visitors what we were trying to do.

A month later we held an Open House in the training room for the neighbors and got a good response. Almost all of our neighbors came, as well as many from the nearest town that had seen the TV report which came as a follow-up to the course. Despite the Scandinavian winter, we tried to keep the development process going with monthly "working weekends" and at the same time continue the communication efforts though Powerpoint® presentations and guided tours whenever asked. And, impressively, people came and helped out digging ditches despite darkness and falling snow.

As spring 2009 approached, it was time for more serious investment, even if we have little money. We planned the development of a huge forest food garden and the vegetable garden. The first-mentioned had to be significant; our wind-whipped land had been flattened after centuries of plowing; the Alaskan latitude demanded tailoring the land to deal with the cold; and the noise and lack of privacy caused by the highway that tangents our western property line had to be mitigated. The solution was constructing seven large sun traps consisting of earthen embankments 6 ft. tall, 16 ft. wide, and installed as 150 ft.-diameter horseshoes forming a chain diagonally across the property. Thanks to the slowdown in the construction industry, we got a good price on the excavation work. The excavations, the large solar cooker reflector from Switzerland, and the velomobile from Germany gave us a swell of media coverage which resulted in a rise in requests for study visits.

So while the community has still not developed as hoped, we continue to develop the site with the funds and labor available. We keep a high profile to attract the right types of members; it also serves to scare away those who do not really share our vision. And a number of candidates are in touch with us. We have seen that subdividing the property and selling off lots would allow us to develop the land quickly. But would it give us the community we were seeking? We don't think so. So we continue the slow route of not adapting to the mainstream demand, and accept that our community will develop in due time. For us, creating a clearer profile of what we are about is the most prioritized investment, so that those who share our ideas will be able to find us. ❋

Robert Hall is a native Californian gone Swedish, father of three, and currently working for the Swedish development aid agency, Sida. His free-time activities include permaculture, solar cooking, and the Swedish cycling movement.

Top: Erik and Fabian carry out seedlings for planting, May 2009.
Above: Work camp meal, September 2008.

SOMERVILLE ECOVILLAGE: Culture and Creating Spaces

By Vida Carlino

In a changing world full of unclear challenges and conflicting viewpoints, people are choosing to re-investigate the ideas of community living. People are looking at their quality of life and asking, "Is this what I really want?"

In my experience a community is a diverse group sharing a common understanding, and the more they share and contribute, the richer the community becomes. After all, community is not something we try to get to or be, it is how we live. People are drawn to community living for individual reasons—social, economic, political, environmental, or any number of others—but once engaged they have the opportunity to share these differences and influence the collective. It is through this kind of sharing that the culture of Somerville Ecovillage emerged.

This page and next: Somerville's wine-making event, February 2006.

Somerville Ecovillage started with people first. In fact, the physical environment is not yet built, yet we have a vibrant community scattered throughout Perth and surrounding areas. After the perfect site for Somerville Ecovillage was located (in 2002), the problem of financing the acquisition seemed daunting. But then the perfect solution manifested, where parties interested in living the vision were asked to loan funds to purchase the land: $1.1 million in total. Not only are community members involved and dedicated, they also have a strong sense of ownership.

In a culture that embraces the wisdom of the crowd, along with a good dose of professionalism, the community gathered to review all commitments and intentions expressed in our documents and publications, to draw out the collective vision and the value statements.

Somerville Ecovillage Vision:
A vibrant village where community flourishes, in which every person is supported and contributes in balance with a sustainable ecological ethic.

This vision and the associated values are the foundation for how we relate to each other, the natural environment, and the world. They are by no means rules. Instead they are set guidelines on how we would like to live. They are a beacon on how to Walk our Talk.

We always believed the topic of cats and dogs at Somerville would be difficult to address. That is why we left it until June 2005. The day arrived, and gathered in a large circle sat 73 members. The question was asked: "Do cats and dogs belong at Somerville?" It was a difficult and emotional gathering as individuals voted "No," knowing that they were saying goodbye to their beloved pets. This selfless decision was based on what is best for Somerville and the natural environment and not what is best for the individual. This moving experience was a living example of common understanding at its best.

As a community we have experienced many challenges. In the early stages of the project, financial constraints could have crippled Somerville, but instead, many individuals with the required expertise restructured their work commitments so they could work diligently on the project. For some, this entailed moving to Chidlow, the nearest town. This was a major commitment and lifestyle change given that success was not assured.

All photos courtesy of Vida Carlino

As we worked together in creating our dream, unseen opportunities emerged, individual skills and expertise increased, and new career paths opened.

It took up to five years for these people to be remunerated for their time and effort.

During this period the community collectively developed the village design, building guidelines, bylaws, and governance model. Our community is blessed with members with diverse skills and expertise and willingness to contribute. As we worked together in creating our dream, unseen opportunities emerged, individual skills and expertise increased, and new career paths opened. Some people who had never previously worked in the areas of sustainability, community development, administration, marketing, and finance were now employed in such positions. It is our strong belief that every person has capabilities and talents, and having a good life depends on whether we have the opportunity to use them. This opportunity has been enhanced for many community members of Somerville.

It is one thing to talk community, but without the opportunity to engage and participate, it is just words. At Somerville we have focused on creating spaces for the community to experience each other. This may be as simple as a place to loiter with intent, or as specific as the "Nemeton," a place for quiet contemplation and meditation.

Our famous yellow shed is the focal point for much celebration and the home of Somerville Sundays, which are held each month and are our main vehicle for project updates, visioning, and dealing with the many issues related to creating a world-class ecovillage. In fact, many events have transformed into rituals and customs, like our February water fight or making Somerville Red Wine. We inevitably have formal committees and a management board consisting of delegated representatives, and all meetings are open to any community member. Somerville operates within an open and transparent philosophy. It is through creating spaces for participation that the community has opportunity to contribute and evolve.

It is through all this "doing" that we have created "The Somerville Way," the living culture of our community. We have walked beside and stood on the shoulders of many, including each other. We have been empowered by the collective wisdom of all those who participate. We have dreamed, shared, experienced, pooled resources, struggled, and celebrated. The Somerville Way (as expressed in our documents) reminds us of where we came from, informs us of where we are and what we are doing, and guides us into the future. In this diverse community, the common understanding provides a platform for dialogue and communication, where doing more of what works is the key.

In this time of continual project delays, employment insecurity, and a tightening financial system, people are being forced

to re-evaluate. Is this what I really want? I strongly believe that community strength is directly proportional to the number of people who contribute their abilities to the well-being of the community, and as this well-being expands, so does the well-being of the individuals. These attributes then integrate into all aspects of life.

It is through community that we have the greatest opportunity and influence to live in a culture that we truly value and respect. ❋

Vida Carlino's experience of 25 years in business and her passion for creating low-impact and inclusive communities are key drivers in the concept and establishment of Somerville Ecovillage. With several years of community research and training both in Australia and overseas, she has used her business, health, and social science skills to contribute to the development of the community enterprise model and the social and governance structure for Somerville.

Somerville Ecovillage:
Statutory Approvals and Finance

By Karen Moore

The idea of an ecovillage just outside of Perth, Western Australia, was first conceived in 2000. As we are now in 2009 and still waiting to commence infrastructure works, the gestation can be likened to that of an elephant! We are assuming that the numerous challenges we have experienced mean that we are giving birth to a beautiful, magnificent, and long-lived creation.

The first challenge was finding a suitable piece of land. After an extensive search and whilst lamenting that the search was not proving fruitful, one of our members told us of a farm at Chidlow that was on the market. This had not shown up during the search process as the land comprised seven separate titles and individually the lots were not large enough. However, the combined lots gave us just what we were looking for, a gently sloping north-facing 162 hectares (399 acres), with water on site, predominantly bush, and walking distance to an existing town. Members completed scoring sheets assessing the suitability of the land with respect to solar orientation, water availability, trees, landscape, and other factors, confirming that this was the right site for us. This process was also a good demonstration of the advantages of "tapping into the wisdom of the crowd."

Now we had found the land (April 2002), the next challenge was to raise the $1.1 million to buy it. This is where our small, existing community rallied. We had numerous information sessions at different locations throughout the metropolitan area, and Open Days out on the land (the then owner was very understanding and sympathetic to the cause). All of this was done with volunteer labour, low cost advertising, homemade goodies, members' talents, and great enthusiasm. I can vividly remember one Open Day where we had to extend the parking area as we were overwhelmed with the number of visitors (over 400 attended); and an information session where, after an interesting method of entry (we had to break the window to get in, then call someone to come and replace the window), we had an incredible day with about 100 people attending. Suffice to say, we (65 families) did it, and with no external funding. People felt inspired, and with a sense of trust in the project and project team, community members loaned money to purchase the land. This was an amazing experience of common purpose and community building.

Now the real journey begins... In April 2003 not only was the first baby born at Somerville Ecovillage but it was the first time the Shire Councillors met to discuss the project, the outcome being that a motion was passed to support the Somerville Ecovillage. September 2003 saw the For-

Review of lots, east of future Village Center.

mal Rezoning Submission lodged with the Shire of Mundaring. Rezoning approval was finally gazetted on 14 August 2007 after the Minister for Planning and Infrastructure at the time, Alannah MacTiernan, overturned the Planning Commission recommendations on two occasions, indicating her support of the project. Mind you, a number of us did "stalk" the Minister at a number of public functions so she became very aware of the project—one way of raising your profile!

Whilst we were waiting for the rezoning approval, and in between "stalking" the Minister, work continued on the Local Subdivision and Infrastructure Plan (LSIP). The LSIP was submitted on 19 May 2006 and was approved at the full Mundaring Shire council meeting on 28 August 2007. The LSIP was subsequently sent to the Western Australian Planning Commission (WAPC) for its final endorsement on 18 September 2007; this endorsement was gained as part of the mediation process through the State Administrative Tribunal (see below).

All photos by Neil Robertson

UNLESS

An opening circle celebrating The Lorax by Dr Seuss. Above: Children at tree planting ceremony in community veggie patch. Top right corner: Open Day, tour of the land, overlooking the dam.

In April 2008 we initiated action at the State Administrative Tribunal as we had been advised that the subdivision application that was submitted on 27 June 2007 had stalled at the Shire of Mundaring. At the hearing in May, the mediator/judge ordered all the necessary government agencies to be a part of the mediation process and indicated that a resolution should be easy to achieve. I found it encouraging that once all the relevant parties were together and gained an understanding of what we are trying to achieve, there was a willingness to assist the process. The result of the mediation was that conditional subdivision approval was granted on 3 June 2008. On 7 October 2008 the Shire of Mundaring issued the approval for commencement of infrastructure works.

celebrations!

Throughout the journey we have celebrated the milestones, big and small, with community events involving food, wine, and music. Events such as the Home-stretch Celebration (in an old shed on the land before we even owned it), Black Tie Dinners, and Bush Dances are fondly remembered and have helped cement the community spirit.

One requirement of the LSIP was to have a lot layout. Ian McHarg's Overlay process was used to exclude areas for development, and assuming that all residents would want motor vehicle access to their homes, a fairly linear lot design was created. The community members were not happy with this design, so another survey followed. It transpired that not all residents required vehicle access, which enabled us to alter the design to the clus-

Left: Olive tree in the orchard.
Above: Tallulah at herb spiral in
community veggie patch.

> *Finally we got all our statutory approvals in place,*
> *civil works contract agreed, contractors waiting to start*
> *on site—and the worldwide credit crisis hit!*
> *Our existing financier withdrew support.*

ter format we have today—another example of the advantages of "tapping into the wisdom of the crowd" and the importance of community consultation.

During the process of amalgamating the original seven titles into one lot required for subdivision, we discovered that there were potentially unexploded ordnances (UXO) on one of the lots. Chidlow had been an army training camp for new recruits during World War II. Experts were called in from Queensland, the property was given the "all clear," and the community soldiered on.

It has been an extremely long process to get rezoning and subdivision approvals, largely due to our development being unique and other parties needing to gain an understanding of exactly what we are doing. Our requirements haven't always been the right shape to get the ticks in the right boxes as easily as wished for. We have engaged in a lot of negotiation to ensure the integrity of our vision is not compromised. Our perseverance has been rewarded with Somerville Ecovillage being awarded a Special Commendation from the Planning Institute of Australia in the category of Environmental Planning and Conservation in November 2008.

As evidence of the commitment of members to something greater than themselves, not only have many members ~~have~~ been involved for seven years, but also from 2002 to 2004 members worked on a volunteer and "conditional fee" basis. This has certainly helped the cashflow. We are blessed to have a deep talent pool of high calibre, skilled professionals including engineers, accountants, and health care professionals on whose expertise we can draw. One community member dubbed 2005 as the year

of "death by Powerpoint®"!

Finally we got all our statutory approvals in place, civil works contract agreed, contractors waiting to start on site—and the worldwide credit crisis hit! This resulted in our existing financier withdrawing support for our second round of funding for the infrastructure works. The community has rallied yet again and provided further short-term funding. I found the experience of sitting in circle in February with members, exchanging different ideas on how we may be able to obtain the finance we need, moving and very humbling. Knowing that there is such a tremendous support base to tap into is food for the soul.

One outcome of the February meeting was to start a veggie patch. So, despite the finance challenge, work commenced and we have a blossoming garden with a Chook Castle (rather than a hen house!). Doing physical work alongside fellow community members and working things out in a team environment has confirmed for me the reasons I joined this wonderful community, Somerville Ecovillage.

We are yet to secure the finance for the infrastructure works, but as the riddle says: How do you eat an elephant? One bite at a time. ❉

Karen Moore has used her 16 years' experience in senior finance roles to assist the Somerville Ecovillage project as Finance Coordinator and Company Secretary. Involved with the Somerville Ecovillage development since December 2001, she has a reputation for "getting things done."

CREATING COMMUNITY WHERE YOU ARE BY BOB GLOTZBACH

Turning a trailer park into a community by buying it cooperatively.

Moon Valley:
A Community on the Horizon?

Moon Valley crowd.

3/20/2010

Can a circumstantial neighborhood, one that has no formal entering process for new residents, become a community? I'm thinking of community as a place where there is a strong consciousness of collective as well as individual rights and where a majority of residents participate in neighborhood issues and programs. There are some examples in both small and large municipalities (with support from these towns), but most neighborhoods in America are not real communities, even when a place with its geography and resources desires it.

An example of the latter is the neighborhood we live in called Moon Valley, a large mobile home park in Sonoma, California. We came here in 2005, soon after moving away from our half-acre farm in rural Glen Ellen, just eight miles up the valley from Sonoma. Now that we were in our 80s, it was a time in our lives for something more urban, but having been community activists in several neighborhoods since the two of us came together in 1987, we were still looking for another community possibility. Moon Valley as a place seemed to have all the attributes of a real community, and it

was attractive to us. The 250-home development built in the 1960s is bounded on three sides by thoroughfares and on the fourth by a well-defined Sonoma Creek. Walking paths connect neighbors so that residents don't have to go across busy streets to meet. The landscaped private and public areas are well taken care of and have a variety of fruit trees; we have a persimmon tree. At the ends of the neighborhood are two clubhouses, each with a kitchen and library, one with a lounge living room and card room. There is a wood shop, laundry, poolroom, an all-year swimming pool and Jacuzzi, two saunas, and some outside common areas where people can sit and talk. You'd think that a strong community feeling would come from these resources, but we found that not to be the case.

Since we've been here, we've made some good friends, and we really enjoy living here even with its community deficiencies. I became the editor of *Whisperings*, the neighborhood newsletter, for two years; Gena volunteered to be a librarian for the numerous books that had been collected. We worked closely with the Residents' Club, a social organization, seeing ourselves as committees that were part of the whole. What we saw happening was a few people were doing most of the community work, and a majority of the people in the park did not involving themselves, being more or less

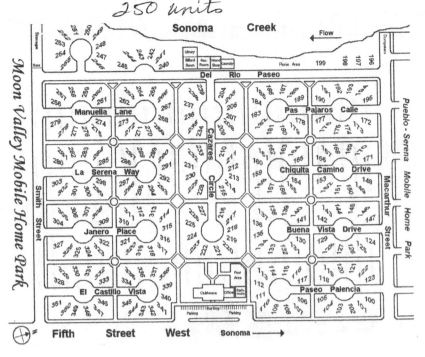

250 units

We won't be able to point a finger at a distant owner when conflict occurs; we'll have to learn how to mediate conflict that's certain to occur among us.

isolates in their living situations. A number of people on the Residents' Club Board had been in their positions for a long time, and with declining interest of residents in social programs, the club board decided to disband in 2007.

Shortly thereafter, a homeowners' association formed to act as a protector of resident interests, to make sure a rent control ordinance stayed in place and to oppose any attempts to subdivide the entire parcel. This process of subdivision is often referred to as condolization. Homes are situated on land owned by a corporation headquartered over 500 miles away in southern California; homeowners pay space rent for use of the land. There has been a trend towards park owners selling properties for subdivision, which would require residents to either buy the land their units sit on or move away. So the homeowners' association came together to defend residents' interests and prevent things like that from happening.

But a new wrinkle came into the equation. Periodically the owners of the park have revised their rules and regulations for resident and management compliance, and most recently this occurred at the beginning of 2010. The residents had minimal input in affecting changes that were made. The most controversial issue was changing the neighborhood into an all-ages park, eliminating the 55-plus age requirement for living here. When the owner made a presentation of the changes in the fall, there was a large turnout of residents and many voiced their opposition to the age change, but the owner representative was not swayed by the dissent.

The homeowners' association has become more proactive lately, and with resident approval by majority vote, is presently going through a process to buy the park from the owners and make it into a cooperative owned by the residents. The park was not for sale, but the owner said that the corporation would entertain an offer from the

park residents. A consultant has been hired to work with the homeowners' association and the owner in developing a fair market value for the park. There has been strong support from the residents for this action and this has brought more homeowners into communication with each other, a necessary step for any community building.

As a cooperative, the homeowners collectively will have ownership of the land, and that raises the question whether we, the residents, will make ourselves knowledgeable about cooperative living in taking the responsibility to oversee the management of a co-op? And, how will we handle the conflict that goes along with making up rules for us all to live by? We won't be able to point a finger at a distant owner when conflict occurs; we'll have to learn how to mediate conflict that's certain to occur among us, now being the owners of the park.

First, a purchase price has to be arrived at and then loans and grants have to be obtained to complete a sale. Forming a cooperative is an exciting prospect for us. It seems to be a good route for us in becoming a real community. Can an action like this by itself help to raise a community consciousness for residents of Moon Valley? It's questionable! It seems appropriate to be working on some conflict resolution program while the sale is being negotiated; Gena and I have some ideas about how to go about that and are inviting our neighbors to participate. We'll have to see how the process goes. ❧

Bob Glotzbach and Gena Van Camp are community activists, both of whom have had some community and "forming community" experiences, as well as being active neighborhood volunteers. They have co-written an unpublished manuscript, "Place, Consciousness, and Participation: the Elements of Real Community."

FORMING COMMUNITY BY MERRY HALL

Illustration courtesy of Merry Hall

Grass Valley

Affording a New Community: a Story of Persistence

We have a dream for AMMA Community. The name, meaning "our Mother who dwells in Earth," honors Mother Nature. The seed of this dream is well planted, fertilized by many hopes, shined upon with great vision, and watered by many tears. For over a year we planned big under the misconception that a multi-million dollar grant was going to become available to somebody willing to seed ecovillages throughout the nation. With high hopes, we submitted a provisional offer for a 650-acre riverfront farm in Turner, Maine. We envisioned an ecovillage of 100 families sharing the land, creating 2.5-acre homesteads and supporting itself and its members with a shared farm, green cottage industries, and an educational facility. We generated impressive documents on a founding vision, bylaws, incorporation, membership policy, sustainability, and conflict resolution

Disappointments could have miscarried our dream. First came a big split over governance styles. Then red tape delayed the funding. Next the land went to another buyer. Then it became painfully clear that outside funding would never materialize.

What were four dirt poor remnant families to do? Give up? NO! Our commitment to our shared vision and the community bonds we had forged were too strong. The seed within us had taken root too deeply. Our plans had become too real to us. Here are the principles that nourish our dream:

AMMA is a community committed to:
- *Sustainability, regeneration, and resilience*
- *Exploration of humanity and nature's potential for co-creation*
- *Homesteads nurturing each member family*
- *Permaculture principles*
- *A resilient, self-sustaining community economy*

- *Community that balances belonging and autonomy*
- *Inclusive governance that honors both self and others*
- *Educational and informational outreach to the larger community*
- *Providing a public demonstration of sustainable lifestyles*

There was no way we could let such a vision wither. It had quickened within us. It became apparent that it would not be born a king, but we are prepared to welcome a peasant.

So we downsized our plans drastically, investigating first a couple of farms on the market in the $200,000 to $300,000 range. These proved unsatisfactory either because of size, soil fertility, or inappropriate location. We also came pretty quickly to realize that we were still reaching beyond our economic means. To be viable, our dreams must be practical as well as visionary.

So we persisted, finding 90 acres in Starks, Maine that spoke to our hearts with good woodlands, fields, brooks, orientation, and a mobile home that would serve as temporary dwelling for each family in turn as we collectively built our affordable green homesteads. The four families that had hung in there through the hardships envisioned a community of up to 18 families, each contributing $15,000 toward the community land and personally financing the materials for permacultural, off-the-grid homesteads we would help one another to build. This plan would necessitate liquidating our current assets. We would have to empty our wallets in order to fulfill our dreams. We became ready to put our shoulders to the plow.

One member said she was willing and able to put down the $65,000 50 percent down payment which the rest of us would pay back to her with our $15,000 shares as we became able. Two other families would immediately put their current homes

(continued on p. 78)

RELATED BACK ISSUES

Power and Empowerment

The following COMMUNITIES back issues speak to various aspects of our current "Power and Empowerment" theme, as do some others not listed here. See communities.ic.org/back_issues for a complete list of back issues and ordering information. You may also order back issues $5 apiece plus shipping using the form on page 13.

AFFORDING A NEW COMMUNITY

(continued from p. 64)

on the market. The fourth family was willing to remain in and mortgage its current home until the remaining 50 percent would be paid off. Only as new families joined us would we be able to afford the barn, greenhouse, and gathering hall we envisioned. Our dream would evolve organically. Great! AMMA Community was regenerated, until...

...the member with the down payment readily available got cold feet and backed out. Now what? We could not allow our dream to be so arbitrarily aborted.

We continue our commitment to our vision. So we are embarking on a membership drive to raise the necessary $65,000 down payment ASAP. We are beginning our educational outreach, even while still unlanded, with a six-session workshop on "Monitoring and Increasing Sustainability." Sessions one to four will focus on sustainability in the areas of ecology, economy, health, and social networks. Sessions five and six will be six-month and one-year follow-ups to monitor progress and plan the next steps. We believe personal and community sustainability is a dream whose time has come. We more than believe it; we are actively pregnant with the idea and now seek competent midwives to help us give birth to it. ☙

Merry Hall, retired teacher and current sustainability activist, is author of the book, Bringing Food Home: The Maine Example, *secretary of AMMA Community, and a member of the Food for Maine's Future Board of Directors. If you are interested in joining, donating, or investing to make the dream of a Maine eco-community manifest at AMMA, please contact her at mainely-organic@yahoo.com, 207-522-2606, or 41 Katherine's Way, Sabattus ME 04280.*

Whole new COMMUNITIES magazine website!
communities.ic.org

Going from Vision to Culture

By Daniel Weddle

My name is Daniel Weddle. I am one of the founders of Dandelion Village, an intentional ecocentric community growing in Bloomington, Indiana. Nearly all of my creative energy for the past three years has been sunk into founding this community. I am the man in the middle of the villagers, city officials, neighbors, and those working for us. I am a politician, speculator, developer, home designer, logger, general contractor, and anyone else I need to be in order to have a place to call home with my friends. My role is beautiful, but exhausting. The story below is about my journey to move out of the center of this project and help it to stand on its own.

Starting with Vision

In January I participated in a panel discussion on a local radio show about the ecovillage movement. A lady called in from a community called Keeping Hill and said, "We have land, a common house, and desire to find more people to live there." She asked me how to find people. The question caught me off guard. I floundered a bit, made some semi-coherent statements, and then spent bits of the last five months thinking about it.

If she were to call me today, I would say: find your vision, make it as clear as you can, and start living and sharing it. Vision is the first step, but ultimately the cross-section of people who are involved in a project at any given time are the culture. Now I want to share some examples of how I have begun empowering others to turn our Dandelion Village vision into our culture. All this work is best viewed through the lens of a young founder working to build community while looking for himself and protecting his sanity.

Handing the Community over to the Community

In fall of 2011, the tension of building a village began pulling me apart and I started to search for ways to dissolve my responsibilities and shift them to the community. I decided to experiment with how much input I had to put into a project before others were empowered to take over. I directed the clearing of a shrubby area of the village, cut garden beds, disked, and cover cropped. Once the land was prepped, I tried to step back and let others take over. But then in January Megan Hutchison approached me about an opportunity to order orchard trees.

We had only a week to decide and I froze up, even though the orchard land was prepped. I communicated to Megan that I was unsure whether the group would be ready to plant trees in the spring without my guidance, and that I was personally overextended in commitments to the village and so couldn't take this on. Megan came to our next public meeting anyway and presented the opportunity. When I said I could not invest in the project but the community had the funds to support it, two people stepped up. This was a big shift; I ceded some control over the project, and others were able to take pieces and make them their own.

Today I can walk through our young orchard and garden even though I did not turn a shovel to make either happen. Enough was provided so that people felt empowered to take on greater ownership of the village and at the same time I was able to move out from some of the burden of being the center. A little preparation energy became big without my help. There is little that is more empowering and beautiful than being trusted. The orchard and garden are the projects of a few that enrich the whole. The work came from their hands and every time they walk through, it is their thing, their individuality in a big communal project.

Going from Founder to Community Member

I've met with my fellow founder, Zach Dwiel, a couple of times to discuss how we could shift our roles from founders to equally contributing community members. We agreed that despite the community's budding energy, it was not yet stable and we needed to choose a metric of stability and push the community toward it. This is where things get muddy, as you can pick an infinite number of metrics. We had already spent a majority of the past two years going through a city rezoning process, and knew that project would come to a close shortly, but it was not enough. Our discussions led us through a 15-bedroom common house, a three-season camping platform called "concrete ruin," and two small community houses. We ultimately realized that all of our conversations revolved around the need for the community to be financially stable. We thus set the goal of Dandelion rental rooms and dues covering the monthly expenditures by the end of 2013.

The push to provide economic stability for the community will be my last contribution above and beyond the norm. If Dandelion Village can't stand as a community then I want to let it fail. Founder syndrome for me is the death of my wants, energy, life-force, as I am crushed by maintaining something that can't carry its own weight. If it can't carry itself it is not community; it is charity. I say with the greatest pride that Dandelion Village feels lighter every day. Thank you fellow Dandelions. ❧

Daniel Joseph Weddle is a founder of Dandelion Village in Bloomington, Indiana. He is currently building his home, Inquisitive Owl, and the home of two other cofounders.

Daniel making hardwood flooring.

The Making of Senior Cohousing: The Story of Wolf Creek Lodge

By Suzanne Marriott

I n 1969, I was driving up Highway 1 just north of Santa Cruz on a warm California day. To my left I saw a farm house and barn. The area was jammed with Volkswagen bugs and buses displaying the usual bright colors, painted flowers, and bumper stickers of the time. I knew there were like-minded people there and that I would be welcome to join whatever party was going on. It turned out to be a hippy wedding, and I was not turned away.

A year later, in the winter of 1970, I was traveling by train through East Germany. We were stopped at a checkpoint when a uniformed conductor tore open the door to my second-class compartment and demanded "Passport!" in a tone that reminded me of Nazi officers from World War II movies. Out the window, I saw a young DDR guard standing beside the track, rifle in tote. On impulse, I flashed him the peace sign. He returned it, not raising his hand, but keeping it discretely by his side. His eyes met mine. The train pulled away.

What do these two stories have in common? They both hold an overarching sense of community—one that transcends place and time. Whether a guard in Russian-occupied East Germany or a California girl looking for fun, we were all connected, all part of one, huge generation—and we knew it. We were a generation that recognized itself, hung together, had fun, and was determined to change the world. And we did.

Theodore Roszak tells us—the boomer generation—that we did it once and now it's time for us to do it again. Change the world, that is. In his new book, *The Making of an Elder Culture*, Roszak writes, "What boomers left undone in their youth, they will return to take up in their maturity, if for no other reason than because they will want to make old age *interesting*." (p. 8) He's talking about us. (Remember Roszak? In 1968 he coined the term "counter culture.") We're still here, and we are going to be here for quite some time. Roszak reminds us that we are still a power to be reckoned with, still active agents for positive change.

Cohousing is part of that change, and *senior* cohousing, in particular, is a social force whose time has come.

My Journey Begins

In the past four years, through my involvement in senior cohousing, I've rediscovered that feeling of connection I had in the 1960s—that feeling of being a part of something larger and nobler than I could achieve on my own. I am once again part of a movement that offers a new way of living, a movement that addresses the social and ecological challenges of the 21st century through sustainable community.

My own journey in senior cohousing began early in the summer of 2006, six months after the death of my husband, who succumbed to complications of multiple sclerosis.

After Michael's death, I began looking for ways to bring new meaning and motivation to my life. Through an online search for "cohousing," a concept both my husband and I had been attracted to in the past, I discovered that a group formation workshop was scheduled that summer in Grass Valley, California. Immediately, I felt drawn to attend that meeting, despite the three-hour drive and the $200 fee it would entail.

As I drove up Highway 80 from my home in the San Francisco East Bay Area, I wondered what I would find. As it turned out, I walked into a workshop with a group of strangers and left knowing

Above: Some members of Wolf Creek Lodge gather at Nevada City Cohousing for a marketing photo session. This photo: Beautiful Wolf Creek flows through the Wolf Creek Lodge property.

they would become my neighbors. That day, 16 households began the long process of building a new and vibrant community. As octogenarian Magdalene Jaeckel, our eldest member, reflects, "Although we are from different backgrounds and didn't know each other in the beginning, I have never found a group that was so spontaneously helpful and fun to be with. It seems to me that the idea of cohousing draws people who are genuinely interested in each other and therefore would make good neighbors."

Starting Our Community

We learned that the cohousing concept was brought to this country from Denmark by Katherine McCamant and her architect husband, Charles (Chuck) Durrett, and these were the people who had called this meeting. One of the things that convinced me to join was their enthusiasm and expertise in creating cohousing communities.

Cohousing communities are small-scale neighborhoods that are planned, developed, and managed by members. With their fully-equipped private units and large common spaces, they provide a balance between privacy and community living. This balance was a major factor for all of us in our choice of cohousing.

Over the ensuing months and years, we grew to become a close-kit community. We named our group Wolf Creek Lodge, after the free-flowing creek that borders our forested property, and embarked on a

Charles Durrett

be in control of our own aging process. Ours will not be our parents' aging. It will be different—vibrant, socially revolutionary, and fun. As one member enthusiastically puts it, "We are cutting-edge!" We are choosing senior cohousing in order to remain independent for as long as possible.

What better way to maintain our independence than through the collective support of our peers? As member Butch Thresh puts it, "We are choosing a place not because we have to, but because we want to. If you have to move because your kids are telling you it's time to move, you have to move somewhere where you don't want to move to. We're making a proactive choice about where

Ours will not be our parents' aging. It will be different—
vibrant, socially revolutionary, and fun.

McCamant guided them thru

multi-year journey to learn about community building. We did not have to create our community from scratch. Katie gave us each a binder that contained recommended procedures, including how to form teams, develop proposals, run business meetings, and make decisions by consensus. Through our team efforts and our monthly business meetings, we adapted all of these tools to our own needs. We had a consultant who led us through the process of crafting our vision statement and learning intentional communication skills. Through a series of workshops with Chuck, we worked on our design for the common facilities and private units, identifying values and priorities and creating the spaces to foster them.

Living lightly on the planet became a primary focus. Our three-story lodge will be compact, the opposite of the urban sprawl many of us hoped to escape. By having a 4,000 sq. ft. Common House at the center of our design, we can reduce the size of our private units and still have everything we'll need. This shared space will include two guest rooms, laundry facilities, a craft area, library, sitting room, and a workshop where we can store and share all kinds of tools. A large kitchen and dining/social/meeting area will provide ample space for community meals and activities. By sharing resources, we will have many opportunities to come together as neighbors.

Our Lodge will be green-built and energy efficient, following ecological construction practices, such as the use of non- or low-toxic materials from sustainable sources, active and passive energy-saving measures, insulation exceeding state standards, low water usage, and responsible landscaping. Our site is walkable to shops and services, reducing our need for cars, and one third of our wooded property will remain open space.

As our dreams became our design, we couldn't wait to move in! We were truly creating a lifestyle revolution—one based on intelligent aging, sustainable living, and community.

Why Choose Senior Cohousing over Intergenerational Cohousing?

Senior cohousing, as opposed to intergenerational cohousing, is our group's choice for many reasons. To begin with, senior cohousing is all about active aging-in-place within a supportive community. We accept the inevitability of aging, and we want to our life goes from here." Many of our members, such as Butch, are planning to move from homes in remote areas, knowing they will not be able to maintain them and their surrounding acreage forever.

Another way to maintain independence is through what we call "co-care." At some point, some of us may need more care than cohousing can provide, but co-care will greatly extend that time. Co-care means that neighbors look out for neighbors. This includes giving people rides to doctors' offices, caring for each other through illnesses, checking up on each other, and, basically, just being good neighbors. As member Pat Elliott says, "I live alone with no nearby friends or relatives. I look forward to knowing that in Wolf Creek Lodge I will be surrounded by friends who will check on me if I don't show up for our morning coffee or walk. And I look forward to doing the same for them. For me, that epitomizes a caring community."

By incorporating "universal design," senior cohousing can accommodate the physical changes that may occur as we age. For example, we will have larger doorways and wheelchair accessible bathrooms throughout. Although our lodge will have three stories, each unit and the Common House will be one-level construction. We will have elevator access to the upper floors.

In intergenerational cohousing, special accommodations are made for children. In senior cohousing, special accommodations are made for adults. For example, we chose to include a crafts area and an espresso bar in our Common House rather than a children's playroom and pool table for teens. Mindful of the realities of aging, our group decided to include designated space for a live-in caregiver. If one or more members should require such a service, they could hire someone to live on site. Remembering the years of caring for my husband when he suffered from MS, I find this provision especially comforting.

Our planning didn't proceed without its opposing viewpoints and difficult discussions, but through these we refined our goals and got to know each other better. A cohousing group doesn't become a neighborhood until members actually move in and start living together, but before that, they do become a community. What holds the community together is the dedication to making decisions based upon what is best for the community as a whole, rather than personal preference. What's best for the community becomes the determining factor.

At the end of our planning phase, Chuck Durrett said of our group: "I'm rather astonished by the level of consciousness the core group participating in the planning develops. When elders spend time talking about the issues of the day and about what it means to be an elder, they get honest and open. They get out of denial. They come to grips with

Left: Wolf Creek Lodge members work with architect Charles Durrett on the design for their lodge.
Middle: The Wolf Creek Lodge community loves to socialize. Here members enjoy a potluck dinner on the deck of members Butch and Virginia Thresh the evening before the monthly business meeting.
Right: Wolf Creek Lodge members are active seniors who enjoy hiking and being out in nature.

Being a part of something larger than myself has given me new opportunities for personal growth, as I venture into new territory and take new risks.

reality." (From an interview: www.secondjourney.org/newsltr/08_Fall/Durrett_08Fall.htm.)

Avenues for Personal Growth

Being a part of something larger than myself—something that calls me to contribute and move ahead toward shared goals—has given me new opportunities for personal growth, and I have been able to venture into new territory and take new risks. For example, as a member of the Process Team, I discovered that I enjoyed facilitating our monthly meetings. As time went on, I became involved with marketing, the last thing I imagined doing. Also, I love to write, and I soon found myself writing articles, ads, and website content, and editing newsletters.

As point persons for the Membership Team, Kirk and his partner, Barbara, have also experienced personal growth and challenges as they work to bring new members into our community. Their stories are unique to their own personalities, yet typical of the type of growth common to all of our members.

Kirk, who had built his own stone cabin far from town, values his solitude and connection with nature. Yet, he realized that isolation has its disadvantages when a neighbor died and was not discovered for days. When Barbara introduced him to cohousing, he was interested, and soon they both became members. He realized that Wolf Creek Lodge offered him a way to combine his need for independence and his love of nature with his growing desire for community. He has come to know our wooded property inch by inch, especially the beautiful creek that flows along its lower boundary. He enjoys showing people the site and inspiring them with his love of the land.

Barbara always saw herself as a support person, not a person in charge. Yet her enthusiasm for her new community drew her into leadership roles, and she became the lead for the Membership Team while also serving on the Process Team and the Financial Team. As one member recalls, "Working with Barbara and Kirk is a lot of fun because they have such enthusiasm for our project."

Recently, Barbara and Kirk have stepped back, as have I, and new members are now in the lead. This is one of the remarkable benefits of cohousing: new people come forward as needs arise. The choice to participate in a cohousing community is an intentional choice, one that is not made lightly. Because of this, commitment runs high and participation follows accordingly.

Problems and Challenges

In creating Wolf Creek Lodge, all was not smooth and easy. We faced our share of obstacles, including the challenges of navigating the city planning maze and the suspicions of future neighbors who feared we were all a bunch of hippies who would hang laundry on our roofs and lower their property values. We embarked on a long process of building a relationship with these neighbors that included going door-to-door for informal conversations, holding "tea and cookies" gatherings at the site, and attending meetings of their Homeowners' Association, where we patiently tried to set their minds at ease. One unconvinced householder insisted that he really didn't understand this cohousing thing and didn't know why anyone would want to live "like that." "But," he added, "You're a bunch of nice people."

Left: Wolf Creek Lodge members gather with their consultant, Annie Russell, for an early community-building workshop at the local Veterans Hall. Middle: The Wolf Creek Lodge Community gathers for their monthly business meeting. Right: Wolf Creeek Lodge members review their design plans.

As our group grew, we gained some members who were geographically distant from Grass Valley and able to attend only a few, if any, meetings and social gatherings. So we took steps to promote inclusion, such as setting up a teleconference line and a listserv where members can access messages and files. Volunteers keep the technologically-disconnected informed through phone calls or face-to-face meetings, and we have a buddy system for new members.

Our Biggest Crisis

In the beginning, we were confident that our construction loan would be approved quickly. We had two-thirds of our units sold. Construction bids were in, and we were ready to build our lodge.

Then the economy collapsed, and banks began requiring much higher equity and collateral. In the fall of 2009, our local bank told us to reapply in the spring of 2010. Meanwhile, we continued to search for other lenders.

Meeting the interest payments on the property loan became another challenge. In September of 2009, we had a special workshop to see if we could come up with the money to cover these carrying costs. It was a long, difficult meeting with a series of discussions followed by secret pollings to determine the amount

each household could commit. In the end, we were able to raise sufficient new funds to meet the carrying costs. We left that meeting exhausted, but with a new sense of solidarity and commitment.

From that point on, marketing became our main focus. We had a workshop to identify new strategies, and we redesigned our website, fliers, and newsletters. Our efforts are paying off, and we are gaining new members. In September 2010, the bank finally approved our loan. We signed a new construction contract, then started working through the title and escrow process. In the middle of October, we broke ground!

Creating the Future

We of Wolf Creek Lodge remain optimistic and enthusiastic about our community and the development of our project. We are one component of a larger movement—the growth of senior cohousing and the quest to find more viable and sustainable modes of living to meet the social and ecological challenges of the 21st century. Our vision is to live the rest of our lives as active members of a vibrant community of elders, dedicated to developing insight and wisdom in order to benefit ourselves as well as the larger community: from our lodge to our city to our state and nation, to the earth that we honor and depend upon. As active seniors, we are once again on the cutting edge of change, pioneering a sustainable and intelligent way to live and actively age in a manner that sustains community and meets the challenges of an endangered planet. We hope to be joined by many others in this venture. To quote again from Theodore Roszak's inspiring new book, *"Urban-industrial culture is aging beyond the values that created it. The revolution belongs to the old, not the young."* (p. 40)

Suzanne Marriott is a member of Wolf Creek Lodge cohousing for active adults in Grass Valley, California and is currently living in Castro Valley in the San Francisco East Bay Area. In addition to writing about cohousing, she is also the author of travel articles and an upcoming memoir. More information about the author and Wolf Creek Lodge can be found at www.wolfcreek-lodge.org.

COMMUNITY LIVING WORLDWIDE BY BILL METCALF

Tasman Village, Australia

Parsons Bay from the deck of the cafe at Tasman Village

"What about cats and dogs?" At last the question that plagues so many intentional communities pops up. Why is it that this question can be so divisive? I look around and everyone in the room who has had any experience with intentional communities either smiles or groans or, in my case, both. People are starting to grapple with one of the key issues of intentional community, the need to regard those around us as community, almost extended family, rather than mere neighbours, so your pet is my business.

I am at the launch of Tasman Village, a fascinating hybrid cohousing/ecovillage project at Nubeena, in the state of Tasmania. I have been invited down by the developer, Ilan Arnon, and his assistant, Lynne Seddon. Two evenings back I addressed a public meeting in Hobart, Tasmania's capital, in support of this project, and today people are meeting on-site to decide whether or not Tasman Village suits their either well-informed or blindly-naïve notions of what an intentional community could and should be.

Tasman Village is on a breathtakingly beautiful 10 hectare (23 acre) site overlooking and having direct access to the placid waters of Parsons Bay, and from there out to the wild waters of Storm Bay and the Southern Ocean where the cold waves and wild winds roll in from Antarctica.

Tasman Village already supports two businesses, a 19-unit motel and resort complex, with heated pool, tennis courts, recreation areas, etc., and a ~~licensed and~~ very popular licensed café, The Hub. Ilan purchased this run-down business several years ago and since then he has negotiated council approval for 65 small, circular blocks on which to build houses, and has strata-titled eight of the existing two-bedroom units, or apartments, all of which are now for sale. At the core of the developing intentional community there is already a communal kitchen and dining room capable of feeding 50 or more people. Most of the core facilities for the intentional community are already in place and it needs only people to become reality.

Why are Ilan and Lynne doing this? There must be easier ways to earn a living? They tell me that they are motivated by social factors such as their desire to live in community, with people from a wide range of ages and outlooks. They want a community with "affordable, sensible, clever and creative homes," on land that "offers abundant natural food," with recreational options, in a strikingly beautiful area with a temperate climate. Sound utopian? Perhaps, but that is Tasman Village.

As with most cohousing projects, the private house sites are quite small, from 114 to 314 square meters (136 to 374 square yards), but this means that over 80 percent of the land will be left available for communal uses such as farmers' market, gardening, reforestation, orchards, sports, or however residents wish to use the site. A small creek crosses the property; there are six dams, and space for several more. Rainwater will be collected from all roofs and reticulated back to houses, while all grey water will be collected and used to irrigate the existing olive groves and stone-fruit orchards as well as any future plantings.

Tasman Village's rural location reminds one of an ecovillage, while the close proximity of houses and the core area with communal kitchen, dining, and recreation rooms is much more like a conventional cohousing project. Ilan deliberately set out to make use of the best features of both cohousing and ecovillage and, in my humble opinion, he has created a remarkable blend. This hybrid cohousing/ecovillage model could be setting new standards of excellence in intentional community design.

The 30 or 40 interested people who have come to the Open Day at Tasman Village have a wide range of questions and concerns ranging from long-term financial returns (probably good) should they invest, and decision-making (hopefully consensus, perhaps with a default vote), to quality of water (very good!)—and, of course, that hoary, intractable problem of pets. In Australian intentional communities many members oppose domestic pets because they kill wildlife and, even if curtailed, their presence will mean that beautiful native animals such as wallabies will stay well away, and their free-range chickens and ducks could be threatened. Other people, however, are just as passionately devoted to their pet cats and dogs, thinking of them almost as family members, and cannot imagine living without them. Every intentional community has to deal with this problem and few manage to do so without a great deal of angst and awkward compromises. At Tasman Village, Ilan suggests allowing pets, under their owner's control, only in the areas outside the Village centre, as well as having strict rules so that the "quiet enjoyment of residents" is not compromised, and with a clear and well-understood warning/policing mechanism. While that is sensible, I doubt it will resolve matters.

Questions arise about employment prospects at Tasman Village. There are already two businesses, a café and motel, operating on site and there is no reason why other small, tourist-oriented businesses could not be developed using the buildings at the core of the complex. Also, within walking distance there are shops, a district hospital and school, and various other businesses, all of which could provide some employment. Tasman Peninsula has a very active tourism industry, largely focusing on the World Heritage site of the ruins of Port Arthur, one of the most elaborate and diabolical parts of the early to mid 19th century British convict system in what was then called Van Diemen's Land. Surely, I think, people moving here who genuinely want work will be able to find or create it, but that takes some faith.

Ilan and Lynne's promotional material waxes lyrical: "The village centre consists of playgrounds, gathering spaces, holiday accommodation, cafe, recreation centre, indoor heated pool, tennis courts and workshop space for live music performances, creative arts and education. The coals are smouldering from last night's fire by the creek, the rhythm of the drums still pulsating in my head."

Have a look at the Tasman Village website (www.tasmanvillage.com.au/location.html) and you'll see what a lovely spot it is. At time of writing, shares are available for $50,000 for a fully-serviced lot, $140,000 for a two-bedroom unit, or $188,000 for land and a house of your choice. This intentional community has been designed to be sustainable and I can see no reason why it will not succeed.

I'll closely follow the bright future of Tasman Village, a fascinating hybrid cohousing/ecovillage intentional community. ☙

Dr. Bill Metcalf, of Griffith University, Australia, is the author of numerous scholarly and popular articles, plus seven books, about intentional communities, the most recent being The Findhorn Book of Community Living. *He is Past President of the International Communal Studies Association and has been* COMMUNITIES *magazine's International Correspondent for many years.*

Photos courtesy of Bill Metcalf

Looking away from the water, back over the rolling fields of and behind Tasman Village.

Cafe in the middle, some of the residential units on left, and newly planted olive grove on the right.

Living the Questions

By Coleen O'Connell

Joanne Moesswilde

Jeffrey Mabee

Jeffrey Mabee

In the small coastal village of Belfast, Maine, an ecovillage is brewing. The ingredients have been steeped, following the recipe of a cohousing project and the dream of becoming an ecovillage. Years in the planning, with designs percolating and group processes filtered through, we broke ground in fall 2011. The first homes are being built as I type this. Move-in for the first residents is slated for May 2012.

Forty-two acres at the edge of town, two miles walking and biking distance to downtown, 36 households will stand. Sandwiched between horse farms, the land is open with hay fields while the Little River defines its southern border. Beautiful views of the coastal Maine hills will greet us each morning as we wake in our south-facing sun-dependent homes.

What are our dreams for becoming an ecovillage? The mission for Belfast Cohousing & Ecovillage is "to be a model environmentally sustainable, affordable, multi-generational cohousing community that is easily accessible to Belfast, includes land reserved for agricultural use and open space, and is an innovative housing option for rural Maine." (www.mainecohousing.org)

Our mission opens many small but significant questions to be decided as we grapple with giving definition to that irascible word *sustainable*. What, exactly, are we trying to sustain? A way of life? The planet? An ecosystem? What will truly make us an ecovillage? So far we answer this with plans for farming, growing our own food, putting food by, shared resources, a neighborhood of the old-fashioned type where the village raises the child, living in harmony with the land, allowing there to be

space for the more-than-human world... an ecological vision for sure, but one that is still only a vision and not yet real.

In the design process, we started with houses, of course. How to arrange them became clear when our decision was to go with a solar design; next came the decision for duplex/shared wall houses. (Now this pushed the psychological boundaries of middle to upper-middle class folks!) Then came a significant pivotal decision to get off petroleum (at least for our homes—we'll deal with cars later...a much stickier issue), and thus the hiring of the local Design/Build team of GO Logic who build to German Passiv Haus design standards. (See sidebar for more information.) Given the climate in Maine, where 90 percent of the winter home-heating fuel is petroleum based, this was a radical decision. Not even gas cook stoves with those telltale propane tanks outside will exist for our homes. Nor will we have wood stoves as back up—we didn't want to breathe each other's smoke. For some of us, imagining a winter without a wood stove as, at the least, back-up heat for a snowstorm that takes the grid down, is akin to heresy. Thank goodness the prototype house that GO Logic built a few miles away is performing to Passiv Haus standards and we have seen the data and are assured that we will be warmed by the sun as we are cocooned within the super-insulated walls of our homes.

With a mission in place to become sustainable, affordable, and multi-generational, we have mostly failed on one account: affordability. By making the decisions we did, we have left out most of the young Maine families that reside in our area. Affordable, we came to understand, is relative. Our prices work for out of state or urban-dwelling prospective members, but are not affordable for most of the young families that already live here. High-paying jobs are not plentiful in these parts, known mostly for its beautiful scenery, recreational summer boating, and organic and conventional farming. The affordability issue also squeezes on the mission to be multi-generational. Because of the costs, we have easily attracted older, close to retirement-aged people who are trading larger homes for a small, energy-efficient homes while we have struggled to retain young families with children under the age of 12. When you look at the demographics for cohousing communities around the country you will find highly educated, progressive folks, with plenty of discretionary time on their hands, and income levels that rank in the middle to upper-middle class range—hardly the demographics for Waldo County, Maine, which is one of the poorer counties in our state. But we do have families with children and for that we are grateful.

These issues have been compounded by the timing of our project. The land was bought in July 2008, with our spirits soaring as months of planning were turning real when people plunked down money to buy the land. August, one month later, the economy collapsed, caused, in part, by a burst of the housing bubble. This project is a testament to the sustained vision held by its members in that we were able to break ground three years from that land purchase with 21 houses sold. Since ground-breaking we have sold three more. We continue to market the remaining 12 units with the goal that the project will be complete with Common House by the end of 2014. Given the bad financial climate, we were also counseled by a former cohousing developer, John Ryan, to do our own self-financing, saving all the paperwork and oversight that shaken bankers would hold us to. Though risky, it has proven to be a way forward in this devastated housing market. As each house is built, the risk becomes less and less. Our final goal is to sell the last remaining houses so that work on the Common House can commence. When the Common House is complete, the main characteristic for a

Photos by Steve Chiasson

Passiv Haus

A Passive House (Passiv Haus in German where it originated) is a very well-insulated, virtually airtight building that is primarily heated by passive solar gain and by internal gains from people, electrical equipment, etc. Energy losses are minimized. Any remaining heat demand is provided by an extremely small source. Avoidance of heat gain through shading and window orientation also helps to limit any cooling load, which is similarly minimized. An energy recovery ventilator provides a constant, balanced fresh air supply. The result is an impressive system that not only saves up to 90 percent of space heating costs, but also provides a uniquely terrific indoor air quality.

A Passive House is a comprehensive system. "Passive" describes well this system's underlying receptivity and retention capacity. Working with natural resources, free solar energy is captured and applied efficiently, instead of relying predominantly on "active" systems to bring a building to "zero" energy. High performance triple-glazed windows, super-insulation, an airtight building shell, limitation of thermal bridging, and balanced energy recovery ventilation make possible extraordinary reductions in energy use and carbon emission.

(See www.passivehouse.us/passiveHouse/PassiveHouseInfo.html.)

Je'frey Mabee

cohousing community will be in place, but then the challenging task of turning all of this into an ecovillage will remain.

As you read this, the first gardens will be producing the first crop of food. The Land Use Committee is deep into its design for the use of the common land: where to put the community gardens; how much acreage to set aside for the CSA farm; how to run that farm; where will the chickens, sheep, pigs go, the soccer field and playground for the children, the campfire ring for nightly sing-a-longs? This part is not a dream; it is hard work and the task of getting 24 households (and eventually 36 households) to agree to the design is a process in and of itself. The growing skill level of managing the decision-making process of a large group of people has brought us from a traditional consensus model of decision-making to moving toward the practice of sociocracy, or dynamic governance. This is both exciting and riddled with obstacles—time being one of them. Distance between members is another. Difference of opinion is always an issue, and issues of power ever present. We have finally scheduled a weekend workshop and are bringing in a renowned facilitator, John Buck, to get us started on dynamic governance.

Sociocracy comes to us from The Netherlands. A Dutch businessman proposed this method back in the '90s as new way of running his business so every person would be respected and included and the interests of the minority as well as the majority would be heard (O'Rear and Buck, 2000). The format and ground rules offer a built-in efficiency such that a large group of people can make decisions together without getting bogged down in trying to come to a full agreement within all its membership. It is a process of consent, where the decision can be made if no one raises a reasoned or paramount objection to going forward with a proposal that has been put on the table. We learn to trust the committees that come up with the proposals and the outcome is that we are all able to live with the decisions. The efficiency factor is most attractive to us, after four years of mostly successful but often slow and stressful consensus processes. We are excited to finally have a clear sense of at least the first 24 household members. Previous facilitation and decision-making trainings have been lost on many people who have come and gone from the project. We have spent money to train people, only to see them leave the project, including most of the founding members. With purchase-and-sales agreements in hand, we can safely move ahead with the new sociocracy training in hopes that the groundwork we are laying now, before we move in, will see us through many years of successful decision making as we collaboratively build the community we have envisioned.

We are slogging through the muck but the vision remains clear. The larger Belfast community is watching us. This is a small town after all, where the networks weave and wind themselves across every sector of the culture. We are under scrutiny. Will we truly accomplish all that we set out to do? Will we be the gold standard for what the word sustainability really means? Will we become yet another example of the growing ecovillage movement? Will we be the hippie village that most folks think we are? Or will we be a group of middle to upper-middle class people living comfortably on a nice piece of land in nice energy-efficient houses?

As Rilke so brilliantly advised, "Be patient toward all that is unsolved in your heart and try to love the questions themselves like locked rooms and like books that are written in a very foreign tongue. Do not now seek the answers, which cannot be given you because you would not be able to live them and the point is, to live everything. Live the questions now. Perhaps you will then gradually without noticing it, live along some distant day into the answer."

Here at Belfast Cohousing & Ecovillage, we are living the questions. ❧

Coleen O'Connell, a member of the Belfast Cohousing & Ecovillage community, has served on the leadership team for the project. Coleen is the Director/Faculty of the Ecological Teaching and Learning MS Program for educators at Lesley University in Cambridge, Massachusetts. Her professional and personal passion has been to explore ecological literacy and sustainability in the context of our personal lifestyle choices. She has traveled internationally with students living in and studying the ecovillage movement. She cofounded a small ecovillage, Ravenwood, in the midcoast region of Maine which has been a teaching laboratory for Lesley University and the Audubon Expedition Institute (now the Expedition Education Institute). She can be reached at oconnell@lesley.edu and welcomes your comments or questions.

References:
O'Rear, Tena Meadow and Buck, John. "Going Dutch," Communities, Winter 2000, #109, pp. 38-43.
Rilke, Rainer Maria. (1903.) *Letters to a Young Poet.*
www.passivehouse.us/passiveHouse/PassiveHouseInfo.html
www.mainecohousing.org

Dandelion Village: Building an Ecovillage in Town

By Maggie Sullivan

It may seem impossible to create an intentional community inside an existing city with all the difficulties in zoning restrictions, red tape, and political jockeying. However, Dandelion Village successfully navigated the legal hoops to form an ecovillage within the city of Bloomington, Indiana and their success can be replicated elsewhere. Their keys to success were understanding the process, identifying allies in positions of power, and communicating with complete transparency about their goals and plans.

While rural ecovillages can provide better opportunities for farming and connecting with nature, urban locations have their own benefits, like car-free living, sewer systems, public libraries, better school options, a market for goods produced by the ecovillage, and a more vibrant social scene. Danny Weddle, one of the founders of Dandelion Village, dreamed of creating an ecovillage in his college town and gathered a group of five people who were ready to make it happen. "We looked for a property that was 15 minutes from downtown on a bike," said Danny. Their original vision was of a 50-member community on a permaculture-designed urban farm with members living in small, minimalist cabins and sharing a communal building with the kitchen and bathrooms. This design would allow higher density than typical single family home developments while maintaining much more greenspace and focusing on "hyperlocal food production."

By scouring the property listings and keeping an eye out for "for sale" signs, they located a potential property just south of town. They held a series of work sessions to produce a 14-page ecovillage development plan. At the same time, Danny, Zach Dwiel, and Carolyn Blank set up casual meetings with a few sympathetic city council members, such as the chair for Bloomington's Peak Oil Task Force. These city council members were very supportive and had many suggestions on how to navigate the planning process. Their chief advice was to start talking with the city planning department immediately to determine their options and the best approach for obtaining approval.

Like many fast-growing communities, Bloomington has extensive development guidelines geared towards preserving the exceptional quality of life valued by its citizens. Simultaneously ranked as one of the best college towns, one of the best places to retire, and one of the best gay/lesbian communities, its local culture is artsy, diverse, environmentally conscious, and progressive. Happily, the staff at the planning department was intrigued by Dandelion Village. "Many of the goals of this project…are things the city has been dictating and encouraging through the Growth Policies Plan," said development review manager Pat Shay, commenting on its compact urban form and its use of an otherwise hard-to-develop lot. However, the project was a challenge because it did not meet traditional zoning requirements. "This was a new issue for Bloomington," said planning director Tom Micuda. "We did not have a code for cohousing and that meant we had to go for rezoning for the land. Essentially we did a PUD." PUD (Planned Unit Development) was

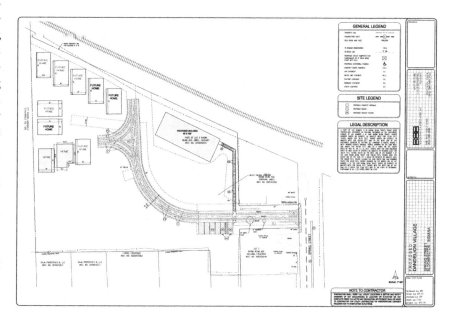

Photos courtesy of Maggie Sullivan

Dandelion Village bees.

Dandelion Village greenhouse.

Daniel Weddle.

a large chicken flock of 50 hens, a small herd of goats, barns, and only two parking spaces for the entire development with the understanding that the members would live largely car-free.

Several plan commission members were skeptical of the idea and many were concerned about having farm animals near a residential neighborhood. However, they were impressed by the group's dedication and preparedness and intrigued by the idea of a project countering the "McMansion trend" seen elsewhere in the city. They did advise the Dandelion group that their PUD request would not be approved without plans developed by a licensed engineer. They also listened attentively to the neighborhood residents who came to the meeting and voiced deep concerns. In response, the Dandelion Village group began canvassing door-to-door to talk with their future neighbors and understand their fears.

Most of the concerns revolved around the idea that a hippie commune would bring in drugs and undesirables, not to mention crowing roosters and loose goats eating their peonies. "It was the issue of 'we're not familiar with this—what will it do to us?'" said Tom Micuda. Many neighbors were also concerned about the impact on existing problems like lack of neighborhood parking and flooding issues. The neighborhood streets routinely flooded during large storm events and there were concerns that any sort of development in the area would make it worse.

The Dandelion group continued to talk with neighbors and even helped relaunch the Waterman Neighborhood Association. They also incorporated water retention structures into their site design. Instead of causing additional flooding problems, their development was designed to improve the situation by holding back runoff from the adjacent neighborhood to the north. "We approached from a permaculture prespective," said Danny, describing how they elected to turn waste into a resource. "Water is one of the most critical flows you can possibly have. There has been a drought for the last three years so we said

designed mainly for developers looking to do large neighborhood developments and allows developers to propose a layout different from the standard pattern. Generally, the idea is that the city gives some sort of concession to the developer (for example, higher density) that is mitigated by the developer offering some benefit to the city, often in terms of subsidizing additional infrastructure costs or helping the city meet one of its development goals like preserved greenspace.

While things were advancing with the planning department, the Dandelion Village group had less success purchasing a piece of land. The owner of the first property raised his price 20 percent, pushing it beyond their budget. Danny, Zach, and Carolyn continued their search via Google Earth and by bicycle. Another promising property fell through before they stumbled on an unusual location that became their ultimate site. It was an odd piece of land sandwiched between a train track, a trailer park, a cemetery, and the blue collar Waterman neighborhood. After conducting environmental studies to determine that there was no contamination from a nearby salvage yard, they purchased the 2.25 acre property for $57,000 and resumed work on the PUD approval process.

Although the Dandelion group had quietly rallied support for months, their first official presentation was to the Bloomington Plan Commission in March 2011. This 11-member board reviews all proposed site developments within city limits and makes a recommendation to the City Council to grant or deny project approval. As part of the process, neighbors were notified of the project and invited to attend the Plan Commission meeting. "In all my years as planning director, Dandelion Village is the most unique project I've ever worked on," said Tom Micuda. "We also had to work through what I would call the fear of the unknown and the fact that ecovillages and cooperative housing are not within the lexicon of standard plan commission members so we had to educate about what that meant."

For the first meeting, Danny and the ecovillage group developed site sketches and proposed development layouts. Their initial strategy was to ask for far more than they thought would be approved, which would allow some room for negotiation. They asked for a density of 15 houses and 75 people as well as site exemptions to allow composting toilets,

(continued on p. 77)

DANDELION VILLAGE: BUILDING AN ECOVILLAGE IN TOWN

(continued from p. 48)

'Let's be selfish and hold that water as much as we possibly can.'"

Hiring a watershed engineer was not cheap but allowed them to present a much more professional set of plans to the Plan Commission at their second hearing. Through the negotiation process, they ended up reducing their density to 30 adults and 10 children with 10 small houses and one large communal building that could contain up to 15 bedrooms as well as a large kitchen and dining hall. They had originally hoped that the small houses could be built without kitchens and bathrooms but that would have classified them as a commercial development (e.g. residence camp) and required the installation of sprinkler systems in all buildings—nearly as expensive as putting in kitchens and bathrooms! They did get permission to have both chickens and goats on the site as well as barns for their agricultural equipment. Composting toilets were abandoned in favor of city sewer connections.

The Plan Commission officially approved their request for a PUD in August 2011. By then, public sentiment was generally in favor of the project and the neighbors who had voiced the strongest opposition began admitting some respect for these crazy young people and their vision. Curiosity replaced concern and the project was unanimously approved by the Bloomington City Council in October as an excellent example of walking the sustainability talk.

By this point, Danny and the other ecovillage founders were worn out but happy. They knew there were still three more permitting steps required and they now had the engineering support needed to develop their final plat for the site. In April 2012, they submitted the final plans for review to get their grading permit, which essentially approves their watershed engineering. Simultaneously, they applied for building permits so that the first two homes could be constructed in the summer. As part of their PUD agreement, they must complete all site grading and basic infrastructure (e.g. storm water retention ponds and main roads) before applying for an occupancy permit, which they hope to acquire in the fall. Once the first founders move in, they will start work on two small community houses and the large community building that will provide a gathering space as well as bedrooms that can be rented out to generate income for the ecovillage and house other members as they build their own permanent homes.

The Dandelion group is thrilled by the location and are excited that they have already formed a bond with their new neighbors. "After a year and a half of politics, it feels great to be through the political process and almost ready to break ground," says founder Zach Dwiel. "I'm super excited to start building and stop politicking." While their community has continued to form over potlucks and planning sessions, the members look forward to working side by side building their new home.

Danny acknowledges that this is still the beginning, for both Dandelion Village and for encouraging ecovillage development everywhere. He will be busy for the next couple of years helping the community develop and take ownership of their property. After that, he plans to return to the planning department to propose that their development be used as the model for a new zoning category specifically for ecovillages. "I feel the greatest effect we can have on the ecovillage movement is to set the precedent of a cooperative housing zoning category for the city of Bloomington," says Danny. He hopes this will pave the way for similar developments in Bloomington and even be adopted in other communities. Perhaps someday his ecovillage zoning category will even become the new normal. 🍂

Maggie Sullivan is a Bloomington, Indiana native with a passion for sustainability and a deep love of the Midwest. She co-writes the green living blog www.greencouple.com with her husband Will and serves as president of the nonprofit Center for Sustainable Living. Her favorite ecovillage is Lost Valley Educational Center where she studied permaculture in 2005, and she looks forward to having an ecovillage in her own hometown.

Women heads of households building their own homes

Nashira:
An Ecovillage from the Grassroots

By Giovanni Ciarlo

Attending the Llamado De La Montaña (Call of the Mountain) Bioregional Gathering in Atlantida Ecovillage in Colombia this last January, and witnessing the emergence of the new Latin American organization, C.A.S.A. (Consejo de Asentamientos Sustentables de las Americas), was one of the most enriching and energizing experiences I've had in recent times. And although I really wanted to visit other Colombian ecovillage projects while I was there, I had time to see only one, Nashira, an urban ecovillage near the Colombian city of Cali.

Nashira, which means "Love Song" in the ancient local language, was one of the most amazing ecovillages I have ever visited. It is run by low-income women heads of households. This reflects a widespread social problem in the outskirts of cities in Colombia, where decades of civil conflict has left many women to manage and sustain the household. A Nashira pamphlet states *"The Nashira project goes beyond offering just housing solutions, it seeks to provide a better quality of life, offering a secure and nutritious supply of food within the compound, an environmentally friendly atmosphere, and a source of income through the development of workshops where women can manufacture their own products."*

I arrived in Nashira just before sunset. I was introduced to some of the residents and shown to a unit where I had a reservation to spend the night. I was met by Osiris, the 30-year-old son of Marta, the head of the house. As a sign of the changes undergone by ecovillage members, Osiris is a social sciences faculty member at one of Colombia's rural Universities, and was visiting his mom for the holidays, something I thought was itself out-of-the-ordinary for people in the lower-income social class. He showed me to my room, a spacious, well-lit single bedroom on the second floor of the 700-900 square foot home that Marta had helped to build during one of the training sessions offered by national and international ecovillage consultants.

I hurried to meet Osiris outside for the last bit of daylight to give me a flash tour of the ecovillage. Nashira was founded by a donor who gave the municipal authorities 30 hectares of land to build an 88-home ecological development for women heads of households with matching donations from government housing development funds. To date 48 units are already built, mostly with the sweat equity of their owners, who formed cooperative groups to learn and help each other to build small, attached, efficient, and durable housing units with the assistance of some additional materials, donations, and capacity training. Both national and international organizations spent time teaching ecovillage design and hands-on skills, from village economics (including small businesses that can operate from inside the village) to food production, decision making for self-governance, natural building, bed-and-breakfast ecotourism, a local solidarity economy, alternative renewable energy technologies, and waste management for recycling and recovering of industrial byproducts. One of the organizations doing the trainings is Change the World, where several ecovillage activists in both GEN and ENA work to bring low tech solutions to indigenous and marginalized people and natural reserves in Latin America. Among them is Beatriz Arjona, one of the organizers of the Llamado de la Montaña event and a member of Aldea Feliz, another ecovillage active

Giovanni Ciarlo

Head of household and daughter at Nashira Ecovillage outside Cali, Colombia.

100

in RENACE Colombia—the Colombian ecovillage network, now C.A.S.A. Colombia.

Osiris showed me the common house, a remodeled pre-existing farmhouse where now there is a computer lab and community center. Across from the common house is the solar restaurant, where one can find pastries and coffee during the weekends, and during special events there are cookouts using solar reflectors to grill, boil, fry, or bake many different local dishes with food grown on site. A dirt drive path passes the communal dry toilet built with bottles, mud, and bales of hay. It is beautiful, with the air of a temple or a pagoda where one would go meditate. Art is everywhere, complemented by well designed landscaping that takes advantage of the location to create gardens and paths around the site.

The shallow pool that children play in during the hot sunny days of the tropics is equipped with a converted bicycle pumping mechanism that is instructive as well as functional—pumping water from the well below to fill the pool and to create a waterfall from about eight feet up a wooden tower. The sound is soothing and children use it as a play station while they shower and enjoy the water and the sun.

We were able to see a number of housing units, and greeted people as they came outdoors to wave at us in the last minutes of dusk before dark. Osiris explained how there are several window-stores in some of the houses that sell snacks and beverages as well as some fresh and canned goods and cooking supplies. He told me that people form cooperatives to have more buying and selling choices. He showed me the partridge egg co-op, the chicken co-op, the cassava processing co-op, the recycling and restoring center, the children's daycare, and the rest of the land.

coop

I was blown away at the achievements of this adventurous group of women. They all came from very disadvantaged sectors of the urban population. Most of them lived in shantytowns and cardboard shacks before getting the opportunity to apply and be selected for the project, creating an ecological community of similar women from the grassroots and poorest families in the Cali region.

Nashira impressed me because it is the first example I have seen of an ecological community, aligned with values promoted by GEN, which has emerged from the bottom up. It is a response and a solution to the housing and poverty issues of the oppressed, in a country that has seen decades of civil strife and violence affecting the majority of people, especially those living in the lower economic rungs. It was created not by a population from the privileged sector of society but by the poor, uneducated, economically distraught women leaders with families and dependents of all ages. Added to this mix was the right combination of aide and guidance of national and international agents, alongside committed activists and individuals empowered to help people from the oppressed sector improve their livelihood, because they believe it is possible and it should be done.

Before going to bed I spent time chatting with Marta, Osiris, and Natalia, his younger sister, about growing up in this village, and the opportunities ahead for them. They were upbeat and

positive all the way. Natalia is also about to start college, where she hopes to study architecture so she can help others build affordable sustainable housing. The next day I took a refreshing cold shower, and as part of the cost for staying overnight, received a hefty breakfast of partridge eggs and toast followed by fresh brewed coffee. They even arranged calling a taxi to take me to the airport in the early hours of the morning. That's what I call *"Hospitalidad Latina."*

Seeing Nashira was like taking a breath of fresh air in the middle of the wilderness. It has given me renewed hope for a new society, that I like to refer to as *the reinvention of everything*, from our worldviews to the way we govern ourselves, the way we relate to Mother Earth, and the way we create local cooperative businesses that aim to provide right livelihoods to community members. 🐦

Giovanni Ciarlo cofounded Huehuecoyotl Ecovillage in Tepoztlán, Mexico in 1982. He is a Board member of Global Ecovillage Network (GEN) and is active in Gaia Education as developer of ecovillage design and education materials. He traveled to Colombia as council representative of ENA (The Ecovillage Network of the Americas). He also performs Latin music in the United States and Mexico with his group Sirius Coyote. Contact him at giovanni@ ecovillage.org. Fostering ecovillage development

Owner built houses and food garden (cassava, bananas, and other local foods) at Nashira ecovillage built after training in Permaculture and self build workshops.

The ENA and CASA group in ecovillage Atlantida, Colombia.

The Adventure of Starting Over

By Kim Scheidt

I'm not sure how much I believe in astrology, in the idea that the movements of the celestial bodies out in space impact me on a personal level here on earth. However, my life recently took an unexpected turn and the timing of it just so happened to match up with the summer Mercury retrograde. According to the explanation I found on the internet, "the fiery energy of Leo activates the winds of change to create events and circumstances that blast us into many new directions. We will find that our life has dramatically changed"...yes, that sounds about right.

For the past seven years I've been living a somewhat "pioneering" life of starting an intentional community on raw land with a few other people. Our sub-community of Dandelion originally formed with three people, one of whom, our best social networker, soon decided to pursue another project close by. We remaining two settled down on 12 acres to create a homestead based around the ideas of permaculture and sustainable living. Our intention was always for more members to join up. We went with the philosophy of "if you build it, they will come," something that, in our situation, did not prove to be true. Those right new members just never seemed to come along.

Chad Knepp

For a while that was okay with me. My partner and I were romantically involved and decided to create a child together. We had neighbors and friends nearby and our larger community regularly met for meetings and weekly potlucks. My social needs were met through my nuclear family relationships and by visiting with friends. However, my desire for a thriving sub-community never dwindled. We continued to host visitors and had a time or two when it really seemed those "right" people had come along. Honestly, after so many years I was at the point where I was ready to give just about anyone who felt aligned with us a try. I so much wanted there to be more people with whom I would share a life, share responsibilities and fun, who would feel a tie to this land and to evolving it into its full potential as a mini-farm and intentional community.

Over time, my partner realized that his personal vision was changing and didn't really include a desire to live so closely with other people. Our relationship gradually degraded to being co-parents and not much else. He felt trapped in our situation and overwhelmed, and he didn't see an easy way out. We talked about splitting up our land and each taking half but concluded that we both had hope and a commitment to try to make it work. We did try, but it just didn't work. And a year later we found ourselves back at the realization that something major needs to shift—we are splitting up and dividing our homestead and our land. My ex-partner will be living close-by on his part of the divided land. We have an amicable relationship and will begin sharing care of our daughter half time on a week-by-week basis as soon as his winter housing is complete.

All that is the story of how I find myself in charge of a seven acre homestead. I am now the sole person responsible for continuing the vision, which I am still committed to, of growing my sub-community into a thriving group. Some days I have complete trust that this is the most perfect situation possible—that Dandelion will now be free to become something so much more amazing than it ever could have under the old existing patterns. Many other days I am scared, so scared...of the responsibility, of the potential for "failure," mostly of the vision of this place being a happy home for me not coming true.

The beauty of this situation is that I have a wonderful foundation on which to build this community, there are already many systems in place, and now there is the potential to tweak it to match my personal ideals. Now when I talk about Dandelion I say we have a strong focus on permaculture, simple living, and **empowering women**. Ending sexism is a key issue for me, and now my community is a spark in the universe doing just that.

I'm still planning to cook and heat using only the sun and firewood, to live

> ## Some days I have complete trust that this is the most perfect situation possible. Many other days I am scared, so scared...

lightly on the earth, and to live in alignment with my core values of simplicity and love. I plan to continually improve on the amount of food grown in the high-tunnel hoop-house, the annual garden, and the young orchards. I have my vision of what I would like for this place to become and it is also completely open to the creative inputs of future members. I feel like the first baby-steps of developing this land have been taken. There is warm housing in the winter and many agricultural projects are going strong. However, seven acres is a lot of land and there is so much room to accommodate the creative passions of whoever else ends up living here. I am a strong woman and am capable of maintaining things for the short term. Perhaps I'll get some interns to help out in the spring. I have confidence that the right new members will come along at the right time for everyone involved. Truly.

At no point in my life up to now would I have predicted that I would take on such a project. At many times I can laugh at this and wonder about the avenues down which life decides to leads us. Even after having some time to process it all, I am still kind of scared. But I am confident that this is a move in the right direction. I am growing into my full potential and also have a wonderful support network of friends living nearby who care about me deeply and want me to succeed.

The future is unknown. Every moment is a new beginning. This is a new opportunity for me to soar. ✍

Kim Scheidt is a member of Dandelion, a sub-community of Red Earth Farms in northeast Missouri. She works part-time for the Fellowship for Intentional Community. She gives loving thanks for her friends at Sandhill Farm and Dancing Rabbit Ecovillage as well as REF.

Greening Your 'Hood

An ignorant kid from the suburbs learns the lessons of living sustainably—from kibbutzes to ecovillages, from cohousing to pocket neighborhoods

By David Leach

When I was 20, I ran away from home to live on a kibbutz in northern Israel. I wasn't Jewish. I wasn't Marxist. I wasn't a back-to-the-lander. I wasn't even seeking (in the words of one volunteer coordinator) the "sun, sand, and sex" that has drawn 350,000 young visitors to the 270-plus communal villages of Israel's famous kibbutz movement.

No, I was escaping both a broken heart and the claustrophobia of growing up in the most middle-class neighborhood, in the most middle-class city, in the most middle-class country in the world. (Ottawa, Canada, if you must know.) I landed by chance on Kibbutz Shamir, near the border with Syria, which had been founded in 1944 by hardcore Romanian socialists.

As a new volunteer, I learned that the kibbutz movement embodied the "purest form of communism in the Western world." (Fifteen years later, kibbutz members would ditch Marxism, privatize Shamir, and list its optical factory on the NASDAQ stock exchange.) I was less impressed by the radical ideals of the kibbutz, however, than its architecture and design. I had grown up in a subdivision where the car was king. Like almost every suburb since Levittown, New York, my neighborhood had been designed to move vehicles quickly from A to B, with walkers and cyclists considered a nuisance or an after-thought. Commercial activity and social hubs had been zoned far from its long crescents of setback homes and double garages. (In fact, the only store you could reach by foot was an automotive dealership.) Cemented into this suburban DNA was an Orwellian message: Two cars, good; two legs, bad.

On the kibbutz, I discovered the simple joy of life on a human scale at a human pace. Like most kibbutzes, Shamir had been purpose-built in concentric circles of small buildings and row houses, linked by pedestrian pathways. A multi-purpose dining hall and an open green space exerted a centripetal force to draw everyone into the community's center. No resident lived more than a 10-minute amble from this hub, where they could share meals, debate issues, and celebrate holidays together.

We wandered down car-free paths to our workplaces every morning, and later to the general store, the bar, the library, the sports hall (which doubled Tuesday nights as a movie theatre), and the swimming pool. These informal gathering sites acted like "third places"—the phrase that American sociologist Ray Oldenburg coined for the casual in-between spaces (like cafés and hair salons, neither work nor home) so vital to a truly democratic society.

On the kibbutz, cars were few, shared among members, and sequestered in peripheral parking lots. Walking formed the fabric of everyday life. So, too, did the conversations sparked by unexpected footpath encounters. Who needed Facebook—still 15 years away—when you could collect the daily news by strolling to the kitchen for an after-dinner snack?

In a quirk of etymology, *kibbutz* (Hebrew for "gathering") and *kibitz* (Yiddish for "chitchat") sound remarkably similar. That confusion contains an accidental truth: At the heart of any community

Kibbutz Degania.

Photos courtesy of David Leach

Street party in Victoria.

Neighbor harvesting produce with author's son.

beats the power of positive gossip, the semi-random conversations that bind friends and neighbors together. That was why the early kibbutzniks built their communities to promote kibitzing.

• • •

Communal life changed me, of course, as it does most people. But the transformation wasn't instantaneous, like a flash from the heavens. I didn't return home to found a commune or live in a co-op. I didn't even join a neighborhood association. No, for the next decade or so, I cut my roots short. Almost every year, I moved (between countries or cities or apartments) for school or work or wanderlust.

Wherever I dropped my backpack, I became conscious of how architecture brings people together or keeps us apart—and how that sense of community impacts the environment, too. I'd grown up in a sprawling Wonder Bread subdivision with the carbon footprint of Godzilla. I later worked for Greenpeace, and my late-blooming ecological awareness nagged at my imagination. Wasn't there a better way to live? Could we design a community to be friendly both to its neighbors *and* to its environment? Could we replicate such eco-'hoods on a large scale, as we'd done with suburbia?

I stumbled across clues to this puzzle in surprising places. My wife and I bought a house in Toronto, Canada's biggest city. It was situated in an odd parallelogram of older duplexes, hemmed in by two busy roads, a subway yard, and a train track. Eco-paradise it was not.

And yet neighbors had turned the geographical constraints to their advantage. They had christened this forgotten corner "The Pocket"—a micro-neighborhood that didn't exist on any official map. One family opened their doors every Saturday to sell fresh-baked bread. Other residents published a regular newsletter to broadcast the history, culture, personalities, and urgent issues of The Pocket. (It evolved into a lively online social network.) A sense of community developed around what had been just another postal code. This common purpose was built, like the kibbutz movement, on a foundation of shared myth. We weren't isolated strangers, powerless and alone; we were the people of The Pocket.

The Pocket felt like an oasis amid the surrounding megalopolis. Eventually, even this micro-neighborhood couldn't keep my family in a city that was losing its battle with Carmageddon: the endless, angry storms of traffic, the summer "smog days"

when simply breathing seared our lungs. A new job and new dreams carried us west. On the Pacific coast, in Victoria, British Columbia, my wife and I moved into a small bungalow on a cul de sac. We could have afforded something bigger and newer on the edge of the city. But we liked the proximity of our new home. It was on a bus route and walking distance to a village-like main street of small shops, two grocery stores, a library, recreation center, a dozen cafes and restaurants, and several schools. We wouldn't need to buy a car right away. (Eight years later, thanks to a car-share co-op, we still haven't.)

Oddly, the house's backyard had a hot tub but no side fence. (Perhaps the old owner was an exhibitionist.) It was assumed we would keep the jacuzzi and erect a fence for privacy. We did the opposite: got rid of the energy-hogging tub and left the yard open.

A funny thing happened: We got to know our neighbors. We didn't need to strain over a fence to chat. When my son was born, he began crawling across the invisible property line and into their strawberry patch. Soon, our neighbor took him under her wing, gave him seedlings, and helped him plant a patch of his own. Over the years, she has become his garden mentor and "shirttail aunt"—closer to him than many of his blood relations. He brings her our old newspapers; she teaches him Spanish and how to prune berry bushes. We look after their house when they're away; they let us borrow their car to run errands. That casual sharing might never have happened had a fence stood between us.

• • •

As I learned to accept the kindness of neighbors, I became aware of a global movement that was taking greater steps toward sustainable living. Soon phrases like "ecovillage" and "cohousing" no longer seemed alien to my ears. (O.U.R. Eco-village, on Vancouver Island, had sprung up not far from where I lived.) I visited a few communities and talked to experts to glean lessons from these new pioneers.

Last fall, I met Charles Durrett, the guru of the North American cohousing movement, when he came north to advise two ecovillages on the mainland of British Columbia. "The most successful ecovillages," he told me, "have cohousing as part of them." On an earlier visit, he had asked residents to face each other in two rows, so they could calculate the ideal distance between their future homes. The car-free commons that would separate their porches had to be wide enough for privacy and yet near enough so they could gauge, at a glance, whether a neighbor needed a joke or a hug or to be left alone.

That weekend, Durrett was helping ecovillagers to plan a common house that, like a kibbutz dining hall, would provide a modern, multi-purpose hub of food and friendship and communal activity. He made living ecologically sound *fun* by insisting that residents don't sweat the details, so they could "enjoy a homebrew on the patio together" sooner rather than later. During a break, he spotted a two-story private house across the street, looming on a huge swath of lawn, with an airport runway for its many vehicles.

"You couldn't build a house with a bigger carbon footprint if you tried!" he marveled. (I blushed: it looked like my childhood home.) "Cooking one big pot of spaghetti is more ecological than cooking 30 pots," continued Durrett. "Where I live, we have 34 houses and one lawnmower." That was the simple arithmetic of sustainable sharing at the heart of his cohousing ethic.

Recently, I read a new book by American architect and community planner Ross Chapin, called *Pocket Neighborhoods: Creating Small-Scale Community in a Large-Scale World*. He emphasizes five architectural features that connect neighbors: a central grassy commons or courtyard; a common building, for meetings and shared meals; smaller homes that don't dominate sightlines; low or no fences; and cars kept to the margins. These "pocket neighborhoods" (Chapin has designed several in the Pacific North-

west) can take many forms, from purpose-built ecovillages, to co-op apartments circling a courtyard, to suburban streets in which neighbors have torn down backyard fences or retrofitted rear lanes to create common gathering spaces. They all rely on what Chapin calls a "web of walkability" to get people out of cars and into casual conversations.

From such kibitzing comes cooperation and a truly sustainable sense of community. I began to think of this effect as a neighborhood's K.Q, or "Kibitz Quotient": the social health of any place, judged by the random conversations you have walking through it.

• • •

I still marvel at the *chutzpah* of pioneers I've met, in Israel and elsewhere, who have sacrificed so much to build a better society from scratch. Whether they are octogenarian kibbutz founders or idealistic young ecovillagers, they've shown more vision and courage than I could ever muster.

But I realize that maybe I don't need to sell my house, flee the city again, and live off the grid to save the planet. I belong to the 99 Percent—the vast majority who make our homes in communities more conventional than a commune, an ecovillage, or cohousing. (You can take the kid out of the suburb, I suppose, but you can't take the suburb out of the kid—not all of it, at least.)

And yet many of us 99 Percenters aspire to live more intentionally, too. With a little inspiration, we can all create our own pocket eco-'hoods by reclaiming our yards, our streets, even our suburbs—*from* the cars, *for* the people. We can weave new webs of walkability and rediscover the power of positive gossip to bind a community together. We can tap into the ecological benefits of simple neighborly sharing. We can broadcast our values through hyper-local newspapers and niche social networks to create new myths, rooted in a rich sense of place, so that we all can feel, whatever we're doing—planting a garden, lending a hand, telling a joke—that we're working toward a common good.

We might not build utopia overnight. But we can move toward a greener future, one less fence and one more story at a time. ❧

David Leach is an associate professor of writing at the University of Victoria and a former fellow at the Centre for Cooperative and Community-Based Economy. He is finishing a book about his kibbutz experiences, called Look Back to Galilee: Searching for Utopia in a Divided Land.

O.U.R. Ecovillage.

New Beginnings at Oakleigh Meadow Cohousing

By Pat Bryan

Nearing retirement, many of us begin thinking and talking about what we want our aging to look like. While many of my friends are drawn to coming together with existing friends to share resources and companionship, I found myself dreaming of living in a multigenerational community. I visited a few cohousing neighborhoods in Portland, Oregon—a few hours from Eugene, where I'd made my home for many years and had sunk deep roots. The city held allure, but did I want to be that far away from my Eugene friends? Then I heard about a new cohousing development starting up less than a mile from my home in Eugene: Oakleigh Meadow—and thus began my cohousing sojourn.

Chuck Durrett and Katie McCamant staged a Getting It Built workshop in Eugene not long after. Filled to the brim with facts, fears, and excitement after the first full day, I consulted the I Ching, which delivered up the image of the wise fox crossing the frozen river, cautious, ears pricked, advancing one step at a time, alert to any impending cracks in the ice. What good counsel, tempering my enthusiasm and allaying my fears at the same time! I left the workshop having agreed to head the membership team.

How does a dream become a reality? I'm finding it takes two things: doing the required work (including lots of meeting and workshops!) while nurturing the first green shoots of community. My first social with other Oakleigh Meadow dreamers took place at Pen and Jim's on Superbowl Sunday, where no one watched the game but all had great fun counting Madonna's costume changes. Kai and Phoebe let me play Chutes and Ladders with them. That day marked the beginning of community for me. That sense of community grew when we spent a day sharing our individual visions of our cohousing community and arrived at four sentences that would become the foundation of our community vision statement. We were becoming "we"!

As my sense of community grew, my personal "must have" deal-breakers began to soften around the edges.

Images as well as words began to shape our sense of "we." Jen, who cobbled together our first website, pulled a photograph of a sunflower off the internet to serve as a bright welcome to our homepage. We all loved it as both a contrast to the gray skies of the Oregon spring and a promise of sunny days living in community. The sunflower has become part of our logo, and we give away packets of sunflower seeds at our marketing events. Jen also posted the first blog, with a photo of an earth-constructed greenhouse that sparked our imaginations. Yes, we definitely want one of those in our neighborhood! Fantasies of neighbors from seven to 70 working together to build it represent the essence of living in community to me.

Then we hit our first bump: a workshop that went somewhat awry. The facilitator mentioned in passing a conversation she had had with our project consultant, who talked about discussing project feasibility with us at some time in the future. We were taken aback, and said so, because we felt we had already been assured that the development was feasible. Unfortunately, the facilitator chose to stick with the workshop agenda rather than allowing us to process what we perceived as a possible setback. We left the workshop with our confidence shaken. One household emailed the community the following week, drawing back from full membership.

At our next business meeting, we spent some time debriefing the workshop. I felt apprehensive, unsettled, uncertain. Then David spoke up. David and his wife Joan had purchased the site, and they dreamed a dream of cohousing which had become our Oakleigh Meadow group. David said, "This is great. Everything we've read told us we'd hit difficult times, and here's our first one. How will we respond to it, I wonder?" I could feel my shoulders and my guts relax as I looked around the room and thought, "Oh, right, it's just us!" After five months of working, eating, and playing with them, I knew these people, knew that we made good decisions together, knew that the wisdom of the group was something I could rely on. (And "feasibility," as it turned out, is an ongoing evaluation routinely done by project managers, nothing for us to worry about. The household with cold feet became full members along with the rest of us on April 1, when the LLC was formed.)

Most of us begin a new venture with ideas about what it must offer in order for us to participate in it: deal-breakers. Mine was wanting a ground floor, single-level unit—not for any immediate reason but "just in case." Other members of the group wanted a development with just a few units and lots of open land, or a community without dogs or chickens. As my sense of community grew, I found my "must have" beginning to soften around the edges. It became a "maybe," something to consider within the context of the larger community. I witnessed the same process happening for others. Those who began by envisioning six or eight households on the site realized that, for many of us, this would make the project cost prohibitive, so their original vision began to yield. Those who abhorred the idea of living in close proximity to other people's animals listened to dog owners willing to take responsibility for their pets' behavior, and they began to recognize possibilities they hadn't considered before. Seeing these shifts in perspective in myself and others inspired the first glimmerings of understanding how commitment to community affects orientation to one's own preferences. They still count, but they now exist in a larger context which counts more.

At one point in our process, we spent some time articulating our values. It sometimes amazes me that what seems like a random group of folks coming together should share so many. Of course, we are not a random group of people. Cohousing and like communities attract people longing for connection and a more sustainable way of living.

Yet the bumps keep coming. Each one is unsettling, at least for me. Sometimes I find myself speaking with impatience and irritation in a meeting while others meet the turmoil with equanimity. Other times, it's my turn to lend some calm and perspective to the group. Somehow, we seem stronger, smarter, and saner as a group than as individuals.

Most recently, the group spent an agonizingly long time choosing an architect for the project. Months of phone interviews with cohousing communities around the country that had worked with this or that architect took place. Many we spoke with wished they had gone with a different architect than the one they had. Some members of our group felt it crucial that we work with someone who would freely collaborate with us on design. These are the artists and architect wannabes whose passions are creativity and aesthetics. Others wanted to keep costs down and focus on moving the project ahead. These are the pragmatists and the business-minded members.

Tense meetings ensued. The process team utilized a number of formats to move our collective thinking forward: a fishbowl, a list of considerations to be ranked by importance, proposal discussions, and so on. Members voiced concern that the group would split, and one member even asked for a show of hands of those who would leave if their architect were not chosen. How did we move through this? I think each of us forged a unique path, yet we took our individual journeys in company with each other, and that made all the difference.

This photo: Vision workshop. To right: Some of us at the site design workshop, an intensive process held over four days to design the overall neighborhood: where the buildings will sit on the land and their relationship to open land and larger neighborhood.

For example, not long ago I became quite frustrated at the seemingly endless architect-choosing process. The group seemed to be swimming in circles. I decided I could not invest further in the project unless "my" architect was chosen. I felt very justified in this, especially because I felt that several other households might also pull out. It seemed imperative to communicate this to the group somehow, but I also did not want to take responsibility for creating a split in the group. I posted a message on our online discussion board stating that I would support any decision the group made and then make a decision about my own participation in the community. I did this hoping it would further the conversation in a useful way. No one was fooled by my crafty dodge, however, and a deafening virtual silence followed. Oops!

The following week at our membership team meeting, Laura very tactfully remarked to the group that some conversations should not be attempted via postings. Since I trust Laura's judgment, I immediately recognized that I had responded to the conflict within the group in a reactive, patterned way—by seeing my well-being as separate from that of the group, by moving to protect my self-interest without considering how that move might affect people I had come to care about. The next few days were uncomfortable ones for me. Was my desire for community a fantasy? Was I willing to stick out difficult times, or was I just in this for the warm fuzzies? What did I really want my life to look like, and how hard was I willing to work to realize that vision? Surprisingly, I eventually found myself feeling MORE committed to the cohousing group than I had before, more aware that I would get out of this venture in proportion to what I was willing to invest—not in dollars and cents, but in faith and effort.

At work recently, I attended a presentation on cross-cultural adaptation (I advise international students at the University of Oregon). The speaker referred to the writing of Young Yun Kim, who developed the "draw-back-to-leap" model to describe an individual's progress in adapting to a new culture. (See accompanying figure.)

Kim sees humans as systems that, when confronted with a new culture, go through "disequilibrium" and then incorporate feedback to bring the "system" back into balance. It occurred to me that this model could be applied to most members of a forming cohousing community. We're coming from a culture which values independence, self-reliance, and individualism, and moving into one of valuing group benefit over personal preference and teamwork over the solitary pursuit of happiness.

Kim's model resonates with my experience in the Oakleigh Meadow Cohousing "culture." Bumps occur, and I feel stressed out, overwhelmed, uncertain of my ability to cope. Over time, and with healthy servings of humor, my perspective evolves and I notice a change in how I think and act. At least until the next bump.

Community: it arises out of a longing for connection and is nurtured through shared work, laughter...and sheer tenacity. In its beginnings, the venture seems quite fragile, and yet its promise keeps us moving ahead. Are we delusional or visionary? Maybe a little of both, huh? ꧁

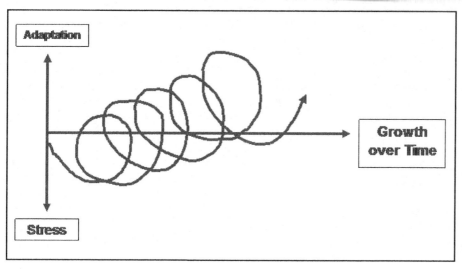

Pat Bryan works in the field of international education. She is a longtime Oregonian and has never lived in community. Oakleigh Meadow is a cohousing neighborhood in formation on the Willamette River in Eugene, Oregon. It is an intergenerational community of independent households committed to finding purpose and a sense of belonging through working, learning, and playing together in a neighborhood designed to make a small and beautiful footprint on the land. For more information, visit oakleighmeadow.org.

Creating a Community of Homesteaders

Land Day Celebration

By Kim Scheidt

This morning I gave a tour to some nice folks visiting our intentional community. They arrived a little earlier than planned so when they called from their cell phone to say they were only a few miles away I brought my breakfast mug of oatmeal with me to eat as I walked the quarter mile from my house to the parking lot where they left their vehicles. I greeted them and as they got geared up for our walk I learned that they were all most interested in taking in information about the styles of buildings that our different members have constructed, and that they were also keen to hear about the overall structure of our community—Red Earth Farms—which is set up as a community land trust.

I usually bow out of giving tours, leaving that task up to some of my more extroverted community neighbors. However, this time I hadn't, and as I walked around answering questions I remembered that there is something extra special about talking with interested people about the intentional community in which I live.

At our community you'll see many passive-solar buildings and some interesting rocket heater stoves, as well as quite a few greenhouses attached to the south side of buildings. There are also rainwater catchment, mouldering toilet, and animal housing examples. We have a wide spectrum of building styles ranging from a two-story strawbale home to small energy-efficient homes built using much more conventional methods.

Moving on to land with no preexisting infrastructure is tough. Doing that kind of thing requires a pioneering spirit. Creative solutions are reflected in the buildings of our different members. We do not have rules about what materials a person can use to construct buildings. Some people went for low-cost, some went for speed of construction, for aesthetics, low ecological impact, or all of the above in different combinations. And keep in mind we are doing this in rural northeast Missouri, a land of few zoning laws or building restrictions. We are granted the ability to construct things as we see fit for the most part and then live with the results of what we've crafted.

Our intentional community formed in the Spring of 2005 with four of us living

Aron Heintz (back center) watches the kids gearing up for sack races at 2012 Land Day.

Aron (back left) with all the members of Red Earth Farms in early 2007.

Valerie Walter

This is Red Earth Farms' Land Day Celebration 2012.

Valerie Walter

We liked the idea of creating affordably priced plots of land where a leaseholder would have creative control over their particular parcel.

The 76 acre tract we purchased was sold to us at a much more affordable price per acre than what smaller plots in the area were going for. However, we did not have the means to pay for it all outright. Aron Heintz, an acquaintance of Alyson's from the communities circle, was our investor who backed the venture. He was a man who had made a fair amount of money at a young age and was looking for socially responsible ways to invest it. I have to confess that it was a little difficult at first ironing out the details. Though Aron didn't desire to live in our community, he had some strong attachments to how we set things up with the thought that perhaps one day he would want to join. He wanted to be more deeply involved than a typical investor might have been, and there were times when his ideas of how we should set things up did not coincide with our own. But it all worked itself out, and on Summer Solstice, with Aron funding the purchase, we closed on the land and had a lovely party to celebrate. (We didn't pick the closing date, it was just chance. Our original closing date had been April Fools Day but the seller pushed it back. No joke.)

Aron's name went on the deed when the land was first purchased. The task was then ours to form the legal entity that would purchase the land from him. Coming up with a name for our intentional community turned out to be a surprisingly difficult part of the process, as did figuring out exactly what type of legal entity would best suit what we wanted to do. It was also quite a task searching for example documents of how to go about setting up a community land trust. Writing bylaws and making decisions about what needed to be incorporated in them took a lot of time. We borrowed heavily from a few sources, blending things together to create exactly what we envisioned. We vowed that when we were through we would always keep our founding documents openly available online for anyone else to use as a model in forming a similar community.

in the '70s era double-wide trailer parked on land across the road from Dancing Rabbit Ecovillage (established in 1997) and three miles away from Sandhill Farm (established in 1974). We were a group of agriculturally minded, independent, idealistic people with a similar vision—homesteading...but not isolated.

None of us had debt. We were all fit and not afraid of physical labor. We had all spent time in places of other culture—Russia, Central America, Alaska. We were influenced by the study of permaculture and wanted to live a low-impact life. We valued diversity and were humble enough to admit we didn't necessarily know what would be the best solutions for living in a sustainable manner—though we were all gung-ho to try our best and put our ideas into action.

We wanted to structure our intentional community so that members could be relatively autonomous on a multi-acre leasehold. We desired that members be empowered to enact their personal visions, whatever they happen to be, just so long as we held similar fundamental values and agreed to adhere to a few policies. We threw around catch phrases like "we can agree to disagree" and have "freedom of choice of implementation."

We structured our community so that a nonprofit corporation, Red Earth Farms Community Land Trust, Inc. (REFCLT), holds title to the land. Only members in the nonprofit corporation can become leaseholders. After making a one-time payment, they hold a 99-year lease on their piece of land. The lease is renewable, inheritable, and salable, the only caveat being that it would have to pass to someone approved to be a Red Earth Farms member. In many ways it is a lot like ownership with the one-time payment for land paid at the current lease fee, the amount that a member would pay to lease an acre of land, which is determined by REFCLT.

It took nearly three years for us to write the documents and go through the steps to transfer title of the deed to REFCLT. Perhaps unsurprisingly, we did not attract many new members during those formative years. Often visitors who were potentially interested in membership stated that they would be hesitant to commit to living in our community until the land trust officially owned the land.

In order for REFCLT to buy the land, we negotiated with Aron a mortgage deal for 73 percent of the purchase price with the remainder being fronted by the existing community members as lease payments. We agreed to a three-year term loan, to be refinanced with Aron when the term was up, that did not require us to make payments on any certain schedule. Payments were to be made as we got incoming members leasing land. And we did begin attracting new members who eventually became leaseholders. It was a gradual process.

In order to prevent speculation and to keep the price affordable, land can be transferred and leased only for the current lease fee amount. This number is tied to the mortgage with Aron and increases over time. As the last acre is leased out we will have paid off the loan. REFCLT does not intend to hold property in common long-term. We encourage co-ops to form if there are groups of people who would like to manage property in a certain way together. We'd like to minimize our time spent in meetings and avoid compulsory cooperation.

I'm pleased to report that the frequency of our group meetings has gone down from once a week to only once a month. And lately the meetings we do have often finish earlier than the allotted hour and a half. Community members now connect in more enjoyable ways such as our weekly potluck dinners and work parties that rotate location so each homestead gets a recurring opportunity to have neighborly help on big projects. We also see each other at less structured gatherings and connect over sharing things such as child care, machinery or tools, and rides to town.

The choice to locate our community of homesteaders where we did brought many advantages. We gain so much from interactions with the vibrant ecovillage next door and from picking the brains of communitarians who've lived in the region for many years. There are social opportunities and work opportunities that would otherwise not exist in such a rural location, and area locals have long been exposed to the idea of intentional community so are less likely to raise their eyebrows at us. Being near other established communities helps immensely to mitigate the feelings of isolation one can experience setting up a household on land where community neighbors are out of eye-sight.

After seven years, with nearly all of the available land leased out, we can say that our project has been a success. We have received a lot of interest over the years in this format of an intentional community of homesteaders. At our last annual board meeting we entertained the idea of expanding so as to accommodate even more people who might wish to join in with our vision. However, we all agreed that we would supportively pass the torch on to new people in other places but not look to increase the size of our holdings at Red Earth Farms. We are happy to no longer be spending so much energy and time on drafting documents and recruiting new members. We're glad to get down to the dirty work of just living our lives. ❧

Kim Scheidt is a founding member of Red Earth Farms in northeast Missouri. She works part-time at the national headquarters of the Fellowship for Intentional Community.

Work party.

Kim Scheidt

Yes, Wealthy People Want to Live in Community in Sustainable Ways Too!
Fourteen suggestions from those who are trying it

By Jennifer Ladd

In this time of peak oil, climate change, and economic instability, many people are looking to build sustainable community close to home and close to their values. This is true for people across the entire class spectrum, including wealthy people. Money can protect one from many things but we ALL feel the effects of climate change, of extreme inequality, and of the breakdown of people-to-people connection, albeit in different ways. Many people with wealth are looking for ways to leverage their resources for good—to help heal the environment and to support the emergence of a new culture based on cooperation and collaboration. And so wealthy people are playing a role, with others, in the growth of intentional communities and other collective working and living projects.

For over two years, I have been facilitating a telephone support group of people with financial resources who have started, want to start, or already live in intentional community-like situations. The conference calls allow people to learn from one another about ownership models, questions of responsibility and stewardship, vision, clear agreements, and power dynamics. The group alternates between having a support group call amongst themselves one month, then having an outside speaker come to the conference call to share information, experience, or expertise the next month.

Members of this group are located in 10 states from around the US. They come from all different kinds of situations: One person has owned land for 20 years and is now interested in attracting others to live, garden, and work together. One person bought land with the intention of living there with community but the community fell apart. Others bought land or buildings with the expressed intention of turning that property over to community over time either in the form of cohousing, land trusts, or cooperatives. Some group members live in the country, some live in cities. One person grew up on a farm that he expects to inherit, at which point he wants to open it up to others. Some have started out with friends to do this, some have started with a spouse, some have journeyed this road on their own with others coming and going along the way.

The taboo of talking about money and class makes this an important topic. Many of us struggle to have these discussions, but in my 20 years of personal and professional experience working on cross-class projects, I have found it is essential to do so. Whether they are made explicit or not, power dynamics, judgments, and fears exist in this area—along with those related to race, gender, ability, sexual orientation, religion, and so on. The more that each person in a community is committed to examining and understanding their attitudes and beliefs about money and class, the stronger that community, or any community-based endeavor, will be.

The individuals who have participated in this group value building a healthy, sustainable world both environmentally and socially. Each person is looking at their particular circumstances and working to understand how he or she can work with others, and with the resource of property, to embody those values.

But it's not always so easy.

Primary funders can be in control but also feel a great deal of vulnerability as they expose their capacity to fund. Many people have inherited their money. They want to do something of service and they are well aware of how people with a lot of money can be viewed in this time of growing inequality—viewed both with envy/jealousy and with antipathy/resentment. Sometimes they can be seen as an endless source of funding. All told there are distances and differences that need to be acknowledged and grappled with.

Suggestions, Ideas, Considerations

This article is not an exhaustive study of how people with money have started or participated in communities. It is a collection of lessons being learned by this particular sample group—lessons that many others have learned along the way.

1. Encourage early and open discussion of class, money, and power dynamics, realizing everyone plays a part.

Tackle money discussions early on in an open and curious way. Clarify your own values around money, land, and control and ask others to do the same, and then find the structure that embodies those values. Share your class and money stories with each other so you have an understanding of the circumstances and conditions from which you come as you deal with conflict and with moving forward together. Spend time really understanding your own needs and desires for community.

2. If you are someone who already owns property and have a close connection to it, read or re-read the section "When You Already Own Property" (pages 23-24) in Diana Leafe Christian's book *Creating a Life Together.*

She writes clearly about the challenges of forming community when there is one sole owner. She writes, "If you're a property owner seeking to create community on your land…be willing to release total control and find ways for people to become fully participating, responsibility-sharing fellow community members. And if you cannot or don't want to release full control but still want to live in close proximity with others, please do so and enjoy it—but don't advertise it as 'community'!"

Why do some people choose to keep control of the land or property? Well, there are a number of reasons but a primary one is that people have history with the land and care for it. One person has owned her land for many years. She knows its valleys, hills, watersheds, and other resources. She has invested in building a house, barn, greenhouse, and other buildings. She has put a great deal of time and money into a vision and place at which she has much history and many ties. She cares for it deeply. This is also true of another woman who owns land. With others, she has made it a model of sustainability and a place for workshops and retreats. She too has put a lot of money, time, and attention into this land.

Even though both of them feel somewhat burdened by the responsibilities and liabilities and are willing to sell some portion of the land, they feel a great deal of concern for its future care and stewardship and are looking for (and also finding) models of ownership that will assure future care for the land. Members of this group are exploring conservation easements, land trusts, and cooperatives, making the ownership not an individual right/responsibility but a group entity.

3. Be very clear what rights and responsibilities everyone has from the very start.

Most people who own the land/property want to live in community in a way that does not highlight the fact they have the control. They long for a sense of connection and camaraderie. They feel this can't be done if they have the power of ownership and all that it implies. But, in an ironic way, the clearer one is about what control in decision-making the owner has and what others have, the more trust can be established. At least three people in the group have written agreements with renters about their own rights and responsibilities.

4. If you already own property and want to start a community, be as clear as you can about what part of the property you want to hold on to and what part you want the group to own.

One person took the time to determine this, and that clarity has been a relief for all concerned. She says, "One way to share some power, if you are not willing to give it all over to the group, is to have long-term leases for members. Having some more long-term security will allow others to engage more and feel more empowered. Making sure there are plenty of things the group and/or other individuals decide will help a lot too."

5. If you have a very strong and clear vision, do your best to be aware of how the strength of your vision both attracts people and potentially disempowers them from contributing their own vision.

Some people have bought land with a fairly well formed vision of building a program, a school, a model gardening place, a place of retreat and renewal. If the land was bought with the express purpose of achieving a particular vision and mission, it can be difficult to maintain a balance between opening the visioning up to others and keeping the main thread of intent. Sometimes founders are so afraid of betraying their own vision that they become rigid, discouraging other potential community members from fully joining in. There may be ways to let others direct some aspect of that vision for which they have passion and expertise.

6. If you are going to start a community, do so with others, not by yourself.

The danger of finding yourself in an almost parental role is high. You will have to hold all the financial and vision responsibility by yourself to begin with and have to navigate the rocky shoals of transitioning and sharing with others. Yes, have an idea, passion, and vision, but start out as early as possible with others if you can possibly do so.

7. If you do start out with others, get to know and form relationships with those with whom you might build community before living in community together. Take your time.

Allen Hancock, who spoke to the group about his experience with Du•má in Eugene, Oregon, said that if he could do it over again he would have spent more time forging relationships with people in the geographical region where he lives—learn what it is like to work together in some endeavor, get to know people over time—then begin the process of visioning and planning together.

8. If you are starting a community with others, find ways to make living together financially possible AND make sure everyone has some "skin in the game."

It seems to hold true in some people's experience that when community members can come in easily, they often can leave easily. Find ways for people to make proportionately similar financial commitments. One person may have more money than another but the degree of stretch or commitment can feel comparable. Look for structures that will enable others to gain some form of equity or share over time as you, the primary or initial funder, lessens your ownership—cohousing, cooperatives, creative LLC structures, and community land trusts are options.

9. Hank Obermayer of Mariposa Grove in Oakland suggests that there are five skills/elements essential in building community: Visioning, Time and Time Management, Financial Knowledge, Organizational Development, and People Skills.

Make sure that either you or other core members have these assets and as Hank says, "Make sure that the entire core group trusts those skills in each other. Sometimes you need to accept what others in the core group say, without understanding why, when the others have the relevant skill way more than you." Very often (not always) the person with the money will also be the person with more time. Be careful about becoming the default primary mover and shaker because of an abundance of money and time. Look for ways that others can also give meaningful time so that the endeavor is more of a co-creation, while being aware that most others need to work for a living.

10. Consider having shared training in decision-making, communication skills, and conflict resolution.

It can be hard to find the time. Whatever is decided, make sure the group who will undergo the training both chooses to do it and finds some way to help pay for it—again this can be done proportionately so that everyone contributes something. Make sure that this is discussed ahead of time.

11. Building a community takes more time and attention than most people imagine when they start the process.

Be aware of what other activities you are involved in and be ready to give up some things so that you have the time and attention to make living together—and whatever project you choose to work on—successful.

12. Have an exit strategy.

Things can change. Every person in a community most likely will have thought about what they might do if they need or want to leave at some point. If you are the sole proprietor or are the one holding the most responsibility for the land, it helps to think beforehand about how you might leave in a way that doesn't damage the community-like living and working situation. Giving this some thought beforehand may lead you to looking into land trusts or other structures that enable you to follow your life path without disrupting everything that you and others have built along the way.

13. Have a way to get support from others grappling with similar questions, challenges, and possibilities.

I have found that when people are living and working in cross-class situations it is very valuable to have caucus or affinity groups where people can air their feelings and sort out their thinking in order to come back to the group with more clarity and energy to engage.

The people on these conference calls do get support from the people they live with, and it is also very valuable to share ideas with others grappling with similar questions of control, power dynamics, and the confusion of how to live one's values in such an inequitable world.

14. It is absolutely worth it.

Everyone in the group has waded through difficult times living and working with others, but they are also well aware of the pitfalls of isolation, which wealth can bring. People want to be connected with others, want to share, want to find ways to work together with others. All these experiments have helped people to learn about themselves, have provided them with joyful times, have helped people to be better co-creators of sustainable living that we so direly need at this time in history.

As noted earlier, this is not an all-inclusive or even original set of lessons, but they may bear repeating. The more we can openly, collaboratively, and sincerely search for ways of stewarding land and property and living in community in life-affirming ways, the stronger we *all* are. ❧

Jennifer Ladd is a philanthropic coach and cofounder of Class Action, a nonprofit organization dedicated to cross-class efforts to educate about and eliminate classism. She lives in Northampton, Massachusetts.

Narara Ecovillage, Australia

Narara Dam creates a lake for swimming, irrigation, and fire-protection.

Members unwind over dinner after lengthy discussions.

O n a sunny Australian winter's day I meet with 40 people who are creating a large, dynamic, and diverse ecovillage about 60 kms north of Sydney.

We meet on 64 hectares (158 acres) of prime coastal land which they already own, and sit in a modern brick meeting room quite obviously of government creation, surrounded by industrial-scale greenhouses, scientific labs and offices, numerous sheds and workshops, plus two large houses. This was Gosford Horticultural Institute, a large agricultural research station that closed recently, and one of the agenda items is to decide what to do with their excess buildings.

I am in Sydney to research and write about Narara Ecovillage as well as to wrap up my research into The Manor, Australia's oldest urban intentional community, established in 1922. On one level, these two are as different as chalk and cheese—while on another level they face similar challenges and offer similar potential.

Narara members have already invested about $7 million to buy this site from the State Government, and pay for the numerous consultancy reports needed by their local government before lots can be sold and house-building commence. This money was raised from member loans, but extra bank financing is now being sought to help develop the expensive infrastructure.

This land became a State Experimental Farm in 1907, having been selected because of its "deep, rich soil, easterly aspect," and its location "close to two railway stations"—features which make it an ideal ecovillage today.

Narara Ecovillage's land is gently rolling, northeast-sloping, partly cleared for agriculture but still with extensive native forest. It has a stream running through it, a large dam creating a lovely lake for swimming, irrigation, and fire-protection, and is within walking distance of a train station, a little over an hour's commute from central Sydney. Their creek flats will facilitate intensive gardening and food production, and there is ample land for other farming activities.

As with many Australian place-names, Narara is probably of Aboriginal origin, but its meaning is uncertain, with suggestions of "black snake," "rib," and "bones."

Occasionally, I wonder about some of this ecovillage's promotion: "Here, there is an opportunity to build with the 'we'/ the 'us' in mind. Not in any self-sacrificing way but in joyful, focused recognition that in what we are developing, the whole is definitely greater than the sum of its parts. The project is fulfilling and quite humbling in its gloriousness." Is this semi-utopian rhetoric? Perhaps. But it *is* true—even if emotive.

Why do people join Narara? Geoff, a scientist in his 50s, and Gail, a woman in her 60s, both tell me it is because their families have left home, they don't wish to live alone, and they see this ecovillage as a positive way forward.

Lesley tells me, "I was attracted to Narara Ecovillage as a community consciously living sustainably, with small water and carbon footprints. After reading about peak oil, climate change, overpopulation, and resource depletion, I'd concluded that moving from city life to a rural, locally-based village economy was 'the answer' to the impending 'unravelling of post-industrial civilisation.' However, after reading *The Great Disruption*, in which Gilding suggests it is too late to rescue our western lifestyle, I question whether it would make any difference. I remain a member of the Narara Co-op, but I'm unsure if I'll live here."

More optimistically, some members are primarily attracted to the land, some want to escape the city, some want to live in community, some want a cleaner environment, some see it as the best place for their family, while others want to design and built their dream eco-house.

At today's monthly meeting, the passionate interactions between members, almost all light-hearted and sincere, suggest a dedicated group of well-educated, astute people who are not yet sure of their direction. Tony suggests they follow council regulations as closely as possible in their Development Application, while John suggests they should be more environmentally strict than required, to demonstrate their ecological ideals and strengthen their moral bargaining position. Some want to enforce small house sizes—but would that perpetuate environmentally-destructive, single-person households? Mark is confused by the agenda process, then Joey objects to the term "rules," instead preferring "guidelines." One of the proposed community contracts is to follow "Permaculture Principles" but Steve asks, "What are Permaculture Principles?" When no one responds he wisely asks, "How can we agree if we do not know what those principles are?" To this, Richard describes inherent conflicts between such principles and other economic, aesthetic, sustainability, and conservation goals. Eckard throws in a joke to which Kate responds. While this might suggest pandemonium, everyone stays polite, good-natured, and on-track.

The story began in 1997 when Lyndall Parris, this ecovillage's undisputed "mother," spoke at a women's function about her dream of communal living. By 2004, Lyndall had morphed this dream into Sydney Coastal Ecovillage, an incorporated association with the vision to "research, design, and build a stylish, inter-generational, friendly demonstration ecovillage near the coast not too far from Sydney, blending the principles of eco and social sustainability, good health, business, caring, and other options that may evolve for our well-being." Attracted to this vision, members joined Lyndall, who then left the workforce to devote herself to its realisation. She toured ecovillages around the globe including Torri Superiore and Damanhur in

Italy, and Sirius, Earthaven, and Ecovillage at Ithaca in the US. Lyndall was particularly inspired by Liz Walker (from Ecovillage at Ithaca) and Diana Leafe Christian (from Earthaven Ecovillage), well-known to COMMUNITIES' readers.

In 2008, members learned that this agricultural research station at Narara was coming up for sale, and opened negotiations to buy it. When the Global Financial Crisis hit, however, their funding collapsed as did negotiations, and the State Government withdrew the property from sale. Lyndall and Sydney Coastal Ecovillage members continued to meet, develop social networks, plans (and dreams) for intentional community, and, most importantly, their own competence.

In April 2012, this land came back on the market and, over a frantic few months, they created a legal framework and raised $5 million from members to buy the land. Interestingly, this is about $4 million less than they had offered to pay in 2008.

In some ways, buying the land has been the easy part. The hardest work then began—to get local government approval for the ecovillage design, create a legal and financial framework, agree on infrastructure design, future governance, and, most importantly, create a cohesive communal group out of the disparate "dreamers" who are attracted to the project. This phase is ongoing, and the meeting I am attending is part of that.

Seven adult members and two children already live in the existing houses on site, and while members own all the struc-

One of the many large buildings left over from when this was an Agricultural Research Centre.

Photo courtesy of Bill Metcalf

Photo courtesy of Lyndall Parris

tures, most can't be inhabited until their development application has been approved. Preparation for this development application has already cost over a million dollars for consultant reports, legal expenses, etc.

Their first stage has 55 lots for sale (mostly claimed), while plans for stages two and three will provide for more homes, increasing both density and affordability. Several members intend opening businesses on-site, using existing buildings. The main building, for example, could provide over 20 large bedrooms plus several large meeting and eating spaces for a conference/workshop centre, after minimal alterations, and their laboratories and greenhouses could be converted into commercial uses. Being within walking distance of regular commuter trains to Sydney means that residents can, if they wish, maintain urban careers.

Lyndall tells me, "I'm so thrilled that we finally own this gorgeous site. We first saw it five years ago and immediately felt it was perfect for us. From the existing research orchards and glasshouses, to the established buildings and dam, and the surrounding State Forest, it ticked all the boxes. It's taken us this long to buy it, and now our plans and dreams have a home."

Members meet monthly as a large group as well as more often in small working parties, as they aim to "transform the site into a model of sustainable living" and "a living resource demonstrating practical methods and technology for securing long-term social, environmental, and economic sustainability." They are exploring the most sustainable ways to generate their own power, provide their own water and at least some of their food, and dispose of their wastes. They are exploring governance models, currently following a modified form of democracy, including aspects of Dynamic Governance.

Narara Ecovillage has attracted world-class consultants. Australian architect Philip Thalis, noted for his sustainability and urban design projects, says, "This is the kind of project we dreamed of as students, so it's just a fantastic opportunity to work with owners rather than developers to create a place that focuses on human needs and aspirations first, rather than, say, car access."

Their landscape architects, McGregor Coxall, base their work on biomimicry—using natural templates and approaches to solve human problems, and this aligns with the ecovillage's "inspired by life" motto—as well as with permaculture.

Narara Ecovillage's Project Manager, John Talbott, who managed major developments at the Findhorn Ecovillage in Scotland, says, "We see this village, so close to Sydney, as the chance to model developments that we hope will become the new 'normal.' And so far we've got over 80 people already on board who want to be part of the village, from young families to singles to empty-nesters."

I wish them well. With a project like this, on an ideal site, with inspiration and guidance from their members and leaders, Narara looks set to establish a new high-water mark in ecovillage development, not just in Australia but globally.

Or will it?

To follow Narara Ecovillage's story see nararaecovillage.org. ❧

Dr. Bill Metcalf, of Griffith University, Australia, is the author of numerous scholarly and popular articles, plus seven books, about intentional communities, the most recent being The Findhorn Book of Community Living. *He is Past President of the International Communal Studies Association and has been* COMMUNITIES *magazine's International Correspondent for many years.*

Members involved in intense one-to-one discussions about future directions for Narara Ecovillage.

Photo courtesy of Lyndall Parris

Photo courtesy of Lyndall Parris

Members and guests enjoy a picnic.

Photo courtesy of Bill Metcalf

Late afternoon shows off rolling landscape of rich colours.

Left over from the research station, these massive greenhouses offer great commercial potential.

Photo courtesy of Bill Metcalf

Opportunity Village Eugene

Pioneering New Solutions for the (Formerly) Homeless

By Alex Daniell

Opportunity Village Eugene is Eugene, Oregon's newest intentional community. In less than three months, in late summer and fall of 2013, for less than $60,000, it went from an empty public works parking lot to a village housing 30 people. There have been many players, major and minor, male and female, straight and gay; organizers, volunteers, and villagers themselves. It is a self-governing village, with oversight and veto power over Village Council decisions by the board of the nonprofit organization Opportunity Village Eugene, which is chaired by Dan Bryant, minister of the First Congregational Church downtown.

Opportunity Village (www.opportunityvillageeugene.org) is governed by the Village Manual and its Village Agreements (www.opportunityvillageeugene.org/p/community-agreement.html). The Village Manual is an improved version of similar documents written by the residents of other homeless camps, like Dignity Village and Right to Dream Two in Portland, Oregon. It is authored by Andy Heben, who is also the urban designer of Opportunity Village.

Nine Conestoga Huts, insulated vinyl-sheathed shelters made from a combination of reused and new materials, were built in the village by Community Supported Shelters (communitysupportedshelters.org). I have designed, and built with the help of many others, all 18 of the solid-walled buildings in the village, including dwellings, a bath house, a kitchen, a front office, and also an outdoor grill. Like the Village Manual, the Backyard Bungalows (hebenaj.wix.com/backyardbungalows) we've built are improved versions of the dwellings erected by residents of other homeless villages. They are modular designs, composed of panels that are constructed in the shop and assembled on site in big work parties.

In July I submitted four of these prototypes, all under 100 square feet, with interchangeable wall and roof systems, to the city of Eugene and the state of Oregon for pre-approval to house the homeless. All four were accepted without any alterations. I now have nearly a dozen prototypes that have passed inspection by the city.

Ted Drummond, a longtime leader in the First Christian Church's annual house-building Mission to Mexico, erected a heated 30-foot yurt for the villagers just days before the early-December snows came. Andy, Ted, and I are partners in the micro-housing business I founded in 2012, called Backyard Bungalows. Our mission is to build Affordable Villages, after the model of Opportunity Village.

When the city of Eugene broke up the Occupy camp in December of 2011, they promised to give the homeless another piece of land. Dan Bryant, a minister who wears a leather jacket and drives a motorcycle, Jean Stacey, a fiery

Our last "Big Build." We've had five so far, all on the last Saturday of the month.

lesbian advocate for the homeless, and Andy Heben, a young urban designer who wrote his thesis on homeless camps around the country which he visited, went around touting the idea of Opportunity Village.

I was working at the time with Erik de Buhr, finishing up one of my Bungalow designs for Jerry and Janet Russell, who have given endlessly to the communities movement in this region. We were also working on the Conestoga Hut, a design that Erik and his partner Fay Carter created in a moment of need at the Occupy camp. At the December 2012 open forum Eugene city council meeting, on the heels of an enraged speech by Jean Stacey, who was camped out with SLEEPS near a Conestoga Hut we had set up earlier in the day, I made a proposal to the city council. I proposed that the Conestoga Hut be permitted as a vehicle in the St. Vincent de Paul car camper program, where homeless people can sleep in their cars in business and church parking lots. Though the city attorney had said that this ordinance would take two months to expand, the council did so in three days. That night they also approved the site for Opportunity Village.

In the following days the Conestoga

Hut got a lot of press and Erik and I had a divergence of opinion. While Erik and Fay wanted to start their own nonprofit professional organization independent of Opportunity Village, called Community Supported Shelters, with the hopes of becoming the village's main housing provider and building Opportunity Village almost entirely out of Conestoga Huts, I wanted to work with Opportunity Village, and to build a village of two dozen micro-houses each of which looked unique—in the process creating a prototype for an affordable village. So I went to an Opportunity Village steering committee meeting.

At this first meeting the group was ecstatic. On the heels of a solid year of pleading with the city to provide the piece of land that they had promised, they were talking of the great popularity they would have, of the micro-businesses they would incubate, of the Academy they would set up. Playing devil's advocate, I mentioned that they had no villagers, no approved structures other than the Conestoga Hut, and no site plan. I proposed that they set up a core group of villagers, and begin orienting them in the philosophy, agreements, and rules of the Village Manual, so that a village culture would be in place before the village itself opened.

Brent Was, father at the Church of the Resurrection, took the lead in this process, and Andy and Ann and several volunteers dove into the paperwork. We began the application and intake process almost immediately. A particular focus was placed on vetting couples and single women, so that there would be a strong female presence in the village. This has proved invaluable, as women have come to dominate both the governance and administrative responsibilities of the village.

At this point I began working with Andy Heben. In addition to producing sketch-ups for my prototypes, working on the site plan, and hammering out the operating agreement with the city, Andy worked tirelessly writing and rewriting the Village Manual, based on the ongoing input of many well-meaning contributors, myself included. It is a brilliant document. I made dozens of copies, and handed them out to everyone. It is a brief, clear set of agreements and rules villagers must understand and agree to before joining the village. Based on simple majority and occasionally two-thirds majority vote at the village meetings, it uses simple clear language that can be interpreted but cannot be corrupted by the board or by the villagers. We read it out loud line by line during our biweekly orientations, with open discussion.

Of particular importance was the village site plan. Despite the difficulties it

Ron and Kathy— married in the village.

Kathy, Rhonda, and Fredricka in the village kitchen.

entailed, Andy avoided orienting the Bungalows and Conestogas in a grid, instead orchestrating them in a series of graceful circular courtyards that maximize a feeling of openness on the small site. By orienting four distinct roof systems thoughtfully, and placing the generous used doors and windows optimally for both light and privacy, we created a village that appears to have grown organically. Each Bungalow is trimmed, painted, and finished individually by its owner. There are distinctly masculine and feminine structures. The most popular prototypes seem to be the Lean To, the Club House, and Dianne's Love Shack, with its purple cornice and black gargoyles.

It's long after supper. I sit with Craig and Randy in the yurt. The flickering light and steady hiss of the pellet stove fill the large, dim space. Chairs and fold-up tables, a coffee pot, and donated food in plastic bags are neatly arranged along the walls. The newest villager, Mandy, drifts by and says hi. Terry comes in and sets up her laptop.

Craig is a quiet, confident hippie, with a bandana over his forehead. He is a father, and a natural leader in the village. "How come no one's in here?," he asks.

"Because it's not below 34 degrees," Randy replies, "so no one thought that they'd be allowed to sleep in here tonight."

The village is full of rules, but they are good rules. The villagers seem to need them. People do file unwarranted complaints, but it's not something the board worries about. It takes time for the villagers to settle in and learn a different way than the Eugene Mission, where a lot of applicants come from. Actually, Craig and I agree, things are going really well. Ernie and Katie and Jones and Matt all have jobs, and two other people just found work too.

"How much more time," I ask Craig "do you have on the Village Council?"

"Two weeks." He smiles serenely.

So far only one person has finished out their three-month term. The only man on the five-person Council, Craig has spoken of stepping down, but the Council has pleaded for him to stay, saying that they need his masculine presence. Craig presented with me at the Central Lutheran Church adult education program recently, answering questions for a half-hour. The Lutherans have donated thousands of dollars worth of materials and thousands of work hours in the shop. They, and Dan Hill of Arbor South, who donated $15,000 worth of materials, were the backbone that allowed us to build Opportunity Village.

"Some people on the board think that it's ridiculous that so few Council members finish out their terms."

"What's ridiculous about that?" Craig asks. "It's not like anyone is getting kicked out of the village. It's a clear sign of the health of the democratic process."

With the stress of a continual influx of new people—living in tents during at least part of their probationary period—and the rest of the village living in unheated Bungalows and Conestogas, Village Councilors have to be steady. When someone is not, they get voted off. No hard feelings.

"The women are much more involved in the administration and governance tasks, and the men are more involved in construction—roofing and finishing the Bungalows. Most of the cooking has been implemented by the women, with much of the infrastructure work being done by their men."

"Why does the Village Council need a male presence? In order to feel credible in the eyes of the male villagers?"

"Probably."

Andy, Joline, and I, along with a half dozen villagers, sit before the warm flames of the fireplace at Papa's Pizza Parlor, eating taco pizza and drinking dark beer at a fundraiser for the village. Every villager needs to come up with $30 a month towards utilities. There is no drinking within 500 feet of the gate but we are farther away than that.

To my left is Anton, a working cobbler, who has repaired two pairs of my shoes and refuses to be paid. He is Greek, so I don't push it. His wife, Fredricka Maximillia Sanchez, a tall beautiful woman, talks of her four daughters, and the honorable lives they lead. Hal, across the table, is a computer programmer. Louis sits to my right, a crafter of wooden inlaid jewelry, who is designing a micro-business that can employ villagers doing piecework. Carl and Dianne have finished out their Bungalows with architectural details and color schemes that we can use as models for regular paying clients. Mark Hubble is one of the original founders of the village.

Ron and Katherine Griffith, who were married at the village, speak of their gender roles:

"It's a reverse relationship," Katherine says, in her North Carolina accent, "and it always has been, ever since Ron tore his ACL. I work, and he does the cooking and cleaning. I don't care if I never wash another dish in my life."

In the last village meeting, in the interests of keeping peace in the community, Richard James and Louis volunteered to wash all the unwashed dishes.

"They make sure we get stuff done," Ron says.

All the villagers are required to do eight to 10 hours a week staffing the front desk, cooking, cleaning, doing paperwork, and/or roofing, insulating, and finishing the Bungalows. Katherine does more than her share, on and off the Village Council.

"I do the electronics, and home improvements. A lot of times when the women try to do the heavier physical labor the men step in and say: 'Let me do that.' I don't care; I let them. Break your back. I don't feel threatened by it. I don't have to do that stuff. If someone wants to do the hard work let them do it."

Mark Hubble, who was the public figure of homelessness at the presentation Dan and he and I gave to the American Institute of Architects, who was the lead speaker at the opening of Opportunity Village, who has been the subject of several articles, and who resigned from the Village Council, shakes his head.

"When we started out it was just a dozen of us, and I liked to take care of my girls. Now everything is different. It's an intentional community."

"I don't think this is an intentional community " Hal chimes in. Hal was voted off the Village Council.

"If this were an intentional community, it would be more intentional about who it let in. Someone else here is footing the bill. We're bringing in outside labor, rather than doing the work ourselves. This is a transitional homeless camp, nothing more."

Craig disagrees: "This is still an intentional community. It's just a different intention. The intention is shelter. What comes through is something very much like the intention of food—the cycle of sowing and growing and harvesting and feasting. This act of building, of cultivating shelter for ourselves and others, builds community like you wouldn't believe. Even those who participate in only part of the cycle still go away with a greater sense of community. The builders of this village are sowing the seeds for another village. The villagers themselves will be the mentors, the seeds for the creation of the next community."

On December 9th, one year after my first presentation at the open forum city council meeting, I spoke again before the mayor and city councilors of Eugene. The homeless of Whoville, a big tent camp jammed in beside the overpass next to the courthouse, threatened with being disbanded in the snow, spoke first. Then Jean Stacey made another impassioned plea. I offered a solution. I spoke of the Conestoga Huts I advocated for last year, now permitted and sheltering 20 people. I spoke of the Backyard Bunglows in Opportunity Village, permitted and housing 20 people. All had come at no cost to the city, state, or federal government. Then I said that we could easily build a second Opportunity Village. The next day an anonymous donor gave $25,000 to Opportunity Village, restricted for the purposes of building a second Opportunity Village, as a challenge grant for $25,000 more. Someone also gave another $12,000 to finish this first village. So far we have spent around $70,000 on Opportunity Village.

The first legal urban camping site in Eugene is about to open across the street from us, run by Erik de Buhr and Community Supported Shelters. Ted and I are visiting Erik and a helper, when Mark Hubble comes up as the welcome party, offering blankets and food for the first residents. He has applied for the job of one of the five property managers who get Conestogas at the 15-person site, which is fenced, monitored, and secure. Mark is the seed of a new village.

Hal says it's time to go home, and leaves. I go to get another beer. When I get back they are playing stupid human tricks. One game, called "Mad Dog," involves holding a plastic ruler with an open box of Tic Tacs taped to either end, clamped in your mouth. You shake your head up and down, and whoever spills the most Tic Tacs wins. Another involves stacking as many Ding Dongs as you can on your forehead.

(Continued on p. 77)

Lean To under construction.

Village Circle at Opportunity Village. Graceful circular courtyards like this one maximize a feeling of openness on the site.

OPPORTUNITY VILLAGE EUGENE: PIONEERING NEW SOLUTIONS FOR THE (FORMERLY) HOMELESS

(continued from p. 61)

First Joline, with five, and then Louis, with six, are in the lead. Then Andy steps up. First he tries the trick while sitting, but we call foul. Then he arranges all the Ding Dongs on the table first, so they will best fit, and then mashes them down on his forehead, to howls of protest. But he wins in the end, by bending the rules.

In a way Opportunity Village itself is bending the rules. But this is because the rules need to be bent. We have to make sure that we adhere to the intention, and not the letter of the law. The city and the neighborhoods do not want shanty-towns. They decrease property values and increase disease. But a nice clean orderly village with rules and sound governance? At $2,500 a person in direct set-up costs? Well, that's hard to beat. The big concern is governance. And that is a big concern. An Opportunity Village board member needs to be at every village meeting. A half dozen people have been kicked out so far by the villagers, with good cause. This is a good thing.

I vetted the first people. Some, I thought, were never going to make it. But it's amazing to see the spirit with which people lift themselves up. The truth is, if you give a homeless person a home then they're no longer homeless. This is the opportunity of Opportunity Village. ❧

Alex Daniell is a designer and builder of small residential structures. He has owned and redesigned six houses, and built several more. He has visited over 30 intentional communities, and lived for two years at the Walnut Street Co-op in Eugene. He consults as a financial advisor and belongs to the Wordos, a science fiction and fantasy writers group.

STARTING A COMMUNITY: With or Without a Recipe?

By Paul Brooks

Each community process has its own group dynamic and its own goals in mind, its own collective vision. Through understanding and patience we weave the web of dynamic and self-governing co-creation. I have been so lucky to have been a part of a handful of different community start-up groups, all being quite different from each other. I have been on the fringe of several others to varying degrees, and have visited and lived in many communities around the world.

A balance between structure and flux is hard to achieve. You might have heard the famous quotes, "That government is best which governs least" (Thoreau) and "Everything should be as simple as it can be, but not simpler" (Einstein). So then, is the task at hand to create a governing system that is elegantly simple in its complexity or just plain simple? Should we use a recipe, or should we just throw something together and see how it turns out?

Solidarity

There is something, I believe, to be said about necessity. If you have a group of people who are struggling independently, they might have a stronger motivation to create community than someone who already has a nice garden, a house, and a decent income. Although they may still desire to live in a community, if it is not absolutely necessary they may not be as driven to make it happen.

In many places in Europe and the UK squatting is not uncommon; communities called squats, or occupied social centers, are established simply by moving into an unoccupied building and changing the locks. This is where the Occupy Movement gets its name.

A group of 13 Polish kids had recently been evicted from an old police station they had occupied, called the Polish Station; now they had occupied a place in Whitechapel, London. They invited me and some friends to be their neighbors, and we took them up on the offer. The protocol for opening a squat in England is that after you have secured a building, you hang a "Section 8" notice on the door to declare legal ownership. So that we did, and soon after we declared ownership of the flat, the police knocked on the door. A male officer cordially and sincerely inquired about our residence. He wanted to know if we were registered to pay Council Tax, and whether or not we were stealing electricity. Although my flatmates were not thrilled about the idea, the police were so nice that I let one of them in to look at our electric meter and assured them that we would be registering our tax status very soon.

Having participated in the opening of a couple of squat communities, having lived in several others, and visited many more, I realize that we usually had no formal governing method, but we also had no budget or big decisions to make. If we did have, in my experience it was by consensus. We ate meals together because we enjoyed it, not because it was suggested we should do so. The fact that we squatters were always aware that this type of community is almost always temporary is an important factor to take into account. The property owners are generally holding these empty buildings as assets and don't plan to use them; however, they still have people evicted. With no money and no other home, this impending eviction creates a strong solidarity and creates a necessity within the squat and the larger squatter community. Therefore, this kind of community is usually successful in terms of its members, but rarely sustainable.

Too Much Structure?

In Lawrence, Kansas I worked with a group of under 10 people with the common interest of procuring land to build a sustainable community. We explicitly decided that we would use consensus for our governing method. I began to see after a few weeks that it is very important not to be too rigid with your guidelines. One of our members was extremely particular about defining minute details about how everything should operate. This ranged from the use of cleaning agents like clorox to how we deal with recycling and compost. Although these are important issues, it was a bit early in our process to create a protocol for things we could not yet actively work with. Every proposal we made concerning cer-

tain areas of the community was blocked by this individual.

Eventually we gave complete power to this person in these areas to keep the process moving. Their response to this was, "Why is this my responsibility?" Under conditions like this, the rigid attachments to structure that was being established in the land project were making progress so slow that we began to lose members and eventually the project lost enough of its energy that it fizzled out.

Too Little Structure?

On the Garden Island, Kaua'i, Hawaii, a permaculture project started. The original idea was to develop a personal estate in a way that provided sustainability at least in food security. On the island of Kaua'i, when you mention free camping and permaculture, it's not long before you have more helping hands than you need. This project and fledgling community kept itself relatively quiet for the first few months, but soon there were eight of us there fulltime plus regular visitors, and the project was becoming a community.

I proposed that we use *Creating a Life Together* as a guide to help us understand what we were working with. Although this idea and others were well-received, they were not implemented due to lack of structure. The property owner and the project manager were eventually both open to the idea of community, but as we all soon realize when we step into a community-creating process, defining "community" is a daunting task. Most of us had lived communally before, but those running the show had the least experi-

ence. This might have worked out fine with regular meetings and a clear method of governance, but neither of these things seemed to be happening. With a budget, and big decisions to make, I feel governance is more important.

The months went by, and we all learned to work together very well. We created kitchen management that was very organized and economic. We built a greenhouse and planted gardens. Some of us were studying massage, some were studying geometry, one was studying traditional Hawaiian planting methods by the moon cycle. We had a breastfeeding mother and an amazing handyman who built us a beautiful artisan outdoor shower. We made raw pies and harvested coconuts and other fruits. At one point we all fasted together, and anybody who has ever done a fast knows how it can make us somehow feel more alive than life. We had all cultivated a quality of life that, probably, none of us had ever witnessed before, at least not in a group. We had fallen in love with life and with each other and it seemed like we had finally found what every human yearns for but never knew how to put to words. We were doing it...but was it sustainable?

> # Community is that which is not monetized, that which is shared unconditionally and without obligation.

Eventually, the property owner offered so generously to pay us for the obvious improvements to the land. Few of us, if any, had been interested in getting paid. As we learn from Charles Eisenstein in his book *Sacred Economics*, community is built upon gift culture, so community is that which is not monetized, that which is shared unconditionally and without obligation.

Even those people who were not doing the physical work were contributing to the community. For example, some people brought the bliss from the beach and one of us was breastfeeding. These things are very important too. Value is not always GDP value; the caring and the cultivation of peacefulness were, to me, just as valuable as building a greenhouse or spending the day behind a shovel. The problem is that nobody knows how to value equality from the perspective of Dollars. We held a meeting where everyone decided that, rather than create a system that would regulate our value within reasonable limitations, we would have a zero governance, anything goes model wherein, if anybody has a monetary need, just ask the property owner for the money.

The free-market ideal proved itself once again when some of us valued ourselves

Photos courtesy of Paul Brooks

independently from the community, and other members valued themselves as the community; some valued themselves higher, and some lower or equal. Most of us asked for a reasonable amount of money on behalf of the work that we had done and even those who didn't ask for anything were offered a little. The project manager, however, asked for a very large sum of money to finish the project on behalf of all of us. He did not get consent from any other members to do so other than his partner. The fact that we had no established governance model allowed him to play this sort of monarchical role.

However, I suppose the property owner was the ultimate monarch, because, after a dispute ensued, the property owner then asked everyone to leave. One of us likened it to a Romeo and Juliet scenario. We had all fallen in love, but we were forced apart, and there was nothing we could do about it. We were all acting in ways that we thought were best and we are all still great friends, and there are no hard feelings, but I hope that we all learned that none of us can see the whole picture at any given time, and that is a good reason to have at least a little agreed-upon structure.

Partnership

In the very first of the Wai Koa Intentional Community meetings it was suggested that we keep a weekly journal that we could use to refine our vision. Each week we could share ideas pertaining to that week's agenda topics. We believed that this would aid in creating a clear picture of what it was that we were trying to create and sponsor active engagement in the community process.

After a few weeks the process was clearly moving along quickly. Not many of us in our group of about 20 had ever lived in community before, so we had a lot of ground to cover. We had land but no buildings and were ready to separate into teams. The governance team began working on agreements and understanding sociocracy, while the design team worked on architectural ideas and layouts.

Things were moving perhaps too fast. When those people with a more clear vision began creating faster than others, some of us began to get nervous and it was obvious that we needed to slow down. We decided that rather than engaging in the creative process, we would continue to meet once a week to work on the vision alone, without actively moving forward. Basically, we were going to start over. This was after several months of meetings. Around half of us stopped attending meetings for the time being and the rest continued in this envisioning exercise which still continues.

It has now been more than a year. Our decision-making process, consensus, is working fabulously with one circle and we don't have a need at this point for multiple consensus circles (sociocracy). We have been so patient with the process, developed a strong understanding of our group dynamic, and got to know each other quite well.

> Sometimes it will be unspoken and nearly invisible, but there is always going to be some sort of structure, whether monarchy, democracy, or consensus.

We now can carefully make the first steps in the creative process such as writing our documents and deciding on how to incorporate.

We were, and are, working together patiently and in partnership. In solidarity, while noticing the importance of structure, but without creating too much of it, we hope to see our process through to fruition.

Conclusion

The purpose of government is not to control the people, nor to protect the people from evil outside forces; it is to provide a framework with which to make decisions together and guide our vision in a balanced and sustainable way that is manageable.

There is always going to be some sort of structure. Sometimes it will be unspoken and nearly invisible, but there will always be a monarchy, a democracy, or a consensus somehow or another. If we liken society to a recipe: in a monarchy, the monarch will decide when and what the rest of us eat, in a democracy at least half of us will decide when and what all of us will eat, and with consensus, all of us will decide when and what all of us will eat, so long as we can all compromise and the process doesn't stop cold and we all go hungry.

We have heard a lot about sociocracy lately. With sociocracy, there is no monarchy, and democracy is only a default mechanism that keeps the kitchen moving when an emergency decision has to be made. It is comprised of ingredients (consensus circles) which allow the recipe to be dynamic. Even when other ingredients are not available, things still keep cooking.

It seems to me that clarity on governance issues is an important first step in creating a sustainable community, and good facilitation makes all the difference. Patience in clarifying the vision is an important ingredient too. Once we understand how we will govern ourselves, we can begin to refine our vision. The journey begins. ❧

Paul Brooks has traveled to communities of various forms in dozens of countries around the world. His primary interests in intentional communities are social structure, governance, and community economics. He currently lives on Kaua'i, Hawai'i, where he is involved with intentional communities there as well as being involved with a community garden and Kaua'i's Food Forest at Wai Koa Plantation.

The Community We Built

By Carly Fraser

We are on our way home from an impromptu day at the farm. The back of the van is filled with sleepy children, half of them wearing their dress-up princess dresses. As we turn the corner onto the street, a small group of people waits on the road between the apartment complex and the big stone house. There are parents waiting for their children, other children ready to play, and new tenants with familiar faces. All of them are friends and community members. As soon as the van door opens, the children scatter, pulling adults into their world of play and storytelling. Later, around a crowded dinner table, this simple story is retold and described as being a magical moment.

This story captures the beauty and spirit of the community that is continuously forming, growing, and evolving in our neighbourhood in Guelph, Ontario. We are a group of engaged people going about the building of an intentional and environmentally conscious community.

Our community is different from a lot of the communities that are typically written about in COMMUNITIES. We live on suburban streets that are like so many others in urban centres. The physical presence of our unique community might be landmarked by the chickens on the roadside hill, or the stone house with the giant park-like backyard that people tend to congregate around and its network of adjoining backyards, but the community spreads down the streets and through the backyards of so many others. Some of us own houses in the area. Some of us rent houses or rooms within houses. Some of us rent apartments, or rooms of apartments, or even beds of apartments! And some of us are WWOOFing, travelling through and trading our time and work to stay

Photos courtesy of Derek Alton

in this community.

There is a place for everyone, no matter the stage of life or financial circumstance they are in. We have found this to be a great strength in the creation of a unique dynamic in the community and for building resiliency. Over time the community expands and contracts as people move in and out, but it does not collapse because it is not dependent on a single space or specific people to keep it going.

A contributing success factor to the community is that it has been built over time in an existing neighbourhood. Slowly the landscape is beginning to change and capture the unique set of characters and personalities that make up the social fabric. Although the physical structure of the neighbourhood existed, the building of community has been sought out intentionally. Community members seek out and find shared experience, connection, and recharge in their neighbourhood.

To do this in a sustainable and successful way, communication is first priority. There are meetings to discuss larger happenings, for voicing concerns and sharing visions. This is the broad-scale communication that occurs. To improve one-on-one communication many members have taken or are currently engaging in a training course that is more personal. Having open lines of communication and a shared language and awareness around the unique needs of others helps this community thrive. Communication ensures clarity and builds trust.

One strength of our community that is continuously brought up is the fact that everyone has some space that they can call their own and define the rules within. Common issues in communal houses include tension over welcoming children or pets into the space, and having to come to consensus over household rules. Since everyone owns or rents their own space, there is enough separation to allow rules to be set to meet personal needs. For example, in certain spaces children are permitted to run freely from home to home. In others it is expected that children would ask permission before entering. The children understand this and the boundaries are respected. It is possible to have community with personal boundaries that meet individual needs; it is important to remember that these boundaries can still allow for connection.

There are spaces and times created specifically to bring the community together. For example last year we started a weekly potluck. Typical attendance ranged between 80 and 100 people! With so many people biking in and children running loose, the street was closed to traffic, essentially making the potlucks a weekly street party. The potlucks also created a pick-up spot for community supported agriculture (CSA) farm boxes and acted as a networking event for all the amazingly skilled people that live in the area. The potlucks will continue this summer.

With so many people to reach, in wintertime it is a challenge to maintain the same level of connection that seems to happen naturally on the streets and in backyards come summertime. But still the intention of maintaining community keeps the spirit alive as people seek opportunities for getting together.

Another thing that unites us is our children. It is very easy to see how it "takes a village to raise a child" living in this community. All of the regular challenges of parenthood still exist—finding childcare for the kids, getting the kids to bed, coordinating the comings and goings of daily activities, balancing work and family time—but working together makes it all doable. Parenting is hard work, no matter what, but parenting together makes it possible to still be energized at the end of the day and to always be present and giving when you are with the kids. The children learn so much from all of the different adult role-models in their lives and it is such a privilege to watch them grow and explore together.

We are creating a functional model for people to live in suburban community wherever we are, in a way that meets and challenges a variety of social, economic, and ecological values. To learn more about

us check out our blog at junctionng.wordpress.com or email us at thejunctionng@gmail.com. 🐦

Carly Fraser was introduced to the benefits of community while living with four wonderful roommates in her undergraduate years at the University of Guelph. She is now giving intentional community a try as a "WWOOFer" at Two Sisters River Urban Farm in Guelph, Ontario (and loving it!). Carly likes to spend her days outdoors learning to garden, playing with children, sorting and thinking about garbage, playing ultimate frisbee, and chasing after escaped chickens. She is very excited to begin studying food waste this fall as a master's student in the Department of Geography at the University of Guelph. You can reach Carly at carlyelizabethfraser@gmail.com.

129

Sharing Stories and Rituals

By SILC Guelph

Over the last two years a core group of people have been working together to explore building an intentional community in Guelph, Ontario. Affectionately called SILC (Sustainable Intentional Living Community just seemed like too big of a mouthful), the group has grown to a core membership of 16 with a listserv of over 60 interested people. Lately we have been caught up in more of the details as we get ready to move forward with purchasing a property and designing our new home, so it was nice to step back for an evening and reconnect with why we are doing this together. The community conversation, part of the 1000 Conversations Campaign, gave us the perfect chance to do this.

We started our conversation by sharing our own stories of community. It was surprising to hear that all of us had experience being in a close-knit community, whether it was an intentional community in Latin America, a small town where everyone knew everyone, or a church family.

Common themes that came out of these stories were the idea of doing things together, whether it was sharing food, chores, or even organizing music festivals. Community seemed to be active.

Mike shared how community was not something that he had been seeking or trying intentionally to build. For most of his life it is just what happened. In contrast we are now intentionally trying to create community with SILC. Some fear that it will feel artificial.

We then had a discussion about the role of boundaries in establishing community. The boundaries are not tied to us as individuals; we can cross them at our leisure, but when we are in these boundaries we feel connected to the community that they define. Bill talked about how this was a natural outcome of our need to relate to our village.

Vicki discussed how some people can be paralyzed by the overwhelming selection of people, which is the case for many people living in urban centers. They are people without community, because they do not have a context to draw a perimeter. Boundaries allow us to build a sense of identity.

We discussed how community enforces conformity. Bill talked about how communities push us to not act in a manner that is detrimental to self or others. He discussed how there are certain limits that you have to stay within to stay a part of the community. Things get off track when those limits become hidden or arbitrarily applied.

Sustainability is a major focus of the Guelph SILC group; we draw inspiration from the natural world and how systems organically ebb and flow, new things are added, old things are discarded. We see the same pattern in a healthy community. When this does not happen, when a community clings on to staying the same, then it starts to become dysfunctional. Despite this necessary dynamism, it is still important to have a central gravity that holds everyone together and keeps a community grounded. We all agreed that this is the role of a set of common values.

Vicki described community like water. She said growing up in a small rural community people did not always get along; sometimes people would fight or not talk to each other for years at a time, but like water they got where they needed to go. People would share farm equipment because that is just what you did, what you had to do to survive. When a disaster struck, the community would band together.

Melanie shared how some communities are about celebrating and having fun together, while others are about getting things done. As long as everyone is clear and on the same page with what type of community you are, then you should all be able to get along.

Mike countered that community does not mean that everyone gets along. It is a group of people who live and do things together and who can more or less rely on each other when things are needed. He described it as the difference between like and love. When you love people you do things for them because they need it. It is not about the warm fuzziness, it is

> ## We draw inspiration from the natural world and how systems organically ebb and flow.

simply a way of relating. It is just what you do.

We then talked about how communities form around needs; but what if there is no obvious need? Can we create a common need? One need that was brought forward for SILC was sustainability. We debated about whether this was truly a need or an ideal. Is it strong enough of a need to pull us together and help form this community?

We see SILC as a way of enabling us to live the values we believe in. But is the fact that we hold more or less the same values sufficient to make a community that works? Bill shared how it comes down to our personal needs and how they will or will not be fulfilled. If they are being fulfilled, then the community can work.

At this point in the conversation, we asked: Why SILC and Why Now? To our surprise the answers varied widely. For Melanie it was a desire to live out her values of a sustainable lifestyle that she felt she could not do on her own. Derek similarly said it was a chance to be fortified in living with integrity to the values he wants to embody. For Bill it was a chance to build more meaningful and lasting relationships that could support him as he got older. For Vicki it was an opportunity to preserve the beautiful garden that she had spent decades making. (Mike and Vicki's property is going to be part of the site for the intentional community.)

Finally we shared ideas of actions that help build community. Bill laid out beautifully how there are three levels for people living in community:

• Personal: Things (ideas, emotions, objects) that lie within ourselves.
• Impersonal: Things we own.
• Interpersonal: Things that lie between/with others and us.

Bill discussed how in community our interpersonal things are on display but our personal things influence it. So in community the personal is really important. We need to develop mechanisms to work on the personal—rituals like meditation. Bill talked about how these practices help communities indirectly deal with issues.

We also added sports, or creativity like art and music, as other spaces to release pent up energy and work on the personal. These activities also create space for us to come and play together. In our hectic life it is often easy to let these things slip away.

Derek talked about rituals, the idea of setting aside a certain time to do a certain set of behaviors that have a deeper meaning. We are able to fall back upon these rituals during times of stress and uncertainty.

Melanie discussed governance as another action that helps build and maintain community. It does this by building a pattern of behavior for decision-making. She noted that governance is not about strict rules but rather an understanding of processes. The metaphor she used was a trellis on which we (the vine) can grow; it helps us keep form but we are free to grow through it the way that is natural and organic.

We also discussed having a common communication method. In the case of SILC we expect that everyone takes nonviolent communication training. This provides a norm of communication.

This proved to be a very rich and rewarding conversation that left us feeling closer to each other. Beyond the emotional experience we were also able to bring forward lots of interesting ideas that forced us to dig deeper into how we are building our community. It will be exciting to see how SILC grows in the months and years to come. ❧

SILC is a Guelph-based group that is in the process of creating an intentional community within the heart of the city. Their values include strong authentic communication, sustainability, and being a community action hub for the residents of Guelph. They have been meeting regularly since the autumn of 2011, and have 16 core members and growing.

Photo courtesy of Derek Alton

SILC members Bill, Mike, Melanie, and Vicki participated in their group's community conversation.

Conversations Take Wing:
The RareBirds Housing Cooperative Story

By Mary Jordan

Y̶ou would be forgiven if you thought RareBirds Housing Cooperative might be a flock of exotic Quetzalcoatl living in a rookery in the Costa Rican rain forest. Perhaps that's not far off the mark as we are a unique group of lively adults who are planning on nesting together. As with any rookery, there has been ruffling of feathers, puffing up and preening for pecking order, some cawing and crowing, strange flight behaviour, and eventually a settling into a place of comfort.

As much as the analogy might fit our chosen name, we are not a rookery at all. Nor are we birds or bird-brained, although there are those who allude to that scenario (unfairly, given the proven intelligence of many birds). We are a group of nine adults, three couples, and three singles ranging in age from 48 to 71, and one beautiful Belgian Tervuren, who have consciously chosen to live differently in the world. By bringing together six typical Canadian households into one, we are able to reduce both our per-person consumption of energy and the duplication of many day-to-day household items and equipment such as household appliances.

The RareBirds can be found in Kamloops, a small Canadian city of 85,000 in south central British Columbia about 400 kilometres east of Vancouver. Kamloops is primarily a resource-based economy and, while our community has diversified in recent decades, exhibiting extraordinary growth at Thompson Rivers University as well as thriving arts and tourism sectors, our conservative roots are still evident. There are many co-op housing ventures across Canada that include both rural and urban models, but in our town, for the most part, co-op housing means government-subsidized, or "not for profit" projects. The idea of a group of mid-life professionals choosing to launch such a venture is certainly suspect.

We could say that our story begins in March 2011 when a couple of friends attended a documentary film: "How to Boil a Frog." It was not a cooking film, but rather a documentary about living more simply and sustainably. It would also be true to say the story began much earlier, through various conversations in a variety of situations about sustainability, shared living, and the realities of aging baby boomers. However, it was on that particular evening in March 2011 that this idea grew wings.

We began by inviting some like-minded friends into a conversation, and the excitement of possibilities was palpable from that first gathering. Although our current group of committed members has had various points of reconfiguration, we have always had the support of those who danced with the vision and flew in another direction. We maintained a core group who enthusiastically upheld these values. As we committed to meeting regularly, emerging ideas gained clarity and scope, further influencing the direction this journey would take.

Initially we developed our intentions and articulated a shared purpose. From this conversation emerged our Living on Purpose document, which continues to guide our decisions and communications to this day, almost three years later.

Purpose:

The purpose of our Intentional Community is to create a model that will enable us to live into the possibilities of social and spiritual transformation.

Intention:

• To create more financial freedom and emotional enrichment for each of us by living interdependently, mindful of environmental responsibilities and sustainable practices in our community living.

• To create an inclusive environment that embraces our extended families and welcomes our friends.

• To create sustainable practices which embody our values.

We spent some months of focused research discovering a variety of options for shared living; there are numerous models out there. Eventually, we settled on a hybrid: a registered self-financed equity housing cooperative, and an intentional community with shared kitchen and various common living spaces rather than independent self-contained units. Our journey has been a series of peaks and valleys; full speed, then speed bumps, and yet with a continuous movement forward. We wonder now as we move into the final stages of our build, choosing paint colours and admiring our view, how we have managed to get here.

In the summer of 2012 we purchased property near the downtown core, on the edge of a ravine with a rushing creek below and boasting expansive views of the river valley and the hills beyond.

With our goal to self-finance, three of us sold our homes, put most of our possessions in storage, and began a nomadic life of house-sitting for friends and acquaintances, who have all been incredibly generous and gracious in their sharing. One of our members recently completed their sixth relocation! Some chose travel for periods of time, requiring us to navigate through difficult decisions by internet conversation and email.

A need to rezone our property required us to garner neighbourhood support and present our project at a public hearing. This process required a long, patient dance with City Planners who initially had little idea what to do with the anomaly of this zoning application. The result was a significant delay in getting the shovels in the ground. Another unexpected and frightening event occurred when one of our members met life-threatening illness which required weeks in the hospital, major surgery, and a long recovery.

As we proceeded to the design and build stage, our desire to include features of sustainable design and sound environmental building practice led us to careful consideration in the choice of professionals. We needed to know that we could trust them with our vision and manage our budget carefully. We have not been disappointed. We know that we have been guided wisely to good choices and best practices.

For example, our home includes active and passive design elements to conserve energy and lessen our ecological footprint. We paid close attention to the orientation of the house and the best use of the land. The house is double-insulated, both within and without, the sheeting of the house reaching values of R-27 in the walls and R-50 in the roof. A solar hot water system consisting of three panels and a 120 gallon storage tank will provide an average of 75 gallons of hot water per day. There are 27 solar panels, each 250 watts, installed on the south-facing roof with an array that is built to eventually provide a total of 45 panels.

We are approved as one of about 270 BC Hydro net metering projects in the province. Our system connects to the distribution system; we receive credit for the 11¼ kilowatts of electrical energy these panels will generate. This equates to about $1,200 (Canadian) per year at current utility rates. An efficient heat pump will be used for heating, ventilation, and cooling.

While we have attended to the business of building a house, we have not neglected the business of building a community. We have been mindful of the need to slow down. Staying on track with each other has been as vital as staying on track with the project.

Photos courtesy of Mary Jordan

Most of this process work has been done in time we have taken to retreat together. We began developing what we refer to as our "Flight Manual," which is basically an outline of our policies and procedures. We view this as the organic document that will guide our living together. We have adopted a consensus decision-making model and use a circle practice in our meetings. This practice is built on three basic principles: speaking with intention, listening with attention, and contributing to the well-being of the group. This process of deep listening, silence, and careful practice is still evolving and fine tuning, but it has served us well.

We incorporated as a BC Housing Cooperative in January 2012, providing us with our integral legal framework. The house and property are owned by the RareBirds Housing Cooperative. We do not, as individuals, have ownership of collective or personal spaces. The cooperative holds six equity shares and each member, either couple or single, owns one share. The question of how to transfer ownership should a member die or wish to sell is a common inquiry and one with which we have wrestled. An individual or estate can elect to sell their share at market value. Any purchaser would be vetted by the community regarding ability and willingness to participate fully. If, after 12 months, the share is not sold, the co-op would assume responsibility for purchasing the share.

As we worked on our "way-of-being together" we researched further aspects of community life and fleshed out our purpose with more clarity. We also knew that if we were to be a model for social transformation, we needed opportunities to increase awareness in our community and encourage others to consider such options.

Our local media has been very keen to support our initiatives by publishing press releases, various articles, and photographs, along with some excellent radio interviews. In March 2012 we hosted our first "Conversation Café" at a local restaurant. While we featured our Co-op project, we also invited other interested groups who could offer experience or research with other models. These included faith-based communities, rural farm-based ventures, a couple with experience living in an urban co-op, and an architect with experience and a passion for intentional community design and building with green technology. We embarked on creating an internet presence—a website, www.rarebirdshousing.ca, along with the Facebook page, www.facebook.com/RareBirdsHousing—and began sharing musings on a blog which is now included as a link on our website.

Interest has built along with heaps of curiosity and questions. While people see the value of what we are undertaking, the concept is for some a large stretch. When we are describing our home, or showing the design, one kitchen is often the stopper. "One kitchen!" we are asked incredulously. "One kitchen with nine people? So, how will you cook, who will do the cooking and who will clean? How will you handle grocery shopping? What happens if you wish to entertain?"

Within this, we often sense an unspoken question: "How will I, as your friend, fit into your new home, and how can I still be your friend when you live in a 'group home'?" We ask ourselves similar questions. How can I maintain my individual friendships? Do people now perceive us being tethered to the "The Birds"? Will my children and grandchildren really be welcome? What will happen if there is a crisis in my family? How comfortable am I with asking for help and offering what I can? How can I step into this with my lifetime of valuing independence? Do I even know what interdependence means and if I don't know, how can I live in an intentional community?

These are huge, exciting, and fearful questions! Not one of us has stepped into this lightly. While we hold the vision and engage in the possibilities, we have learned to wrestle together with our shared doubts and fears because we know we must. The business of building our home has taken time and energy from each of us. The decisions have seemed endless and it has not always been easy to know when to step up or step back.

Early on, one of us remarked, "This will stretch us in ways we can't even imagine yet." This has proven true so far. Old patterns of control and deferment, assumptions and judgments, differing needs and expectations have been wrestled with both individually and collectively. We have each retreated to our "cave" now and then but we are learning to let things go, trust the process and each other. We are curious birds! Yet we tend to prefer the word "wonder" over "curiosity."

Curiosity is very valuable. It is a mental process of trying to know more and understand more—this is all good. Wonder, on the other hand, is more of a heart word. Wonder holds some of the mystery of life. One of our touchstones we use during group process is this: "When the going gets rough, turn to wonder." We ask that question first of ourselves: "I wonder why I am reacting in this way to what is going on?" Curiosity and wonder have been gifts to us along the way. Communication within the group is essential. Facing miscommunication and owning it is a crucial piece. No relationship, family, or community can thrive without that, and we know it.

One of our members recently shared a reading by American writer and social thinker Peter Block, a reflection on what it means to create community. He believes that when people truly collaborate they are accessing latent resources that already exist among them. It is not just making decisions. It is an energy release, an activation of gifts hidden from view or ignored or underestimated. This has been our experience as we navigated through a myriad of decisions.

Three years ago life was first breathed into this vision. Soon we will inhabit our creation and begin a whole new way of being in the world. We still step back from time to time, shrinking from the immensity of this undertaking—bigger, more challenging, and more awesome that any of us could have envisioned. We have learned together, laughed and cried, flapped our wings and flurried about, and, at times, flown off completely.

We sometimes see ourselves as crazy birds that have learned to fly in formation like the Canada Geese. As "The Story of the Goose" tells us, as each bird flaps its wings it creates an updraft for the bird following. Their V formation adds 71 percent more flying range than if each bird flew alone. They honk from behind to encourage those in front to keep up their speed. When the lead goose tires, it falls back in the V and another goose flies point. When a goose gets sick or is wounded, falling from formation, two other geese join their companion to lend help and protection. We, the RareBirds, are cultivating this same sense and as all sensible birds know, the rest is in the rookery, that collective place where we find our perch. ❧

Mary Jordan is a single senior, with daughters and two delightful granddaughters. She is also a counselor working part time. She loves adventures, travel, and people. She is curious about interdependence in a culture that values independence and fears dependence. The value system she embraces includes living cooperatively, sharing resources, skills, and time.

FROM CONVERSATION TO COMMUNITY:
How a Bunch of Mates Bought Some Land Together

By John Hepburn

Have you ever found yourself sitting around with a group of friends saying "wouldn't it be great to buy a block of land together in the bush?" For years, my life partner Jemma and I found ourselves having the same dinner party conversation, yearning for something more than nuclear family life in the suburbs.

Eventually, we decided that we should actually do something, or else stop talking about it. This is a story about what unfolded. I say "a" story, because each of our co-conspirators has a different one as our lives have come together to share the exciting journey and our connection to the beautiful place that we call "Black Bulga."

Our first step in taking this idea seriously (sometime in 2006) was to organise a Sunday lunch with the friends we had been discussing the idea with. Out of that lunch came an agreement to spend a weekend away together in the country to kick the idea around. We were explicit that there was no pressure, and no expectation that this group of people would do anything together other than exploring a conversation.

After two separate weekends of staying in lovely farmhouses, eating delicious food, drinking too much wine, and traipsing around the countryside looking at properties, it was clear that this was a group of people with very different ideas and expectations. Out of the seven of us who spent those weekends together, only three of us seemed to be looking for similar things.

Michael, Jemma, and I kept the conversation going. We shared a common connection to the Hunter Valley and over the course of the next couple of years, spent a number of weekends exploring the foothills of the Barrington Tops World Heritage Area. We read books on intentional communities, visited as many communities as we could find, reached out to friends of friends who lived in the Barrington Tops area, and began to get a sense of what kind of properties were out there. All the while we kept floating the conversation with other friends who we thought might be interested in the idea.

Our friends James and Danielle decided to come down from Brisbane for a weekend of exploring places and ideas. They both had Newcastle roots and had a long-term dream of rural landsharing and intentional community. James has spent much of his life as an environmental campaigner and activist educator and had a strong vision of creating an activist training centre. Dan works as a communications professional with a passion for visual arts, and she was excited about the creative potential of this kind of project. Other friends dipped in and out of the conversation over this time but by the start of 2008 our group of three had grown to five.

Jemma and I moved up to Newcastle to be closer to her family when Rosa, our first daughter, was born. We were infected with the madness of first-time parents and bought an old terrace house in Cooks Hill, which we proceeded to renovate. During winter, when we had no bathroom, our friends Geoff and Deb came to our rescue and offered hot baths and warm soups. I had known Geoff for years through his work with the Minerals Policy Institute and Greenpeace, but it was through this

Jemma, Deb, and Rosa: first visit on the ridge.

period that our friendship deepened and we got to know Deb. Geoff had just completed his Ph.D. into how to develop a "just transition" away from coal dependence to sustainability in the Hunter Valley, and Deb was embarking on her own Ph.D., exploring the challenges of educating boys. Over the course of many lovely evening discussions (in between having hot baths and soothing a newborn baby) we discovered that they were also seriously interested in the idea of co-owning a block of land in the Hunter Valley. Our group of five grew to seven.

It was during this time that Jemma and I met a young carpenter by the name of Steve who was passionate about sustainable building. We asked him to help us with some of the structural work on our renovation and Steve and I spent a few days working together. It turns out that Steve shared a similar dream of buying land together with like-minded people, but he felt he was a long way off being ready for that kind of project.

Sometime in 2009, after Jemma and I were back in Sydney, our group of seven spent a weekend up at Wangat Lodge, near Barrington Tops, to explore the land-sharing idea and to look at properties. We shared our dreams, hopes, and fears, discussed criteria for land, and explored the kind of legal arrangements that we would need to do this kind of project. By this time, Jemma, Michael, and I must have looked at every rural property for sale in the entire district, and the local real estate

agent was starting to get pretty weary of us. But all of a sudden we found ourselves looking at a property that ticked all of the boxes. It was magnificent: stunning views, a creek, cycling distance from Dungog and the trainline to Sydney and Newcastle; it had a six bedroom house, large shed, and two rental cabins already built. The only problem was that it cost close to a million dollars.

We quickly figured out the maximum that each of us could afford and worked up a business plan. We needed 16 people to make it work financially. We put the word out to our closest networks. James called a friend and colleague from Brisbane. After hearing about the place and who was involved, John (Jmac) pretty much said he was "in" over the phone. Another friend (James A.) from Sydney did the same thing. I called Steve, who by this time had become a good friend, and he came up to check the place out. Geoff and Deb reached out to their friends Matt and Sarah who also came up to see the property.

All of a sudden we had reached critical mass—we had a vision, a great group of people, and fantastic block of land. We scrambled to make it happen. We put up $2,000 each and engaged a lawyer from northern New South Wales who had experience setting up rural landsharing projects. We started negotiations to buy the property. Our dream was about to become reality. In our minds, Jemma and I had moved to the land and built our dream house already…until we got gazumped. While we were rushing to get our constitution in order, somebody else bought the property from right under our nose. It was gut wrenching.

In the weeks after we had found the property, we had rapidly turned an idea into a serious project with a clear vision, a legal structure, and a business plan—but with no land and a great deal of disappointment. We regrouped and kept looking.

Without a real place to ground the project, it became increasingly difficult to maintain momentum. Intellectually, it seemed far more sensible to develop the group, the legal structure, the plan, and a clear set of criteria before finding a block of land, but practically speaking, it was all starting to feel a bit too abstract. The financial model and the vision

Black Bulga Celebration.

The first garlic harvest.

Strawbaling at Black Bulga.

Easter at Black Bulga.

Photos courtesy of Danielle Nelson

Early days at Black Bulga.

Rolling the header tank up the hill.

Rosa at the garlic harvest.

Geoff and Deb.

Exploring the land together.

were invariably going to be different for each different property, depending on cost of the land and the existing infrastructure. We had a long list of agreed "criteria" but Jemma and I kept on coming back to "the vibe" as being the most important thing.

We soon found another property that seemed to fit the bill and we once again started to develop a vision for how our project could fit that piece of land. We ended up in the awkward situation of having half of our group really keen to buy it and the other half not. We spent a weekend there together (where the cicadas nearly drove us all mad) which ended with the difficult and quite stressful decision not to buy it. We began to doubt that we'd ever find another place that everyone liked.

In the aftermath of that weekend, I was up late one night scouring the online real estate listings once again and came across a new listing that looked too good to be true. Jemma, Rosa, Deb, and I headed up there the next weekend to take a look.

We arrived at the property and the real estate agent took us straight to one of the most beautiful swimming holes we'd ever seen, at the confluence of the Karuah and Telegherry rivers. And it just got better from there. From the ridge we could see dramatic wilderness for miles and a landscape that invited us to explore the valleys and folds of the rolling mountains. The river flats of rich alluvium had an abundance of water from a gravity-fed irrigation system coming out of the neighbouring conservation area. And the rivers… oh the glorious rivers…where you could swim with your mouth open and drink deeply of the crystal clear waters.

As we left the sun-drenched ridge on that first visit, we knew we had found the place we had been looking for. An eagle soared overhead, and Rosa grinned a delicious blackberry-stained grin as the wallabies hopped away through the paddock. And so we began the journey to becoming custodians of the land that we have come to know and love as Black Bulga. ❧

John Hepburn is a founding member of Black Bulga Intentional Community in the Hunter Valley, New South Wales, Australia (www.blackbulga.org.au). Black Bulga is currently looking for new members; email Hepburn.john@gmail.com if interested. This story is adapted from an article John posted on his Facebook page in March 2014.

Oakleigh Meadow Cohousing
Hard at Work "Building Community,
One Conversation at a Time"

By Cindy Nickles

"*The Sneetches and Other Stories," "Hatchet," "The Happy Hollisters," "The Secret Garden," "The Little House," "Henry Reed, Inc.," "A Child's Garden of Verses," "Paddle-to-the-Sea," "Bone Games," "Black Beauty," "Nancy Drew mysteries," and "Native American chief histories."*

Were Oakleigh Meadow Cohousing members and friends at a book club meeting?

Not exactly. Reminiscent of grade school students at circle time, we were answering this two-part question: "What book did you read as a child that was important to you, and how did it affect you?"

That opening exercise served double-duty as ice-breaker and group introductions at a Communications Workshop facilitated by Anita Englise in Eugene, Oregon.

As we took turns sharing our favorite childhood books and their impacts on our lives, we were already well on our way to "Building Community, One Conversation at a Time"—the title of the workshop designed and facilitated by Engiles, a local mediator and trainer.

It was also a trip down memory lane. As individuals talked about their favorite books, we found ourselves nodding our heads in agreement as we remembered the stories too.

"I got a sense of adventure from reading those books," one cohousing member said about the *Nancy Drew* mysteries. "I also read every *Hardy Boys* mystery there was." Ditto for another member.

When one cohousing member was 13, he read *Hatchet*, a book about a kid his same age who survived a plane crash, left with only a hatchet to survive. He said, "I thought it was the coolest thing in the world to be out in the wilderness. Somehow he found wood, food, etc."

Each of us in turn shared similar fond recollections.

• • •

Oakleigh Meadow Cohousing will be Eugene's first multi-family development designed and built using the cohousing model. In April 2012, we formed a Limited Liability Company (LLC), and we expect to break ground this year. Our "new, old-

Oakleigh Meadow Cohousing members Barbara Boylan and R.C. Cross participate in an interactive exercise about their favorite communication style: accommodating.

Photo courtesy of Cindy Nickles

fashioned neighborhood" will feature 28 individually owned flats and townhouses built around shared facilities, including a Common House and gardens, on 2.3 acres alongside the Willamette River and bike trail.

Vision

We're an intergenerational community of independent households committed to finding purpose and a sense of belonging through working, learning, and playing together in a neighborhood designed to make a small and beautiful footprint on the land. Our shared values include the importance of neighbors and community as well as learning to live with a light impact on the environment.

team

We are currently working hard learning the ropes of cohousing, including holding biweekly business meetings and third-Sunday orientations, site visits, and community suppers. Teams—including Marketing, Membership, Landscape, and Finance and Legal—also meet biweekly.

process

On an as-needed basis, the Process team meets. Among other responsibilities, it is tasked with team-building activities and workshops, including the Communications Workshop that was held Saturday, April 27, from 11 a.m.-3 p.m., at the environmentally friendly Stellaria Building in downtown Eugene.

The objectives for our workshop, which had previously been discussed and aired by all of us:

- Opportunity for more full interaction than what takes place at meetings and meals;
- Welcoming and integrating membership, new, old and in-between; and
- Building communication skills and ease.

Topping the priority list was tools on how to deal with confrontation. Specifically we wished to learn how to understand and communicate with people without it being confrontational. We wanted to learn how to diffuse confrontations.

In the words of a fellow cohouser, her workshop goal was "improving my ability to receive feedback without getting my hairs up."

Also on our "to-do" list was to learn the different styles of communication. As a cohousing member said, "There are different styles in the way we process and sometimes there's a disconnect."

Empathy vs. Sympathy

Anita led us on a Q&A that turned into a heartfelt discussion on what we felt were the differences between empathy and sympathy.

On empathy, our comments ranged from "feeling with the person," "walking in that person's shoes," to being "open to all the different facets—to have as much understanding as possible." This contrasted with sympathy—"pitying" or "feeling sorry for" the person.

Anita explained to us: "If we *can't* empathize, we can say, 'I have no idea how you must feel.' Have the person recognize that you're not faking it. We can certainly sense that lack of authenticity."

"When we can empathize with people, we can make stronger, more meaningful connections," she said.

Before asking us to pair off to practice, she advised, "When we try to listen empathetically, it's really hard not to try to problem-solve. It's very powerful when the other person gives you the space to solve your problem."

When it was my turn to listen, I worked on not making judgments and not offering an opinion or interrupting, but being present by making eye contact and silently acknowledging what my friend had to say.

Positions and Interests

As a group, we went through an exercise of three case studies to glean an appreciation and understanding about peoples' "positions and interests."

For example, we learned how to word our questions in the best way to resolve issues and problems. "Opened-ended questions can help, so people can tell us what their experiences are," said Anita.

Also important are self-awareness of judgmental tendencies, withholding our own judgments, using an approach of phrasing your impression as a question rather than a conclusion, and meeting the person and making the connection.

"That connection is the first thing people need," said Anita.

Conflict-Handling Modes

Concluding the workshop was an interactive exercise about the five conflict-handling modes. We all have a favorite communication style that we fall back on.

In a nutshell, the different approaches to handling conflict include accommodating,

> **Different approaches to handling conflict include accommodating, avoiding, controlling, compromising, collaborating.**

avoiding, controlling, compromising, collaborating.

Around the room, Anita hung up poster-sized paper for us to choose our most comfortable style of communication. Then we defined the response style we selected, gave several examples of when we might use this style, and discussed the benefits and challenges, pros and cons, of using this style.

Afterward, we gathered as a group, and shared what we'd learned.

In her wrap-up at the event's end, Anita left us with this take-away question: "What does this mean for me as a member of the Oakleigh Meadow Cohousing community?"

In our hearts, we believe that cohousing is built by individuals in relationship with one another and we are committed to improving our communication skills. So, it's practice, practice, practice for all of us. ❧

Cindy Nickles is moving to Eugene, Oregon, from Sacramento, California, to be part of Oakleigh Meadow Cohousing, which she joined as a full member in December 2013.

Jewish Intentional Community Building in the US

By Rachael Cohen

The Jewish Agency for Israel, Hazon (America's largest Jewish environmental group), Isabella Freedman Jewish Retreat Center (Falls Village, Connecticut), and Pearlstone Retreat Center (Reisterstown, Maryland) joined together to convene the inaugural conference for a growing national Jewish movement of intentional community building, November 14-17, 2013 (www.jewishagency.org, www.hazon.org, isabellafreedman.org, pearlstonecenter.org). The following article is adapted from a speech given at the first plenary.

My passion for intentional Jewish community building is likely a result of the social isolation I felt in my early years. I was a child of suburbia. My mother went back to her job when I was six weeks old and I went off to a babysitter each day. My father spent most of his waking hours at work. Both sets of grandparents lived out of town. My sister was five years younger and, in my opinion, an unacceptable playmate. We were minimally affiliated Jews. I went to Hebrew school, but we had no connection with synagogue life. We rarely, if ever, had guests. What if the house wasn't clean enough? The food tasty enough? We gave cursory waves to the neighbors, offered quick smiles to people we passed in the supermarket, made perfunctory exchanges with gas station attendants and bank clerks. I observed: be pleasant but detached.

I felt a loneliness and lack of connection that I could not adequately voice to my parents. As I matured, I had windows into other people's lives: friends whose families took vacations together, my large pack of cousins who all lived in the same distant town, kids who went to one summer camp year after year, families with many children. These groups were building a shared sense of belonging and I felt envious.

When I was 15 I worked at a small, rural, Jewish day camp. For the first time I felt held and supported through a sense of deeper meaning and connection to community. That fall I joined my synagogue's youth group, and again, felt the tenderness of intimate communal belonging I had never known but so instinctively craved. As I gently allowed myself to feel relevant and purposeful in these chosen communities, I saw myself defined not just by my own individual qualities, but by who I was in relation to the community. It was a revelation. Who I am is directly linked and impacted by who I am to you and who you are to me.

It took me 15 years to find that sense of belonging again. I attended five colleges, nine programs in Israel, made Aliyah [immigrated into Israel], left Israel, and was a resident of more municipalities in America than I have fingers to count. I dragged first my husband Yishai, and then our kids, around with me to numerous conventional communities, gauging the social climate, measuring, calculating, computing, and assessing all aspects of the prevailing social systems and interpersonal patterns. And over, and over, and over again I was disappointed—sometimes despondent—over the inherent lack of intention and substance. Yet I could not give up my search. I was compelled to address the insistent demand I felt within—to belong to something bigger than myself; to define who I was in the context of something greater than my individual experience alone.

Despite finding a handful of secular intentional communities that seemed absolutely perfect for our family, when I seriously considered our ultimate life in one of them, I realized a non-Jewish community could not serve our purpose of social sustainability. We would not be able to participate fully or authentically in community life without the aspects that define a Jewish community and resonate so profoundly for us. Regular communal prayer, shared holidays and life cycle events, acknowledgment of Shabbat [day of rest], awareness and consideration of kashrut [dietary laws], and the collective consciousness of almost four thousand years of shared history are all imperative to me.

Finally, last year, when a seasonal job was advertised with Teva, the Jewish environmental education program, at the Isabella Freedman Jewish Retreat Center, I knew we had to seize the opportunity.

Isabella Freedman is first and foremost a retreat center, hosting transformative theme-based Jewish retreats and rentals. But for those lucky enough to find themselves a position there, as staff of the retreat center or Teva, or as participants in the Adamah farming fellowship, it also serves as a Jewish intentional community. It is a short-term, cyclical community in that most people stay seasonally, for three to four months at a time. There are approximately 50 people living and participating on-site at any given time, most of whom are single and between the ages of 20 and 30.

Communal meals provide the setting for powerful relationship-building opportunities.

Yishai interviewed for the position and was offered the job. We were met with some raised eyebrows and questioning expressions from family and friends. Were we crazy? How would we survive on so little? Where would we live? There was no on-site housing available for families. No Jewish day school for our five-year-old. No regular synagogue services. Only three other families with children.

By moving to Isabella Freedman, we have chosen a lifestyle based on ideals. Despite some very real obstacles, we are more content and fulfilled than we ever have been as a family. Our children are growing up in a social environment much larger than we alone can provide. They have many aunts and uncles who love them, teach them, discipline them, and watch over them. The depth and meaning in the relationships that they are creating is palpable, and the single most important reason we live in community. Authentic access to other human beings is sorely lacking in society today.

We have had to use savings and live frugally, but the rewards have been life-changing. We have opportunities to develop deep, authentic relationships based on shared values such as environmental stewardship, a progressive stance on Judaism regardless of affiliation, Jewish farming, mindfulness and personal improvement, and commitment to communal living. The friendships we grow and nurture with members of our community serve to strengthen and enhance our own identities, interests, and independence as individuals, and ultimately, improve our relationships with each other as family members.

I would like this type of community experience to be available to any Jew who desires it. In order to proliferate the creation of Jewish intentional communities, my husband and I created New Jewish Communities, an internet forum where ideas and views on Jewish intentional community building can be exchanged for the purpose of 1) connecting people with existing, forming, and conceptualized projects of intentional Jewish community; and 2) establishing the first Jewish Ecovillage in America: an intergenerational community of people who are consciously committed to living Jewishly, in the same geographic location, with the intention of becoming more socially, economically, and ecologically sustainable.

As a part of a growing global movement for a more sustainable world, the communities we envision will integrate a supportive social environment with a low-impact way of life. They will aim to strengthen and repair the individual, the family, Judaism, and society by developing a system of mutual support that is becoming more difficult to achieve in conventional social systems. In this way, I believe New Jewish Communities have the capacity to change the face of contemporary Jewish life, and I look forward to being a part of that transformation. ❧

Rachael Cohen is a big-picture thinker, captivated by social systems and social change. She believes in the process of community building as a means to remedy social disintegration and repair individual well-being. Rachael has a masters degree in macro social work and community practice, as well as a certificate in nonprofit management. She is currently working on relationship-based social change through the internet forum New Jewish Communities (directory.ic.org/23150/ New_Jewish_Communities), and in Falls Village, Connecticut, both at the Isabella Freedman Jewish Retreat Center and within the local community. Rachael's full-time job is raising two marvelous daughters.

Photos courtesy of Rachael Cohen

Loving Earth Sanctuary
Two Women's Quest for a Low-Tech Life

By Gloria Wilson

A newly forming community and innovative rural homestead in the hills of California's Central Coast, Loving Earth Sanctuary is based on the principle of "nourishing ourselves in a way that nourishes all life." Members will reside in their own simple dwellings and together work to pursue a life of land-based sustenance, inner growth, and service/sharing with the broader community.

A central tenet of this project is "radical simplicity," the effort to become more independent from fossil fuels, industrial mining, sweatshop labor, and other modern production systems that harm the Earth and people's health—while also cultivating a sense of abundance and contentment with life's simple joys. A rural life of material simplicity is also intended to free up more time for personal spiritual practice (of any faith or background), creative expression, and voluntary service to others in need. The project's two main founders, Gloria and Dori, are excited to build an egalitarian, consensus-based community on the land, and are open to new prospective members interested in this lifestyle.

In the following article, visionary and cofounder Gloria Wilson shares her own journey and reflects on the decision to live mostly free from modern technology.

My partner and I had a natural inclination toward Luddism from the start. We spent our childhoods dreaming about the "old days" of hand pumps, hen houses, and candlelight. While enamored with stories like *Little House on the Prairie* and *Caddy Woodlawn*, we also were motivated by our own sensitivities to modern life. We both recall how, as children, it was tragic for us to watch stars being consumed by street lights or to see a television replace jovial family dinners; we connected the dots early that technological advancements came with costs.

Nevertheless, culture has a way of ensnaring even the best-intentioned budding visionaries. In spite of our childhood fantasies, it didn't take long before we relied on computers and the internet for networking, information, creative outlet, and to some degree entertainment. Although we hadn't yet met each other, our ideas about technology were evolving on a parallel track. What had begun as hardcore "Amish" sensibility was now morphing into a more con-

ventional reliance on modern gadgets. Although still aware of the detriments posed by industrial life, we found momentary solace in the neo-environmentalists' solution for a greener future: solar panels.

At 15 I moved with my family onto 40 remote acres in the hills, where we put up a yurt and, after a year of mostly electricity-free living, set up a photovoltaic system. Living off-grid in a rural setting, I came into young adulthood optimistic about solar and other high-tech solutions to the myriad of current problems spiraling about my awareness. Convinced that solar provided the only realistic answer to climate change and peak oil, as well as a viable form of resistance to violence in the Middle East, I was able to reconcile my new-found love of internet chat forums and indie movies with my desire for world harmony.

It was, however, a tenuous relationship. On quiet nights in the crevices of time, when cricket sounds oozed through window screens, when I felt whole and complete simply being, I sometimes wondered if I really needed the modern world at all. I contemplated the losses: the mental fluster I felt from an overload of information, and the time spent in a virtual reality rather than the vibrant world around me.

• • •

Illustrations by Dori Stone

While I spent balmy nights in the hills writing poetry by candlelight, my future lifemate was going on a journey. After graduating college with a degree in International Agriculture, she went in search of sustainable alternatives to the American Dream. Based on experiences at small farms across the continent, Dori was reaching the conclusion that small-scale local sustenance was one of the most effective means of resisting violence, whether in the form of sweatshop oppression, warfare, or environmental devastation.

But it wasn't until visiting Stillwaters Sanctuary (a project of the Possibility Alliance) in northeast Missouri that she began to question more deeply the role of technology in society and in her own future. Greatly influenced by Ethan and Sarah's commitment to a petroleum- and electricity-free sanctuary, she discovered that independence from computers, electric lights, power machinery, and all the modern appliances we take for granted was not only possible but also deeply gratifying.

At Stillwaters, Dori learned that even solar panels take a toll on the planet, from the mining of raw materials and routine dumping of toxic sludge, to the discarded batteries that store solar energy. She also learned about high cancer rates among computer factory workers, and how the mining of coltan (a component in nearly all electronics) is contributing to regional wars and environmental destruction in Central Africa.

This information was hard for Dori to confront. As a passionate writer, her relationship with computers was a strong one. Not only did the computer serve as an artistic medium, but she also relied on it as a tool for communicating important messages to a world in need of change. Like myself, she had come to believe that the benefits of using such technologies could outweigh the costs.

But after a seven-month internship at Stillwaters, Dori emerged

with a different perspective. She'd witnessed a community of people living a beautiful, abundant, deeply meaningful life without using any electronics at all. Dori returned home to the Central Coast of California with a vision for founding a similar project in the region where she'd grown up. It was here, after over 20 years of living in the same circle of progressive local artists and activists, that our paths finally crossed.

By this point, I had started thinking seriously about living in a self-sufficient intentional community. Inspired by Gary Snyder's *The Four Changes*, I began to envision a self-sustaining village model for human life on planet Earth. I was already aligned with Dori in her effort to cease consumption of fossil fuels, but it wasn't until hearing about her experience at Stillwaters that I began to question my own views on "green technology." We discussed the impacts of solar panels and computers, from the depletion of rare earth metals to the hazardous e-waste resulting from planned obsolescence (products designed to break down and be replaced).

Ultimately, as much as we both appreciate the value of high technology for art and activism, we had to confront the fact that the "green tech revolution" is just another guise of the industrial revolution, a sly mask for the same oppressive system. Together we reached a shared conclusion that creating a life as free as reasonably possible from electricity is essential to our pursuit of a gentler life—one that not only enriches ourselves but nourishes the health of the planet and other people.

• • •

We know what our ideal looks like: using only materials we can acquire ourselves sustainably from the land where we live, harvested by our own hands. We feel that any system in which resources are extracted in far-off places or assembled by laborers obscured

behind factory walls is too vulnerable to corruption to be preferred over localized production, where we can truly know what we live on.

You may be wondering what I mean by "as free as *reasonably possible*." The truth is, we aren't sure yet ourselves. Having recently bought land (with the help of generous collaborators/supporters John Powell and Aron Heintz) in the Santa Lucia Mountains of coastal California and now on the verge of building community, we've been asking ourselves this very question: What exceptions to the low-tech ideal (if any) are reasonable, appropriate, or necessary for our lives?

Like our friends at Stillwaters, we face unique challenges posed by our land and local region. The criteria for affordable property, near our families and without strict building code enforcement, meant that any land we found would also have certain drawbacks. Our 40 acre parcel is beautiful, off-grid, and has usable wells, but unfortunately is located 35 miles from the nearest substantial town (Paso Robles) and 13 miles from the tiny community of Lockwood.

This presents a transportation conundrum. My parents and brother live up the road and carpool to Paso Robles five days a week for work. Although Dori and I use bicycles and public buses for getting around town, we've been hitching a ride there and back with my family about once per week. (With the exception of this trip between Paso Robles and our land, Dori is basically "car-free" and abstains from riding in personal vehicles, and I only accept rides when the driver is traveling to a particular destination already and has extra space in the car.) It burdens our hearts to be dependent on anybody's ongoing expenditure of fossil fuels, so we're actively considering alternatives. How can we engage with people in the nearest sizable population center, where many of our close family members and friends live, while also staying true to our deepest values?

Determined to try, we recently attempted a bike trip to Paso Robles from our land. The typical car route is 35 miles and takes an hour, but we've deemed that road too dangerous for cycling, so we took the

longer but safer 52-mile route. After more than half a day pedaling over rugged terrain and country roads, we stopped 10 miles short of our destination due to a flat tire and intense summer heat. Although it was a fun adventure, we realized that bicycling as our sole form of transportation between the land and town (even just once per week) may not be realistic on an ongoing basis, especially when we consider long-term knee health and other factors in the equation.

This left us to contemplate more creative options. We've pondered the idea of riding to Paso Robles on motorized bicycles fueled by our own homebrew ethanol. We also could pedal from the land to Lockwood in just under two hours and catch a bus there. (Of course we're aware that public buses do run on fossil fuels, and this weighs on our consciences. However, we still consider public transit an acceptable "transition technology" during the shift to more sustainable and localized communities. In spite of its drawbacks, we believe that public transit could reduce modern society's ecological footprint substantially if utilized by more people.) We're also considering a team of mules to carry us to the rural community hall six miles away, and for picking up visitors in a mule-driven cart from the bus stop in Lockwood. One way or another, we're committed to be creative and adapt our lifestyle as necessary in order to live in a rural place with minimal reliance on gasoline or personal vehicles.

Another drawback of our region is the aridity. With no summer rainfall, the only way to establish fruit trees or grow warm season crops is by pumping groundwater for irrigation. Our property's main well already had an electric pump (to be powered by a generator), which we've reluctantly used a couple times for our initial work to restore and clean the well. This summer, we plan to build and install a simple hand-pump and windmill, in order to obtain water with no further use of fossil fuels. We're also eager to set up rain catchment barrels for the roofs of our house and barn.

An additional challenge of our location is that it's completely off-grid, which means no phone lines. (The folks at Stillwaters, although virtually electricity-free, still use a basic land line telephone.) Like our friends in Missouri, we feel that a telephone is a reasonable exception—in lieu of a computer—for coordinating logistics, connecting with others, and getting help in emergencies. Unfortunately, we don't have the option of a land line on our property, so we've resorted to a cell phone instead. We plan to build a cob phone booth with a small salvaged solar panel (and no batteries) to charge the community's phone during daylight hours.

Our phone calls are already kept in moderation by the steep hike to our call-spot, the only area on the land with phone reception, which helps keep the rest of Loving Earth a true sanctuary where people can remain present in their surroundings without the distraction of text messages or ringtones. While owning a high-tech, factory-made cell phone doesn't sit well with us, it's the best way we can think of at the moment to meet our needs for safety and for staying in touch with the broader world.

• • •

Despite the obstacles I've mentioned, the land is full of blessings. Every day I am joyfully reminded of the popular permaculture saying, "the problem is the solution." The fiery heat of the sun cooks our food in a homemade cardboard box solar oven. We've also been utilizing the waste of modern society by cooking on a fuel-efficient rocket stove made from salvaged aluminum cans, which can quickly boil a pot of water by using just a few sticks. Areas of dense brush on our land provide a source of rocket stove fuel, plant medicine, and good fodder for honeybees and native pollinators.

Our rural isolation has also allowed us to develop a more intimate relationship with the land. Recently somebody on the bus advised us to get a TV, unable to fathom how we could be content living "in the boonies" without one. We explained that our land is so rich in beauty it isn't necessary. At dusk we rush to the ridge to catch our favorite evening show—the sun flaming as it sets in a swirl of pinks and amber over the mountain tops. And every night we lie beneath the cinema of the night sky, fading into sleep amidst meteor showers and moonlight.

Yet even in this place of pristine natural beauty, the struggle to define our relationship with modern technology is an ever-present reality. It's a challenge each of us must face, exploring our values and setting our own boundaries. Throughout history the adoption of technology has happened without much thinking; new innovations merely get absorbed into a culture for the convenience they allow in daily life. I believe it's the responsibility of all thinking and compassionate human beings to question the ways we convenience ourselves, deeply considering the costs and benefits each new tool presents.

We live in a time when the benefits are far more discussed and championed than the costs, especially when it comes to "green technology" like electric cars or solar panels. A culture that forgets to watch its own progression is like an elephant with a bag tied over its head, bound to be a force of destruction, not by ill-will but by ignorance. This is what gives me courage to engage in the ongoing struggle for a better way. Like a salmon pushing against the weight of its stream, this struggle is one for life, a struggle we make for future generations. 🐦

Gloria Wilson is a philosophy student, writer, naturalist, and cofounder of Loving Earth Sanctuary. To get in touch or request further information, please call 805-235-5547 or write to PO Box 2813, Paso Robles, California 93447.

CREATING THE IDEAL INTENTIONAL COMMUNITY
(OR REVITALIZING AN EXISTING ONE)

I, Sahmat, grew up in intentional communities and have lived in 10 of them. I have been so dedicated to Community with both humans and Nature that I've been called "The Community Guy". The communities I grew up in shared a fairly strong "sense of community". I call this deep and sustained sense of community "Common-unity" because it's a state of unity we share in common, with the unique individuality of each human and each species still honored. It's this state of Common-unity that I've found most valuable in life and to me it's the main reason for living in an intentional community. When a group is deep in Common-unity together, there's a shared sense of love, joy, and peace that tops any other group experience.

However, I've found that in all the communities I've lived in, the sense of community is not nearly as deep and sustained as it could be. It's precisely this lack of Common-unity that is the root cause of the catastrophic global suffering of racism, wars, child abuse, abuse of women, environmental and species destruction, etc. So the ultimate goal is ending global suffering through "Global Common-unity": the spreading of Common-unity throughout the world by forming a global network of Common-unity-dedicated Communities.

So I've spent my life learning how to create Common-unity-dedicated communities that share true Common-unity: a deeper and more sustained sense of community. There are two keys to starting a Common-unity community (or moving an existing community into deeper Common-unity):

1. The first key to Common-unity is for everyone to be "Common-unity-dedicated" as their top common priority. This doesn't seem to be the case in any existing community, which results in focus and energies being bled off into other priorities. So maintenance of Common-unity doesn't get enough time and energy.

2. The second key to Common-unity is to learn "Common-unity Skills", skills that must be practiced to maintain Common-unity: Speaking from the Heart, Empathetic Listening, Emptying of Ego-attachments, Conflict Resolution, Consensus, Heart Wound Healing, Cooperative Housing, and Cooperative Economics. Modern culture does not teach us these skills.

We at the Alliance for Global Community have developed free workshops that train you in these Common-unity Skills. The workshops contain the Sharing Circle process developed by M. Scott Peck, a Nature connection exercise developed by John Seed and Joanna Macy, healing exercises developed by Byron Katie and Richard Moss, and exercises in creating Cooperative Housing and Cooperative Economics. We've tested various versions of these Common-unity Skill Building workshops over the past 25 years, and we've found them to be quite effective in teaching Common-unity skills that can help maintain Common-unity. If you'd like to start a Common-unity-dedicated community, or if you'd like to bring more Common-unity into an existing community (perhaps through a Common-unity sub-community or "pod"), you need to learn or improve these Common-unity skills as soon as possible.

To find out how to sign up for a free public Common-unity Skills workshop or schedule a free workshop for an existing group or community, please go to my website thecommunityguy.org There you can also find out how to get a free copy of the book "Skill Building for Global Common-unity". You can contact Sahmat directly at info@thecommunityguy.org or at 434-305-4770.

COMMON-UNITY WITH HUMANITY AND NATURE

The Power of Community

By Charles Durrett

Today we can text our sibling to find out what they are having for lunch in Paris, but we don't know the name of our next-door neighbor, nor probably their birthday—unless we've looked him or her up on PoliceReport.com...because, you know, we should know who our neighbor is. It's only prudent to be cautious.

Similarly, the increased need for police surveillance, emergency rooms, assisted care, after-school tutoring, out-of-the-neighborhood childcare, psychological therapy, and so many other institutionalized care activities that we have created reflect a waning of true community—for community can render these institutions much less necessary, if even necessary at all. There are so many pathologies in our society, and so many attempts to remedy them through institutions, graduate degrees, research, police, fire departments, social services, and every conceivable method other than personal engagement.

Many people are familiar with the idea that if the neighbor next door cares, or better yet, if an entire covey of neighbors that surround you really care about who lives next door — and who can act to support them—then the need for external behavior control mechanisms (from outside the community) diminishes immensely; likewise, the need for outside care or support, like psychological therapy, are less frequently outsourced from the community or not outsourced at all. Every one of these line items is immensely affected.

When folks feel accountable to their next-door neighbor, and don't call the police just because someone parked in their driveway, then the costly police are less required. The number one call received by the fire department where I live in Nevada County, California, is a "pick-up and put-back" call (i.e. a senior has fallen in their own house and needs to be helped into bed). A huge portion of our county's millions and millions of dollars of fire department budget goes toward providing services that a neighbor could do.

Last year the Paratransit shuttle for seniors (the big lumbering bus carrying usually one or two seniors, but capable of carrying 12) made 64,000 trips in western Nevada County for about 2,000 seniors to go to the doctor, to the pharmacy, to the store, or to visit a friend. Some people say that 30 trips per year per senior just to get them out of the house is far too few—others say far too many. Needless to say, there were zero pick-ups needed for the 20 seniors living in our cohousing community. Neighbors swing by to offer assistance if needed—"I'll just pick up your medicine when I'm there"—and their best friend lives next door. Last year Americans drove five billion miles to serve seniors at home, mostly meals on wheels and nurses on the go. At Nevada City Cohousing, that didn't happen at all.

We know that this is not sustainable when the funding necessary to provide these services shifts all the time: Kansas City just went from 14 provided senior meals per week to one, because of lack of gas money. Paratransit also just went from 64,000 trips per year to **zero**, because of a $247,000 shortfall.

But: What's in community living for you? Why would you want to live in a community? What would you get out of it? Before I say more, allow me to tell you a couple of relevant stories.

First, recently our local newspaper's

Cohousing comes in all forms.

headline read, "17-year-old boy passing an 80-year-old woman has a head-on collision with 76-year-old man. 76-year-old man perishes." That reminded me that, in the new senior cohousing community just two miles from that "accident," a 77-year-old resident recently told me at common dinner that he went from using four-to-five tanks of gas per month before moving into cohousing to less than one tank per month after moving into cohousing. That was no accident. *That* same evening, an 80-year-old resident said that after moving in she sold her auto altogether. Less driving equals less collision risk, and *that* is no accident. Both of them now meet with others at their convenience, have dinner with others at their choosing, and often have coffee with their neighbors in the mornings. Most mainstream senior living is no accident either, but more of a set-up: a set-up for either isolation or institutionalization.

My late father once visited us in our community for 10 days. Before his visit he kept saying, "Ya Chuck, I'm coming up. But now please explain to me one more time, why do you live in cohousing? You could have your own house." I could only respond, "Ya, well we do live in cohousing and we still hope you visit. Oh, and by the way, we do have our own house, but in the context of a high-functioning neighborhood."

Long story short, he was the last one out of the common house every single night for all 10 nights—while sparing Katie and me the travel and construction stories that we had heard many times before. During those 10 days he cooked common dinner twice (without being asked once)! Then, once back in Sacramento, he lamented incessantly, "Why doesn't anyone ever visit me?" And "I don't know my neighbors."

Finally I asked him, "Dad, you had so much fun in Nevada City. Why don't you just move into cohousing?" He retorted, "What would my friends think?" I was bewildered! "You mean the ones living in Colorado and Florida?" I asked him, hardly believing my ears. "What would your friends think? Dad, you're 73! What are we, in high school? Besides, just don't change your email. They'll never know!" His words reminded me of Steven Covey's sentiment, that one of the worst things that you can do to your own well-being and growth is to stereotype yourself: "Oh, that's not me!" or "I couldn't do that!"

I share these stories with you because for me they were a rude awakening. They made me realize—in a very close and personal way—that we *ARE* living according to nonsensical social restraints. And those are the same social restraints on which people base their "reasons" *not* to embark on senior cohousing. The number one of these "reasons"—or excuses—is the time it takes to put together a project. To which I say, nonsense! It doesn't take long when there are homes available in a number of existing cohousing projects that people can just buy and move into immediately, and it's OK to take advantage of the hard work of your predecessors and the profound community that they have already built there.

Community is what made my grandmother's final years worth living. She lived in a small town of 325 people and was mostly bedridden in her waning 10 years. Fifteen locals looked after her; she didn't spend a day in a nursing home. But she had that kind of small town caché. Cohousing is just that kind of reconceiving; the kind of reconceiving of community that we have been waiting for. It's time to stop boxing ourselves into narrow parameters and face our realities. Many of us don't have extended families nearby, we don't have stay-at-home daughters to take care of us anymore, and we have few high-functioning small towns. According to *Harper's Magazine*, 6,000 small towns have evaporated in Kansas since 1970, bought out by agribusiness. But if we look up, we do have cohousing, and cohousing-inspired communities, within our reach.

We have all heard it said, "People have to pull themselves up by their bootstraps." Have you ever actually seen anyone do that? What we all need is support, companionship, to feel needed—part of something—and we need to have fun! My concern is: are people doing the best they can to achieve these goals that really aren't that far off? As a cohouser myself, I'm motivated to make the lives of my neighbors as easy as they make mine. We are each other's stewards in the ebb and flow of our living landscape, which allows us to know, therefore care, and therefore support each other without it hindering my life or theirs. To

Growing old is timeless.

These residents are musicians. They have to practice somewhere; their neighbors love it!

Cohousing comes in all forms.

We say in our office, "if it doesn't work socially, why bother?"

Photos courtesy of Charles Durrett

Work days are also fun days.
See the new book by Charles Durrett, *Happily Ever Aftering in Cohousing* (bit.ly/HEAiC).

learn how to grow old together is a natural part of life, more of a freeing experience than an encumbering one.

Let's look at the issues at hand in a broader scale, a scale that lets us see the big picture. In Nevada County, we are collectively considering what to do with a couple of million dollars of federal Community Services Block Grant funding. It looks like the money will mostly go to seniors' meals and rides: food sustenance and social sustenance. Although there are in fact a lot of other needs—like drug counseling, childcare, suicide prevention, homeless shelters, and halfway houses—still the seniors' needs seem to get the nod. Not that there's anything wrong with that, but that isn't the most efficient way to ensure that seniors have a healthy life. Nevertheless, this CSBG grant at most will provide a tenth as much money as necessary to even support the elder needs. A supporting community allows seniors to be part of the solution, without consuming the lion's share of the already thin resources.

At the other end of the spectrum (from community to disconnection), I find it disturbing when I read that the suicide rate of seniors is up to all-time records. According to the *New York Times*, suicide in citizens over 50 increased as much as 60 percent from 1999 to 2010. The social restraints, excuses, and myths that we let rule our lives produce an isolation that demonstrates that all of the current social norms are unfortunate at best. Perhaps suicide has come to be the ultimate individual statement: you really are all by yourself. Which reminds me of a young local homeless woman who told me once that her grandfather committed suicide while alone in his big house. It made me ponder: who was better off? At least she had a community in her homeless camp.

The time has come to work harder for community. So what's holding us back? What's the elephant in the room? Is it ignorance? Decreasingly so. You can find information and articles about cohousing published almost every single day. Is it shame? *"I would be giving up my ranchette."* Are we talking about the same *"ranchette"* you work on until the waning moments, as the myth goes, and then they take you out boots first? Is it fear of commitment and obligation? If so, then you really don't understand cohousing. Cohousing is not that you *have* to do things for others, rather it allows you the opportunity to *grow* to do what you want for, and with, them. For example, I received an email from the Mountain View Cohousing group about how they spent a couple of hours reconsidering the heating system, and telling me about what a profound, inspiring community building conversation that was.

Our society isn't conducive to making choices that contradict what is "normal." Choosing cohousing isn't normal, but it's smart. And sometimes we have to make choices that are the best for us, even if they aren't the easiest thing to do. That is what we tell our children, but we need to listen to the advice ourselves.

When I think about the amazing support the 20 seniors in our community receive, I realize that these were the few willing to look around and ask: What will *really* make my life easier? More convenient? More practical? More economical? More interesting? And more fun? I'm inclined to respond that it is the obvious ease of relationships, knowing that you're not alone.

I certainly do not want to overlook the 50- and 60-year-olds who move into cohousing because they want to live in a healthy and fun environment. For example, I went to a concert in Nevada County a

Seniors in cohousing elder each other, which is exactly how to have a successful elderhood.

month ago, only to meet two cars full of senior cohousers who had carpooled over. Having neighbors that you can break bread with—community—is simply essential to your wellness. Contrast this image of wholeness with how wasteful and deleterious to the well-being of most people the alternatives are, and ponder the self-imposed restraints. The myths that we live by keep many from considering cohousing and cohousing-inspired communities as an alternative to traditional housing models.

Can I say that growing older is timeless or is that a non sequitur? If you're lucky you grow older. But having a good time with it

is no accident. You have to plan ahead—to "grab the fun" as my daughter Jessie would say—to enjoy what cohousing does for you. Like, going to a restaurant for dinner and all your friends are there; like, when you get sick, having warm chicken soup brought to you; like, having more help than you need for lifting something heavy; like, enjoying plenty of space for your family to comfortably stay when they come to visit; like, several real belly laughs at every dinner. Sometimes people annoy you, but you come to realize those are beautiful people, and you realize that they prepared this incredible dinner last night, or they drove to the concert and got you out the door. What's in community living for you? Real life, and a lively life at that.

This is a call to break free of the self-inflicted *"Oh, that's not me!"* This is a call to action. Many resources—workshops, books, and opportunities to visit—are available. You too can achieve the kind of community cohousing seniors enjoy every day. ❧

Charles Durrett, noted architect and author of Senior Cohousing: A Community Approach to Independent Living, *introduced the concept of senior cohousing to the US from its success in Denmark. He has designed over 50 cohousing communities in North America and has consulted on many more around the world. His firm, McCamant and Durrett Architects, is known for its affordable and community-based senior cohousing communities, intergenerational cohousing communities, as well as mixed-use neighborhoods and neighborhood centers, town planning, and for its expertise in sustainability in the context of budget.*

Dinner in the common house at Wolf Creek Lodge.

Off-Grid, and In Community:
'TIS EASIER TO FIND THAN TO FOUND

By Dan Schultz

I had no epiphany or precipitating event that sent me out of the suburbs toward off-grid life. As it has been said: "The day came when the risk to remain tight in a bud was more painful than the risk it took to blossom." I think that's what took place, except that my edit would read: "A time came when it took more energy for me to stay in 'the system' than to leave it."

Probably aside a grocery list or a refrigerator note to my kids, I penciled out a few mildly appealing steps to acquire some land and do what Henry David Thoreau suggested I do. "Simplify, simplify, simplify," he said, and "I wanted to live deliberately."

Soon I found myself signing a deed on a 160 acre plot in California's Siskiyou Mountains—an unlikely parcel for the endeavor of creating an organic farm and community. It was densely forested with steep, rugged terrain. I had never started a chainsaw in my life. Never grown a tomato. I had never known community at all, living alone for the lion's share of my days, avoiding roommates as often as possible. I just knew what I wanted to do and who I wanted to be.

Seven years later, with two handfuls of calluses, eight buildings, orchards and gardens, five full time members plus wwoofers and interns, and a bank account that perpetually hovers about zero, I confess that I have learned a few things. Starting from scratch was a massive and often overwhelming task. I do not exaggerate when I speak of 70 hour work weeks during the first few years. I began to see everything around me as an unfinished project (and sometimes still do) as the land was transformed from beautiful, raw native forest to a construction site. One can learn to ignore, as best they can, material piles, slash, and clutter. Not many show up when it's like that, so mostly you're on your own. When it all comes together and starts to look more polished, more like a retreat, that's when more people take interest.

From inception to today, I've always been a little surprised at the shine people take towards the subject of off-grid living and community. I suspect few of them are willing to actually make that leap, but they're still quite interested, even intrigued, which seems to be something of a zeitgeist. Amongst wwoofers, interns, and visitors of all kinds one of the most common sentiments expressed is an ardent desire "to start their own thing like this." I understand the appeal.

But I often recommend against them "starting their own thing," mostly because that's what too many want to do. I appreciate my fellow dreamers and drivers, and yet I see the movement (and I definitely see a movement gaining way) getting a little ahead of itself. Isn't it the case of too many chiefs and too few Indians? Too many head chefs in the kitchen, captains on the ship...pick your metaphor.

People in the West need to learn to work together again, co-creating a new existence even as the old system fails, and one of the most important steps in replacing the old paradigm is the abandonment of our rugged independence. I hear that independence in their enthusiastic voice even while speaking of community ideals, and I shrug a little.

Excepting of the two wonderful children I have raised into this world, my most satisfying achievement has been to integrate my life into a landscape, build something special with people and the earth. But would I do it again the same way? Actually, no.

I didn't mind the blood, sweat, and tears, nor the long hours and messes that came from starting from scratch. And while I am pleased to have been a part of creating something grand and beautiful, I think now the opportunity cost could have been too great and my priorities sometimes upside down. Knowing what I know now about finding true community and a healthy, potent place in the world, I would do it differently. If I had to do it all over again, I would probably search for an existing, congruent community that works, and find a place for myself there.

Nearly every day something at our mountain village reminds me that co-creation trumps individual vision. Applying the principle on a larger scale: if everyone were primarily focused on cooperative culture most all of the world's problems would vanish, while the every-man-for-himself M.O. hasn't been working out so well. While this country will indeed need more community places, I try to steer most of the idealistic visionaries in the direction of first joining the collective, because I believe they will find a more humbling and empowering purpose in becoming part of something bigger than themselves.

Dan Schultz is co-director of Maitreya Mountain Village (www.maitreyamountainvillage.com), which creates intentional, caring community and farming in an off-grid, wilderness setting. Dan hosts and produces a talk radio program called New Culture Radio focused on sustainability, and together with his partner Jane leads Transition Del Norte in Northwestern California.

151

Photos courtesy of Dan Schultz

Senior Cohousing in Canada:

How Baby Boomers Can Build Social Portfolios for Aging Well

By Margaret Critchlow

The news that household debt is on the rise in many parts of the world is usually cause for anxiety rather than celebration. But in the southwest Pacific country of Vanuatu where I have lived and worked as an anthropologist, household debt reassures people that they can relax and not worry about the future. Indebtedness is their best insurance. Some of their debts are financial—they may owe a fellow in the next village who contributed a pig to their mother's funeral or be indebted to a brother for paying a child's school fees. But what is important to understand is that financial debt follows social pathways, and that social indebtedness ensures enduring relationships.

To be fully human in Vanuatu is to live in a community of relationships. If exchanges are square, like a cash transaction in which both sides end up owing nothing, there is no relationship. Social investments—a pig given at a wedding, a chicken to appease a grudge, cooked rice for a toothless elder—are always slightly imbalanced—I owe you or you owe me—and our indebtedness ensures that the relationships continue. In crisis or as you age, you can call on those relationships and be confident that you will receive what you need. There are few doctors, scarcely any pensions, little cash, but also no starvation and a lot of joy. In fact, Vanuatu topped the first Happy Planet index in 2006.

In Vanuatu, everyone ages in place because there are no alternatives—no retirement homes, assisted living, etc. Like the people of Vanuatu, most of us want to age in place. In North America and Western Europe, most don't want to move to "The Home" until they are ready. Often people don't think they are ready until it's too late. So we may stay in our homes for "as long as possible" or sometimes longer. Eventually, perhaps our children move us into a place they select for us.

Aging in Place

In Canada, it is fortunate that most of us want to age in place, because we may not have many other options. The demographic bulge as baby boomers age will tax our health care systems. In a decade, 30 percent of the Canadian population will be retirement age. Our state-supported health care system is challenged to keep up with the demands of our aging population. Meanwhile a sluggish global economy, not fully recovered from the recession that began in 2008, inhibits state support even as it reduces personal savings and increases household debt.

Aging in place may be necessary but it is not always the ideal choice that it appears to be. First, retrofitting a home to meet the needs of aging occupants may be financially unaffordable. Second, once a home is adapted for aging in place, the cost of maintenance, taxes, and bringing in outside help may be unaffordable, especially to seniors on a fixed budget. The wealthy can afford these costs. The poor can receive basic services at little or no charge. The middle class may be out of luck.

A third reason that aging in place may not be an ideal choice is this: Rich, poor, or part of the middle class, no one can afford the social isolation that often accompanies aging in place. Recent research suggests that stronger social relationships are associated with 50

Kids in Vanuatu are some of the happiest on the planet.

Douglas Campbell

Douglas Campbell

To be fully human in Vanuatu is to live in a community of relationships.

Douglas Campbell

Course participants learning new ways to play.

Margaret Critchlow

Harboursiders hosting pizza night.

Margaret Critchlow

Weekend "Aging Well in Community" participants, September 2013. The course appeals to young people, too.

Margaret Critchlow

Andrew Moore leads course participants in learning new ways to play.

Margaret Critchlow

percent greater chances of longevity. Surprisingly, the mortality risk posed by social isolation is as great as other risk factors such as smoking.

Building a Social Portfolio

What if building a **social portfolio** had the same importance as building a financial portfolio? Could you act like you live in Vanuatu? Invest in relationships? Diversify? You probably won't need a lot of support to age in place, just a little. The baby boomer generation has a chance to take charge of the next chapter of their lives as they did the earlier ones. What a great opportunity to reconnect with youthful dreams of changing the world by living values of cooperation and sustainability!

A rich and diverse social portfolio is much easier to build if one is not car-dependent. Imagine living in a beautifully designed home in the centre of a town that is walkable to everything you need. A home that has few steps, little maintenance, and lots of connection with cooperative neighbours. It is compact but shares a large common house with guest rooms for visitors and a suite for a caregiver when needed. Not an institution, but a home you own in a sustainable neighbourhood you help organize and manage. You work with the architect to design it. It is built green to keep energy costs very low, maybe even at zero. You don't have to be "old" to live there but you have to endorse an "aging-in-place-friendly" vision and be willing to cooperate with your neighbour.

This kind of place exists—it's called senior cohousing.

Canadian Senior Cohousing

Our nonprofit Canadian Senior Cohousing Society raises awareness, applies for grants, and conducts research. In partnership with Royal Roads University in Victoria, British Columbia, we offer a two-day course called "Dare to Age Well in Community." Our society promotes the development of senior cohousing communities in Canada. Ronaye Matthew, an experienced project manager who created Wolf Willow, the first senior cohousing in Canada, is working with us to create Harbourside Cohousing, the first in British Columbia. We believe that this can be a prototype for a made-in-Canada model for aging, not just in place but in community. For me, it is a model for a Canadian solution for aging in place, inspired by one of the happiest places on the planet.

Senior cohousing creates socially, financially, and environmentally sustainable communities for the second half of life. Common facilities include housing for a caregiver whom residents hire as needed. Members provide voluntary mutual assistance for each other (co-caring) that encourages well-being and aging in place. Like multi-generational cohousing these are intentionally cooperative neighbourhoods where each household owns a small but complete home and spacious common facilities are shared. Well-established in Europe, especially in Denmark where it emerged from multi-generational cohousing in the 1990s, senior cohousing is new to North America.

"Dare to Age Well in Community":
Day Two flip chart.

Margaret Critchlow

The Right Place at the Right Time

Senior cohousing is about being in the right place at the right time in one's life. The creation of Harbourside exemplifies that serendipity. After lecturing about cohousing for years in York University anthropology courses, I left Toronto in 2004 for a sabbatical year on Vancouver Island off Canada's west coast. The small town of Sooke, self-described as "where the rainforest meets the sea," captivated me with the beauty of its place and its people. I soon knew that if there were ever a place to walk my cohousing talk, this was it. A group of

Harboursiders enjoying the deck of the resort
building that became the common house.

Susan Eyres

Some Harbourside members on the cohousing's wharf with common house in background.

Margaret Critchlow

like-minded people formed and went so far as looking for land, but, as is so often the case with such ventures, when it came time to put money on the table, no one was quite ready.

By 2010, the time was right. I moved my mother into a "very nice" retirement home back east and knew in my heart it was not what I wanted for myself as I grew older. I wanted to have a say in the location and design of my home, be car non-dependent, choose who was hired to provide my care, and most of all, give and receive mutual support that would enable me and my neighbours to flourish as we aged well in community. My friends and I talked, and discovered this was what they wanted as well. We could see the pressure our baby boomer demographic was about to put on the health care system. We decided to get creative and look after our own old age. A friend and I called a meeting above a grocery store to gauge local interest and 30 people showed up. Our journey into cohousing had begun.

Meanwhile, in 2009 *The Senior Cohousing Handbook* was published. It clearly outlined the many steps for a grassroots group to create a senior cohousing community. The author, Charles Durrett, had brought the cohousing concept to North America in 1988 from Denmark where he had observed its success, especially as housing for young couples with children. For these families, supportive neighbours, economies of scale from shared ownership of resources, and the privacy of a single family home all made cohousing very attractive. In the 1990s, Durrett had seen the adaptation of this model to a way of housing people in "the second half of life" in Denmark. He called it "senior cohousing." In these communities, members' priorities shift from raising children to aging in community. Both the physical and social design reflected these priorities.

A group of teachers in Denmark who wanted to help seniors age in place recognized the critical role that social connection plays. Even then, the dangers of social isolation were apparent. More recent research, mentioned above, suggests that the mortality risk posed by social isolation is as great as other risk factors such as smoking. The Danish teachers created spaces for seniors to talk about the issues of aging in place.

One of several design workshops at Harbourside.

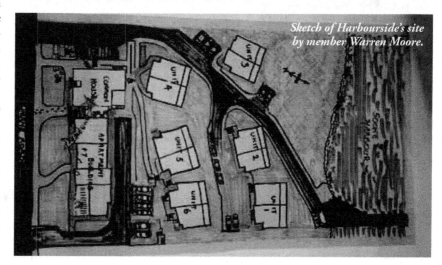

Sketch of Harbourside's site by member Warren Moore.

Harbourside's Groundbreaking Ceremony, September 2014.

Durrett calls these meetings Study Group One. He developed a 10-week Study Group One to prepare North Americans for aging in community and he began training facilitators to offer it. In the spring of 2011, fellow Sooke resident Andrew Moore and I took Durrett's training at his Nevada City Cohousing where he lives in California. We then offered the 10-week study group twice in 2011 to a total of 44 participants. By the completion of the second study group it was clear that there was plenty of interest and commitment to the idea of senior cohousing.

Settling on a Site

The next challenge was to find a suitable site. (See "When Do We Begin to Flourish in Cohousing?," COMMUNITIES #157, Winter 2012). Our group considered six sites before settling in 2012 on a two acre waterfront property in the village where we could walk to everything as well as enjoy a spectacular view and the use of our own wharf. The property was operating as a small resort. The 3,900 square foot resort building included a common area for cooking, dining, and entertaining, three guest rooms and baths, and ample multi-purpose space. It could easily convert to a common house for the cohousing group.

To purchase the property, a group of eight households committed to pool equity of $C 20,000 each, creating a limited liability company for the development phase with the help of an experienced cohousing project manager, Ronaye Matthew. The property was purchased subject to preliminary feasibility studies (e.g., environmental, geotechnical, archeological). Once these were complete the seller became a member of the cohousing group, which came to be known as Harbourside.

While development proceeded into preliminary design and a rezoning application to build 30 (later 31) units of housing on the site, our educational outreach changed tacks. From the beginning we had required that all potential members purchase a copy of *The Senior Cohousing Handbook* and complete the study group. As interest in Harbourside grew, Andrew and I lacked the capacity to offer the 10-week study group as frequently as required. We also felt that the experience could be just as effective, perhaps even more so, if condensed considerably. We redesigned the curriculum and we developed a relationship with nearby Royal Roads University so that they handled registration and local arrangements for a two-day course called "Aging Well in Community." We offered this course eight times in 2013 and 2014, revising the curriculum again and changing the name in autumn 2014 to "Dare to Age Well in Community."

Co-Care

A crucial part of the course prepares participants for "co-care," which is central to senior cohousing as an adjunct to the medical system in Canada. The idea of co-care is as old as good neighbours, but the concept has yet to be defined—there is no co-care entry in Wikipedia. In our course, we define co-care as a grassroots model of neighbourly mutual support that can help reduce social isolation and promote positive, active aging. It encourages independence through awareness that we are all interdependent. In a cohousing

community, giving and receiving co-care is entirely voluntary. We may choose to support each other through such activities as doing errands, driving, cooking, or going for a walk with our neighbour. We believe that being good neighbours helps us age well in community and have fun doing it.

While co-care is customary in cohous-

> ## Co-care is a grassroots model of neighbourly mutual support that can help reduce social isolation and promote positive, active aging.

ing communities, in senior cohousing it can be essential to living independently. Studies show that seniors need relatively little support as they age, especially until they are older than 85. Co-caring neighbours can provide much of that support. A caregiver, living in an affordable suite in the cohousing and paid for by the members who need him or her, can help with dressing, medications, bathing, and other activities that are more than neighbours say they are willing to do. Economies of scale are possible as one caregiver can tend to multiple residents. Other medical and housekeeping services can be provided to our central location.

Harbourside Cohousing gets building permit, November 2014. From left: Margaret Critchlow (Harbourside), Ronaye Matthew (Cohousing Development Consulting), Aimee North (Campbell Construction).

Peter Treuheit

Ellen Candlish

Lessons Learned and Prospects for the Future

It is clear from the enthusiasm for Harbourside that senior cohousing is an idea whose time has come in British Columbia. Harbourside, with its caregivers' suite and reliance on the Royal Roads University course, has taken a different approach than that taken by its sister community, Wolf Willow in Saskatoon. We believe that these aspects of Harbourside have made it more attractive to potential members by raising awareness and increasing acceptance of issues that can occur in the aging process. It is also encouraging that Harbourside has sold all units so quickly. A fearlessness, adventurousness, and sense of community arise that bode well for our success.

What else have we learned?

• There is a pent-up yearning for community that will come as no surprise to readers of COMMUNITIES. Senior cohousing appeals particularly to baby boomers who had an agenda for social change in the '60s but did not often live communally for their child-raising years. Now that they're in their 60s, the desire to reactivate youthful values is palpable, especially as boomers respond to the state of the world and the planet. Can we be the change we want to see? Are we the people we have been waiting for? Many seem eager to find out.

• Affordability is highly valued and difficult to achieve. There is a dance always between values of affordability, aesthetics, designing for physical accessibility, and building "green." Harboursiders, like many baby boomers, want it all.

• A personal and community commitment to combine co-care with a potential caregiver gives members confidence that they can age in place in senior cohousing and enjoy healthier, richer, more active lives than if they lived in conventional housing, or in the institutions they dread. One of the hardest things to learn, apparently, is the obligation to receive. Participants in our course are eager to share what they would offer to their neighbour but find it much more difficult to agree to request or even accept the same care. We recognize the challenge of learning to accept help in a culture that values individualism so highly.

• We have benefited greatly from retaining an experienced project manager with a strong commitment to cohousing. This adds to the development cost at Harbourside but we know that without her, the cost of our inexperience would be far higher and the results less successful. At present, only a handful of people in North America have this expertise, which is a major constraint on the ability to scale up senior cohousing to meet demand.

• Finally, Harbourside Cohousing is a prototype. If well-documented and if the lessons from our experience are learned, Harbourside can lead to the creation of other senior cohousing projects. Increasing capacity to facilitate the "Dare to Age Well in Community" course, and to develop senior cohousing, could allow for scaling up senior cohousing as a radical social innovation to respond to the "silver tsunami" of aging baby boomers. Who

knows, perhaps like the people I learned from as an anthropologist in Vanuatu, we will soon be cheerfully indebted to each other and topping the Happy Planet index ourselves. ~

Margaret Critchlow is Professor Emerita of Anthropology (York University). She lives in Sooke, British Columbia where she is a director of the Canadian Senior Cohousing Society and a founding member of Harbourside Cohousing. This article is substantially revised from a presentation to the 11th International Communal Studies Association conference in Findhorn, Scotland. The conference proceedings were published in the UK in Social Sciences Directory 2(4), 106-113, October 2013.

Progress at Harbourside Cohousing

The course and the participatory development process at Harbourside Cohousing are creating community long before move-in. As Harbourside's membership has grown, so has the sense of community. Shared experience helps create solidarity (see "On the Ropes at Harbourside Cohousing," COMMUNITIES #164, Fall 2014).

All 31 units at Harbourside sold before construction began in autumn 2014, and demand continues for what Harbourside offers. We are taking a waiting list, but also supporting other senior cohousing groups to succeed in meeting the growing interest in this form of housing for an aging population.

Not everyone who wanted to join us has been able to do so. We are building in affordable operating costs through construction to Built Green Canada/Energuide 80 standards. But this adds to the initial cost, so only people with equity in a home (or other net worth) have been able to purchase a unit at Harbourside. We have active participants who do not intend to move in immediately, and others who want to rent from them, but this has its own complications, including insecurity of tenure for renters, different commitments to the community, and the potential for a socioeconomic gap to appear between landlords and tenants.

—M.C.

Construction begins for 31 units at Harbourside Cohousing, November 2014.

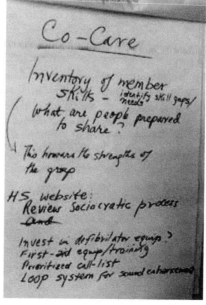

Belfast Ecovillage Produces Farm

By Sarah Lozanova

Sunday mornings at Belfast Cohousing and Ecovillage begin with Swiss chard, green onions, and piles of kale. Once a week, neighbors harvest veggies from Little River Community Farm, the three-acre on-site community supported agriculture (CSA) farm at the ecovillage. It is a worker-share arrangement, so neighbors dig in the dirt, snip, wash, and bundle the farm bounty together, while discussing recipe ideas.

Belfast Cohousing and Ecovillage is 36-unit multigenerational community in Midcoast Maine that has attracted members from all walks of life, including musicians, gardeners, educators, and naturalists. The 42-acre property was formerly a dairy farm, but is slowly turning into an ecovillage, with gardens, walking paths, bird watching, and many more ideas for the future.

Despite being a rural property, the homes are clustered to preserve open space and the built area is limited to six acres. Many of the super-energy-efficient homes are near net zero, with solar panels powering and heating the homes. The construction phase of the project is nearly complete, and only two units remain unsold.

"To me, a really important part of being a member of Belfast Ecovillage is the farm, where we raise food and work together," says Jeffrey Mabee, an avid gardener. "The CSA has really answered my prayers about that. Having young farmers using the land in such a responsible way feels right. The farm feels like the heart of any intentional community. It has a much greater significance than merely producing food."

The farm cofounders, Brian Hughes, Jenny Siebenhaar, and Amy Anderson, are all members of the ecovillage, and founded the farm last year. Hughes and Siebenhaar were farm apprentices in Europe in the early '90s, where they learned about permaculture and organic methods. They have managed three other CSA farms in recent years.

The farm at Belfast Ecovillage is unique because the current 22 farm members collectively own the land as members of the ecovillage, reside at the community, and contribute to maintaining the farm. An additional share purchased by community members is donated to the Belfast Soup Kitchen weekly.

"Little River Community Farm is the coolest CSA out there," explains Hughes. "Because the members also own the land and will have a long-term relationship to it, we can plant perennial crops like asparagus."

In the fall months, Belfast Ecovillagers start to notice the scarcity of cool storage space for fall crops. With slab-on-grade construction, the homes do not have basements. The common house, however, will have a root cellar, helping to alleviate this limitation. For now, many members can or freeze surplus vegetables.

It is common to see children at the farm workdays and harvests, where they develop a deeper relationship with their food and find an opportunity to learn. "I didn't learn where food comes from growing up," says Hughes. "I grew up in the suburbs and I was in my 20s before I knew what potato, beet, or carrot plants looked like."

Because Belfast Ecovillage is just completing the construction phase, farm projects have given members the unique opportunity to connect with the land and do physical labor together. Until this point, much of the community work has occurred in meetings—in planning and setting policies.

Some community members really appreciate how Belfast Ecovillage helps promote a healthy lifestyle. The weekly harvests help keep members active as they pick and haul the veggies. The community farm promotes culinary exploration and a high content of vegetables in the diet. Of course there is also a challenge associated with using a new vegetable such as kohlrabi or consuming all the kale that might arrive with a share.

"It is as fresh as you can get, like getting it from your own garden," says Hughes. "That impacts nutrition and taste. We're avoiding most of the carbon footprint of the food and we don't use packaging except for recycled bags."

In addition to the farm, there are several other multi-family farming initiatives in the community. There are two multi-household egg clubs, where members raise hens, while sharing the eggs, labor, and expenses. There have also been three multi-family flocks of meat birds during warmer months. Many Belfast Ecovillagers dream of having an orchard and then canning the harvest in the common house that is currently under construction. There is also interest in having livestock in the community, but the visions for the land are limited to the 36 acres available.

There is a widespread passion at the ecovillage for homegrown food. "Somehow when you are part of growing food, it feeds you more than just physically," explains Siebenhaar. "It feeds your soul and spirit and there is a beauty to this. It goes beyond calories, vitamins, and minerals." ✍

Sarah Lozanova is an environmental journalist with an M.B.A. in sustainable management from the Presidio Graduate School. She has lived in several intentional communities and now resides in Belfast Cohousing and Ecovillage (mainecohousing.org) in Midcoast Maine with her husband and two children.

Photos courtesy of Sarah Lozanova

The Balancing Act of Farming in Community

By Coleen O'Connell

*Cedar Mountain Farm's hay barn
at Cobb Hill Cohousing.*

Today started with sun but the sky has clouded as a major February northeaster blows into New England, promising a much-needed snowfall to deliver us from paths coated with treacherous ice. The children of Cobb Hill are anticipating a snow day and the best sledding conditions they have had yet this winter of 2014/15. A foot of new snow on our steep hillsides will delight not just the young, but a few of us old ones as well.

Meanwhile the cows, horses, sheep, and llama are nestled warmly in the barn. Calves are due so we'll see if any of them make their way into the world during the storm. The chickens probably won't venture out of their hut on wheels, but they will lay their eggs as usual. The car ballet (moving cars from lot to lot) will begin when the plow guy arrives to clear us out. We'll be in trouble if the electricity goes down and we can't chatter back and forth on our listserv advising where to move cars and when. The hustle and bustle of life on "the Hill," as we call it, will not be stopped by a mere snowstorm.

In 1991, Donella Meadows, coauthor of *The Limits to Growth* (1972), wrote in her nationally syndicated Global Citizen column, "Though I didn't grow up on a farm, I've been attracted to them all my life. When in 1972 I finally came to buy my own home, it was a farm. My psychological roots grew instantly into its cold, rocky soil. I have tried several times to leave it, reasoning that I could write more if I didn't spend so much time shoveling manure, that I need to be where the political action is, that I'm not a very good farmer anyway, that New Hampshire is a terrible place to farm. But I've always come back. Something deep in me needs to be attached to a farm."

She would eventually leave that farm in New Hampshire and move across the Connecticut River to the rural Upper Valley of Vermont, buying two adjacent dairy farms. With friends, she set out to found a "farm-based" community that would integrate principals of sustainability into all aspects of design and practice. The cohousing movement provided a useful model to help self-organize rather than re-invent the wheel. One of the original farmhouses became the headquarters of The Sustainability Institute, now the Donella Meadows Institute in Norwich, Vermont, and the process of planning and developing a cohousing community on the side of Cobb Hill went into full motion.

Moving with her to Vermont were her farming partners, Stephen Leslie and Kerry Gawalt. Choosing the rocky hillside to plant the homes left the prime agricultural fields available for farming. Kerry and Stephen and Donella would arrive on the property in the fall of 1999 with seven Jersey heifers, two Norwegian Fjord workhorses, and a draft pony named Bill. More people joined the development, moving closer to the community as the homes were being built. Stephen and Kerry began milking in 2000, and a group of Cobb Hill members began making cheese shortly after.

Farming Enterprises at Cobb Hill

Cobb Hill residents are co-owners of 270 acres of forest and farmland. Early in the development of the community, an enterprise system was started, allowing members to use common resources of land and buildings to bring sustainable agriculture and forestry

159

products not only to the Cobb Hill community but also to the surrounding community and beyond. It is a free lease system with the idea that best practices will result in continued productive farmland and forest, with sustainability at the forefront of everyone's products. Money from sale of the development rights to the Upper Valley Land Trust and funds from the Vermont Housing and Conservation board were contributed to help make one of the homes qualify as an

rooms, and Frozen Yogurt (six flavors). Pigs and broiler chicken enterprises are in hibernation and might emerge again in the future. There are dreams of adding a few more enterprises. Local food is booming in Vermont and Cobb Hill is proud to be part of this movement.

Of the 23 families (40 adults, 16 children) living at Cobb Hill, few make their living through the enterprises at Cobb Hill. Most are hobby enterprises that might net participants a small profit in any given year. Most enterprises are co-operated by various members of Cobb Hill, which can change membership from year to year. Some have investment capital that can be put in or taken out; others are standing operations that need labor only. At last count, there were 18 adults involved in the enterprises of Cobb Hill, and one high school student who oversees the Community Chicken enterprise.

Your first impression upon turning into the drive of Cobb Hill is that you have entered a working farm. The large red barn with a Farmstand sign greets you, the silo stands tall against the sky, and the machine shed yawns at you showing off its riot of tools, farm equipment, pails, fencing, and countless miscellaneous gadgets. Once past the barn you have only to look up the hill to see the passive solar homes perched solidly on the shale

At Cobb Hill, you quickly discover that you are not on a typical working farm.

"affordable" housing unit. It was written into the Land Trust Agreement that an affordable unit should always be available for a farm family.

Gathering momentum, the enterprise system has operated at Cobb Hill for the past 15 years now boasting many enterprises—CSA Market Garden, Jersey Dairy Milk, Cobb Hill Cheese with two Artisan cheeses, The Farmstand, Hay, Maple Syrup, Icelandic Sheep, Chickens, Honey, Shiitake Mush-

bedrock hillside. You know you are not on a typical working farm.

Cedar Mountain Farm is the enterprise started by Stephen and Kerry when they first moved to Cobb Hill with Donella. They produce sustainably grown vegetables, fruit, hay, flowers, milk, beef, and Jersey heifers. They use the Community Supported Agriculture system to market their vegetables, along with direct sales of their products through the Cobb Hill Farmstand (open every day for the passerby or local Cobb Hill or Hartland residents), private sales, mail order, and local farmers' markets. Wholesale accounts are set up with Cobb Hill Cheese and Cobb Hill Frozen Yogurt, Dairy Farmers of America Coop, area restaurants and farms, and 12 gallons a week of direct raw milk sales go to residents of Cobb Hill and the surrounding community. The Jersey heifers are sold through Jersey Marketing Services to supply the national milk market.

Making artisan cheese at Cobb Hill.

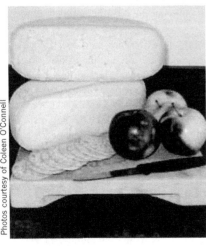

Photos courtesy of Coleen O'Connell

Plowing with Fjords at Cobb Hill.

Halloween harvest at Cedar Mountain Farm.

Cows grazing at Cedar Mountain Farm.

A fall day on the farm.

The farm business demonstrates the viability of using horses for traction power on the farm and to educate the public about the value of local-sustainable agriculture. The farmers have 17 acres in hay, 35 in pasture, and the balance in garden and greenhouses...altogether about 60 acres of Cobb Hill land. They feed an average herd of 50 young stock, steers, bred heifers, and milking cows, plus four working horses. (Cobb Hill Enterprise report, 2013.) Stephen is also an author, having published *The New Horse-Powered Farm* through Chelsea Green Publishers (2013); another book specifically on market gardening with horses is due to the publisher in a few days. He's not your typical farmer either.

Value-added products have enhanced the opportunities for this small-scale farm to gain recognition. Award-winning Cobb Hill Cheese and Cobb Hill Frozen Yogurt are products of the raw milk, rich in butterfat, of the Jersey cows. Owned and managed separately by other Cobb Hill residents, the cows are fed specifically to elicit the kind of milk needed to make the artisan cheese. A symbiosis is in play—without the quality Jersey milk, the award-winning alpine cheese would not be possible. Without the cheese, and the frozen market, the farmers would have to sell their milk on the larger volatile milk market.

Dairy farms in America have been on the decline for the past century. Vermont continues to support a small cadre of small-scale farms, but in the agribusiness world that has taken over, doing agriculture is a rare thing these days. Less than two percent of the US population now makes any of their income from farming and less than one percent makes all their household income from farming. Stephen and Kerry are committed farmers, loving what they do, doing it the best they can with what they have, yet struggle to support themselves and their daughter.

Struggles, Tensions, and Conflicts

So from all that you have read so far, you might conclude that the experiment at Cobb Hill is not only successful, but is a model for how one can do community and farming cooperatively. To some degree that is true, but taking off the rose-colored glasses, there have been struggles, tensions, and conflicts that have plagued this farm/community system over the years and continue to do so.

In the larger economic world of agriculture, as mentioned above, there is little support for the small-scale farmer. When Cobb Hill set out to do farming and community together, they devised what seemed like a wise and cutting-edge system to support a small farming enterprise. Fifteen years later, we are learning and growing from the conflicts and tensions that have surfaced time and again over the course of the community. The community support has come in the form of lease-free land, use of existing farm buildings, maintenance of those buildings over the years, and help with major tasks of hay and some field work.

As a newcomer to this community, I experience a lack of physical participation of the community in the farm for various com-

(without the investment expenses that keep many young farmers from fulfilling their dreams), they also have to contend with market prices for grains, hay, supplement, as well as the unstable prices for milk. They are too small to qualify for the subsidies that larger corporate dairy farmers might enjoy, but in truth most of the subsidies these days are going to mega farms growing soy and corn. So they must make their way through the small Vermont-focused agriculture grants that come through the state, and scale back any investments in infrastructure or stock to just those that they can afford from year to year.

Even though the Cobb Hill cheese and yogurt enterprises pay above-commodity prices for their milk, when you add vet bills, machinery, vehicles, gas, pasture upkeep costs, and other items to the list, you shortly begin to see that a 24-head milking herd and several acres of vegetables do not net you much in the end. A seven-day-a-week regimen of milking twice a day means the farmers must hire farmworkers in order to not exhaust themselves completely. By the time they are finished paying all the bills, there is little money left for Stephen and Kerry's salary.

Income variations among those who live at Cobb Hill can make farming among a cohousing community socially challenging. While Kerry rises at 5:00 each morning to milk, I personally work only half-time, and online, so I can pretty much do my work whenever I want during the day and week. I hear her crunch through the snow outside my window each morning as I turn over and thank my lucky stars I am not needing to milk in the dark at -21 degrees F, as was the case for Kerry this morning. I make a very modest salary but it is still more than what Kerry and Stephen make working 16-hour days on the farm. How

Income variations among cohousers can make farming socially challenging.

plicated and complex reasons. Some have to do with people's busy schedules and commitment potential for tasks, some have to do with insurance and what the farmers can invite people to do, some have to do with personalities and how communication happens. Ultimately this lack of participation remains a source of stress in the community that needs tending to on a regular basis.

From my interviews with residents it seems that most were attracted to Cobb Hill because of the farming aspect of the community. What a great place to raise kids and have fresh homegrown food! Most people at Cobb Hill know little about farming, however, and less about dairy farming, and have little knowledge of the market forces that drive agribusiness in this country. It is difficult to escape the larger economic systems that control agriculture in our country and world.

Though Kerry and Stephen can feel grateful and blessed to have lease-free land to farm

does a community manage and deal with income inequality? How do we talk about this without being whiney or eliciting guilt or shame? It is a conversation we are due to have.

Managing 270 acres, 125 of which are forest and a maple sugar bush, plus trails, and the infrastructure of maintaining 20 households plus a common house with three apartments, takes the time and energy of the larger Cobb Hill community. Tensions in the community can arise because there is much work other than farming to be done in a land-based cohousing community, and Stephen and Kerry have little time for anything beyond keeping the farm going and raising their young daughter.

How does a community that prides itself in the working farm balance its desire for broader community engagement, while accepting that farm life may not make community involvement possible? How do we accept that Kerry and Stephen are adding a great contribution to the community even without showing up? This stress is one we spend a good deal of time talking about and grappling with. Kerry and Stephen are beginning to see that though they are stretched for time, showing up makes a huge difference. Life at Cobb Hill

A waffle morning.

and in any intentional community is a balancing act.

Many could argue that the community could be more engaged in the farm, allowing for shared workloads, thus relieving Kerry and Stephen of some of their duties. Many would love to do this, actually. But it's nice in theory, harder in practice. As is often the case, it is more complicated to have volunteers than just do the work yourself. Certainly large actions such as putting up hay bales or weeding the corn patch can benefit from volunteers. But when raising animals, you want only those trained well or those in training to be the ones who deal directly with your most valuable resource. These cows are not just taken care of, they are nurtured here at Cobb Hill. Kerry is proud of her Jersey cows and she runs a tight ship in the barn. She holds to high standards and will not compromise on many things. You want a farmer in your community farm to have this work ethic and commitment. Running a farm by consensus or volunteerism is a recipe for disaster...and not just for the humans. Yet people like myself can continue to romanticize how wonderful it is to be living in a community with a farm, while I plan my two-week upcoming vacation to Hawaii.

An Evolving Vision

Almost 14 years since her death, Dana Meadows' spirit resides here at Cobb Hill, as do her ashes. Her dying at the beginning of this experiment left a community of people, overtaken by their grief, struggling with the task of figuring this all out without her extraordinary vision and collaborative spirit. Her words continue to guide us as we begin to take stock of the system we have created here for farmers and community to be in collaboration with each other.

We still hold out a sustainable vision for our world...hopefully using the definition that she spoke of in a speech in Spain in the fall of 1993: "I call the transformed world toward which we can move 'sustainable,' by which I mean a great deal more than a world that merely sustains itself unchanged. I mean a world that evolves, as life on earth has evolved for three billion years, toward ever greater diversity, elegance, beauty, self-awareness, inter-

relationship, and spiritual realization."

Life at Cobb Hill continues. The car ballet went off without a hitch. We didn't lose power. We begin in 2015 to take stock of what has been created here. It is time to re-examine our assumptions, expose what isn't working, create some new dynamics, always looking for ways to intervene in the system. Dana would be proud to know that we are evolving this farm/community she loved. ❧

Coleen O'Connell recently moved to the Cobb Hill community from Belfast Cohousing and Ecovillage in Maine, where she served on the leadership team in developing the project. Coleen is the Director/Faculty of the Ecological Teaching and Learning M.S. Program for educators at Lesley University in Cambridge, Massachusetts. Her professional and personal passion has been to explore ecological literacy and sustainability in the context of our personal lifestyle choices. She has traveled internationally with students living in and studying the ecovillage movement. She can be reached at oconnell@lesley.edu and welcomes your comments or questions.

Coop on wheels w/ moveable fenced pen.

Summer at Cobb Hill

ZONING NIGHTMARE:
Hartford's Scarborough Street House

By Dave Rozza, Hannah Simms, Josh Blanchfield, Julia Rosenblatt, Kevin Lamkins,
Laura Rozza, Maureen Welch, and Simon Raahauge DeSantis

Somehow or another, our smallish urban intentional community of 11 has found itself at the center of a zoning brouhaha that none of us could have anticipated.

We are longtime friends who have been involved in community activism over the years. As our bonds deepened through our collective work and struggles, we developed a plan to live together as an intentional community in our city of Hartford, Connecticut. Over time, the concept of our extended family evolved and the core group solidified. Several of us lived first in an artist community, then in a purchased home together elsewhere in the city. We celebrated the births of our children and suffered the deeply painful loss of a community member to lung cancer.

When we began looking for a bigger house to fit all of us, we realized that we needed a total of nine bedrooms, a rare find in our city. We were committed to staying within Hartford city limits, and as we scouted for houses, there simply weren't many homes that fit the bill. In the spring of last year, we found the foreclosed mansion on Scarborough Street, a home with exactly nine bedrooms and two acres of land. It was still well outside our price range, but over the following three months, the price dropped $100,000. The stars aligned and we bought the house.

The house on Scarborough Street was, by far, the largest purchase any of us have ever made. We are "all in," both financially and emotionally, and it was important to us to make sure all *i*'s were dotted and *t*'s crossed, legally speaking. Though only two of us could be on the mortgage, we worked with a lawyer to draft a partnership agreement that makes us all legal owners of the home. We have a shared bank account and we make household purchases like food collectively.

As we moved forward, we were aware that the city's zoning codes could have been an issue for us. But any person who takes the time to really pore over the zoning regulations would find the exact same thing that we found: ambiguous zoning language that doesn't make any sense in a modern context. One of the main selling points of the house was that it resides on over two acres of land. This section of the city is designated as R-8, a "single family zone"; however, there is a density clause within the language that allots for 3.6 families per acre. Though we live and operate as a single family, we figured that if issues arose, we would be covered under that portion of the code.

The Hartford zoning regulations' definition of family reads:

"Family means, one (1) person; a group of two (2) or more persons living together and interrelated by consanguinity, marriage, civil union, or legal adoption; or a group of not more than two (2) persons who need not be so related, occupying the whole or part of a dwelling unit as a separate housekeeping unit with a common set of cooking facilities. The persons constituting a family may also include foster children; the number of which shall be in accordance with general statutes as amended and live-in domestic employees. For the purposes of determining density, a roomer, boarder or lodger shall not be considered a member of a family."

This definition allows for an unlimited number of domestic servants. So clearly, the code was not written with the sole purpose of controlling population density within the neighborhood. Dating from the late 1960s, its design seems to have been more about controlling who could afford to live there.

At no point in the buying process did we try to hide the makeup of our group and at no point did anybody advise us not to purchase this property because of the zoning ordinances.

Family photo.

Fixing a window.

Kid committee game night.

Working in the back yard.

We moved in and began the difficult work of fixing the house up. Renovating a nine-bedroom historic home that had been empty for at least four years took all the time, energy, and money we had. We brought the electrical up to code and began to repair the plumbing. We went out of our way to consult with our neighbors about outdoor aesthetics and checked with them about the type of fencing we wanted to install for the dog. Studies demonstrate that empty houses contribute to neighborhood decline and reduced property values. We hoped that because we were purchasing and caring for an abandoned home, our neighbors would be happy to have us, even if our family structure isn't quite traditional. Interactions with the neighbors were very positive and we breathed a sigh of relief and let our guard down a little.

The first inkling we had that some of our neighbors were less than pleased with our arrival came about two months in, when a neighbor told us that there were "phone calls going up and down the street" about the number of cars we had. We had eight cars when we first moved in, one for each adult in the house. We had always planned to downsize and share vehicles but with the chaos of moving and renovation, we hadn't made it a top priority. Our driveway was small and we had been parking cars on the street (a call to Hartford Parking Authority confirmed that this is, in fact, legal, though apparently not the neighborhood norm). As soon as we were told this was an issue, we started parking only in our driveway. We sold two cars and moved driveway expansion to the top of the repair list. Although we remedied the situation, the damage had been done.

The neighbors convened a meeting to discuss our house (we were not invited). At this meeting, attended by 20 or so people, they decided to send a letter to the City of Hartford. Although we moved in wanting only to live quietly and happily, we are not ones to shy away at the first sign of trouble. We love each other, we love our home, and we will do anything we need to do to keep it.

We received a letter from the city stating that we "may be in violation of zoning." As requested, we contacted them right away to set up an inspection date. In the meantime, we drafted an email to our neighbors introducing ourselves and our living situation. We sent it to some neighbors who had been friendly towards us and asked them to forward it on to others on the street. This email was then forwarded to the city and we received a cease and desist order, stating that they had completed an "inspection via email."

Snow day.

Halloween.

Setting the Record Straight

A few things we've been wanting to share:

• It's not lost on us that we are fighting to stay in our beautiful mansion while others among us struggle each day for their lives, living under racism and other systems of oppression. White privilege plays a huge role in every aspect of our situation and we never forget that.

• Though some have drawn parallels and we are honored by the comparison, our struggle in no way compares to what our LGBTQIA brothers and sisters have endured and continue to endure. Marriage equality is only the first step on the long road to equality for all people.

• While we are not polyamorous, there are many poly families out there who have been forced to live in the shadows. Nobody should ever have to hide their consensual, loving relationships. Family is who you love, who you care for in your everyday life. If, collectively, we as humans stopped looking at the nuclear family as the point to strive toward and instead, began shaping our own definition of family and healthy relationships, what would the world look like?

• It is important to mention that a few of our neighbors have been absolutely wonderful to us, bringing us welcome baskets and inviting us over to their home for drinks. Their kindness means more than we could ever say.

• There are effective ways to allow for "functional families" while disallowing boarding houses, frat houses, and the other fears that our neighbors have. The Town of Bellevue, Washington just passed fantastic updates to their zoning ordinances that accomplish just that:

Bellevue, Washington's Definition of "Family":

Not more than four adult persons, unless all are related by blood, marriage, or legal adoption, living together as a single housekeeping unit. A group of related persons living in a household shall be considered a single housekeeping unit. Provided: a group of more than four unrelated adult persons living together in a dwelling unit may also be included within the definition of "family" if they demonstrate to the Director that they operate in a manner that is functionally equivalent to a family. Factors that shall be considered by the Director include whether the group of more than four unrelated persons:

A. Shares the entire dwelling unit or acts as separate roomers;

B. Includes minor, dependent children regularly residing in the household;

C. Can produce proof of sharing expenses for food, rent, or ownership costs, utilities, and other household expenses;

D. Shares common ownership of furniture and appliances among the members of the household;

E. Constitutes a permanent living arrangement, and is not a framework for transient living;

F. Maintains a stable composition that does not change from year to year or within the year;

G. Is not a society, fraternity, sorority, lodge, organization or other group of students or other individuals where the common living arrangement or basis for the establishment of the housekeeping unit is temporary; or

H. Can demonstrate any other factors reasonably related to whether or not the group of persons is the functional equivalent of a family.

The Director shall issue a written determination of whether a group of more than four unrelated adult persons are operating in a manner that is functionally equivalent to a family.

Bellevue's "Rooming House" Definition:

A non-owner-occupied dwelling that is subject to multiple leases or in which rooms are offered for rent or lease on an individual room basis.

—L.M.R.

We hired an accomplished attorney who is also a fellow activist and friend. We had a number of options before us:

• We could try to get a variance, which is essentially an exemption from the zoning law. Variances are difficult to obtain, at least in Hartford, and it wouldn't improve the situation for anybody else affected by outdated zoning regulations.

• Adult adoption is legal in Connecticut, but the judge who would decide the case lives in our neighborhood.

• We could have hired each other as servants, but we were worried about tax implications, not to mention that we don't want to hide behind a technicality.

Ultimately, the zoning regulations as they are currently written affect far more people than just us. We decided to challenge the definition of family within the city's zoning regulations.

There has been a great deal written about how zoning laws have been, and continue to be, used to oppress communities. There are many others in situations similar to ours who are forced to fly under the radar. In our city, which is one of the poorest in the country, many families are forced to remain silent while their landlords keep their homes in deplorable conditions, because the first question landlords ask is how many people are living within the dwelling and whether they are related by blood.

It is far past time to change Hartford's definition of family, not just for us, but for people in our city and beyond.

Simultaneous to the city's actions, our neighborhood civic association, WECA, convened a hearing to discuss our house. The WECA hearing kicked everything into high gear and made our situation very public. Op-eds and editorials starting appearing in the newspaper and local news stations took notice. From there, national news outlets picked up the story and it was shared widely on social media. We were, and continue to be, completely surprised and overwhelmed by all the attention our situation has received.

We then faced the zoning board of appeals. The board was able to rule only on whether the cease and desist order was issued appropriately, not whether the definition of family itself should be changed. All eight adults and one of the three children spoke at the hearing. We shared how we live as a family day to day, how we love and care for each other, how we support each other in happy times and hard times, how we live as more of a tight unit than most "typical" families do. At this hearing, many neighbors spoke against us, arguing that we are changing the character of the neighborhood and if they allow us, it will open the door to boarding houses which are—without question and for many reasons—a big problem in our city. These arguments are all easily addressed with well-written, thoughtful zoning language, and there have been attempts made by friendly folks within the city to do just that (attempts that were quickly shot down). Out of the five who heard our case, three board members were fully on our side and believe that the ordinance needs to be changed. They were saddened that they did not have the power to do so, and that they could not, in good faith, find the grounds to dismiss the cease and desist order. Two of those three were moved to tears that they couldn't help us.

With heavy hearts, we took the next step of filing a lawsuit in federal court against the city.

The day before we were set to announce our federal lawsuit against the city, the city, in turn, filed a preemptive lawsuit against us in state court.

Around this same time, the zoning board quietly changed the code to limit to three domestic servants, clearly an attempt by a few on the board to make our court case harder to pursue.

In a city where zoning violations are routinely ignored, where the blighted properties list is pages and pages long, and the slumlords who own properties in Hartford's low-income communities of color routinely get away with ongoing and repeated violations, why was a minor infraction to an unclear zoning ordinance enforced so heavily?

The case is currently in court, with our lawyer and the city's lawyer battling it out behind the scenes. We don't anticipate that there will be any significant progress made until the fall and in the meantime, we are not facing any mounting penalties and we are thrilled to have a little quiet time to simply enjoy family dinners, garden, celebrate birthdays, and play some epic games of hide and seek in our giant home.

We are worn out and exhausted. But at the same time, we are deeply hopeful. The amazing support we have received from friends, loved ones, and fantastic strangers gives us strength. We are sustained by the fact that our situation has allowed us to share with the world how joyful, fulfilling, practical, and sustainable intentional community life is. What keeps us going is the hope that we can change the definition of family for many more than just us. In the end, it's not the house that's the prize, it's our community. This is worth fighting for and we aren't going to let anyone tear us apart. ❧

Dave Rozza, 37, likes things and stuff. Dave is super proud of his two awesome kids and adores his smart, beautiful, talented partner in crime, Laura...without her he would likely be lying in a ditch somewhere.

Hannah Simms, 31, is (as Tessa likes to remind her) the household's youngest grown-up. She works with Julia at theatre company HartBeat Ensemble, does a bunch of freelance theatre gigs and projects, and grows an overabundance of zucchini.

Josh Blanchfield, 37, is a social studies and history teacher, husband to Julia, and father to Tessa and Elijah. LOL is a literal term for Josh and his sense of humor keeps us snarfing our juice.

Julia Rosenblatt, 40, is (as Tessa likes to remind her) the household's oldest grown-up. She is the Artistic Director of HartBeat Ensemble, the mother of Tessa and Elijah, the wife of Josh, and a lover of sleep.

Kevin Lamkins, 38, is Associate Professor of English at Capital Community College in Hartford. He loves playing and listening to music, hockey, bikes, and zombie stuff. He also loves animals, especially his 13-year old calico, Rosa.

Laura Rozza, 37, works in the grants department for the Town of East Hartford. Things that make her happy include her partner Dave, who is amazing in every possible way, her son Milo, her step-son Joshua (not Josh Blanchfield), and her fluffy kitty Tater Tot.

Maureen Welch, 34, is a therapist and general feelings enthusiast. She enjoys drinking coffee with Simon, wearing rompers, and playing drums in the indie rock band The Lonesome While.

Simon Raahauge DeSantis is a 34-year-old Latin teacher originally from Massachusetts. His passions include rowing, bicycles, retired racing greyhounds, Mazda Miatas, and Maureen Welch. His loyal and lazy dog is Sofie.

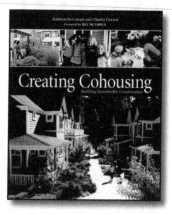
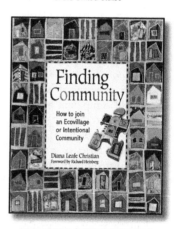

NEIGHBOR NIGHTMARE in Northern California

By Chris Roth

Editor's Note: *Some details in the story below have been altered to preserve anonymity.*

Joan and Michael (not their actual names) have been cultivating community for most of their adult lives. A decade ago Joan moved to a rural intentional community in California's redwood country, where she met Michael, who'd been a long-term resident and facilitator of workshops focused on self-awareness, communication, and group connection. After a couple years of life together in community they moved into the nearest town to co-create a socially and ecologically responsible business, one of whose core values was also cultivating and giving back to their broader community. They eventually sold the business to another local couple and moved back to the country, finding a piece of rural land just outside of town where they started to host occasional gatherings and workshops at their house.

They soon decided to create a separate gathering space inside an old equipment barn. A core team created the design and did much of the work, and a series of work parties enlisted hundreds of people in helping build the earthen structure. Many artists, artisans, and eco-builders lent their touches to the central circular space and its outer rooms. It became a vibrant gathering place for an extended network of people interested in the offerings presented there—music, yoga, meditation, and workshops on communication, personal growth, and various forms of spirituality. Hundreds of people participated in events in the space during its first year of use, and it became an important force for "community" among those drawn there.

However, those golden days did not continue; use of Om Space (an initially half-facetious name which stuck) is now on indefinite hold.

I interviewed Joan over the phone recently. We hope her story will offer a cautionary tale and valuable lessons to others sharing similar visions who may aspire to enact them more easily.

• • •

What was your vision when you bought the land?

We wanted to go back to our roots of having a land-based lifestyle and being in community again. We had gotten very used to hosting and giving, because we developed a lot of abundance with the business in town. When we chose our place, we saw that it had a beautiful house that seemed great for hosting, and the land was also beautiful. We were feeling very confident and excited to be in the position to have a community and to host gatherings.

Our biggest priority was to be close to town, so distance would not be a barrier for most people to come. We went around to the neighbors before we bought it and said, "Hey, this is what we want to do: we are social, involved in the community, and we want to have some gatherings, house concerts, workshops, and things like that, but we recognize that could have an impact and we want to know how you feel about our hosting these kinds of things."

And the neighbors that we visited said, "I think it's great—thank you so much for talking to us." They also had some harsh things to say about the previous owners. At the time we were thinking, "Oh, wow, well of course we're not going to be like that." But now I understand more the phenomenon of when meeting somebody new and they start talking about other people and how things have been bad or hard, it's kind of a red flag—though it is easy to dismiss it as, "Wow, they just haven't had someone to talk to about this."

We had blinders at that point, we really did. We thought, "How could anything go wrong?" Things had been going so well in our lives and we're so steeped in the philosophy of open-hearted, honest, transparent communication, we must have been assuming unconsciously that if we're that way, and we're drawn to this land, it meant that things would go well. You could call it denial, or magical thinking, and in looking at it now it seems that way. But it did feel OK at the time.

We actually did not visit the one neighbor we're having the most difficulty with, because we couldn't even see his house; it was so far away and he has lots of land between it and us. We approached neighbors if we could see them. Looking back, we made some big mistakes in not understanding that a lot of people move out of town to the country because they want a particular way of life that usually involves having more control or more privacy—which is understandable.

Did you look into the legalities of what you were allowed to do on the land? Or how many people were allowed to live there, things like that?

We really did not look into that very much, to be totally honest.

Was that because of the general culture where people do a lot of things that aren't technically permitted? That was part of the culture of the intentional community you'd been in as well.

I think so, I think we had a lot of trust in ourselves for being caring and considerate, and our experience with that is with this bubble of community in which we all have a trusting understanding that even if something is difficult, we work it out. We didn't recognize that some people have no interest in doing that. And not only that, if they get rubbed the wrong way, they are going to be antagonistic, for reasons that don't make any sense to me.

We were also imagining being low-key. Then, when we started creating the gathering space, several people involved were masterful designers and builders and it became a really incredible community project. It created something for the community that was very beautiful. As we went along we got swept up in that and didn't pay attention to what could go wrong.

Had there been any problems before you built Om Space? And what was your vision for it? How did it come about?

No, there were no problems. We were having gatherings and workshops in the house. But when Michael's aging mom moved in with us, we considered her health concerns and how large groups of people in our house impacted her, and realized it would be much better to have some separation between the home space and these other things that we wanted to do. So we decided to have another space on the land—an Om Space.

We got involved with a friend who was a very dynamic designer, and our creative juices all started to merge in a fun and exciting way. In our minds we thought, "Well, you know, we talked to the neighbors before we bought the place, and everyone we talked to was supportive." We did a lot of research in terms of talking to designers, builders, architects, other community people, but we didn't actually research or understand all the laws, because we understood that there's a bunch of gray area. Everyone always said it's all about the neighbors, and so in our minds we thought, "Oh, we did that."

Looking back on all this recently, we have been grieving together about our naivete. Michael was afraid that our decision-making had come from a lot of arrogance in him, and maybe there is some, but overall I think it came from positivity, and trust, and naivete for sure.

Were there any problems as Om Space was being built?

One of the neighbors who is closest expressed concern that there were people driving by and not saying hi—they found that really offensive, and requested that we ask our guests to say hi when passing neighbors on the driveway. They also asked that people drive slowly, that we put a stop sign at the end of the driveway, and also that we plant a screen shielding their property from ours. So we had a friend come who is very experienced and skilled and we planted over 300 trees. No matter what happens, I'm so happy that we planted that forest.

I feel we had a good relationship at that point with that neighbor; that was a good communication.

Later, once the space was completed, that same neighbor told us there was a complaint. We don't know who it was from—we're pretty sure it was from this one neighbor who is going gangbusters on shutting everything that we do down in every way. Then the County got in touch with us and said, "Hey, it's been brought to

Illustrations by Anna Helena Jackson

our attention that you're having stuff going on here and that there's money being exchanged"—which there was; we had a couple of concerts and we collected money and paid the musicians. Apparently, to do that you need what is called a Home Occupation permit. We had not known that, and so we found this great guy who is a land use specialist and hired him to start applying for this permit. As part of that process, the permit application goes out to all the neighbors.

And the neighbors who complained about the stop sign and the driveway and all that stuff said that once it became formal, once it became a matter of its potentially being certified as legal, they stopped feeling good about it. If it had not become a legal issue, if they had not gotten a notice saying we were going to do this, they would have been totally fine with it. But they felt that they were in danger because if it became legal, and they agreed to anything, then we would not feel the same need to communicate with them any more.

We thought, "Oh my god, we're all about communication, we even lead workshops in it, and we want everything to be cool—but they don't know us or have that experience of us." And once they made their decision, it seemed set in stone. They became kind of unfriendly at that point.

That was the first indicator that we and our neighbors were operating in really different ways. A lot of neighbors were frightened when they got that application request, and wrote in opposition to us having a Home Occupation.

One problem, when we applied for the Home Occupation, was that the notice to neighbors from the County specified what we'd be *allowed* to do. We'd be allowed to have 70 people this many times a week and to have this many cars, and that was all spelled out. But that wasn't the level of activity that we intended; it was just the maximum that was allowed by law. We explained this afterwards to the neighbors but by then they already seemed to have made up their minds.

Feelings also started to be relayed to us about the nature of what we were doing. People were pretty careful about how they said it, but basically they reacted to the fact that we were doing yoga, and chanting, and that we had *murtis*, which are deity statues, and things like that.

I think we still were in this bubble of thinking, "God, there's just got to be a way to connect about all this," so we decided to have an open house and invite everybody over to our place to see it and talk about it. I tell you, that was so hard for me. I did not like that ex-

perience. I understood why were doing it, and Michael felt open to it. But all these people were looking at Om Space who had no understanding or appreciation, and it felt really strange to me.

Some of what we wanted to do was to open to all these people that we didn't know. So it became really ironic that our neighbors, our literal neighbors, were starting to dislike us and feel threatened by what we were doing. It was the opposite of what we wanted.

You were hoping to contribute to the neighborhood or build the neighborhood.

Yeah, and when we had the open house I was thinking, "*Yes*, we're doing this for our community." We invited them to have their own gatherings in it too. I feel stupid now in some ways. We were just so clueless as to how some people were really feeling about it— they were like, "God, I don't like this." There was a lot of judgment or just not being able to relate.

When you put in for the Home Occupation permit, you got all these objections. What was the next step?

Well, we tried addressing all the concerns, but it seemed like the feeling was not very good, so ultimately we withdrew the Home Occupation application and concluded that "Yeah, OK, we got excited about this because we have this incredible space, but people are really not wanting it. So let's just permit this beautiful building and we'll be able to use it and have gatherings and not have it be a business in any way. It'll just be something that we can still enjoy and do yoga and kirtan and some concerts in." So we started pursuing that route.

Our neighbors were starting to dislike us. It was the opposite of what we wanted.

When you built it, you built it without a permit, expecting that you would have to get a permit at some point?

Yes. The building that contains it, the old barn, already existed, so it was kind of a build-out situation. We decided that we would do it and then get it permitted after—but not before, because of the timing of the creative process. We asked a lot of people and it seems that the County does of course want you to do the permitting first, but that can take a really long time, and lots of people do something and then get the permit. So we paid very special attention to doing everything to code.

One of the things that this one very antagonistic neighbor is saying is, "You have to be punished, because you did something without a permit, and now there's just no way that this can happen." I mean we didn't know that we needed a Home Occupation permit. We were aware that when you do a building project you need some building permits, but we also thought, "This is an existing building and we're doing something inside the building."

And it was really only while it was happening that we started thinking of it as a possible business. We thought, "Wow, we're spending a lot of money on this, more than we expected, way, way more—and why not? It's a great resource for the community and it could help us reclaim some of the money we put into it." And actually the land use specialist told us that we're allowed to have a Home Occupation; the zoning is totally fine for having that. We just decided to withdraw it because it was becoming really intense.

So you withdrew it but that wasn't the end of the problems.

Nope. At that point I think whatever feathers were ruffled were still ruffled, especially in the case of one neighbor who, you know, the words that come out of his mouth are "This is not going to happen, I'm sorry, but this is not going to happen," whatever that means. I think he thinks that he has more power than he does, but he also has deep pockets and is willing to move forward in his opinion.

How did the other neighbors feel?

The other neighbors seemed a lot less willing to talk to us about what was OK or not OK. Our driveway has an easement on one of the neighbors' land, and actually that's a huge other piece... looking back, considering just even that alone, we would choose a different site. Basically we were advised that we had a 50/50 chance of getting the Home Occupation permit. It's allowed and legal in our zone, but the only reason it wouldn't be granted is because of the easement with the driveway, if that neighbor objected. My advice now is: if there's a driveway easement, don't have a community there.

So we decided to just go for getting the building permitted, and now this one especially antagonistic neighbor is hiring attorneys and filing appeals, which he has to pay for—because it seems like he does not want to us to be able to save and use the building at all, for anything. It really has become a power struggle at this point.

We're applying for the building to be permitted as an accessory structure to the house, and it's a little bit farther away from the house than is normally approved as an accessory structure. Before we can get the actual building permit, we need to get this accessory structure permit. An accessory structure can be a workshop space, a dance space, a studio, a play room, a place where people sleep over... It's not a residence, but you could think of it as another room of your house—it's just not attached to your house.

The neighbor is saying that it was an existing barn and that there's a law that says you cannot convert an existing barn to an accessory structure. But that is a new law that passed recently, and I think it's because people have been converting their barns into huge wedding venues and things like that. In any case, it turns out the building was never permitted at all, as a barn or anything else. So the land use permitting board recommended that they pass our application; they said yes, it's an accessory structure, and yes, it's farther away than normal but we see no good reason not to approve the application. But the neighbor is really going for it now with the lawyers and he showed up at the hearing and said because the board is not doing their job we all have to show up here and spend money and time doing this.

> # My advice now is: if there's a driveway easement, don't have a community there.

Has there been any pushback against this neighbor?

Well here's the thing. I have a little studio that happens to be 204 square feet, where I play my music and prepare for teaching. The legal limit of a studio is 200 square feet. He decided that this space is a schoolhouse, and he reported it, and said there's a schoolhouse here that's being operated. He also reported the other storage building that is near Om Space, that our friend uses as a studio—he claimed it was a residence. So he's really reporting us, and every structure...it's like a nightmare.

It's true that our friend was sleeping in the storage building, but not very often. And it's OK for someone to sleep in there occasionally; it just can't be a residence, which means it can't have a bathroom and other things like that, and it doesn't. The point is that he's looking at these structures and he's turning them in. And meanwhile the other neighbors all have structures that are being used as residences but not legal ones. My opinion is that he's in a position where he's being a bully, and these other neighbors are thinking, "Whoa, he's turning them in, he sees our places too, he has a perfectly good view." And now they don't want to say anything...they're scared.

They're afraid of opposing what he's saying and doing.

Exactly, why would they oppose him? They will sort of go along with him so that he doesn't report them.

It's gotten into the realm of harassment, for me, to have this person who is watching, and keeping track, and then saying these things about us that aren't true. I talked to our lawyer about it, and he said it is harassment: he's slandering you and making things up about you, and I can send him a letter.

So you have a lawyer who is attempting to stop him?

Yes, we have a lawyer and a land use specialist who work really well together, and we like them and trust them. They keep reassuring us that what this neighbor is claiming and how he's going about it don't have much to stand on. At the hearing this neighbor and his lawyer presented a really, really thick—like phonebook-sized—document about us, and I think part of his claim is that we had a business in town, and so our intentions are...well, what they kept murmuring and muttering behind us was "bait and switch, bait and switch." They think that we are just trying to get away with something surreptitiously. It's a complete lack of trust, and I don't see how we could gain that trust at this point. So it's been a lot of emotional stress and grief and regret, really. I feel like if we could do it all over again we wouldn't have done this.

You would have chosen a different place.

Yes. And then we would have done it a different way too.

What would you say to someone who doesn't want to end up in this situation? One is: don't get a property with an easement through someone else's land.

Right. And I think we would buy land where the neighbor presence is pretty much nonexistent—where you don't really see the neighbors or interact with them or share a driveway with them. And then we would do things low-key. Maybe we would still make a building like this but I think we wouldn't be as trusting; we wouldn't think that we could just put this out to all the neighbors out of town and they'd all be like, "Great, this is great, yea!" It's sobering that a lot of people don't want change, they don't want something new, and they don't care about the same things that we do. That's just part of how it is.

Have there been any complaints about noise?

No, you can't hear anything coming from inside the space; it's totally sound-insulated with earthen walls. The biggest effect, and it is a real effect, is cars, coming and then parking when we have an event or gathering. We totally understand that. I wish there was a way that we could say, "Hey we're really sorry, we get it that you don't want this here, but what *would* be fine?" But we've basically tried that, and

so far the neighbors aren't willing to say they're fine with *anything*. So now we're in a position where our neighbors are dictating our lifestyle. Because the issues got raised and it has gone through the permitting and the County, everyone has a say now in the lifestyle that we're living. That feels really weird to me. If we lived in town, we could hold parties and have people over and do yoga and not worry about the neighbors stopping that.

I've heard that you have a couple neighbors who blast really loud music for long periods of time...

Yes, and there's absolutely nothing to say about that, legally. They blast very loud music, just broadcasting it out to the whole valley, and those same neighbors and others nearby have dogs that bark incessantly, and some other neighbors recently cut down the whole forest of trees on their land—and they are all allowed to do those things. Meanwhile, it feels like our activities are open to total scrutiny, and that feels terrible; I hate it. It's definitely not what I was imagining.

> # Because the issues got raised, everyone has a say now in how we're living.

My hope at this point is that we'll keep slogging through and we'll get the accessory building permit and we'll be in a position where there's not this constant attack; that we'll just be able to use the space again and then hopefully the issue will just kind of fade away.

Do you still see any possibilities for cultivating residential community on your land?

We are allowed to have five unrelated adults living in the house, and we also have another lot on the same land and are allowed to build another house. We spent so much money on this project I'm not sure how we'd go about that, but there probably still is a way to have community and to grow more food and do more permaculture projects. My sights have been turning more towards the land and how we can use the land, because I'm just not interested in living in a big house out in the country with my small family—that was never my intention. I want to have community in some way, but I've been told that using that word isn't always so good, it's like a red flag a little bit...

"Community"?

Yeah...that's just incredible.

Remember LHT in Livingston

So that's a red flag among the kind of neighbors you have? →

Yes. I just didn't think that this would happen. ❧

Chris Roth has been witnessing, navigating, and occasionally running smack up against the legal obstacles to living in community (especially ecologically responsible community) for nearly three decades now.

The Changing Landscape of the Law:
EXPERIENCES IN COHOUSING

By JT Hinds

David Clements rents out the apartment above his home at Westwood CoHousing, but current laws limit the number of renters he can have in a 30-day period.

When individuals choose to live and work with others, they give up a degree of autonomy and agree to abide by certain restrictions on their behavior so that the group can function smoothly and accommodate the needs of all its members. How the balance is struck between the needs of the group and the preferences of the individual members differs from one community to another, but this tension is inherent in a free society.

Laws, rules, and agreements are attempts to codify expectations (e.g., we don't steal from each other), anticipate problems (e.g., health and sanitation requirements designed to prevent food-borne illnesses due to improper handling), clarify our intentions (I agree to provide certain services and you agree to pay me a certain amount), and send would-be offenders a message about the severity of the offense (a sentence for murder is more severe than a fine for a parking violation).

Depending upon the nature of our activities—operating a business or nonprofit, practicing in a field that requires a license, raising a family, or hosting large gatherings in our homes—we are subject to a variety of rules and regulations that dictate which activities are permissible, that set forth requirements for permits and exceptions, and that prohibit certain behaviors and conditions.

People who live in intentional communities are expected to comply with the laws of the country and region where they live as well as any additional agreements imposed by the community. Members may agree to duties and restrictions that contribute to creating a certain kind of environment, even though no external laws apply to the behavior—a spiritual community might expect members to actively participate in a regular group practice like meditation or yoga, whereas an ecovillage might expect residents to refrain from using products that pollute the environment.

As people's needs change—individually and collectively—laws and behaviors also change. Small communities can often respond to changing circumstances faster than governments and institutions that are responsible for the welfare of large and diverse groups of people. The careful and considered approach to rule making, which may require studies by experts and input from the people likely to be affected by the proposed rules, results in a process that can be slower than we might like.

When new approaches don't fit easily into old categories, the flexibility of the system is tested. Can the system allow an exception, expand its definitions, or alter its procedures? If not, the project may fail—or need to relocate, if that's an option.

Planned Unit Developments (PUDs) allow an entire development to be planned from the outset (instead of houses being built lot by lot) and offer flexibility in site design, permitting a mixture of single-family and multifamily dwellings that may otherwise be prohibited by zoning ordinances.

Westwood CoHousing was the first PUD in Asheville, North Carolina. "The PUD designation allowed us to take the number of units that were permissible within the zoning in this neighborhood and cluster them together rather than spreading them out each on its own lot as was required before," said founding member Elana Kann.

The number of units per acre remained the same, but the cluster design, which allows for the preservation of communal green space, was new at the time.

Some governments will be more receptive than others to cooperating with entrepreneurs and trendsetters to find workable solutions, but even the most repressive governments will ultimately fail if they attempt to impose overly restrictive regulations that stifle creativity and innovation.

A Pioneering Spirit: Cohousing

As cultures evolve, some people seem destined to be at the forefront of change. Their ideas, services, and activities spawn new industries and practices that revolutionize the way we live, interact, and do business. They recognize opportunities and are willing to take risks. They explore uncharted territory, often making up the rules as they go.

Early adopters are excited by the possibilities presented by these leaders and visionaries; they see the potential of new approaches and technologies and are open to change. If the venture is successful, it can serve as a model for others to replicate. When the essential features are better understood, variations can add unique characteristics while still embracing the main concept and overall design, and nonessential features can be tailored to suit the specific needs of different groups.

The cohousing model is an example of a form that allows for flexibility in design while still retaining the essential features of a cohousing community. Cohousing is characterized by private ownership of homes (including apartments and townhouses) and collective ownership of common spaces and shared facilities. Homeowners and residents develop the policies that govern the use of common space and join together for recreation and other collaborative endeavors, including accomplishing the tasks that keep the community functioning.

More than 100 cohousing communities have been built in the United States, with many more in the planning and development stages. The common house generally serves as the hub for community life; it often includes a kitchen and dining area for use by residents, laundry facilities, accommodations for overnight guests, a play room, sometimes a teen room or tv room, and an office area. A workshop may be housed in the common house or in a separate building. Some cohousing communities plant gardens and keep chickens or goats; others build swimming pools and tennis courts. Multigenerational communities are likely to include a playground, and families may share childcare. Neighbors look out for each other and learn to cooperate as they find solutions to the problems and challenges they encounter.

The cohousing model encourages interaction and sharing but allows for variations to suit different conditions. A group building a community in a rural area might prefer more space between houses than would be possible in a trendy urban neighborhood. Many communities require community service by members and residents, but a community with wealthier residents might decide to hire workers to take care of the lawn and clean the common house. Some cohousing communities are designed and built by professional development companies, but a group of energetic and skilled craftsmen could form a legal entity, purchase a plot of land, and build their own homes from the ground up.

The people drawn to cohousing communities are often interested in sustainability and an energy-efficient design, but the needs and interests of residents in a senior cohousing community may differ from the needs and interests of young families or busy professionals. A group could incorporate a focus on artistic or holistic endeavors or be committed to permaculture or spiritual development if the founders design the community with specific goals and intentions and are able to attract enough members to join the project, but the typical cohousing community brings together a diverse group of people who were probably strangers before undertaking to build (or join) a community.

Questions arise—and obstacles must be surmounted—when new designs and methods such as cohousing are introduced into society. Can a new form of community obtain funding or insurance? Is it permitted by zoning laws? If public hearings are part of the approval process, will the would-be neighbors oppose the development?

Approximately a quarter of a century has now passed since the first cohousing commu-

nity was built in the US. Individuals who are interested in joining an existing community and groups looking to build new communities can benefit from the experience of the communities that have been in existence for years. Laws—and lawyers—are involved early in the process, as group members choose a form of organization, sign legal agreements, and research local requirements and regulations. Members are bound to each other for the duration of their memberships, and legal issues continue to affect various aspects

If a neighbor—or your group's governing body—is breaking the law, do you report it?

of community life after the building phase is complete.

Westwood CoHousing

West Asheville's Westwood CoHousing was completed in 1998. Twenty-three townhouses plus the original farmhouse are clustered around pedestrian walkways, gardens, and a common house. Owners are members of the Westwood CoHousing Homeowners Association, which owns the common house and common property. A Board of Directors oversees the community's legal and financial affairs.

I spoke with several members of Westwood about some of the legal challenges and hurdles faced by the community, both past and present. As with any multifamily development in Asheville, zoning regulations and building codes specify requirements for the building phase (e.g., the size of the spaces in the parking lot) and regulate residents' activities (e.g., requirements for operating a home business).

Community member David Clements noticed a potential hazard to pedestrians after settling concrete created a two-inch step along a walkway near the common house. He brought his concerns to Westwood's general maintenance team, and a ramp was installed to remedy the problem, but David thought the slope of the ramp was too steep to be accessible to people using wheelchairs. When the deck around the common house was expanded several years later, David expected city inspectors would require modification of the ramp to meet handicapped accessibility requirements, but the deck passed inspection.

David again brought his concerns to the general maintenance team, requesting that adjustments be made—a fix that he thought would require only a minimal additional expenditure. The team agreed to consider his request, but no action was taken.

David thought about contacting city inspectors to determine whether the slope of the ramp was in compliance with building codes. "I would have been able to get my way with the community by taking that action," he said, whereas he believed that internal procedures for raising issues through community meetings or by contacting the appropriate team were likely to be ineffective.

He decided to let go of the issue. "I didn't really like the idea of me as an individual strong-arming my way to get what I want just because it happens to be the law."

Ensuring that common spaces would be accessible to individuals with physical disabilities was not a priority at the time Westwood was designed and built, and local laws didn't require handicapped accessibility features in order to pass inspection. Any new construction, however, has to comply with current building codes and regulations, including accommodations such as wheelchair access.

As residents age (more than half of the adult owners and long-term residents of Westwood are age 65 or older), modifications may need to be made to ensure the safety and ease of access by all residents when using common spaces. And if the community decided to, say, make the guest rooms in the common house available to travelers through a site like airbnb.com, the building's classification could change and modifications to comply with regulations governing handicapped accessibility might be required.

Complaints, Compliance, Complicity

Many ordinances and regulations are enforced only when someone complains about a hazard or violation. Nothing prevents citizens from reporting to authorities the nuisances or hazardous conditions their neighbors are creating, whether actual or imagined, but the close relationships that can form in an intentional community may cause a member to think twice before doing so. After all, people join cohousing communities because they want to share resources and participate in the life of the community. Members of Westwood CoHousing, for example, join together for meals (organized weekly meals that are prepared at the common house as well as potlucks that are held at members' homes), work days, and other social events and business meetings.

If one of your neighbors—or the governing body of the community—is breaking the law, whether through action or inaction, do you report the offense to outside authorities and risk creating resentment, divisions, and alienation within the community, or do you tolerate the behavior and look the other way?

A Westwood homeowner who wished to remain anonymous had discussed the issue of neighbors policing neighbors with other community members, some of whom shared her concerns. "It would feel like a Gestapo, if I had to live like that, with people saying, 'Here's where you are breaking the law.'" *neither. You go to the person.*

Yet that same homeowner considered calling health inspectors to complain about a roach problem that developed, she suspected, because of conditions in the townhouse adjoining hers. (The neighbor subsequently moved away, eliminating the need for action.)

A concerned resident needs to consider a variety of factors in determining whether to contact government officials about a potential violation occurring within the community. Does the behavior or condition endanger any person (or tree or animal or the community as a whole—including the community's reputation)? What is the likelihood of obtaining a remedy through procedures set up for resolving conflicts and complaints within the community? Has a reasonable amount of time passed since the concern was raised? How imminent is the threat or danger? How strongly does the person feel about the issue? Is he (or she) willing to put principles above popularity in pressing the point—and seeing it through to a conclusion?

Laws change; we may or may not be aware of the changes when we make judgments about what "the law" does and does not require—if we ever really understood the requirements to begin with. Some laws take an individual's intent into consideration; some regulations create obligations that apply whether the individual is aware of the regulations or not. (Try telling an agent for the Internal Revenue Service that you didn't realize you were supposed to pay taxes and see if your debt is excused. More likely, you'll be fined and interest will be added to the total!)

Emerging Trends: Short-Term Rentals

Though their property boundaries may be clearly defined, intentional communities are not completely separate from the larger social, economic, and environmental forces that

The guest room the upper floor common house handicapped acc

affect other individuals and communities in the region and, increasingly, the world, as the interconnectedness of financial markets increases and the ease of international communication, travel, and commerce transforms the way we live, work, and obtain goods and services.

Asheville is a popular tourist destination, and several residents of Westwood are interested in offering guest accommodations in their homes through sites like airbnb.com. Currently, local laws prohibit short-term rentals* (less than 30 days) in residential areas, unless the home qualifies as a bed and breakfast operation. ("Homestays" are the exception to this prohibition, but only homes of at least 2,500 square feet are currently eligible, and property owners must obtain a permit to offer rooms in homes they occupy. None of the dwellings at Westwood qualify.)

Like many municipalities throughout the US, the City of Asheville is considering how to regulate homestays. Commercial lodging establishments such as hotels and inns object to the unfair competition that exists when homeowners who are (illegally) offering rooms for overnight stays do not pay occupancy taxes, and policymakers are concerned about the adverse impact of homestays on the availability of affordable housing in the area (as well as the safety of visitors staying in homes that don't satisfy building code requirements).

Some residents of Westwood have raised concerns about the potential for negative impacts to the community if short-term rentals are permitted on an ongoing basis. The Westwood CoHousing Homeowners Association invited interested individuals to discuss the issue in a series of meetings.

Not all of the City's concerns are shared by residents of Westwood, but parking is a consideration when short-term rentals are permitted in residential urban areas, and Westwood is no exception. (Currently, several spaces in the communal parking lot are allocated to visitor parking. Resident parking is assigned by the parking team.) Other concerns include increased traffic (which may result in additional noise) and the introduction of outsiders who have no connection to the community and who may or may not have any interest in the cohousing philosophy and way of life. Because the expense of heating water is shared by all residents—as is the water bill—the cost of additional water usage by short-term renters is also a consideration.

As the City of Asheville grapples with the question of how to handle homestays that don't meet the current requirements, Westwood adopted its own policy on short-term rentals, requiring homeowners to notify the community of their intention to offer a short-term rental—whether a room, an apartment, or an entire house—and to track the number of days they have renters so that their utility bills can be adjusted accordingly. The common house, including the kitchen and laundry areas, is off limits to short-term renters unless they are accompanied by a member of the community. Hosts must notify the parking team if renters will be staying for more than two weeks.

Homeowners who offer homestays recognize that, until the City of Asheville changes its regulations, they run the risk of discovery if anyone complains to local authorities. Violators are subject to a fine of $100 per day if they continue renting their property after receiving a notice of violation. That's a risk that David Clements and Evan Richardson, and some other members of Westwood, may be willing to take.

David and Evan have sometimes rented out the (separate) furnished apartment above their home. Thus far, they have limited rentals to one per month in an attempt to comply with city regulations prohibiting stays of less than 30 days when the owner does not reside in the home. Now that the community has decided in favor of allowing short-term rentals, they are considering making the apartment available for shorter stays.

Like many other regulations, enforcement by the City is complaint-driven. Knowing that the City's policy is under review—and that the risk of a complaint is low—alleviates their main concerns.

"We were waiting to see if short-term rentals would be acceptable to the community," David said.

The Westwood community, that is.

Westwood residents are encouraged to bring any complaints and concerns about short-term rentals to the community. If problems arise, limits on the number of renters permitted each month—or the number of homes that can offer short-term rentals at any given time—might be imposed. Many of the same considerations (i.e., parking, noise, traffic,

cost of utilities) would arise if some homeowners had frequent *non*paying guests; an intentional community might decide to impose restrictions on behaviors, or require fees (e.g., for parking), even if the behavior is not "illegal."

Finding Balance, Moving Forward

Overly restrictive regulations can inhibit the development of creative approaches to the challenges that accompany a society's growth and evolution, but the lack of planning and oversight can create its own problems, such as urban sprawl and environmental pollution when individuals haphazardly undertake activities without considering the long-term consequences or the impact on the larger community.

Policymakers attempt to balance competing interests by passing legislation that imposes requirements and restrictions on businesses and individuals. Sometimes laws favor development and commercial enterprise; sometimes the balance is struck in favor of preserving the environment and safeguarding the rights of individuals (and municipalities—local governments are not always free to pass and enforce laws that contradict state and federal laws). Incentives such as rebates and tax deductions can motivate people to adopt practices and behaviors that policymakers want to encourage, like installing energy efficient appliances. Experimentation allows for innovation, and successful programs can serve as models for other groups and communities as we collectively identify the methods and designs that are most effective.

The idea of a "sharing economy" is not new to members of intentional communities, but its widespread adoption by large segments of the population signals the dawn of a new era and requires governments to adapt to changing times. 🐚

JT Hinds, J.D., M.A., has lived in several intentional communities (and visited many more) but is not a member of Westwood CoHousing.

*The definition of "short-term rental" used by the City of Asheville differs from that used by Westwood CoHousing in developing its policies and procedures. The City uses "short-term rentals" to mean property rentals for overnight stays of less than 30 days when the owner does not reside in the home. For Westwood's purposes, "short-term rental" refers to overnight stays of less than 30 days, whether the home is owner-occupied or a vacation rental.

Getting to Community and Life *after* Community: COLLECTIVISM VS. INDIVIDUALITY

By Lisa Paulson

Here is how I got to community, was in it deeply for over a dozen years, how I came out the other side—and what happened then.

My perspective on the community idea is a long one—roughly spanning the last 40 years. But before that I'd lived in Italy in the 1950s, joining an inspiring humanitarian project started by my future husband, Bel Paulson, to help sort out an appalling postwar scene of starvation and homelessness. I'd served as logistical backup for his surprisingly successful refugee resettlement experiment on the island of Sardinia. And I'd done the same in the dustbowl of northeast Brazil where he was researching village dynamics. But these were specific assignments, focused around dire political, social, or economic crises, and I zeroed in mainly on my particular supportive role within that larger context.

I came of age in an era when women married young and took it for granted that any career based on personal creative expression was sublimated to caring for a husband and children. I got that—for about 10 years after we'd settled in Wisconsin. But then came the national ferment of the 1960s, and I began to seriously question this role. I left the housewife job to help run a school teaching altered states of consciousness.

Findhorn: Introduction to Community

Then, in 1976, while organizing conferences around consciousness and paranormal research, I happened on the mesmerizing legends coming out of Findhorn, the renowned spiritual community in a remote corner of Scotland—tales of people so attuned to enigmatic forces in their gardens that they began growing improbably large vegetables. I determined that I had to go and see for myself.

By some miracle I managed a solo voyage to Findhorn. There, a dream—a mission—began to take shape as I plunged into the vibrant life of this utopian enclave, whose primary purpose was to redress the balance between people and nature.

At the end of my stay, I was seemingly pushed by some mysterious cheerleader to take the Findhorn ideas from the blustery North Sea and sand dunes home to Wisconsin. These were imperatives to live in connection, in community, in mutual compassion with each other, and with all life they touched.

It was a message coming at exactly the right time in our part of the world. The passion that had been ignited for me in Scotland turned out to be contagious. People flocked to my talks from across several Midwest states. They were hungry to hear about alternatives to tired belief systems. They wanted to learn about new, different ways to think, organize their own lives and society, and to plan constructively, not only for the survival of human civilization, but for the very survival of the earth. Remember that this was a couple of decades before "sustainability" became a familiar buzzword. I think

Circle dance in the High Wind farmyard.

Tim Conner

everyone was astonished at how quickly and deeply the ideas caught on.

I did manage to stick with my initially skeptical family while, at the unlikely age of 50 (with the help of an escalating number of enthusiasts) I started to implement some of those far-out imperatives. Eventually I was able to draw in my husband to be my lifelong, essential partner in creating our own intentional community.

And so it was that for the next 20 very earnest, alternately frenzied and epiphany-like years with my fellow pioneers, we put everything aside "for the good of the whole." Our purpose was to implement the grounding and outworking of the venture we called High Wind—blending the spiritual vision of Findhorn with the ecological goals and experiments of the New Alchemy Institute in Massachusetts.

Here is our High Wind credo that laid out a comprehensive approach to living together sustainably and designing education around these concepts:

> *To walk gently on the Earth;*
> *To know the spirit within;*
> *To hear our fellow beings;*
> *To invoke the light of wisdom;*
> *And to build the future now*

Epiphanies as Well as Power Issues Surfaced in the Community

My Findhorn experience reflects what I think often happens in mid-life—when one's ideas and maturity are peaking, as well as energy and flexibility, and an inner sense of personal power, savvy, and confidence takes hold.

High Wind attracted mostly folks a generation younger than Bel and me. As we discovered, especially in situations where community founders are older than their recruits (and perhaps more financially viable), a dynamic develops where the founders find themselves the "parents" and the other members the "children." And, as in mainstream families, there's a natural tendency for the kids to test their muscle against those they perceive as authority figures, and to rebel. Bel and I frequently saw our ideas and proposals challenged, especially when people arrived and discovered that the fixed ideas about community life they had brought were not the reality at all. Despite our insistence that we all held equal authority and made decisions by consensus, fingers were predictably pointed at Bel and me as the "power" figures. Members thought that if we didn't like an initiative they put forward, it had little chance of materializing.

As the self-appointed "vision-holder," I especially found myself to be the prod to remind others of the particular lofty purposes and standards that had been articulated initially—the ideas that had excited and attracted everyone. My problem was that because I cared so deeply about this fragile organization I saw as my "child," I suffered when I saw it tilting away toward another track (as to a closed homesteading model instead of reaching out—"serving the world"—through education and demonstration). Often, our very lengthy, sometimes heated meetings ended with me limping away, fully inhabiting my thin skin, doubting myself and distrusting those who had joined High Wind. I wondered what had happened to erode such a compelling, important goal. Over and over I was knocked down just because I was in a position to be perceived as a leader—exactly what I didn't want. A pretty big comedown from my Pied Piper image upon returning from Findhorn!

Of course the community was right. Bel and I *did* embody a certain power. We were the founders, High Wind was our idea, and it began on property we had owned. We had an income because Bel continued to teach at the university, not an easy juggling act. Our recruits had abandoned paying jobs and rushed to give their hearts and energy to an ideal as volunteers. They found, though, that High Wind had no money to

Seminar attendees learn the intricacies of our organic vegetable garden.

Indian drumming at the sacred fire circle.

Women at High Wind sometimes take on the heaviest work.

Visitors tour the two small High Wind Styrofoam domes.

Photos courtesy of Lisa Paulson

Staff meeting during High Wind/Lorian summer seminar.

Sunday morning discussion group in the bioshelter greenhouse.

support them, and they had to scramble to provide their own sustenance.

In intentional community, where egalitarianism is a central tenet, such a collection of factors might have been a pretty deadly deterrent at the starting gate. Bel and I didn't always succeed in diminishing some people's unease around this reality, but we found that after members left, those who had often struggled and grumbled the most about money issues, about fitting in, or realizing their goals, came back to tell us that High Wind had been a pivotal growth experience. Being here had set a compass direction for the rest of their lives.

Besides the issue of who held the power, and a subtle hierarchy of haves and have-nots, there was also the fact that High Wind was unfolding in a larger community considerably more conservative than we were. With a flock of young singles, we didn't fit into the traditional rural family structure surrounding us. When I encountered a couple of young hunters on a walk in the nearby woods, they lit up when I told them where I lived: "Where do you keep your animals for sacrifice?" they wanted to know. Or when Don collected a pile of scrap wood after building his house and invited the rest of us to come to his bonfire to lift a few celebratory beers, the rumor went out the next day that we were dancing around a ritual fire in black robes reciting Satanic incantations. Much more fun to believe juicy gossip than to realize we were hardworking, boringly straight, ordinary mortals! But this, of course, pinpointed a major flaw in our calculations: we hadn't done the essential political spadework of getting to know our neighbors better, blending in, allaying unnecessary fears about alien influences. We relied for support on the hundreds (thousands over the years) who flocked from Milwaukee and from across the country who were already believers. It was a lot harder to convince those unacquainted with our perspectives.

Gifts of Community

We should have realized that introducing values and practices that ran counter to those of the dominant culture was going to be a hard sell. Such is the lot of pioneers. High Wind certainly felt the brunt of this divide, but on the other hand every one of us grew stronger and took away a huge array of new skills. We got to wear a lot of hats.

My personal takeaways: how to dig

French intensive raised planting beds, nail up sheetrock or a roof, split wood, construct a wigwam, cook for groups, lead tours, talk about solar buildings, put out a newsletter, and handle outreach and fundraising. At High Wind workshops, I became familiar with everything from Permaculture design and indigenous healing methods to weighing the wisdom of the Perennial philosophy. Probably the most valuable lifelong skill was learning to negotiate the emotional shoals of living with other people. And, as well, we would always carry with us the ideals and aims projected by the wider communities movement.

The Tyranny of Ideals

However, when you have some 20 people doing *everything* together for months or years on end, everyday life and relationships can get to be challenging. When our folks, who'd been fiercely motivated to install their own images of what the ideal community *should* be like, started to experience what our community *was*, some pretty intense dynamics were bound to surface. Emotions became fragile, and we began to realize that, ironically, the most precious (and scarce) commodities, and what we longed for, were more privacy and the right to indulge in personal pursuits—the antithesis of community?

At a certain point, all of us at High Wind saw that our personal zeal for the cause was being eroded by creeping burnout. Besides our regular jobs in construction, the vegetable and flower gardens, the grounds, kitchen, and office, we were servicing increasing numbers of visitors and participants in many educational programs. We decided to step back, take a deep breath, and reassess.

For a dozen years we'd been living and working in lockstep, aspiring to what we believed was the highest and purest of what a community could be. Then some of us (certainly I was one) began to realize how badly we were also craving an independence from what had come to be the tyranny of our ideals.

In the early 1990s there was a momentous, unanimous decision to let go of our intentional community image. Opting to relax our dogged earnestness (which sometimes had threatened or puzzled townspeople), we agreed to become a considerably looser "ecological neighborhood." To our surprise, those of us who remained found that we actually related better and took more pleasure in caring for each other and organizing group events than when such togetherness was obligatory. Eureka moments!

Togetherness or Individualism: Is That the Question?

In the founding of the United States, freedom and independence were mandated. Individuality was prized and protected. It's irrefutably in our bones, in our DNA as citizens and as a country. It's been our history from the beginning, unlike much of the rest of the world with its kingdoms and fiefdoms—rulers and serfs. It's what compels us to struggle to shine as autonomous beings.

There's the wisdom now that we *do* need to function with far greater consensus and community—to see ourselves as citizens of the earth where every being/life form has rights and must be protected. Where cooperation for mutual survival of all species is more imperative as threats of extinction loom. Yet within that realization there also

> # When some 20 people do everything together for years on end, everyday life and relationships can get to be challenging.

needs to be acknowledgment of the birthright of individualism that requires freedom to break free, to express, create, and develop without guilt.

In retrospect, High Wind can feel that it has influenced and inspired legions of supporters, regionally and nationally, and ultimately has made a bit of a positive dent in our surrounding area. Those of us who remained in the eco-neighborhood, as well as the residents who left, were indeed changed. Those going back into "the world" usually sought new paths with more meaning and significance to fit their talents and personal proclivities than they would have if they'd never risked dipping their toes into community.

For me, there were mixed emotions. I felt an enormous sense of satisfaction at what we'd collectively pulled off and the legacy now in place. It also came as a blessed relief to step off the merry-go-round of togetherness and responsibility. I felt as though I'd been on a treadmill 24/7, trying to move the world—my smallish world at least—into a better, saner place.

After Community

With this weight lifted, in the next years I stepped back to reflect and revisit what had been a lifelong touchstone—Nature. I've always had a connection to the magic of land or place, and have felt compulsively driven to create visual images and words

Digging French intensive raised beds for the new vegetable garden.

to describe all this. I caught the spirit embodied in meadows, forests, mountains, streams—whole communities of elements conspiring to capture human sensibility, if only we'd pay attention. Post-community, I resumed the delicious, solitary exploration of wild places, much as I had long ago.

In 2008, definitely an elder, I began to write and publish the first of four books that unpacked some of my most vividly remembered experiences of the last eight decades—experiences that shaped what I ultimately believed in and became. I've written of our concerted attempts at social change, as well as remembering and recording personal adventures throughout the past 70-odd years.

Here in our High Wind neighborhood I can initiate leisurely interactions with my near neighbors. (As I write this, I'm about to amble next door for a potluck house concert that will involve not only our former community members, but also friends from the area.)

I look forward now to several months a year living out-of-state where I become simply one more villager, seen around town with my easel and paintbrushes (that I resurrected after 40 years). I don't carry a label (positive or negative) that screams "radical" or "revolutionary" or "ideologue."

Ethnobotany field walk during summer seminar.

dividual projects with a community of just two?

I may have moved beyond intentional community, but it's still my tribe. Of all my adventures, creating community was undoubtedly the most meaningful. It was my central life mission. I'm still *of* it, but not *in* it. Some of my close friends remain with me on the still-active High Wind board that now gives grants to regional groups for sustainability initiatives. (Check the other articles by some of these extraordinary board members in this issue.) And I love sharing our experiences with groups and individuals who seek us out at the threshold of starting or joining their own communities: I talk about the satisfactions, opportunities, pitfalls, and our painful learning curves. People also come to inspect the environmentally sensitive home we designed in 1986—a design now superseded by more efficient technologies, but which can still keep us toasty without backup heat when it's zero out and the sun is shining.

At this stage I can relax and accept the opposing pulls of dual forces within myself: a messianic call to promote community and a lifestyle imperative for the continuance of civilization—and also the absolute need to be alone, quiet, independent. I know that both are possible and that I can open doors at will to either. I've finally learned that moments snatched for deliberate loafing and ruminating are not only possible but essential. We don't always have to keep running to catch up with the Red Queen.

> # Of all my adventures, creating community was undoubtedly the most meaningful.

My circle of friends can include those who may oppose my political, spiritual, or societal views, but these differences might not even come up. I can step through now permeable barriers, which is really freeing. It's trickier in my area of Wisconsin (though for the past dozen years I've been getting together regularly with a diverse, thoughtful, often wonderfully outrageous bunch of women from neighboring towns).

Togetherness *and* Solitude, Action *and* Reflection

I think how one approaches this dichotomy depends on what stage in the arc of life one is. How is it that I could relinquish the most important and fulfilling happening in my life, shared with a group I loved, and trade it in for a life filled with silences and very in-

Note: I've touched only briefly on some of the dynamics of our community experience (focusing more on the challenges instead of on the times that were absolutely glorious and rewarding—which were many). Some readers may recall that several of our thorny problems were aired in much earlier issues of COMMUNITIES. Both the difficulties and the very positive impact or significance of the community are spelled out exhaustively in my 2010 book: *An Unconventional Journey: The Story of High Wind, From Vision to Community to Eco-Neighborhood* (available through the FIC Bookshelf). Information about the other books both Bel and I have written can be found on our Thistlefield Books website (thistlefieldbooks.com). ❧

Writer and artist Lisa Paulson met her husband, Belden, in the slums of Naples while backpacking through Europe. She joined him to help alleviate the dire conditions among homeless Neapolitans living in ruins following World War II devastation—and also to provide relief for Iron Curtain escapees interned in refugee camps there. After work in Sardinia and Rome, they settled in Wisconsin. Then, inspired by her trip to the Findhorn community in 1976, she and Bel cofounded the High Wind community north of Milwaukee.

Words of Experience:
STARTING A COMMUNITY

By Kim Scheidt

One gorgeous sunny day last fall I was set up at an informational table as a representative of the FIC (Fellowship for Intentional Community). This was at the annual community open house event put on by the local ecovillage. Since my table was located right near the entrance I got to be one of the first people to interact with the hundreds of guests who came out for the event. Some were neighbors or people who had been to the open house in years prior, but most were folks who had never before traveled to the area and were seeing it all with fresh eyes. Quite often that day, as people milled about waiting for their scheduled tours to begin, I found myself engaged in conversations many of which focused on people wanting information on setting up an intentional community back at home where they lived. Some already had land available for such a project, others had a core group of interested friends, some had a well-developed vision of what the as-yet-unformed community would one day become, and a few special folks had all those things but were still unsure where to go from there.

I genuinely enjoy listening to people talk about their visions for community life, and often I find myself in situations where I am given the opportunity to pass on knowledge and wisdom stemming from my involvement in community. As a cofounder of a 10-year-old intentional community (ours focuses on homesteading) I have insights into what some of the challenges can be and lots of empathy for people who are going through the start-up phases of setting up a community, seeking one to join, or trying to decide if they want to join one that's already in existence or begin one of their own. I want to share my perspectives with others so they can avoid pitfalls and hopefully learn from my experiences. Setting up a legal entity, figuring out financing, having a committed core group, preventing overwhelm and burnout, anticipating population turnover, and dealing with power dynamics are a few of the myriad topics to ponder when making the decision to launch a community venture.

Now usually my first piece of advice goes something like this: "It is a LOT of work to start an intentional community. A LOT. If you can possibly find a community already out there that seems to be mostly aligned with what you envision for yourself, then I recommend you try out living there. Just give it a try. And by the way, intentional communities are an incredibly varied phenomena; each has its own different flavor. So if you have the means and resources to travel and visit different ones before settling down, then I totally recommend that too."

On the other hand, I personally have never been one to follow the usual way of doing things—or even my own retrospective advice. I am a peace-loving rebel at heart, and after limited experience of a few days visiting one ecovillage in the US and a handful of eco-farms in Central America I decided to join a group of three other people in creating our own intentional community. At the time we were starting it certainly felt like the right thing to do because no other community we knew of embodied enough of the values we were holding to be a good fit, we wanted to be located in a particular geographical area, and we figured that it really would be an attractive community model for others in the future. We were visionaries with pioneering spirits and a lot of dreams and excitement, so we took the plunge and decided to become community founders.

We spent many hours together clarifying our vision and mission statements as well as researching how to set up the legal entity. The book *Creating a Life Together* by Diana Leafe Christian proved to be a great jumping-off point. After examining our legal options we eventually settled on establishing a community land trust corporation. We then spent many more hours poring over the bylaws, articles of incorporation, and lease documents from sources we could scrounge up—other intentional communities or land trusts that had been similarly established. We took bits from many sources, as well as some of our own original input, to eventually craft our founding documents; upon completion we showed them to a kind lawyer knowledgeable about intentional communities who recommended a few tweaks. It seemed that our number of four founders was probably the bare minimum to successfully handle such an undertaking. It was a struggle at times not to feel burned out or overwhelmed with all the details. And when life kept us busy, progress on the technical aspects moved at a snail's pace. Although having a smaller group was probably conducive to more easefully crafting a workable combined vision, having a larger group would have helped to spread out the burden of all the research and wordsmithing.

Part of our research involved finding possible sites in our area on which we could develop the community. Cold-calling names listed on a county plat map resulted in success—a local landowner agreed to sell his tract of pasture land at a reasonable cost. But although the four of us came with some savings, our pooled money would cover only about a third of the purchase price. Choosing how to finance the rest was another somewhat complicated process for us. We contemplated a few different loan options and also the possibility of recruiting other founder-investors. We finally negotiated borrowing from a friendly acquaintance who, although he did not want to join as a member of the community, had definite attachments and opinions on what we should be doing which at times was tricky to navigate.

We pushed forward and got things settled to buy the land. We celebrated and began camping on the property. Life progressed until the next little bump in the road for me personally as well as our newly formed community. Approximately three months after we purchased the land, one of the founders decided to leave. He and I had been involved romantically for over four years and as our romantic relationship declined he recognized that he needed to move on and travel to other places. So among other challenges of that time,

Darien Flores

this also meant our forming community had lost a quarter of its membership during this delicate beginning phase.

Most intentional communities are familiar with the concept of a high turnover rate in population. It was not surprising that someone would choose to leave and more people would come in as residents. There were folks who had not been part of the visioning stage but who were there with us early on. Each time it was a learning experience. Our first new resident was a charismatic guy who was going through a break-up and had kids in the area for whom he shared parenting responsibilities. He was friends with us and we were wanting more people to join. Although not a perfect values match it seemed like it would work out beneficially for all. The membership group gave approval for him to construct a "tiny house" on the property as well as a small shed and some animal housing. After some months as a resident he then decided to move on. In the beginning we had not foreseen all the possible complications that could arise with such a situation. Things eventually worked out fine; however, our experience with this resident and the structures he left behind led us to come up with some policy norms that we didn't have in place prior to that. Namely: a person has to be a resident on the land for six months before becoming a member, and during that time the expectation is that they will not make any permanent changes to the land or construct permanent dwellings (we have made rare exceptions to this by full group consensus). Also, when an individual or family begins camping on unleased land, they are to pay a monetary deposit to help ensure that the site gets satisfactorily remediated in the event of their departure.

One topic that has come up with the advent of additional people in the community is the power imbalance that exists between members and residents. For our group, this dynamic is something to acknowledge and simply accept as unavoidable as part of the process of creating a functional and healthy community. The understanding is that this power imbalance exists as a temporary phase while the community and resident get to know and trust one another. It can help ease relationships if the existing members make a concentrated effort to integrate and support new residents rather than leave them flailing on their own feeling isolated. We've tried our best to do this by appointing each resident a liaison to the community and by offering to help the residents organize work-parties for settling in or tackling projects that seem daunting. We set aside time in our meetings to have a resident check-in with the full group at least once a month to provide space and a scheduled format to address any issues that arise.

To a lesser degree an imbalance of power also exists between founders and those who join later. Members who did not help to craft the founding vision will perhaps be holding some different core values or ideal ways of being together in community. The default will be the position of what has come before, and once a rule or norm has been instated it can take substantial effort to create a change. Though not impossible, it takes a lot of momentum to shift the status quo, and it can feel like an uphill battle—that those who crafted the vision have their desires incorporated into the basic structure of the community, and those who join later hold valid and useful preferences which are not necessarily upheld by community norms. Therefore it can be very helpful to make certain from the outset that both the current community norms and the longer-term community vision are explicitly communicated to incoming visitors, residents, and members so as to make sure everyone is clear about what they might be getting into.

And how do we attract those new people best suited for joining the community? That is a question that nearly all communities wrestle with at some point. In fact it is one that I continue to spend a fair amount of thought energy on even now. "If you build it they will come" only goes so far. Getting people involved who have a propensity for networking can come in handy. Listing with the FIC Directory, creating an attractive website, and using social media can be great. There are conferences to attend and a multitude of ways to get the word out. When contacted by community seekers I ask them pointed questions to attempt to quickly determine if their intentions are serious and if their vision would be something that could practically happen within our particular framework. At times we have been nearly overwhelmed with people wanting to live at our homestead community and at others we go an entire season without serious interest. At one point we were considered full and then about a year later we have leaseholds available again as members decide to explore other life adventures. I believe it is important to keep in mind that it is natural for a community's population to wax and wane. I have hopes that this intentional community of ours will continue to function long after I am gone. And I know that frequently people who come for even a short visit are impacted in ways that can be life-changing. I try to keep an open mind and open heart and trust that what we are doing is making a difference. ❧

> It is very helpful to make certain from the outset that both the current community norms and the longer-term community vision are explicitly communicated to incoming visitors, residents, and members so as to make sure everyone is clear about what they might be getting into.

Kim Scheidt lives at Red Earth Farms in northeast Missouri at the egalitarian sub-community homestead of Dandelion. She works part-time doing accounting for the Fellowship for Intentional Community and other area nonprofits. She is excited by the ideas of simple living, feminism, spirituality, permaculture, and open communication. She can be reached via email kim@ic.org.

Building Community and Learning from Failure

By Jenny Pickerill and Ruth Hayward

Many have dreamed of living in community but have struggled to know where to start. You can read all the books out there and still flounder. Both of us had explored the possibilities of starting a community, and feared that we were repeating the same mistakes others had already made. Despite a long tradition of eco-communities in Britain, there are relatively few successful examples, and among our friends many had experienced failure. More than that, most successful eco-communities are full of people who have endured multiple failures on their way to finally building a project that worked.

We didn't want all that experience and knowledge to go to waste so we started a small research project where Ruth interviewed members of groups either in the early stages of a project or who had decided to abandon an idea. We worked with five groups in Britain: two cohousing projects, a cooperative, an eco-community, and an emerging group. Talking about failure is not only emotionally difficult but stirs up all sorts of accusations about who, how, and why things didn't work out. As we don't want to make this personally difficult for those involved, we have had to anonymise who we are talking about. We want to share stories about three of these groups and the lessons they learnt about starting a community.

In the west of England people started meeting about the possibility of setting up a cohousing community in the region. There were lots and lots of meetings and various visits around the country to other communities and cohousing projects—like LILAC in Leeds—to learn from what worked. The group spent two years discussing and evolving their plans; they also had support from the local Council and a government agency who were both keen to facilitate community self-build projects in the region. The group had significant expertise and knowledge amongst them, including an architect, an academic who had worked with numerous communities worldwide, members of previous housing cooperatives, and a trained group facilitator. Many participants noted how much they had enjoyed meeting new people who shared their goals and politics, and the optimism of feeling like they could build a new way of living.

Yet after years of meetings little progress had been made. The main problem, it seems, was that the group was too open to new members and every time new people arrived the discussions would repeat. As one member argued: "It seems a shame but had there been a small core group with clear ideas, a possible location, and an agenda, a stronger group might have formed earlier and those with a different intention might have gone off and formed another group rather than too many disparate people hanging on together for too long." This lack of clarity about, for example, whether this was an urban or rural project and everyone being too polite to argue over points of potential disagreement eventually led to the group fizzling out. Rather than simply celebrating points of commonality it is also necessary to explore the detail and different perspectives around which people might diverge. It eventually emerged that some members wanted the group to be a support network, others an information sharing point, and others still a practical building project. While it can be hard to start a community with a clear vision, especially when you want to be inclusive and democratic, it was obvious in this instance that the lack of agreement on what the purpose was and the turnover of people involved used up the energy of the group. As one member suggests, "don't open the group out to all and sundry until you have a firm base of understanding in the core group...different people dipped in and out all the time and affected the dynamics."

Further south a group began with public meetings and quickly a large number of people were interested in building an urban cohousing community. They worked out a finance plan only to realise that although they all had money to invest they did not all have capital immediately available and they could not, therefore, purchase the land they had found. They connected with a Housing Association (a nongovernmental social housing provider) who was keen to work with the group and very quickly the land was purchased. It was at this stage, when the group was tied into working with this third party, that things got complicated. The group began to lose control of the project as the Housing Association began to act like a private developer. The quick success of the group also attracted more people, each with their own agenda. The Housing Association started, as one member described, "making conditions on the cohousing project" so that "finally we didn't feel we could [afford] the cost of each unit." Also, "we had all said we wanted intergenerational" but the Housing Association said it would be only "over 55s." It became unclear to the group what the final houses would cost. Eventually most of the original group withdrew from the project, with those remaining setting up a new group to continue working with the developer. The new group is going ahead and cohousing with a shared common house is due to be completed by January 2017.

Another group of people participated in several attempts at starting communities in the south west until just four of them decided to set up their own rural eco-community. The initial attempt, a cohousing community, suffered from a lack of clarity, as one of the group recalled: "it was very, very difficult to create...you can't really create a vision out of an amorphous group. I think it is better to have a smaller, better defined group than larger amorphous groups." There was a fear, by some of those involved, of limiting the group, and yet "they're going to have to learn to say no to some people," for practical reasons if nothing else. Having decided to leave that project, the four of them went on to work with another group that was working with a Community Land Trust. Much like the group in the south, once this outside agency got involved, the members began to lose control of the project. The group got sidelined as the Trust negotiated with planners in development jargon and "the whole thing was going so fast, we were running to keep up with it." Eventually people walked away from the project, disheartened at the way it had been co-opted by others with different agendas, feeling "exhausted...I'm going broke...I'm quite anxious." Now the group has purchased a small piece of land and is establishing a rural eco-community.

These stories share several common threads: from frustrations with ideas being co-opted by others, often external organisations, to the difficulty in balancing a clarity of vision with being inclusive. The entrepreneurial drive needed to push a project through to realisation requires determination and spirit and to grasp opportunities as they arise, but this very drive can take groups into alliances with those they ultimately do not wish to work with. Perhaps stereotypically for the British, some members felt that people were too polite to each other, not identifying points of disagreement until they became highly divisive.

> **Eventually people walked away from the project, disheartened at the way it had been co-opted by others with different agendas.**

Avoiding disagreements does not strengthen a group; rather, there needs to be space to discuss and resolve conflicts, with agreed conflict resolution processes This is especially important as the need for an entrepreneurial spirit to get a group off the ground means that groups are full of initiators, people with lots of skills and passion, who also tend to be strong characters. This is a good thing, and necessary, but it can result in quite serious personality clashes and differences in approach that can result in groups splitting up.

It is better to work out conflict resolution processes before being in conflict. While strong characters can help a group move forward, disruptive personalities can undermine the ability of people to work well together Without some ways in which to minimise disruption, people who you would like to keep in your group will walk away, probably without telling you why. If you are in a group that works well, then develop a membership policy to help it stay like that. Also, everyone involved could ask themselves periodically, "is my behaviour helping or hindering the process?"

Moreover, being inclusive is not about assuming everyone brings the same expertise and skills, and yet feelings of unease around certain members overplaying their expertise can lead to conflict. There are productive ways to acknowledge and identify different skills in complimentary ways and often naming them lessened people's anxiety about them.

People also have differing levels of knowledge around cohousing, which can become an issue when the group remains open to all, and new people have to catch up very quickly in order to be able to make an informed contribution to discussions—or else feel they don't have the knowledge to contribute and so drop out.

Although we focused on attempts at starting communities that did not quite work, many involved went on to be part of other successful projects. In getting members to reflect upon what worked and what didn't, many felt that they had actually been too willing to compromise too quickly. Finding land, funding, or a project partner (such as a Housing Association) had blinded some

While part of the point of community is to work in common with others, it is just as important to identify, discuss, and resolve points of difference.

to the risks involved. Balancing levels of pragmatism, and knowing what is worth fighting for and sticking to your principles was ultimately more important than progressing a project quickly.

There is a truism shared by those who have successfully built communities: building houses is the easy bit, building community requires all the work. The groups we worked with were emotional on their reflections of wasted hours and energy on projects that did not materialise, but none regretted their involvement. They had not just learnt personally from being involved but had hugely enjoyed the humour, laughter, and friendships made in the process. Not wanting to simply list how things can go wrong, we would like to end with 12 lessons that the groups we worked with identified as important in starting a community:

1. Start small: Starting with a small core of people helps build a firm base of communal understanding and enables key principles to be agreed more quickly.

2. Decide purpose early: A lack of a clear purpose wastes people's time and energy. Deciding early on that, for example, the project is for urban senior cohousing or rural low-impact development helps people decide if it is something worth investing in.

3. Decide decision-making processes early: Without clear governance structures through which it is clear how decisions are made, recorded, and checked, problems will emerge when people seek to challenge already-made decisions. If decision-making is unclear groups can end up in loops of repeating debates endlessly.

4. Create space for informal sharing and conversations: Taking the time to get to know each other is vital in building trust and in helping people decide if they want to live together. Sharing regular meals, beers, dancing, etc. enables one-to-one conversations and friendship building. Having fun is vital to a successful project and keeps people wanting to be involved. You could also develop a "friends group" through which people can get to know each other without necessarily formally committing to the group.

5. Good practice in meetings: Hold regular meetings in a neutral space and agree who will facilitate and who will take minutes. Most groups rotate the roles around different group members. Within meetings try out different communication techniques to ensure that everyone is heard. These practices should help prevent power struggles in a group and reduce misunderstandings or assumptions.

6. Find points of commonality and difference: While part of the point of community is to work in common with others, it is just as important to identify, discuss, and resolve points of difference. Only by articulating differences can their importance be understood.

7. Use structured activities to help group progress: Few people have time and energy to waste in endless meetings. Structured group activities (such as visioning exercises or sharing workshops), especially those that allow small-group work, enable people to see progress being made, their views included, and momentum sustained. These activities can be within regular business meetings or held separately; as long as sufficient time is given to them. However, it is hard to find group activities that are tailored to the needs of setting up communities, with groups having to invent their own each time. The sharing of activities that work is something the support networks could do to help emerging groups.

8. Develop a robust and clear system of communication: This might be a group email list or posting of minutes online, but it needs to be available to all.

9. Develop a standing agenda for meetings: This saves time and helps in consistency. This could include: greetings, icebreakers, apologies, minutes, matters arising, current issues, reports from the task groups, any other business. Some groups also end with a short period of silence.

10. Share case studies: By exploring other examples of community self-build projects and sharing information and knowledge, groups can reach a collective understanding of what housing they are interested in and the detailed issues involved. Be aware that all projects have their strengths and weaknesses, so look closely at more than one example.

11. Use external agencies, training, and expertise: Using third-party help brings additional knowledge and fresh perspectives to your project. Through this process you also build good support networks. You will also need, eventually, to have access to professionals, such as lawyers, preferably those who understand what you are trying to achieve.

12. Find an external project manager: Some of the most successful groups had an external project manager. Ideally you need someone who can help with people processes and someone else who understands the technicalities of building. Having someone external also means that the group does not become reliant on one individual; assuring that no one person is indispensable gives the group more resilience. ❧

Jenny Pickerill is Professor of Environmental Geography at Sheffield University, England, and lives in a self-built eco-house. Her new book Eco-Homes: People, Place and Politics, *about eco-communities worldwide, is published by Zed Books.*

Ruth Hayward is an environmental organiser, teacher, and researcher based in Newcastle Upon Tyne, England.

Reflections on Setting Up an Intentional Community

By Arjuna da Silva

Editor's Note: Every quarter, we post and distribute a "Call for Articles" describing the theme of the issue to be published a half-year later, and supplying prompts to stimulate the creation of articles. Here, an author from Earthaven Ecovillage in Black Mountain, North Carolina responds directly to some of those prompts:

NikiAnne Feinburg via Earthaven.org

What are your experiences starting or attempting to start a community?

I imagine founders are just as clueless as new parents about what their "offspring" will be like, even though they haven't a clue that they haven't a clue! Life is like that in general, but when what you're doing involves other people, including people you don't know yet, well…perhaps in terms of disappointments over time, it might be helpful to expect the best and plan for the worst!

I like to tell folks who come on the community tour that if they're thinking of starting a community, they should get their founders to commit to being together for a minimum of five or (better yet) 10 years, depending on how much prep they have to do to move in. Sure, no one can be forced to stick it out, just like a marriage, but one of the hardest things for me at Earthaven is that most of the original people with whom I committed to building my long-time home in community were gone within five years. Why? Here's my sound bite: visionaries aren't necessarily pioneers. Know your people and the odds!

What led you to start a new community rather than join an existing one?

This was the third or fourth time I was involved in the inception of an intentional community. Twice before they were rural, and short-lived (two years) but full of rich experience. Once it was an urban, guru-inspired intentional community connecting many households, much more autonomous in so many ways than sharing land or long-term worldly goals. It lasted a decade but was dependent on reasons other than being in that particular town. As locational focus shifted, the community dissipated.

Interestingly, I got involved with Earthaven's founding because two of my best friends from the urban community moved to the Asheville area and got involved in the founding group. We had often dreamed of starting a land-based community together, and we felt the combination of spiritually-focused folks among the founders, albeit from a variety of traditions, wrapped in a cloak of permaculture, had a good chance of making a valuable difference.

(And it does!)

What preparations are necessary or helpful for those aspiring to found a community?

Visit and interview others who lived through it! Learn how to dialog well in conflict situations; in fact, decide what kind of internal justice system you will have. Practice some sort of meditation (not necessarily sitting still). Never lose sight of the importance of celebration. Get superb legal advice, even if you have to look out of town, and be willing to pay for it!

What resources have been helpful to you in starting a new community?

Having tried many times before. Being with a brilliant group of people in the beginning, particularly folks familiar with community among the founders. Permaculture trainers and trainings brought confidence to a land-based project, and the spirit of adventure allowed us to experiment with so much that was new to us: consensus, solar technology, natural building…. Connection with and through the FIC was especially beneficial early on.

What advice or guidance would you have for others starting a community?

All of the above. Don't overdo the idealism!

What do you wish you'd known when you began that you know now?

More about the legal implications of land ownership in our area. How to do better new member orientation and education. 🐾

Arjuna da Silva helped found Earthaven (see www.earthaven.org) 21 years ago and watched this dynamic ecovillage become something quite different than she had thought was being built, thus learning that while the satisfaction of your own vision may not be as important as the survival of your offspring, the vision itself can live on, evolve, and look for fertile ground. These days she finds it in and beyond Earthaven, practicing and demonstrating facilitation of Restorative Circles, a restorative justice community dialog process on the long arc to freedom.

The Rocky Road
TO ROCKY CORNER COHOUSING

By Marie Pulito

Rocky Corner will be the first cohousing community to be built in Connecticut. That seems strange, considering how many cohousing neighborhoods exist in New England. Being the first in our state has presented unique challenges. Dealing with those challenges makes for a good story, but it's the more common challenges that we've really learned from and that other cohousing communities can learn from.

Key decisions and actions over the past few years have helped us in creating our new community. When we started meeting back in 2007, we worked hard on becoming a cohesive, fair-minded group. We found guidance in Diana Leafe Christian's book *Creating a Life Together*. We used activities from her book and from *Heart and Hands*, by Shari Leach, to learn more about each other. We did our best to hold meetings where all were encouraged to participate. Having members who were Quakers and Unitarians was helpful at first. But those early meetings never had agendas or designated facilitators.

Hearing that many cohousing groups used consensus to make decisions, we hired C.T. Butler, who offered training in formal consensus, based on his book *On Conflict and Consensus*. We rented a local B&B and spent a full weekend with C.T. learning directly from him. He taught us the process of formal consensus and how to base decisions on our shared values. More important, we learned from C.T. how to hold a meeting. He demonstrated and had us practice how to create an agenda and how to facilitate a meeting. This is a process we still use.

Formal consensus was not easy. We realized early on that we needed a written statement of our shared values to direct our consensus decision-making. We knew that people could block decisions if any proposal conflicted with our values. But we had never decided as a group what our common values were. We generally knew that we were all looking for lives that were more sustainable, energy-wise and community-wise. In retrospect, it's not surprising that it took us more than a year to write our vision statement. It was difficult to get a group of 10-plus people to agree on a statement because we had different dreams for our cohousing neighborhood. But on top of that problem, how does a group agree on proposed values when all consented decisions are supposed to be based on values already agreed upon? What a crazy Catch-22! After many versions and much wordsmithing, we have our vision in a document that has helped us attract more people (see rockycorner.org/our-vision).

I'm sorry to say that having a written vision statement and practicing formal consensus did not solve our internal conflicts. Now that most of us had invested money and years of hard work into this project, tempers often flared and feelings were hurt during meetings. We were still struggling with the work needing to be done. Which of us could do this work? Which of us knew how? How do we buy land together? Do we incorporate? How do we protect our investments and assets? Were there loans or grants available that could help us?

These questions led us to our next key decision—hiring a housing consultant. His name is David Berto, and his company, Housing Enterprises, Inc., is here in Connecticut. We interviewed a few people but David seemed perfect right from the start. We love him and he loves our project, as well. With nearly 35 years of experience helping organizations

Rendering of construction plan.

vision statement first, then values then consensus building.

build affordable housing, David had never worked on cohousing. He immediately understood what we were doing and what we wanted. He understood how much we needed to be a part of the process of getting our neighborhood built. Without Housing Enterprises, we can honestly say we would have given up. With his help we have found a property, designed the neighborhood with a nationally known local architect (see centerbrook.com), worked with lawyers to get zoning approvals, written condominium documents, obtained loans for the pre-development expenses, and applied for (and won!) a Connecticut Department of Housing affordable housing grant to subsidize the prices of 13 of our 30 homes. He has done all of this while fully respecting our vision and our ways of making decisions.

The decision that I personally believe has helped us the most has been adopting dynamic governance as our decision-making and organizational model. Again, we wanted to learn directly from the experts. Our first training was run by John Buck, who was instrumental in bringing sociocracy to the United States. He and Sharon Villines wrote *We the People: Consenting to a Deeper Democracy*. Jerry Koch-Gonzalez, from Pioneer Valley Cohousing, and Diana Leafe Christian, from Earthaven Ecovillage, assisted with the training. We invited other cohousing communities to join us and had participants from Nubanusit, Belfast, Burlington, Pioneer Valley, Cornerstone, and Legacy Farms. Since that weekend training in January 2012, we have had a follow-up workshop with Jerry Koch-Gonzalez and one with Diana Leafe Christian. We have learned that we need ongoing training.

Dynamic governance has helped us organize committees in a way that we were never able to achieve under formal consensus. Our general circle, consisting of leaders and delegates from all our committees, meets twice a month to review committee progress, consider proposals that affect the whole community, and select leaders for new or existing committees when needed. By using the selection process we learned from John Buck (which we all seem to love, by the way), we have ensured our ability to choose effective leaders. The general circle consents to the vision, mission, aims, and authority (VMAA) for each committee. This basic charter clarifies what the committees are charged with and what they can do under their own authority.

We have stopped using formal consensus and now make decisions using the consent model we learned from our dynamic governance teachers. The two are similar, and we still bless C.T. Butler for all we learned from him. Consent decisions are made with a planned time for reevaluation. "Good enough for now, safe enough to try" is usually said aloud by at least one of us whenever we consent to a new proposal. We have been repeatedly surprised how well this decision-making process has worked for us even for difficult matters like deciding on our pet policy and our firearms policy.

I personally place so much value on dynamic governance that I have become critical of every other organization in my life. The redundancy of work done in the department where I am employed is horrendous. The congregational meetings of my Unitarian society, which are run using Robert's Rules of Orders, make me cringe. The annual town meetings in my small New England town, where the budget is "discussed," fall far short. Where is the equivalence of voice, the power of many minds coming together to find a solution to a problem? *I want every organization in the world to convert to dynamic governance.* I must admit, however, that the energy needed to get Rocky Corner built leaves us with little energy to bring conversion to others. This article is the closest to spreading the word that we can manage right now.

Just like formal consensus, dynamic governance is not easy. We have not been good at timely evaluations. We work so diligently at getting our neighborhood built that there are some processes we have not found time for. We struggled at the start just to consent to the terms we wanted to use: dynamic governance vs. sociocracy, committees vs. circles. Every committee, every leader and delegate, has to stay focused on correct practice. Otherwise, members of Rocky Corner don't feel fairly treated, don't feel heard. Correct process builds respect. As Diana Leafe Christian taught us: Plan, do, measure...and trust will follow.

I am one of those who believe that cohousing can save the world, one neighborhood at a time. Working toward a built neighborhood has taught us how important good will and collaboration can be to building relationships and community.

So if you skipped ahead to this last paragraph, that's OK, because here is the big advice:

• If you are a newly forming cohousing group, I highly recommend that you look into hiring a housing consultant.

• If you are a cohousing group at any stage of existence, discuss your common values and write your vision document.

• Learn how to run a good meeting with a planned agenda and skilled facilitation.

• **Most of all, adopt dynamic governance to organize the ongoing work you need to do and to make good decisions that are safe and smart and build trust.** 🍂

Raised in suburbia, in love with rural living near a small city, Marie Pulito is proud to be a long-time active member of the first cohousing being built in Connecticut on the outskirts of New Haven (see www.rockycorner.org). She works as a lactation nurse specialist at Yale-New Haven Hospital. She is looking forward to a shorter commute to work, a farm right outside her door, a small energy-efficient home, and neighbors she knows well.

Land.

Leaps of Faith

By Rebecca Reid

I t all started three years ago when we took a leap of faith. It was one of those moments when you knew your parents would not have approved, but you were going to do it anyway. Except that we were in our late 60s, and our leap was out of a cohousing community and into a duplex farmhouse in need of renovation on a nine acre farm, to live with a young family with two small children.

The Story

My husband Michael and I were living in Pioneer Valley Cohousing Community in Amherst, Massachusetts with 31 other families. I was a founding member, deeply entrenched in the community. We were pretty happy with our situation there. I thought I was at the culmination of a life in search of community and had finally found one where I could live out the rest of my days. I was born into a Quaker family, went to a Quaker school that was a cooperative farm, lived in cooperative houses most of my adult life, and worked in a consensus-run nonprofit organization. The balance of public and private in cohousing seemed ideal: I could be part of a healthy community and have my own private (read clean) kitchen. I believed (and still do believe) that consensus decision-making is an elegant, inclusive, and powerful way for human beings to relate to each other.

Then a young pregnant couple with a small child moved into the unit across the path as temporary renters, considering membership. We became fast friends as we discovered how much we had in common in spite of being of different generations. We had the kind of personalities that work together well, and we enjoyed each other's company. We respected each other's skills, which were many. We all valued simplicity, good work, and living as lightly as possible. We all wanted to grow as much of our own food as we could and find local sources for the rest, and to raise animals for meat and milk. They wanted to raise their children to be connected to the land and to where their food comes from. Because of my relationship with this new family, I began to be aware of what I was missing at Pioneer Valley: close connections based on deep common values and common purpose, and I wanted a farm. It gradually became clear that Pioneer Valley Cohousing was not the place to begin. There was not enough land for all of the uses the community had in mind, and there was considerable resistance to farming and farm animals.

It wasn't easy to do. I was still attached to the idea of cohousing, and a little afraid to leave such a safe environment on the cusp of my old age. At some point I realized that to be in a small close community with people who love me was much safer than the idea that "someone" in cohousing would step in if I needed help. We talked about starting a new, smaller cohousing community, but abandoned the idea because of the time it would take, and the difficulty of finding other members. We decided to look for land with living space for both families.

A two-family house with nine acres and two barns came on the market, and without looking back, we leaped off into the unknown. We spent six months doing a deep energy retrofit, creating an energy efficient house from scratch out of a series of sheds in the rear for the other family, remodeling and insulating the large old colonial front house for us. We set aside rooms that would always be owned in common: a large pantry

We started small with chickens, a small garden, a hedgerow, and the beginnings of an orchard, and gradually expanded to include two hoop houses for season extension, a small herd of goats, more gardens, and lots of projects in the planning stages.

We were hoping for another family to join us, but knew that they had to be kindred spirits, not just people wanting to farm. A year and a half into our adventure, another young couple, friends of our farm-mates, bought a little house right across the road from us and joined us as equal partners in the farm. We became a community of six adults and three children, now ranging in age from two to 71. We made conscious effort to integrate the new family, since they were coming in after we had established ourselves, and their house was not connected the way our houses were. We wanted to be sure that we broke down any barriers before they arose. It is still more difficult to include them, since so many conversations happen naturally at random times during the day as we wander in and out of each other's houses, but we have regular farm meetings after dinner once a week to make sure to catch each other up on our lives and farm business.

> ## I realized that to be in a small close community with people who love me was much safer than the idea that "someone" in cohousing would step in if I needed help.

on the first floor between the two kitchens and a guest room on the second floor and a common front porch. During the entire renovation, we never had an argument. Plenty of decisions, some disagreements, but all peaceful. It still felt totally right.

We moved in in June of 2012 with great ideas. A permaculture farm, with gardens, goats, chickens, meat chickens, turkeys, pigs, a pond, hedgerows, rainwater system, compost system, sugarbush. We designated an area around three sides to go wild and provide habitat for local flora and fauna.

We all share the work of the farm, but each of us has an area we are most drawn to and know most about. I am a longtime gardener; Seth devises systems, builds and fixes things, and loves the goats. Jason knows all about engines, and loves the garden as much as the animals. Jess is my garden buddy. Bethany manages the orchard. Michael is the grease that makes it all flow smoothly by running errands and helping with any manual labor that needs doing. The children, being very social creatures, love to help out and are learning real-world skills. Since many of our projects are new to us, we are constantly searching out information and skills and we research in our area of expertise and then share it. We have work days, usually a half day, when we all work together on some project. Recently we reroofed a portion of one of the barns in preparation for solar panels. We have work days to plant the garden and to prepare it for winter, to tend the orchard, to get in the hay. We struggle, however, with getting it all done, as you might imagine. Four of us have full-time jobs, but two are teachers and have the summer off. Michael and I are retired, and have lots of time, but limited energy. We are all constantly excited about starting new projects and have to rein ourselves in with practical considerations.

Rebecca Reid

Photos courtesy of Rebecca Reid

Alina and Seth.

We don't sell our produce, but hope only to feed ourselves as sustainably as possible. We are not aiming for self-sufficiency. We believe that sustainability can't be achieved without the wider community. We are cultivating interconnections, first among our three generations, then outward to neighboring farms, farms in our watershed, and to local and regional businesses. Barter and sharing labor are an integral part of our philosophy: we share, lend, and trade with several nearby farms for manure, seeds, tools, equipment, labor, and produce that we don't grow. We participate in Valley Time Trade (a local labor/barter system). A neighbor pastured his geese and ducks on our land, fertilizing our pasture, and gave us some meat in return, and two geese to guard our chickens. We traded two oil tanks left from the renovation for manure from the horse farm nearby, spread by a neighbor with access to a manure spreader. We save and share seeds. We hope to create a web of interconnections that will be resilient in what may be difficult times to come.

Our finances are separate, but we have a farm account that we all contribute to every month, which pays for the things that we buy in common: fencing, animal feed, tools and hardware, fuel for the tractor and mowers, supplies of various kinds. Bulk food we pay for as we go, splitting the cost. We transformed the ownership of the duplex house from co-ownership to condominium ownership, in a nod to the fact that one or the other (probably us) will one day leave and need to sell. Jess and Jason own the house across the street, and we are working to find some legal arrangement that recognizes their commitment to the farm.

The door between the houses in the duplex is always open, unless there is a specific reason. We eat dinner together almost every night, unless one family needs solo family time, or someone has guests and wants quiet dinner conversation. There is no meals schedule, no payment for meals; generally someone will come up with an idea for dinner, and tell the rest by email in the morning and serve it up at night. Often others will contribute some side dish to the meal. The cost of food evens out over time, especially since we grow most of our food and buy together in bulk what we can't produce. My husband and I have the largest dining table, and the biggest space, so dinners usually happen in our house, the downstairs of which functions somewhat like a common house in cohousing—everyone is free to walk in any time. I come home

sometimes to cheery small voices greeting me from my living room. When I get up in the morning, small footsteps run through the pantry that connects the houses and it is Case, five years old, with his cheerful and charming smile come to see if I am ready to play. Alina, seven, had a little desk in my study for art projects, until she outgrew it. Alina and Lyla, who is now two, have a big/little sister relationship that is very sweet to see.

The kids are learning all about food, and acquiring a sense of place that is rare in the world. They are also seeing adults collaborate and work through problems.

I asked Alina what was the best thing about being a kid here. She replied that because we are on a farm, there is always something good to do, and sometimes kids can do things that grownups can't do, like milk the goat with little teats. The kids are learning all about food, and are acquiring a sense of place that is rare in the world. They are seeing adults collaborate and work through problems. They have a chance to learn to use tools and be part of a working team, and to develop confidence and strength.

Seth and Case building the chicken house.

Alina.

What Makes It Work?

I also asked Alina what makes the farm work. She said (not in these words) that we know each other very well, we generously share things without feeling territorial, we don't keep score, we all work together as a team, and we talk to each other about important things at dinner. She's right. Since we are a small community we can get to know each other in depth. We all believe that community rests on generosity, communication, and openness. Because we are so small, and know each other so well, accountability is built in—there is no anonymity. If we agree on a decision, it is because everyone has thought about it, talked about it, and genuinely agrees to uphold it. If we need to change our minds and do something different, we can easily do that. We have no disgruntled minority. We give each other the benefit of the doubt, knowing that we are all doing the best we can because we are all committed to our adventure.

Since our farm mates are younger than our children, it might have been easy to treat them like children and to be constantly aware of the age differences, and for them to see us as parent figures. But somehow we don't think of them as anything but farm mates, with their own unique skills and personalities. They don't see us as parents, but respect us instead on our own merits. To the children we are essentially surrogate grandparents, and when the real grandparents come, we take a back seat.

Our struggles center around communication—with three small children and four jobs, it is difficult to find time to talk over all of the things that we need to, both farm business and interpersonal issues when they arise. For the same reason, the time line of many projects is not what we hoped, and that sometimes causes tension. Our priorities are not always the same. Why are you cleaning the barn when the tomatoes need to be staked? Should we get pigs or meat chickens next year, or just do a better job with what we are already doing? What can we realistically expect to be able to do? *values*

We also struggle with the finer points of some of our values and with our attitudes toward money: a riding mower would enable us to spend less time mowing and more time growing, but it uses fossil fuels and emits pollution. Is it better to hay early for the sake of the health of the hayfield, or do we wait until the ground-nesting birds are gone? When there is not enough time, what is it ok to let go? Do we buy what we need, or try first to make or borrow it? How strictly do we try to vote with our money? Do we buy it from the big box store because it is cheaper and available sooner, or support the local hardware store no matter what?

We do manage to navigate these more perilous waters with the spirit of community as our guide. Our relationships and connections with each other are more important than our differences of opinion. We would rather have a happy community than be right. We find solutions to our problems that work for everyone because if we win only individually, we lose as a community.

We were incredibly lucky to find the right people and the right land, at a time in our lives when we could take advantage of the opportunity. I think it would be very difficult to set out to create something similar with only the idea and the desire. But what is possible is what I did: Take time to find and build your community. Nurture your connections. When you find it, don't let it get away; leap into it and give it your whole heart.

I wake up in the morning to the sun streaming in the east window, making the hallway glow. I hear Seth's and Jason's voices in the barn, and the soft bleating of the goats. I hear children's laughter downstairs; I smell coffee and hear the rattling of dishes as someone enters our kitchen to put last night's supper dishes away. I am filled with gratitude every day, and I have only one question: What do you do when you have everything you've always wanted? ❧

Rebecca Reid is a grandmother, a farmer, and a photographer who thinks that community is the answer, and has been trying to prove it for years. She lives in Leverett, Massachusetts with her chosen family, and is very happy.

Kids reading.

Living in a Multigeneration Household:
HAVEN OR HELL?

By Maril Crabtree

A few years ago, my husband and I moved from our down-sized 1200 square-foot townhouse with no outdoor maintenance to a five-bedroom, three-and-a-half-bath suburban home surrounded by green lawns, decks, and leaf-shedding trees.

No, we didn't have to acquire new furniture or a new lawnmower. We chose the house along with four other "new" household members: our son and daughter-in-law, both in their 40s, and our two teenage grandchildren.

Heart arrhythmias that made stairs difficult for me started the whole conversation. Added to that was the fact that Jim, Tiffany, Jamie, and Jessica yearned for a bigger house with a little more room for everyone. The two families lived just a block apart when one day my son said, "Why don't we sell both our homes and buy a house where we can all live together?"

Many of our friends shook their heads.

"Sounds like a nice idea, but I don't think I could ever live in the same house with my children," they said. They cited personality conflicts, too much noise, and different lifestyles as the big stumbling blocks.

Some of Jim and Tiffany's friends were having similar reactions.

"What happens when your parents start giving you advice about how often to clean the kitchen or take out the garbage?" one said.

Even the grandkids' friends expressed doubt.

"Won't it be like living with two sets of parents? Yuck!"

All valid objections. The six of us sat down one evening to discuss the idea seriously. Each of us in turn spoke about doubts, fears, and hesitations.

"I need a certain amount of privacy."

"Will I be able to watch my favorite TV shows?"

"Will we still be able to entertain our own friends?"

Then we looked at the positives.

"There'll be more people to share the chores with."

"By combining households both families can share resources and maybe save some money."

"The dog won't be so lonesome during the day."

"I won't always have to be the one to go to the grocery store."

We decided to look for a house that might fit our needs. There were some things we weren't willing to compromise on: the grandkids wanted to stay in the same school district; both couples wanted a master bedroom suite with their own bathroom; my son wanted plenty of deck space for his barbecuing and grilling passions.

Astonishingly, the first house we looked at, an older home that had been renovated and updated, fit all those needs and more. The main floor had a large kitchen and dining area with floor to ceiling windows that looked out on a large deck. We had a master bedroom suite, another room that we could use as a sitting room with our own TV, and a guest bedroom and bath. Upstairs was another master bedroom suite and a room Tiffany could use for her home office. Downstairs, a finished basement beckoned as a teen hangout with space for a lounge area and two bedrooms.

Seven years later, we're all still happily living together, although life has continued to change. Jessica has finished college and moved to another city for graduate school, so she'll be home only during holidays. Jamie is also away from home at college, and he's living full-time in another city for residency purposes.

The house seems much emptier without the grandkids. I have as much quiet writing time as I could possibly want, with only Stevie, our dog, to keep me company on many weekdays.

What are the key ingredients for our success? Simple things like communication and respect go a long way. We respect differences in lifestyle preferences and honor the need for privacy. Just because we

(continued on p. 77)

LIVING IN A MULTIGENERATION HOUSEHOLD: HAVEN OR HELL?

(continued from p. 51)

live together doesn't mean we have to eat every meal together or like the same movies. (We made sure to subscribe to a TV cable company with enough room—and cable boxes—for all of our recording preferences!) We let others know what our needs are with respect to the use of common appliances like the washer and dryer. And we have ample room to spread out.

Having also lived in community households with nonfamily members, I think it helps to have basic values and goals in common, such as resource-sharing and living with environmental awareness. But if different values do emerge, it's more important to understand one another than to aim at changing one another. If compromise is needed, it often happens more readily in an environment of love, trust, and acceptance.

It helps to have a little training in, for instance, making "I" statements that communicate as factually and clearly as possible. "I feel angry and upset when I don't get enough sleep." "I dislike loud noises early in the morning." It takes some practice to communicate like this all or most of the time. But it pays off in the long run.

Perhaps most of all, it helps to be living with people you genuinely *like*. Even if Tiffany weren't my daughter-in-law, my heart would lift when I heard the sound of her car in the driveway. Even if Jim weren't my son, I'd look forward to hearing about his day's adventures practicing law or his latest photography coup. They're wonderful human beings and pretty easy to live with. *And* they don't expect me to do the yard work! (I try to make it up to them in other ways.)

Those casual moments when we're all making a meal together or watching an exciting baseball game are times when we all reap the benefits of sharing a home together. The bonus is knowing that we can also live out our values of resource-sharing and give each other support when it's needed.

Maril Crabtree is a writer and editor who has lived in several forms of intentional community in Kansas City. For more information, go to www.marilcrabtree.com.

Reflecting on a Quarter Century
of O.U.R. History

By Brandy Gallagher

Photos courtesy of O.U.R.

In the 25 years of O.U.R. (One United Resource), first as an urban intentional community house with city-based projects, and then as O.U.R. Ecovillage, a 25 acre Sustainable Living Demonstration Site and Education Centre on Vancouver Island, British Columbia, we've learned much about how community shows up in the wider world. We are now known globally for our work in regulatory reform and legitimate development of ecological design, and yet there is still so far to go in transforming the notions of what "cooperative culture" might mean. That transformation will require all of us, and so we have become evermore inclusive in our approach to change-making.

Over 17 summers as a living research project, we have had the privilege of hosting some of the top sustainability experts in all fields: local and international teachers, facilitators, community development experts, natural builders, permaculturalists, and many professionals from key stakeholder industries (e.g., waste, energy, and regulatory systems). And yet the challenge of incorporating all perspectives is still a dance.

Flashback: imagine the early days of working with all levels of government, business, and academia in your local community. What would the neighbours say if you proposed creating an ecovillage in their local area? For O.U.R. Ecovillage we imagined it would be a "shoe-in" to bring a green project home to a community where most of us were from. And yet, the reception was not what we imagined. In 1999, not only did local folks never utter the word "permaculture" (and had no construct to relate to what we were describing), many never even stated the term "sustainable." A fast track to being ignored or shunned is to use language that is not used as common culture, with no one relating to your dialect.

Moreover your experience might be that at educational events, folks will stand two steps back from your information table and wonder if you are safe to interact with because 1) you are a "hippie commune" (and goodness knows, there goes the neighbourhood, given that hippie folk drive down the price of your Real Estate and make big messes); or 2) everyone knows what you really mean by the "Green Economy" in your educational presentations, especially in British Columbia, and you are faced with being seen as potentially being a "grow operation"; or 3) clearly if you describe yourselves as an altruistic organization, you might be a *cult!* (given the assumption that anyone who does something for nothing must be hiding something—and is probably a religious order of folks who are trying to persuade others that they could organize around a seemingly dysfunctional model of living in service to humanity).

Despite these obstacles, the O.U.R. team persisted, and 10,000 folks per year are now involved in our efforts, through visiting, living, working, learning, and/or collaborating together with us. We've experienced a steep learning curve ourselves. Any model of social experimentation attempting to move people from mainstream consumer culture to alternative culture is going to awaken conflict in its participants and visitors. It is not easy to persuade either the Next Generation or the mainstream generation who are now leaning into intentional communities and the ecovillage movement to give up the culture of addiction which is prevalent in the larger world.

We continue to promote change, social justice, and community development with a range of K-12 programs and alliances with 11 universities and colleges, with business and corporate interests, and with stakeholders we would never have imagined in our wildest dreams when we started 25 years ago. Neighbours are buying food box programs and learning about the the nature of organic farms which are intercultural, intergenerational, and interfaith. We have a basic commitment to being all-inclusive folks who wish to build unity in our community. One of our messages is: we all can become champions of what we believe in.

In our early days, we were radical changemakers. These days, we no longer "act now and ask for permission later." We open ourselves to all possibilities of partnerships, not just "the likely suspects"—we invite everyone possible to the table. It is socially just and practical to craft a team of invested players who wish to see real-life change manifested. We are no longer "eco-kooks"; we are "eco-consultants"; and the process of change continues. ❧

Brandy Gallagher works with Sustainable Community Solutions Consulting (SC2). She is also Education and Outreach Coordinator of O.U.R. Ecovillage (www.ourecovillage.org), a 25 acre sustainable living permaculture demonstration site, education center, and learning community on Vancouver Island, British Columbia.

KINDLING NEW COMMUNITY:
Village Hearth Cohousing

By Pat McAulay

Listening to the steady drum of rain on the roof as I write, I'm reminded of our first big tabling event: North Carolina Pride. Thankfully, in anticipation of fall sunshine and high humidity, we'd reserved a spot under a big tent. That day, the rain was mostly gentle but persistent, making the grounds a soggy mess. But my optimistic side likes to say that we joined 10,000 of our closest friends that day to celebrate Pride. We had a good day, talking to a steady stream of interested folks who took this flyer, that card, this brochure, and did or didn't sign up for our email list. As importantly, two of our members joined us and turned out to be formidable marketers!

My wife, Margaret, and I are the "burning souls" behind Village Hearth Cohousing. We're gathering with LGBTs, friends, and allies to create a caring community in Durham, North Carolina, with the intention to age in place in a community of "good neighbors." Our vision has followed a long path originating 15 or more years ago with long weekends and, eventually, weeks at the beach. We fell in love with the sound of women laughing, the aroma of brewing coffee, the sight of souls braving the ocean currents in November. We thought we wanted to create the ODH (Old Dykes Home): what turned out to be a shared housing concept. When our gang started to retire, we faced the reality of *actually living together under one roof permanently*, as well as the standard reply, "I'm going to stay in my home until I can't." That forced us to seek out other solutions. Having the close-knit community with a balance of privacy in cohousing is where we landed.

We read the cohousing canon, Coho/US, COMMUNITIES, the cohousing listserv, and we knew that we were blessed with several existing communities in our area. Well, let's figure out which one we want to move to. Oh, wait! We're talking about this being the last home we move to. That means we need the community to be totally accessible and visitable. What good is an accessible home if one is kept prisoner there by not being able to visit neighbors or go to the Common House? Wait! We don't need a second story; we won't be able to do the stairs. Wait! We already live in an apartment building with an elevator that doesn't work when the power goes out. Wait! We don't want to be so far from downtown Durham that we'll choose to stay home because the drive is too far. Wait! I need some green space. Wait! What? Well, hell; we're going to have to build our own community.

We chewed on that concept for awhile. I spied the Boulder regional cohousing conference, Cohousing: The Good, the Bad, and the Ugly happening in September 2014. I convinced Margaret that we needed to hear these realities of cohousing and then could make a decision about moving forward to create community or give up the idea and figure out where else to build or buy in Durham. So, we drove to Boulder, where we were struck by the golden glow of the aspen. The conference was hosted by three communities, including a senior community, Silver Sage, and was well-attended with around 90 participants. Succinctly, the best thing about cohousing is the people, and the worst thing about cohousing is the people. We came away fired up and ready to start. On our way home, we toured three additional senior cohousing communities: Valverde Commons in Taos, Sand River in Santa Fe, and Oakcreek in Stillwater, Oklahoma. Cohousers are generous people and want to spread the good news, so we spent several hours among the three communities and learned a lot. But we fell in love with the McCamant & Durrett single-story attached cottage design of Oakcreek, and that community became our touchstone.

Next we had to figure out who we wanted in our community. We knew we wanted an adult-centered community—not that we wouldn't welcome the occasional visiting grandchild, but we don't have children and don't want to live among them. The complexities of ownership structure steered us away from saying women only or lesbian only, as the Old Dykes Home would have been. We decided we want to be around people who have had a

similar path. We know that just because one is gay or lesbian doesn't mean we'll be fast friends, but we want to be around people who can relate to our past: not having any role models and thinking there was something wrong with us; struggling to come out again and again and again to oneself, one's best friend, one's parents, one's coworkers, one's faith community; experiencing discrimination and being marginalized by society; maybe even being the victim of a hate crime. With this shared experience, we hope we'll have a basis for coming together in community. We're welcoming friends and allies to join us—anyone who has witnessed our paths and supported us throughout—and, frankly, we can't exactly check sexual preference IDs at the door.

At the Boulder conference, we heard from at least three different communities from the US and Canada that they strug-

Margaret and Pat celebrate on the land after closing. Holding the boundary survey, Land Day 8/28/15!

Paul J. Stinson

Pat McAulay

Fifty-five people attended Katie's public presentation—half of whom we'd never met before!

Village Hearth Cohousing

ohousing

for LGBTs, friends, and allies

Welcome home

NC Pride. Margaret's ready for the 10,000+ who braved the rain.

Long winding road leads back to a secluded area where we'll build.

Terri Murphy

gled to get going and keep going because members were sure they could save money by foregoing the "experts." They related that as soon as they brought in a professional, the project began to move along and move in is slated for "_____." With that level of sharing, we decided to bring in the experts as soon as we hit a snag. We want to do this as fast as possible and not have any expensive missteps along the way. The first bump in the road was the water department referring me to a 232-page document to figure out what size sewer pipe and water lines I might need for this 22-30 unit development. Luckily, the 2015 national cohousing conference was coming up right in our home town! There we connected with Katie McCamant of CoHousing Solutions and Chuck Durrett of McCamant & Durrett Architects, who worked with Oakcreek, and they agreed to provide consulting to our group.

We've been holding Outreach meetings since April 2015, and we had a small group bonding over the concept. We cajoled Katie into providing a preliminary home price, and half our group had to drop out because of anticipated cost. This was a very difficult blow for Margaret and me: we'd spent months developing and deepening relationships, and we really *liked* the people we'd gathered. The hard facts are that we can't build what we want where we want it and come in at a comparable market price. The common amenities and land, the higher grade sustainable materials and better than standard fixtures, the things that are really important to us just cannot be produced at a price comparable to a development of 300 homes. We expect energy savings with our attached homes built well with proven materials. We must learn to communicate the value of community—the people—to ameliorate the shock of the initial investment. We need more than just our vision and a few pictures of Oakcreek.

"More" means land. We looked for land for months. Dozens of MLS listings daily, trying to figure out the zoning, the watershed, the buffer, the "this," the "that" from the GIS maps. Printing maps, enlarging maps and printing them and taping them together. Killing trees left and right to get the right view to decipher the alphabet soup that would add up to the right piece of land. With a house; without a house? Finally a word from Chuck at the conference, "It doesn't matter if there's a house on the property or not. We'll figure out the best way to use the land either way." Generous Ann Arbor folks told us on a visit there to look for commercial, office, or industrial land with a land broker. We tried that on our own, and finally were just about to get hooked up with a land broker...then the MLS listing came through. Fifteen-plus acres, relatively flat (tough to find in Durham), next to a subdivision with city water and sewer, less than 20 minutes to downtown, zoned at two dwellings/acre, but with future land use at four dwellings/acre. City water guy said, "Yeah." City planning guy said, "Yeah, with x, y, and z, it's doable." Price well under $200,000. After a few days of going back and forth with the owners and getting nervous about a builder sniffing around, we jumped with a full price offer to close in 10 days. Since the land appears to have been underpriced, we're pretty sure we could turn around and sell it if it isn't right for the project. Now we had the motivation to move forward and something to "sell."

Must gather more people. We'll talk to anyone, anywhere, about cohousing and what we're doing. More Outreach meetings, individual meetings, a "friend" sponsorship for the big arts festival, materials to pass out at the Gay and Lesbian Film Festival, an ad in the Pride guide, tabling at Pride. Then, a connection to a couple we used to know casually, an invitation to join them for a common meal in their cohousing community, a couple we don't know at the table who had heard about us from "so-and-so": you know "so-and-so," don't you? No, we don't. Finally, evidence that the word has spread beyond friends and friends of friends. We have a member in Athens, Georgia; a couple in Virginia. We're just thinking about dipping our toes into national advertising. This week we've had inquiries from Asheville, North Carolina, and Golden, Colorado. Coho/US, Katie, and Chuck have all promoted us to their mailing lists. One sweet man from Tennessee mailed us a box of cohousing books since he'll never be able to talk his partner into it. A lot of people are interested in the concept, but we find that most people think they don't need to do it now.

When Katie and Chuck brought cohousing from Denmark in the 1980s, they also brought along a class for elders about successful aging known here as "Study Group I." Chuck says we need to get people out of denial. It's tough. The Department on Aging person who worked with me to set up the class at the senior center said, "Oh, don't call it Senior Cohousing: Successful Aging [which is what the book is called]. Successful aging has the connotation of climbing mountains and zip lining. We need another term to describe what most people do. Something with 'thriving' maybe." While I appreciate that she's trying to find terminology that works, I find it very frustrating that we can't use the words "senior," "elder," "aging," "aging in place," etc. We don't "die," we "pass" or are "not here anymore." Walking this terminology minefield is an impossible task. We can't wait until someone invents a new word to call one who is older. At any rate, the 10-week class was wildly successful, precisely because no one feels safe to talk about aging in any other setting. The course led us right up to this last weekend when Katie came to town.

All the while the course was going on, we marketed Katie's visit. She came to do our first weekend workshop with us, but also planned a public presentation on senior cohousing. (Back to, "What do we call it???") We did paid ads and press releases, resulting in a lengthy article in the real estate section of the newspaper. Fifty-five people attended, and we had never seen at least half of them! None decided to join us for the weekend workshop, but the seed is planted. This is a slow-growth forest, and yet, look how far we've come. Katie led us in an informative weekend explaining the timeline, the budget, what impacts both, best practices of other communities, walked us through our shared values, and sent us on our way with committee assignments. We come together again tomorrow, and we're waiting with bated breath to see who's in and who's leaving us this time. It will be hard if it's the latter, but we believe in our project, we're riding some good momentum, and, after hearing Katie talk about living in cohousing, we understand even better now just why we want to live in community. ❧

> ## We believe in our project, we're riding some good momentum, and we understand even better now just why we want to live in community.

Pat McAulay loves her adopted home of Durham, North Carolina, and can't wait to get settled into Village Hearth Cohousing with her wife, Margaret. They are both looking forward to fun and new experiences while living in community, as well as being and having good neighbors. Pat can be reached at naturepat@aol.com, and you can follow Village Hearth Cohousing on Facebook, Meetup, and on their website, www.VillageHearthCohousing.com.

Looking back from the rise.

Terri Murphy

YARROW ECOVILLAGE:
Cohousing as a Building Block to the Ecovillage

By Charles Durrett and Katie McCamant

Following the first cohousing community in the United States, Muir Commons in Davis, California, cohousing has not only continued to expand throughout the US and Canada, it has also become a model for other housing types (senior housing, nonprofit affordable housing), and a building block for other larger communities, ecovillages in particular. Yarrow Ecovillage is one such project. True to the cohousing concept in general, it aims to re-establish many of the advantages of traditional villages within the context of 21st century life.

The site of this community is a former dairy farm, left inactive in the 1980s. Quite conveniently, the site is also on a main road that connects the small town of Yarrow (drained by decades of suburban sprawl, and now incorporated with its neighboring town of Chilliwack) with both urban Vancouver (to its west) and the natural beauty of the Fraser Valley. Yarrow Ecovillage offers the possibility of creating a new town center for Yarrow, a place for living combined with commerce. The 25 acre site on Yarrow Central Road in Chilliwack, British Columbia, includes a 33-unit intergenerational cohousing project, a 30,000-square-foot mixed-use area (commercial, rental units, learning, etc.), a 20 acre farm, and a 17-unit senior cohousing community.

Yarrow Ecovillage is designed to offer an exceptional combination of cohousing, sustainable living, farmland preservation, a live/work community, a learning center, and a mixed-use town center. Three main elements—living, working, and farming—along with many other activities and amenities such as learning, socializing, sharing, teaching, playing and visiting, are designed to come together to provide a model for environmentally, economically, and socially sustainable lifestyles. In order to accomplish the many objectives of the ecovillage, the city of Chilliwack worked with the resident group and its architects to establish an entirely new custom zoning code. The result is an Ecovillage Zoning designation that includes residential, commercial, cottage industries, work space, public open space, recreational space, and farming.

The "town" of Yarrow has a population of about 3,000 people. It once had a concentration of commercial buildings and houses along its main street, and twice the population. It was a rural but functional small town surrounded by farms. Like too many rural towns, Yarrow's commercial viability is eclipsed by big box stores scattered between farmland, new residential developments, and previous downtown corridors. As a result, it is nearly impossible to shop, dine, be entertained, or go to school, the library, or the park in the area without getting into a car.

Although technically part of the city of Chilliwack, Yarrow is about nine miles away from Chilliwack. (For financial reasons, the town of Yarrow was incorporated in 1980 with its larger neighboring city, population 80,000, because it could not afford its own in-town infrastructure—sewer, water, schools, police, fire, administration). The community's disparate but numerous fruit and vegetable markets and smattering of small retail stores are too spread out to have any long-term commercial viability, much less culturally create any sense of place. Their dispersed locations do nothing to contribute to the kind of personal relationships that stitch a town together.

Ecovillage Zoning:
A New, Sustainable Land-Use Concept

In the winter of 2010, MDA and a few of the members of the Yarrow Ecovillage development team met with the city manager of

The ecovillage is filled with fun!

Photos courtesy of Lindy Sexton

Chilliwack, as well as the heads of planning and public works and other staff—nine city officials in all. To begin the discussions of the site, the officials opened the zoning map, the parcel map that designates the allowable land uses for all of Chilliwack and the surrounding incorporated areas. Parcels were designated for farming, residential and commercial, or a park, a school, and so on. Then we came to the 25 acre site on Yarrow Central Road, the address of Yarrow Ecovillage. Its zoning was (in capital letters) ECOVILLAGE—the first site in Canada that we know of, and perhaps in North America, that is a zoned ecovillage.

Cohousing as Essential Building Block to Ecovillage

The 33-unit intergenerational cohousing community completed in 2015 is the first building block of the ecovillage and plays a critical role in creating the culture of the place. In building it, the group learned co-operation and development skills, as well as how to brainstorm, discuss, and decide; it is the place where well-intentioned citizens learn to make consequential decisions together to accomplish their environmental and social aspirations. It is also where the relationships built during the design and development process carry over to everyday interactions and relationships now that the community is complete.

The Getting-It-Built workshop, an essential piece in starting cohousing communities, was a large catalyst in this process, taking the group from being $700,000 in debt for seven years with four houses, to finishing the 33-unit cohousing community in two years. Cohousing is the foundation upon which other players at Yarrow Ecovillage (such as merchants and farmers) model their legal structure to achieve a cooperative corporation. That is, they have learned how to invest together and, most importantly, how to get things done by working together.

The second and most public component of Yarrow Ecovillage is a 2.5 acre mixed-use area (commercial, learning, etc.)—effectively a town center. It includes 30,000 square feet of commercial space offering services, and places for work and creative opportunities, to the greater neighborhood. Yarrow Ecovillage and its new commercial area—including a yet-to-be-built 17-unit senior cohousing community, a refitted classic old dairy barn, and a completely walkable environment—functions as a small town center. Its co-developer, the Yarrow Ecovillage Society (YES) Cooperative, continues to bring clarity of vision to the process. YES originally owned the site and works with new entities such as the Mixed-Use Development group (MUD) to best create the synergy on-site that will continue to set everyone up for success. Many of the original organizers of YES moved into the cohousing on-site.

The ability of the group to work together effectively yields the best strategy for accomplishing the sort of new town center that redevelopment agencies dream of. Yarrow Ecovillage is already a high-functioning hub and will grow to be a place where people can purchase locally grown organic produce (some grown on-site), park once and shop at four or five locations, meet a friend for coffee, work, get to know their neighbors, or take a class or two. It will be a place where families, seniors, and even teenagers will want to congregate. The goal is to not only enhance commercial viability and create a quality living environment, but to create a culturally viable and culturally vibrant place.

A 20 acre organic farm is located adjacent to the cohousing community. Some of the people who live in the cohousing community co-own and operate the farm, and like the commercial area, the farm is a separate partnership, managed by people with agricultural expertise (the business of farming), while remaining an important part of the larger whole—Yarrow Ecovillage.

Cohousing Site Design

In January 2010, we held a site design workshop with the group to plan and focus on the cohousing site. The outcome was a site plan that achieved the group's objectives. It added a diagonal pathway that links the cohousing site in the middle with the mixed-use site at one end, and the other end serves as a sight line, giving the residents a view of an existing silo that will continue to be preserved in the redevelopment, along with the heritage barn.

The cohousing site includes 33 private residences with a variety of housing types (duplexes, flats, townhouses, and shared houses), a common house, and ample programmed and unprogrammed open space. A new 3,900-square-foot common house is built at the intersection of the pedestrian pathways alongside the parking area on the east side of the site. This central area accommodates a terrace (connected to the common house) and a children's play area (across from, but separate from, the common house terrace). The location of the common house contributes to the overall functioning of the community as a gathering place. It is visible from private homes and the path that links them to the parking area. In this way, residents pass it on their way home and are likely to drop in.

Yarrow Ecovillage is designed to foster a sense of community along the pathways and

A view of Yarrow Ecovillage.

The original barn still exists.

Gerry

Gerry, one of the village sages, with a couple of young residents.

The group planned their ecovillage together.

The Common House is centrally located to bring together the community.

YARROW CENTRAL ROAD

MIXED-USE AREA

(E) BARN

(E) SILO

COMMUNITY FARM

Yarrow Site Plan.

in the various outdoor spaces, balanced with adequate room for privacy in more secluded areas, such as private backyards. It is also well suited to passive and active heating and cooling possibilities, and overall sun control.

Reviving the Town Center

The town center is almost as old as human settlement. Members of Yarrow Ecovillage understand that the combination of positive, usable public space, combined with commercial activity and spaces for creativity and learning, activate the environment. Such public space doesn't just provide retail opportunities; it provides opportunities for meaningful human interaction. Over time, these spontaneous, informal interactions may grow into more formal friendships. You get to know the person who bakes your bread, grows your carrots, or relaxes in the public square on a sunny day, and he or she gets to know you and your children. The variety of relationships and diversity of people, skills, and interests will likely establish a vibrant culture of learning, doing, and being—as a functional, interrelated society.

Cohousing Design to Facilitate Community

Yarrow Ecovillage, while a model project in its own right, is part of a larger, growing trend in neighborhood design in which cohousing has played an important role.

(continued on p. 77)

YARROW ECOVILLAGE:
COHOUSING AS A BUILDING BLOCK TO THE ECOVILLAGE

(continued from p. 43)

We have seen many cohousing communities, like Yarrow Ecovillage, that begin as small infill projects and, over time, bring new life to an entire neighborhood. Yarrow Ecovillage is no different and has the potential to catalyze other developments nearby, helping to stem the tide of sprawl in this beautiful valley. As an infill project that reinvigorates a former, under-utilized site with a variety of uses, it is a model to be expanded upon in similar rural settings.

The Yarrow Ecovillage group has successfully completed a design and construction that captures a true *genius loci*, the spirit of a place that is memorable for both its architectural and its experiential qualities. This combination also allows for a wonderful balance of economics, ecology, and positive social space. This type of calculated diversity assures flexibility and longevity for Yarrow Ecovillage. The cohousing, first in the development process, is really the kingpin of the larger whole. It is the cornerstone or the incubator for thoughtful and efficient processes and investment models in the future. It not only catalyzes the Yarrow Ecovillage larger whole, it also helps to synthesize the three separate endeavors to accomplish the overall goals of the ecovillage.

In Conclusion

At one point, we were talking to the city about adding the 17-unit senior cohousing community. We asked, *can this work?* The city replied, *we don't know, it's zoned as an ecovillage—you tell us. We don't claim to know anything about ecovillages.*

And they were correct. It was up to the residents to come up with what made sense from an ecological, economical, and social point of view. Where is the synergy that will make it an ecovillage? What the group has designed couldn't be more sophisticated, more synergistic, likened to the organic villages of old that you find in southern France. Those villages were created before development became big box and big subdivision. Like when human environments were human scale—that's Yarrow Ecovillage. ❧

McCamant & Durrett Architects | The Cohousing Company is an architecture and consulting firm with offices in Nevada City, California. Principal Architect Charles Durrett and his wife, Katie McCamant of Cohousing Solutions, have become well known nationally and internationally for the design of cohousing communities, sustainable design and development consulting. Since 1987 the firm has provided complete architectural services for a wide range of clients. Charles and Katie have published many essential cohousing books, including Cohousing: A Contemporary Approach to Housing Ourselves, Creating Cohousing: Building Sustainable Communities, *and* Senior Cohousing: A Community Approach to Independent Living. *MDA has adapted its cohousing design experience to affordable housing developments and senior neighborhoods. Other projects have included custom strawbale homes, mixed-use developments, town planning, commercial projects, and childcare centers. MDA's Lindy Sexton helped with the editing of this article.*

CLOUGHJORDAN ECOVILLAGE:
Modeling the Transition to a Low-Carbon Society

By Peadar Kirby

Photos (all taken at Cloughjordan Ecovillage, Ireland) by Davie Philip

While Ireland was living through the most severe economic collapse of its history since independence, a group of pioneering people were sowing the seeds of a new society through founding the ecovillage of Cloughjordan. Seeking to model sustainable living for the 21st century, the ecovillagers conceived their project during the boom years of Ireland's Celtic Tiger in the late 1990s and early 2000s, but by the time the infrastructure was being laid in 2008 and the first houses built in 2009, the Irish banking and construction sectors were in freefall and the ecovillage became the country's biggest building site.

Now with 55 houses built and a population of around 100 adults and 35 children, Cloughjordan has been recognised as one of Europe's most successful "anticipatory experiences" showing the way to a low-carbon society. As an educational charity, it draws thousands of people a year to learn the lessons of this pioneering community. Central to those lessons are the combination of some modern technologies that help lower emissions, embedded in a resilient community that seeks to foster a rich sense of interdependency, not without its tensions.

Among ecovillages, Cloughjordan is unusual in that its founders decided to integrate it into an existing urban settlement. They chose the small village of Cloughjordan (around 500 people) in county Tipperary. A site of 67 acres (27 hectares) was available on the south side of its main street, on a train line, and some leading people in the local community recognised it as an opportunity for regenerating a village that was in decline. Before buying the land, members of the ecovillage project worked with children in the local schools and with the residents of Cloughjordan to win support for developing the project.

Cloughjordan ecovillage therefore models not just ecological sustainability but also rural regeneration, drawing visitors to the existing village and fostering a new social, economic, and cultural dynamism. Readers of *The Irish Times* voted Cloughjordan one of the 10 best places to live in Ireland. The ecovillage embodies the important message that low-carbon living does not mean reverting to the privations of the past, but can be the catalyst for drawing together a diverse group of people who, through their wide range of talents, make it a lively and interesting place to live.

Integrating with the Natural Environment

The greenfield site that was bought behind Cloughjordan village was developed in a way unique for an Irish urban settlement. The

205

village's planners confined the residential area to about one-third of the site closest to the main street, while devoting a further area beyond that to support services and amenities including a district heating system, an eco-enterprise centre, allotments for growing food, and a community farm. Ecovillagers have planted native varieties of apple trees in this area; throughout the village, various varieties of herbs and fruit bushes create an "edible landscape." An area of 12 acres (5 hectares) devoted to farming in a biodynamic way constitutes one of Ireland's few Community Support Agriculture (CSA) projects.

On the final third of the site, devoted to woodland, villagers planted 17,000 trees in 2011—mainly native species such as oak, ash, Scots pine, birch, rowan, cherry, hazel, and alder. This is regarded as an amenity area for visitors and a contribution to promoting biodiversity. A labrynth, built according to an ancient Celtic layout, provides a quiet space for reflection amid the woodland. According to the ecovillage website (www.thevillage.ie), "the community's land use plan is based on the principles of environmental and ecological diversity, productive landscape and permaculture." The design of common and private areas includes corridors for the movement of wildlife, and the composting of organic matter to regenerate the soil and avoiding toxic or other harmful substances is strongly recommended to all members. Since all are responsible for the upkeep of the common areas, the community organizes regular periods of communal work on the land (the Gaelic word "meitheal" is used for these, recalling the traditional practice of communal work among Irish farmers).

Central to the success of the project is the combination of low-energy technologies and robust community living. The Village Ecological Charter, drawn up by members, contains the guidelines for the development of the built and natural environments so as "to reduce the impact of the project on the natural environment and so promoting sustainable development." This includes detailed and specific targets for energy supply and use, plans for land management, water and solid waste, construction (including materials, light and air, and ventilation), and community issues such as transport, social and communal facilities, and noise and light pollution.

Towards Low-Carbon Living

Combining both cutting-edge technologies and some traditional technologies gives a rich and unique mix to the ecovillage. One of its most innovative features is its district heating system, the only one in Ireland powered by renewable sources of energy. This supplies all the heating and hot water for every house in the ecovillage, using no fossil fuels as primary energy sources and emitting no greenhouse gas emissions. (Electricity supply to drive the pumps and for other purposes is taken from the public mains at present, but there are plans for on-site generation in due course.) It saves an estimated 113.5 tonnes annually of carbon that would be emitted by conventional heating systems for the number of houses served. Though the ecovillage has the largest bank of solar panels in Ireland, these haven't yet been commissioned due to faults in their installation; the district heating system relies on waste wood from a sawmill about an hour away.

Members buy sites from the cooperative which owns the estate (of which all site owners must be members), building their own houses to their own designs, in keeping with the principles and specifications of the Ecological Charter. As a result, many different building types have been used, including passive timber frame with a variety of insulations and finishes, Durisol blocks (blocks of chipped wastewood bonded with ecocement), sheep's wool, cellulose (shredded newspaper), hemp-lime (lime is a tradi-

tional Irish form of finish but the addition of hemp, a fibrous plant material, gives it strength and insulation), cob (clay, sand, and straw), a Canadian stick-frame house with double stud walls (with no cold bridging), and kit houses, while natural slates or recycled plastic roof tiles and "green roofs" are widely used. These provide a colorful variety of different designs and finishes that gives the ecovillage a very distinctive look compared to other residential areas in Ireland. It also has some of the lowest Building Energy Ratings (BER) in Ireland.

The ecovillage includes Ireland's first member-owned and -operated CSA farm. Some two thirds of ecovillage households are members and the rest come from the wider Cloughjordan community. Currently it grows 4 acres (1.6 ha) of vegetables, 1 acre (0.4 ha) of cereals, 1 acre of green manure (humus building), and 6 acres (2.43 ha) in permanent pasture. Members pay a monthly fee (around €130 for a household of typically two adults and two children) and can take what food they want from a central distribution point that is supplied three times a week, all year around. Two part-time coordinators act as the main producers, are paid from the farm budget, and are answerable to the farm board which is elected by members. They rely on WWOOFers (Worldwide Opportunities on Organic Farms) and interns as well as on the voluntary labour of members when called upon.

Not only does the form of food production and distribution link the producer and consumer in a deeply interactive relationship, but it changes practices of consumption since members rely on whatever food is available according to the season, the weather, and the amounts planted. The farm also contributes to the resilience of the ecovillage itself, lessening reliance on commercial producers (often very distant), improving greatly the quality of food consumed, and enhancing skills and practices among members. It recently returned to the use of horses to plough the land to avoid the compacting that resulted from the use of tractors, and has hosted public demonstrations of horse-drawn ploughing.

The farm also links in with other projects through which ecovillagers earn a livelihood, such as the award-winning Riot Rye bakery and baking school, members who turn the food produced in the farm into tasty wholesome meals for ecovillagers and visitors, and the Green Enterprise centre with Ireland's only community-based Fab Lab (fabrication laboratory with 3-D printers). Ireland's largest cohousing project is being developed in the ecovillage to offer low-cost accommodation to those who want to come and sample life or live in the ecovillage. All these exemplify the "ecosystem of innovation" through which synergies grow, enhancing each of the elements of ecovillage life.

Finding a governance structure that reflects its values is a particular challenge for any intentional community, particularly one as complex and multifaceted as an ecovillage. By 2007, the existing organisational structure of Cloughjordan ecovillage based on multiple committees was under strain, unable to deal effectively with the many tasks and challenges facing the project. This led members to turn for support to consultants Angela Espinosa and Jon Walker, who promote the use of the Viable Systems Model (VSM) in cooperatives and large communities looking for alternatives to traditional hierarchies. This resulted in the restructuring of the ecovillage governance structures according to the principles of VSM, identifying the primary activities (PA) of the project and establishing groups to promote them. Two PAs exist in early 2016, one on education and the other on land use. A Development PA, looking after the development of the built environment, has recently been disbanded as it wasn't working well, and a replacement is being put in place. Each PA has a number of task groups within it responsible for different aspects of the primary activity.

> ## Horizontal rather than hierarchical management ensures that bottom-up initiatives flourish while preserving the coherence of the project as a whole.

The PAs are known as System One groups in VSM. Supporting these are what are called the meta-systemic management functions, Systems Two to Five, each of which fulfills essential functions in the organisation. These include a Process group to oversee the smooth functioning of the whole structure and to resolve problems as they arise, and a coordination team drawing together the activities of all the various groups and providing a monthly reporting mechanism to members. System Four involves keeping a close eye on what is happening in the wider society so as to strategically relate to developments. This led to the establishment of a Navigation group. Finally, System Five involves oversight and direction of the whole project, and includes the Board of Directors and the monthly members' meeting supplemented by an Identity group which deals with issues of membership and purpose. VSM allows a horizontal rather than a hierarchical management of the project, which ensures that bottom-up initiatives flourish while at the same time the coherence of the project as a whole holds together.

Community Resilience

Beyond the technologies, both ancient and new, what is essential to the character of the ecovillage is that it is an intentional community. The dense web of interconnectedness that characterises relationships is strengthened and at times tested through a myriad of different kinds of activities, from the often tense discussions attempting to reach a community consensus on key issues to the enjoyment of community meals and parties where rich encounters take place. A special Process group exists to facilitate community interactions, and the monthly community meeting establishes a period in which any member can voice any issue that is troubling them, including issues of grievance and pain caused within the community. Successful community, then, depends not on avoiding or minimising pain and tensions but rather on facilitating their expression in an atmosphere of mutual respect. A diverse membership, which includes professional facilitators, counsellors, and psychotherapists, helps this process.

Communication

Ecological Footprint

Having put in place the means to transition to low-carbon living, the ecovillage needed evidence that it was succeeding. This required measuring its ecological footprint and comparing it to other similar communities in its locality as well as nationally and internationally. The concept of the ecological footprint (EF) is widely used internationally to quantify

the amount of carbon emitted by a household through measuring energy consumption, waste assimilation, food consumption, water consumption, built land area, and travel impacts. Aggregating household measures allows an estimate for a community to be produced. In mid-2014 all households in the ecovillage received a survey that gathered data to measure the EF of ecovillagers. The survey used a measure developed at the Centre for Environmental Research at the University of Limerick and implemented in communities in the region by Tipperary Energy Agency (TEA), which compiled and analysed the results. The survey covered the following areas:

• Household characteristics (number of dwellers; size and type of house)
• Household energy use and its sources
• Household waste (amounts and disposal)
• Food consumption and its origin
• Transport (modes and frequency)
• Water use, including water-saving measures and water harvesting

The questionnaire achieved a 94 percent response rate, indicating a high level of interest. Based on the survey, an EF of 2 global hectares (gHa) was estimated for the ecovillage, the lowest recorded for an Irish settlement. This compares to an EF of 2.9 gHa for the nearby town of Ballina after a four-year campaign to reduce its footprint, 3.9 gHa for a commuter community, and 4.3 gHa for 79 settlements throughout the country. Apart from measuring the ecovillage's EF, the results also allow the sources which constitute each of these EFs to be compared. The Global Footprint Network, an NGO which has developed and implemented the methodology for measuring EFs internationally, estimates an average EF of 4.6 gHa for Ireland (www.globalfootprintnetwork.org). It recognised the significance of Cloughjordan's EF by including an article on it in its newsletter. Globally, it is estimated that the maximum EF for each human being that allows them to live within the planet's biocapacity is 1.8 gHa. Based on this, ecovillage residents would currently need 1.1 planets to continue living the way they do. A plan for the systematic reduction of the ecovillage's EF with targets and periodic measurement to establish progress is being developed in early 2016.

International Recognition

Cloughjordan ecovillage faces many challenges. It is still only in its early phase of growth with more than 70 sites yet to sell, which will draw in new members and more than double its population. Yet already it is winning national and international recognition. Cloughjordan won the National Green Award for Ireland's greenest community three years in a row from 2012 to 2014 and won a gold medal award at the 2013 International Awards for Liveable Communities (LivCom), also known as the Green Oscars, hosted by Xiamen in the People's Republic of China and supported by the UN Environmental Programme (UNEP). The Milesecure consortium of 15 research centres throughout Europe was funded by the European Commission to learn the lessons for European policy of how to transition to a low-carbon future. As part of its research, it examined 1,500 projects all around Europe to identify the most successful "anticipatory experiences" to help guide EU policy. Among the 23 finally selected was Cloughjordan ecovillage and it was the only project to be highlighted in the "manifesto for human-based governance of secure and low-carbon energy transitions" that the consortium wrote as one outcome of its three-year project (see www.milesecure2050.eu). In these ways, the project is helping establish itself as a beacon for the challenging future that confronts humanity.

Peadar Kirby is Professor Emeritus of International Politics and Public Policy at the University of Limerick. He is the author of many books on models of development in Ireland and Latin America. His recent books include Adapting to Climate Change: Governance Challenges, *co-edited with Deiric Ó Broin (Glasnevin, 2015) and* Transitioning to a Low-Carbon Society: Degrowth, austerity and wellbeing, *co-edited with Ernest Garcia and Mercedes Martinez-Iglesias (Palgrave Macmillan, forthcoming in 2016). He is writing a book on pathways to a low-carbon society to be published by Palgrave Macmillan in 2017. He was one of the first residents of Cloughjordan ecovillage in 2009 and is currently chair of the Board of Directors of the ecovillage.*

Roger Ulrich: A Founder Reflects

By Deborah Altus

Roger Ulrich, the octogenarian founder of Lake Village Homestead, a 44-year-old intentional community near Kalamazoo, Michigan, has been on a lifelong community journey. From an Amish-Mennonite background, he learned as a child what tight-knit Anabaptist church community is like. Then, after rebelling from his pacifist roots and spending a couple of years in the Navy, he learned about military community. Finally, he ended up immersed in academic community, earning a Ph.D. at Southern Illinois University and later chairing the psychology departments at Illinois Wesleyan University and Western Michigan University—the latter where he served for many years as a research professor.

Ulrich pursued the study of behavioral psychology with the fervor of a convert. As chair at WMU, Ulrich recruited well-known behaviorists in an effort to turn the department into one of the top behavioral psychology programs in the country. But he wasn't content simply to study behaviorism or to apply it to others. Rather, he wanted to live what he was studying in an authentic way. This quest led to his longest and most personally meaningful exploration into community: the building and sustaining of a cooperative farm community.

Spurred by B.F. Skinner's 1948 utopian novel, *Walden Two*, Ulrich was drawn to creating an intentional community based on behaviorism. After meeting with a group of *Walden Two* enthusiasts (including folks who went on to start Twin Oaks community in Virginia), Ulrich went on to found Lake Village Homestead in 1971 on 265 acres along Long Lake, just outside of Kalamazoo.

Trying to put *Walden Two* into practice was at first eye-opening and eventually paradigm-shattering. Although he was still at WMU as a research professor, Ulrich felt an increasing pull to experiment with his own life—not only through behaviorism but in ways ranging from psychedelic drugs to Native American spirituality. Doubts about behaviorism started creeping, then pouring, in.

Despite his far-reaching fame as a scholar and author of articles and books on the control of human behavior, Ulrich came to the difficult realization that he couldn't even solve everyday problems at Lake Village. Kids were cleaning up by sweeping cat litter under the carpet and he didn't know how to stop it. The more he tried to experiment with his life, the less he realized he knew. To say that it was a humbling experience for him is an understatement.

Skinner's views, which Ulrich had held in the highest esteem, felt increasingly false—not the principles of behavior (he still buys into the science upon which behavioral psychology is based)—but the idea that control of human behavior is easy or even possible. Skinner was telling others to experiment with their lives in *Walden Two* but he wasn't doing it himself.

Ulrich finally concluded that *Walden Two* was a fairy tale. He knew he'd need to find other teachers and other ways to help Lake Village move forward. So he started searching in earnest. He drew sustenance from Native American spirituality and was drawn, in particular, to the ideas of Rolling Thunder. Surprisingly, though, he found that his previously cast-aside Amish-Mennonite roots provided the clearest direction.

Ulrich began to see that his forebears weren't quaint relics of a bygone era but were full of practical wisdom on how to live in a more self-sufficient, sustainable way. He realized that they "were in many ways attuned to the Native American way of life that I

Try positive reinforcement—oops, it hadn't been invented yet!

> **Skinner's views, which Ulrich had held in the highest esteem, felt increasingly false—in particular, the idea that control of human behavior is easy or even possible.**

later came to know in greater depth." Their focus was on living on, and learning from, the land that nourished them. This focus felt truthful and authentic to Ulrich and was a path he wanted to follow.

To Ulrich, the bottom line is that "you have to live the truth to understand it." But this piece of wisdom did not come quickly or easily. "For years as a research professor," Ulrich notes, "I ran experiments, but I kept finding that there is no experiment other than the real situation." His message is reminiscent of Skinner's words in *Walden Two*, advice that Ulrich is quick to note that Skinner never followed except in superficial ways: "I mean you've got to experiment, and experiment with your own life! Not just sit back—not just sit back in an ivory tower somewhere—as if your life weren't all mixed up in it" (Skinner, 1948, p. 5).

So Ulrich lives day to day with around 20 Lake Village members on close to 300 acres of land—with another 20 or so former members living on an adjacent 100 acres. The community refers to itself as a "pasture based, beyond organic, farm cooperative" where they offer sustainably grown local food, farm education, recreation, and community living (see www.lakevillagehomestead.org). Ulrich estimates that about 400 people have called Lake Village home at one time or another over the past 44 years.

Ulrich has a take-charge approach, honed in roles ranging from student-body president to university department chairman, and he is the first to admit that there have been power struggles over the years. He says that coping with his own stubbornness and "tendency to act like a god" has created challenges for him and others. But now that he finds himself "on the other side of 80 years on the globe," he is better at taking life's challenges in stride. And while community life has not always been smooth sailing, he is glad he's stuck with it and pleased to see Lake Village move into its fifth decade—no small feat in the annals of intentional community living.

Having once referred to himself a "Behaviorist Amish Indian," Ulrich quips that his current alias might be "Amish Indian trying hard to behave." While he feels that he has learned infinitely more

> Once a self-described "Behaviorist Amish Indian," Ulrich quips that his current alias might be "Amish Indian trying hard to behave."

from the land than from the lab, he nonetheless honors his behaviorist roots and adds that "I most certainly cherish the memory of my friendship and the fun I had hanging out with Fred Skinner."

He's also learned to cherish the piece of the earth he has settled on, and to cherish the surrounding community. In return, he says he has been cherished in even greater ways. He is learning to practice "the art of living comfortably with the inevitability of change" and doing his best "to make heaven here on earth"—a process that he finds "exciting and extremely meaningful."

As he grows older, Ulrich's thoughts sometimes turn to what is next for him. Ever curious about what he calls the experiment of life, he says he finds himself "considering the possibility that death is perhaps nothing more than just another change of perspective during the eternal trip."

When asked what's next for Lake Village, he responds as you might expect from someone who greatly values diving into life and learning from whatever comes your way: "Veremos. We'll see!" 🐦

This article is based primarily on an interview by the author with Roger Ulrich from Spring 2015. Other sources include:

Altus, D. "Roger Ulrich & Lake Village Community: 'The Experiment of Life'." COMMUNITIES: Journal of Cooperative Living, no. 98 (Spring 1998): 52-54.

Ruth, D. "An Interview with Roger Ulrich." COMMUNITIES: Journal of Cooperative Living, no. 30 (January/February 1978): 12-18.

Deborah Altus' interest in Walden Two *communities dates back to living in a* Walden Two-*inspired co-op in college. She lives, loves, and plays in Lawrence, Kansas, and is a professor at Washburn University in Topeka. She is on the editorial review board for the FIC.*

Building an Ecovillage in the Friendly Islands

By Philip Mirkin

Community members build the author a cottage as a thank you for the gift of a new boat. Here they are plastering Hybrid Adobe over the woven bamboo walls.

Our deluxe bure (cottage) has woven mats, handmade bed frames, and traditional building techniques.

We began Fiji Organic Village (FOV) in 2006, and a year later built a sustainable lodge we named "the Flying Fish."

As cofounder I faced the challenges and joys in cross-cultural community. On a tiny island in the Blue Lagoon, happy Fijians became family. Many ask me how we started and sustained an Ecovillage in paradise. They have no idea how crazy and wonderful this funny adventure truly was.

Bula Vinaka! (Big Welcome!)

I left Waiheke Island, New Zealand, for Fiji in early 2005. Known as the Friendly Islands, Fiji is home to people who earn the moniker. Camped on a remote backpacker outpost in the Yasawa chain, I kayaked the warm turquoise sea around the tip of the island to a rocky shore, exploring coral reefs with a snorkel. Afterwards I took a lot of wave-born rubbish off the beach, roped it down, and kayaked back (as we did in NZ). Impressing the locals, word spread in the nearby village. In the morning two Fijians marched me down the loveliest beach to a stunning cove to the local Chieftain (Ratu), at his request. At my welcome feast, they served me heaps of food and strange delicacies. Obliged to eat more, I did. Then I made the Sevusevu offering of kava. We drank, sang songs. Magic. Serendipity.

With the respect I showed the Islanders, strong, smiling Ratu, a fantastic fisherman with a crippled hand, told me I couldn't camp at the outpost. I was now his guest on the island; later he adopted me as his brother. The locals wanted to build a Fijian style lodge, needing help and leadership. I became "uncle" to a hilarious crew of Fijians, staying most of six years.

Early Days

At first, we lived a traditional Fijian lifestyle, simply, without electricity, on a 68 acre Native-owned organic farm: fishing, farming, carrying water, using kerosene lamps. Their tired little boat leaked. Adorable children played in the flower gardens and loved me like a grandfather. Clan land was apportioned out for garden plots. Other lands and resources managed by community elders were joined together. Tired of working for $1.50 per hour at overpriced resorts owned by cheap, greedy foreigners on nearby islands, they wanted to bring their family back together and create jobs for themselves.

Coconut groves and old growth breadfruit trees already grew there; we planted cassava (manioc) fields, garden veggies, four kinds of bananas, papaya, pineapple, yam and pumpkin

patches, spinach, and a chestnut tree nursery.

People power! Happy, singing, smiling locals, they had the experience and skills, but not the business savvy, nor international connections, they explained. They didn't know I designed sustainable buildings and ecovillages, or delivered humanitarian aid on Native American reservations. They respectfully asked me to join them: "kerekere Tai Felipe?" How could I say no? Founded on the simple philosophy of sustainable living and sharing, from their loving cultural perspective, we began.

Elder respect is part of the culture. Traditional practical wisdom guided the chief and me in our leadership roles. We listened to all; younger members and clan members voiced their feelings, and were heard, as respect and patience are Fijian traits. In fact, Chiefs' coalitions can be voted down by others. Women too are Chiefs (Adi).

A basic societal premise guided us: you give first, generously of your spirit, your smile, home, food, and ask for anything later. Guest hosting and loving childcare comes naturally to the soft, sweet Fijian personality, men included. Given so much I asked for little.

I purchased and transported much needed medicine, tons of food, fresh clothes, a wheelbarrow, and heaps of building supplies. They honored me. A year later we bought the village a new community boat. They built me a home as a thank you. Our gift exchange grew.

Who builds you a lovely cottage as a gift? The gift economy indeed works!

We did the physical work together, building traditional huts and a large building with kitchen, dining room, office. The community grew quickly when lodge guests arrived, as relatives wanted to join us. I would visit relatives on other islands, and ask their employers if I could take them back with me as they were needed at home. I thanked them before I paid the needed boat fare and we departed. Locals jokingly called me "the Kidnapper."

Our relaxed pace revolved around gardening, meals, farming, land management, joking, fishing, cleanup, singing, and kava. We helped other Fijians, while enjoying the visitors to our shores. All religions and nations were respected, including LGBT persons. In the background, a sweet murmur soundscape of guitar, song, laughter. Our mantra: "seqa na leqa" (no problem).

We built with natural plant fibers, hardwoods, and earth (we rarely used dimensional lumber, just for custom doors and storm windows). Four-star chefs also used machetes in the cassava fields, prepared breadfruit, harvested yams and seaweed, and collected firewood. I shipped over a solar panel from NZ and wired the buildings with 1.5w LED bulbs. All done with happy human power.

After lunch: afternoon nap. After work: volleyball, frisbee, games, kayaking, fishing, or swimming. Tea time brought fresh baked treats, endless smiles, and sometimes a walk down the beach to support the neighbor's tea house.

Many modern things were unnecessary.

Village elders didn't want TV and its violence, etc., due to a strong morality about what children might see. A rare exception: to watch Fiji play international Rugby. Otherwise music was our world: guitars, lovely voices, and ukuleles. Church too was always a singing sensation.

Most importantly, we were guided by what would be best for all, as a true community, renewed in song and story around the ceremonial Tanoa (kava bowl).

Ultimately success came from simplicity, and not taking things seriously. Visitors felt part of an extended family that lovingly included them.

A couple dozen overseas friends helped, some joining us in Fiji for a few weeks. Michael Freeman of Durango, Colorado taught permaculture in free workshops. Email updates to hundreds gained grateful overseas support. Big-hearted Aletha McGee of Oakland, California did research/outreach for years, hosted fundraising benefits for hurricane relief, inspiring many others, even before her visit!

Logistical Challenges

Fiji is 333 islands (two thirds of them uninhabited) in the tropical cyclone belt of the SW Pacific, two and a half hours' flight from NZ, the nearest bigger country, and 10 hours from LAX. Imported goods in Fiji's cities were very expensive. There are no shops or nurse on our small island, and only rare, intermittent cellphone coverage. No local businesses or governmental agencies existed within the three to four hour boat ride to the big island, only tourism outposts in a similar situation, or a small village. We had renewable resources and items to share. If the sea was rough or the tide was low we couldn't go anywhere except on foot or kayak. For internet connection, I loaded my laptop in a waterproof bag, strapped it to my back, and kayaked to the next island. There the Italian owner allowed me to email prospective visitors and overseas support.

My week-long shopping missions to Lautoka (Sugar City) were often dependent on unreliable supply boats. I'd have to check with three different captains about available space for our supplies and departure dates. With help from big island relatives, we prepared 15-20 boxes of supplies each trip plus tools/hardware while waiting for a boat home. I learned some Fiji Hindi to deal better with the Big Island merchants and establish relationships as a regular local customer.

Why It Worked:

- We respectfully trusted each other to get our jobs done without supervision or judgment.
- Humor and lightheartedness. We laughed at ourselves and with each other.
- Always saying gratitude at meals.
- We focused on solutions and blessings, not problems.
- Little conflict or pettiness. No control-freaks. We "agreed to agree."
- All were included in village life; feasts were joyous celebrations!

Father Dan prepares kava with clan and community members in our Grand Bure meeting room

The community eats all their meals together, Fijian style; with smiles from Alesi, Nabola, and Simeli.

A formal gathering to honor a few long-term visitors before they leave the island.

Photos courtesy of Philip Mirkin

• We sang together most nights, often around a bonfire.

• We stayed relaxed and present. No fears of the future nor grudges to hold onto. Resolution came quickly and lovingly with hugs.

• No Fijian quibbled about money, rules, or having it their way. We gave gifts.

• We talked about things openly at the kava ceremonies and at meals. If something came up later we could walk over to talk about it.

• We worked in harmony. Appreciation was freely given.

• We shared common abilities as natural builders, cooks, farmers, and fishermen, interchanging jobs, both men and women included.

• Most of us had special skills as carpenters, mechanics, electricians, etc., allowing the village a high degree of self-sufficiency.

• We were all used to hard work.

Best of the Village: Expertly prepared fresh organic food, calm, relaxed atmosphere, incredible snorkeling, shady park-like beach, kava parties, harmony and peace, daily laughter and singing.

Worst of the Village: unflushed toilets in the morning, cutting feet open, scary fishes, boils, sand fleas, cyclones.

Some of Our Successes:

• Dozens of visitors/communitarians expressed that these were the most peaceful and enjoyable weeks of their lives.

• We built a fully hurricane-resistant 4 meter x 6 meter bathhouse (three toilets, three showers) using Hybrid Adobe blocks with local pumice. The structure itself cost less than $1000 to build.

• We built a huge community water tank with solar powered pump for the larger village (with British funding).

• Concrete was not used; no generator running for hours; no cars or roads; weekly boat fuel consumption was only 6-12 liters, making for a tiny carbon footprint.

• We integrated traditional farming styles with permaculture principles and methods, using a hand-dug well.

• At capacity we hosted 35 people with flush toilets, solar power, and four-star cuisine (Ratu's sons had been chefs at Turtle Island Lodge).

• We hosted nurses from NZ who gave free health assessments and treatments to hundreds in four nearby villages at no cost.

• We provided free first aid, hurricane response, and local ferrying to Yaqeta Island.

• We prepped the village for flooding, then evacuated 30 people to high ground, all in 90 minutes before the Japanese tsunami struck our island.

• We kept the quiet peace there (usually singing was the loudest sound).

• Projects were done using human power, including hand saws.

• The back-up generator was rarely used (just for large feasts). A small pump was used to fill water tanks from the well.

• Our little shop provided basic goods to islanders at cost.

A Cultural Bridge

I learned the local dialect, songs, ceremonies, and customs. The Fijians rightly saw my efforts as respect and appreciation, enjoying their life-ways. As a cultural bridge between the hardworking Islanders and idealistic westerners I could explain Fijian culture, their community values, and a high level of sharing (including sandals).

Back in the 1980s and '90s I led geographic wilderness trips teaching Native American culture in German and English, and leading humanitarian aid trips on reservations at Natives' request. At FOV I explained Fijian life in cultural terms familiar to residents of Germany, Canada, France, NZ, Australia, US, UK, etc.. I went "Island," wearing a Fijian Sulu (sarong), a nice button-down shirt, barefoot, just like locals. Fijians in other parts of the nation laughed and clapped when I sang Fijian/Yasawan songs. Still, each year I traveled to California and NZ to work on the business end of our venture, the website, etc., gaining support.

I spent three weeks of every month on our island, before going to the big island for a week of shopping, resupply, business communications, outreach, etc. The cultural and lifestyle changes were harder for new arrivals. Some made mistakes: they got infected, sunburned, or ate a forbidden plant. The responsible geographer in me prepared

Community members sing the traditional farewell song "Isa Lei" before a family leaves the ecovillage on our boat for the Big Island.

Outdoor dining with community members always brings smiles.

The chief teaches an Australian visitor how to weave Tabu, or palm frond shingles, for the roof.

Three women of the village sharing a hammock for the evening singing.

Father Dan carries our old boat motor to the boat in preparation to transport visitors.

Feasting on fresh fish and organic farm produce, community members grow 80 percent or more of our own food.

12-page practical briefings sent before their arrival to smooth and guide their cultural integration. I overplayed the annoyances: how massive coconut crabs came into the cottage at night if you left the door open. Plus the real danger of giant stingrays, lion fish, sea kraits, and other poisonous sea monsters.

Communitarians could be invited to live with us for up to a year. Some stayed a few months, most a few weeks. Many had never been to a place this remote. Those who stayed for the rainy months dealt with skin problems, bothersome insects, or ran out of money. Still it became hard for them to go back to their "other," noisier lives.

We dealt with unforeseen, surprising, and crazy situations:

• The 2006 Coup in Fiji!

• I led the tsunami evacuation, collecting medical/surgical supplies, other emergency/communications gear, organizing teams.

• I spent long nights putting out international appeals for hurricane recovery.

• As the authority on the south side of the island, we also stopped illegal fisherman using dynamite.

• I treated intense infections, a stroke, wounds, and dental emergencies.

• Sometimes Fijians woke up the village at 4 a.m. loudly cleaning fish.

• Plus drunken revelers, a few insane Americans, and some truly difficult visitors!!

• And as the "concierge"/shopper I had to deal with everyone's requests: tobacco, birth control, underwear, medications, cellphones, shoes, and so on.

• I had five pages of shopping lists each time I left the island.

Humour

Joy was a guiding principle; we all joked. Fijians waited behind bushes to scare me; we hosted a kava party in lingerie. At a church fundraiser we hosted, all laughed when I suddenly climbed out the window. We played Bocci ball with coconuts. Hilarious! Our Grand Opening party was legendary fun: a quarter of the nearby village celebrated at FOV, some 'til dawn.

Our clumsy attempts to bridge the culture gap also brought laughter. Early on, as the appropriate thing to do, I brought a ceremonial Tabua to Ratu. Rather than be offended, laughter ensued when it turned out that this whale's-tooth was a clever fake made from a bulamakau or bull's horn; we caught the culprits later. Obliged to drink many high-tide bowls of kava at a funeral, I fell backwards, snoring in front of chiefs. At the wedding, a huge white guest wearing only a skirt danced wildly in a conga line.

Fijian nicknames kept it light-hearted: I became "Grandma," a Colonel in the Fijian Army (Ratu's brother) became "Mr. Bullshit." "Father Dan" was an island-style Jim Carrey with a rubber face, fast and funny antics, and excellent English skills...as a former wannabe priest/boat captain he left the sermonizing behind, entertaining us with his funny impersonations.

Decisions

In council, everyone was respectfully listened to when speaking. My advice was often asked before decisions were made. We didn't cater to western ways nor shove them into Fijian faces. FOV remained a nascent Fijian village that just happened to have a white-faced elder. Fiji is the most inclusive society I've known.

We agreed to add boat radios, life jackets, cellphones, and other emergency gear. Most of this I carried from the US or NZ in my suitcases so we had to decide priorities; it became very important after some neighbors' boat motor broke down and they spent 17 days drifting to Tonga. Otherwise I brought over large tents, which were needed to house those wanting to join us.

Responsible for communications, leadership, marketing, funding, supplies, outreach, hosting, and snorkel guide, I wore four hats too many. I interpreted Fijian culture for newcomers' understanding, carefully choosing respectful words.

Ecovillage Details

We built the ecovillage with less than $60,000! Fijians had no money, but put in serious sweat equity. My job was to find seed money. We started with $8000 of my own, and Mum put in 10K. Later we each put in another 10K. A friend donated about 15K paying for structures like the Hybrid Adobe bathhouse, kitchen, and toilets. I was receiving $450 a month for the Hybrid Adobe home I built and sold in Colorado and donated the money for the building and operations; I lived as simply as the Fijians. After a year of hard work we opened the lodge. Revenue from guest stays was shared with community members and used for maintenance and supplies.

Fortunately, I booked the grand opening of the Flying Fish for eight days, with a wedding party of 11. Their prepayment gave momentum, paying for the linens, beds, furniture, dishes, etc. Another 5K in donations came in from the appeal following a hurricane. Gueststays rebounded after recovery, providing some revenue to start to pay back small loans after the cyclones...some loans were kindly forgiven. (Unfortunately I was stuck with a few of the loans and maxed out credit cards.)

Infrastructure included: a large dormitory/meeting space, five cottages, a simple solar system, 10,000 liters rainwater collection, and a septic tank.

Building materials were almost entirely hardwoods, natural materials, pumice, and earth. Guests donated $30-50 per night, four gourmet meals a day included. Average stays

Natural disasters, due to extreme global weather, can undo a lot of work. However, the community is people, not farm nor buildings. We repaired and replanted so the infrastructure remains for all island residents' use. Many visitors experienced an authentic, healthy, timeless life in a harmonious village for their first time.

Few of the visitors were prepared for real community living, so be careful who you let join.

Ultimately, the atmosphere/lifestyle was as compelling as the golden sand, palm tree paradise. The locals cherish our village. Isa lei. We miss you. And we thank all our supporters.

Life after the Ecovillage

With my elderly parents' health deteriorating, I moved back to the US. In Fiji I had given my shoes away, so I bought some new flip-flops for the airplane adventure, arriving to immense culture shock in California. Where were the joyous gatherings? I felt the social poverty of the States and saw how important it is that we do create intentional community here.

It was very difficult to keep in touch with FOV, since no one there had real email access. Telephone calls were merely brief pleasantries. I was swallowed up by this overwhelming, alien life in California. Things had really changed in just a few years.

The ecovillage is still there, sometimes just the extended family, as a small, simple village with few jobs, so fewer people than before.

It's good I came back to spend the last year of my father's life near him. This became possible since the Fijians taught me the value of family, and I still had one. I practiced forgiveness. We thrive through community—our chosen extended family, sharing smiles even during the rough times, and disaster.

The nearby village suffered heavily in Super Cyclone Winston, an EF5 that roared through Fiji with 250+ kph winds (February 20, 2016), as the worst storm ever in the Southern Hemisphere. Forty-two people were killed and thousands made homeless. Eight homes were completely destroyed and many heavily damaged, leaving some locals homeless; FOV fared better.

> # We thrive through community— sharing smiles even during the rough times, and disaster.

went from four nights to two weeks. Some guests became residents. Residents mostly did work exchange plus donated cash towards supplies. We bought yams, fish, etc. to help create an economy for island neighbors.

Supporters were amazed at how much we built with limited funds. Exposure from our website complemented the valuable listing on www.ic.org.

Our low-cost website gave a lovely, accurate description of the sweetness of the lifestyle. Connections to the local ferry, travel bureaus, and other lodges helped get the word out. We literally spent no money on advertising, except a simple brochure.

Real upset seemed rare: hurricane damage to our old growth forest and roofs, nasty racist visitors, or a dental emergency I could barely treat. Sadly the lodge business ended when European cyber criminals hacked our website, stealing funds/support and creating divisions. They were deported.

Lessons

Easygoing, joyful ecovillage living is sustainable with skillful, hard-working people. As the founder, I couldn't have anticipated the surprises inherent in this wonderful adventure. Nearly every moment was truly lovely.

However, the people on our little island are the lucky ones, as the wealthy resort nearby, that often employed them at low wages, is now employing them to clean up the mess at their resort. The village will be repaired and the 8th grade schoolhouse rebuilt after it was literally blown off the bluff to the beach below. Our concern now is with those villages in the north of Fiji that have no wealthy neighbors and little help on their own remote islands.

By the time you read this article I may have already returned Stateside after helping devastated communities rebuild, while also planting the seeds for a new intentional community: a community to provide a sustainable home focused on the safety of women and children. ✍

Donations can be made to FOV's recovery fund by sending PayPal donations to philipmirkin@hotmail.com, or see their crowdfunding page at gofundme.com/fijirebuild.

Philip Mirkin, founder and designer of Hybrid Adobe, authored The Hybrid Adobe Handbook *(Soaring Hill Press, 2003) and has taught over 120 workshops on sustainable building and design (at Solar Living Institute, University of Puerto Rico, for the American Institute of Architects, etc.). Philip was a keynote speaker at the San Francisco Great Outdoors Adventure Fair, the Auckland Ecoshow 2005 (in NZ), Native American Awareness Month at Whitman College, and Ho Ka He in Germany. Last year he taught the Sustainable Sculptural Building course at UC Santa Cruz, where he founded the Navajo Project in Sustainability. Philip cofounded Fiji Organic Village and has designed ecovillages and buildings in New Zealand, Puerto Rico, California, Colorado, Native Reservations, and Fiji. For 15 years he led geographical and humanitarian aid expeditions to remote parts of Native American reservations, while supporting traditional ceremonialists and delivering humanitarian aid to needy families. Current projects include developing tiny house communities in central California, teaching homeless mothers and veterans sustainable building, and designing new forms of lightweight hurricane-resistant relief housing. He also manages a 40 acre off-grid ranch. Philip consults on new ecovillages and sustainable buildings, in the US and overseas. Contact him at philipmirkin@hotmail.com or visit www.EasyAdobe.org, www.HybridAdobe.com, and www.ic.org/directory/flying-fish-organic-village.*

The First Ecovillage in Palestine

By Frederick Weihe

Ecovillages are not always founded. Sometimes people are simply together, doing what they feel is natural, necessary, and right—loving their communities and the natural world, working for justice and sustainability—only to discover after a few decades that people are calling them an ecovillage. That's the story of Farkha, a town of about 1500 people in the Salfit district, not far from Ramallah in Palestine's West Bank.

In a way, it is also the story of Findhorn and Tamera, two other projects that existed long before the words ecovillage and Permaculture were invented. They are two of the founding members of the Global Ecovillage Network (GEN). And as part of GEN and Gaia Education, representatives of both were present to support the first Ecovillage Design Education (EDE) course in Palestine—and the first in Arabic—in November of 2015 in Farkha.

So this story is about Farkha and the EDE, and what makes a village an ecovillage. But even more, it's about the synergy of networking, about friendship and knowledge-sharing. It's about how when human beings discover the shared vision that unites them, the details that separate them become much less important. It's about the universal truth that when you offer solidarity, you also receive it in the same gesture.

• • •

The town of Farkha is just outside of Salfit, a small city once nicknamed "little Moscow" for its communist politics, and still known for its Marxist leanings. The only road to Farkha passes through Salfit and then follows a ridge to the center of the village, which is perched on a hilltop and surrounded by terraced slopes that roll off into the distance. Farkha is home to the Palestinian Organic Olive Growers Association, and this is only the most visible of many ecological and community-minded initiatives: There are a number of women's associations which, for example, manage a kindergarten and cultural center in a shared building. There is another association that makes cosmetics from organic olive oil. The village has been hosting an international cultural festival for 23 years, and through this has a long history of cooperation with supporters in Central and South America. The murals and graffiti around town often include portraits of Ché Guevara and Hugo Chavez. The town has mixed-gender schools—a rarity in contemporary Palestine—and a high rate of graduation for both young men and women. There is a new, 6 hectare demonstration site for organic farming named for Simon Bolivar. The village has a full-time employee who picks up trash, and the council encourages chemical-free home gardening and rooftop rainwater harvesting.

In other words, Farkha is a concentration of progressive thought and action, and would be a great role-model for small communities anywhere on earth...but it's not just anywhere. It's in the middle of Palestine, under a brutal and illegal military occupation. Although Farkha is quiet on the surface, Palestine is a small country; it's not possible to be very far from the terrible reality. Traveling even short distances means checkpoints, delays, and roadblocks; daily life is marked by negligent or punitive power- and water-cuts; many of the EDE's students and teachers have been in Israeli prisons, witnessed terrorism and state-sanctioned murder, and all have experienced the racist violence of the occupation. This doesn't only bring logistical difficulties and the likelihood of having large infrastructure—water tanks and cisterns, for example—destroyed by the IDF (the Israeli military); it also means operating in a culture where fear and despair have been so normal for so long that anger and victimhood have become habits. Fortunately, more and more people in Palestine reject both violence and resignation, and realize that autonomy and sustainability are among the most effective tools of nonviolent political resistance.

Qambaz Baker—mostly just called "Baker"—is the mayor of Farkha, but this official role is simply one consequence of his natural qualities as a leader and visionary. He is accessible, quirky, and endlessly energetic. A true egalitarian, his house is open to the constant flow of supporters; he seems uninterested in the suits and polished desks that small-town politicians so often hide behind. He and his sons—especially Mustafa Baker—were always with us, working on the fields and earthworks, singing, serving food,

A view of Farkha on the hilltop, from the ecological farming demonstration site.

The terrace-swales emerge during a group work party.

sharing knowledge, and thinking together about the future. While we were there, Baker announced that the town had just received a grant to install a complete, autonomous photovoltaic system, to completely fill the town's electricity needs. Farkha has the vision, the knowledge, and drive to move towards real ecological sovereignty, sustainability, and justice; they are a role model not only for Palestine but for the world. We are fortunate to have this friendship; to be there to witness, to learn, and to offer support.

An important bridge between Farkha and the international community is Saad Dagher, an agronomist and permaculture teacher...and yoga instructor, Reiki master, peaceworker, and lover of animals and all living things. He grew up in a village near Farkha, and now lives in Ramallah with his very international family. He speaks Arabic of course, as well as fluent English, Russian, and Spanish. He knew that something special was happening in Farkha, and brought it to the attention of the wider world.

Aida Shibli is a friend of Saad and a key representative of the global community of ecovillages. Herself a Palestinian political activist and peaceworker, she lives in the Tamera Peace Research Village, an intentional community in Portugal. She has long carried the dream of one day seeing an international peace community arise in the Middle East, and in the last years she has focused on network-building in Palestine, putting different activists, visionaries, projects, artists, experts, and students into synergistic and creative contact. This has been within the framework of the Global Campus, an initiative of the Tamera community. One of the many fruits of Global Campus Palestine has been to bring Farkha into contact with GEN, and to bring the EDE and other international networking events to Farkha. Most of the students and experts who participated came as a direct result of this effort.

Many of the teachers came from projects just as remarkable as Farkha, and the EDE also marks a continuation of the cooperation among them. The Bethlehem-based teacher of nonviolence Sami Awad was there; as was activist and author Mazim Qumsiyeh, a professor at the University of Birzeit, and the founder and director of the Palestine Natural History Museum. Permaculture expert Murad Alchufash came from his project Marda Farm to teach. Samera Asafadi came from the animal protection league to talk about her work—also with Saad—to change the often difficult fate of wild and domestic animals in Palestine.

Long-term friend and frequent host of the Global Campus Palestine, Fayez Taneeb, came from Hakoritna Farm, with his special knowledge of how local agriculture and the political situation interact. His family's land in Tulkarem was mostly lost to the apartheid wall, and what remains has been flattened by the IDF's bulldozers many times. But his commitment to nonviolence and resilience is strong; he rebuilds and replants every time.

There are many other innovators and activists who were not present, but who are part of this increasingly solid and coherent network.

There were 31 students, 25 Palestinians from the West Bank, Gaza, from within Israel, and from the diaspora. Twelve came from Farkha itself. There were six internationals participating as well. It was mostly men, but with every event in Palestine we make steps towards parity. Being in Farkha, with its strong women's groups, was a help; we had more women present than ever, as students and on the team.

The EDE curriculum was designed by Gaia Education, and covers the different dimensions of sustainability: Worldview, Social, Ecological, and Economic. Of course, our group was a little different. Our students mostly had backgrounds in natural agriculture and a direct lived experience of the political reality of the world, and we worked to match the content to the needs of our group. To put the local experience in a global context, there were also instructors from the international network, including Aida Shibli, Kosha Joubert—executive director of GEN, and Findhorn resident—and Alice Gray. Alice is a British national based in Palestine, an activist and a certified Permaculture instructor. Thanks to the networking efforts of the last years, the other experts were locals, able to offer the content in Arabic. One of the lasting benefits of the EDE, and the whole process around it, was to put the different experts, activists, and visionaries in contact with one another. Great things are already arising.

One important expert from outside Palestine was the natural rainwater management expert Bernd Müller, who was in Palestine for a series of watershed management (continued on p. 78)

The EDE group during a tree-planting at the Cultural Center in Farkha.

Muhyiddin Sultan

Saad and Aida during a visit to Hakoritna Farm in Tulkarem, in front of the separation wall.

Frederick Weihe

Baker, Murad, and Fayez in Farkha.

Muhyiddin Sultan

Terrace-building with Baker.

Frederick Weihe

THE FIRST ECOVILLAGE IN PALESTINE
(continued from p. 63)

consultations with the Palestinian Authority, local governments and farmers, and NGOs. The course had many classroom hours, but also days of hands-on action, and one of the most exciting was when we began to rebuild the neglected—but centuries-old—fieldstone retaining walls on the ecological-farming demonstration site. Baker brought his knowledge of traditional terracing, which fit beautifully with Bernd's contribution from Permaculture; what emerged was an innovative and aesthetically-pleasing hybrid of terracing and swales. Among Saad, Baker, and Bernd, there was so much collected expertise, so much love for life, water, and the land...how could anything but deep friendship emerge?

For the student group also, these days working outdoors were a high point of the course: two joyful days of work towards food and water autonomy, cooperation with nature, and community-building. What we accomplished exceeded our expectations. Not only was a lot of stone and earth moved, but—as if by magic—time expanded to allow plenty of stories, ad hoc language and history lessons, abundant conversation and Arabic coffee, spontaneous song and poetry, and the occasional nargile. Some came to teach, some to learn...but everyone came to connect.

• • •

In the last few years, the definition of ecovillage has expanded beyond agricultural collectives and intentional communities, to include traditional villages and other projects that support a new human relationship with the natural environment. The 2016 EDE marks the moment when the growing scale and complexity of the projects in Farkha began to overlap with the growing global network of ecovillages.

For me it's a real source of hope to find people who, despite living in a small village under such constant challenges, nevertheless wake up every day and take a global perspective: They know very well that when they move towards autonomy and sustainability, they are working not only towards their own liberation but towards the liberation of everyone, for example their friends in South America, where farmers are driven off their ancestral lands by mineral speculation and industrial agriculture.

When I leave Farkha and pass through the checkpoints and borders; through traffic, cities, airports, and highways, I don't have the impression of leaving an oppressed people and stepping into the "free world." I have rather the feeling of leaving an island of joyful hope and beautiful resilience, and re-entering a culture of distraction, plastic, and hidden exploitation. Truly, my main thought is not "I'm glad I could help." Rather, I am humbled and grateful that the people in Farkha are working so tirelessly for my survival and liberation—as they are also working for their own survival and liberation, and for yours—by helping to build a world in which community, sustainability, and peace are possible. ༄

Dr. Frederick Weihe lives and works in Tamera (www.tamera.org), an intentional community and peace research center in southern Portugal. His main professional activity there is in sustainable technology, especially decentralized energy systems. He blogs occasionally at www.physicsforpeaceworkers.org.

INNISFREE VILLAGE:
Lifesharing in a Service Community

By Nancy Chappell

I have lived and worked at Innisfree Village for most of the last 24 years. I raised my son here. I have enjoyed a lifestyle of sharing, learning, caring, and laughing with people from around the world as well as with people with Intellectual Disabilities. We all have things we need and gifts we can give.

I can cook a meal for 20 with little effort and give some decent haircuts. I am not very good at measuring carefully and cutting things in a straight line. That's where my friend Willy comes in. He can be very exact and very literal. He challenges me to think in other ways or at least to consider the world from various people's viewpoints. I can practice a foreign language here, get help with my computer, or car, or bicycle. Hugs are free here and given quite freely.

This is a full, rich life that is not for everyone, but could be for many of you. We have quite a few similarities to egalitarian communities: we share resources, grow many of our own vegetables, have a pool of vehicles for our use whether "work"-related or for personal time. We are free to go in and out of each other's homes. We get fresh bread and granola delivered to our house twice a week. We have movie night, birthday parties, dances, and potlucks. There is always someone to be with. Finding alone time is possible but requires a bit more effort.

Some of the ways we are different from egalitarian communities: we have a Board of Directors, an Executive Director, and are bound by the License granted to us by the Department of Social Services for the State of Virginia. The population with Intellectual Disabilities, whom we call Coworkers, pays tuition to live here. Or more precisely their families do. In a more perfect world (and perhaps in more socialist-type democracies) this would be free to all who need it and a birthright of being a citizen. Unfortunately, we don't live in that world here in the US (yet?).

Innisfree Village is a Lifesharing community with adults with Intellectual Disabilities. We are a Service community in that we serve adults with disabilities. We were established in 1971 by some parents of young people with disabilities wanting a place for their children to grow and thrive in a community of respect and beauty.

Our mission includes:

1. Being a model therapeutic environment with people with intellectual disabilities, emphasizing empowerment, interdependence, and mutual respect of all community members.

2. Evolving with the changing needs of the individuals with intellectual disabilities within the Village community and beyond.

3. Valuing work and fostering creativity through artistic crafts, stewardship of the land, and daily community life.

4. Promoting efforts in the stewardship of our land to acknowledge the reciprocal relationship between our human health and our natural environment.

5. Encouraging the integration of community members into the larger society through participation in cultural, educational, recreational, religious, and volunteer programs.

6. Relying for its financial resources upon family support, the spirit of volunteerism, and private funding.

7. Supporting and encouraging the talents and individuality of community members from diverse educational, national, ethnic, and social backgrounds

We are a community of about 75 people, 60 of whom live here. It is a dynamic community, as people do come in and out on a regular basis. The 40 Coworkers make up the foundation of our community. Philip, Bee, and Marny all arrived here in the 1970s. Kevin, Sian, Corinne, and the two Brookes arrived in the past five years. We all arrive from various places and bring differing problems, needs, and gifts. The more dynamic part of our community is the Residential Caregiver Volunteers who come from around the world to serve for at least one year within our community. At the moment, we have Volunteers from 20 to 68 years of age who have come from Germany, Maine, England, California, Alabama, Zambia, Michigan, Spain, New York City, and Japan.

We have 10 houses spread out on our 550 acres. Each house has one to six Coworkers living there, with one to three Volunteers who live together. This is what Lifesharing means. Our day starts with breakfast in our homes and we need to "get to work" by 9. One of my favorite times of the day is between 8:45 and 9 a.m. when everyone is heading out and walking to work. I lovingly refer to this as our morning rush hour.

We have seven main workstations where we might work. The Farm is where we collect and wash eggs from our 300 or so chickens. We consume this within the village and usually have enough to sell to some local restaurants and health food stores. We also have about a dozen mamma sheep. We are just learning how to shear the sheep, then clean, card, and spin the wool into a workable product.

We have two gardens; one is the Vegetable Garden, which grows veggies on about five acres of land. We have a CSA about six months a year, that is mostly for our use, with a few select customers outside of the community. We also have an Herb Garden which grows herbs and flowers. We sell flower bouquets in a local grocery store and once or twice a year will provide flowers for weddings. Our herbs also yield fresh (in season) or dried (out of season) basil, oregano, sage, dill, parsley. We make a variety of teas that get put into tea bags and also we make an assortment of soaps.

Our weavery and woodshop have both been up and running since the early '70s. We are especially known for our beautiful cutting boards, placemats, and scarves. We sell to some local craft stores as well as various artisan fairs.

Our bakery produces about 50 loaves of bread twice a week, for our own consumption. In addition, we make granola that is enjoyed by the Village and sold in some local stores, including Whole Foods. The making of our communal lunches is one of our workstations. All 70 of us join together for a delicious vegetarian lunch four days a week. We have some excellent—and possessive—garlic peelers and cheese graters, so we probably eat more than our share of garlic and cheese at our lunches, thanks to Heyward and Katie.

Is it paradise, you ask? Some days yes and some days no. As in most communities, we have to deal with difficult personalities. There are people in community that we may not like but need to find a way to live with. Because we are looking for the best in our Coworkers and try to work with people's strengths, that can also help in dealing with the Volunteers and Staff who live or work here. Our Coworkers can have challenging behaviors above and beyond what the general population has to deal with. Fortunately, having a large property means that people are free to move about and take long walks when frustration or anger is our motivator.

Folks with seizure disorders need a vigilance that most of us do not require. At Innisfree Village, we work long hours and may have little time for ourselves. It is necessary to be flexible, have patience, and enjoy a healthy sense of humor.

New Volunteers are joining and leaving our community every few months. This keeps a dynamism but is exhausting, as we are continually offering thorough training for the life and the guidelines here, as well as constantly saying goodbye.

Coworkers might come to the end of their lives here and that can be difficult, powerful, and sad. Can we keep someone here or do we need to find another end-of-life situation for them? The most we can do is to consider each situation on its own and join with their families for the best option.

On a lighter note, a colleague just piped in with these "hardest aspects of our community": working 24/7, allergies, Virginia summers, cohabiting with spiders and snakes. I can say that this challenges me regularly. I just walked home to put away some of our eggs and meat in my fridge, to find a black snake wiggling on my kitchen floor. Not fun for me. For many people, especially for those not used to our climate and life in the country, these are the biggest challenges.

One needs to **want** to live with people differently-abled in a rural environment and to be willing and able to share of themselves in a community that is big and sometimes messy, but where smiles and hugs are plentiful too.

There are many opportunities to experience life in a Service Community, whether one commits for one year or 24 years. The benefits of Lifesharing are limitless. We welcome visitors and more importantly, Community Members. ❧

Located in Crozet, Virginia, in the foothills of the Blue Ridge Mountains, Innisfree Village welcomes visitors and new Community Members (see www.innisfreevillage.org). Nancy Chappell is Innisfree Village's Associate Director.

THE GESUNDHEIT! INSTITUTE:
A 45 Year-Old Communal Hospital Experiment

By Patch Adams

I entered medical school in 1967 to use medicine as a vehicle for social change. I immediately saw that hospitals were expensive, hierarchical, frantic, unhappy places easily causing burnout to all levels of staff. I saw nothing "healthy" about a hospital setting. There were high levels of racism and sexism where the rich "elite" were treated so much better than the disadvantaged poor. I decided to spend my four years in a medical school studying hospitals with the idea upon graduation to create a hospital that addresses all the problems of care delivery, not as the answer, but to show that answers to these problems are possible. Two years into medical school, in 1969 I went to visit the Twin Oaks community. After having wonderful words with Kat Kincade and others, I realized I was a communal person—part of the great tribe called human.

When I graduated in 1971 no one gave us a hospital, so I decided to form a commune that was a hospital open for 24 hours a day, seven days a week for all manner of medical problems from birth to death. For 12 years we did this experiment, mostly with 20 adults and our children (three were physicians) in a large six-bedroom house. In the peak years we had 500-1000 people in our home with from five to 50 guests a night. We did not distinguish the patient from the "non-patient." Instead, our focus was to try to have a relationship with everyone who came. If one came "as a patient," our ideal was to have a three- or four-hour-long initial interview (instead of the 7.8-minute one we were taught) and to visit their home. By 1980 we had gathered enough resources together to purchase 321 acres in West Virginia (the least served state for healthcare).

Everything was given freely. We didn't feel like a charity since our focus wasn't on helping the "poor." We simply didn't want people to think they owed us something in return. We wanted them to be excited to belong to something called community, a nest of care.

In this same flavor, we never heard anyone praise insurance companies. They are, after all, one-quarter to one-third of the cost of care created by the practice of medicine. So, we never had anything to do with them. One can never know before a treatment what the effect of that treatment would be, so we need the right to make a mistake, so we are the only hospital in the United States that refuses to carry malpractice insurance.

In medical school, we never had a single lecture on health and so had to discover how to spark interest and give examples of exercise, diet, love, and spirit. For example, we would host all-night dance parties, and yoga sessions during the day, as examples of exercise. For dieting, we kept extensive gardens and learned to feed lots of people. We showered everyone we met with love and affection; my longest hug was 12 hours! To encourage spiritual growth, we allowed all practices to show themselves, and generally feel that spiritual means love in action.

At this time the only complementary medicine that was legal in our state was chiropractic medicine, so we welcomed it. Then, we broke the law by welcoming acupuncture, homeopathy, naturopathy, and so many more—even some that others may think are profoundly strange.

We were all so well known for our integration of human and play that others began calling us "the Zanies"! For me, it was so thrilling and enchanting to be alive every day for those 12 years.

Since those early days I have been constantly, relentlessly raising the funds to build a hospital. This ideal hospital will be a technologically modern hospital that will show a happy, funny, loving, cooperative, creative, and thoughtful atmosphere. A hospital that will run at only 10 percent of typical operating costs.

In those early years, we never asked for money. And so, we ran with little support for those 12 years. In fact, our staff had to work outside jobs—imagine having to pay to

In March of 2002, we took 22 clowns from six different continents and 10 tons of aid to Afghanistan for five weeks. This is outside of a pediatrics hospital in Kabul.

Here we are working in our community site in West Virginia, summer 1990.

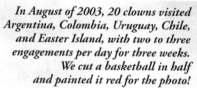

In August of 2003, 20 clowns visited Argentina, Colombia, Uruguay, Chile, and Easter Island, with two to three engagements per day for three weeks. We cut a basketball in half and painted it red for the photo!

The crew dresses up at our hospital building site in West Virginia, 1988.

A home-grown 1975 performance of Friedrich Dürrenmatt's The Physicists.

practice medicine! And yet, no staff left in the first nine years. I believe this is because the playful, deep, friendly practice of care is such an enchanting experience that it is worth paying to do. No one was making a sacrifice to be there. Love, play, and care are so seductive of appreciation.

All these years later, I'm still raising money for our dream hospital—even though a majority of financial promises have fallen through, and we may have asked over 1400 foundations for a grant. With all the setbacks, we still look to the successes that have sustained our effort.

We are a political project. And, as a political project, we realized that our style had become so intense, we would soon run the risk of burning out many people. It was then that I realized that to continue our project, we have to build a communal ecovillage to protect this dream of a hospital. It became clear that every staff person must have a room for their own and the other projects that hold their interest (like the arts). The way we had been was no model to show possibility—we had to actually have a hospital, albeit our style of hospital. We had refused publicity up to this point. We realized that if we were to raise the millions of dollars we need to build and endow our hospital, we would have to bring in publicity. In order to raise this money, I would become some sort of a celebrity. So, we closed our doors in 1983 and held a press event. Shortly after we closed the hospital, I was invited to lecture and perform all over the world. We tightened up the communal home for six to eight people for the next 15 years—waiting for that chance to build our fantasy.

By 1985 I was feeling such an emptiness from not being able to do direct care that I started our clown trips to foreign countries. This was a second wonderful exploration of communal living because the clown trips were a totally random collection of people. People have ranged in age from three to 88, from over 50 countries, and many come with no prior experience. We started in the Soviet Union and we have gone there usually with 35-40 people for two weeks. Our Russia trip is now in its 31st year! Using the same six qualities—happy, funny, loving, cooperative, creative, and thoughtful—complete strangers become a coordinated team of beautiful clowns. Over 150 trips have happened since the initial outing, involving over 6000 people; maybe only five or six did not work out.

Of course, the big trick was that all were going to human suffering with love and fun, which extracted these six qualities out of whoever came. The trips have been universally enchanting. Twenty-three years ago

received such donations that as I write we are putting the roof on our first big building.

In 1987, at a conference of the International Cybernetics Association, I met a radical group of artists and activists who put the conference on, and I instantly felt a connection. The next five years we got closer and they changed their name to the School for Designing a Society (designingasociety.net). We invited them to do the school in the summer on our land in West Virginia because it was like the missing piece for our project. We are here to teach and show social change. So right was this union, that we decided that the first big building we would build will be a school building. We had agreed from the beginning that our medical and clowning work would be free, and our educational work would be how we would raise our funds. By educational work, I mean

We've taken clowns into war zones, refugee camps, and horrible disasters all over the world.

we were touring some orphanages in such an unhappy state that we were overjoyed when we met our astonishing friend Maria. Maria began work that has continued all these years with over 600 orphans, exceeding our wildest dreams.

In these years we've taken clowns into war zones, many refugee camps, and horrible disasters all over the world. Eleven years ago we were touring the Peruvian Amazon with a group of clowns when we came upon an unsettling number of children (ages three to five) that have been afflicted with gonorrhea. Our shock has emboldened us to return there every year since then and help out in any way we can. Now we team up with 100 clowns from all over the world for a two-week extravaganza filled with humanitarian projects and clowning for all. We will return this August! For this past year we have also maintained a year-long presence in the area with four women who moved there to see what can happy: a doctor, a psychologist, and two musicians. A similar project was started in Nepal eight years ago by our dear partners, Ginevra and Italo.

In 1999, Hollywood released a film about my life called *Patch Adams*. I agreed to do this foolish thing because they promised to help us build our hospital. The film made hundreds of millions of dollars—but we made no money from the film. We are here to end capitalism after all. However, the film did make my speaker fees go way up, and so another kind of communal project developed where I could give a talk, and with volunteers we could build a clinic or school in a poor country. The fees also made it possible to build three beautiful buildings on our West Virginia property in preparation for the big buildings we want for the hospital. In the last few years, through three bequests and some sweetly eccentric people, we have

lectures, speeches, workshops, and classes. Here was an in-house way to raise funds and to teach nonviolent revolution. What may be interesting to communal societies is that we have combined our communities, but kept the styles for each community as they are. The School has also created clown trips that have clowning in the morning, and education in the afternoon and evening. They have annual trips in Ecuador and Costa Rica. They have also returned recently from a clowning event in Mexico.

So yes! We have failed to build the hospital that I began in 1971, and was sure it would be funded in four years. Imagine my glee when I realized that the delay has been a great gift! The design of the hospital is a lot more intelligent now than we ever dreamed at the beginning. For

In Peru, clowns perform a sex-education skit, with Patch as a spermie.

Following a series of hurricanes in Cuba, clowns partner with the National Children's Theater group, "La Colmenita" to bring cheer to the disaster area.

Clowns from 15 different countries parade in Belen, Iquitos, Peru.

Participants in annual "Laughing Body" seminar enjoy the mud pit.

Patch's wedding, the community's first, in 1975. The theme of the wedding was Louis the XIV with all dresses and garments made in the community.

Every year since 1985, 40 clowns travel to Russia for two weeks and take a picture at this location.

Our annual Commune Christmas Picture, taken in 1978 in Charles Town, West Virginia.

example, environmental consciousness and desire have really progressed these 45 years. So we will have 120 staff, all living together in our communal ecovillage. This will eliminate 85 percent of the village's ecological footprint. Permaculture and other ideas have leapt into our concept. With our global outreach and fame we are connected all over the world in our project, and those of other countries. It is thrilling! Clowns are now going into hospitals in over 130 countries, and in Argentina laws have been passed to require pediatric departments in every hospital to hire clowns. I lecture 300 days out of the year, and have done so for over 30 years in 81 counties, spreading seeds of a love revolution of enlivening community and a call to end capitalism. I have corresponded with letters to 130 countries so it feels like a global family—each with their own special directions of care.

I have never been discouraged; in fact the pursuit has given me a vigorous life. The smartest thing I ever did was be communal. This was the sweetest gift to myself. The hospital, the clown trips, the lectures and correspondences have made me feel that the earth is my commune, and all of us are truly brothers and sisters. Let's get to work!

Our funding must be right around the corner!

In Peace, Patch

Patch Adams, M.D., founder of the Ge-sundheit! Institute, is a doctor, clown, activist for peace, justice, and care for all people, and lifelong reader of COMMUNITIES *maga-zine (since its birth in 1972). See www. patchadams.org.*

ACTIVISM AND SERVICE AT BLACK BULGA COMMUNITY: Inspiring, Nurturing, Challenging, and Not All Hard Work

By Geoff Evans

Our small rural land-sharing community, Black Bulga, comprises 13 people and is located in the forested, healthy, and clean headwaters of the Karuah River in the Hunter Valley in Australia, near the city of Newcastle, which is about 100 miles north of Sydney. We have been forming together as a community for seven years and have owned our land for five years.

We formed as an explicitly "service" or "activist" community having gotten to know each other mainly through social change activist networks. We are very fortunate. We enjoy a healthy environment in a country where there is relatively little violence or war. Being aware of our special luck, we were determined when we formed our community that our purpose was not to retreat from the world. Rather our purpose is to create a community that will sustain us, and inspire us to engage with the wider world to help make it a better place for our generation and those that follow.

Our shared commitment to activism gives Black Bulga a distinct purpose, and our commitment to service and activism is written into the vision and values sections of our bylaws: "Our vision is to act as custodians of the rural land upon which we live, working together to create a sustainable and just future in our immediate community and in the wider world." The values written into our bylaws include commitments to use our collective resourcefulness and creativity to care for the land, and for each other, our neighborhood, region, and the planet. While we subscribe to no particular ideology, our politics is informed by ecological libertarian socialist values. We pay attention to how we can support each other to sustain our activism in the spirit of these values.

Our members' activist work spans multiple roles and locations, including as frontline defenders joining local residents blockading proposed gasfields in the nearby town of Gloucester and elsewhere; as managers of social change organizations; as activist trainers, community organizers, and facilitators; as mentors and elders to a wide community of activists in multiple fields and in different places and age groups; as educators and researchers in a wide range of academic and activist programs including in family wellbeing and sustainability; in international community development and medical aid work; as practitioners in community arts and sustainable food growing; and as parents and allies to fellow parents, Our collective and individual activism inspires us, exhausts us, nurtures us—and challenges us.

The youngest and oldest Black Bulga community members (and friends) marching for climate action in Sydney in November 2015.

We have found that our social change activism builds local community and connects us with our neighbors as well as the wider world. In fact, we did not need to go far to find opportunity to put our individual and shared passions for social change into practice. In our local valley, our service work gets literally "down amongst the weeds." We are

and other residents from the length of the Karuah River catchment together to learn about and fight the proposal. We formed the Karuah River Protection Alliance and together we spoke out strongly through local and national media, to government officials, and directly to the company. Following our extensive lobbying the proposal was dropped, and by winning the campaign, we helped secure the future of the valley for nature-based tourism and sustainable food growing.

Before the campaign we were known rather disparagingly as "The Commune," but through the campaign our neighbors got to appreciate the campaigning skills of the "new kids to the block," while we admired their skills and capacity to organize locally. The campaign sped up the process of us being accepted as part of the community. We now share farming knowledge, host our neighbors' horses and cattle on our land, regularly have meals together, and celebrate family events such as children's birthdays, Spring

Balancing social change work with building a strong community poses many challenges.

and Autumn (Fall) Equinox, and New Year's Eve.

While our valley is mining-free, thousands of residents and farmers in neighboring valleys across the Hunter Valley are fighting the devastating impacts of vast open-cut (open-pit) coal mines and the threat of gasfields with severe impacts on their environments and health. The Hunter is one of the world's largest coal-exporting regions, with hundreds of millions of tons of coal exported from the port of Newcastle annually to North and East Asia. The region is also the home of coal-fired power stations that have historically been the major source of Australia's electricity. Together these industries make the Hunter region one of the world's climate change hot-spots. Many times our members have joined frontline action against coal and climate change including blockading gasfields in the nearby town of Gloucester with local residents, and other peaceful blockades and lock-ons at coal mines and coal export terminals in Newcastle and elsewhere.

Balancing externally-oriented social change work with building a strong and viable intentional community poses many challenges. Our service and activist work takes our focus away from building our relatively new community and from working on our land. This challenge is compounded by the fact that actually living and working on our land is very difficult as it is quite remote and there are few jobs in the local area. We have had to find ways to transition from careers in large cities to work that we can do from the land or in nearby towns. Jemma, who manages a small international development organization as well as co-parenting three children under eight years old recently moved from Sydney to Newcastle, as part of her family's strategy to be closer to the land and spend more time at Black Bulga, highlights the tension;

"To make Black Bulga to grow and thrive in the long-term, it needs people there, planting through the seasons, working together, creating a hub. But it is a tricky tension to manage—how to be on the land while still being an active part of social change campaigns. At the moment, we are all in the transition to spending more time at Black Bulga. We have monthly community meetings, regular all-in working bees, and big social gatherings. There is a real network of friends and family—many of whom work in social change—who have a genuine connection to Black Bulga, who visit regularly, talk politics, get their hands dirty, dream and replenish. I love that the Black Bulga community is bigger than just the group of unit holders."

The heavy demands and occasional heady excitement that comes from activist work—which in some cases allows us to travel the world, be in the national media spotlight, and confront powerful political and corporate interests—makes a stark contrast to the work of building community and caring for food crops, stock, and buildings. John, who is often away supporting local coal and gas campaigns around Australia and globally, reflects that "It is too easy for me to live in my head but Black Bulga helps to keep me grounded. The place has a wildness that replenishes the soul."

Another member, James, who develops education programs for activists, also grapples with the challenge of balancing his external community and Black Bulga community focus: "I try to meet my own and my intentional community's needs by being at Black Bulga as much as possible and when here, I get stuck into a hands-on project such as building work, and

proud to have been instrumental in forming a local Landcare network to protect our river catchment from weed infestations. In Australia, this Landcare movement has been a powerful social movement that has brought farmers and environmentalists together at grassroots and national levels, with government funding support. As Landcarers we've worked and sweated in hot sun and along riverbanks with our neighbors, removing weeds and creating space for local native plants to regenerate. John Mac, the Black Bulga member who leads this work, reports the benefits:

"This service work builds local community networks to collectively protect our local environment. We have in our valley, between us, hundreds of years of land management knowledge. We share stories of about what is effective and efficient land management, and what doesn't work and is a waste of time and effort. We also share lots of cakes and cups of coffee."

We have among our members some very experienced activists who have spent decades campaigning around mining, environmental protection, and human rights, working with mine-affected communities locally and globally. When a gold mine was proposed upriver in upper reaches of the Karuah River in 2011, soon after we had bought our land, the mine-owners may not have realized who they were taking on. The whole catchment community saw the mine as a threat, with the risk of sediment pollution and, potentially, cyanide contamination jeopardizing local farming and tourism industries and the rural lifestyle and amenity.

We were quick to act, and with our neighbors, we used the extensive networks throughout the valley to bring farmers, ecotourism business operators, oyster farmers, joining in the cooking and sharing of great food, and reading and playing with the children. Black Bulga helps me keep the relentless demands of work in its box. It's not easy, but my fellow community members help me meet this challenge."

As individuals, and as a community, we are still in transition when it comes to combining our activism with a rural farm-based lifestyle. We are trying to work part-time rather than full-time. We use internet, Skype, and email technologies as much as possible so we can work from the land. Our aim to make Black Bulga an arts and ecology education center is part of our community's purpose but, like living on the land permanently, we recognize that this vision is long-term and is happening in small steps. Dan, who recently held a successful solo exhibition of paintings inspired by the vast and ever-changing Black Bulga skies, comments:

"The arts and ecology project is part of a lifelong journey of the community. We are giving effect to the vision by organizing arts and ecology events and activities on the land, even though we don't yet have a building specifically for this purpose. Our community celebrates the equinox and solstice with gatherings that involve rituals that range from reverent to ridiculous. We have raced down the river on inflatable rafts, built clay pizza ovens and cooked seasonal feasts to eat under the stars, made beautiful lanterns and ugly effigies of 'baddies' to set alight, woven baskets from weeds, and healed a gully with plantings. Already many friends and community come here to draw, paint, and take photos; some have learnt blacksmithing; others have come to write, take nature walks, go bird-watching, and more."

The community consciously works on integrating the service elements of our lives with the personal and community care elements of our lives in an intentional community. Deb, who works in family studies and relationship research programs at the region's university and across Australia, as well as with academics and family relationship professionals and activists in India, Southeast Asia, and the US, identifies the need for balance here: "At Black Bulga we work hard at supporting each other to pay good attention to both our work and personal lives. The demands of managing complex decisions about the future of the community requires care and a strong commitment to listen to and support each other. We look out for each other. This work on building positive relationships helps us be whole, well-balanced people at Black Bulga and in our family, professional, and activist lives as well."

Prue, mother of two-year old Blake, is a campaigner supporting communities trying to stop fracking for gas in various parts of the state. She is often away from home: "Activism work can be hard on the family. Luckily I have a very supportive partner, but the activist life requires a strong and constant focus on our own well-being individually and collectively, particularly on our work as parents. All members of the Black Bulga community are great support and allies to us as parents, and to Blake as a young toddler."

As individuals and as a community we at Black Bulga know that service and activist work is incredibly important, rewarding, and challenging lifelong work. Our community is a vital support foundation for us being able to go out into the wider world as effective change agents. As many of our friends are also activists, we recognize they have the same challenges balancing service and personal lives as we do. We encourage them to get "out of the city and into the bush" and to use Black Bulga as a place to enjoy nature, and to swim, walk, and play together with family and friends. Reconnecting with the rhythms of nature—and enjoying collectively-grown and cooked food, fireside conversation under starry skies, and being woken by the sounds of the dawn chorus of birds—helps us see that service and activist lives are not all hard work. 🐦

Geoff Evans is a wannabe farmer. He keeps the Black Bulga dream alive through activism on mining, climate change, and community development, and working with the community to build a small house and grow an organic garlic crop each year on the land.

Black Bulga hosting a celebration dinner for the Community Organising Fellowship in our big strawbale shed in July 2015.

NOT the Last of the Mohicans:
Honoring Our Native Predecessors on the Land

By Jeff Golden

Let it not surprise you my friends, when I say, that the spot on which we stand has never been purchased or rightly obtained; and that by justice, human and divine, it is the property now of the remnant of that great people, from whom I am descended. They left it in the tortures of starvation and to improve their miserable existence; but as a cession was never made, their title has never been extinguished.

—Mohican Chief Quinney
from a speech delivered the 4th of July, 1854, in New York

For the 98 percent of us in the United States who are not Native American, what does it mean to live in this country today, to live in the shadow of what was done to the native people? What does it mean to be living on and trading in land and resources that were taken from the native people through intense and chronic violence and deceit?

The Common Fire Housing Co-op was created in 2005 in New York's Hudson Valley with a vision of providing a home for people who wish to be very intentional about living in a just and sustainable way. One of the four core principles was Aligning Our Lives with Our Beliefs. We shared a sense that much of the violence and destruction in the world today arises not from malice, but from people being invested in the current systems and contributing to them in small ways that add up and give the systems power. And so we sought to think and act together to try to weave greater integrity into our everyday lives and into our work and service in the world.

That showed up in a number of ways, many of which will not be new to other community-minded people. Community members were selected specifically with an eye to their commitment to making a difference in the world, in whatever ways that showed up in their lives. The building that housed the co-op was built to be extremely environmentally-responsible, and earned the first Platinum certification in New York from the US Green Building Council. The food that residents bought and prepared together was primarily local and organic. Residents organized and participated in regular trainings on important issues and critical skills related to living in community and being effective in the world. And so on.

We also sought to grapple with those fundamental questions about the history of the land and the people who once lived there, and what was done to them and what became of them.

To do that, it was first necessary to find out just what that history was, and even who those people were. Asking other locals about it revealed that most people had no idea what tribe had lived in that area, and the town's website and the few individuals who did offer answers turned out to all be wrong. None of the basic histories of

New York or of the local area had any solid information, so the residents had to dig deeper into histories and primary materials specifically focused on Native Americans.

The History and the People

But the history and the people did reveal themselves with some persistence. The first people arrived in what is today known as New York's Hudson Valley some 12,000 years ago. Their descendants lived in the area for about 600 generations before the first Europeans (led by Henry Hudson) arrived in 1609. At that time the Mohicans lived where the housing co-op would be built nearly 400 years, or about 20 generations, later. And it turns out the story of their interactions with the Europeans is as grim in its own way as any tale told by other native people in America.

A huge percentage of the Mohicans died from diseases that came with the Europeans. Another large number of them died from violence with other Indians that escalated with the arrival of guns and trade with the Europeans. And a large number of them were intentionally killed by Europeans. Those who survived were forced from their land and driven away. The pre-contact population of the Mohicans is unknown, but was somewhere between 5,000 and 12,000. Within a mere 50 years that had dropped to less than a thousand, and there were virtually none left in the Hudson Valley.

Some 50 Mohicans took refuge at a Protestant mission near the border with Connecticut where the missionaries were very helpful, exposing traders who illegally sold the Mohicans alcohol, and offering legal support in their dealings with the Europeans. The local settlers spread rumors of atrocities committed by the Indians, they prevented people from visiting or trading with the mission, and they eventually petitioned the governor for permission to kill the Indians at the mission. The petition was denied, but it sufficed to drive away the remaining Mohicans in 1746.

Many of the survivors found their way to western Massachusetts and tried to survive by adopting the customs and occupations of the Europeans. In the 1780s they were forced to relocate to

229

western/upstate New York with the Oneida tribe. In 1818 they were in turn driven from that land to Indiana. And in 1822 they were forced to Wisconsin. The 40,000 acres they were given there was reduced to 16,000. The land was not generally suitable for farming, so much of it was turned over to logging companies who clearcut the land. With very little food or shelter, some of the Mohicans moved into the abandoned offices left by the logging company. Many of their children were sent to boarding schools run by non-natives that forbade the

some 750 out of about 1500 enrolled tribal members today—live on that same reservation today. The forests have returned, along with the wildlife; housing has expanded greatly; there is a health center, a meeting hall, and more. The largest employer in the county is a tribal casino, which generates a large degree of the income on the reservation. In the words of one Mohican, Molly Miller, "The road from colonization is long and painful but we continue to work at it."

What To Do?

Which brings us back to those initial questions. What does it mean to "own" a portion of this land that was so violently taken from those people who had lived there for 600 generations? What does it mean to live on that land, to enjoy it and so many of the benefits and riches that have flowed from these lands, benefits and riches largely denied to the children and grandchildren of those people? And what does it mean to go about our daily lives in a larger community and society while this massive violence and injustice is largely ignored, unacknowledged, and even unknown by so many, and on some levels continues to be perpetuated against those people?

> What does it mean to "own" a portion of this land that was so violently taken from people who had lived there for 600 generations?

For those of us in the co-op, it meant writing up and sharing publicly what we had learned about the Mohicans, as well as what we learned about other aspects of the history of the area, including a significant use and abuse of black slaves, and sharing that history with all who visited the co-op, and making it available on our website.

kids from speaking their native language and practicing their native customs. Their population at one point fell to 600.

Contrary to what James Fennimore Cooper might have had us believe, however, with his fictional book, *The Last of the Mohicans*, the Mohicans did survive.

A large number of their descendants—

It meant creating an initial pool of money. Without knowing for sure what we were going to end up doing or what kinds of resources we would need, everyone in the co-op agreed to pay an extra $10 a month towards the "Mohican Project."

It meant reaching out to a number of Mohicans both in New York and on the reservation to discuss with them what they thought the residents could or should do. Once again, a little legwork was required. Who to reach out to? And how? We read through the tribe's

The author and others helping with the construction of the Tivoli Co-op.

Photos courtesy of Geff Golden

website and found that they have a couple committees that felt related to our efforts and concerns. One is the Historical Committee, the other the Language and Culture Committee. (The last fluent speaker of Mohican died in 1933, and many aspects of the traditional culture were intentionally stamped out by the Europeans, so nurturing the cultural and linguistic roots of the Mohican people, in a sense the spiritual roots of the people, is an important focus for some in the tribe.) So we wrote to those committees.

We also read the tribe's biweekly newspaper online and subscribed to it. There we gleaned a few other names of people who seemed like good contacts for us—one who writes a regular history column; another, apparently the only enrolled tribal member located in the Mohican homeland, who was a Masters student in history; some people involved in the local museum.

We wrote these people, sharing a little about who we were, and seeking whatever thoughts they might have about ways we could help to heal this history and take responsibility for the legacy we had inherited. Some people we never heard back from. Some very kindly referred us to other people. And a couple of them fully engaged us, sharing deeply of their own experiences and suggestions, and reaching out to other tribal members for their own thoughts.

The history of what had been done to the Mohicans and what had become of them was obviously well-known to those people, but the questions we were asking were generally new to them; they hadn't been asked them before. The 400-year anniversary of Henry Hudson's arrival in this area was about to be commemorated a year later and some of their initial ideas included providing a place for people to stay if they were able to organize a trip back to their home-

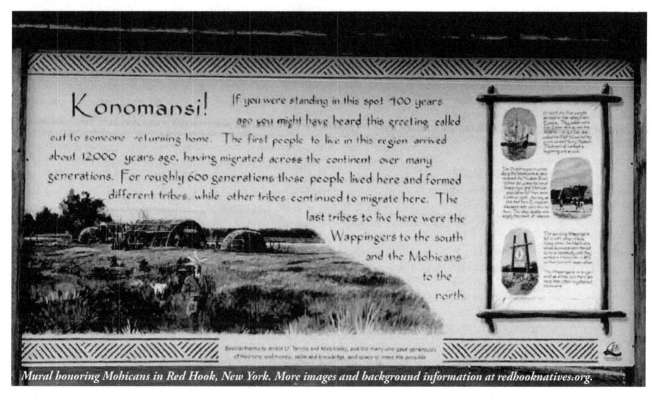

Mural honoring Mohicans in Red Hook, New York. More images and background information at redhooknatives.org.

land for that, supporting them doing some kind of "wiping of the tears" ceremony, and helping them with their land claims, as well as continuing to educate locals about their history and who they are today. They were all very supportive of what we were doing as a co-op, both in relation to the Mohicans and in general, though one person courageously added, "To be really true to your thinking, if there comes a time that the co-op were to be no longer, then will your land back to the tribe."

We had the Mohican who lives in New York come and speak at one of the annual Harvest Festivals held at the co-op. We

look like, including some of the history and some key images. We scouted possible locations and decided that the most popular ice cream shop in the county was hands down the best place to really get our images and information before a lot of people, and in a positive, familiar environment.

We asked around about the owner and were told by one person that there was zero chance, that he was politically not at all the kind of person who would support us. But we reached out to a couple prominent people in town with whom we had relationships and who were of the same political party/perspective as the owner of that land, and they helped us connect with him. We sent him our request along with the draft image. We had a meeting on-site and found him to be really supportive of the idea. We discussed the location and he ran it by some of the store owners in the plaza there. He asked for just a couple changes to the language and gave us a green light.

We then took the images and text to our main contacts among the Mohicans for their feedback. Again, with a couple minor but meaningful changes they felt good about it as well.

We got in touch with a prominent muralist in the region who advised us on what kind of wood, paint, and finish to use. We got someone to project the image and paint it for us on a piece of 4'x8' high quality plywood. Another person donated some rustic posts; other people donated the labor of putting them in the ground and erecting the mural. Using our pool of money and fundraising from locals and friends and family, we raised the $1,000

> ## We focused our educational efforts on getting a mural about the Mohicans erected in town.

tried to get the local town to correct its website to acknowledge who the real native people were in that area and what became of them, though there was some defensiveness and uncertainty about whether what we had discovered was true, and the website never was changed. There are a couple "Welcome to Red Hook" signs at the edge of town. We also requested that the town add to those signs, "The Southern Boundary of the Mohican Homeland." That required going through one of the local clubs, and we didn't get too far with that. We also considered trying to get some information about the Mohicans in the local school curriculum, but the process for that seemed very daunting.

One of the co-op residents helped us really focus our intentions by posing the simple but powerful question: "Today almost nobody knows who the native people were here. What do we need to do to make sure that a generation from now almost everybody does?"

We decided to focus our efforts on getting a mural erected somewhere very visible in town, but on private property, where we really would only need to deal with one person, the owner. Using images of Mohicans from a painter in the region who seemed to have an informed and not stereotype-based or derogatory sense of the Mohicans, we created a draft of what the mural might

that the mural ended up costing us on top of the volunteer labor and donations. And we created a companion website to the mural, sharing what we had ourselves learned about the Mohicans. You can see that at www.redhooknatives.org.

The mural turned out beautifully, and it is seen by so many people!!! We couldn't be happier with that part of our journey.

The End of the Co-op

For a variety of reasons, in 2013 we decided to close down the housing co-op. The question of how to be in right relationship with the Mohicans through that process was important to us. We owed a lot of money on the building in the form of a mortgage with a local credit union, so we couldn't just "will the land back to the tribe," as that one Mohican had suggested. But we were willing to sell the land to the Mohicans for the rock bottom amount of money we needed to cover that mortgage. And we reached out to some friends who are native and very active in their communities, and we discovered that there are a couple organizations that donate money and offer loans in support of native people regaining access to their original land.

We wrote the person who was our main contact on the reservation about what we were thinking, and about those two organizations, and about our willingness to do our best to help with fundraising as well through our own networks. Our contact forwarded our letter to the tribal government for them to consider. We weren't sure how important taking ownership of this land would be to the Mohicans, or whether they would feel it was worth whatever effort or money it would take to pull off this purchase. But we never heard back from them one way or the other, even after following-up a couple times.

So we did what felt to us like the next best thing. We sold the property and committed to in some way investing any money left over to supporting the Mohicans. We took the responsibility of shepherding that money very seriously. Tribal governments are often not particularly effective. We did not have any reason to believe that was true in the case of the Mohicans, but by that time our relationship with our main Mohican contact had deepened, a couple of us had actually met her and visited the reservation in Wisconsin, and so we had a lot of trust in her and felt very good about her helping guide us in terms of how to direct that money.

So far we have donated $28,000, with a little bit of money still tied up in legalities around the property that will hopefully be freed up at some point for us to add to this amount, though that is uncertain. The money has been donated to the Historical Committee, which is part of but has separate finances from the general tribal government. The money has been used to support a gathering of native people on the Mohican reservation, a gathering of native people near the Mohican homeland, and efforts to reconnect with the Mohican language.

In the letter we wrote that accompanied our last donation, we wrote:

"It's a strange and cruel thing that we have had the opportunity to live in the Mohican homeland, to enjoy many of the blessings of this land, and to have even 'owned' some of this land by the laws and customs of the United States, knowing full well that these laws and these opportunities rest on a foundation of profound violence, disrespect, and oppression that killed and drove off the Mohicans and other native peoples who had lived here for thousands upon thousands of years.

"We are clear that we are returning a very tiny portion of so much that is rightfully the tribe's to begin with—riches that were stolen long ago. This is not a gift or donation from us to you, it is that tiny portion finally finding its way back to its proper place.

"It is our hope that this money and the spirit in which we offer it help to bring greater joy, peace, and health to some in the Mohican community."

In that same vein, I offer this article, not because I think we got everything "right" or others need to do exactly what we did, but in the hope that it is helpful and inspiring to you on some level, and does help to feed greater joy, peace, and health in relation to the native people of these lands. ❧

Jeff Golden cofounded Common Fire and played a central role and lived in its two communities in New York's Hudson Valley, including the Common Fire Housing Co-op in Tivoli. More recently, he contributed the article "Common Fire's Top Ten Hard-Earned Tips for Community Success" to COMMUNITIES #170.

The Tivoli Housing Co-op was a new construction project.

People gathered at the grand opening of the Tivoli Co-op.

A gathering of residents and friends at the Tivoli Co-op.

The author (in background) with daughters visiting the Stockbridge Munsee reservation.

AGING IN COMMUNITY:
How an Older Couple Helped Launch a New Multi-Generational Ecovillage Neighborhood

By Wallace Watson

Getting Here

Nine years ago, my wife Shannon and I decided (at ages 65 and 71) to downsize from our roomy Victorian house in Pittsburgh, Pennsylvania and head north—in spite of the admonition of my daughter in South Carolina: "But Daddy, when people get old, they move south."

We were drawn northward by a small vacation property on the Canadian side of the Thousand Islands of the St. Lawrence River, a retreat that Shannon had acquired through her family many years earlier. We wanted to live closer than eight hours to that magical place after Shannon joined me in retirement. A friend had handed us an issue of *Time* magazine with a story on cohousing featuring EcoVillage at Ithaca, New York (EVI). "This might interest you." It did indeed. At that time we were fairly serious about living sustainably—recycling, composting, gardening, replacing inefficient old windows, adding home insulation, even buying a hybrid car. But we knew little about cohousing and had never heard of an ecovillage.

A short time later, we briefly visited EVI. We were impressed by what we saw as we wandered through its two neighborhoods, "FROG" and "SONG," which were completed in 1997 and 2003. There were 60 small-to-medium sized duplex homes of modern-rustic design tightly clustered on walking paths free of automotive traffic, with large south-facing windows, and a lot of rooftop photovoltaic and solar hot-water panels. Nearby were two organic farms, community gardens, a swimmable pond, and several miles of paths leading through fields into thick woods. All this was just four hours from our island cottage.

We heard that a group was planning a third neighborhood, which had just been named "TREE," and decided to get involved, even though that meant making a six-hour drive up from Pittsburgh every few weekends. We soon came to both understand and appreciate the group's commitment to the principles guiding the first two neighborhoods: both older and younger residents living together lightly on the land, taking responsibility for finances and maintenance, self-governing by consensus, living cooperatively while respecting privacy—not at all typical of the few retirement communities we knew about. Our growing interest in EcoVillage at Ithaca was now motivated by much more than its closeness to our Canadian vacation spot.

Early in 2008, we put down serious money ($1,000) to become charter members of a newly formed TREE Joint Venture. This, with the increased payments that soon followed, constituted a fairly serious financial risk for an elderly couple with moderate fixed incomes and no guaranteed return if the project should fail. We hoped we could help it succeed.

Planning the New Community

Shannon and I took on major responsibilities early in the planning process. A retired attorney, she coordinated the Legal Committee, which developed bylaws and guided the group's evolution from Joint Venture to Limited Liability Company and then Cooperative Corporation. As a former professor and academic administrator, I was inclined toward organizational processes and soon found myself convener of a new Co-ordination Committee, among other tasks.

We sold our Pittsburgh house in July 2011 and spent most of the next three years in rented apartments near Ithaca, anxious to know when we would be able to move into our new home. That finally happened in July 2014, shortly after my 78th birthday. By then, I had begun to wonder if I might be getting too old for this kind of adventure.

Like our predecessors in FROG and SONG, the TREE planners were intent on building not just a physical neighborhood but also an intergenerational community of people who knew, trusted, cared for, and co-operated with each other. We accomplished this in large part by resolving increasingly difficult strategic and financial challenges.

The author, Wallace, and his wife Shannon, in front of their house in TREE, fall of 2015.

Residents of TREE and the two other neighborhoods at a goodbye party for a couple returning home to Austria after a short-term residency in EcoVillage at Ithaca.

James Bosjolie

What TREE Built

Construction of the first seven standalone homes and two duplexes was completed in the fall of 2013. The remaining 10 singles and two more duplexes were finished in 2014. The Common House was occupied last fall. It contains a large dining room, kitchen, and other common spaces on the ground floor, as well as 15 private living units ranging in size from efficiency to three or four bedrooms.

Early in the long TREE planning period, we realized how many in our group were at or near retirement age or would soon be dealing with physical challenges. So we identified "aging in place" and "accessibility" as major considerations. Thus the Common House includes a four-story elevator, and all its living units and common areas are wheelchair accessible. So too are the entrances and first floors of the 25 stand-alone homes in the neighborhood; only the eight duplex units do not have bedrooms or complete baths on the ground level.

Our house, just one door down from the Common House (and thus, happily, close to the neighborhood laundry room), is one of 10 similar free-standing homes: a story and a half, with 1050 square-feet of living space, bedrooms and baths upstairs and down, a flexible living-dining area, and modest storage space. If Shannon or I ever need to use a walker or wheelchair, we can live on the first floor; a resident caretaker, if it comes to that, can use the second floor bedroom and bath.

All the homes in TREE are Energy Star certified; the houses have met LEED Platinum standards, and the Common House

As in the two older neighborhoods here, our major decisions were made through unanimous consensus. When on occasion this method didn't seem workable, Shannon and I found it hard to disguise our impatience. Given our ages, we didn't have that long to wait! Still, the consensus process did help us all to listen more thoughtfully and eventually come to agreement, rather than to fight for narrow majoritarian victories likely to leave the losers embittered. (Last June, TREE changed its decision-making process to "Dynamic Governance," a much more flexible way of making decisions in community.)

Delays, Cost Increases, Solutions

At times, the planning process moved along fairly quickly, as on one memorable afternoon when we planned the general layout of the neighborhood by arranging small wooden blocks on contour maps. At the west end would stand a large Common House containing living units; from there, double rows of single-family homes and duplexes would extend eastward and northward.

It took several months, however, to agree on a detailed Architectural Program, and several years to work through increasingly difficult financial challenges. Those money problems were exacerbated by the Great Recession, as well as serious construction delays. We lost about two years' progress because the first two construction managers we hired didn't fit our needs.

Those delays of course meant increases in construction costs. The price of my and Shannon's shares in the Corporation (which gave us modified ownership of our house) rose inexorably—increasing from the architect's initial preliminary estimate of $195,500 for the base design (to which

> ## On one memorable afternoon we planned the general layout of the neighborhood by arranging small wooden blocks on contour maps.

we added over $14,000 in optional features) to the final base cost of $248,000, which is approximately in the middle of the range of TREE house prices.

Those increasing costs created considerable tension within the group. But TREE weathered the storm in creative and empathetic ways—including implementation of a turnover fee of three percent on future sales of TREE homes; purchase of second units by a few members for rental to those unable to secure mortgages; donations of tools, furniture, kitchenware, etc.; and extensive (in some cases heroic) sweat equity.

is expected to be so certified soon. All the homes are equipped with very thick outside-wall insulation and unusually energy-efficient glass in windows and doors; when necessary, the interiors are warmed by a few small electric baseboard heaters. Large windows on the south allow us to shut down the heat during even the coldest days in winter when the sun is out. In the winter, air is circulated by a sophisticated energy recovery ventilating system; in warmer weather casement windows (opening from either the top or the side) make possible natural air circulation that has virtually eliminated the need for air conditioning in any TREE homes.

Affordability

Early on, Shannon and I hoped we would be able to pay cash for our new home, after selling the Pittsburgh house. But rising costs

However, our costs are significantly less than those in some similarly energy-efficient communities I have heard about. Moreover, many TREE members hope, with Shannon and me, that in the not-too-distant future we will figure out ways to make it possible for more lower-income people to share the TREE-EVI experience—perhaps by applying some of the proceeds of the three percent sales fee we have instituted.

Living in TREE, EVI, Ithaca

In spite of the long wait to move into our house, Shannon and I are very happy with our decision nine years ago to undertake this challenge. Outside of EVI, she has been able to continue her lifelong participation in choral singing, through her Unitarian Church choir and a large community chorus. I've become fairly active in the Quaker Meeting here, as I was in Pittsburgh. We enjoy, often with EVI neighbors, an unusually rich variety of cultural and entertainment opportunities in Ithaca and environs: excellent movies, music, and theater; an impressive Museum of the Earth; hiking trails near dozens of waterfalls in our gorgeous Finger Lakes region ("Ithaca is gorges"); and a surprising number of good eating opportunities for such a small city.

> ## We who helped plan TREE have not yet fully reached the third of our goals: "Sustainability, Accessibility, Affordability."

required us to get a mortgage. Nevertheless, our monthly payments (mortgage plus monthly maintenance fees) are only moderately higher than what we paid for the modest two-bedroom apartment we had shared before moving into TREE. Moreover, those monthly fees cover property taxes and part of our home insurance—and of course we are now building home equity.

Our energy-saving measures, including both the tight home construction and solar panels that we added during the first year after move-in, are definitely paying off. The average monthly cost for electricity (hot water, heat, all appliances) during the final year in our small ground-floor rented apartment was $192. That expense dropped to $73 during our first year in the TREE house (including one of the coldest winters on record). In our second year, the monthly electric bill has averaged $33. We expect the cost of those photovoltaic and hot-water solar panels (totaling $12,800) to be fully recovered within six or seven years of their estimated 25-year life expectations.

All in all, living in the new TREE neighborhood of EcoVillage at Ithaca is definitely "affordable" for Shannon and me. We realize, of course, that living in this community—even renting a small apartment—is an option available almost entirely to middle-class households. Thus we who helped plan TREE have not fully reached the third of the goals we so often invoked: "Sustainability, Accessibility, Affordability."

Within EcoVillage we have hiked many nearby trails and Nordic-skied them occasionally; cooled off in two swimmable ponds; picked organic berries; regularly joined in delicious and healthy common-house meals; and enjoyed a variety of spontaneous or planned events such as the winter-solstice "Spiral" ceremony and the "Sparkfest" celebration of village talents. As an amateur stargazer, I have attended many astronomy programs at nearby Cornell University (where the spirit of Carl Sagan is still alive) and have often taken advantage of the intentionally low outdoor lighting in EcoVillage for nighttime viewing. I am usually joined by Village neighbors old and young—including the young boy I was pleased to hear shout one afternoon last summer: "Hey, Wallace, the sky's clear. Are you getting your telescope out tonight?"

Environmental Education and Inspiration

EcoVillage is by no means a "gated community." Many of the residents are actively engaged in important local, state, and national issues—political, economic, social, and (of course) environmental. Just living here constitutes for Shannon and me a substantial senior-citizen education on ecology and sustainability. The Village email server regular sends messages about recycling and garbage disposal, work parties for tree-planting and

Wallace Watson

Several generations of TREE residents gather for a special breakfast in their Common House.

other ecological improvements, environmental workshops and seminars, and ride-sharing. Some of our residents have taken leading roles in the (so-far) successful effort to ban fracking in New York State. At least a dozen have joined protesters at the site of proposed gas storage facility in the fragile salt caverns underneath nearby Seneca Lake—for which some have willingly been arrested.

Intergenerational Living

One of the most appealing features of living in EcoVillage at Ithaca as septuagenarians has been the opportunity to share our lives with an amazing mix of people of many ages, backgrounds, personalities, and lifestyles, in an intentional community committed to sustainability.

Of the three neighborhoods, TREE has the highest proportion of older residents. A recent informal estimate indicates that there are 30 people over 60 years old in the 40 TREE households, compared to 19 and 13, respectively in FROG and SONG (each of which has 30 households). Even so, we in TREE encounter younger people continually. Our neighbors on both sides are couples with six of the 16 young children in TREE; several other households include teenagers full- or part-time. We regularly join younger adults, and sometimes children, in social events, meetings, and work-team projects. We particularly enjoy watching younger folks' outdoor activities through our large kitchen windows (which, as in all the EVI houses, are deliberately placed to look out on neighborhood pathways): parents and children hurrying to and from school and jobs or appointments downtown; kids rough-housing or having tea-parties on the grassy swale out front, and building snow-houses in winter.

The Challenges of Aging

In many ways, our experience in TREE and EVI confirms the saying "60 is the new 40." Most of the post-60 EcoVillagers lead relatively active lives; many hold leadership positions in local and regional religious, civic, and environmental activities. I think of one resident slightly younger than I am who paused only briefly after having a second mastectomy before resuming her volunteer advocacy work opposing extraction of fossil fuels and promoting use of solar and wind energy. Seniors are major contributors to committee work and social events—as well as physical labor, from snow shoveling and grass cutting (in both of which I have been a regular participant) to preparing the new TREE common garden.

Still, an aging population will inevitably face physical and other limitations. One of our friends in TREE died of long-term cancer last spring, before she could move into her apartment in the TREE House. I know of two other residents who are dealing with cancer, and a third with serious lung disease.

Although EcoVillage at Ithaca does not provide formal medical assistance, there is a long tradition here of neighbors helping neighbors—particularly so for elderly and physically impaired residents. When I needed to make an emergency trip to the hospital one afternoon last year, I was relieved to see a dozen or so neighbors appear in our front yard

as the ambulance was parking; one of them drove Shannon to the emergency room, and several others came by to check on us later. A village Community Health and Aging Team (CHAT) is making such help more systematic. The group meets monthly to discuss present and anticipated needs of individuals in EVI, review relevant books and video presentations, and plan information-sharing events. Using a free website called "Lotsa Helping Hands," the team coordinates volunteers who provide meals, grocery and medicine pick-ups, and trips to doctors. Last year for CHAT I organized a team to help residents in health emergencies; members of the team stand ready to guide ambulances to homes, contact family members, and temporarily take care of children and pets as needed.

Shannon and I, the oldest couple currently living in TREE, have lately had to limit our participation in neighborhood and village activities because of medical problems. In 2010, Shannon was diagnosed with likely early-stage Alzheimer's disease. Shortly afterwards, she bravely explained in a TREE meeting why she could no longer chair the Legal Committee and would have to limit her other work within the community. Happily, her short-term memory loss has proceeded very slowly, and she has so far been able to continue most of the other activities she has enjoyed in EVI and the surrounding area. It is possible that her high level of social, intellectual, and physical activity at EcoVillage and in the wider community has slowed the progression of her cognitive impairment.

I too have been obliged to cut back on my participation in the community, because of

(continued on p. 77)

Two women on the TREE snow-shoveling team pause from work during the hard winter of 2014-15. The unfinished Common House is in the background.

Wallace Watson

Ecovillagers gather to greet new TREE residents in the fall of 2015.

James Bosjolie

AGING IN COMMUNITY:
HOW AN OLDER COUPLE HELPED LAUNCH A NEW
MULTI-GENERATIONAL ECOVILLAGE NEIGHBORHOOD

(continued from p. 62)

my increasing responsibilities as Shannon's care partner as well as a cardiac arrhythmia that required insertion of a pace-maker last spring. I am now intent upon making most of my contributions to our community life through less psychologically and physically stressful tasks than those I took on earlier. I am happily involved in committees dealing with land use, gardening, and composting, and Shannon and I frequently join in spontaneous projects meeting unanticipated needs of the community. I will still enjoy joining others in clearing light snow from our paths, but I won't be lifting the heavy, wet stuff anymore.

It is frustrating to have to limit my contributions to our community life in these ways, and to have to start saying "no" increasingly to the many social and cultural opportunities available in EVI, Ithaca, and the surrounding region. But it's good to see how many younger people have taken increased responsibility for major tasks in the Village and are taking the initiative for organizing pleasurable activities here and outside.

Elderhood

Of course, those of us who have to limit our more active work in the community can feel good about contributing in quieter ways. I think we have a lot to offer younger people. We can share the breadth and depth of understanding that comes with having lived long, and the serenity that many of us often feel as we contemplate the coming end of our lives. In the final chapter of *What Are Old People For?* the well-known writer on aging, Dr. Bill Thomas, describes three "late-life developmental tasks" of Elders (as distinguished from more action-oriented Adults): "peacemaker," "wisdom-giver," and "legacy creator." I can't say that I aspire to all of those roles. But I have noticed that I speak up a lot less often in TREE meetings than in my earlier years here. I now find it easier to look upon whatever current issue is raging within our community with a sort of benevolent detachment, taking a long-range view. Others have told me they find this valuable. I expect to devote myself increasingly to writing, astronomy, photography, and music—in general to slowing down and to spending more time getting to know well the extraordinary people who live here (young and old), paying more attention to the natural phenomena so close at hand, and sharing these experiences as I can with Shannon and others.

In spite of all the volunteer support and assistance that is offered by our friends and neighbors in EcoVillage, Shannon and I (as well as others here, I am sure) are trying to be realistic about our present and future needs and the limits of long-term health care available here. We fully recognize that a community such as ours cannot provide the kind of medical care that would be available in a continuing care retirement community.

We are doing what we can to prepare for what may come. Of course, we regularly see our primary physician and specialists. We have taken advantage of support programs in the outside community sponsored by the Alzheimer's Association, the county Office for the Aging, and a senior resource center. In consultation with our children (all of whom live a considerable distance away), we are beginning to look into residential health care facilities in and near Ithaca, and elsewhere, in case we need to make such a move.

Meanwhile, we look forward to living as long and actively as we can in the very stimulating and satisfying intergenerational neighborhood that we helped create over many years—and in the larger community that includes it. We are convinced that we did the right thing in undertaking this late-life adventure in EcoVillage at Ithaca. And we are grateful for the stimulation and support we expect to continue to receive from our age-peers as well as our younger neighbors here—up to and beyond the point at which we may have to make the difficult decision to leave this community.

Wallace Watson and his wife Shannon Wagner joined the planning group for the TREE neighborhood of EcoVillage at Ithaca (NY) in 2008 and have lived in TREE since July 2014. Wallace was formerly a professor of English and college/university administrator, most recently at Duquesne University, Pittsburgh, Pennsylvania.

Affordable, Developer-Driven Ecovillages:
MEETING AN UNMET NEED

Ecovillage at Ithaca - EVI [handwritten]

By Mac Maguire

Member-driven, bottom-up ecovillages around the world epitomize the "think global, act local" insight that humans can understand and respond to undisciplined human consumption—and do it where we live.

Because our communities were gradually shaped by the dreams, designs, and compromises among a diversity of people, each village has become a unique creation. This is part of our charm and could not be otherwise. Yet having been created along distinctive historical trajectories, the resultant physical configurations of our communities prevent them from being globally replicable—not at scales sufficient to shelter the millions of humans relentlessly moving into already overtaxed urban areas in the teeth of equally relentless climate change.

The deep-rooted knowledge we embody of how generations can thrive together in community harkens back to millennia of human experience. In recent decades much of this experience, withered by a century of heat from the atomizing furnace of industrial demographic concentrations, has been recovered in cohousing cultures like the one I live in. While these evolving patterns of liberating experience cannot be reproduced on a robotized assembly line, the physical components that permit them to thrive sustainably can be. And they must be if we want our culture to radiate globally.

It is by economies of scale that the devices of modernity we often love to hate have "trickled down" through all social levels. Systems far more complex than those that compose a fully outfitted ecovillage have become the ordinary trappings of our daily life. But they have become so only when actually exposed to a market-driven discipline of evolutionary redesign and cost cutting.

Consider the gradual social diffusion of automobiles, piped hot water, flush toilets, gas and electric ovens, refrigerators with freezing compartments, telephones, radios, airlines, air conditioning, televisions, microwave ovens, personal computers and smart phones. These were restricted to the few until increased production numbers and competitive engineering reduced costs so they could be afforded first by a solid middle class and finally by folks of modest and low income.

Now consider a couple of questions. What social-economic level is typically represented in today's member-created ecovillage—shaped as they have been by current construction and technology costs? On the trajectory of economic accessibility, what social range cannot be served at these costs? My own answer is that at current costs ecovillage projects are almost exclusively the preserve of solidly middle to upper class folks and that others of modest to low income are excluded. And absent the prototyping of a technically integrated and mass-replicable alternative, I think they must remain so.

The relative lack of affordability inherent in member-designed and built communities is a moral dilemma much discussed in my community—EcoVillage at Ithaca. Even when dramatic steps are taken to keep our communities from going the way of exclusionary gentrification, a painfully obvious fact remains. To date there is no way that folks of modest income can plan and build ecovillages. So far there has been a missing link in the evolutionary trajectory of the ecovillage movement. This article will argue that that link is a developer-driven prototype for a technically integrated and maximally autonomous ecovillage and that such a model has recently emerged—RegenVillage.

What is the RegenVillage model?

It is a developer-driven, replicable, global-scale ecovillage model. The Venice Architecture Biennale in May 2016 generated a flood of interest in the RegenVillage conceived by James Ehrlich and his associates at Stanford and designed by EFFEKT Architects of Copenhagen. A prototype of this model is soon to begin at Almere in the Netherlands. Lund, Sweden and other northern European locations appear ready to follow. I try to see this development in the light of the last century and a half of economic history. As such I regard it as a necessary first step in making the ecovillage culture an affordable, social option for all classes.

The RegenVillage project has self-consciously set for itself the task of designing and prototyping autonomous ecovillages suitable for all the world's climatic regions. It will initially focus on adapting its design to the rigors of the colder climates of Europe and the more arid climates of the Middle East. It reasons that proof of concept at these extremes would also ensure success in more forgiving regions.

It plans to build "autonomous, regenerative villages powered by renewable energy, and managed by machine learning MEMS (micro-electrical-mechanical-system) inputs. Energy-efficient, aesthetically pleasing and comfortable homes capable of producing redundant high-yield, organic food and energy sources for self-sustaining communities." (Stanford RegenVillages Initiative, www.youtube.com/watch?v=PN67HuUtrSo)

Global challenges and the Regen response: the re-villaging of mankind

The historian Arnold Toynbee argued that societies grow by creatively responding to challenges and then successively transcending any unanticipated consequences that result.

This section looks at some of today's challenges and the RegenVillage effort to play a serious part in addressing them at a global scale. A self-monitoring component is part of the Regen business model. From the outset, the RegenVillage project intends that each local village should become an open-source, information-sharing venue. These will provide continual input to advance overall curriculum development, research, incubation, and innovation. The goal is to meet the following challenges.

About 40 percent of Earth's land surface area is now deforested, biodegraded farmland. Every acre devoted to Regen's integrated system of fish, livestock, and vertical aqua farming could replace 10 of these conventional farmland acres, while producing a biologically diverse yield of food in equivalent amounts. The other nine acres could be regenerated using permaculture techniques that would gradually sequester carbon naturally.

Today 70 percent of global water consumption is used for terrestrial farming, causing rivers and lakes to dry up. Every gallon of rain water harvested and stored or grey water recovered and cycled into a RegenVillage's integrated system of fish, livestock, vertical aqua-farming, and seasonal terrestrial farming leaves nine gallons in the aquifer to regenerate rivers and lakes.

Globally, the manufacture of fertilizers, along with current farming practices, food transport, and refrigeration accounts for about 30 percent of all greenhouse gas emissions as well as causing nitrogen and phosphorous contamination of groundwater, rivers and lakes. In the RegenVillage model livestock consumption of food scraps and composting displaces those fertilizers. Phosphorous and nitrogen no longer wash into the environment. Black Soldier Fly larvae digest human waste and scraps and become protein-rich fish food whose detritus then enriches the water mediums of aquaponic and aeroponic systems for growing organic food. Farm-to-table, doorstep-accessible food eliminates transportation costs and is the only definitive cure for hunger since it empowers its erstwhile victims to become self-sufficient where they live.

Traditionally, humans work in large part to pay for their shelter. The Regen project aims for the shelter to provide rather than absorb personal income. It would embed human life within a self-reliant community of asset-producing dwellings and infrastructure. This would ultimately reverse the flow of income. Redundant energy, water, and food produced would become mortgage-eating income assets. A smart house that is also embedded in a smart community creates valuable assets. Meanwhile, regenerative residency not only restores its actual footprint but also de-stresses that portion of the world beyond that is no longer required to supply its needs.

Today 842 million people cannot produce the food they need to live active, healthy lives. They are mostly rural farmers in climatically challenged areas. While one in every seven

people in the world suffers from hunger, one in every three pounds of food is wasted in storage, transport, and undisciplined disposal of scraps. Food transfers from other regions are currently the only backups when transient weather or long-term climate change turn on challenged farmers. Would it not be more helpful to empower them where they are now? A truly unassailable form of food security would require empowerment through local self-sufficiency. It requires that sunlight, water, human waste, food scraps, and technology close a virtuous biological circle with gardening and fish and livestock husbandry.

Regenerative basal metabolism replacing unprincipled human consumption

It is not any particular level of human consumption of natural and manufactured goods that has compromised our Earth. Rather it is the undisciplined acquisition of their components and the indiscriminate dispersion of their waste that has so compromised our life on Earth. Transforming the outputs of human consumption from being waste into becoming value-added inputs in the natural circle of life is the regenerative circle that autonomy embodies.

The RegenVillage model mixes rainwater and sunbeams with human waste to produce potable water, organic food, and power in a sustainable self-reliant circle. Its community metabolism displays embodied energy constantly shape-shifting through multiple channels. Since a given category of human leavings might economically enter different processing streams at different times, their flows will be monitored with MEMS sensing and triggering devices that will channel them efficiently to meet community needs.

Regenerative flows of waste, food, water, and energy characterize the metabolism of the Regen Village prototype. Except for the critical inputs sun and rain these flows form continuous cycles within the community:

- Human "waste" starts to become an asset as it is being sorted into compostable and non-compostable leavings.
- Compostable lawn and garden cuttings can stream toward compost bins or biogas digesters.
- Compostable food scraps can stream toward compost bins, to a biogas digester, to livestock as food, or to feed the larvae that emerge from the eggs of black soldier flies.
- These larvae then become a protein-rich food for pigs, fowl, or fish.
- Fish water becomes a nutrient-rich soup channeled into aquaponic tanks or mist in aeroponic vertical farming.
- The fish and the livestock can be harvested as protein-rich human food.
- Non-compostable human fecal matter can stream toward either soldier fly larvae for fish food or a biogas digester for energy and water recovery.
- Urine can stream toward a bio-digester or be diluted for direct use as a terrestrial garden fertilizer.
- Biogas processing recovers water that is channeled to a water storage facility.
- It also produces gas that is fed into a smart grid to be used directly as combustible fuel or indirectly by generating electricity for local use or regional trade.
- Electricity is also harvested from rooftop solar panels for similar dispositions.
- And adjacent to these are solar thermal devices that directly transfer heat energy into maintaining water and room temperatures within homes.
- At the water-storage area, grey water from homes is separated toward a holding tank for irrigation of the seasonal farm whose soil has been enhanced by manure-enriched compost.
- Meanwhile, potable water harvested from rain or separated out from the bio-digester effluent will provide community drinking water and irrigate aquaponic and aeroponic organic produce as needed.

> # We may not have more than a few decades left to re-village an entire planet's worth of urban and rural neighborhoods.

Summing up: Why the urgency?

My own home of EcoVillage at Ithaca required an entire generation to build a community for 100 families in three neighborhoods. EVI grew within the warp and woof of families knitting their lives and their dreams together. Its particular patterns of dwellings, infrastructure, agriculture, and self-governance and management are deeply sustainable by today's standards. EVI's achievement is an against-the-odds accomplishment that honors the imagination and endurance of the generation who created it.

But we may not have much more than the time of another such generation to re-village an entire planet's worth of urban and rural neighborhoods with a community metabolism based on locally produced food and harvested energy—if we are to slow and stabilize climate change and provide definitive food security for all humans.

Here's how I hope folks in the ecovillage movement see the RegenVillage model. It is a blueprint for a tightly integrated and constantly evolving group of building and farming techniques that can produce a strategically autonomous community about the size of a neighborhood or village. It transforms sunbeams through food into smiles.

Many of us spent years and tears designing and building sustainable communities. We know where bodies are buried. So, here's what I suggest. Draw upon your own heritage and having read through this essay, now go to the EFFEKT RegenVillage website and study their model. Then ask yourself this question: "If this model had been available to me when I joined a group in search of a just and sustainable community, would I have insisted that we design our own model or would I be trying to persuade my partners that we aim from the outset for the autonomous patterns of EFFEKT's RegenVillage model?"

And here's another more critical question. Which model, a member-designed and built village like yours or mine or a RegenVillage model, is most likely to bring meaningful security to those whom an earlier generation often referred to as the "Wretched of the Earth."

In an article by Sheila Shayon, James Ehrlich addresses meeting the needs of marginalized rural populations: "While ReGen chose Almere [in the Netherlands as its first prototype] for its upper-middle class potential, the bigger prize is in developing countries as billions migrate from rural communities in search of better living conditions. Half the world's population lives in cities today and projections are that 2.5 billion people will be moving to cities in the next 50 years....

"'Our intent from the very beginning is global scale, and bringing thriving, regenerative and resilient platform design thinking into peri-urban and rural areas where it's frankly needed the most....

"'With the inclusion of high broadband access into each ReGen Village, along with other managed services at the neighborhood scale, it is our ambition to encourage families to stay in their local villages, and eventually to attract city dwellers back into these areas....for the future of humanity.'" (www.sustainablebrands.com/news_and_views/cleantech/sheila_shayon/regen_villages_behind_design_self-sustaining_eco-communities)

The return to a form of community life locally sufficient in food and energy, but enhanced with modernity's option-expanding innovations, is not a radical idea. It seems radical only from the perspective of our addictive dependence on a globally trafficked web of energy and food that, not unlike those for outlawed drugs, services us by despoiling the natural order of life on Earth. I would add that the above-mentioned "wretched of the earth" also dwell in the hollowed-out cities and in the rural backwaters of America. 🌿

Mac Maguire lives at EcoVillage at Ithaca; contact him at larremag@gmail.com.

Neighborly Questions and Critiques

After reading an earlier version of this article some of my brothers and sisters at EVI were kind enough to reply to my request for their thoughts. Since I take them seriously, the article has morphed a bit where my writing may have misrepresented. Their questions and views can be summed up as follows:

Questions:
- If this model is prototyped among educationally underserved communities must there not be some instructional component to develop the skills necessary to deal with the technology involved?
- How would this model deal with transportation issues?
- Is there a place for social gatherings and common meals in this model or is it more like a super-green condo franchise?

Views:
- The Regen Model does not seem to fully appreciate the social muscles and instincts that can only be honed in a community of folks intentionally sharing their lives in meaningful ways. These are critical to the success of any community no matter how technically savvy the physical side may be.
- If the Regen Model as described actually did succeed on the scale described it might have the unintended consequence of undermining local economies and regional solidarity.
- However green and regenerative, some folks would be excluded from what would likely become more gated communities that cut themselves off from the needs of the ambient region.

—MM

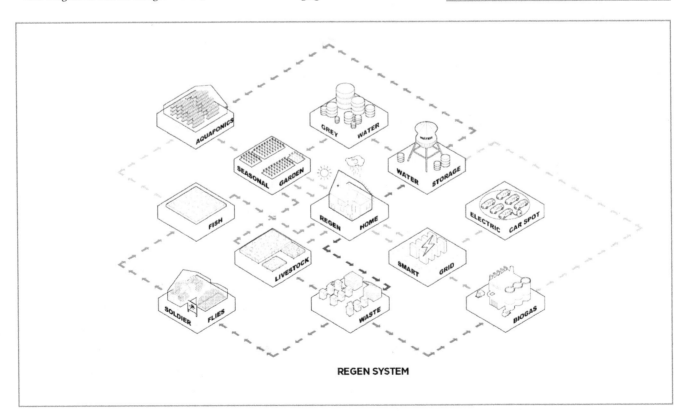

REGEN SYSTEM

242

HOME OWNERSHIP IS DEAD!
Long Live the Permanent Real Estate Cooperative!

By Janelle Orsi

Imagine that a group of people works hard to fill their neighborhood with urban farms, bike lanes, parks, murals, community services, and education programs. Next, imagine that those same people are forced to move away. Ouch, that bites.

Sadly, this is real: Improving the livability of a previously disinvested neighborhood creates opportunities for speculators, landlords, and developers to increase rents and drive up the cost of property, often causing displacement of the very people who made the neighborhood livable to begin with.

It's paralyzing to realize that the positive changes we make in our communities can do more harm than good. We eventually arrive at the most difficult-to-answer question: What will stop the pattern of displacement of low- to moderate-income communities and communities of color?

I believe that only one solution will make a true and long-term difference, and you rarely hear anyone utter it, because it so radically challenges everything we've been told to do as responsible adults pursuing the "American Dream." So brace yourself...

We have to stop profiting from property. We have to treat homes as homes, not as investment vehicles that we hope to later sell to the highest bidders. If the privilege of property ownership determines who builds wealth, then the wealthy will build wealth more quickly than everyone else, white people will build wealth much faster than black people, and we'll continually deepen inequality and racism in this country.

This reality has settled in to the point where I'm ready to declare: I can never, with a clear conscience, buy a house and feel entitled to the capital gains generated by the housing market. I wouldn't feel proud if my method of building wealth is to participate in the pricing out of lower-income families. But I do not want to remain a renter and be victimized by the same dynamic. So, now what?

Now I believe that the most important thing the Sustainable Economies Law Center (SELC)—and everyone else, for that matter—can work on is creating and spreading a different model of property ownership.

This is where the Permanent Real Estate Cooperative (PREC) comes in. "Permanent Real Estate Cooperative" is the name SELC has given to a model we have been working on for land and housing acquisition, management, and ownership. The PREC model employs similar tools to those used by limited equity housing cooperatives (LEHCs) and community land trusts (CLTs): Residents buy homes and feel much like homeowners, but the equity that they can build in a property is limited to what they put in (purchase price and improvements) plus a strictly limited rate of return, usually tied to inflation rates or a consumer price index. Capping the resale value and putting land into community control helps ensure that it won't be sold back into the speculative marketplace.

In addition, the PREC model brings multiple innovations:

1) It's for everyone: Unlike most affordable housing developments and 501(c)(3) community land trusts (CLTs), which are often limited (by tax exemption or their funding sources) to providing housing to low-income households, the PREC is a cooperative corporation spreading the notion that everyone—high-income and low-income—should stop profiting from property and live in limited equity housing.

2) It's self-help: PRECs are platforms for mutual aid and self-help, not charitable assistance. Charities can create a disempowering divide between the helpers and the helped. The cooperative structure transforms the relationship to create groups of people working together to provide for their own long-term housing needs. That can make it motivating and empowering, and it sets the stage for communities to engage in mutual support in many forms beyond housing.

3) It's self-organizing and scalable: Our vision is to design the governance of PRECs to enable bottom-up organizing by hundreds or thousands of members, rather than top-down management by a board and staff. A household or group of people can self-organize, find financing, and identify a property to shepherd into the cooperative. The cooperative will serve as a container to hold title to land and enforce limited equity. The cooperative board and staff support members in this process, but generally do not drive decisions about what properties to buy and who will live in them. Because all members will be responsible for organizing to acquire properties, we believe that a PREC can grow quickly to involve many people and homes.

There is much more to say about the PREC model, how properties are financed, how governance works, how to ensure permanence of affordability, how we can grow a movement of PRECs, how PREC members build economic security outside of the conventional housing market, and so on. SELC has put a lot of thought and research into it, and we feel satisfied that this is a viable and powerful path forward.

So, while a short article cannot do it justice, a SELC project to pilot PRECs in the Bay Area will hopefully illuminate a way out of the gentrification and displacement trap. Stay tuned as we develop this model, and let us know if you recommend any resources or potential support for our work. Note: We have not received funding to do this particular work, and we are just beginning the process of fundraising while we use unrestricted funds to lay the groundwork. Stay tuned, and let us know if you have suggestions.

Janelle Orsi is Executive Director of the Sustainable Economies Law Center. To contact SELC or find out more, visit www.theselc.org. This article is adapted with permission from www.theselc.org/homeownership_is_dead under a Creative Commons license, creativecommons.org/licenses/by-sa/4.0/.

243

WURRUK'AN:
An Experimental Intentional Community

By Bill Metcalf

What is an *experimental* intentional community? Surely every intentional community is an experiment? So why does Wurruk'an merit that adjective?

I'm in beautiful rolling green hills a couple of hours east of Melbourne, Australia, with a group of enthusiastic young, would-be communards. However, it is cold and windy, and I'm hungry and thirsty, helping to lay a timber floor at Wurruk'an. I need to plane the edge of several recycled boards to make them fit, but not one of their three planes works! This epitomises the good and bad of life in this dynamic, new "experimental" intentional community.

In 2013 Dr. Samuel Alexander, from University of Melbourne's Simplicity Institute, wrote a book entitled *Entropia: Life Beyond Industrial Civilisation*. This utopian novel envisioned a radically simple and satisfying life emerging on a South Pacific island after the "Great Disruption" brought on by climate change, i.e. economic and environmental meltdown. In writing this book, he felt driven "to expose and better understand the myths that dominate our destructive and self-transforming present, and to envision what life would be like, or could be like, if we were to liberate ourselves from today's myths and step into new ones. We search for grounded hope between naive optimism and despair. Without vision and defiant positivity, we will perish."

Much to Dr. Alexander's surprise, soon after publishing *Entropia* he was contacted by a family who offered eight hectares (20 acres) of land on which to develop an experiment to test the utopian communal lifestyle which his book had posited. Being a true scholar, Sam accepted the challenge and set out to create what we now know as Wurruk'an, an experimental intentional community.

We finish working on the floorboards just on dark; a lovely meal of homemade vegetarian lasagne and homegrown salad from their abundant gardens awaits us, along with a glass or three of local red wine. All my aches and pains—and frustrations about planes—slip away and I enjoy the evening with these charming and committed young people.

Members ask about my research with intentional communities around the globe—what works and what doesn't. They fully realise that communal living can be tough, and want to make the best of it.

I mention that in the late 19th century there were several communal groups in this area, such as Aurelia and Moe Village Settlement, and Erica Commune in the mid-20th century—but they had not heard about them and, perhaps correctly, doubt if knowing about their predecessors would help at this time of climate change.

Dr. Alexander sought to create an intentional community that would be "explicitly political, engaged and inclusive" and, because of climate change, have an ecological footprint so low that it would set a benchmark for other ecovillages. Fortunately, he found plenty of people who resonated with this aspiration.

With the project promoted online and through the media, 42 people came in December 2013 for a workshop to build an Earthship, which they dug into a hillside, and made

Yurt and latest tiny house.

Wurruk'an members.

Members discuss outside yurt.

Cob baking oven.

Yurt at night.

First tiny house.

from glass bottles and old car tyres filled with clay, with large glass doors facing the sun. Two months later, Sam organised a workshop to build a mud hut, attended by 25 people. Later that year he organized two more workshops, one

oped organic gardens, planted an orchard, and installed water tanks and composting toilets. They built a large enclosure for ducks and chickens, brought in bees, and made a cob pizza/baking oven. Referring to that time, Sam tells me that "something very interesting was happening, even if we weren't exactly clear what it was."

"What it was" became the small but thriving intentional community of Wurruk'an, the name deriving from *wurruk*, a local indigenous word meaning both earth and story, and *k'an*, a Mayan word meaning seed. They chose the term to signify their "attempt to seed a new Earth story."

As expected, Wurruk'an's biggest challenge was not the provision of food or shelter but managing social relations.

Having created basic infrastructure, Sam advertised for people to live at Wurruk'an during a year-long experiment, with 52 stepping forward. Out of these, a dozen young men and women were selected and moved there, committing to stay during 2015. Most had not met before and were "linked only by the desire to explore a life of radical simplicity and

to build an "earthbag" shelter and the other to build a "tiny house" from recycled timber and tin. They also purchased a secondhand yurt—the floor of which I am helping to install today.

As well as these building projects, they developed

to help raise awareness about the necessity of transcending consumer culture and its underlying growth fetishism" because of climate change. And that turned out to be a surprisingly strong link.

While Sam and the owners helped select members they then stepped back and let them get on with developing a community.

Some members slept in the buildings previously described while others slept in a caravan or tents

Rachel and Liam harvesting

Workbreak, common house.

Liam scything grass.

Common house, breakfast cooking.

Common house cooking area.

Earthbag house.

Common house lounge area.

until the cold weather drove one couple to build their own tiny house, using recycled timber and tin, for $420. Everyone ate together and socialized in an old shed. The group grew as much of their food as they could, went dumpster-diving, and thrived on a simple but highly variable diet. They tried several models of balancing work/money contributions to the collective endeavour.

An Australian filmmaker, Jordan Osmond, offered to record this experiment and create a documentary. Jordan became so interested that he moved onsite and, over the year, interviewed members, filmed their work, meetings, problems, and social events, and, with Sam, created a unique chronicle of this experiment: *A Simpler Way: Crisis as Opportunity,* a film well worth watching on YouTube.

The tin shed where they had created a common kitchen and lounge proved unsuitable as winter set in so members insulated it, found cast-off glass doors for the front and, for about a thousand dollars, created a comfortable communal space. Individual spaces are only for sleeping and having time out—the real living takes place in their communal kitchen and lounge. To that extent Wurruk'an is closer to an urban commune, or even cohousing, than to most ecovillages with individual homes and their associated higher costs and ecological footprints because everyone has their own stove, hot water system, washing machine, etc.

As expected, Wurruk'an's biggest challenge was not the provision of food or shelter but managing social relations. Few members had communal experience. I had met with Sam in the planning phase for this experiment and recommended being as selective as possible and accepting that conflict is inevitable and can be either productive or destructive. The drive within any communal group must be to creatively deal with and resolve conflict—it can never be avoided. And this Wurruk'an members have done remarkably well.

Members learned to be realistic, to compromise, to do their best and not stress about the impossible. Sam recently wrote, "Wurruk'an has not been comprised of eco-saints but human beings. Some pushed the boundaries of ecological practice more than others—and they are to be admired...but at various stages, for various reasons, everyone found themselves making certain ethical compromises.... Exploring simplicity in an overly complex society is riddled with contradictions and challenges. So much for voluntary simplicity. Sustainable consumption rather implies involuntary complexity. This is one of the many paradoxes of the simple life."

The year-long experiment ceased, as planned, at the end of 2015 although several "experimenters" remain there. Others have since joined and the membership is increasing, they hope to about 10.

Members are still collecting scrap building supplies and creating new and dramatic small sleeping and meeting spaces—hence me helping lay a timber floor in their yurt.

Each member contributes a mixture of labour and money, both on a sliding scale and under frequent review. They strive to use consensus, but for deciding on new projects each member has three votes to allocate as she/he wishes. Sam and the owners continue to offer support but, as far as I could see, are not directive; members make their own decisions.

Ownership is an issue, the land being held by the original family, who do not live there and who are happy for the communal group to continue. This has caused no problems so far—but inevitably this will need to be legally clarified someday.

There are no children, yet, so that might be their next big challenge. Childbearing can be very destructive to communal living because parents often opt for more space and their own house, for *private* over *collective*, and that dramatically increases costs and ecological footprint—and promotes rather than offsets climate change.

Wurruk'an's members are all in their 20s and 30s, and it would help to have several elders. It would also help were they to regularly visit and learn from long-standing intentional communities in their area such as Moora Moora and Commonground.

They have so far avoided admitting any sociopaths—and I hope they will continue to be vigilant.

I was deeply impressed by members' willingness to work hard, to make the best of what is available, to create a comfortable living without increasing their ecological footprint.

It is worth remembering that Twin Oaks, in the US, now in its 50th year, was loosely based on B.F. Skinner's *Walden Two*; so too might Wurruk'an, loosely based on *Entropia*, also be thriving in its 50th year.

The next morning we finish the yurt's timber floor—my small contribution to the success of this Wurruk'an experiment.

I was deeply impressed by members' willingness to work hard and to create a comfortable living without increasing their ecological footprint.

Ten members is probably too small to be sustainable as a community, although they are perhaps better thought of as a "commune." To remain at this size they would probably fare better were they to become even more communal, sharing ever more. For example, they now share costs but not income. Greater sharing would probably help in their drive towards greater consensus—or could blow them apart.

Was the experiment a success, however we might define that?

In looking back, Sam admits that one cannot call this a successful intentional community after only one year but, he proudly points out, "I would be surprised if there are many ecovillages on the planet that have a smaller ecological footprint. In the material sense, life was simple but sufficient." And because they learned to deal creatively with conflict Wurruk'an thrives.

One member, Dan, tells me, "when the community is passionately working together towards a mutual goal, that can be magic," and he appreciates the empowerment "from learning homesteading skills and living more autonomously"; but, he admits, it "can be demoralising and eats up a lot of my mental space" when members resist working through problems.

Beth, another member, tells me that her biggest challenge is avoiding the "individualistic, self-centered mindset" with which she was raised, instead "having to actively cultivate a more egalitarian and holistic mentality"; but she welcomes those "growing pains" which are what she has "enjoyed the most."

What is the future for Wurruk'an? Unless something drastic unexpectedly happens I anticipate Wurruk'an will continue to thrive for many years, and grow to an optimum size of 15-20 adults. As long as they can maintain communal eating, and a common budget, they should be fine with that number on that land, and be able to provide most of their own food.

Dr. Bill Metcalf, of Griffith University, Australia, is the author of numerous scholarly and popular articles, plus seven books, about intentional communities, the most recent being The Findhorn Book of Community Living. *He is Past President of the International Communal Studies Association and has been* Communities *magazine's International Correspondent for many years.*

Resources

Entropia: Life Beyond Industrial Civilisation, by Dr. Samuel Alexander, 2013, is available from www.e-junkie.com/249897 and www.createspace.com/4294895 on a "pay what you wish" basis.

Dr. Samuel Alexander's account of this experiment can be found at *Prosperous Descent: Telling New Stories as the Old Book Closes* as published in Griffith Review, 52, 2016 (griffithreview.com/wp-content/uploads/GR52_Alexander_Adcock-Ebook.FINAL_.pdf).

To watch Jordan Osmond and Samuel Alexander's film about Wurruk'an, *A Simpler Way: Crisis as Opportunity*, go to www.youtube.com/watch?v=XUwLAvfBCzw.

Earthship house.

MOBILE HOME PARKS:
A Fast and Inexpensive Path to Cohousing

By William Noel

*I*t's been my experience that people who love communal living still want to maintain a level of independence in their household. My wife Brynn is one of them. Eight years ago, before we were married, I rented a two-bedroom house by the beach with seven friends. We built queen-size bunk beds in the garage and our friend Mac lived in the driveway in an RV. When Brynn moved in with us she lasted six strong months before needing a less populated and more controllable space. We now live in a flat in San Francisco with Mac, and I often think about living again with more people and how I could balance that with Brynn's desire for privacy.

I own and operate a real estate investment business. Because I've spent most of my life happily living in group environments, I can't help but keep one eye open for buildings and land that would provide housing for people who want communal living while maintaining ownership of their space. Two years ago, Brynn and I started working with a type of real estate that could provide a solution to the lack of community housing in this country: mobile home parks.

Key Ingredients

Mobile home and RV parks have similar physical structure to cohousing communities. In each, residents own their own homes, share common ground, and have plenty of opportunities for daily interaction. People live closely together while each maintaining their own space in their own home.

I don't love the formality of the term Intentional Community, but in this case it fits as there is a glaring difference between most mobile home parks and cohousing projects. The lack of intention can be seen when you enter a mobile home park where the land is neglected, the homes are in disrepair, and a welcoming community is nowhere to be seen.

My hope, and a hypothesis that we're testing now in Dayton, Ohio, is that if we give the land attention, fix up the homes, and help create a vision for the community, we can transform a distressed mobile home park into a vibrant mobile home neighborhood that is physically similar to a cohousing community and 10 times more affordable.

Last year a prominent cohousing developer told me that a typical cohousing community takes about seven years to create, from idea conception to moving in. The seven years of struggle, frustration, and ultimate elation creates strong group bonds that help form the foundation of the community.

With parks, the land is already zoned and approved for multiple dwellings, the infrastructure is al-

...me - A charming ...le of what can be done ...an 8' wide RV or small ...ile home.

Singlewide southern - Manufacturers can add inexpensive custom touches to your home. This front porch adds $1,000 in cost and adds ten times that in character.

ready in place, and the homes are pre-fabricated. A community formed within a mobile home or RV park could be ready for habitation within a few months. While mobile home parks offer a quicker and more affordable option, the group may miss the bonding that happens during the longer formation process of a cohousing community. Personally, I'd rather bond over a sunset BBQ or planting a garden than a date with the city planner!

Jumping Financial Hurdles

Buying an entire mobile home park may seem impossible to somebody who doesn't have mountains of cash. Here is a secret: it is possible. Mobile home parks are famously difficult to finance through a bank. Sellers know that many buyers don't have enough cash to buy the park without financing, and that many banks refuse to loan on parks. Enter Seller Financing.

Seller financing (also called owner financing or seller carry) is common in the mobile home park industry. It works like this:

• Buyer talks to Seller.
• Seller thinks that Buyer is an honest person with a good business plan.
• Seller accepts a down payment on the park and lets the buyer pay the rest of the purchase price over the next number of years in monthly payments with interest.

People can buy parks from Sellers with as little as 10 percent down, sometimes less. Pick your location, find some smaller or poorly run parks, and call the owners. You'll be surprised how many are willing to sell their park to you and carry the financing. Small parks and poorly run parks often don't make money, and sometimes the owner is paying each month to keep the park afloat. These Sellers are highly motivated. Find them.

Banks will finance parks too, but it is a dreary process. If you can find seller financing, that's the preferred way to go.

Do I Have to Buy the Cow?

There are two types of residents in mobile home parks: lot renters and house renters. Lot renters own their own homes and pay the park owner to keep their home in the park and hook up to utilities. House renters rent mobile homes. Both of these options are less expensive than apartments and offer the benefits of having a yard, no shared walls, and a house you can drive up to. For friends who are craving community, but don't have the time or money to purchase a park, buying or renting mobile homes on adjacent lots would be one of the cheapest and fastest ways I can think of to begin a community.

Those with more money could buy a small park and move in all their friends. That's what the billionaire founder/CEO of Zappos, Tony Hsieh, did in Las Vegas. He was lonely in his penthouse apartment so he purchased an RV park and invited his friends to move in. Here are the two options that I see:

• **Rental:** Find the closest RV or mobile home park to where you and your friends want to live. Each person rents a space. Put out picnic tables, potted trees, and a good vibe. Seed the feelings of community within the park as you live right next to your best friends.

• **Purchase:** Buy a small park. Use the existing homes at the park or bring in the caliber of homes you desire, from $5,000 fixer-uppers to $120,000 triple-wide ranch homes. Alter the landscape how you see fit.

Community Creation

My wife and I currently own and manage mobile home parks in three states. I don't think the way that we're building community in our parks is necessarily the best or most effective. We buy existing parks, host BBQs, fix up vacant homes, and try to create the best neighborhood with the ingredients that we're given. That is a top-down approach, where the change happens from the property owner.

The ground-up transition happens as the old residents move out and new residents move in. We look for people who will be good neighbors, with clean records, good communication skills, and the ability to afford living in the park. Because we aren't starting with a group of like-minded individuals, it usually takes two years for us to turn a neglected park back into a full and vibrant community.

Buying or renting a nearly empty park with an existing group of friends, you could make this transition in months instead of years. Compare that to the seven years is takes to form a group, buy land, and plan, permit, and build new homes and infrastructure in a traditional cohousing community. Not only is the time reduced, the costs are cut dramatically compared to building a community on raw land.

Identifying Your Future Community

There are two types of mobile home park communities:

• **Lifestyle Communities:** These parks are clean and expensive and have nice amenities, like pools and clubhouses. Think of the perfect place to retire with your friends where you ride golf carts around have short white picket fences. That is a lifestyle community.

• **Affordable Housing:** Most parks fall into this category. The price to live here is about the same as a Class B or C apartment building. People live in these parks because they don't have to share

Doublewide big - A nice doublewide will set you back $60,000 or more. The inside looks like a normal "stick-built" home. A few custom touches and people won't be able to tell it's a mobile home.

Photos courtesy of William Noel

Uninspired park - A clean park. With the right residents this could be a vibrant community. Notice on lady in her side yard reading. That's the idea!

walls with neighbors, they can drive right up to their house, and they have a yard.

Lifestyle communities don't need your help. The social scene is good and people are happy to live there. If you want to create a strong and positive community where one doesn't already exist, let's assume that you're going to buy an affordable housing park.

To find an affordable RV or mobile home park you can either work with an agent or DIY. For those who have never bought property before, the real estate agent is almost always paid for by the person who sells the property, not the buyer. Even if you're planning on doing all of the hunting yourself it won't hurt to have an agent look for you as well. A good agent will use her network to uncover properties that you might not find on your own.

Ready to start looking? Go to www.mobilehomeparkstore.com and start to get yourself acquainted with the parks in your area. This will give you an idea of the parks that are for sale in your state, near your town, and in the price range you're looking for.

Whether you decide to use an agent or look for yourself, you need to know what you're looking for. Most of these principles apply to houses, apartment buildings, and other forms of real estate. Grab a glass of water, we're about to get into the gritty details.

Utilities

With parks, there is much more land and more infrastructure than single homes or apartment buildings and you should be aware of how everything in your park works. Here is a very brief introduction to park utilities.

• **Water:** If the water is provided by the city it will either be billed directly to the park residents or there will be one large bill to the whole park. If the water is directly billed then each lot will have a separate bill from the city and the city is responsible for maintaining the water lines. If there is just one meter for the whole park, or if you have a well, you are responsible for maintaining your own lines and fixing leaks. Direct billed is preferable from a maintenance standpoint, but it means that your park will be somewhat urban. If you prefer to have a remote park, you will be on a well. Be sure to talk to everybody you can about the well, from the EPA to the park maintenance man. Wells are great and cheap, until they aren't. Know the age and condition of your well and water lines.

• **Sewage:** Everyone's favorite topic! City sewer is preferred. If the water is direct billed and city sewer is included in the bill then you will not be responsible for maintaining the sewer lines either. Whew! Septic tanks are the second best option for sewage, and the best option for rural parks. Almost everyone who lives in the country has septic tanks and many people know how to maintain them. Much less desirable are Lagoons and Wastewater Treatment Plants. Avoid these at all costs, they are one of the only things that can single-handedly destroy your dream if something goes wrong.

• **Trees:** Trees are beautiful and give a park some character. The tree roots are bad for water and sewer lines and septic leach fields. Tree limbs can also break and fall, crushing homes and cars. I love trees; just make sure that you have some time and money set aside for them.

• **Roads:** Pay close attention to the roads in your park because they are expensive to re-pave. Most people do not re-pave the roads in their affordable living parks. They patch potholes, keep the drains cleared, and keep the roads in decent working condition. Other than that, a road is there so that we know where to drive. It doesn't have to be pretty. Most people pave roads only when they refinance their bank loan or list their park for sale.

• **Electricity and Gas:** Try to get these utilities directly billed to each house. If there is one meter for the whole park then you are responsible for the electrical lines and gas lines. You do not want to be responsible for the gas lines. The electric lines are less of a problem, but can still be scary. If you're responsible for their maintenance, make sure you know the age of the lines and condition and budget for their repair and replacement. Keep a friendly relationship with your local electrician too!

If you understand how the utilities work at your mobile home park you will be much better off than I was when I purchased my first park. A major utility problem is one of the few things that can shut down your park. A minor utility problem can still be expensive and usually involves sewage or explosions, or, god forbid, both. Lagoon (large open settling pond for sewage) can become flooded or contaminated, gas lines can leak and be shut down, well water can contain illegal levels of Uranium, electric lines can fray and spark. Know your utilities. The replacement costs, if they aren't in your budget, will be an unwelcome surprise.

(continued on p. 74)

In 2003, "La Cité Écologique" was founded, in Colebrook New Hampshire, on 315 acres of beautiful land surrounded by forest and mountains. Our ecovillage gives priority to education, optimal living to its members, a cooperative culture with resilience in its development and social entrepreneurship. So far, we have built one single family building, two large community residences, where people live in a kind of condo arrangement, and one community building (all powered by solar). We are expanding new building projects, to give a home to growing families and/or new members. We've created businesses, non-profits, a nonprofit school, and an organic farm, that helps better serve ours, and the local community. Visitors are welcome to our annual Open House in June, and Harvest Celebration in September. Guided tours, and internship programs are also available from May through October.

Contact: Leonie Brien (603) 331-1669
www.citeecologiquenh.org

La Cité Écologique
of New Hampshire
An Ecovillage since 2003

MOBILE HOME PARKS: A FAST AND INEXPENSIVE PATH TO COHOUSING

(continued from p. 43)

Management

When you buy your park it is very likely that people will be living there. If there is nobody living there, you can start your community from scratch but beware, a park with no people may have infrastructure issues or worse. If people are living there you are now responsible for providing them a safe place to live and in return, they pay you rent. Don't worry! You don't have to call yourself a "landlord" or feel bad that you are exploiting your position. Just treat people fairly and be strict about your park rules.

If you clean up your park and create good bonds with the new and existing residents you will begin to attract more people who care about their homes and neighborhoods. This is a good first step toward building community in your park.

There is a lot to learn about park management, much more than can be covered in this article. If you find yourself in the position where you own a park and want to better the neighborhood, please give me a call and we can discuss different places you can go to learn the trade.

Go Get 'Em!

We've covered some of the basics you will need to evaluate a mobile home or RV park. In addition to what is listed, you can do research online, talk to local real estate professionals, call manufactured housing dealers, and start to visit some local parks to imagine what it would be like to create your community using mobile home and RV parks as a foundation. Parks will require less work, less time, and less risk than building your community from scratch.

Today, mobile home parks house six percent of the US population. When people like us realize the potential that mobile home parks have for inexpensive community living, I believe the concept will become one of the most popular forms of communal housing available. ☙

William Noel owns and operates mobile home parks throughout the country and is a lifelong community builder. Will invites you to contact him at Noel@ElkhornGroup.org to learn more about using mobile home parks to achieve your communal housing dreams.

Permaculture Design
Regenerating Life Together

Information & Inspiration

- Natural building
- Ecovillage design
- Intentional communities
- Perennial vegetables
- Community gardens
- Natural health
- Appropriate technology
- Forest gardens— and much, much more!

www.PermacultureDesignMagazine.com

BUSINESS CO-OPS
as a Prelude to Intentional Community

By Werner Kontara

LA Ecovillage +
LA Coop Lab

Many intentional communities struggle not only with learning how to get along (group process), but also with financial constraints, which add a lot of stress. While some communities have started one or more businesses, these usually come more as an afterthought rather than being part of the initial overall plan. Wouldn't it be better to develop a successful business as a prelude to the residential community, rather than the other way around?

A pre-established business that already shows its worth can then be evaluated for the financial potential it would provide to the community. Planning the community becomes much more realistic. And a business that is already up and running can support a more vigorous community from the outset.

The indigenous businesses that do exist in intentional communities (ICs) take the numerous forms that exist in society in general, i.e. sole proprietorships, partnerships, LLCs, nonprofits, and worker cooperatives. Some were formerly owned by individual members. Others have been started along the way. Each has its pluses and minuses. The one type that most closely resembles an intentional community is a co-op.

Cooperative businesses have been around for a long time. Indeed, the International Co-operative Alliance (ICA), an umbrella association, was established in 1895. According to Wikipedia, there are today more than 100 million people in the world working in co-op businesses. (See en.wikipedia. org/wiki/International_Co-operative_Alliance.)

Mondragon Corporation, located in the Basque area of Spain, is a leading organization that started out in 1956 with five people manufacturing paraffin heaters, and, later, bicycles. Today, the corporation is nearly 75,000 people strong. They have branched out into many kinds of things: electronics, grocery stores, banking, and insurance. (See en.wikipedia.org/wiki/Mondragon_Corporation.)

While there are a number of kinds of co-ops—housing co-ops, consumer co-ops, retailer co-ops, producer co-ops, worker co-ops, and even to some extent some types of employee stock ownership plans—I am mainly going to be referring to the type exemplified by Mondragon, which some call individualist or worker co-op.

I see a number of parallels between intentional community and co-op business. Both are owned, organized, and managed by the people who participate in them. Both tend toward more consensus-oriented decision making. Both prefer to be more socially interactive. For these reasons I refer to these as Intentional Businesses (IBs).

The methods, and therefore the learning curves, of establishing IBs and ICs are also similar. As is true for forming ICs, business startups need to discuss and develop a realistic business Vision, Mission, and Goals. Follow-on agreements on how to handle the strategic and day-to-day affairs are also needed. A good book on IC development is Diana Leafe Christian's *Creating a Life Together*. Much of what is in there, I see as equally applying to IBs. And Chapter 14 should be an eye-opener for many, in the context of a need for IB within IC, or at least adjunct to it.

While I personally do have interest in ecology and "getting back to the land," I also have aspiring interests in things futuristic. Being that my background has been in technology, industry, and information research, that is where I am "coming from." And I see these areas as potential sources for more sustainable lifestyles as well.

Here I am not just talking about alternative energy, but a whole gamut of possibilities, including what is called "New Space"—commercial development of industry off the Earth. How about joining Elon Musk and his SpaceX corporation in developing an Intentional Colony (IC) on Mars?

One would of course have to start with something more down-to-Earth, like everyday computers and internet stuff. Those other dreams may be in our 100-Year Plan. But between here and there covers a LOT of territory, and therefore opportunity.

My description would include things like manufacturing solar panels, wind turbines, and other related devices, dealing in and/or repairing farming equipment, operating a vehicle repair shop or computer repair shop, manufacturing tools, assembling electronic or mechanical equipment, research and develop-

Member-owners of Pacific Electric, an IB connected to an IC.

ment, and safety testing. I can envision these examples being compatible with some ICs, as they are considered "light industrial." And even in heavy industrial, there are areas where we could set a better example, at the very least in a fair-trade sense.

In the non-technical sphere, there are opportunities in medical/dental clinics, accounting services, entertainment services including stage shows, eco/wilderness tours, veterinary clinics, credit unions and financial advisers, edible landscaping services, unique and practical furniture, legal services, marketing services, therapy, and life coaching services.

You might want to try a Preliminary Business Plan of your own with both work and home in mind. Here is a basic template. Mine is filled out below it:

Vision

(one paragraph—what would it look like?)

Mission

(one to three paragraphs—what is its intended purpose?)

Goals (can be chronological or by priority)

1) (First accomplishment)
2) (Second accomplishment)
3) (Third accomplishment)

My Possible Business Plan:

Vision

Establish, be part of, and run a technology-based cooperative business that operates in the mechanical, electronic, and computer industries. This business becomes the basis for inten-

tional community that organically grows up around it.

Mission

To supply high quality hardware and software to the high technology industry, in an ecologically, ethically, and financially sustainable manner.

To provide meaningful, satisfying work for communitarians and non-communitarians alike. This satisfaction can come in the forms of intellectual, financial, social, and personal fulfillment.

To set an example to industry of a more ethically progressive way of doing business that is a win-win-win for all of society.

Goals

1) Get a business established, or purchase an existing one, dealing with everyday computer technology—install, maintain, repair, move, migrate, etc.

2) Get into manufacturing of supplier-level wares, both hardware and software.

3) Venture into "New Space."

How IBs Can Grow ICs and More IBs

Initially, people can rent or buy housing in the area. After the business has enough of its own momentum, some could plan and implement Intentional Community housing nearby.

The first company can become an incubator for others. For example, the accounting department could begin doing bookkeeping for other businesses in the area. As it grows, so it then can be spun off as an independent company. Same can be done with the maintenance department, and the landscaping group. And in fact, why not the design group and the manufacturing department too? What about the cafeteria and legal departments, public relations, project managers, janitorial, IT? Janitorial can expand into recycling. Maintenance can get into renovation, construction, or small-scale manufacturing. Legal can also venture into political, social justice, or land use issues. HR can get into career coaching, wellness, life coaching, and human development. The possibilities are limited only by the imagination (and money, of course).

As college has become very expensive recently, set up training programs that include an educational component for apprenticeships and internships. These also apply more real-world scenarios to education, rather than just pure classroom book learning. This approach can be extended to include interaction with Regional Occupational Programs (ROPs) and Regional Occupational Centers (ROCs), as well as local colleges and universities. Eventually, these programs may even become accredited themselves.

Cooperation between the IB and the IC could establish daycare facilities. These could be based on such educational methodologies as Montessori and/or Waldorf. Over time, schooling could be developed to progress up through the grade levels to finally meet with the IB educational programs.

One challenge, however, that I have come across is well described by Laird Schaub in his article on mixing entrepreneurship with intentional community Please see www.ic.org/entrepreneurial-dilemma (featured in COMMUNITIES #163) for his views on how integrating entrepreneurial energy into cooperative communities often proves difficult as well as necessary.

I hope this stimulates discussion and especially then action toward a more financially sustainable intentional communities movement. To get more involved in the topic of Intentional Business, I invite you to join our IB email list by emailing me at IB@kontara.com. You can also contact me directly there.

Pacific Electric is associated with LA Eco-Village. LA Coop Lab, a group that helps coops get started, assisted Pacific Electric.

Werner Kontara's work background has been in the technology industry, aerospace, and IT. He has also recently established a home as a residential program with personal recovery in mind. It is called the "Recovery House for the Inner Child," emphasizing self-improvement via attention to Inner Child and Codependency issues. Professional therapy and life coaching are integral parts of the business, which is intended as the seed for establishing an Intentional Community.

Sunflower Cohousing en France

By Martin Prosser

Our journey into community living started one evening in the Summer of 2009 when we were grouped around a campfire with friends discussing possible future lifestyle alternatives. We (Barbara, Martin, Alan, and Maria) jokingly agreed to buy a residential home between us, so that we could dictate to staff, and not the other way around, as to how we would spend our days in later life. Then we stumbled across "cohousing," which completely changed our thinking, and decided that was the route that we wanted to take—a group of like-minded people sharing and assisting one another in day-to-day events.

We had initially looked at joining a forming or established community in the UK, but were not happy with all of the ideals of those communities that we looked at. In one forming community we were being asked to invest a large sum of money, but the existing group members were unable to tell us who would be responsible for saying how that money would be spent—neither could they give us any ideas of the accommodation that would become ours. At another flagship established community, the organisers admitted that one of the houses had just been sold, and new people were moving in, but nobody in the community had met with those people. Whilst this latter community was held up in the press as being very forward-thinking in respect of the building and site design, there was no evidence of any community spirit.

We believe that there are problems with forming a new community in the UK associated with the high cost of land, and planning controls which essentially revolve around an initial "knee-jerk" reaction of planning. It can literally take years for a group to find a suitable and affordable site, and as a consequence, the make-up of the group, and the ideas as to how the community should evolve, have, in the meantime, changed out of all recognition as members drop out and new members join, the focus of the group keeps changing and becomes aimless. Another option is to go with developers, but this leads to high cost and high-end housing. Another option is to borrow, which none of us wanted to do.

We therefore decided to try to start a community in France, where the cost of land is much cheaper and planning controls are much more relaxed. After we found our site, we received an approval in principle within weeks, and whilst we did later have more protracted negotiations with planners over the external appearance, we knew that the initial approval of the concept could not be overturned. The cost of the site was also such that we could afford to purchase this, and develop the first of the proposed new houses, without resorting to borrowing. Our initial experiences in the UK also led us to purchase the site as an SCI (Société Civile Immobilière)—essentially a nonprofit, limited liability company with shareholders. We have all invested equal amounts into the community, we all have an equal shareholding, and we all have an equal say.

One of the potential problems with cohousing is trying to determine what happens when people, for whatever reason, decide that they want to leave. It is all very well saying that disposal of shares, or a leasehold or freehold interest, has to be approved by the remaining members, but how do you enforce that stipulation, and, perhaps even more importantly, what are the consequences if the remaining members do not approve of the proposed new members? Will financially responsible people looking to join a community commit to joining you if there are potential problems of realising their investment in the future?

We have decided that, in addition to any initial financial investment, community members would also have a rental agreement in respect of the property which they occupy as their own. The rent would need to be a market rent, and one idea which we propose to adopt from our UK research into cohousing is to make an annual dividend payment to an investing member which would be equal to 50 percent of the cost of renting the smallest house on the site—as such, there would be no net additional cost to investing couples unless they chose to live in one of the larger houses which will become available, and where we propose to adjust the rent pro rata to suit the increased floor area.

In the event that people do wish to leave the community, we have proposals for a contingency fund which could be used to buy back the shareholding of an individual member. Whilst we believe this to be a laudable step, this could in itself create financial problems for the rest of the community if more than one member (or couple) wished to leave in the same time frame, and we may need to temper this proposal with the community instead having the first option to buy back shares of members which come up for disposal—to date, we have not found an easy "catch-all" solution.

This, in turn, has highlighted a problem that we had not envisaged. The majority of interest shown in our community to date has been from single people, not couples. Our houses are intended to be occupied by two people, but you cannot force two people to live together, and what happens when a couple split up, and only one of them wishes to leave, or if they both wish to stay, but in separate accommodation? At present, we have no plans for dedicated accommodation for single people who wish to invest in the community—it is something that we will need to address, but it is another thorny problem.

One of the principles of cohousing is that you should downsize, and, owing to the footprint of the existing stone barns within which we are building the new houses, we cannot realistically make the new properties any smaller without possibly constructing apartments—but would people want to live in an apartment on an upper floor which has no direct access to external private space? As our ideas stand at present, a single person living in a two-person dwelling would effectively need to pay rent on one half of the property, but that proposal will need to be revisited when new members join, as they would then also have an equal say as to how the community should evolve.

Our proposals will mean that the original investing members will give up some "control" of the community when new members join—we welcome that situation, but have built in "rules" to protect the community which we hope will be acceptable to incoming investing members as these will also serve to protect future investors.

I am disappointed in the attitude of cohousing.org.uk—they profess to be interested in cohousing in Europe as well as the UK, but, unlike the FIC, they refuse to allow us to register our community on their website. Coupled with the fact that the French, unlike the rest of Europe, also refuse to assimilate the word "cohousing" into their language (we have to refer to ourselves as "habitat groupé" or "habitat participatif"'), this means that it is difficult to advertise our presence to attract new members. The interest that has been shown to date has been solely generated by our presence on the FIC or GEN websites.

We hope to complete the first of our new houses this year (timber framed, terraced-style dwellings, built within the footprint of existing stone barns), and further development of the community site will then need to be put on hold until we can attract new members and additional investment. We do not intend to profit from our physical or monetary investment to date, and are only asking that new members match our financial investment in return for an equal shareholding, and an equal say, in the community project as a whole.

Additional investment will allow us to build a further house for the new members, and will also allow us to commence work on converting another barn into workshops with offices and additional visitor bedroom accommodation over—we also have plans to convert a further barn into a community building, thus freeing up the original house on the site for alternative uses (possibly ambulant disabled accommodation). On the positive side, we will now have more time to spend on developing our potager (vegetable garden), where our ecological approach to the growing of vegetables requires increased hours on weeding and tending plants, although we are also introducing permaculture principles. We will also be implementing wastewater recycling, solar electric, and solar hot water systems as part of our ecological approach to the community.

Following two working-party weeks (thanks to all involved) we now have two high quality composting toilet cabins, and we also compost kitchen waste by way of worm bins. The new houses will also be fitted with "Aquatrons" (a Swedish design which uses a conventional flushing WC, but which then separates solids from liquids, allowing the solids to be composted, and the liquids to be recycled). We have also developed an aquaponics system (a permaculture arrangement whereby fish poo is used to feed vegetables) which we intend to put into full production in the coming year in order to provide us with fresh fish at the dinner table.

One of our working-party volunteers is a horticultural student, and for her final year dissertation she is developing proposals for landscaping of the communal courtyard around which our buildings are constructed, and again, we hope to start work on this aspect of the community project over the coming year.

We have tried to keep our French neighbours abreast of our proposals, and we have had an "Open Day" (to be repeated this year), when a French architect, Mathilde Berthe, who has previously worked with the American architectural practice of McCamant & Durrett, gave a talk on the future of cohousing in France. Our neighbours remain firmly entrenched, but we hope to attract interest from French (and other European nations) as well as the UK—over the years I have come firmly to the conclusion that you can give your child no better start in life than encouraging them to become bilingual, and we also have plans for larger houses for family accommodation.

Over time we have given a lot of thought to our proposals, and to date, the only real setback that we have had is with the French Notary whom we had employed to oversee the purchase of the site, and who completely failed to understand what it was that we were trying to achieve—we had to completely rewrite the articles of our SCI.

We are now looking forward to the next stage in the community development, in particular to receiving further expressions of interest from potential investing members, when we will have the first of our new houses to demonstrate. We will also need to give serious thought as to how we might want to approach accommodation for single persons and/or for members who might wish to rent as opposed to investing in the SCI.

Vive la France! ☙

Martin Prosser is a founder member of the forming intentional community Sunflower Cohousing in France (www.sunflowercohousing.org.uk, www.facebook.com/groups/505483079482490). He is a retired consulting structural engineer who has always been interested in developing practical solutions which are "out of the box." He has extensive DIY skills, and is largely responsible for the design and construction of new timber framed houses being built within the footprint of existing stone barns at Sunflower Cohousing.

Why The Farm Collective Failed

By Melvyn Stiriss

Guatemalan Mayan man in field.

Stephen Gaskin blowing horn to start Om.

The '60s spawned widespread pockets and tribes of people attempting to break away from the military-industrial complex, materialistic, conformist society to get back to the land to create a better lifestyle based on spirituality, simplicity, and sharing. Collective communities and hippie communes popped up all over. The Farm in Summertown, Tennessee was "the ultimate hippie commune."

The Farm was an amazing tribute to the power of human spirit and human energy working in harmony to manifest what we thought would be the best of all possible worlds—affordable Paradise on Earth, a gracious, fun, peaceful lifestyle the whole world can afford. At The Farm's peak in the late '70s, 1,450 people enjoyed Zero Unemployment, Universal Healthcare, and all necessities on a little more than $100/person a month!

Over the collective's 13 years, a total of 5,000 people lived and worked together as "voluntary peasants" sharing labor, life, and friendship—living a path with heart—working labor of love without pay, manifesting a grassroots, 24/7 peace demonstration.

We built our own town nestled deep in Tennessee woods—a village complete with an FM radio station, solar-heated school, crews of people dedicated to farming, construction, and infrastructure. We had a soy dairy, clinic, doctors, midwives, bakery, cottage industries, a dozen satellite communities around the country, and our own hippie Peace Corps working humanitarian outreach projects around the world.

First, I hasten to make clear: The Farm did not fail, completely. The Farm is still around. It was only the original collective phase that proved unsustainable. First there was The Farm collective, the community's original incarnation—the "Stephen Gaskin as spiritual teacher" version—which existed between May 1971 and October 1983, when The Farm collective community threw in the towel, conceding the collective experiment was not sustainable.

Next came The Farm Cooperative which still exists to this day on the same land. People now pay dues, have their own money, own their houses, but not the land those houses sit on, because the land is still held in its original trust.

In 1980, Plenty International, our own hippie Peace Corps, was awarded "the alternative Nobel Peace Prize," the Swedish Right Livelihood Award—"For caring, sharing and acting with and on behalf of those in need at home and abroad." I myself worked as a volunteer with Mayans and a crew from the community in remote indigenous villages after a devastating earthquake in Guatemala. We built schools, clinics, houses, and a clinic for Mother Teresa in a Guatemala City slum.

We did some good, helped some people; even saved lives. We made a difference in the world, shared great adventures, made dear friends, and demonstrated that we can escape the humdrum pedestrian. We learned people can get "out of the box," leave behind soul-sucking jobs and lifestyles to live out dreams and be happy. So, what happened?

Why did the collective fail? It was certainly not for lack of trying. Typical residents were dedicated, hard-working people who contributed their blood, sweat, and tears in a labor of love. There is a concatenation of causes as to why it failed, but it boils down to:

• The Cult Effect
• Terrible Money Management
• Hierarchy and Denial of Hierarchy
• Ego
• Lack of Intergenerational Continuity
• Marijuana
• The Living-in-a-Bubble Effect

The Farm guru, Stephen Gaskin, was a charismatic, six-foot-five, long-haired, marijuana-smoking, magic-mushroom-and-peyote-eating, self-proclaimed tripping guide and spiritual teacher, who held free "tripping, energy, and telepathy" classes in San Francisco and Sunday morning meditations. A hundred colorful buses followed Gaskin on a 'round-the-country-save-the-world bus caravan/speaking tour. Over time, the former college teacher and US Marine Corps combat veteran became an adored life coach and guru to hundreds of hippies. In the beginning of The Farm, everyone was Stephen's devoted, enlightenment-seeking, out-to-save-the-world spiritual student, and The Farm was Stephen's ashram, school, and monastery.

With the wisdom of hindsight, it seems The Farm could have made it financially if we were not supporting Stephen's expensive travel and celebrity habits, all done in the name of "getting the word out." There never would have been a Farm without Stephen, but, in the end, Stephen unwittingly undermined the whole experiment with his ego and bad financial decisions.

While the community struggled to stay afloat—everyone working overtime to keep the community covered for food, medical, housing, and

257

clothes, Stephen spent thousands of dollars of community money to buy a used Greyhound Scenicruiser, retrofit it, take 25 talented people out of our workforce and go out on national and international tours with our band, to give free concerts and for him to speak, recruiting additional community members, overtaxing all our systems, especially housing.

Another major flaw was the existence of hierarchy. Though we agreed in the beginning to create a "classless society," Stephen not only allowed hierarchy, but he himself created a class system that had him and his immediate family at the top, followed by his inner circle who traveled with him on tour. Next on the ladder came married couples. Singles made up our low class. Hierarchy was counter-unity, and it got to be like George Orwell's *Animal Farm*: "On the farm, all animals are equal, but some animals are more equal than others."

About the cult effect: Groupthink is rampant all over, not just in cults. Groupthink is that situation in which we overlook flaws in our leaders. We make excuses for them and rationalize all negativity. And, over time, we sacrifice judgment and critical thinking. Groupthink took its toll and also led to the end of our collective agreements. Once proud of our group intelligence, we were stumped on how to right our ship.

About marijuana: Though marijuana slowed us down at work, at the same time, marijuana kept our spirits high and often gave carpenters and farmers a "second wind." So, it was a tradeoff, and I don't think marijuana use cut into production significantly.

However, I think using marijuana engenders contentment and a pleasurable feeling that "all is right with the world." Sometimes, we need a little relief from everyday stress, but everything was not all right with our world on The Farm, and the populace was lulled into a false sense of security and failed to act appropriately to deal with real problems that were taking a cumulative negative toll on the very underpinnings of our community.

Other contributing factors that weakened the community and undermined success include the 1981 election for the Council of Elders. Exercising Farm-style all-inclusiveness, the election was open to everyone, regardless of age. You could vote for anyone you thought was an elder, meaning a rock solid citizen, a pillar of the community, a wise, exemplary Farmie.

What happened was that the burgeoning, juicy teen population, feeling its collective power, conspired to organize and vote as a bloc, and the teens won 16 seats on the council. Our clever, rebellious teenagers hijacked the election, got some power, had their joke, and effectively shortchanged the community of a basic ingredient in any successful, sustainable society—elder power.

About living in a bubble: We were living a big, beautiful energy bubble—a bubble we consciously created and sustained with synergy, the combined energy of our daily shared labor of love.

We loved our bubble—our beautiful land, our beautiful people, our beautiful ideals and spiritual intentions. We were having an ongoing, mostly good time in our bubble. But there is a downside to living in a bubble, remote and insulated from the outside world. Precious little information gets in. For example, we totally missed out on Watergate and other major national and world events. I learned of Watergate years later. Most of what we knew about the outside world was what we heard from Stephen at services. Also by living in our bubble, content with homegrown entertainment, we missed out on experiencing art, theater, classical music, opera, Shakespeare, and popular culture like TV.

What are my qualifications to offer an educated opinion on why The Farm collective failed? I am a founder of The Farm. I was there Day One. I lived and worked on The Farm the entire 12-and-a-half-year collective period. Before The Farm, I was a member of the community of followers of Stephen Gaskin at Monday Night Class in San Francisco and on the great, 'round-the-country, save-the-world, hippie school bus caravan.

I am a journalist. Before my hippie days, I worked as a newspaper reporter and as a reporter, editor, and announcer for United Press International. For the past 30 years, I have been writing *Voluntary Peasants*—anecdotes, vignettes, and objective reflection about the community—and

this process of writing has helped me better understand what really happened back there. ☙

This article is excerpted and adapted from Voluntary Peasants—Sharing Life, Land and Love at the Ultimate Hippie Commune—The Farm in Tennessee, *available in ebook and print editions. Visit www.voluntarypeasants.com.*

Now 74, Melvyn Stiriss lives in upstate New York, enjoying his "senior career" as an author, publisher, storyteller, and aspiring movie maker. He speaks at colleges, organizations, and groups around the country. He loves hiking, playing keyboard, photography, travel, movies, and great literature.

Mel baking bread.

258

Why The Farm Survived

By Douglas Stevenson

A group photo. Today The Farm is home to approximately 200+ people, a mix of members, provisional members, children, and visitors or guests.

I t could be said that there's a million stories about what happened during The Farm's great change in September of 1983, and although the principal components of those stories may overlap, each interpretation is filtered by the individuals and their personal experience. So, while my friend Melvyn and I did live on The Farm at the same time, the conclusions or opinions we have are not entirely the same. Because I came to the community a few years after it started and stayed through "The Changeover," the transition from "The old Farm" and its communal economic structure, to our current, cooperative economy, and continue to live on The Farm today, I have a different perspective on how and why The Farm survived.

I joined the community in 1973, and was not part of The Farm's early beginnings in San Francisco or the bus Caravan that left California to find land in Tennessee. This meant that we, my wife and I, and many others like us, had much less of our commitment to the community based on a relationship with Stephen Gaskin. From my observation, often those who were with Stephen from the beginning became more disillusioned, lost faith, and left. Many who stayed in the community after The Changeover were those who came later.

Cult or Cultish?

The first time I saw Stephen on a speaking tour to promote The Farm, he explained that anyone you give your attention and energy and use as a role model, is filling the role of your spiritual teacher. Better to be aware of how you are directing your energy and make the conscious decision to support someone with a positive message. In my mind, I was able to place Stephen in the role of preacher, someone who brought us together, but early on I also saw him as a man with shortcomings and ego. Ultimately, I recognized the community as my true teacher, defined by the people I bumped up against every day who helped me grow and change.

A Hierarchal Power Structure

There is no question that Stephen was the "abbot of the monastery." This gave him the power to fire people who had risen to roles of responsibility, which frequently seemed more to do with conflicting egos than qualifications or abilities. He could make decisions that affected The Farm's econ-

The ambulance crew. During the communal period, The Farm had many services that did not generate an income for the community, but employed a large staff of people, such an ambulance service on call 24 hours a day.

After "The Changeover," most community businesses were privatized, owned by their former managers, such as an electronics manufacturing facility that produces devices for monitoring nuclear radiation, otherwise known as Geiger counters.

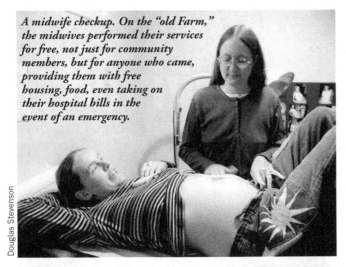

A midwife checkup. On the "old Farm," the midwives performed their services for free, not just for community members, but for anyone who came, providing them with free housing, food, even taking on their hospital bills in the event of an emergency.

Douglas Stevenson

Douglas Stevenson

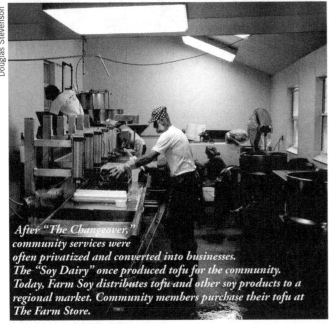

After "The Changeover," community services were often privatized and converted into businesses. The "Soy Dairy" once produced tofu for the community. Today, Farm Soy distributes tofu and other soy products to a regional market. Community members purchase their tofu at The Farm Store.

omy, but was not wise in the ways of money. There is no question that he spent money on promoting himself as the messenger, at times inappropriately. However, most of us who have shared this Farm experience were brought to the community through those efforts. Even though these expenditures may have had a negative impact on our bank account, they alone were not responsible for the financial debt that ultimately brought down the communal phase of the community.

Poor Money Management–Young and Inexperienced

In many ways, during the communal period, Stephen played a very "hands-off" role in managing the day-to-day operations of the community. We could have become more organized, employed better financial management, but overall, we were young and inexperienced. Rebelling from our parent's generation, we did not have and were not open to advice from elders.

Our disorganization meant that there were many different entities within The Farm that had their own income, checkbook, and relationship with our local bank, such as the farming crew and all of the different business start-ups. This meant they were able to take out bank loans, using the land as collateral, without the oversight of a central government. It wasn't until the months leading up to The Changeover, that we pulled all of those checkbooks and bank accounts together and created a broad financial overview, revealing the enormity of our debt.

Our dream of supporting the community as vegetable farmers crashed when a blast of arctic air froze and killed a huge crop of green beans we'd planted in Homestead, Florida, south of Miami. This created $100,000 in debt overnight.

The Farm did not buy nor could it have afforded health insurance. We took care of own healthcare, with a clinic, doctors, nurses, a pharmacy, and were able to care for most needs on our own. However, emergency runs dealing with life and death situations eventually built up overdue bills of well over $100,000 to various hospitals.

There are many other examples of our financial mismanagement. A large crew of people operated and maintained an antiquated internal telephone system. Even though we were installing water systems in other countries, many homes on The Farm did not have running water, but had water delivered each day by two guys driving a truck with a large tank on the back, something we called a "temporary emergency expediency," that went on for years.

Living in the Bubble

When people joined The Farm, they wanted to live and work inside the community, not turn around and get a job in town. The vast majority of the Farm's population did not generate any income. It relied on about 100

A circle of residents, 1970s. At its height The Farm had a population of between 1200 – 1400 people, but not the necessary infrastructure to support them. Most homes provided housing for 30-40 people, but did not have running water or electricity.

The Farm Archives Library

"basic budget boogie boys" who went out every day doing construction work. Unfortunately, the recession of the early 1980s brought a stop to much of the construction work.

There were a few other sources of income, some guys who ran a trucking company, a couple of doctors working emergency room shifts, but it simply wasn't enough. There were numerous additional business start-ups, but they weren't generating sufficient cash flow to make contributions to our communal bank account. At the time of The Changeover, the community was bringing in only

placed its Council of Elders, who had no real power, with an actual board of directors. This shift also meant that Stephen Gaskin no longer had the authority to make any financial decisions for the community.

An overview of The Farm's finances and all its operations was performed, followed by a democratic vote to determine the operating budget for running the community. Each adult member was able to vote for the services they deemed essential and the allocated cost. This included operation of our water system, hiring bookkeepers and accountants, maintenance of roads and public buildings, plus the cost of community services such as our clinic and lifeguards for our swimming area. The total amount was then divided between all of the adult members, establishing the amount each adult was required to pay every month. Altogether, it added up to about $100 per person, plus an additional $35 a month per person to go towards paying down our debt. Within four years, the community was debt-free!

All of the businesses in the community (with the exception of The Book Company) became privatized, owned by their principal managers, the people with the skills and knowledge to actually run the business. These companies had to start paying their employees, so that these folks would have an income to cover their personal needs, feed their families, and pay into the operating budget. Right away it became clear which businesses were generating real money.

> # The teachings that have held the community together really did not come from Stephen, but were broader truths, the fundamentals of hippie culture.

around $6,000, but spending $10,000 a week.

Because of the communal economic structure, our businesses did not pay their employees a salary. This meant there was no real accountability, or financial oversight to determine if a business was running efficiently or showed any true potential for making a profit.

Although not expected to generate an income, work crews for various services within the community, such as the clinic and the motor pool, were also tremendously overstaffed. The extra hands could not make up the difference for a crew short on adequate tools and supplies.

Everything became radically different after The Changeover.

Becoming Financially Sustainable

With onset of The Changeover, The Farm re-

Those not employed by a community-based business were forced to seek employment outside—that is, get jobs. A large number of people went back to school, getting two-year nursing degrees at a local community college. Over time several of the community's business start-ups became solid and provided employment. Once unfinished, overcrowded houses with 30-40 people became beautiful single-family homes.

The Farm survived because the vision of intentional community was much greater than the cult of celebrity, including a hippie spiritual teacher. The teachings that have held the community together really did not come from Stephen, but were broader truths, the fundamentals of hippie culture:
• Peace and nonviolence
• Respect for nature, understanding our role as stewards of the land
• A responsibility to treat each other with respect, and to honor each person's path

The journey is not over. The community is in a new period of transition, from the original founding generation to the next. Survival is never a given, but comes from perseverance and the result of great effort. May the members of The future Farm carry with them the wisdom of what we have learned from the past, and the vision to keep the spirit of community high and vibrant! ✎

Douglas Stevenson is the principal volunteer media interface and spokesperson at The Farm, once recognized as the world's largest hippie commune, now one of the most widely known ecovillage intentional communities. His interviews have appeared in countless newspaper and magazine articles, documentaries, and TV news programs such as CNN's United Shades of America. *Douglas is also the author of two books,* Out to Change the World *and* The Farm Then and Now, a Model for Sustainable Living, *where he shares insights developed from over 40 years of life in community.*

Douglas, Deborah, Jody, circa 1975. My wife Deborah and I were both 21, and our son Jody was 1 ½.

Douglas Stevenson

Th Farm survived because many of those who remained after The Changeover were able to successfully transition into a spirit of entrepreneurship, establishing businesses (including this mail-order that provide employment for other members.)

Douglas Stevenson

The Start of Ravens' Roost—Ravens Unite

By Mary Miner

When my husband and I were newlyweds, we lived in a small town called Fort Defiance, on the Navajo Reservation. Fort Defiance was so small that people walked wherever they needed to go. In the evenings we had pickup games of soccer or gathered at someone's house for dinner and when times were tough we looked after each other. When my neighbor Cezanne was on bedrest for six months or so, we all stepped up and helped with meals, books, and music.

It was a really tight community.

In 1990, we came home to Alaska and settled in Anchorage on the Hillside. Instead of walking everywhere, we drove our car. Our main encounters with the neighbors were as we waved hello or goodbye while clicking the garage door opener. But I never forgot our first neighborhood in Fort Defiance. As I was driving around Anchorage, whenever I'd see a neighborhood that might have a community vibe, I'd stop and knock on doors, asking if anyone was interested in selling, but no one was.

This went on for 20 years.

Then, in 2011, I was at Title Wave used bookstore and found this book called *Creating Cohousing*. It's a how-to manual for regular, non-developer folks to go about building neighborhoods that are designed to support and encourage community.

In cohousing neighborhoods, the houses are clustered together and the parking is kept to the periphery so people can see and talk with each other as they go about daily life. Cohousing includes a common house where people can get together for potlucks, and shared features like play areas for kids, common gardens, and a workshop so everyone does not have to have their own power saw or snow blower.

WOW! This was an epiphany for me. A neighborhood designed for people and not cars! I was so excited. I began talking about this to anyone who would listen. Most people I spoke with thought it was a great idea, but not for them...maybe somebody else. Then one day, this woman named Terri called me. She had been traveling around the US and Europe visiting cohousing and thought it was a great idea AND she said she would do this with me. So we put on a Getting It Built workshop and more people got involved. We formed a company and came up with a great name: Ravens' Roost. But we needed land to build the project on.

We looked all over Anchorage, and talked with lots of property owners; some laughed at this crazy idea, some were irritated with me for wasting their time.

Then one day I was driving up Abbott Road and I saw this gorgeous tract of land next to a small farmhouse. I pulled into the driveway and knocked on the door. It was February and this little white-haired woman with wire-framed glasses opened the door and the first thing she said was, "Honey it's cold out, would you like to come in and have some tea?" Well, would I ever!

I was so overcome, I said "I would love some tea and could I give you a hug?" She looked at me cautiously and said, okay. I went in gave her a hug and had a cup of tea, at her kitchen table.

It turned out that she and her husband owned the land and wanted to sell it. That was how we found the site.

At that point there were seven households in Ravens' Roost. We were working on this when, one day, my phone rang. It was this guy named Tom, who said (to paraphrase), "I've been interested in cohousing for a long time, and, yes, I know where the land is, I live across the street. My wife Marilyn and I would like to join you, and by the way, I'm an architect and Marilyn is a midwife."

Holy Tomatoes!! Who better to help deliver this project than a midwife and an architect? When Marilyn and Tom joined and we had the land, the project really took off.

Our next step in developing Ravens' Roost was to get a design done and approved by the city. This involved a public hearing before the Planning and Zoning Commission. In preparation for this hearing, we went to the local community council a half dozen times, with information, hoping they support our project.

Well, this backfired. It turned out that the president of the local community council was much more comfortable with the conventional suburbia-type subdivision and we were not doing that. We were building 35 homes clustered with the parking to the periphery. This president had a lot of concerns about our project, to the extent that he sent a snail mail letter to every household in that CC's catchment area, advising them of our public hearing date and encouraging folks to attend and express any concerns they might have about the project.

When we got wind of this, the Ravens put our heads together and wrote a letter of our own, and in the spirit of community, we decided to deliver it in person, to every house that bordered our land. This was in December, and we had a ton of snow that year, so nights and weekends we bundled up, climbed over the snow banks, and introduced ourselves to our future neighbors.

The public hearing was held the first week of January 2012. When we got to the Loussac library, the room was packed, standing room only. When I saw all the people in the room, I thought, "I hope we don't get clobbered." Our case was presented, and during public testimony, people spoke for and against the project. Then the Commission grilled us about the project. When the Planning and Zoning Commission voted, and the votes were tallied, they had unanimously approved our project. That packed room erupted in cheering, whistling, and applause. It was a great moment for community.

Five years have passed. Ravens' Roost Phase I has 29 homes compete with 27 households moved in. We have two more buildings with six units to complete, and will be doing those as new reservations allow. The common house is busy, with community meals four nights a week, guests in the extra bedrooms, and the snow got shoveled all winter. The shop is seeing a lot of use and the new bee hives are humming. Life is good! ❧

Mary Miner is a wife, mother of three, and retired civil engineer who served as the burning soul and project developer/manager and construction administrator for Ravens' Roost Cohousing in Anchorage, Alaska.

Communal Studies Association

Encouraging the study of
Intentional Community since 1975

Our Mission: * Provide a **forum** for the discussion of Intentional Community
* Help **preserve** America's Communal Sites
* To **communicate** the ssuccessful ideas and lessons learned from
Intentional Communities

We hold an **Annual Conference** each fall at an historic communal site. We encourage all to come and participate, learn and contribute to the discussion.

We also publish a **journal** and a **newsletter**, both issued twice-yearly.

Special registration and **membership rates** are available for community members.

For more information or to join us, visit our website
www.communalstudies.org

Five Things We've Learned BEFORE WE'VE EVER BUILT

By Mairéad Cleary

It's amazing to watch how community can be created and enthusiasm generated from a twinkling of an idea. I believe this is because people are craving community and connection in this increasingly disconnected world.

Bruns Eco Village in Byron Bay, Australia is rapidly forming, spurred on not only by the desire for shared living, but by a desire to trial a model that can be affordable, ecological, and enterprising.

The ecovillage on Australia's east coast has been started by Kelvin and Skai Daly and a strong working group of professionals with various expertise. The working group formed in mid-2015 and with the project being in the forming stage at present, they have been working weekly on building the foundations that the ecovillage will rest on—legal structure, planning, design, investment, communications, social fabric, and renewable resources.

Not a sod has been turned but already we have learned many lessons.

1. Sustainable isn't enough

Since the very inception of Brun Eco Village in January 2014 it has been almost taken for granted that the ecovillage would be designed, built, and maintained with sustainability principles at its core. The definition of sustainability is "the ability to be maintained at a certain rate or level." It is a term that is bandied about liberally these days and the credibility of environmental sustainability is in fact dependent on many factors.

In February 2017 Shane Sylvanspring, who runs the Village Development Program for Bruns Eco Village (more on this later), organised a workshop with Jamica Stevens, author of and project manager for *ReInhabiting the Village: CoCreating our Future* (see reinhabitingthevillage.com/product/reinhabiting-the-village-book). During the one-day workshop Jamica carried the focus beyond sustainability, pointing out that it's time to move past organic and sustainable to embrace regenerative methods. As she states in her book, "regenerative describes processes that restore, renew or revitalize their own sources of energy and materials, creating thriving systems that integrate the needs of society with the integrity of nature."

Jamica's workshop served as a turning point in how we now view our environmental responsibility in creating this ecovillage. Sustainable measures are no longer enough. We have refocused our concept to incorporate restorative and regenerative approaches that can leave the land better than we found it.

2. Experiencing community before living in community provides a reality check early on

All too often ecovillages and communities fail. Community living, as many are aware, can be romanticised and idealised; however, in reality, joining a community is a significant commitment and a lot of things need to be considered.

In an effort to avoid the disillusionment that often comes when romantic ideals aren't met, Shane Sylvanspring, an ecovillage designer, created a Village Development Program for Bruns Eco Village. Shane drew from the Global Ecovillage Network's Ecovillage Design Education Curricu-

Photos courtesy of Mairéad Cleary

lum, a storehouse of up-to-date knowledge from intentional communities around the globe.

The program is a series of workshops that exposes its participants to the various elements of living in community. It kicked off in September 2016 with a full house of 125 participants and has covered topics such as social design, invisible structures, and nonviolent communication as a method for conflict resolution. It has hosted well-seasoned ecovillage figures such as John Talbot, former Director of the Findhorn Ecovillage, Scotland and currently Project Director of Narara Ecovillage in Australia, whose real life experience provides an invaluable learning for aspiring ecovillage creators.

This process is allowing interested potential residents to engage with the village in a meaningful way without the full commitment and financial risk of moving into a communal living arrangement.

As of May 2017 the year-long program is half way through completion and is facilitating the intended experience. Participants are being challenged in all sorts of ways, some to speak up for themselves, others to be quieter and make space for others. Many are still in the slightly uncomfortable process of finding their place in the forming community. For some participants (albeit very few) the program is revealing that Bruns Eco Village is not what they thought it would be and cannot provide what they need. Rather than this being a negative outcome, however, it can be seen as a positive result. Far better for would-be residents to realise early on that the shoe does not fit than to walk several miles with sore feet!

The remainder of the program will cover ecological design, innovative economics, and will formulate the values and ethics of the village community.

An imminent workshop will host a discussion regarding "Pet Policy." This is a topic that many in the Village Development Program are divided on. In Australia wildlife are particularly vulnerable to domestic animals. The majority of national parks across the country prohibit dogs and cats and many living communities have followed suit by adopting a similar policy within their boundaries. The outcomes of this discussion will mark a milestone in the community's development and provide a test of the community's cohesion.

3. Innovation attracts attention

The Bruns Eco Village approach is pretty unique in Australia. We're challenging the mainstream concept that *success = ownership* and are advocating for the concepts of *success = connection* and *success = energy*, but also *success = interdependence.*

Bruns Eco Village has developed an innovative concept called an Alternative Ownership Model that means the 129 houses built in the ecovillage can't be sold on for profit later. Instead the houses will be owned and managed by a village cooperative that oversees the village homes, renewables precinct, commercial zone, school, and wellness centre. This keeps the houses "affordable" in an area that is highly unaffordable, even for earning professionals.

It's not always easy to convey this alternative concept considering mainstream society has trained us to think of houses as commodities. However for those who are actively seeking solutions to the affordable housing crisis in the country, the Alternative Ownership Model is inspiring closer investigation.

Since launching the ecovillage's website in July 2016, the Bruns Eco Village working group has been invited to speak at a Byron Shire Council Affordable Housing Summit in February 2017 and further afield to a Bellingen Shire Council affordable housing meeting in July 2017. Both councils are facing critical housing shortages in their communities for both renters and buyers.

Whether the Alternative Ownership Model can be adopted to suit potential housing initiatives elsewhere is yet to be seen.

4. Affordable is a relative term

Byron Bay is not unique in the fact that it is experiencing a housing crisis. This is a phenomenon that's sweeping the globe, particularly propelled by high income-generating holiday letting, such as AirBnB.

In June 2016 the median house price in Byron Bay reached $1.24 million. Rent for a two-bedroom house in 2017 has reached a phenomenal AU$480 per week. In comparison, the median household income in Byron Bay is $871 per week.

Bruns Eco Village wants to offer homes to residents at rates that are affordable and lower than the area's current rates. But what is "affordable"?

This very question was raised in a working group meeting as recently as May 2017 where Ella Goninan, one of the working group, challenged the use of the term as potentially misleading.

Since the conception of Bruns Eco Village, land steward Kelvin Daly has been adamant that the land upon which the proposed ecovillage is to be built remain the property of the future ecovillage cooperative and not be susceptible to land speculation. As such each house built will not have freehold title and cannot be sold on by its inhabitants. In this way the value of each home cannot increase individually in value beyond the reach of Byron's residents. This measure is intended to keep the homes "affordable" for those who wish to become members of the cooperative and live in the ecovillage long-term.

The proposed rental rates will be below Byron's market rates, but those rates are still very much outside the reach of many Byron residents. For those people, the ecovillage is far from affordable. This makes the term potentially problematic.

The solution for now appears to be to define "affordable" in context so as to avoid disappointment when people realise that Bruns Eco Village may not be "affordable" for them. Time will tell whether this can avert the dashing of hopes for those craving community but lacking sufficient funds.

5. Dynamic governance is seriously productive

We have seen that unclear leadership and governance can be the undoing of a project and a community. Which is why we have considered various governance structures early on in the forming process of Bruns Eco Village.

Our working group meetings began around shared meals and continued that way for several months. These were a friendly and casual opportunity to catch-up as well as to work on the tasks at hand.

In February 2017 the working group decided to adopt dynamic governance (also known as sociocracy) as a method of governance. The intention was to trial dynamic governance within the core working group and as that has proven successful we are now expanding that governance structure to include other people and groups (or circles) as the project progresses. Each circle has two representatives who meet with representatives of other circles.

One of the refreshing things about holding a meeting under a dynamic governance structure is that every member of the group gets an opportunity to both facilitate and record the meeting but more importantly, every voice is heard. It eliminates the hijacking of a meeting by one or two dominant voices and empowers the quieter members of the group to include themselves.

Round-table discussions are held on every important subject, which makes for rich and often incredibly productive meetings.

The main challenge of course is that this is a new way of interacting and while the initial motivation kept the working group on track, it can be very easy at times to fall back into popcorn meetings where everything is discussed at once and very few matters are fully resolved.

Feedback from other communities that have adopted dynamic governance has been that there is a danger of important tasks failing to be accomplished because no one person takes responsibility for their completion. Perhaps this awareness will be enough to keep us on track for the foreseeable future.

• • •

This process is only starting and each element of the ecovillage project carries with it the excitement of innovation and shared learning along the way.

Bruns Eco Village is on a steep learning curve, the curve that each intentional community must travel as it forms and establishes itself. Our working group members are leaning on the experiences of other communities to learn what has worked and what has failed in the past, and is taking a slow and purposeful approach in order to establish a solid foundation beneath it from which to progress the project.

We are continuously reaching out to other intentional communities to form important bonds so that we can support each other and also hear firsthand about other communities' experiences. Locally we have visited established communities. Internationally we have had conversations with both successful and not-so-successful villages. Atamai in New Zealand is one such community which unfortunately ground to a halt in late 2016 due to financial and governance difficulties.

We are recording the process as we go along, in both written and video formats so that we can in turn share our wins and our challenges with other groups that wish to start an intentional community. Our hope is that capturing this information in the moment can provide a realistic fly-on-the-wall perspective for others.

Pictures paint a thousand words, so seeing our ecovillage in action, even though only forming, will go a long way to attracting like-minded people to the project and providing valid guidelines for others starting their own project.

We are all looking forward to seeing where the road will lead us next. 🐾

Mairéad Cleary is an engineer by profession but a researcher and writer at heart. In 2016 Mairéad published Byron Trails, *a comprehensive walking trails guidebook for the popular Byron Bay region (byrontrails.com). Mairéad is completing a Masters in Gestalt Therapy with a focus on ecopsychology. She has a passionate interest in how people relate to their environment and to the environment and how that relationship impacts them. Mairéad is a member of the Bruns Eco Village working group.*

> ## Round-table discussions are held on every important subject, which makes for rich and often incredibly productive meetings.

Back to the City!

By GPaul Blundell

An early meeting introducing Point A in DC.

There's an abundance to the city, an almost overwhelming abundance. Today this abundance showed up as 20 rolls of sushi. A couple weeks ago it showed up as about 30 lbs. of filet mignon. Before that it was a gross of eggs (a dozen dozen) and a crate of organic grass-fed heavy cream and a case of fair trade black Himalayan chia seeds. All free. All pulled out of a dumpster in the middle of the night and brought back to the main house of Compersia, the commune I call home in Washington, DC.

As anyone who has moved to the country to pursue the simple life will tell you: the simple life is not so simple. The dream of rural abundance, of growing all your own food and fashioning all your own tools, is more often a reality of long hard work and making do with less. Unless you're independently wealthy, there are not many places you can live where everything you might want comes easily and abundantly.

Fundamentally there is one difference that separates rural areas from urban ones: population density. Many communes and intentional communities settle in the country. Insofar as they desire to build a new world divorced from mainstream society this makes sense. With fewer people occupying the land there's more room to build and more room between you and your opinionated neighbors. Over the decade that I lived at rural Acorn Community, in central Virginia, this is certainly the reality that I experienced. The abundance of space, both physical and cultural, provided a lot of room to grow a little utopia and keep it insulated from the corrosive effects the mainstream would have on it. However, there are abundances in many places if you can appreciate and cultivate them.

When I first moved to Acorn in 2005 I came looking for proof that a better world was possible. My political blossoming in college, during the peak of the anti-corporate globalization movement and the run-up to the Iraq War, saw me immersing myself in the history and theory of anarchism. But in conversation after conversation my passionate insistence that we could, as a society, thrive without constantly brutalizing and dominating each other was met with skeptical requests to cough up the proof that my nice ideas could stand up to harsh reality. When I discovered Twin Oaks and then Acorn, all quite by accident, I knew immediately what I had stumbled upon and that the egalitarian communes movement was my life's work.

And the communes did not disappoint. Acorn Community, an egalitarian income-sharing commune, member of the Federation of Egalitarian Communities, and daughter of older larger commune Twin Oaks Community, was founded in 1993 and at the time of my joining listed "anarchist" as one of its self-applied labels. Acorn operates by consensus, runs a fairly complex and highly

seasonal mail order garden seed business, and does it all with a minimum of formal structure. While there we saw the business quadruple in size (rising to over $1 million in revenue by the time I left), helped two other nearby communes to form, built a giant eco-groovy new headquarters for the business, and weathered an arson and a whole string of health, mental health, and interpersonal crises by various members. My time at Acorn and getting to know the other rural social laboratories of the FEC taught me or confirmed several important things:

• Prosperity and organization are possible without heirarchical domination of each other. People are, as it turns out, really good at managing complexity.

• Complex organizations can be run democratically with relatively small overhead. This is related to the above point but the distinction I'm making is that a business or organization can be both directed and managed in a non-heirarchical, democratic, and cooperative way.

• Motivation is available without individual or private reward, like wages. Human motivation is more complex. I found that people could be motivated to apply themselves to valuable labor by the prospect of collective enrichment as well as less tangible things like their values, personal curiosity, or simply love of a good challenge.

• Intense cooperation/communalization/socialization significantly boosts quality of life relative to cost of living. In short, a middle-class quality of life is achievable at sub-poverty levels of income. And it comes with a lighter and less rigid labor burden than is required by almost all full-time jobs! A corollary of this is that intense communalization brings ecological impact down to ballpark global sustainable levels with relative ease.

• The socialized economy of the communes provides a supportive healing space for people dealing with various forms of mental illness (from simple things like anxiety to more complex things like psychotic breaks) as well as being flexible enough to make mental differences that were a problem in the mainstream not a problem in the commune.

What I noticed about all these is that none of them seemed to be a result of the communes' rural locations. In fact, for all the advantages of living in the country there were several glaring problems. The work that could be done in the country was generally pretty low wage. Low population density means commune life could feel isolating, particularly for minorities of any sort. Undeveloped land means that population growth is limited by the speed at which new residences can be built. Their remoteness made visiting them difficult for interested people. Perhaps most striking of all, though, is simply that there are a lot of people who want to live communally but do not want to live in the country.

Our society is run by the few at the expense of the many. It is consuming and degrading the environment we depend on. Inequalities of wealth and power are accelerating. The world is on fire. I thought I had found some ways to help put it out but now those tools needed to spread.

In the summer of 2014 I had the good fortune to be able to take a trip to Europe both for pleasure and discovery[1]. In Madrid, I visited the comrades of the Red de Colectivos Autogestionados[2] (RCA). Most of the members of the RCA were also members of the CNT, Spain's famous anarcho-syndicalist trade union which is remembered as the most successful anarchist organization in history, having fought off Franco's fascist coup for several years and controlled large areas of Spain at their peak. After Franco died and his fascist regime was dismantled, membership in the formerly illegal CNT exploded. However, despite sky-high membership the CNT did not display the strength or resiliency that it had historically and had been fading ever since. The RCA arose out of a very material analysis of this situation. Spain has a long deep history of cooperatives, long predating the Rochdale Society in England and with a stunningly high and widespread membership. It was this community of cooperatives that provided the material base and support for the combative and often embattled CNT during the decades leading up to the fascist coup. By the time Franco died (peacefully in his bed) he had largely succeeded in co-opting the cooperative movement and cleansing it of its leftist politics. Looking at this history the comrades who started the RCA concluded that for the CNT to regain its power they needed to rebuild the network of radical cooperatives that had fed and supported it.

There's an example of this closer to home and closer to now in the Movement for a New Society (MNS). A Quaker peace movement-derived organization that started in 1971 and lasted until 1988, MNS saw the world as being on the verge of a revolution and made it their mission to research, educate, train, and prepare the new society that could arise after the old one tumbled. To support their work and their activists they established a nationwide network of cooperatives and urban communal houses, often sharing income. In interviews I conducted with several veterans of MNS the value of the communes and cooperatives in supporting the work was reiterated again and again. This support came not only in the form of material support (to avoid bankruptcy) but also in social and emotional support (to avoid burnout) and as laboratories and testbeds for the ideas that MNS' activists were developing.

So here we were. The world clearly needed changing. We had some proven strategies for building effective movements. The rural egalitarian communes had done good work but had also clearly shown their limitations. The need to develop a network of urban egalitarian communes to support radical social change work was clear. In the Fall of 2013 several fellow communards and co-conspirators and I decided to try to do just that by launching a project called Point A.

Of course, we are not the first ones to try such a thing or things like it. Specifically on the urban egalitarian communes question, since I first joined Acorn there's been one or two urban communes in the FEC. When I first joined there was Emma Goldman Finishing School in Seattle, Washington, and a few years later they were joined by The Midden in Columbus, Ohio. Both shared the same general model and in the last two years both have devolved into simple group houses or co-ops and left the FEC. This is a sobering recent history but there are counterexamples if we widen our gaze a bit. Ganas, an intentional community with a smaller income- and asset-sharing commune at its core, has been thriving in New York City for 35 years. Over in Germany there are a bevy of income- and income- and asset-sharing communes located in major cities, some of which have been going for over 30 years[3]. In Spain (mostly) there's Las Indias, a nomadic but very stable income-

An early meeting introducing Point A in DC.

Photos courtesy of GPaul Blundell

sharing commune that's been going for 14 years. In Israel, a new generation of urban kibbutzim has arisen. In light of this, it's easier to consider the dissolution of Emma Goldman Finishing School and The Midden as something peculiar to that model or an accident of circumstance.

Point A took on the mission of working to cultivate ambitious and engaged egalitarian income-sharing communes in the urban centers of the American East Coast. Ambitious and engaged—to connect them to the wider work for social justice and liberation. American East Coast—because that's where the FEC has the most resources, and the FEC is a natural ally for this work. When we started working we went in every direction we could find at once: Researching examples of successful urban communes. Finding and forging contacts with collectives, cooperatives, and organizations that might make good allies. Conducting research into legal and tax options for urban communes. Conducting research into financing options for urban communes. Organizing public talks, workshops, and events. Building out a website and blog to point people to.

We started the work in one city: Washington, DC. This is the city in whose suburbs I grew up and where I had the densest network. It's where I wanted to get a commune started. And it's where I have stayed and worked, but the project didn't stay there. Soon after starting in DC we were enticed to NYC by some exciting prospects, and other Point A organizers started working there. Then we got involved with some collectives in Baltimore that we thought might be interested in converting. Then we were contacted by a new, and sadly short-lived, commune in Richmond, Virginia. Then a collective house in Binghamton, New York. Various Point A organizers have tried various tactics in each of these cities.

In DC, meanwhile, the project, as I was organizing it, maintained a laser-like focus on getting a single commune started. The general strategy was to start by recruiting potentially interested people from our existing network. These people would start the conversation that is the first phase of any cooperative project. One caution we had heard again and again was that the people to start the conversation would likely not be the people to start the commune. Keeping this in mind, we thought of each phase as a sinking island, a platform we could find temporary purchase on but that, if we wanted to continue, we would need to be planning to move on from. That first meeting had about 20 people. Of those, 12 ended up coming to our monthly meetings. After a little less than a year, a group of eight likely founders had identified themselves. Together those founders, of whom I was one, finished hammering out what we hoped was the bare minimum of policy and structure that we needed to start and put each other through our newly designed membership process. Of those potential founders, five made the jump and actually started the commune: Compersia, the first egalitarian income-sharing commune in DC (in a while, at least).

After that I stepped back from Point A work. My fellow Compersians and I had a lot of work cut out for us continuing to build out the agreements and policies we didn't have, figuring out how to live together, and figuring out how to run this urban commune we had created. Now, a year and a half in, we're still around. We're even growing! With any luck we'll need a second house before long to fit all our members. ❧

To learn more about Compersia visit compersia.community or better yet email contact@compersia.community. To hook up with the Point A crew check out frompointa.org or send an email to info@frompointa.org.

GPaul Blundell is a member of Compersia Community in DC and an enthusiast about egalitarian community. He enjoys long easy bike rides, nerdy board games, and building the new world in the shell of the old.

Some of Compersia's founders crew at first retreat.

1. I visited a number of urban and suburban egalitarian communes in Europe and the results of my interviews, observations, and analyses eventually made it into a one-off podcast called "Income Sharing Across the Pond" available free on Soundcloud.
2. English translation: The Network of Self-Managed Collectives.
3. I personally visited Kommune Niederkaufungen in Kaufungen outside of Kassel and Villa Locomuna located in Kassel.

Cinema Hearts.

The Split Seconds.

Paul J Mangano

1605 COMMUNE, Washington DC

By Bryan Allen Moore

My introduction to people living together purposefully, as opposed to circumstantially, did not occur until I moved to Washington, DC four years ago. My home, our community, is located one mile north of the White House. This gives us a unique view of national issues and places us squarely in politics, intentionally through work and activism or through a forced viewing by proximity.

Sometimes we have activities, hobbies, and careers or jobs that keep us separate from each other more than together. Even the term roommate implies that we are separate in some ways, because we do not typically speak of each other as a unified community. We always share a modest amount of financial burden that living in a house in the city requires, but the frequency of house meetings fluctuates. Perhaps the efficiency we have achieved over the years has allowed for the financial freedom to travel more often for some of our members, or the trust formed through our situation has made it easier on all of us to live without the necessity of regularly scheduled renewals of commitment to each other.

After reading about our house, I hope readers take away the notion that an intentional community does not always go through rigorous planning. There have been, and will be, unique opportunities and problems that arise from forming consensus as we go, as opposed to making an agreement before taking the first step.

Our particular community is formally referred to as The 1605 Commune, but I have only become interested in a thorough history in recent months. Shorthand monikers have been used over the years to identify our house, home, music venue, and community center. This identity brought us to the attention of the

Right Wing Safety Squad in December of 2016. This group found us through its targeting of DIY music spaces and politically active communities, and we made the 4chan list of places marked for disruption in the wake of Oakland's Ghost Ship fire and our own local Pizza-gate conspiracy. This incident is too complex to expand on for the purposes of our story, but is a starting point for my own exploration of our collective identity.

For an extended weekend, I searched the internet for all traces of events that had occurred in our home with the hope of being able to manage, if not remove entirely, our digital presence. Other homes, venues, and artistic spaces were more successful at either re-branding or moving into obscurity, but the diverse nature of what we had been involved in over the years was too extensive. Thinking back on my futile efforts, I desperately wanted to protect everyone, perhaps at the expense of our legacy. As a private residence we were largely unaffected by physical manifestations of this movement, but it put me in touch with our past.

We did not start as an intentional community, but have slowly though not always permanently integrated intentional community concepts into how we approach living with each other. We have no charter, no mission statement, and not even a written agreement with the owner of our home. We dabble in consensus-based decision making. I have seen former roommates intimidated or uncomfortable with the kind of structure required by the more earnest collectives in our area. Although we do not share incomes, we maintain a robust "house fund" which I see as a gateway for more radical ideas. I have personally been able to escape a monotonous career and 40-hour work week through this shared living environment, but some of us are dependent on full-time employment and it is difficult to incorporate another set of guidelines into our lives, as would be required if we were to collectivize more.

I could not point to any specific criteria we look for in new tenants, but the aesthetic of our house is old, has funky remnants of former residents, and probably attracts a specific type of individual. My version of the guided tour starts in the basement, to remove all doubt as to the nature of our building. If you can make it past that, we conduct group interviews of prospective tenants. An adventurous spirit, focused on saving money, could be drawn into an appreciation not of the aesthetic but of the challenge living in a house built at the turn of the 20th century. Even if such a person had no awareness of intentional communities, their having to interview with upwards of 20 other people gives us an idea how they would react to living in such a crowded environment.

In my experience, the upside of this process is that we usually end up choosing a strong personality with great individual willpower and enthusiasm for life. The downside is that we potentially miss out on the more subtle gifts of quiet intellects, and those may be better suited to daily maintenance and balance.

Despite our best efforts laying out some general philosophy of living together, it is easy for potential residents to be enthusiastic about the benefits of our situation without understanding the work involved. The benefits are easily quantified. However, the reality of living with new people as they become tenants can be somewhat discouraging. Without a concrete set of guidelines, rules, procedures, or specific intentional mission, it is difficult to find potential roommates who can fully commit to and appreciate the differences between intentionally living with others and simply sharing the same space.

The implication of moving in with us should be a vision that is ambitious and idealistic, but the reality is that it is impossible to expect the kind of loyalty and commitment to intentional living ideals without trust earned over time. On a few occasions, we have been deceived by individuals who expressed interest in intentional living to get in the door, literally, and then became impossible burdens on the community. Momentum has been lost through these deceptions, but nonetheless they presented opportunities for hard lessons for those truly invested in living together.

Beyond the lives of current occupants, I wonder how much "community" is derived from a credible thread of former members keeping in touch with each other. Change has occurred in waves, mostly, and our home was generally unwelcoming in the beginning. The arrival of new roommates sometimes coincides with the departure of less compatible roommates and this is when we usually see drastic changes in house policy. Some policies get handed down and altered a little bit. Some roommates have such strong, individual visions of communal living that they simply cannot accommodate others, also causing significant shifts in policy.

The first efforts on the part of tenants to transform six bedrooms into a community occurred in August of 2009, when a few individuals got together and decided to work together on chores. There was not, in the beginning, 100 percent participation. An interesting solution to this problem was the concept of the "seventh" roommate. There were only six living in the house at the time, so the idea was that this extra "person" was incapable of contributing to the house in any way except to add to the clutter, the refuse, and wear on the house. In addition to chores, a couch-surfing profile was created online to allow the home to be open to sharing community with this imagined, temporary extra roommate. The idea behind these combined efforts was that we have a lot, so it is good to share. Dance parties and art projects followed shortly after, and it is at this point in our history that

I begin to recognize our community that still keeps in touch eight years later.

How much former members identify with this intention is dependent on their interaction with house contemporaries. Some members of our community in the past, who otherwise held strong beliefs about shared communities, had disagreements with other members strong enough for them to withdraw or move out of the house entirely. We have no concrete expulsion policy, but we have discussed the subject twice in the four years I have been a resident.

Our members rotate frequently, numbering as few as five, but as many as 12 have been accommodated by the multi-purpose nature of our common spaces. The turnover rate of members ranges from one month to seven years, but given the age of our house the lifetime of our community is finite. Our age range spans between 19 and 38, and I suspect that is related to both the gentrifying neighborhood and the short-term opportunities our capital city

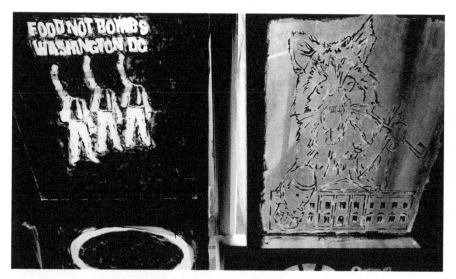

Maulrat.

Paul J Mangano

Erin White and
Marshall James Kavanaugh.

Local punk band
(BBC) playing in the
basement.

The house.

Stephane Ott-Hauville

The Smirks.

Herschel Hoover

provides. Not everyone has contributed to the presence that our community takes, which is somewhat different from other intentional communities. While I would not judge our roommate configuration as ever having the properties of a set of cliques, it is difficult sometimes to get everyone together as a unified body.

We have two conduits for opening minds to ideas about collective living. The first is providing space for the Washington, DC

are formally promoted. We use the spaces we have, whether it is intimacy from hanging out in our living room with poetry and acoustic music or celebrating the DC punk rock tradition of a basement show. It is no coincidence that many in our community are musicians, and it is known in smaller circles that there is often a vegan meal waiting for bands that load in early.

While our FNB chapter may technically have 30 regulars, there is a broader group to which the donations it receives are shared. This eases the financial burden of everyone who participates, allowing those of us who engage completely some benefits of financial independence. I have seen the awe that food recovery creates in the minds of individuals who realize that they do not need to depend only on themselves and their occupation for their existence. The expansion of our mission is exponential because it also includes bands from an equally diverse list of international locations. Between the local, immediate sharing of food and the word-of-mouth experience of traveling musicians, it is difficult to estimate the impact our home has on the causes that are important to us.

Finally, I will end as I began; by trying to figure out how to protect the community. I wonder if my interest in our history as a group, combined with the friendships I have made, is enough to sustain participation in something bigger than ourselves after I am gone. The owner of my home is in the twilight years and almost as venerable as the structure itself. I plan to go down with the ship, so to speak, but should things change

I have seen the awe that food recovery creates in individuals who realize that they do not need to depend only on themselves and their occupation for their existence.

chapter of Food Not Bombs. For more than two years, we have used our kitchen and living areas to host one of the many global, autonomous collectives focusing on food recovery and feeding the hungry. Each chapter has its own identity; for example, most choose to focus on vegan advocacy, animal rights, or local progressive causes. While the DC chapter prepares 100 percent vegan meals, we receive such generous, diverse donations every week that we are able to use this food to supplement many individual household groceries and supplies. When our core group meets, because we are located in the nation's capital, there is a sharing of information about a multitude of groups and initiatives that promote causes or correct injustices too numerous to recognize here.

The second access point is equally diverse and often happens the evening after our FNB chapter meets. Hosting music and performance art events is an important component to our community, transformed over eight years from those original dance parties into events that

in my life I still want people to be able to access our couch-surfing profile or talk about the 1605 mythology with enthusiasm.

Some barriers to this are becoming more familiar to me as I participate, and they all relate to the concept of privacy. Several members have withdrawn, physically or emotionally, when living in close proximity causes friction. I have experienced these symptoms myself during the two aforementioned periods where an expulsion policy was discussed. There can also be an irreverence towards established norms and prior decisions, or an unwillingness to honor agreements made in the past. I have fought several policies that I felt were outdated or did not recognize the limitations of individual schedules and life circumstances. Roommate fatigue can set in, when becoming too familiar through a sense of "knowing" how someone would think or feel is either repetitious, or causes someone to proceed without consent because a roommate's thoughts or feelings are anticipated. If the language I am using seems familiar in some way, it is because I have gained an understanding of the intentional living condition not just through experience, but through contact with other communities.

Meetings, dinners, message boards, email chats with people I have never met, and putting these words in order have given me temperance towards sharing my privacy with others. When someone comes into my home, shares a meal, hears some music, listens to a discussion, and then hears that we are all doing this on purpose, I understand that then they are invested and our efforts are protected. 🖎

Bryan Allen Moore is a Washington, DC-based artist. In addition to volunteering, Bryan facilitates and consults for several arts/cultural organizations in the National Capital Region. He is a recent convert to freeganism, dedicated to spreading the word about food recovery.

Problem: In the face of rampant greed and short-sighted self-interest, it's so easy to lose connection to the extraordinary creativity displayed around this planet.

Response: Establish a centralized access point to sources of social and environmental inspiration — enabling activists and organizers, students and citizens to identify and amplify what might help our own acts of creation.

EXEMPLARS!

a free, searchable, living library of what is hopeful,

fascinating, and sustainable.

Visit **www.exemplars.world**

your portal to designing a sustainable future

Browse the 4 domains of **www.exemplars.world** For each Exemplar, the initial insight, the organizing strategy, tools, outcomes, and a link to websites.

View relevant essays and videos.

Submit Exemplars you have created or know of, as we expand the data base.

1. Cities, towns & communities   **2. Businesses and organizations**

3. Systemic interventions   **4. Cultural sustainability**

Curated by Paul Freundlich, pfreundlich@comcast.net

Founder, Green America

273

ENRIGHT RIDGE URBAN ECOVILLAGE:
A 13-Year-Old Retrofit Ecovillage in Cincinnati, Ohio

By Jim Schenk

Last year we bought a bar. It had been a family bar for over a hundred years, until about eight years ago. The bar had become a haven for drugs, shootings, and police runs. The Enright Ridge Urban Ecovillage had the chance to purchase the building and liquor license, and so we now own the greenest pub in Cincinnati. It went from Paradise Lounge to its new name, Common Roots. We select local and organic drinks as much as possible. We are now open three nights a week from 7 to 12. Open mic night is on Thursdays, and other events happen on many other nights. This was a major purchase, made in our 12th year.

I'm getting ahead of myself. Back to 2004 when we began the ecovillage...

Imago is an ecological education organization founded in 1978. We reached a point at which we felt that we needed to live our values. After a number of attempts, we decided on developing an ecovillage on Enright Avenue, where Imago has its center and where we had a number of residents who supported our work. We also saw this as an opportunity to create an example of how we can live ecological lives in the city.

Our belief is that humans need to stay in the cities. Moving out of the cities would destroy the ability for other species to have places to live and would reduce the farmland that we require for food. We also have numerous houses and established infrastructure already existing in the cities. For ecological reasons, we need to keep these structures and use them rather than tear them down and start over with virgin lumber and other materials. We need to convert our present cities.

As an ecovillage in an existing neighborhood, with existing housing, we had the potential to form the ecovillage fairly quickly. The night we met in June of 2004, the ecovillage began. We didn't have to wait and find a site or plan for the site development or find financing and then build—we just started. The buildings were all here. The people who came together already lived in the neighborhood. So, we could just begin.

The first evening we brainstormed ideas of things we would like to see in the ecovillage and decided to focus on five areas: potlucks, marketing houses in the ecovillage, signage, developing a walking path around the ecovillage, and a youth group.

This isn't to say that everything was easy. We live in a neighborhood with many other people.

We had to convince them that it was a good thing for this to be an ecovillage, even if they weren't interested in ecology or in community. To this end we put out a monthly newsletter and did an exercise called "Treasure Mapping" as a way to help people realize we weren't trying to pull the wool over their eyes.

The newsletter consisted of a "gossip column" about people in the ecovillage, coming events, what the ecovillage committees were doing, educational pieces, and problems that might exist in the neighborhood. Many people contributed to the newsletter. It wasn't fancy, but it was informative.

Treasure Mapping is a way of encouraging people to give input. We took two sheets of 4' x 8' plywood, cut them in half and made a 4' x 4' box. Each side had a different question in terms of what they wanted to see in the ecovillage, in regards to: Housing, Marketing, Family, and Greening the Ecovillage. In the newsletter and then two handouts, we let people know about the event, the date and times. Enright is 3/4 of a mile long, so a little hard to communicate within. We loaded the box on the truck. In advance we had divided the street into eight sections with eight to 10 homes in each. We had "ambassadors" who passed out the fliers about the event, and when we came to their section they went door to door to encourage people to come out. On a Saturday morning we went around to each section, pulled the box off the truck, put it on a table with magazines and scissors, marking pens and blank sheets of paper so that people could create a collage around what they would like to see within our four topic areas. Over 2/3 of the homes were represented. When completed we took the box back to the Imago Earth Center, and invited people to help decipher the information on the collage. From this we developed Task Forces to work on specific areas.

This was our beginning.

We were incorporated as a nonprofit in 2007. We needed a board of directors. Since 2007 we

have gone through two board structures. The first was to invite everyone in the neighborhood to be part of the board. While this was a good idea on paper, few people came to the board meetings. The second structure saw elected officers and the chair people of our Task Forces (now called committees) making up the board. Anyone could come to board meetings and be part of the meeting. However, if there was a controversial item, the board members alone would decide, by consensus, on this decision.

The neighborhood has become a desirable place to live, so there is little opposition. A rough estimate gives us about a third of the ecovillage involved in the ecovillage, about an additional third open to thinking of themselves as part of it, and about a third indifferent.

But there are struggles...

Most of the people who live in the ecovillage have lives outside the ecovillage. When moving to a rural ecovillage, people give up most of the previous lives and the ecovillage becomes the new center of their lives. Most of those who lived in the ecovillage when it began had jobs, recreation, spiritual practices, etc. outside the neighborhood. The ecovillage is just another thing on their agenda. Most of the people who moved to the ecovillage moved from within Cincinnati, which meant they too had their lives outside the ecovillage. We have struggled with how to make the ecovillage more of a center of people's lives. While we have a simple membership fee of $25 per year, we recently started membership categories where members are required to make an initial financial commitment and for each year following, along with a yearly work requirement. While this seems to help some, there is still a feeling that we need to create deeper relationships among members. This is still on the drawing board.

We have had a good number of young families move into the ecovillage. This has been exciting. However, with family demands it is hard for some families to really get involved. We also have the struggle of separation and divorce with families in the ecovillage. This is especially difficult when the families have been deeply involved in the ecovillage. In most cases both parties are loved and respected. Figuring out how to relate to the two parties is especially challenging when they have become a major part of the community. We aren't aware of any formula for this. It seems to be different in each case and relationships are different in each case both within the family and within the community. It does create major stress in the community. While we haven't had a big problem with people siding with one or other of the couple, experiencing their pain and filling holes that are created by their frequent withdrawal from their role in the community are

> ## About a third of the ecovillage is involved in the ecovillage, about an additional third open to thinking of themselves as part of it, and about a third indifferent.

huge. The board especially has had to struggle when members of the board have chosen to leave or take a leave of absence.

We have also struggled with people working for other residents in the community. People have hired their fellow community member to do work for them, and sometimes they are

Part of the 2-mile hiking trail in the urban forest beginning at the Imago Earth Center and wrapping around the Ecovillage.

Ecovillage's weekly potluck at the Common Roots Pub.

Jerry Ropp is a resident contractor who has helped rehab 19 houses in the Ecovillage.

Photos courtesy of Robert Johnson

CSA shareholder pickup day at the greenhouse; workers separate the week's harvest for collection on Saturday mornings.

acres of woods and greenspace surrounding us, with a mile-and-a-half trail leading through it.

We also have Imago in the ecovillage, which was the impetus to starting the ecovillage and remains a mainstay. Its 40 acres of preserved land and building are key assets for the ecovillage.

We offer a monthly tour of the ecovillage as well as offer consultation to other neighborhoods interested in forming their own retrofit ecovillage. I have just finished, with the input of other ecovillage residents, a book on the ecovillage, which is now in the process of finding a publisher. I see it as a kind of "how to" book on creating a retrofit ecovillage in a city neighborhood.

These are a few of the things that make our ecovillage a good place to live. At this time only our head farmer in the CSA is paid, with most all work in the ecovillage carried out by volunteers. While there are always opportunities for more people to be involved, we have established a solid group of people who are passionate in helping make the ecovillage work.

The urban retrofit ecovillage is one way we can recreate our cities. While there are some other urban retrofit ecovillages in the US, we would like to see more of them formed within neighborhoods throughout all of our cities. We don't claim to have the only answer to living ecologically in our cities, but it is definitely one of the possibilities. ❧

Jim Schenk helped start Enright Ridge Urban Ecovillage (www.enrightecovillage.org) and is an avid promoter of the retrofit urban ecovillage. As mentioned in the article, he has completed a book on the Enright Ridge Urban Ecovillage as a model for making our cities sustainable, and is seeking a publisher. (Any suggestions?) He is available for consultation. Contact him at jschenk@ imagoearth.org.

not pleased with the work done. There have been cases where mediation was used, while other times feelings of resentment fester. At one point the housing committee decided not to hire people in the neighborhood to do any of its rehab work. Although this seemed like the opposite of what one would want in an ecovillage, where we should be providing for each other and supporting each other, there is little doubt that this will remain an issue that needs to be dealt with on an individual basis, especially in an ecovillage where the majority of people have not bought in to being directly involved in the ecovillage.

While there are major issues, the majority of residents of the ecovillage revel in the gathering of such wonderful people forming the village. We believe it is a huge improvement in the way people live over most neighborhoods in our cities. It both forms community and provides an ecological framework for living in the city. Many of us see our efforts as a real demonstration of how we can live better in our cities. A lot of exciting things have happened:

The purchase of the Common Roots Pub: the pub is as green as we can make it, and is run totally by volunteers.

Our ecovillage CSA provides households with food every year. We are now in our ninth season and are running strong. The CSA food is grown in backyards, lots, and any other available land in and near the ecovillage. The trip to pick it up isn't far for the shareholders, just up the street.

Our monthly newsletter, "The Ridgerunner," keeps people in the community informed about what is going on. It is particularly important since a good number of people aren't actively involved in the ecovillage. The website (www. enrightecovillage.org) serves people inside the

ecovillage as well as beyond. There is also the Community Earth Alliance website (www. communityearthalliance.org), a place you can find out about houses available in the ecovillage and other information.

The weekly potluck—at the pub—is an opportunity for people to come together to share in great conversations, good food, and green drinks. It is also on Thursday evening, which is Open Mic night at the pub. Once everyone is full, they can stay and listen to some great music.

The woods around the ecovillage provide a wonderful place to hike or just sit and connect with the other residents of the ecovillage, our non-human residents. We are only seven minutes from downtown Cincinnati, but have some 200

Open Mic night at the Common Roots Pub.

The Dolphin House, Looking Forward

By Brittny Love

W e are living in powerful times where the desire for community and a regenerative lifestyle is at the forefront of most of our minds. We've watched, and been a part of, a world that allowed greed and corporations to take over, and where sustainability and the best interests of the whole have taken a back seat. Many of us have felt the urge to uproot ourselves from the city and settle on a plot of land out in the country, but we've wondered, *what about the cities and all the people we know back home?* This has been the dilemma for my friends and me in the desert valley of Arizona.

Our intentional community began about a year ago, when a dear friend was killed in a car accident. Kelly was an incredibly special and ambitious woman, who dedicated much of her time to nonprofit organizations, art, and making the world a kinder place. Her sudden passing was especially difficult on our close friends, and her boyfriend opened his home for the Dolphin House to embark on intentional community living. We had 10 people living in a four-bedroom house, with a couple toddlers in the mix. The members ranged in age from early 20s to early 30s and varied in ethnicity. Although I lived at my own place nearby, I attended weekly meetings where we would touch base and address issues and concerns.

It always impressed me to see how well this group of friends managed to coexist together, maintaining a tidy home, cooking healthy meals, and spending most of their time dedicated to creating art and music. They also dug up the back lawn and replaced it with a permaculture-style garden, where we've been experimenting with different edible plants and learning the art of growing our own food. Some of the issues that arose were learning to deal with so many people in a shared space, and handling relationship challenges as we learned to humble our egos and listen to one another. Our evening circles were very productive in maintaining a mature space for everyone to speak and be heard.

We've known that living at the home wouldn't be permanent, but an experiment for what we want to embark upon with establishing an ecovillage. Everyone in our group is very involved with community events and passionate about bringing awareness and education to the surrounding cities such as Tempe,

Mesa, Chandler, and Phoenix. The numbers of "awakened" young adults in the state are strong, and there is a strong desire to build a better world, but there is lack when it comes to places to hang out and be productive together.

The Dolphin House has hosted several block parties in which we've held workshops on backyard gardening, jewelry making, and guided yoga and martial arts practices. The intention for our block parties has been also to reach out to those in the neighborhood and create a stronger human connection.

Our community is currently considering land that's not too far from the Phoenix area, but still puts us more in the forest. One of the concerns we've had for building in the city is the stricter regulations and zoning laws. For example, Heathcote, near Baltimore, Maryland, has been forced to close its outreach programs due to unexpected zoning issues they've faced with the county which have taken several years to try and get resolved. Our intention is to build an ecovillage where we can continue to host workshops while helping those who visit remember how to connect with the Earth. I believe one solution leading to a better world is taking the wisdom and knowledge of nature back to urban areas and implementing it.

While I was visiting Denver, Colorado, I met an organic farmer who lived in the heart of the big metro area. "I used to be afraid of the cities. I didn't like being in them at all, but a lot of people live in these dense areas, including my friends and family. If we were all to run off to the woods, there would be no one here to help the places that really need it," James said.

"Have you faced any issues from the city for being an organic farmer?" I asked.

"There are a lot stricter codes and zoning laws. For some reason, the city of Denver doesn't like greenhouses, which I find odd. I also can't label my produce as organic at the market unless it's certified, which entails paying money," James added. "I feel like if people knew how to build shelters and grow their own food, we wouldn't need to spend so much time developing and strengthening a system that doesn't serve us as a collective."

We live in a country where our voice counts. If we can get people to care about growing food, strengthening community, and being self-reliant, I believe there will be a big change in our politics and how we function as a society. Money needs to be put toward creating food forests, community gardens, sustainable building, and creating places that human beings can enjoy together. Imagine if we could have creative control over our cities again? What amazing art would we create? How could we design our buildings better and to be more exciting? What if we could include more rooftop gardens and edible landscaping? What if we stopped saturating our soil with weedkiller and other toxic chemicals?

As human beings, we are more capable and stronger than we usually give ourselves credit for. We can't sit back idly, waiting for someone to come fix things; we must be the ones motivated to make change. We have incredibly creative minds and the ability to transform our world; the only thing that holds us back is fear and the belief that we won't be supported in our endeavors. This is the time to come out of our shells, to take risks, to be motivated to initiate new projects, events, and gatherings—to share our skills with one another and inspire the younger generation who will eventually take our place as the leaders of this world.

If you're reading this, please know that you're not alone and you're never too small to make a difference. Start a small garden, inspire your neighbors… Reach out to those in your community and have conversations! We are at a choice point of doing what's right for our evolution, or choosing to stay the old course. What will motivate us to step up and be the change we want to see in the world? 🍃

Brittny Love is the author of the inspiring travel series, Diary of a Starseed. _Her books and videos are available at StarseedStory.com._

Photos courtesy of Brittny Love

COMPACT COMMUNITY
at Maitreya EcoVillage in Eugene, Oregon

By Robert Bolman

Robert Crumb's iconic illustration, "A Short History of America," starts with its first panel depicting a pastoral country scene. The next panel introduces the railroad to this setting; the next panel, a telegraph line, a small house, and a dirt road. Subsequent panels add more and bigger buildings, more utilities, pavement, etc. By the 12th panel, our bucolic country setting is choked with cars, pavement, and all the ugliness that has characterized the suburban "growth and development" that followed WWII.

The final three panels depict three possible future scenarios: ecological collapse, the techno-future with flying cars, and the ecotopian future with bicycles and trees. We all wish to avoid ecological collapse; I feel that the financial and energy resources are not going to be there to support the techno-future; which leaves us with the ecotopian future. It is that scenario that I would like to see urban planning strive for.

Social and architectural critic James Howard Kunstler laments that suburban sprawl has been "the worst misallocation of resources in human history." Countless cheap, flimsy tract houses, strip malls, burger joints, and big box stores fan out in most directions from our cities—all of it built with the full expectation that we will always drive around in cars. Meanwhile, US tourists flock to European cities for the pleasure of vacationing in a humane, pedestrian-scale urban environment: Taller, mixed-use buildings line the street, defining it as a large, outdoor room. Flowers, parks, and trees combine with sidewalk cafes and corner markets to create a festive, lively environment where people walk many places, public transit is fast and convenient, and community flourishes. After their European vacation is over, US tourists return to their own wretched US cities where the downtown is commercially comatose and all serious shopping is done by driving to the Walmart on the edge of town.

It will be more challenging than most people understand for US-style automobile culture to survive the end of fossil fuels (a whole other essay). Urban planners consider 15 dwelling units per acre to be the minimum density necessary to support reasonably fast and efficient public transit. Most suburban sprawl development in the US falls woefully short of that. So, in terms of land use, we've painted ourselves into a corner.

In 1991, I sold a single house in San Francisco and bought five contiguous city lots with a smattering of older houses about one mile west of the center of Eugene, Oregon. Already a builder, I soon discovered green building. That led me to permaculture, intentional community, appropriate technology, and renewable energy; all of it culminating in the ecovillage and broader ecocity concepts. Owning vacant city land, I experimented with various green and natural building techniques. The more interesting things I built, the more interesting people moved in. Upon completing a triplex in 2002 and with a regular meditation group, we named the place Maitreya

EcoVillage. It has continued to organically grow and change ever since. Much of that change has been focused on density—density of dwelling units, density of food production, density of uses and activity, density of fun and laughter.

In a nutshell, where urban development is concerned, we need to have sufficient density to support functional public transit, bicycling, and walking, and yet have it be so beautiful, fun, green, and rich with community that people will enjoy being there—not yearning to jump in their cars to get away.

Many historical cities were dense for security purposes. The oldest part of Barcelona has some streets so narrow that a car can't physically fit on them. Not coincidentally, this is arguably the most fun, vibrant, and lively part of the city—the streets filled with people walking places and never a dull moment. I would argue that nowadays our cities should densify again—also for security purposes. Like a threatened turtle, pulling its legs and head into its shell, we must pull our urban extremities inward in preparation for life without fossil fuels and the approaching "Long Emergency," as Kunstler calls it.

With some residents having bought an adjoining property, Maitreya EcoVillage now houses about 30 to 35 people on 1.25 acres. In addition to about 10 dwelling units, there is also a Cascadian anarcho folk grass band, a brewing cooperative, a wood shop, a steel fabricating area, a koi pond, a sauna, a strawbale and earthen community space, a cob guest cottage, a biogas digester, a free food distribution area, and lots of gardening. Currently under construction are an octagonal meditation sanctuary, a 4000 gallon rainwater cistern, an outdoor kitchen and an 8.5 ft. x 16 ft. tiny house complete with bathroom and kitchen that I wish to Airbnb—bringing an educational, ecotourism component to our village. Next year I want to build a permanent greenhouse to experiment with aquaponics.

I built a new house on top of an existing, single story 1940s-era house—an example of what could be done to millions of dreary, energy-wasteful US homes: making them all into creative, net-zero-energy, eco-trophy duplexes. I have a few rooftop decks in mind. The idea is to go up rather than out—wanting to make Maitreya as full as possible of fun and interesting activity all within its limited urban footprint. Richard Register's ecocity vision includes rooftop gardens and rooftop cafes with bridges joining rooftop to rooftop. An important aspect to stacking up the urban fabric is that the farmland surrounding our cities is more precious than we've understood. When the tractor trailer rigs stop bringing our food from 1500 miles away, we'll appreciate the tragedy of having paved over so much farm land.

While it's still a glorified landlord-tenant arrangement, I like to think that I'm the world's coolest eco-landlord. We have business meetings at least once per month where decisions are made by consensus. (How many cats are acceptable in an urban ecovillage setting?) Having gotten to be 61 years old without producing any children of my own, I have a standing offer among those here that upon their organizing a credible financial entity to assume ownership, I will bequeath it a substantial percentage of the equity. Thus, Maitreya EcoVillage will hopefully continue boldly into the future with a life of its own. ✒

Robert Bolman is a green builder and artist. In 1991 he bought one acre of land west of the center of Eugene, Oregon that is now Maitreya EcoVillage.

The north side of 1623 West Broadway, with new house built on top of 1940s-era structure. The cistern will feature a star-gazing platform.

Starting a Community: Wisdom of Communities, Volume 1

Making a Case for Urban Cohousing

By Grace H. Kim

A view of Capitol Hill Cohousing's rooftop garden and neighborhood context.

William Wright Photography

While cohousing has traditionally been established in rural or suburban contexts, as a cohousing consultant I am seeing an uptick in those who are interested in building urban communities. There are benefits to urban cohousing, many of which are mirrored in the reasons my husband and I chose an urban location in Seattle to start our own cohousing community. While our reasons for choosing this urban lifestyle are personal, I believe they resonate with many other families, seniors, and individuals, such as those who found and joined us on our cohousing journey. Here, I will make a case for urban cohousing, and discuss how our community has benefited from our densely urban location. Please note that I use "community" to describe our cohousing community and "neighborhood" to describe the greater neighborhood that surrounds it.

Why choose an urban site?

There are some simple yet practical reasons to choose urban cohousing. Urban sites usually have the zoning in place to build multifamily housing, whether it be stacked flats or clustered homes. This translates to reduced time and expense for land use approval, there are no rezone applications or hearings, and there is a reduced likelihood of neighborhood opposition. Fewer hurdles to development can mean fewer expenses and a faster development process.

Urban sites also have the added benefit of convenient access to coffee shops, grocery stores, and restaurants. But because of our society's reliance on cars, one's ability to drive and maintain a driver's license can stand in the way of the convenience that walkable neighborhoods afford. For many, including the young and elderly, walkability should also be considered interchangeable with independence. Walkable neighborhoods allow everyone of all mobility and ability levels to enjoy the freedom of meeting with friends, running errands, and going about one's day without relying on another person to shuttle them to and from the activities of daily life. The same is true for individuals who choose to live without a car, families with one vehicle, and others who might otherwise be homebound without access to a vehicle.

Walkability, in conjunction with the abundance of services made available by an urban site, makes urban cohousing an attractive option for many cohousers.

How "urban" is urban?

"Urban" means different things to different people. For those who are used to living in rural areas, urban is anything within the city limits. For others urban is a single-family house in a residential neighborhood within walking distance of coffee shops and a grocery store. For still others, urban means living in a multistory building within a dense urban neighborhood with shops and services at the street below. When starting a new urban community without a site determined, it's important to define what you mean by "urban" so that newcomers are clear about how urban you intend to be.

Our site is located in Capitol Hill, one of the densest neighborhoods in Seattle and purportedly among the densest west of the Mississippi. Our community was built on one-tenth of an acre, just 4,500 sq. ft. The conventional single family lot in Seattle averages 5,000 sq. ft. The building is five stories tall with nine two-to-three bedroom homes that range in size

Diagram showing circulation spaces of building, as well as common house, courtyard, and rooftop farm activation.

roof deck

rooftop farming

401

301

303

302

shared outdoor stairs
and balconies

201

common house

203

202

alley

shared courtyard

103

102

12th ave

schemata workshop office

Capitol Hill Urban Cohousing
Schemata Workshop

Schemata Workshop

Common house activity after an event.

Schemata Workshop

View of courtyard from above with resident children playing.

Schemata Workshop

from 810 sq. ft. to 1,300 sq. ft. My architectural office is located on the building's ground floor, and our street brings restaurants, coffee shops, and neighborhood services within steps of our front door. This is how we defined "urban."

Who does urban cohousing attract?

Urban sites attract a diverse set of people for many different reasons. Use our community as a case study of this fact: Our community is made up of singles, retirees, empty nesters, and families. We are 17 adults and 11 children, all full-time residents. The adults range in age from mid-30s to late-60s, the kids from one year to 16 years. We have four school teachers, three university professors, three architects, a graphic designer, a computer scientist, a web designer, and a finance director from a local nonprofit. Three of our nine households are comprised of people of color.

Every family and individual had different reasons for joining us. One woman moved from another local cohousing community because she wanted to be closer to the performing and visual arts venues where she attends events two to three times a week. A couple of retirees lived on Capitol Hill for 30 years before joining us. They had looked into cohousing before but didn't want to relocate to a more residential part of Seattle. Our site is halfway between their two previous homes, and gives them the urban density they desire. Many of the families in our community already lived in the neighborhood but were renting and, in addition to community, liked the housing stability cohousing provides.

Our location has the added benefit of proximity to city transit, such as Seattle's Light Rail. Our residents who work at the University of Washington appreciate being one stop away from the campus by light rail. This is a community in which my husband and I plan to age in place, so we wanted to live in a neighborhood that was vibrant and diverse, with all of my daily needs within walking distance.

Just within our community, there are varying and unique reasons for being attracted to cohousing in an urban environment.

Engaging the neighborhood at large

Our urban location makes neighborhood connections possible by proximity and daily reminders of these pressing community needs. Many in our community are involved in our neighborhood. Several members are involved with a local homeless youth advocacy, job training, and housing services organization. I serve as the chair of Seattle's Planning Commission and am involved with the Chamber of Commerce and my daughter's public school PTA. I also serve on the board of an advocacy organization for affordable housing in our county. My husband chairs the Capitol Hill Ecodistrict and the Disaster Preparedness committee for our professional association. Two of our community's teenagers are very involved with an LGBTQ youth organization.

We have a rooftop farm that provides produce for a farm-to-table restaurant located about six blocks from our building. And we have been talking with the local community college to engage their sustainable agriculture students in internship opportunities.

Our urban location makes these connections possible by proximity and daily reminders of these pressing community needs.

What does urban cohousing look like?

Urban cohousing looks a lot like suburban and rural cohousing, just concentrated in a smaller footprint. In our building, we reimagined the idea of the pedestrian path vertically, connecting our homes with a common staircase and shared balconies. Instead of a large outdoor recreational area, we have a central courtyard that serves as a dining area for meals, play area for children, and gathering space for meetings or events. Our Common House anchors one side of the courtyard and provides a common kitchen, and more eating and meeting spaces. The large glass, French doors that connect the Common House to the courtyard give us flexibility in using the two spaces.

The three homes per floor share access to a balcony that overlooks the courtyard. This exterior space means we can see each other come and go and has the added benefit of reducing our heated and conditioned spaces.

When he visits, my father says our building "feels so alive." There is life and activity all around to remind us that we are not alone. This is true for all cohousing, and possible in an urban environment when we consider traditional cohousing elements in new and imaginative ways.

How does community come together in urban cohousing?

Cohousing in an urban environment doesn't make creating community any more difficult than in rural or suburban cohousing. Depending on goals or values, different cohousing communities will come together for different reasons and in different ways.

In our community, we come together for meals. We have dinners three times a week—just about every other day. Our meal program has mandatory cooking participation, and, because of the ease of our system, we have high participation. There are times that the teenagers don't come, or that one of us has an after-work meeting, event, or are simply out of town but there are often guests—sometimes several—and it generally feels like a dinner party. While people are welcome to take a plate to go, it is more typical that people in our community linger after dinner to share in continued conversation.

We also come together in our civic engagement. In the Common House, we host events for the nonprofit organizations that we support. Sometimes we have sign painting parties for rallies and marches, and we'll host friends and fellow marchers for dinner after those events.

And, of course, we love to come together to celebrate birthdays, anniversaries, or weddings. We never have more fun than when we get to eat cake and to dance.

But I need a garden!

When we were recruiting for our group, and even now when I make presentations about our urban community, I often hear "but I need my garden." And to address this concern, we talk about all the many ways we bring nature into our homes and community.

While most people think they need dirt in the ground, we know that in urban locations, the dirt in the ground around us is sometimes contaminated from spills, or leaching, or simply car pollutants like oil, lead, and brake dust. In our community, we garden with raised bed planters, we import clean soil, and we control what goes into it by farming organically with no chemical pesticides or fertilizers. In our rooftop garden, we produce food for our community dinners but also for our neighborhood restaurant partner. On our balconies and private terraces, we plant fresh herbs and flowers.

We each have a chance to garden in the way that works for us, and we can bring the natural world indoors. Urban sites can also provide easy access to parks and other green areas, so the children in communities like ours rarely want for space to run around and play, even without a traditional yard.

Conclusion

Urban is not for everyone, but for those who are interested in cohousing without losing access to the amenities, conveniences, and vibrancy of city life, it can offer a unique alternative to other types of housing. Our urban community is far from perfect, but we all feel quite lucky to have the community and quality of life that we have found living here.

Grace H. Kim is a member of the American Institute of Architects and co-owner of Schemata Workshop, based in Seattle, Washington. She is also the cofounder of Capitol Hill Urban Cohousing (for whom Schemata Workshop served as architect). Grace is an internationally recognized expert in cohousing, with a special expertise in Common House Design. She has served on the board of the Cohousing Association of the US and has visited over 80 communities in Denmark and North America. Grace gave a TED talk on cohousing which can be seen at www.ted.com/talks/grace_kim_how_cohousing_can_make_us_happier_and_live_longer.

Meal prep for community meal in the common house.

Mark Hipple

The building's street-facing façade at an open house event.

Danny Ngan

William Wright Photography

View of residents' shared balconies from inside a unit.

Community-Building in the City

By Sheila Hoffman and Spencer Beard

We have lived in the heart of Seattle, on Capitol Hill, for more than 35 years. This is the story of how we landed in an intentional community.

We love the density, diversity, and walkability of our neighborhood. The idea of intentional community always interested us. When we explored cohousing in the early '90s everything seemed to be out in the country. Living in a rural setting seemed isolating to us. After 20 years in a large house where we spawned two all-volunteer community groups, but had no children and didn't know our neighbors despite efforts, we decided to downsize to a new, nearby 150-unit condo that was marketed as community-living. For the first few years it was "cohousing lite" because we did many things to foster community. But when community isn't "intentional" it really is not sustainable. We soon felt isolated again because no one shared our vision for community. In 2010 we heard about a forming cohousing community with property located in our neighborhood. And that is where our story begins.

Challenges We've Faced

1. Finding the People, and Developing Community

We began with regularly scheduled introductory meetings promoted through the neighborhood blog. We joined the group after that first meeting and got to work by publishing a website with our vision and values to help attract folks who would be a possible fit. During this process we "kissed a lot of frogs." Many folks were excited about cohousing and/or our project, but for an assortment of reasons it didn't work for them. Barriers included timing, size of units, cost, and lack of parking. Of course in some cases it just wasn't a good fit. It was a "self-selecting" process with no application form, background checks, or community approval. Potential candidates simply came to more and more events. And it worked. After several years we had all nine of our families committed and participating. Everyone involved was drawn to living in community AND specifically to this urban Capitol Hill location.

Our intention to build our skills as a community was an integral part of our success. Early on we had several all-day, professionally facilitated workshops which included creating our vision and values, learning to make decisions by consensus, conflict resolution, communication styles, and power dynamics. From the beginning we had monthly business meetings with potlucks, and sometime before construction started we added biweekly Supper Club. We organized social events such as roller-skating, going to baseball games, bowling, game nights, pumpkin carving, and post-Thanksgiving potlucks to create connections and a sense of community. There were also numerous team meetings to devise plans for our common meals, integrate the kids into the community, draft our legal structure and operating agreements, and most importantly design and develop the building and how it would all get financed and maintained.

2. The Property

Property in the city is at a premium. Generally developers buy it and then sell condos to make back their money with a hefty profit. Of course since we were not building to sell at a profit we had to factor in the higher property costs.

The site itself is one city lot, about 4500 sq. ft.—40 ft. wide and 113 ft. deep. Original plans explored buying adjacent lots, but we were unable to make that happen. To maximize floor area we chose to build lot-line to lot-line, which meant no windows on the north and south. To include windows would have meant a 3 ft. setback, which would mean lost living space and a higher rent per square foot.

We were required by the city to have commercial space on the ground floor and the site topography allowed for a maximum height of five stories. This limited the number of units we could create in our space. Combined with the limitations of a single lot, we ended up with nine apartments ranging from 810 sq. ft. to 1300 sq. ft. plus 900 sq. ft. for our Common House.

Fortunately parking spaces were not required because our location is in an "urban hub" with a myriad of transportation options including bus, light rail, bike and car shares. This saved us hundreds of thousands of dollars for the cost of underground parking. We're in walking distance of hospitals, library, groceries, parks, farmers' market, restaurants, entertainment venues, and colleges.

3. Time and Money

The rule of thumb we'd heard going in is to expect the process to take about five years. When we started in 2010 we thought that having a site and cohousing-savvy architects already in place would save us time. Our project actually took longer. We lost a full year due to the lawyers who couldn't comprehend that the founders didn't want to make a big return on their original investment to buy the property or that the LLC we formed wasn't motivated by the capitalistic idea to maximize profits.. That delay put us on the back side of a construction boom in Seattle, which meant we had difficulty finding contractors and subcontractors within our budget for the project.

In 2014, as we neared closing on our construction loan, our developer realized we had a $700K shortfall in the equity our group was bringing to the table. She helped us brainstorm a way to raise the money, a seemingly impossible task. Within a month we raised all the funds through low-interest loans from friends and family—including those who didn't know us personally but lived in cohousing and wanted to see us succeed. Our developer mistakenly believed that once the building was completed we could get a large enough mortgage to pay off these loans. Sadly, the new loan amount came in lower than expected. The final amount was based on the LLC's net income and since we want to keep our rent low, our loan was correspondingly lower. So it will take longer than we planned to retire our debt.

4. Unique Financial Model

Why didn't we just build condos? Due to the 2009 crash, no one was lending for new condo construction and we learned that the national Coop Bank was not interested in financing any new cohousing projects. We developed our own model. We formed an LLC which owns the building, which is how many apartment buildings are owned. Since we are all members of the LLC, we essentially rent from ourselves.

Being both landlords and tenants was unconventional enough to make the bank underwriters nervous at first. But actually it offers advantages to the community. For one thing it allowed younger families and those without liquid assets to remain in the community—we didn't require each family to have a large down payment for a home. It also means when families downsize, they can change the unit they occupy without changing title and without the associated costs of selling and buying into another more expensive one which would be a typical condo scenario.

5. Construction Delays and Quality

We started with a big vision and high values around sustainability and construction quality. But once again monetary realities created challenges and compromises. With all the construction in town, prices skyrocketed for everything from labor to materials. Along the way we had to scale back some of our green building plans. We still retained many sustainable features which also enhanced our community interaction such as taller windows, higher ceilings, and wide walkways.

One setback was when our electrical contractor went belly-up mid-project. The General Contractor had to find a replacement. Then the new contractor had to review and fix a lot of what was thought to have been already completed. Construction delays ultimately ate up any budget that might've provided some of the comforts of home such as rooftop furniture and Common House furnishings. One way we have addressed it is with occasional anonymous funding sourced within our community for the things removed from the budget.

Notable Successes

1. Meal Program

We decided early on that meals would be the glue of our community. Therefore our Common House kitchen and dining areas were designed to accommodate our whole community and guests, including having a pantry, guest room, and laundry.

We consider our food program a huge success. In fact, a cohousing visitor from Australia declared it was "brilliant!" It provides a variety of tasty meals. It frees up busy parents and professionals from almost half their evening meal preparation. This simple system where everyone participates requires no bookkeeping. The head cook decides the menu, buys the food, then leads the prep with two assistants. The cook spends what they want, recognizing they will enjoy 17 meals free over the next six weeks. Everyone's special dietary needs are accommodated along with a commitment to being nutritious and delicious.

We've had fun with figuring out interesting menus—some simple and others much more elaborate with specialty cocktails and desserts. Plus, guests are always welcomed.

2. Decision-Making

We've learned there is a great power in community we might call Trusting the Group's Wisdom. On many occasions we've been to the edge of throwing in the towel because a problem seemed insurmountable. We've found that when we hit an impasse the best approach is to remind ourselves of these two important points:

1) Keep an open mind rather than being attached to the idea you came in with AND...

2) Remember it's about what is best for the community.

With these points guiding us, we consistently come out the other side with a better solution than any one of us started with.

3. Rooftop Farm Partnerships

The city requires a certain amount of greenspace in every urban project. Rather than grass, trees, or flowers, we opted to create a working farm to support our goals of sustainability and community partnerships. Since most of us have full-time jobs and/or children, we partnered with Seattle Urban Farm Company (SUFCo) to design, construct, and operate our farm. We held a web-based "BarnRaiser" to raise the donations to pay for the build-out of the raised planters, the additional structural system to support the roof, and the irrigation system. Then we partnered with a nearby white-tablecloth restaurant that is paying the on-going maintenance costs directly to SUFCo. In return they get a large percentage of the harvest for their upscale "farm-to-table" menu. The community also gets some of the fresh produce for community meals. And best of all, our kids learn where their food comes from, how it grows, and can get their hands dirty.

In Closing

We have now lived in Capitol Hill Urban Cohousing for more than a year. We love living in community with adults and children, sharing meals three times a week, being available to each other's needs including walking children to school, pet sitting, repairs, outings, etc. Recently we all attended the wedding celebration of one of our resident couples. We clearly have built not only an apartment building but a true sense of community.

Sheila Hoffman and Spencer Beard have had "founder's energy" for decades, having founded and led the local chapter of EarthSave International in the '90s as well as founding the Evergreen Tandem Club in 2001 and of course being part of founding Capitol Hill Urban Cohousing on Seattle's Capitol Hill (capitolhillurbancohousing.org). Sheila develops WordPress websites and Spencer is a retired elementary school teacher. At 68 and 65 respectively, they are the elders in CHUC.

Photos courtesy of Sheila Hoffman

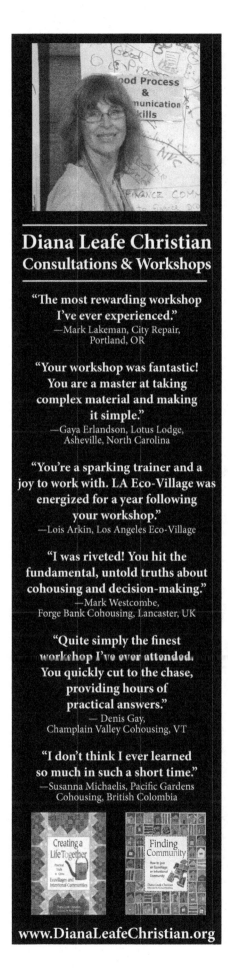

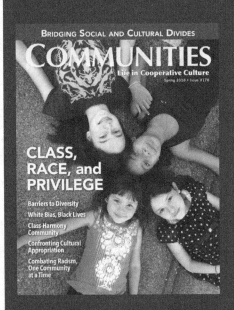

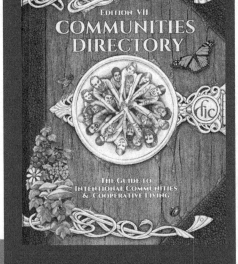

III

CULTIVATING NON-RESIDENTIAL COMMUNITY

Chicken à la West Birch Avenue

Flagstaff

We used to be a typical neighborhood. People were friendly enough and we waved to each other on our way into and out of our houses. We had the occasional chat on the sidewalk while shoveling snow or doing yard work. But that was where community ended on our block of West Birch Avenue in Flagstaff, Arizona. Our shady, tree-lined, historic downtown neighborhood mirrored countless neighborhoods across the United States: polite, but disconnected.

Knowing how valuable a connected neighborhood is, I had always wanted to create more meaningful neighborhood relationships than just small talk on the sidewalk. For one reason or another it never happened until one day when our neighborhood started a process that enabled us to connect in real ways. It began when my husband Pete and I consulted with a permaculture landscape company that was creating a design for our backyard. When they suggested we get chickens to eat our food scraps, make fertilizer, and provide eggs, I dismissed it immediately, thinking that chickens were far too ambitious for us as a single family with a five-year-old, a baby, and two cats. We had our plates full already.

I mentioned the landscape plan to our neighbor Jessie and suddenly a concept began to germinate: we could create a neighborhood chicken co-op! The idea had brilliant energy and momentum. The project gelled during a neighborhood potluck hosted at our house. We talked with more neighbors (Mark, who is also Pete's brother; his partner Jamie; Jessie's partner Brin; Sara; and Eric). We realized that we had five households of people on our block who were excited about the project. As we sat at our dining room table we discussed our collective ignorance about chickens, our fears about being able to care for them effectively, and our concerns that they would be noisy and smelly.

Despite these obstacles, Jessie decided to join because, in her words, "it was an opportunity to regain a relationship with the food we eat, and in the process a deeper connection to the natural world and our neighbors." Sara was dubious but decided to go along with it because we were proposing housing the chickens in her backyard and she didn't want to stand in the way of the project. For Pete and me, it was an opportunity to give our kids an experience that would highlight our values of sustainable local foods and community. By the end of the potluck, we were all committed.

It took shape quickly. One of the best things about the project was how each neighbor applied his or her unique skills. Jes-

sie was the only one of us who had any experience with chickens, so she volunteered to keep the tiny chicks in her kitchen for their first couple weeks of life. She spearheaded the task of checking the chicks' vents several times each day to ward off pasty butt and keep them healthy. Our daughter Gemma and Eric's daughter Ellie were enamored with the chicks and Jessie left her back door unlocked during the day so the kids could visit them.

Eric had a friend with chickens, so he kindly arranged for us to borrow supplies we would need, like a large tub to house the chicks as they grew. At this stage, the chicks moved to our garage, where Pete used an old door from our basement and some chicken wire to rig up a "roof" to the tub so the chicks would be safe from our cats. Everyone in the neighborhood had the code to open the garage so they could visit the chicks during the day. I loved seeing how effortlessly the boundaries of private space began to open as the neighbors united in this common endeavor.

Mark owns the duplex where Jessie, Brin, and Sara are tenants, and he suggested that we use the old horse barn behind the duplex house for a coop. Pete and Mark developed a design for the coop that would keep our chickens warm in winter, cool in summer, and safe from foxes, skunks, and raccoons. Again, Pete harvested old windows and building supplies from our basement to create the coop. We were all so excited when we located some paint that was being given away free by the city to paint the inside of the coop.

The chicks grew rapidly and Pete, Mark, Eric, and Brin worked diligently on the construction of the coop. When it was time to put netting over the chicken run to protect them from predators, Jamie and Sara helped watch our baby Angus while other neighbors put up the netting. Gemma helped construct and paint a hot pink ramp for the chickens to go in and out. Meanwhile, I hosted another neighborhood potluck so we could enjoy our success and "talk chickens." Eric organized a chicken rotation and each household now cares for the chickens a week at a time. Of course, if anyone ever needs someone to cover their shift, help is easy to find.

In this project, we have gained much more than fertilizer and eggs. We now have a shared commitment to these little beings that brings us together in satisfying ways. The chicken coop has become a sort of neighborhood commons where impromptu gatherings occur as neighbors stop by to drop off their kitchen

Top left: The chicks. Top middle: Pete and Brin working on the coop. Right: Gemma holding a chick. Bottom middle: The chick are starting to get feathers. Bottom left: Jesse adding the finishing touches.

scraps, give the birds fresh water, or brainstorm about how to fix a hole in the fence. It's a great conversation piece when friends and relatives come to visit; we have been able to meet more of each other's extended networks around the coop. The chickens also make us laugh as we watch them peck over old pieces of lettuce, moldy grapes, and pizza crusts.

Pete and Mark both put gates in their fences so we now have a corridor that runs across the back of three houses, linking us together. I like to see how this has increased our daughter's sense of freedom within the neighborhood. She is now free to run back and forth between the yards and I don't worry about her being alone in the front of the house by the street. Sometimes when Eric brings his daughter over (they live across the street) I'll find that the girls have struck up a spontaneous playtime that may focus around the chickens or extend into our house. It has also increased Gemma's ability to have independent relationships with the adults in our neighborhood. I'm glad that our children have this really cool project to do together and with other adults that enables them to feel freer in the world.

Taking care of these birds has created a shared sense of compassion and responsibility. Sara and I have both been surprised at how much we have come to like the chickens in the process of caring for them. One night, a ringtail cat got into the chickens' yard and frightened one bird literally to death. Several of us heard the "ladies" squawking at 5:00 in the morning and Mark came to their rescue. During that day, I noticed how we all shared concern for our birds' safety as we pieced together the details of what happened. Gemma took extra care with the chickens, visiting them often and making them "soup" of weeds and water that she hand-carried to them to help them recover from the scary event.

Another surprise along the way is how easy it was to create a miniature model of sustainable food production in an urban area. Jessie says, "the chicken co-op has helped me to realize that it's not hard to build community or affect our food system. There isn't any special formula or checklist to follow. A simple potluck is all it takes to bring people together to make a positive change."

I love how this project is also teaching us and our children about the cycles of nature in a tangible way. Daily, we see our kitchen scraps devoured and transformed into poop for our gardens. We are just now starting to get an egg or two each day. For those of us who eat meat, we've had the opportunity to connect to that particular source of food in a real way.

In our neighborhood, we are allowed to have only hens and not roosters due to a city ordinance. So when we discovered that two of our original 16 chickens were roosters, we decided to slaughter and butcher them. This decision was something most of us felt squeamish about—a testament to how disconnected we are from the meat we eat. Most of us did not feel up to the task, but Pete and Eric volunteered and went through the process together from start to finish. Afterward, Pete and I cooked the roosters into broth and stew meat, which is in our freezer. The kids (who were not as squeamish as the adults) later saw pictures and heard the details of how it all happened, creating an important link for them in understanding where meat comes from, and seeing how their care and nurturing can contribute to the food we eat.

The next neighborhood potluck is due in a couple weeks, and we will be enjoying chicken soup à la West Birch Avenue, and perhaps a quiche or an omelet, homestyle. ✽

Hilary Giovale is a mother, writer, and belly-dance instructor in Flagstaff, Arizona. She holds a Master's degree in sustainability from Northern Arizona University.

In 2003, "La Cité Écologique" was founded, in Colebrook New Hampshire, on 315 acres of beautiful land surrounded by forest and mountains. Our ecovillage gives priority to education, optimal living to its members, a cooperative culture with resilience in its development and social entrepreneurship. So far, we have built one single family building, two large community residences, where people live in a kind of condo arrangement, and one community building (all powered by solar). We are expanding new building projects, to give a home to growing families and/or new members. We've created businesses, non-profits, a nonprofit school, and an organic farm, that helps better serve ours, and the local community. Visitors are welcome to our annual Open House in June, and Harvest Celebration in September. Guided tours, and internship programs are also available from May through October.

Contact: Leonie Brien (603) 331-1669
www.citeecologiquenh.org

La Cité Écologique
of New Hampshire
An Ecovillage since 2003

Support the FIC
Become a member today!

When you join the
Fellowship for Intentional Community,
your contribution supports projects like the
Communities Directory, Communities magazine,
and the Intentional Communities Website
(www.ic.org)

VOLUNTEER NOW!

8th Life
PANAMA

ECOVILLAGE IN FORMATION

@8thLifeAstoria
HTTP://8THLIFEPANAMA.ORG

CO-WORKING CO-LIVING SPACE &
21 HA OF ROLLING HILLS BORDERED BY RIVERS

NINE TRADITIONS THAT DRAW US TOGETHER: How a Small Town Nurtures Community

By Murphy Robinson

I've been a part of many communities in my life, many of them ephemeral: summer camp staff teams, wilderness trail crews, and urban houseshares with an ever-changing parade of roommates. Four years ago I moved to the tiny rural village of Worcester, Vermont, and found a unique and vibrant community that welcomed me immediately. After a decade of subscribing to COMMUNITIES and scheming to start an intentional community one day, it struck me that I'd just stumbled into one by accident—one that was cleverly disguised to outsiders as a regular small town of just under 1,000 people.

Why do some towns and neighborhoods seem to embrace you in the arms of community, while others don't? Let me share a few of the things that make my village feel this way:

1. Community Lunch

Every Wednesday I head down the hill to the Worcester Town Hall for Community Lunch, as does just about everyone else who's in the village at noon on a Wednesday: young mothers, senior citizens, the local loggers, and people who work from home. While the meal is officially sponsored by the Vermont Food Bank, people from every economic class attend enthusiastically. This is where you see your neighbors every week, talk to the guy you want to buy your firewood from, find a friend who can lend you their truck, wish someone a happy birthday, and hear the local news. A core group of volunteers does the cooking every week, and they always lavishly decorate the hall for every major and minor holiday they can think of. Community spirit is palpable, and every newcomer is welcomed in without hesitation. Before you know it you've learned everybody's name and feel right at home.

2. Gathering Place

Worcester has a tiny gas station, a post office the size of a closet, and a little café that closes at noon. This "commercial district" (two small neighboring buildings) is home to the morning banter of all who rise early and work hard. You can find tradesmen grabbing coffee, commuters gassing up, and local hunters displaying their take. When it's not yet time for Community Lunch, this gathering place is where you go to see your friends and hear the latest news.

3. Online Forum

Vermont is the home of Front Porch Forum, a local online discussion board for each town. You must have a valid local address to be a member, and a summary of the posts lands in your inbox every day at 6 p.m. Whether you are selling a chest freezer, renting your cabin, announcing an event, or reporting a lost dog sighting, you know your neighbors will hear your words and respond.

4. Volunteers

Worcester's sense of community is founded on the village's volunteers. Community Lunch, the Fire Department & Fast Squad, the After School Play Group, the Community Garden, the twice yearly Clothing Swap, and the Fourth of July Committee are all run entirely by unpaid community members. These labors of love allow residents to serve their town and be proud of what they achieve together.

5. Long-time Residents

People tend to come to Worcester and stay. Many folks who started as renters love the community so much that they buy a house and settle down. When friendships and alliances form, they get to deepen and ripen over time. This is something I really missed in high-turnover communities, and it gives the town traditions deep roots.

6. Economic Interdependence

While plenty of people commute to work in the nearby capital city, lots of folks make their living right in our town. The loggers supply everyone with firewood while being thoughtful about forest sustainability on the small private woodlots they manage. The

ladies who run the café give us a place to meet and connect. I'm proud to live on one of Worcester's two community farms, where CSA members often volunteer in the fields to harvest the vegetables. Worcester is big enough to provide a living for those serving the community, and small enough that we all know these people by first name.

7. Celebrations of Community Pride

The Fourth of July is Worcester's day to celebrate itself. The town proudly puts on the best fireworks display for miles around, and everyone lines the street for the tiny parade. The winters are long here, so at the height of summer we come mingle on the public field in the center of town and smile giddily with community pride.

8. Direct Democracy

Like many New England towns, Worcester is governed by a town meeting. All registered voters may attend to elect town officers, approve (or challenge) the town budget, and

discuss the school board. Even if it's only one day per year, this participation in direct democracy reminds us all that we collectively decide what Worcester will become.

9. Accepting Our Differences

Worcester has a very rural character, but it's close enough to Vermont's liberal capital city that values of acceptance prevail. It's very okay to be gay (thank goodness, because I am!), neighbors of differing economic classes tend to rub shoulders with relative comfort, and the United Methodist Church co-exists peacefully with the Green Mountain Druid Order. We're a very white town, but racial diversity is embraced when it finds its way here. Since the '60s and '70s Vermont has faced an influx of back-to-the-landers who sought a place in the traditional rural communities, and here the integration seems to have enriched both groups. It's as if everybody has decided, "Well, you choose to live in our wonderful little village, which shows good sense, so I guess you must be alright."

Reading over this list, I recognize many of the core traditions that support the success of most intentional communities. Indeed, aren't many of our intentional communities seeking to reclaim the lost small-town solidarity of yesteryear? So I suppose Worcester is an unintentional community that has partially retained its rural heritage of community traditions and partially been enriched by fresh ideas from beyond its borders.

These nine methods of community-building could be applied to any small town or city neighborhood where the residents are willing. If you're a communitarian soul living in the non-communitarian world, give one of them a try in the place where you live and see if the seeds of community take root. While intentional communities are crucial laboratories that teach us so much about how the human social fabric can work, the art of creating community spirit within mainstream towns and neighborhoods has at least as much potential to change the world for the better. Now, if you'll excuse me, I have to go to Community Lunch!

Murphy Robinson is a wilderness guide and hunting instructor. When her wandering years came to an end she founded Mountainsong Expeditions in the wild forests of Vermont, where she helps people learn to be in deeper relationship with the land and each other. Your can learn about her work or send her a message at www.mountainsongexpeditions. com. She has also published Communities *articles in the past under her former legal name, Mary Murphy.*

ALTERNATIVE MODELS BY RUDY M. YANDRICK

A Virtual Retirement Village:
Combining Independent Living with Community

In historic downtown Lancaster, Pennsylvania, where city dwellers commonly live in townhomes on compact, tree-lined streets, intentional community drifts through the air. Here, members of a "virtual retirement village" called The Lancaster Downtowners are nestled among the neighborhoods of the "Red Rose City" that reflect 1700s colonial architecture.

The key word in understanding the Downtowners is "virtual." This group of about 100 retirement or near-retirement age people doesn't fit the traditional shared-living model of intentional community. You won't find a common room, permaculture how-to manual, or food co-op anywhere—and members generally are not next-door neighbors. Yet this village's spirit, enthusiasm, and common interests were inspired by intentional community ideals.

The Downtowners, who first began to form in 2004, are bonded by three things: the transition from working life to retirement, a strong sense of independence, and an aversion to condo or assisted living. In practice, Downtowners is a member network that operates as a non-profit organization. It provides home management services, extensive opportunities for social interaction, education on life skills, provider networking, and liaison with special interest groups.

These are among the tangible benefits—either presently offered or in the works—but it is the intangibles that are priceless to some members, such as getting a lift to the grocery store from another member and together doing the week's shopping.

It took a creative and persistent individual to herd individuals with diverse lifestyles, interests, and ideas about retirement into a virtual village. His name is Rod Houser, the Downtowners' founder. Some 40 years ago, Houser was an inhabitant of a shared-living intentional community out in the hinterlands of Lancaster, Herrbrook Farm, which today is a spiritual retreat center. "It reached the point where all the care and attention of a rural intentional community was no longer practical. When

I started networking in Lancaster, I found lots of other people my age who wanted to stay connected with the city and not be resigned to eventually enter a 'gated' retirement center."

In a curious use of the "Kevin Bacon rule"—in which somebody knows somebody who knows somebody until they find that any one person is connected with anyone in the world by no more than six people removed—kindred spirits found each other and coalesced surprisingly quickly. Numerous retirees and near-retirees—as well as some others as young as their mid-30s, far from retirement—are now in its fold, some of whom serve on its board of directors. As for Houser, he still lives at Herrbrook Farm, but plans to turn over daily management of the property to family members and join his city contemporaries. In the meantime, as a biking enthusiast, when the weather cooperates he bikes to and from the inner city.

Diverse Personalities

Downtowners is loaded with diverse personalities who have had fascinating life experiences. Bob Ibold is a 71-year-old former advertising agency executive now enjoying his hobby of collecting and selling ethnographic masks. "My wife, Regine, and I decided that we wanted to continue living in our townhouse on a quiet little street. It's a lifestyle that suits us, and we enjoy the rich cultural life of downtown. Retirement communities tend to be homogenous with respect to age, income, and ethnicity. That's not for us, at least right now."

Mimi Shapiro, 62, an art instructor, believes that social changes across the United States have boosted the practicality of the virtual retirement village. "Cities like Cincinnati and Annapolis have really been at the forefront of the city renaissance movement, but small cities across America are becoming more and more livable," she says. Shapiro is more than a little enthusiastic about her urban lifestyle. She likens Lancaster, with its city population of 55,000, to European cities, where peo-

Lancaster, Pennsylvania: the view from Holy Trinity Lutheran Church Spire.

ple commonly walk to where they need to go. Here, the city's downtown parks, farmers' market, and myriad shops are highly accessible on foot. "This morning, I walked to Central Market, which is open three days a week. I get to know the growers, the farmer, the butcher. One family makes Ethiopian foods. This is the heart of Amish country. If retirees can have it all and not have to leave our homes and neighborhoods, then that's great for us. We have the best of what city life has to offer."

For board member Ken Nissley, 65, and his wife, Elizabeth, it's about the true spirit of cooperative living. "I have some expectation that if the time comes when I need assistance, I might get some," says Ken. "While I'm still able to, I'm more than ready to go to the aid of others."

> *"If retirees can have it all and not have to leave our homes and neighborhoods, then that's great for us. We have the best of what city life has to offer."*

Tea at the Macks'

One priority for members is feeding the social appetite. A six-week stretch from last October to December featured a menu of nine social events, including home gatherings for informal dinners and afternoon teas, dining in ethnic restaurants, and educational programs. One of the gatherings was a social tea on a Sunday afternoon at the home of Marcie and Jim Mack. Just as the common meal is a staple of intentional community living, food and drink are the centerpiece of most Downtowners social events, whether they be held in a member's house or a downtown restaurant.

At the Macks' residence, a snug 1700s corner rowhouse, eight members, mostly from a part of town known as Musser Park, shot the breeze about everything from banking to baking, leaf raking to art appraising. In an ambiance created by art motifs that vary from one room to the next, high ceilings with rich crown molding that lends an air of refinement, and the sound of Bach wafting along, they found out how much they have in common. For example, three who came talked about having lived in Lancaster only a few years and finding Downtowners a great way to network socially, as others indicated they have done through their church. All in all, it was a great study of the invisible threads that form bonds in community.

The Business Side of a Virtual Village

The Downtowners' board has recognized that knowing its members' needs and interests goes hand-in-hand with success. For example, most Downtowners are computer literate and life-long learners. In fact, both attributes are increasingly vital to late-stage independent living. So over the last two years, Downtowners has been expanding its information-dissemination capabilities, posting a website, and sponsoring a listserv that lights up with frequent conversation. As for the educational programs, members cannot get enough of them. For example, the representative of a local hospice center recently held an educational seminar on end-of-life issues and the Five Wishes document. Another time, a local historian told attendees about the history of Lancaster, and still another seminar instructed them on how to make homes safer by rooting out danger spots.

Of course, the more services and benefits that are offered to meet demand, the greater the need for organization and business structure. The Downtowners has a financial sponsor in a business development group, the Lancaster Alliance. Through that relationship, the Downtowners has 501(c)(3) status and can receive tax-deductible contributions and grants.

Additionally, the Downtowners hired its first staff member last fall, a program director, who is enabling it to meet increasing member demand for services. She is responsible, for example, for compiling a list of plumbers, electricians, and others into a provider network. Eventually the Downtowners would like to introduce health care services for members, but this calls for "real big picture thinking," says Houser, because it will require pooling financial resources, agreeing on a health care delivery model (single- vs. multiple-provider), and other steps that will test the village's capacity to build consensus.

So far, Downtowners has been able to hold annual member dues at $40 for individuals and $60 per couple. Meeting additional needs, such as health care delivery, will require creative financing in some cases and perhaps à la carte services in others. One of the decided advantages of the virtual form of intentional community, however, is that it doesn't have the monetary tripwires associated with physical housing that so often are encountered in shared-living residences. "Our model doesn't involve buying real estate," explains Houser. Still, Houser says the Downtowners could accommodate a subgroup that wishes to, for example, buy a warehouse and build six units within.

> *One of the decided advantages of the virtual form of intentional community is that it doesn't have the monetary tripwires associated with physical housing that so often are encountered in shared-living residences. The model doesn't involve buying real estate.*

"We Didn't Reinvent the Wheel"

After Lancaster Downtowners began to form, they quickly learned that they were not the only such group in the country. In fact, there are currently 13 such villages throughout the country—in locations including Washington, DC; Greenwich, Connecticut, Bronxville, New York; Palo Alto, California, and elsewhere—with another 50 on the drawing board.

"We didn't reinvent the wheel," says Houser, choosing instead to turn to the original village, Beacon Hill Village (BHV), for help with some of the technical aspects of formation. BHV, which formed in 2001, figuratively and literally "wrote the book" on this model of intentional community. (Please see the sidebar article.) Its 450 members dot the Boston neighborhoods of Beacon Hill, Back Bay, West End, South End, North End, Charlestown, and the Waterfront. BHV, which has a staff of seven to meet membership need, is busy forming an online network to link the actual and prospective villages together. According to recently hired village-to-village coordinator Rita Kostiuk, "We all have so much in common, yet are so different from one another in terms of geography, needs, and grassroots activity. There's a lot we have to learn from each other, and the resources are coming into place that allow us to do it."

For the Downtowners, the quaintness, the homeyness of small-city life puts a sparkle in the eye of its members. "Retirees here are able to connect with the city. The more isolated we feel, the more we're afraid," says Shapiro. "The Downtowners helps us to be integrated."

Rudy M. Yandrick is a freelance writer who resides in Mechanicsburg, Pennsylvania. He has a longstanding interest in intentional community and has visited several in south-central Pennsylvania.

Want to Build Your Own Village?

Beacon Hill Village (BHV), which began the virtual retirement village concept in 2001, has received over 3000 inquiries in the last three years. On their website, www.beaconhillvillage.org, they provide advice on starting a village, with steps including:

- Form a core group of people passionate about staying in their own homes
- Research your village: number of elders, income, geographic area, other programs
- Implement a market survey to see what people in your area want and to determine interest

- Contact health and other providers; get discounts from vendors for your members
- Write a business plan
- Raise seed money
- Form a board and hire a director

Additionally, BHV has published a how-to book, called *The Founder's Manual*. It provides advice and experiential information on the village launch, successful business model, community surveying, marketing, business planning, fundraising, publishing a newsletter, and so forth.

CULTIVATING THE NEIGHBORHOOD

What Are the Boundaries of an Intentional Community?

An Experiment in Geographically-Dispersed Community-Building

By Don Schneider and Elin England

Where and How it Began, and How it Went
In a rural community in the beautiful Cascade foothills just outside of Eugene, Oregon, a group of community-minded families joined together for a number of years to talk, share, cooperate, and eat. Elkdream Farm, an eight-acre parcel with good agricultural soils, good sun, and good water, was the primary host-location for what we came to call the Pleasant Hill Progressives—a group of mostly progressive and environmentally-oriented, secular, middle-class, and middle-aged individuals.

Many of the group's members had lived in communal households during college and for a number of years (in some cases decades) afterward. But over time, the pull of the broader culture toward individual pursuits had lured us all toward separate lives. Our family moved to Pleasant Hill just after our second child was born, drawn to the area by the promise of good schools and dreams of establishing a large kitchen garden and orchard. As we got to know the community, we discovered that we were surrounded by a mix of very conservative, old-school rural Oregonians with good hearts and rigid views; wealthy professionals busily buying up old mobile homes and replacing them with McMansions; and an assortment of young and old hippies with more alternative mindsets.

What we did not find, however, were avenues to connect with our fellow Pleasant Hill residents in ways other than attending one of the many churches or involving ourselves with the school sports programs. In an attempt to establish some community for ourselves and find others of a like mind, we instigated a discussion group based on the Northwest Earth Institute's (nwei.org) format. Starting first with Voluntary Simplicity, we went on to explore several other topics in the NWEI series revolving around environmental and social change issues, before launching onto our own path. We found our way through a Peak Oil phase, reading and discussing works by Richard Heinberg, James Howard Kunstler, and other notables of that genre. We also began discussing the question, "What does it mean to be a community?"

It became clear that we were, in some ways, functioning in a conscious, intentional way as a self-declared community. To be sure, we all lived in our own geographically-dispersed homes, none of them on the same tax lot; we had our own separate lives, and paid our own separate bills. We weren't sharing a bathroom and kitchen with each other, one measure of living communally—nor, separated by several miles, could we hope to consider ourselves a cohousing community. But we were, in fact, meeting with some regularity, sharing food, and developing our own culture, customs, and closeness. We were cooperating as an intentional-but-dispersed, rural "virtual" community.

At the peak of our group's membership, 43 people gathered for a summer potluck. But more typically, there were about 12 to 15 at any particular meeting, unless it was a special occasion. We had an email newsletter for a while that helped maintain cohesion among the larger group by reporting what we had discussed at the last meeting, what was on the agenda for the next meeting, what was on the horizon in terms of action items, and any other reminders or follow-up issues. We visited and hosted speakers from other intentional communities in our area. We had a calendar of seasonal events including bonfires, labyrinth walks, coordinated plantings among households for sharing at harvest time, coordinated bulk food purchases from local food producers, food preservation and holiday parties, and even a collective chicken harvest—an educational if somewhat grisly affair.

Because many of us had school-aged children, we were a "kids welcome" community by default. We found that Sunday gatherings at 3 p.m. worked best—discussion from 3 to 5, potluck from 5 to 7. Everyone went home on Sunday evening fed and feeling good with no need to cook dinner and plenty of time to get ready for the work and school week ahead.

We met successfully for several years twice a month from September through June. Summer vacation schedules proved too scattered to make regular meetings feasible during July and August. However, as the kids got older and busier, and as the increasingly frenetic pace of modern-day, middle-class con-

Left: Community campfire at a gathering of the Pleasant Hill Progressives. Right: Summer games.

sumerist lives took its toll, the group began to lose focus and momentum. We began meeting just once a month for what we called our "Second Sunday" gathering. And finally, at our summer break in 2008, we decided to discontinue our regular meetings. Now we mostly just get together informally, often in smaller subgroups, or for special occasions.

What Worked, What Didn't Work, and What We Learned

First, we learned that a sense of community and a feeling of belonging are not limited by geography, and that a positive aspect of having geographical distance between households is that many of the usual communitarian concerns—pets, chores, noise, and so forth—do not become issues. And we reaffirmed our belief that eating together is good, natural, healthy, human behavior and essential to feeling connected and nourished as community.

However, we also learned that it is hard to maintain momentum and move forward in a coordinated manner when you don't live within walking distance of each other. Maintaining community cohesion seems harder in a rural area than in an urban or suburban neighborhood, because you don't cross paths or see each other on the street coming-and-going as often—you have to get in a car and drive several miles after a long day. Ugh!

We also learned that it is hard to keep motivation, commitment, and leadership going unless people really grasp the concept of what it means to be a self-organizing group. *Everyone* has to take responsibility for making the group happen, or it will fizzle out. In the early stages of the group, meetings were held at various members' houses on a rotating basis. Although this was difficult when families with children came to meetings at homes that were not childproofed, it did facilitate more of a shared sense of responsibility for the group by those serving as the host.

Connected with this, we found that while some people have issues with structure and leadership, in fact, having some structure is helpful—it brings continuity, coherence, and meaning to

time spent together. When there is a predictable schedule that can be planned around, a set number of meetings so there is an end in sight, a specified ending time that is respected, and tasks assigned in between meetings having to do with specific topics or agenda items, then cohesion and satisfaction are strengthened and people are more willing to make time in their busy schedules for the group. This was evidenced in the early stages of the group, when we were utilizing the structure provided by the eight-week Northwest Earth Institute discussion courses. The expectations were clear, the beginning and end points were clear, and structure was provided, even if we strayed from it at times. The group seemed to flow very well, and meetings were well attended. In contrast, when we moved away from NWEI, guidelines and expectations were hazy, and participation dropped off.

In addition, in our desire to be egalitarian about steering the direction of the group, we also suffered from a lack of leadership, particularly after we moved away from using the NWEI courses. As a result, the aim or purpose of the group, other than coming together as community, was not always clear. Without more leadership and structure to mobilize the potential of the group for satisfying and effective action, the focus faded and people began to drift away. We were not, it seems, able effectively to move the group focus from being a social gathering back to having a greater purpose, despite our attempts to encourage the group to engage in self-reflection and refocus.

We knew that working toward emotional closeness and strong relationships is essential to realizing our vision of a better world, but we were unable, except on rare occasions, to provide an effective context conducive to talking about deeper emotions. As a result, on the occasions when discussion turned, for instance, to deeper feelings of concern about the state of the world (e.g., despair, frustration, fear, etc.), these expressions were too often met with a somewhat cynical, joking attitude, or other interjections which tended to derail the discussion and prevented deeper exploration that might have led the group to a stronger level of commitment. We also lacked a specific, agreed-upon

Photos courtesy of Don Schneider and Elin England

process or method for resolving conflicts. These factors, along with the natural pull to socialize and seek pleasure rather than explore and possibly experience discomfort, led, over time, to stagnation and kept the group from evolving. Our collectively conditioned middle-class tendencies to keep things pleasant conflicted with the possibility of greater depth and closeness. The cultural tendency toward individualism prevailed over the ideal of communitarian pursuits. People drifted off and the group disbanded.

We began the group with a rather relaxed attitude of "Come if you want, hope you can make it," without requiring any sort of commitment. And out of a desire to be inclusive, we had a policy of "taking all comers" without any sort of pre-screening or criteria for inclusion. These were errors and proved to be detrimental to group cohesion and progress in numerous ways. The constant churning of new faces resulted in frequently having to go back to square one in terms of information that had been presented. Not being more selective resulted in some amount of interpersonal discomfort that kept interactions at a more superficial social level and was disruptive to the formation of a solid, committed core group. Comments from established

members such as "I'm sorry, but I'm never coming again if that person is going to be part of this group" revealed just how important the screening process is.

So What's Next?

We are still interested in cooperative community and cooperative economics. There is still interest among several of the past members in building a community group with more commitment, depth, and focus that is outcome-oriented. What that will look like is, as yet, undetermined. But we are very clear about the importance that community has in our lives. ❀

Don Schneider and Elin England have been together through several life-chapters over the last 27 years. They hosted the Pleasant Hill Progressives at their home, Elkdream Farm, in western Oregon for eight years. They are currently looking into prospects for developing a senior-friendly (though not exclusively elder) cohousing community in the south Willamette valley of Oregon. They can be contacted at elkdream_farm@yahoo.com.

Eating Close to Home

Eating Close to Home: A Guide to Local Seasonal Sustenance in the Pacific Northwest by Elin Kristina England. 2009, 232 pages. ISBN 978-0-578-00069-5. elkdream_farm@yahoo.com.

The author collected recipes from her own kitchen and from gardeners, farmers, and food-lovers in her local community (including some of the Pleasant Hill Progressives) to create a bioregional, seasonal cookbook intended to help Pacific Northwesterners eat close to home year-round. Sections take readers through Winter, Spring, Summer, and Fall, describing both familiar and almost-forgotten vegetables and fruits and how to prepare them into delicious "nibbles," salads, soups, main dishes, side dishes, baked goods, and tasty treats. Additional chapters contain dishes that fit any season, instructions on putting food by, and resources for going more local. The following are excerpted from a list of helpful websites on pp. 220-221:

The 100 Mile Diet. **100milediet.org**. A website started by Alisa Smith and J.B. MacKinnon, authors of *Plenty*, the book detailing their year of eating only what food could be obtained within a 100 mile radius of their home in Vancouver, BC. The website has stories from people all over the world interested in eating locally, lots of suggestions for how to make your diet more sustainable, and a mapping tool to help you figure out the parameters of your local foodshed.

Chef's Collaborative. **chefscollaborative.org**. A national net-

work of chefs, food producers, educators, and food lovers who come together to celebrate local foods and foster a more sustainable food supply. On their site you can find restaurants all over the country that serve locally grown foods.

Eat Local. **www.eatlocal.net**. An extremely informative, easy-to-use website with links to many great resources across the US. It also has lots of great recipes, inspiring articles, and lots of support for those who want to make their diet more sustainable.

Eat Well Guide. **www.eatwellguide.org**. A guide for finding fresh, wholesome, sustainable food in the US and Canada. The site lists farms, stores, restaurants, and outlets.

Edible Communities. **www.ediblecommunities.com**. Their mission is to transform the way communities shop for, cook, eat, and relate to the food that is grown and produced. Through printed publications, websites, and events, they connect consumers, from a variety of regions across the country, with local growers, retailers, chefs, and food artisans, enabling those relationships to grow and thrive in a mutually beneficial, healthful, and economically viable way.

Urban Edibles. **urbanedibles.org**. An intriguing site created by a cooperative network of wild food foragers. Based in Portland [Oregon], their ideas could well be expanded to include other areas. The site includes a map of where in Portland one can find various wild edibles, plus information on identifying and harvesting edible and medicinal plants, preservation techniques, and other useful tidbits.

By Lawrence Siskind

Two and half years ago, P and M, a couple close to me, put out a call to a few friends. They asked if we would be willing to meet regularly, one night a week, to support them in their partnership by helping them communicate and process thoughts and feelings with which they had been struggling. Six of the invited responded, and we quickly decided to make the Thursday evening gatherings about all of us, rather than just the one couple who had inspired us to meet. The rest is history, at least for eight of us, plus D, who joined us earlier this year. We continue to meet every Thursday night, and our connections to each other, already deep and growing at the beginning of the experimental meetings, have grown to such a degree that we unabashedly use the f-word, "family," to describe what we are doing.

It certainly is difficult to use any other word since each of the nine of us would describe differently what we might be up to. Though we are all, to varying degrees, polyamorous and intimate with each other, we have no particular intention when we meet other than to honestly connect and to support each other in whatever ways to which we are moved. We gather in one of our living rooms—we live, three couples and three individuals, spread out over six houses, in compact Eugene, Oregon—and we usually begin with short check-ins during which each of us shares (holding our red, polished heart-shaped stone) what's been going on for us that day or that week. After we hear from each person, we decide who wants more time and attention, or occasionally, we decide to

experiment with some process or activity that one of us wants to offer, a meditation or an energy work modality. For example, recently, we went around the circle telling stories from our lives that the others were not likely to know with the intention of revealing more about ourselves, and another week we expressed gratitude for each other in a completely darkened living room. At the end of two hours, or thereabouts, we indulge in desert (homemade cobbler and ice cream are our favorites), and often repair to the hot tub. Though several of us are lovers, in varying degrees of intimacy, sex is not a part of Thursday nights (except there was this one time...).

Although Thursday nights made us the family we are, we are much more than some "poly" folks who meet on Thursday nights to process their relationship baggage. We suffer the weight of many other varieties of baggage which can often make

> *We are much more than some "poly" folks who meet to process their relationship baggage. We struggle with how honest we want to be with each other, how much we want to share and receive.*

for some heavy lifting. We struggle with how honest we want to be with each other, how much we want to share, how much we want to receive, and whether expanding the size of the group to others in our lives will raise our collective energy or dilute our intimacy. Since we have no particular goals for our meetings, no personal growth agenda, we have to face whether we really want to consistently show up and be with each other, because each other is all we can agree to. Early on, we floated the idea of learning Nonviolent Communication (NVC) together, but a few of us were less than enthused. Nothing, other than being present with each other to the best of our abilities, has inspired us to get serious about something, and I doubt anything will. We simply love each other as a family. But in this family, we strive to uncover our secrets, to expose our deep behavioral patterns in order to prevent the building up of petty resentments that undermines connection.

Although we socialize in many ways other days of the week, and with a wider circle of people, we have trouble doing much together as a group, other than meet on Thursday nights. Seven of us went to Burning Man together a couple years ago, and it was a strain to do much, other than the arduous set-up of our camp. Four of us, my partner S and I and another couple, L and M, spent some time together in New York during the holidays, and we had trouble getting along. For example, S and I like to walk a lot, even in the cold, but L and M wanted to jump on a bus, subway, or in a cab whenever possible. We like abstract expressionistic paintings, L and M, figurative works, so even museum visits led to separation rather than connection. Because we are a group of people with

Courtesy of Lawrence Siskind

The G8...or is it G9...or 10?

such varied interests and needs, it is particularly important and challenging to communicate clearly.

I do think it's unlikely that we all will live together any time soon. We're far too eccentric and set in our ways, and we're a bit old to start building residential community; I'm the youngest at 45. I imagine us, in our old age, living more closely and sharing more resources. At the present moment, we remain very independent souls. We came together in an attempt to try to

help a single couple stay together. (They're still together, despite ups and downs, both economic and emotional, and we're still working at it.) That said, I truly believe that our group is stronger than the individuals and couples it contains.

At the Network for a New Culture Summer Camp, at which we all met (at different camps over the years), we're an exciting item to other Campers. Questions are asked: What are you G8 folks up to? Can we join you? How can we create a group like yours? And isn't it all about sex? The answers to the questions, I believe, are actually quite simple: We connect in whatever way is true in the moment. To join us, you would have to fall in love with each of us, then we would demand (actually we're too lazy to demand, but we would be unable to resist) your presence. You can create a group like ours by assembling those individuals who you think love you, and seeing who keeps showing up. And no, it isn't much about sex... but we can still dream. ✸

Lawrence Siskind, despite having lived his entire adult life on the West Coast, considers himself a New Yorker in exile. He currently lives in Eugene, Oregon, where there is more opportunity for loving connection than there is for teaching high school English. He and his partner are involved in a "committed," "open," "codependent" "experiment" that they call a "relationship." They reside at the Du•má community, where he loves to empty the dish rack and hone his backgammon skills. He spends much of his time and energy processing and funning with the G8, and participating in the planning of the Network for a New Culture Summer Camp.

Smoker and Mirrors?

"Well, I could probably see it the way you do if I were an a••hole!" P remarked to me. I had been curious as to why P was so much more attached, felt so much more betrayed, by his partner M's admission that she'd been secretly smoking cigarettes away from home for months. P read in my objective-sounding curiosity a lack of concern for his partner M's health, and he was angry because I wasn't more understanding about his disappointment in the dishonesty of her behavior. My reaction to getting called "an a••hole," when my intention had been to try to help shed light on the emotions we all were feeling about M's coming clean, was to shut down emotionally. When the discussion about P's feelings continued on with others in a pretty heated manner for our group of lovey-dovey "family," I requested that we simply stop trying to talk further at this time about the issues. For me, the heated emotions were too painful to witness. I was that upset, and I am the one of us who almost always wants to push and push in the group, to get us to share more deeply. The intensity of the emotions showed us all how difficult it can be, among partners, lovers, and deep friends, to even try to disentangle loving concern from emotional codependency. Do we care so much about our loved ones' behaviors because we are concerned for them, or because we believe their behaviors are a part of ours? If M risks her health by smoking and fails to be honest about it, is my health at risk? If I were her partner, would I be able to remain civil while others wondered why I was so upset? These complex issues of intimacy are the kind with which our group is dealing on Thursday nights, and beyond.

—Lawrence Siskind

LESSONS IN BUILDING RESILIENT NEIGHBORHOODS:
Reflections on the PROUT Institute Community SEED Program

By Ryan Dubas

To the common passer-by, River Road in Eugene, Oregon looks like typical 1950s-1960s suburban development. Traveling north on the five-lane arterial road, tucked amidst the stately Douglas Fir trees, one encounters many hallmarks of modern industrial-consumer culture: heavy motor traffic, convenience stores, a gun shop, a Wells Fargo bank, and an intersection pock-marked with chain eateries such as Hardees, Wendy's, and Domino's Pizza. But if one observes carefully, off the beaten path, only a few blocks west of this thoroughfare, a different type of development is being realized.

Scattered throughout this quiet neighborhood, residents are working together to manifest a vision of a sustainable community inspired by permaculture design principles, localized economics, and respect for all living beings. Their neighborhood resiliency project is focused on developing a network of properties producing basic necessities, particularly food, and fostering an ethic of compassion and resource sharing. In addition to sharing healthy organic food, tools, materials, and know-how, the community also offers social events, education in permaculture and local economic planning, and instruction in yogic practices and philosophy. The established touchstone properties include the beginnings of a food jungle, several small gardens, an evolving village for volunteers and interns, and a spiritual and social center. This network of small suburban farms, none bigger than one

acre, demonstrates how small sites and connected people can carve a viable niche in the shadows of an outmoded paradigm.

This past summer, members of this River Road community extended their influence and shared their vision with roughly a dozen interns participating in the Community Sustainable Economics and Ecological Design (SEED) Program, sponsored by the PROUT Institute. A diverse group of young and curious minds from locations spanning the country—Maine, Vermont, South Carolina, Louisiana, Missouri, Ohio, Michigan, Nebraska, Montana, California, and Oregon—congregated for the program. Living in community at the Dharmalaya Center for Human Development, home of the PROUT Institute, interns studied yogic philosophy while offering 25 hours of labor per week developing neighborhood infrastructure, which, in turn, taught them useful lessons in permaculture, gardening, natural building, and community development.

The interns' work this summer focused on a dramatic transformation of a single acre back yard from a litter-riddled, blackberry-infested, and largely unproductive lot into the beginnings of a food-producing village. Interns helped clean the property, fell a 20-year-old Douglas Fir tree, raise and plant garden beds, construct a greenhouse, clear and set camping spaces, deconstruct and remodel a garage, erect a strawbale kitchen/bathhouse, create adobe bricks with local

Neighbors and interns share food from the garden at a potluck.

Photos courtesy of Ryan Dubas

soil, build an adobe wood-fired barrel oven and adobe canning stove, design and construct a composting toilet outhouse, and more. The property will be used to house volunteers and interns in the future, perhaps becoming the center for a neighborhood food cooperative.

I signed up for the internship program with only a vague conception of what I was to learn. Emerging from four years of teaching English at midwestern colleges, I was eager to immerse myself in physical work and purge my consciousness of hastily-written essays conveyed through small typeface on flattened wood pulp. And being raised in a household where my connection to food production had been obscured, I wanted to experience the magic of growing and consuming local food. I knew that the material world was more than keyboards, paper, pens, restaurants, and markets but I wanted to feel that truth. So, when I discovered the PROUT Institute internship, the ideas—construction, organic gardening, and yoga—were enough to inspire my participation. The experience of living in this community has been far deeper and more complex than I anticipated. It has been flavored with challenges, discoveries, and successes.

SEED Program interns celebrate after a hard day of work.

a moment of silence. "New people are arriving, more will be joining. A sort of flow will be developed. You see, large organizations are looking more and more to chaos theory to inform their organizational structure. They adopt certain minimum specifications—core values—as their guidelines. Instead of enforcing a rigid top-down systems management, they instill a cultural ethic in all members. This allows for a certain flexibility and empowerment for individuals in groups. Keep this in mind as more people arrive. It is perhaps analogous to a flock of birds. As more members of the flock join the flight, the formation takes shape."

The tone of ambiguity in this speech set the stage (or skyscape) for the summer program. Paradoxically, this was one of the most difficult yet fulfilling aspects of the program. While there was guidance from staff members, the interns were given the space to figure out logistics of community living (such as the food system and cleaning schedule) on their own. In a group of 12 people, many of them living in community for the first time, having access to varying levels of financial support, and being exposed to a new Sattvic diet (vegetarian, no onions, garlic, or mushrooms), this was not always simple. Interns were tested with the demands of figuring out, together, how to make perhaps the most essential and nourishing elements of communal living—food—work for the whole group. Lacking explicit top-down

I was struck by the apparent intention in all things, ranging from garden design to words spoken.

When I arrived in mid-May, the program was not yet in full swing. I was one of five people in a flock that would eventually grow to 12. Immediately, I could see that I was entering into something both intentional and flexible, something still very much in process. Indeed, at the first morning check-in meeting, PROUT Institute Executive Director Ravi Logan launched into a brief aside about chaos theory.

"We are entering a new phase," he said after tuning into the meeting with

instruction, importantly there was space provided for open communication amongst interns and staff. Successful systems were eventually developed, unfortunately some not until later in the program, yet it was valuable for interns to feel both the tension and resolution of collective decision making. In fact, the whole exercise was empowering because throughout it all, sincere respect was given to individual voices.

This respect for all voices is one of the minimum specifications, part of the cultural ethic shaping the systems at the PROUT Institute and in the broader River Road community. In the same way that each neighbor contributes to the community according to her or his skills and abilities, and each species contributes to the ecosystems in these permaculture-inspired gardens, each individual person offers a valued perspective and voice. Probably this is why upon my arrival I was struck immediately by the apparent intention in all things, ranging from the garden design to the words spoken. Everybody

Author Ryan Dubas at work in the garden.

SEED Program interns learn how to make cob.

SEED Program interns at work installing a garden.

seemed to speak slowly, and with attempted precision; and all others listened through long pauses—patiently. My mind was accustomed to less thoughtful, knee-jerk phonic projections. For a moment, I considered the communication too sensitive, but quickly I softened into it and appreciated the respect paid to all speech and the sense of empowerment it provided for speakers. Empowerment, not coincidentally, is one of the critical imperatives of the PROUT paradigm of development.

PROUT is an acronym for the Progressive Utilization Theory, a new paradigm of socioeconomic development and political organization based on the fundamental assumption that all people have potentiality in the physical, mental, and spiritual spheres, and should be given opportunity to develop and express their potentialities. PROUT is a comprehensive approach, with its own foundational values and planning principles, economic and political structures, and social and cultural systems. All of these are designed to work in synergy to meet everyone's basic needs and to promote the progressive enhancement of people's potentialities at the individual level, within the collective society, and in balance with the more-than-human world that sustains all life. PROUT offers hope, vision, empowerment, and a solution-oriented approach to people and communities that are seeking a viable, life-affirming alternative to global capitalism and the various contradictions and crises inherent to it (see www. proutinstitute.org for more information).

The summer internship program is a part of a larger effort by the PROUT Institute to create a PROUTist model on a neighborhood level. Indeed, as the internship program ramped up, I began to see in practical terms how the values of PROUT informed the work we were doing. For example, to imagine the idea of "progressive utilization," consider the manner in which goods and services are exchanged in this community development project. Neighbors know that they are in an exchange, but the exchange isn't defined, so each person can contribute—money, food, labor, construction materials, expertise, social connections—according to his/her own skills or resources. An artist in the community might paint a mural to enhance the aesthetic beauty of a building in exchange for labor deconstructing a patio. Or a gardener falling behind on weeding might exchange some of his/her harvest for labor. Tools circulate as needed, knowledge is shared, seeds are spread. It is a sort of cooperative economics, more or less informal at this stage but certainly the foundation of different kind of approach that, over time, will become more structured. Individuals don't depend entirely on this cooperative system, but having it there connected to and supplementing the individual home economies makes life easier.

For me, learning from and observing the more collective mentality of this community was the most profoundly educational aspect of the internship. To see a vital community in action was not only inspiring, but a lesson in information exchange. With every week of participation, I was introduced to new community members, each with vital and intriguing knowledge to share. Interns were sometimes dispatched to other properties in the neighborhood in the spirit of community service, allowing them to learn from a variety of designs and ideas. The information and skills shared through this network in this way—face-to-face, feet-to-earth, hands-to-tool—was exceptionally deep and enriching, especially for one coming from a desk-centered, indoor career path. It was like surfing the internet, but more focused, multisensory, and without advertisements. However, I couldn't have learned all that I did with keyword searches for construction, organic gardening, and yoga; I did it by helping plant a literal and figurative community SEED and nurture it from the ground up. ❧

Ryan Dubas was born in Colorado Springs, Colorado and raised in central Nebraska. He studied English and Cultural Studies and taught as an English Instructor at Hastings College and Kansas State University. He now lives in Eugene, Oregon and is pursuing interests in natural building and energy management. Contact him with questions or comments: ryandubas@ yahoo.com.

CREATING THE IDEAL INTENTIONAL COMMUNITY
(OR REVITALIZING AN EXISTING ONE)

I, Sahmat, grew up in intentional communities and have lived in 10 of them. I have been so dedicated to Community with both humans and Nature that I've been called "The Community Guy". The communities I grew up in shared a fairly strong "sense of community". I call this deep and sustained sense of community "Common-unity" because it's a state of unity we share in common, with the unique individuality of each human and each species still honored. It's this state of Common-unity that I've found most valuable in life and to me it's the main reason for living in an intentional community. When a group is deep in Common-unity together, there's a shared sense of love, joy, and peace that tops any other group experience.

However, I've found that in all the communities I've lived in, the sense of community is not nearly as deep and sustained as it could be. It's precisely this lack of Common-unity that is the root cause of the catastrophic global suffering of racism, wars, child abuse, abuse of women, environmental and species destruction, etc. So the ultimate goal is ending global suffering through "Global Common-unity": the spreading of Common-unity throughout the world by forming a global network of Common-unity-dedicated Communities.

So I've spent my life learning how to create Common-unity-dedicated communities that share true Common-unity: a deeper and more sustained sense of community. There are two keys to starting a Common-unity community (or moving an existing community into deeper Common-unity):

1. The first key to Common-unity is for everyone to be "Common-unity-dedicated" as their top common priority. This doesn't seem to be the case in any existing community, which results in focus and energies being bled off into other priorities. So maintenance of Common-unity doesn't get enough time and energy.

2. The second key to Common-unity is to learn "Common-unity Skills", skills that must be practiced to maintain Common-unity: Speaking from the Heart, Empathetic Listening, Emptying of Ego-attachments, Conflict Resolution, Consensus, Heart Wound Healing, Cooperative Housing, and Cooperative Economics. Modern culture does not teach us these skills.

We at the Alliance for Global Community have developed free workshops that train you in these Common-unity Skills. The workshops contain the Sharing Circle process developed by M. Scott Peck, a Nature connection exercise developed by John Seed and Joanna Macy, healing exercises developed by Byron Katie and Richard Moss, and exercises in creating Cooperative Housing and Cooperative Economics. We've tested various versions of these Common-unity Skill Building workshops over the past 25 years, and we've found them to be quite effective in teaching Common-unity skills that can help maintain Common-unity. If you'd like to start a Common-unity-dedicated community, or if you'd like to bring more Common-unity into an existing community (perhaps through a Common-unity sub-community or "pod"), you need to learn or improve these Common-unity skills as soon as possible.

To find out how to sign up for a free public Common-unity Skills workshop or schedule a free workshop for an existing group or community, please go to my website thecommunityguy.org There you can also find out how to get a free copy of the book "Skill Building for Global Common-unity". You can contact Sahmat directly at info@thecommunityguy.org or at 434-305-4770.

COMMON-UNITY WITH HUMANITY AND NATURE

CULTIVATING THE NEIGHBORHOOD BY ZANE HAMM

Creating Family Where We Are Now
Building sustainable communities with the next generation

When I think about my most vivid memories growing up, two ideas spring immediately to mind. First, I recall times with my grandparents, who showed me how to plant and harvest a garden, gave us the space and tools to make tiny boats out of scraps of wood in the shop, and took a team of joyful kids to feed cattle with a horse-drawn sleigh. I am choosing to share these memories now because with a new little boy in my life, I'm embarrassed to admit that I hit a wall a few months ago. The good news is that I emerged on the other side with a new understanding of what it means to find ways in which to jump into community experiences with a child, and perhaps more important, to create a new way of being part of a community if you notice a gap. I was seeking a community to join that could include—but more than include, *embrace*—this new, very active member of our family, and to share the highs and challenges of child care. The immediate absence was a lack of part-time childcare.

In this article I share the challenges and lessons learned as I created childcare exchange with another mother and her son. I'll highlight the steps I took to start a shared childcare system, and illustrate the benefits of involving this young generation in local opportunities. I underscore the importance of creating family and community for the next generation by reflecting on how my own experiences growing up informed my commitment to building a vibrant community.

Rock Bottom

In conversations I've had with numerous parents now that I've started a childcare exchange, it's clear to me that there is a growing need for these community supports. If only I had known this—or had what my sister calls "faith in timing"—when I felt I was crashing. Maybe I'd have been able to envision a solution sooner, or known that I wasn't the only one facing these barriers when I sat in our vintage VW Jetta at the side of the road, listening to "Just a spoon full of sugar" while my toddler sobbed between breathless utterings of "all done, all done" in the back seat. I too fought back tears of frustration and what felt pretty close to desperation. "What am I going to do now?" This question was spurred after driving across town to pick up my one-year-old son from a dayhome that had graciously agreed to take him one day a week to help me out while I tried to find a longer-term solution. The young woman was a gentle and capable caregiver, but was trying to manage my scruffy little rag-tag of a boy who just wanted to be outside while supervising five other older children. The look in her eyes said it all, "He's a lovely boy, but there are just too many of them. I'm *done*."

I felt like I was *all done*, too. After we'd remained on numerous waiting lists for a year, none of the daycare or dayhome options seemed to have space available any time soon, and it is especially challenging to find a part-time option of three days or less per week. Understandably, it is easier for the caregivers and the child to gain momentum and establish a routine with five days, and filling full-time spaces is a high priority. I'd joined a childcare cooperative when my son was four months old with some reservations about caring for another babe this young, but many of the women involved soon returned to work and had their children in daycare full-time, or had a family member who was available for care. The co-op that had been so thoughtfully created fizzled before it had a chance to take off. If it was an option, I'd have jumped at it now.

As a Ph.D. student, what I needed to find was care for two to three days per week, or full-time if that was the only option. I know now that many new parents face this same challenge, and the problem extends to other urban centers and rural communities. Although I'd committed to balancing family and work, and to working from home when I could, it seemed impossible to progress (or focus on professional responsibilities) with no viable childcare options in sight. Others echoed my frustration, and daycare managers even voiced their concerns to me about the challenges of limited resources and growing waiting lists. I look back at this time now and find it hard to imagine the despair I felt at the time. A peek at my journal brings it back into focus.

Digging Out of the Hole, or So What?

Feeling like I needed to pull out all the stops and find respite for even one day a week, I recalled an email message from an acquaintance from a network for new mothers that I'd joined at a local health center. She was looking for an option to trade childcare two to three morning per week. The problem? I could not imagine taking care of two children—the same age—at the same time. Thinking back on my experiences babysitting as a teen, I could not even fathom how brave I'd been to take care of five young children when I was just 11 years old. What was I thinking? Had I no concept of the level of responsibility this required?

Despite my reservations and fears, I contacted the other woman, and proposed a one-month trial. In my mind I thought that this would allow us both to find other options if sharing care did not work out. Had I no faith? To be honest, this was the least confident I had felt about any aspect of my life in a long time. I'd known how to make and defend decisions in a professional environment, but taking care of our children felt like shakier territory, and more ambiguous to me in terms of "right" and "wrong" choices. I want to share with you what I wish I'd known then. It seems intuitive and pragmatic now that I know how well

it works—and when there is not the feeling of dread or debilitating sleep deprivation attached to it, with the little voice that sneaks in, "what if this doesn't work?"

The Surprise

What surprised me most, and what I eagerly share with anyone who will listen now, is that it is possible to successfully create this new form of community. Once I was open to trying it, the logistics flowed. I highlight here a few key lessons I learned:

1. Communication: Being able to communicate about scheduling and being somewhat flexible on occasion is the key. For example, the other mother will call and tell me if my son is still sleeping at 4:00 and say, "Why not come at 4:30?" Time to have a latte or visit the public library? Yes, please! I return the favor.

2. Strategy: Being ready for the day, and having some easy systems in place—favorite spots with a snack, or toys and music on arrival for transition; snack and change just before 10 AM; nap or walk/nap at 10/10:15; change and lunch at noon; playing and music, books, outside plucking at things in the garden; changing as needed, of course; change, snack, and nap or nap/walk again around 3:00/3:30; change and little snack or more playing and music around 4:00 before pick up. This rhythm also helps me to relax into our time together and maximize the joy of my time with my son on those days.

The other steps that really helped were to 1) Write out my ideas for a proposed plan, suggesting we get together for coffee and see how the boys did together at our homes for a few hours with us there together; 2) Write out a possible schedule—and a few ideas of how to try a few shorter days first; 3) Talk up front about their routines and how we might be able to work with them; 4) Decide on a trial—reserving judgement until the boys got settled, but trying it for a month with willingness to revisit if it was working on all sides; 5) Meet anyone else who was going to be implicated—our partners in this case, but I'd also introduce friends or anyone else who would pick him up.

Finally, I have found a drop-in community group on Wednesday mornings. The group is within my community, has about 20 child-adult pairs, and is welcoming and diverse. Around the snack table there are more than six languages spoken. It is a destination to go with the two boys, where they are happy and I feel supported and part of a vibrant community. I've shared my challenges and successes with starting a childcare exchange with others there, and it reinforced my intention to pass on to COMMUNITIES readers that it is not only possible, but might even exceed their expectations.

How to Evaluate Success

The bonus with this arrangement was that it doesn't require any more emotional energy than ensuring it's a match, and of course monitoring how you feel about the separation. Seeing our sons just jump right in and start playing assured me that they would be fine once they were settled. Another strategy for overcoming the challenge of anxiety was to say "Just give it some time—even a few weeks—to let everyone get

(continued on p. 77)

Gardening Two by Two

Four grubby little hands reach up and pick snap peas for a snack, their faces still wet with strawberries from their first ripe course. I grab a handful too and revel in the fresh green pods still warm with sunlight. It's a gritty, mucky affair, but the sheer joy in these simple acts is undeniable. As the pint-sized helpers threw seeds in the ground last spring in a colourful "heap" rather than in rows, I had my doubts. Gardening with small children—especially two toddlers—requires flexibility and patience, but what better way to connect directly to our food? Hearing them rattle off the names of plants and show visitors around the garden fills me with hope, even if it means a few edibles yanked out unceremoniously, and weeds gleefully dug out and tossed together with sand. They call it "salad."

CREATING FAMILY WHERE WE ARE NOW

(continued from p. 61)

settled, because that's how long it takes sometimes to adjust to change." My goal was not to get too frazzled, and to take a little space and time to navigate the new roles and relationships.

Celebration

Knowing that both boys are being very well fed, and cared for with lots of attention and an understanding of their individual needs and preferences, helps immensely, and is reason enough to celebrate. With just two, we can adjust to "no nap," or later nap, or needing a bit more holding or one-on-one time without any other pressures. The flexibility also extends to beginning our days later, or working it out between two families how we will handle vacation time. In daycare we would have to continue to pay during these times, whereas we just work this out between our families.

This childcare exchange has meant a new clarity for me, to be able to have some time to work and gain valuable perspective during two days a week, while enjoying the balance of time with the boys, and time with my family. Although, paying for the care if you know that it is the right match would certainly be worth it in some cases, mathematically speaking, there is a huge financial savings of thousands of dollars—a major bonus.

Final Reflections

If our children were members of a bluegrass band, my son would be wildly "faking it" on the fiddle and switching erratically to the mandolin mid-trill, while the other young man, age one, no less, would be solidly holding the tune with the stand-up bass. Part of why it works is that there are real characters involved in our new little community. It is easier to laugh at our inexperience and reservations now that we've seen results. The other reasons for success are less easy to pin down. Our commitment to taking a risk together, born from necessity or a creative way to solve our problem, was a key. Our vision for what *could be possible*, beyond the challenges of *what was*, or *what if*, was necessary to move the concept into action. And now? I keep thinking that something will shift. They'll move to Oklahoma, or they'll decide to hire a nanny. But it's working, and I would be willing to try again. The lesson I've learned is this: We're committed, and we have faith, but more important, we have a plan. And a back-up plan, because it matters that much to us. We're building this new community together with purpose and intention. ❧

Zane Hamm is an educator in Edmonton, Alberta, with a passion for community health. Between gardening and photography, she's completing a Ph.D. in Adult Education.

Earthsong Eco-Neighbourhood—
Rebuilding Community within the City

By Robin Allison
architect

Turn off busy Swanson Road in the western suburbs of Auckland, leave your car in the carpark to walk between clusters of houses into the heart of this urban community, and you find yourself in an oasis of calm, beauty, and abundance. Neighbours stop for a chat on the path, children race past on their tricycles, and the loudest sound you hear is the birdsong. This is Earthsong, home to 69 adults and children in 32 homes nestled amongst gardens, paths, and a village green on only three acres of land.

Earthsong is an eco-neighbourhood based on the twin principles of cohousing and permaculture. The founding vision, still strongly held by residents today, has three equal components: sustainable design and construction, respectful and cooperative community, and education by demonstration. At Earthsong we are relearning the skills and benefits of belonging to a community, and rebuilding a healthy interdependence with each other and with earth.

Launched at a public meeting in 1995, the project grew as people joined and worked together over several years developing the foundation agreements of effective group procedures, legal and financial structures, and site and design criteria. In 1999 they purchased the land (a former organic orchard), then worked with consultants to design the whole development, and contracted with builders to build the project in stages. While the first residents moved into their homes in 2002, the last homes and siteworks weren't completed until 2008.

Communities such as Earthsong add another layer of belonging into the standard suburban model—a layer of community relationships and governance, that doesn't reduce our personal autonomy in our own homes but adds the enormous richness of a cohesive neighbourhood within the more impersonal wider suburb and city.

Design for Sustainability

What makes Earthsong an eco-neighbourhood? Earthsong itself doesn't have the shops, businesses, school, or other facilities suggested by the term "village," so we are happy to be known as a housing neighbourhood. However we are a short walk to the shops, library and community facilities, bus stop, and train station of our local suburban centre.

Within our neighbourhood the site layout, buildings, and services are designed to work with the natural landform and climate. Rammed earth and natural timber give the houses a solid and timeless feel, with plenty of windows to let the sun warm the coloured concrete floors for passive solar design. Solar water heaters, nontoxic materials, natural oils and paints all add up to low-energy and healthy houses.

Clusters of two-storey attached dwellings are arranged along the common pathways and shared courtyards, surrounded by old fruit trees and lush new plantings. Homes range from one-bed-

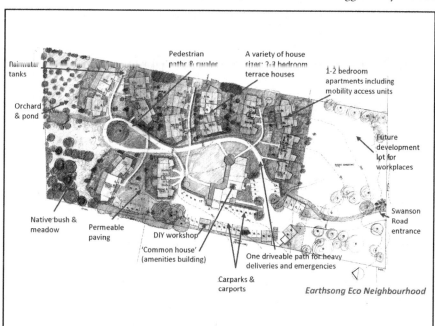

Rainwater tanks

Orchard & pond

Native bush & meadow

Permeable paving

'Common house' (amenities building)

DIY workshop

Carparks & carports

Pedestrian paths & swales

A variety of house sizes: 2-3 bedroom terrace houses

1-2 bedroom apartments including mobility access units

Future development lot for workplaces

Swanson Road entrance

One driveable path for heavy deliveries and emergencies

Earthsong Eco Neighbourhood

Earthsong common house.

Pedestrian pathways: people space, not car space.

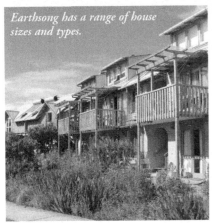

Earthsong has a range of house sizes and types.

Neighbours gather on the path.

Photos courtesy of Robin Allison

room studios to four-bedroom houses to suit all ages and different household types. Easy gradients on all paths allow full accessibility, and seven single-level houses are designed for those older or less mobile.

Roof water is collected for reuse in the homes. Surface rain water flows into densely planted swales (shallow dish drains) beside the paths, and down to the large pond, home to frogs and ducks, reducing water runoff from the site. A comprehensive permaculture site design includes gathering nodes and children's play areas, vegetable gardens, native bush and orchard areas, water management, and composting.

We couldn't include everything we wanted at the time of building due to cost or regulatory obstacles, so we built in the ability to upgrade later. There are cables inside the walls of each house to assist later installation of photovoltaic panels, land area is set aside for more water tanks, and networks of spare conduits in the ground allow for future

internet upgrades. Sustainability includes affordability, and our approach has been to achieve as much as we could across the full spectrum of environmental and social sustainability and to be willing to let go of perfection in any one area.

Community Aspects of Sustainability

What we have learnt at Earthsong is that social and environmental sustainability are complementary and mutually reinforcing. Many of the sustainable design aspects of our neighbourhood were made possible not only in *addition* to a social and cooperative structure, but *because* of our social cooperative structure; the two have always gone hand-in-hand.

One example is our car-free neighbourhood: we place a higher importance on our relationships with one another than with our cars, so we designed the carparks at the edge of the site. This has both social and environmental benefits—land area that would otherwise be driveways or road is freed up for productive gardens and community living space, for children to play safely and neighbours to interact as they come and go from their houses.

By sharing resources, we have access to increased facilities and "common wealth" while we use less overall. At the heart of the neighbourhood is the common house, our much-loved community building owned jointly by all the house-holders and providing shared spaces including the large dining/meeting hall, sitting room, large kitchen, childrens' room, guest room, and shared laundry. The individual houses are well-designed but compact (100 square meters for a three-bedroom home) because they don't need a spare bedroom for occasional guests, or a living room large enough for large parties or meetings. Even eco-friendly construction uses significant energy and materials so building smaller houses and having shared facilities makes good environmental sense.

Living within a diverse and supportive neighbourhood makes it easier for individuals to make low-energy, sustainable choices. With good systems of management, equipment such as lawnmowers, garden tools, and workshop tools can be shared. Carpooling and car sharing are much easier to organize and manage when we already know and trust one another.

Working alongside my neighbours on a cooking team for a common dinner or a working bee in the garden is a great way to build the social glue of relationships that maintains community. Cooperation also happens on a daily informal basis, from child-care arrangements to moving furniture or watering the garden when a neighbour goes away. It's all about building connections between people and valuing the sense of belonging.

Another powerful way that being part of a cohesive community can facilitate environmental responsibility is that we learn from each other. Designing eco-friendly buildings and neighbourhoods is an important first step, but the behaviour of the occupants is at least as significant when it comes to the overall impact. It takes extra effort to live a more sustainable life, to resist the gravitational pull back to doing things the "normal" and therefore easier way, but in community we can help each other with information, support, and accountability.

One example is electricity use, which can vary widely even between identical houses with similar numbers and ages of inhabitants, because of the habits and behaviour of the residents. As a cooperative neighbourhood we can facilitate

behaviour change in a number of ways, through information exchange and education, sharing ideas and tips about how to manage the systems more efficiently, internal pricing plans that reward low users and discourage high use, built-in feedback mechanisms, and accountability by making individual house use transparent to all. All of these mechanisms are in place in some form at Earthsong, with the result that 32 homes and the common house are functioning with an electricity supply of the size that usually supplies six houses in New Zealand.

"Through living at Earthsong," one resident told me, "I have become aware of permaculture and have seen it work in practice. With the support of neighbours I am now implementing permaculture principles in my garden."

"My education focused strongly on decision making and producing 'optimal' results," another said. "Our consensus decision-making process here at Earthsong makes me realise how much learning we lose by reducing decisions to numbers. In the beginning I just wanted to get done with the rounds and the meetings; now I value them for providing insight in the thought processes and mindsets of my neighbours."

And another: "I buy much more organic food for myself because it seems strange to live in a healthy house on a certified organic property and fill the fridge up with non-organic food."

Eco-Neighbourhoods within Eco-Cities

Earthsong has become a catalyst in the rejuvenation of the wider suburb. The

front portion of our site will be developed as eco-friendly shops and offices, to link the housing with the wider neighbourhood, enhance the adjacent commercial centre, and provide work opportunities for both Earthsong residents and the wider community. Several residents have been deeply involved in local community development projects, working towards a more socially, culturally, and environmentally sustainable suburb or "ecovillage."

Like a healthy organism with healthy organs made up of healthy cells, sustainability needs to operate at all levels: the individual, the household, the neighbourhood, the village, and the city. A flourishing, sustainable "eco-city," by definition, would include many flourishing, connected ecovillages and neighbourhoods, of an appropriate scale to encourage cooperation and healthy relationships. It is increasingly apparent that we are all part of one vast, complex planetary system or organism, and eco-neighbourhoods and villages offer fertile environments to re-learn the skills of interdependence and cooperation that will contribute to the health of our beautiful earth home. 🐦

An architect, Robin was the initiator and development coordinator and is now a contented resident of Earthsong Eco-Neighbourhood (www.earthsong.org.nz). She is a fellow of the New Zealand Social Entrepreneur Fellowship, and is profiled in the recent book How Communities Heal. Her chapter is available at tinyurl.com/hchallison. Contact robin.allison@earthsong.org.nz.

The pond: home of ducks, frogs, and herons.

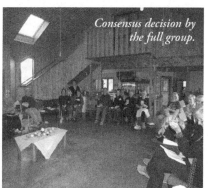

Consensus decision by the full group.

Kawsmos:
The Unintentional Community

By Mary Wharff, Elizabeth Schultz, and Deborah Altus

In 2003, a couple dozen people were invited by Doug Hitt of Lawrence, Kansas to watch and discuss Brian Swimme's *Canticle to the Cosmos*, a video series about the connection of humans to the Universe and all living things. Hitt didn't set out to do anything more than that. But now, 11 years later, that gathering has evolved into Kawsmos: 15 people who meet monthly to deepen our knowledge about life, to celebrate being part of the cosmos, and to understand our place along the Kansas (Kaw) River.

In March 2014, Kawsmos devoted an evening to participating in the Tamarack Institute's conversation about community. The conversation fit neatly into our planning process for the immediate future: in fact we had just begun to discuss whether or not the term "community of practice" fit us. Our conversation revealed appreciation for the community we've gained from Kawsmos, as well as some resistance to any term which would define what we are. Resistance to definition is just one of the ways our group has avoided structure, guidelines, and rules so common in many organizations. But as we talked about community, it became clear that this resistance, as frustrating as it can sometimes be, is a key part of the organic structure that keeps us interested, connected, and coming back for more.

"Community" was not the goal

When our group first convened, some of us had known Hitt a long time, but others were relatively new acquaintances. Some of us knew each other, some of us knew no one but Doug. We knew we would meet once a month that year and be exposed to new thinking about science, ecology, and theology.

But we did not know we would decide to keep learning together after the first year ended, and that our gatherings would give new shape to our calendars with celebrations for each solstice and equinox. Nor did we dream we would sing together, write poetry

together, dance together, tell stories and paint together, walk through woods and wetlands together, perform "science theatre" together, sled together, and watch the sunset in the rain together. We didn't know that we would bring food we had prepared to every gathering and break bread together before we began the evening's activity.

The more we talked about our shared experiences during our community conversation, the more obvious it became that "community" has happened to us, whether we planned for it or not.

"No rules" was the rule

We've come to where we are today with no mission statement, no set goals, and no set rules. Why? A partial answer is that we are a diverse and rebellious lot—we wouldn't be attracted to a new story about life if we weren't! We range in age from 16 to 78, are married and single, gay and straight, humanists and scientists, members of faith communities and atheists.

We couldn't talk about community without remembering the rebellious participants in our early years who felt strongly that even a name would lead us down a slippery slope to mission statements, formal rules, and obligations. As a result, our first years were name-free, leader-free, and expectation-free. We chose our yearly program by consensus. We took turns, voluntarily, planning program content. This planning process was, and is, extensive and time consuming, but it is not governed by rules.

Like the cosmos, however, we evolved. The name nay-sayers moved away, and at about the same time, we added new participants from a second group that Hitt had introduced to the *Canticle to the Cosmos*. Suddenly, the make-up of our group changed, and interest in a formal name grew. Up to that point, many of us had developed nicknames to write on our calendars—"cosmology," "earth literacy group,"

Kawsmos members enjoying the outdoors before their Community Conversation, March 22, 2014.

Jerry Jost

314

"eco-lit," and creative combinations of the Native American name for our region, *Kaw*, in combination with the word "cosmos," such as "beKAWS" and "Kawsmonauts." But no particular name had stuck.

After six years of avoiding the issue, we were ready for a real name. We wanted consensus, as usual, which meant discussions about the value of names, along with the limitations. Why, we considered, is *Echinacea* called "coneflower," but not "purple-petal thistle head"? Is "Mars" made less wondrous by its name? How could our group find a name that would be spot on tomorrow as well as today?

allotting an entire year to study each of the Four Elements. During each year, we engaged in activities which illuminated our understanding of these elements from the cosmic, planetary, and Kansas perspective.

During the Year of Water, we not only toured our local wastewater plant and took a canoe trip down our lovely and badly polluted river, but we also each created art expressing our need for and love of water. During the Year of the Sun, a Kawsmos artist allowed us to take over her studio floor so we could imagine in colors and design the creation of radiance. To study Air, we considered wind globally in mythology, poetry, and fans! We also discussed a video on wind farms and engaged a local dancer to lead us in breathing exercises and wind-tossed dances. In our year about Earth, we returned to the artist's studio, this time seeing it as a cave and ourselves the first visual artists. This year also involved a trip, led by a professional geologist, to a beautiful local woodlands area, marked by a creek and stunning limestone cliff.

We enjoyed remembering many of these activities during our conversation and we discussed the value of shared learning and celebrating community. We also became more mindful of how we have helped each other take action. In the Year of the Sun, for instance, we agreed to reduce energy in our individual homes. One of our group designed and built a stunning three-dimensional model, using miniature coal cars, so we could visually demonstrate our energy usage and its reduction, month-by-month. Naming our experiment "Lighten Up," we brought our model to our city's Earth Day celebration to demonstrate the impact of reducing energy consumption.

We joined hands and experienced unity like never before...until someone suggested we have a logo to go with our new name!

Rather easily, as it turned out. One of our new participants suggested "Kawsmos," and right away, we loved how this name captured our reverence for the cosmos and our attachment to our Kaw Valley home. We said yes. And in a ceremony that was mentioned repeatedly during our community conversation, we took turns smudging the cheek of the person next to us with mud we had made with Kansas soil and Kaw water. We added glitter to represent stars. We joined hands and experienced unity like never before.

Unity, that is, until someone suggested we have a logo to go with our name! A banner was suggested, too, which led to T-shirts which led to mugs which led to... *dissent!* And, once again, we chose to back away from any more organized organization. A name was enough. Perhaps it still is.

Organic evolution deepened our connections

Openness and flexibility were mentioned again and again during our community conversation. We have proceeded from year to year in the same way that cells and more complex organisms have evolved—trying this, trying that, learning from failure, sticking with what works. After our initiatory year, Kawsmos embarked on exploring Water, The Sun (Fire), Air, and Earth,

Our conversation also took us to memories of shared grief. One time, we gathered around an immense hole, dug on prime agricultural land ostensibly to create sewer facilities for an existing airport, but probably to initiate a development project. We brought bouquets of wild flowers, grasses, feathers, and bizarre debris found near the construction site and set up cairns of resistance as well as of repair, restoration, and reverence along the rim of the hole. We also grieved together in the Wakarusa Wetlands, a wild area seething with infinite animal and plant life within our city limits and under threat from the development of a massive highway project. In 2010, we met there to mourn the loss of life caused by the Gulf of Mexico BP oil spill and to honor the ongoing life in all watery

Kawsmos holding a Council of All Beings at a beloved local wetlands.

Doug Hitt

places in the world.

Mourning together is just one of the ways that Kawsmos offers spiritual support to many of us. In learning a new world view, we have also been learning new ways of expressing that view. And to be able to do this with others has been illuminating and moving.

We once met at the wetlands for the Mirror Walk, in which one person guided another who was blindfolded into the breathing, sensual world. When the blindfold was removed, we "opened our eyes and looked in the mirror," seeing ourselves in the prairie grass, cattails, red-winged blackbirds. On another occasion at the wetlands, we held a Council for All Beings, with each of us creating a mask of a beloved and respected fellow being.

Many of us also cherish the memory of our Cosmic Walk in the Hitts' outbuilding. There we walked a spiral, illuminated by candles marking the significant developments in the cosmos' 13.7 billion-year history, moving outward from the Big Bang in the center to our solar system and planet, cells, plants, animals, and humans on the periphery. The Cosmic Walk allowed us to experience, body and soul, the wondrous journey of creation.

Now, after two years of monthly meetings and intense engagement with Mary Evelyn Tucker's and Brian Swimme's *Journey of the Universe* series, Kawsmos continues to feel our collective way forward, examining and questioning in a mindful way. With a deep shared memory of journeys, rituals, experiences, actions, conversations, discussions, and celebrations, we are a community in process, a community evolving.

Flexibility has its downsides

We would be disingenuous if we were to pretend that Kawsmos has been all smooth sailing. The organic and flexible nature we love about Kawsmos, that which provides the glue that binds us, also makes us vulnerable to conflict. While we do invest much energy each year as a group in planning our topics for the next year, and we have a volunteer subset of participants who devote significant time and effort to prepare content for monthly gatherings, we do not have formal policies or procedures for governance, planning, hosting, and participation. As a result, we have had to rely on communicating often and well in order to address needs as they arise.

Several times we have had to discuss whether to add participants because we do not have a set policy for selecting new members. We also do not have an agreed-upon way to ask members to leave. Nor do we have a set rotation for hosting gatherings or for ensuring that work is shared equitably. While we sometimes use a talking stick at gatherings, we don't have a consistent method that ensures voices are heard in equal measure. And as result, some of us have felt misunderstood or ignored at some point. Mostly, our hurts and misunderstandings have been processed individually or in small groups. Occasionally they surface at a full group level, usually on our email listserv. Yet we don't have an agreed-upon method for addressing these issues as a whole. As a result, hurts have sometimes lingered.

Our absence of formal structure, then, both helps and hurts us. We are loath to formalize rules for fear of being constrained in our creativity and hampered in our pursuit of new ways of being. Yet our recent community conversation helps us see that greater attention to group process may be valuable—or even essential—to our future together.

Community is a journey

Our recent conversation about community was a new experience for us despite our 11-year existence. Somewhat paradoxically, discussing community allowed us to focus on each other as individuals—our wants, needs, and desires—in new ways. We learned that some members want more community in their lives while others have plenty. We discovered that many of us desire more group adventures and additional time for communal art and theatre. We found that one of us continues to have a deep need to grieve the loss of nearby wetlands. We learned that another wants gatherings of a more practical nature—how to parent, how to engage in financial planning, how to plan for retirement, how to plan for death. Several expressed a yearning for more shared silent time. Yet another wants more opportunities to eat together. In typical Kawsmos fashion, this discussion led to ideas for future programs and adventures together.

And so here we are, 11 years into a fascinating journey—a journey that has been about the universe and, unwittingly, about community. We are grateful to the Tamarack Institute for providing the impetus to explore what this journey has meant to us. Through this exploration, we see more clearly that our "no rules" approach is not why we come together. Rather, this approach allows us to change the "why" into new and different questions. It allows a group of individuals to retain a fair amount of that individuality, and at the same time, to come together in community to share knowledge, strengthen convictions, and discover new ways of being—not only with each other and other humans, but also with the much larger community of beings with whom we share this planet.

From being strangers to one another, through time, work, thought, disagreement, imagination, exploration, experimentation, Kawsmos now creates and mourns and celebrates together as a community, caring for each other, our bioregion, and our planet. ❧

> # Greater attention to group process may be valuable—or even essential— to our future together.

Mary Wharff writes short fiction. She lives in Lawrence, Kansas with her husband and their adopted four-legged family.

Elizabeth Schultz, retired from the Kansas University's English Department, now enjoys life as a poet and an arts and environmental activist in her adopted community of Lawrence, Kansas.

Deborah Altus lives, loves, and plays in Lawrence, Kansas. She is a professor at Washburn University in Topeka and a member of the FIC's editorial review board.

Kindista:
Technology for Living More Freely

By Benjamin Crandall

Today I gave a tent to someone I don't already know. That in itself is somewhat unremarkable. People give away free stuff all the time on Craigslist, Freecycle, or on the side of the street.

But this gift tells a story about using technology to build community. My friend Lal gave me the tent to offer up on Kindista, an online gift economy network that I helped create. I fixed the broken zippers and posted it as an offer on Kindista. Within a day, six people had requested to receive it. I logged onto Kindista and drafted a group message to everyone who had replied. I asked if someone would be willing to be the caretaker for the tent. They would keep it and use it whenever they wanted. But I requested that they leave it posted on Kindista to lend out to others as they saw fit. That way it could serve everyone who replied instead of just one person.

I ended up giving it to Belle, a young lady I had seen posting somewhat frequently. I looked at her Kindista profile and saw that we have a number of mutual connections who would probably vouch for her if I took the time to contact them. I could also see that she had already shared with someone I knew. Turns out Belle was going to be WWOOFing in California and Hawaii during the winter, a time when the tent was unlikely to get much use in cold and rainy Oregon. She was deeply grateful for the tent and happy to lend it out upon her return to Eugene in a few months.

As with most Kindista transactions, I received nothing material in return. But the appreciation I experienced from Belle felt far more valuable. She also posted a deeply touching statement of gratitude on Kindista; an indication to others that she has received from the community and that I have given. The gratitude shows up on my Kindista profile, so others can see my contributions to the community when deciding to share with me in turn.

Gift economy is nothing new, of course—quite the contrary. Before money, most of the economy was gift. Communities were small. Everyone knew each other's contributions to the whole and shared their abilities and resources freely. Cooperation, not competition, was the norm.

Eventually society grew to the point where people wanted to exchange resources with people they didn't already know. Money was created to facilitate these exchanges. Over time, money came to dominate our economy to the point that we forgot how to share freely with each other.

But now, with the internet, we can have the best of both worlds. Kindista enables people to share freely with those they already know and trust. And its social reputation system enables trust between people who don't already know each other.

The tent example gives a taste of what is possible when we bring gift economy online. Tools and equipment can be shared by whole neighborhoods instead of everyone having to own everything themselves.

But Kindista isn't just for sharing tools. Kindista means "one who practices kindness"; and kindness takes many forms. In addition to lending out my wheelbarrow and ladder, I also use it to offer T'ai Chi and meditation classes, saxophone lessons, computer programming mentorship, help with natural building projects, and a variety of household goods I no longer need.

Kindista is also great for group collaboration. I recently used its event calendar to schedule a work party to spread earthen plaster on the walls of the wooden yurt my partner and I are building in our back yard. It also has group accounts for intentional communities, businesses, neighborhood organizations, and faith communities. Group accounts enable their members to see what is available from each other, what is needed, and the sharing that is happening between them. Groups can also use Kindista to share with other groups. In time group accounts could even be used to coordinate supply chains so that, for example, solar panels could be manufactured, transported, and installed on rooftops by a variety of groups of people, all coordinated through reputation.

Speaking of collaboration, all the preexisting software we used—the operating system, programming language, the webserver and mailserver—is open source. Decades of work and countless hours spent by thousands of programmers went into the software we built upon. And it was all given freely, for the benefit of all.

In the same vein, Kindista is open source and run as a 501(c)(3) nonprofit. We will never have advertisements or sell data; it will always serve the interests of its users first. Although we do need monetary gifts now to grow, Kindista has been given as a gift. We've spent thousands of hours on it and no one has made any money from it.

I do hope that my work on Kindista will eventually support my basic needs, monetarily or otherwise. But it is my devotion to a vision of what I see as possible, along with the gratitude I receive for my contributions, that sustains my work.

Although Kindista prohibits barter and commercial transactions, gift relationships naturally encourage a desire for reciprocation. Tara, another Kindista member in my neighborhood, has been keeping our house stocked with kombucha. And I am happy to lend my car out to her when she needs it; not out of any sense of obligation, but because I appreciate what she gives me and my community.

> ## If anything, Kindista encourages more time interacting with people, face to face, in the real world where gifts are actually given.

I know many folks are apprehensive about adding yet another website into the routine of their lives. But Kindista isn't designed to be a time suck. I go on Kindista when I need something or I have something to offer. Then I post gratitude after I have received something; usually just a quick note of thanks from my smart phone.

If anything, Kindista encourages more time interacting with people, face to face, in the real world where gifts are actually given. And many times these interactions happen between people who don't already know each other. With each positive interaction, trust is built. And that trust is the fabric that weaves true community.

Kindista is still pretty new. Unless you live in Eugene, Oregon, you may be the first one to sign up in your community. If so, no worries, it's pretty easy to get a network going where you live. Just post what you can offer, request what you want, invite your friends, and spread the word to groups you are a part of. Let it come up naturally in conversations and in no time you'll have access to a wealth of latent resources hidden within your community.

No technology, Kindista included, will save humanity from itself. Humanity must evolve, and that comes down to each of us. If we can become inspired enough to see that change is possible, then we can apply technology intelligently towards the changes we wish to see in the world.

We can move from an economy of debt, obligation, and entitlement to trust, appreciation, and giving from the heart. A global culture of sharing is within our reach; let's work together and we can all live more freely! ❧

Benjamin Crandall is a computer programmer, social entrepreneur, community organizer, musician, and martial artist. He founded CommonGoods Network, an Oregon 501(c)(3) nonprofit organization, and co-authored Kindista, an online gift economy network (kindista.org). He lives in Eugene, Oregon, with his partner Christine.

November, 1963. In the middle of the Pentagon's grey corridors, the inner courtyard is a green haven for civilians and military on their lunch break. On a crisp fall day, an attractive young matron waves to her navel lieutenant husband. It is 12:15 pm, and Kay has nothing on her mind except the small picnic basket she has brought. Along with the rest of the United States, she is oblivious to preparations in a Dallas office building, perhaps on a nearby grassy knoll, which at this moment remain suspended in time, subject to intervention and choice, if we only knew.

If we only knew then what we know now...

Plunked down in the middle of the 20th century, reverted to his childhood body, but his memory intact, Joshua Leyden takes a run at revising his own life, and changing a future that needs some tinkering.

"Held me every step of the way. A great read, challenging ideas, fascinating and seductive." – David Kahn, Harvard Faculty.

Consider two trains heading in opposite directions, but stopped in a station. While the trains wait, it is possible to change between them. Transferring passengers would then head down their own timelines, reviewing past images incrementally. So it is with memories. So it is with dreams.

"Wonderful, touching characters, reworking our fate." – Hazel Henderson, Economist.

...and the most outrageous, yet logical path for time travel ever.

Each night, the sun went down, Nora to bed, and Josh prowled around her soul, searching for a key to unlock their mystery. While Nora slept beyond a narrow wall, Josh fought the need to break on through to the other side – replaying every mistake he'd ever made in either life. Rising, hitting the brandy, writing in a notebook lest the typewriter wake the girl. He couldn't even feel sorry for himself when he knew Nora had it far worse.

It's about time: A love story, both provocative and playful...

Paul Freundlich, Founder of Green America and Dance New England; for a decade an Editor of "Communities"; filmmaker, essayist and activist has created a journey that transcends time and reworks reality. **Available from Amazon**.com **[search: Paul Freundlich]**

The Community We Built

By Carly Fraser

W*e are on our way home from an impromptu day at the farm. The back of the van is filled with sleepy children, half of them wearing their dress-up princess dresses. As we turn the corner onto the street, a small group of people waits on the road between the apartment complex and the big stone house. There are parents waiting for their children, other children ready to play, and new tenants with familiar faces. All of them are friends and community members. As soon as the van door opens, the children scatter, pulling adults into their world of play and storytelling. Later, around a crowded dinner table, this simple story is retold and described as being a magical moment.*

This story captures the beauty and spirit of the community that is continuously forming, growing, and evolving in our neighbourhood in Guelph, Ontario. We are a group of engaged people going about the building of an intentional and environmentally conscious community.

Our community is different from a lot of the communities that are typically written about in COMMUNITIES. We live on suburban streets that are like so many others in urban centres. The physical presence of our unique community might be landmarked by the chickens on the roadside hill, or the stone house with the giant park-like backyard that people tend to congregate around and its network of adjoining backyards, but the community spreads down the streets and through the backyards of so many others. Some of us own houses in the area. Some of us rent houses or rooms within houses. Some of us rent apartments, or rooms of apartments, or even beds of apartments! And some of us are WWOOFing, travelling through and trading our time and work to stay

Photos courtesy of Derek Alton

in this community.

There is a place for everyone, no matter the stage of life or financial circumstance they are in. We have found this to be a great strength in the creation of a unique dynamic in the community and for building resiliency. Over time the community expands and contracts as people move in and out, but it does not collapse because it is not dependent on a single space or specific people to keep it going.

A contributing success factor to the community is that it has been built over time in an existing neighbourhood. Slowly the landscape is beginning to change and capture the unique set of characters and personalities that make up the social fabric. Although the physical structure of the neighbourhood existed, the building of community has been sought out intentionally. Community members seek out and find shared experience, connection, and recharge in their neighbourhood.

To do this in a sustainable and successful way, communication is first priority. There are meetings to discuss larger happenings, for voicing concerns and sharing visions. This is the broad-scale communication that occurs. To improve one-on-one communication many members have taken or are currently engaging in a training course that is more personal. Having open lines of communication and a shared language and awareness around the unique needs of others helps this community thrive. Communication ensures clarity and builds trust.

One strength of our community that is continuously brought up is the fact that everyone has some space that they can call their own and define the rules within. Common issues in communal houses include tension over welcoming children or pets into the space, and having to come to consensus over household

320

rules. Since everyone owns or rents their own space, there is enough separation to allow rules to be set to meet personal needs. For example, in certain spaces children are permitted to run freely from home to home. In others it is expected that children would ask permission before entering. The children understand this and the boundaries are respected. It is possible to have community with personal boundaries that meet individual needs; it is important to remember that these boundaries can still allow for connection.

There are spaces and times created specifically to bring the community together. For example last year we started a weekly potluck. Typical attendance ranged between 80 and 100 people! With so many people biking in and children running loose, the street was closed to traffic, essentially making the potlucks a weekly street party. The potlucks also created a pick-up spot for community supported agriculture (CSA) farm boxes and acted as a networking event for all the amazingly skilled people that live in the area. The potlucks will continue this summer.

With so many people to reach, in wintertime it is a challenge to maintain the same level of connection that seems to happen naturally on the streets and in backyards come summertime. But still the intention of maintaining community keeps the spirit alive as people seek opportunities for getting together.

Another thing that unites us is our children. It is very easy to see how it "takes a village to raise a child" living in this community. All of the regular challenges of parenthood still exist—finding childcare for the kids, getting the kids to bed, coordinating the comings and goings of daily activities, balancing work and family time—but working together makes it all doable. Parenting is hard work, no matter what, but parenting together makes it possible to still be energized at the end of the day and to always be present and giving when you are with the kids. The children learn so much from all of the different adult role-models in their lives and it is such a privilege to watch them grow and explore together.

We are creating a functional model for people to live in suburban community wherever we are, in a way that meets and challenges a variety of social, economic, and ecological values. To learn more about

us check out our blog at junctionng.wordpress.com or email us at thejunctionng@gmail.com. 🐦

Carly Fraser was introduced to the benefits of community while living with four wonderful roommates in her undergraduate years at the University of Guelph. She is now giving intentional community a try as a "WWOOFer" at Two Sisters River Urban Farm in Guelph, Ontario (and loving it!). Carly likes to spend her days outdoors learning to garden, playing with children, sorting and thinking about garbage, playing ultimate frisbee, and chasing after escaped chickens. She is very excited to begin studying food waste this fall as a master's student in the Department of Geography at the University of Guelph. You can reach Carly at carlyelizabethfraser@gmail.com.

MKP Weekend training! Bill Kauth is a cofounder of MKP
He + wife Zoe live in Ashland.

Starting a Community: Wisdom of Communities, Volume 1

Time for Tribe:
Boomers Get Connected

By Bill Kauth and Zoe Alowan

Tribe on holiday together on the Pacific coast.

We are a tribe of 21 people mostly born in the 1940-50s and a few in the 1960s. We are clearly boomers edging gracefully into geezer-hood. Lightly we refer to each other as "tribalites," a play on the word tribe and trilobites (fossils). Humor is not formally one of our core values, but perhaps it should be as we laugh a lot.

We are group of people who share specific values, hold each other as a priority, and formally commit to each other. We become each other's dear, trusted friends, social safety net, and extended family. The old story of "fear and scarcity" is giving way to "love and sufficiency" as together we are transformed into a new life.

Our "new tribe" model is different from the usual "intentional community" as we live in our own homes and not on shared land. "Bicycle distance" is our metaphor for living close enough to meet face-to-face with weekly consistency.

Over the years, we have experienced many living situations and know that living together does not automatically lead to intimacy and deep trust. Without property considerations, we are able to come together quickly to build our intimacy. We can imagine a wide range of possibilities, including living together, but it is not our main focus.

If this vision of your own tribe intrigues you, we boldly suggest that your tribe will become the ones you spend the most time with, trust the most, and will become your dear friends. These people will cover your back as you will cover theirs. They are the ones with whom you co-create your life and have made commitments; they're the ones you think of first in joy or emergency. You will know these people for the rest of your life, or their lives.

Learning how to engage people in our "New Tribe" model took us seven years of devotion and focus. There were some dramatic fails, like repeatedly calling a group of people together saying "Let's build community!" They were always wildly enthusiastic, but for some reason that was the last time that group ever met. After too often "expecting a different result from the same action," we remembered that classic definition of insanity. We learned the big lesson that tribe forms one person at a time, as a series of one-to-one relationships. This was almost too simple for us to grasp right away.

Once we learned what actually worked it took less than a year to have the first wave of our "tribe" committed and bonded around shared values and commitments in a workable ongoing structure. We meet eagerly at least every week!

What has been a most difficult and important part of building a co-creative tribe has been navigating our old conditioning. Often we have had to acknowledge and name our "recovering patriarchal male" and "recovering angry unseen female" aspects. Formative times have been when Zoe would challenge Bill's very masculine structures and also be able to honor the masculine focus—and when Bill has let go of protocol to follow Zoe's wisdom in listening to the group's need for organic flow and inclusive language. Both of us have been called by our commitment to each other and this work to mature and gently transform.

The process of transformation or evolving as a new human is something we know about from powerful weekend training events like the ManKind Project work and similar women's work. In tribe we see constant transformation in ourselves and others catalyzed by the week-after-week process of being together in powerful mutual support and love. We see the flowering of each other's genius!

Please note that we choose the word "tribe" very deliberately, as the word "community" has proven to be too big, with too many meanings. Tribe by definition is face-to-face, bound by kinship (chosen in our case), reciprocal exchange, and strong ties to place. Also tribe (not the family) is the essential social unit and is hard wired in us. We say "you can take the people out of the tribe, but you can not take the tribe out of the people."

Tips on Getting Started

Here is how we evolved the model we have found works. First and most noteworthy, we underscore that tribe starts with one person. This is a most important detail! One person must be committed to making it happen. And so it begins when the

"champion" or one who founds the tribe talks with friends she/he has come to trust over the years, about intentional friendship.

After enough conversation there comes a time to formalize the acceptance of an invitation. In our case, Bill invited Zoe and presented her with a written document to formalize her intention. Upon completing and signing her "Testament of Intent" she dramatically presented Bill with the same opportunity. This created a movement from thought to action and established a base for expansion. Now we could reach out, and present the shared vision, values, structure we held as essential, to one person or one couple at a time.

Some friends liked what we offered and accepted our lead. A small core group of men and women formed. Beginning with a commitment of three years we called this our family of choice. A small core group can become an energetic cooking pot and source of nourishment. This wonderful caldron of support catalyzed the next steps of building our tribe.

We eventually learned that for a larger body of people to stick together as tribe, they would need to enter a formal process of shared intention and belief. We needed a tribe training.

The Orientation and Initiation

Next—and this is BIG—we invited four trusted friends as "initiates" into a 15-hour training over five weeks, every Tuesday for three hours (though it could all be done on one weekend), to learn to feel safe and build trust. Here we shared in depth our values and structure, a practical conflict resolution process, and, very important to us, a way for men, women, and those of gender fluidity to be together in deep safety.

Everything we do is absolutely by invitation and mutual respect. Our ceremonies and rituals are such fun and often surprise people. Arriving the first day, they come up our steps to find two of us welcoming them with a feathered fan spreading sweet smoke around them with a special heartfelt welcome. They are asked to enter in silence past a transparent silver cloth, and are greeted with music.

We create a safe space for initiates to consciously practice intimacy skills. In one process we like, we invite each person to take the time to be with each other person, one at a time, and looking eye-to-eye, one says, "I am here to be seen." And the other responds from the heart, "I see you." (Then reverse. Move to next partner. Try it in your core group.)

The training is an experiential orientation where they begin to find their own place in the tribe. They learn our values of living near each other and staying put, meeting face-to-face every week, long-term commitment, the deep importance of gender safety in our tribe, how to resolve conflict in a safe way, and how the membership sequence unfolds.

The "tribe training" brings everyone onto the same page as to who we are, what we be-

Tribe members dance.

Part of the tribe just after an initiation ceremony.

The tribe circles-up in a park to share some delight together.

Photos courtesy of Bill Kauth

Mindful thanksgiving.

Tribe hikes to a mountaintop on Bill's 70th birthday.

lieve, and how we function. At the end of the training they are "initiated" into the tribe as provisional members for three months to a year. It's a bonding time of mutual observation, and when they are ready each creates their own initiation ceremony into full membership. They may then sponsor their trusted friends as possible members.

Our Commitments Reflect Our Values

1. To Place: we choose to stay put, to not move on.
2. To Each Other: seasoned friends growing together.
3. To Gender Safety: clear boundaries and transparency.
4. To Personal Integrity: we're accountable and tell the truth.
5. To Long-Term Intention: we imagine a lifetime together.
6. To Celebrate Relationship with Divine Presence: spirit.
7. To Cultural Co-Creation: action toward sustainability.

Unlike some communities, our tribe fully exercises our right to choose who joins us. Here is why. Robert Putnam, author of *Bowling Alone*, offers us a most useful distinction as he identifies "bridging" and "bonding" groups. Bridging groups focus outward, including different types of people in order to be of service to them in some way. Bonding groups are people of like mind, focused inward, working together with the intention of personal growth and evolution. Our tribe is designed as a bonding group, therefore we choose carefully whom we invite. The beauty of this is that once people have a safe place to grow and thrive, they naturally find themselves bridging out in service to others.

As founders we designed our roles to move from leaders to co-creative equals. Thus, once our group was of adequate size and competence, they felt ready and released us as founders. In a wonderful, blessing "de-role-ing" ceremony, the first dozen or so stepped up to be more fully responsible for the co-creative tribe process, and we as founders no longer had to hold so much responsibility.

Now as peers we are wrestling with how to make challenging group decisions in a good way. We have been exploring a Nonviolent Communication/Sociocracy Consent Decision-Making model. With each new challenge we are enjoying the dynamic process of building the plane as we are flying it.

The Process in a Nutshell

In summary, here are the specific steps of the process we developed that actually works:

1. Start with a Champion, the ONE who gets it started.
2. Identify others choosing this physical place, open to the adventure and possible commitment.
3. Carefully invite one person or one couple at a time.
4. Training in values, structure, and skills. This is the glue that bonds the tribe.
5. Ceremony and initiation, with formal commitments.
6. Develop a decision-making process.

7. Founders are de-roled and tribe runs itself.

A final closing story: this fall we had a tribal event relevant to our boomer status. One of our newer members was informed after a routine physical that he had a growth on his heart valve. Suddenly he was scheduled for open-heart surgery. His wife was away for the weekend. Within hours of this discovery, men from the tribe stayed with him in the night prior to surgery. In the morning some others joined his wife at the hospital as he underwent the procedure. A large portion of the tribe adjusted their schedule and held a song circle for him—singing and holding space until the surgery was complete. The surgery took half the time expected. Once he was home we regaled him with more song, and his recovery has been remarkable.

The biggest challenge when several of us visited him in the days following was to not make him laugh too much while he was recovering. Pretty tough for a tribe that should have humor as a core value. 🍂

Cofounder of The ManKind Project in 1984 and author of A Circle of Men *in 1992, Bill Kauth has launched literally thousands of support groups (mostly men), many of which have become communities. He met multi-talented artist Zoe Alowan at Burning Man; they married in 2008 and live in Ashland, Oregon. Together they have been working with men and women building long-term, committed, non-residential community. They wrote the book* We Need Each Other *(Silver Light Publications, 2011), and their new book,* Toolbox for Tribe: How to Build Your Own Community, *will be released in 2015. See giftcommunity.net.*

IN LAND WE TRUST
for the Lake Claire Community Land Trust

By Stephen Wing

" I don't want to go to school,
I want to stay here!"

When you come to the gate with no fence,
relax. You're safe here.
We've all come looking for the same thing.
Not shelter, exactly,
because it's the same sky everywhere, but
sanctuary. "Peace and love"
laid out in wood-chipped paths among the trees,
gardeners kneeling
beside their beds, children on the sandpile
and the swing,
Big Lou the Emu gulping grape after grape
through his fence . . .

One day someone wondered aloud
what lay hidden
under the blanket of kudzu and trash on that hill
of Georgia clay
overlooking the commuter traffic and the railroad
tracks.
A generation later
we're still excavating, still exploring, still in search
of a definite answer.

Sunset deepens over the downtown skyline
from the tall chairs
on the deck, the hidden tank beneath us slowly
filling with water
to irrigate the gardens as the sun gives
the day's last kiss
to the south-facing panels that power the pump
down in the dark well . . .

Colored lights tint the corrugated tin overhang
above the stage
where raucous picking and fiddling and singing
entertain an empty
amphitheater of old granite curbstones while
invisible voices rise
in ceremonial laughter from the dark sweat . . .

Flames burst skyward as the firetender heaves
a dried-out Christmas tree
across the roaring coals, and the circle
of dancers and drummers
whoops the ritual response to that dark infinity
between the lights
of skyscrapers and jet planes and galaxies . . .

It's the exact center
of the known universe—a humbling honor
when you consider
how much of the universe remains unknown,
and how much beyond that
must be orbiting completely unsuspected around
this insignificant little
asylum for the sane and all-ages playground.

The stubborn red clay
underneath these trees and gardens and pathways
must have soaked up
so much joy and delight and loving attention
over the decades—
so many running footsteps of children who grew up
playing here—
so many boots and sneakers and bare feet,
trowels and rakes,
wheelbarrows of wood-chips or drums and
guitars—
so much that by now
the land just can't help radiating it all back out
again
in continual waves
which even the smallest visitor instantly tunes in
like a compass needle
seeking the exact center of the human heart . . .

"You don't have much
in the way of playground equipment here,
but after we go home,
my kids are happy for hours!"

The Lake Claire Community Land Trust celebrated its 30th anniversary in 2015. Founded by a group of visionary neighbors whose visions sometimes conflicted, this 1.5 acre greenspace in the heart of in-town Atlanta became a 501(c)3 nonprofit in 2008 and is now protected from future development by a conservation easement. No one lives on the land, but several surrounding communal households give it a village atmosphere. It has become a place where multiple communities cross paths, hosting gardens, workshops, scout troops, drum circles, sweat ceremonies, yoga and meditation classes, pumpkin-carving, Easter egg-hunting, music festivals, and more. Its lack of off-street parking and ever-growing popularity continually reinforce the motto: "Every neighborhood needs a Land Trust!" Learn more at www.LCCLT.org.

Stephen Wing is a neighbor, secretary of the Land Trust board, and the most famous poet on his block. He has written for COMMUNITIES *on the topic of the Rainbow Gatherings. He is the author of the novel* Free Ralph!, *two books of poetry, and the Earth Poetry chapbook series. Visit him at www.StephenWing.com.*

325

YOU ARE HERE:
Finding the Feminine Energy that Cultivates Community

By Beth Ann Morrison

In March 2014, I uprooted myself from the community I had been cultivating in Jersey City for over 12 years and relocated to Los Angeles. It was major step in a long-term vision. I'd been creating sculptural spaces meant to encourage intimate conversation between strangers for years. Now it was time to become central to those conversations myself—to shift from singular to collective and begin to build the world that I want to be a part of.

As an undergrad, I came across Suzanne Lacy's book *Mapping the Terrain: New Genre Public Art,* and found a description of how I want to function as an artist: one who works with people, effecting real change in society. I knew I would move out west to learn from this woman, and spend time in the desert building homes with the earth. I just didn't realize it would take me 15 years to get here.

Now I am a second-year student in Suzanne's Public Practice MFA program at Otis College of Art and Design. I found a kindred spirit in my small cohort, Jenny Kane, and the two of us set out to find and define a sense of community. We built a transformable trailer that met multiple needs of people in the desert towns of northeast Los Angeles County: *You Are Here* was a platform for education, commerce, conversation, and celebration. Its recognizable yellow and white umbrella became a symbol for finding oneself in relationship to the land and each other.

I began working with Elektra Grant, a lecturer at Otis with degrees in fine art and sustainability, who helped ensure the values of permaculture and regeneration were woven through the process of creating *You Are Here*. We discovered a shared interest in intentional community, as Elektra is a former resident and I am trying to shift my lifestyle more in that direction. She turned me on to the Transition Movement and began an exponential chain of introductions that continues to grow.

One of the first people Elektra connected me with was the mentor of her Human Ecology class at Otis, Joanne Poyourow: author, educator and environmental activist. Joanne partnered with Peter Rood, a rather progressive Episcopalian priest, to launch the Environmental Change Makers (ECM) 10 years ago, in my new neighborhood of Westchester. Together, they fought to help the public understand that global warming existed, pre-*An Inconvenient Truth*. The team enhances our community's post-peak sustainability in stages, focusing on low-hanging fruit: solutions that people can put in place in their own lives, right away. They have been instrumental in the creation of many community food gardens, the advancement of the sharing economy, the fight for food justice, and the movement against GMOs in the city.

The Environmental Change Makers brought Rob Hopkins to Los Angeles in 2008 to introduce the Transition Movement: a replicable model of the efforts that groups like ECM had been doing to build community resilience in the face of climate change, peak oil, and economic crisis. I found my tribe when I realized I have long shared the international movement's stated goal of co-creating "a life that is more abundant, fulfilling, equitable and socially connected" (quoted from www.transitionus.org). Apparently this area is filled with like-minded folks, as eight local Transition groups and outliers have since become active.

Elektra knew that ECM was planning to build a cob bread oven at Peter's church, a site that the group has activated as a hub for like-minded "changemakers." My interests to learn the skill and build collectively made this project an uncannily good fit.

When Joanne and Peter invited me to envision the oven sculpturally, eyebrows were raised. There was some friction among the members of ECM who were already knee-deep in planning the oven when I came along. They had an architect, a landscape architect, and an engineer already on board; why did they need an artist? I was honored to be included in the process, though, and as the weeks proved ECM's prowess in fluid group decision-making, delegation, and fundraising, the team grew to embrace me as a member, outlandish designs and all.

More than 100 people came together throughout the process of building the cob oven during the summer. The daily mud-covered collaborations—with conversations that ranged from the southern California sunshine to the mystery of creation—were a balm to my transplanted soul that so longed for connection.

It was my esteem for the deeper conversations that led Peter and Elektra to introduce me to Swami Omkarananda and the chai talks of Transition Mar Vista/Venice. Swami lived in ashrams for years, easily sharing her space and possessions, before being asked to relocate to Venice and assume the role of director of the Sivananda Yoga Center. Though she muses that her initial impression of Los Angeles was as socially warm as her idea of Siberia, Swami began to recognize an opportunity to in-

A potluck gathering brings together women who are building the resilience of Los Angeles' west side.

The You Are Here trailer: a mobile, transformable platform for community building.

Beth Ann Morrison

Nearly 100 people created over 280 adobe bricks for the cob bread oven at Holy Nativity in Westchester.

Peter Rood

Peter Rood

Peter Rood and Joanne Poyourow, cofounders of Environmental Change Makers.

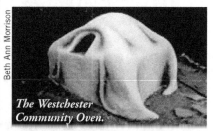

Beth Ann Morrison

The Westchester Community Oven.

Jennifer Kane

Oven in progress: volunteers form the glass bottle thermal layer just below the fire brick surface.

tentionally create the community she was accustomed to. She became involved with the emerging Learning Garden nearby and helped to found Transition Mar Vista/Venice in May 2009.

The chai talks (named for Swami's delicious contribution to each session) represent the "inner transition" process for this group of roughly 10 core members: supporting each other as we work to shift our own beliefs and behaviors toward those that will regenerate harmony between all life forms and the earth.

I was so drawn to Swami as a mentor, and to these discussions, but found myself in a holding pattern as the small group debated my membership. "Chai" had become so personal and productive; one small energetic ripple could potentially damage the safe space they had created. I practiced patient observation and respected Swami's efforts to create community through *communion* in contrast to the onslaught of "communication" in today's technological society. Chai presented a chance to slow down, enjoy each other's presence and insight, and, somehow beyond language, gain a deeper sense of connection than text messages and social media updates will ever provide.

A series of deeply engaged, one-on-one conversations at cafes, potlucks, and an ice cream social turned out to be a sort of Chai vetting process that I greatly enjoyed: I felt solidly anchored in community when I was finally invited into this intimate discourse about *The More Beautiful World Our Hearts Know is Possible...* (Chai has been discussing Charles Eisenstein's book that happens to perfectly address the inner transition).

As this epic summer continued to unfold, I made plans to establish a meetup group for people who share my desire to experience a deeper sense of community in their lives. Elektra agreed to co-organize the meetup as a means of exploring the possibility of turning her home into an intentional community. We joined forces with Carla Truax, who had already compiled a group interested in cohousing in Los Angeles. The three of us discussed learning what it takes to be a community by visiting others who are "getting it right." We needed to find an identifiable form that would tie our experiences together as we traveled around the region: enter the bright yellow You Are Here symbol and the values it stands for!

The You Are Here: Intentional Community

(continued on p. 75)

YOU ARE HERE: FINDING THE FEMININE ENERGY THAT CULTIVATES COMMUNITY

(continued from p. 29)

Los Angeles meetup group now has 65 members. I have found myself as a facilitator, leading circle conversations on intergenerationality, community beyond property ownership, diversity, the shape of our surroundings, and more. We visit intentional communities and talk about the steps we can take to build community where we already are. Many projects and side groups have already begun to form as a result of our discussions. I am grateful that the meetup has become a clearinghouse for those of us who choose to reach beyond consumer culture toward a more humane future.

Bringing the meetup group under the umbrella (no pun intended!) of You Are Here has not been an easy step in Jenny's and my collaborative process. Together, we are learning how to create a structure that is flexible enough to grow indefinitely—embracing any community that aligns with our core values and creating a global network. This polycentric system will hold space for ultra-local experience, shared dialogue between communities, and aggregated learning. We want to experience home wherever we go.

Coming together to prepare this article was a community-building experience in itself. As each of these sage women described her actions toward the cultivation of community in Los Angeles's west side, I began to see the ripple effects of their efforts on the national scale. It also became clear that these women are helping me claim my role in the lineage of mentorship. In deep gratitude, I will continue to seek the knowledge needed to co-create the radically alternative, socio-economically diverse, interdependent, sculptural urban ecovillages that I want to call home. ‿

Beth Ann Morrison is an artist, community organizer, and professional grant writer living in Los Angeles, California. She is learning as much as possible about living sustainably in community so she can be of service as our society shifts in that direction.(See www.meetup. com/You-Are-Here-Intentional-Community-Los-Angeles, www.facebook.com/youarehere. av, www.bethmorrison.com.)

How to Create New Nature Reserves

By Dr. Adrian Cooper

Felixstowe's Community Nature Reserve encourages gardeners and allotment owners to allocate at least three square yards of their land for wildlife-friendly plants, ponds, and insect lodges. As a consequence, we are developing a "community nature reserve" composed of many pieces of private land, but between which insects, birds, and other wildlife can fly and develop sustainable biodiversity. In three to five years' time we hope to have 1,666 people involved, each having allocated their three square yards. The result will be a community nature reserve of 5,000 square yards, i.e. the size of a soccer field. This article tells you our story so far.

Getting started

The original idea behind Felixstowe's Community Nature Reserve was born out of my frustration with politicians during the 2015 UK General Election debate. None of them even mentioned the catastrophic decline in bee and other wildlife populations. Clearly, action from local grassroots was needed.

After the election result was announced, I started talking and listening with people from local government, as well as everyday people from the Felixstowe community. In fact, I spent the months until October 2015 listening and learning about what might be possible, and gathering a small team of volunteers.

Most people understood that wildlife populations in Felixstowe were falling, and they wanted to help, but they simply did not know how.

It also became clear that getting hold of a single plot of land for any kind of nature reserve project in the Felixstowe area would take too long, and would be too complicated.

I therefore decided to make participation in this initiative as simple as possible. First, I redefined what a nature reserve could be. Instead of it being one area of land, I suggested to local people that each of them only had to allocate three square yards of their gardens and/or allotments for wildlife-friendly plants, ponds, and insect lodges, and then aim for 1,666 people to take part. That combination would give us a total area of 5,000 square yards—the area of a soccer field, an image which everyone could imagine.

Creating our new nature reserve

By the end of October 2015, I was certain that enough local people understood what I was trying to do. I therefore started a Facebook page with my partner Dawn Holden to advise local people about wildlife-friendly plants. It can be found at www.facebook.com/FelixstoweCommunityNatureReserve.

Three times each week, a new plant was advised to our rapidly growing readership. That plant list comprised: rowan, barberry, firethorn, foxgloves, thyme, sunflowers, lavender, honeysuckle, ice plant, buddleia, evening primrose, and purple loosestrife. In other words, something for everyone!

For local people who don't have access to the internet, I wrote an article for one of our local advertiser magazines. I also did an interview for our local community TV station, as well as BBC Radio Suffolk. One of the volunteers took it upon herself to print off information posters about our work and aims. Those posters ended up on just about every community notice board in Felixstowe! Over the months leading up to Christmas 2015, it was difficult to miss the name of Felixstowe's Community Nature Reserve! By this time, we received messages from 92 local people, saying they had bought and planted at least one of the plants which we had recommended. We were thrilled with that early take-up of our ideas!

Our work continued by highlighting plants which have berries and other seasonal fruit. Here the plant list was composed of hawthorn, yew, alder buckthorn, elder, berberis, holly, rowan, spindle, dogwood, and wild privet.

Where are we now?

At the time of writing (March 8, 2017), we've had 714 messages from local people, telling us that they have bought and planted at least one of the plants we have recommended. But the good news hasn't stopped there.

In the Leicestershire villages of Cosby and Burbage, local people decided to copy our model to develop their own community nature reserves—all thanks to the internet, and Facebook in particular! So now, there is the Cosby Community Nature Reserve, and the Burbage Community Nature Reserve. We've also had several enquiries from people all over the UK,

Photos courtesy of Dr. Adrian Cooper

asking about the details of how we set ourselves up, and how the initiative has developed. That's why I wanted to write this feature—to inspire and help other communities to take responsibility for their local conservation in a way where everyone can get involved.

Even window box owners are encouraged to take part! After all, they can grow herbs, crocus, snow drops, and much else. So, no one is excluded.

The BBC presenter Chris Packham found out about us, again through the internet. Chris's tweets to his 145,000 Twitter followers produced a small avalanche of enquiries about our work and achievements.

We've also started to work alongside Suffolk Wildlife Trust's Community Project's Officer to help them with their grassroots conservation initiatives, but also to raise our profile. In April 2017, we helped Suffolk Wildlife Trust in Felixstowe with the presentation of a swift walk—to raise awareness of falling populations of swifts, and what everyday people can do to help. In September, we will help the Trust to raise awareness of hedgehog populations in the Felixstowe area.

We often recruit more volunteers. With them come new ideas which we like to introduce. One such innovation has been a Plant Swap Scheme, to keep the cost of buying and growing wildlife friendly plants as low as possible. We have also recently met a local poet who hopes to organise a summer poetry competition on themes related to the work of Felixstowe's Community Nature Reserve. The benefit to that poet (Tim Gardiner) is that we raise the profile of his work, while he contributes his beautiful poetry to our Facebook page. Overall, awareness is raised about wildlife-friendly gardening.

Moving forward, some lessons

The most important lesson which we can offer other groups who may wish to start their own community nature reserve is to listen to as many local people as possible. Be patient. Don't rush into the Facebook phase until your local community feels comfortable with what you plan to do.

The next lesson is to keep listening, so fresh new ideas from the community can be fed into Facebook and other social media as often as possible. We like to use Streetlife.com because it's a great way to get discussions going among local people who otherwise might not get involved in community engagement.

Finally, we recommend that you use as many different types of local media as possible to spread the message about what you're trying to achieve. To give you some idea about our media work, we have so far used Facebook, Streetlife.com, LinkedIn (including multiple LinkedIn posts), three local magazines, our community radio and TV station, BBC Radio Suffolk, and Twitter. ✑

Dr Adrian Cooper worked as an Associate Research Fellow in the Department of Geography, London University between 1992 and 2013. His principal research interest is the public engagement with conservation spaces. He is a Fellow of the Royal Geographical Society, and a Consultant to the BBC TV.

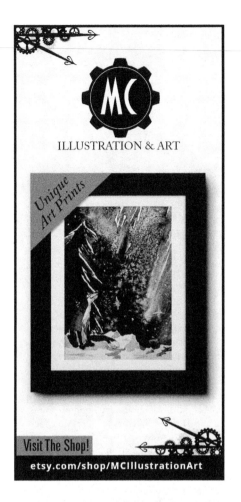

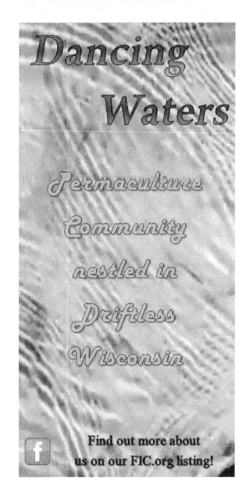

HONORING THE CONVERSATION:
Turning a Neighborhood into a Community in Intown Atlanta

By Stephen Wing

"To change the world, you have to change the conversation."
—Tom Blue Wolf, Ani-Coosa (Muscogee Creek) Faith Keeper

1

One April evening, a small group of neighbors gathered on a big sunny back porch to begin a conversation. Some of us were meeting for the first time. Others had worked together for years on the board of the Lake Claire Community Land Trust. The topic was the level of sound at the Land Trust's bi-monthly drum circles and occasional music festivals. This had become a point of contention when a young couple moved in directly behind the Land Trust and found us an unexpectedly noisy neighbor.

We began the conversation as we begin our monthly board meetings, with the recitation of a blessing, followed by the lighting of a candle and the chime of a bell: *"We come together in peace to share our visions, honor our differences, and create community. Let us embrace the notion that the words we speak and the actions we take begin with good intention. This may help us listen with generous hearts and open minds."*

The issue was not resolved that night, but steps toward compromise were made. And something else occurred, something at once magical and mundane. The evening began with neighbors becoming acquaintances, and by the time it ended we knew a little about the minds and hearts behind the faces and the names. By putting conflict to the test of peaceful conversation, we were acting on our commitment to turn a neighborhood into a community.

The conversation continued on a Sunday afternoon in May when a larger gathering convened in the Lake Claire Cohousing Common House, across the cul-de-sac from the Land Trust's main entrance. This time each household on the three surrounding streets received an invitation, and we hired a professional mediator to facilitate. About 25 people came. This was a broader conversation that was long overdue. We heard from neighbors who had been silently putting up with us, formed new relationships, and opened avenues of communication for the future.

People all over Atlanta know instantly what you mean when you mention "the Land Trust," even if they never heard of a neighborhood called Lake Claire. Technically we are not even a land trust. Our 1.7-acre greens-

View of the stage and amphitheater from the highest point on the Land Trust.

pace contains no housing, just trees and paths, 60-plus garden plots, a playground, a solar-powered well, a Japanese meditation garden, a tiny farmlet, a pond inhabited by a large tribe of frogs and turtles, and one beloved emu. Amid the greenery are two gazebos, a sauna, a restroom, a deck with a view of Atlanta's downtown skyline, a small wood-heated structure for winter gatherings, and a stage and amphitheater. The land is owned by a 501(c)3 nonprofit made up of neighbors, and is protected from development by a Conservation Easement. It is the result of 30 years of volunteer efforts, a handful of grants, and a multitude of modest donations from neighbors and a wide circle of supporters.

People who move in next door to a high school know they're getting football crowds, stadium lights, school buses, and chattering teens. People who move in next to a city park know they're getting picnic and playground sounds, soccer or tennis matches, and (in our neighborhood, at least) an annual over-the-top music festival. People who move in next to the Land Trust don't necessarily know what they're getting.

What they're getting, above all, is an opportunity for endless conversation. We aren't City Hall or the school board, just a neighborhood greenspace trying our best to be a good neighbor. For better or worse, becoming a neighbor of the Land Trust sometimes requires joining the conversation and getting drawn into the vortex of community. That's what happened to me when after living down the street for over 10 years—and after surviving a bout with cancer—I decided to trade in my long-distance commitments for a nonprofit endeavor right in my neighborhood.

This ongoing conversation, I slowly realized, is an end in itself: a sort of group spiritual practice that is the true heart of community. It has been going on since well before my time, when a small group of neighbors first began to discuss what might happen to three empty lots the transit authority was using to build a new rail line along Dekalb Ave. It's a conversation that will never reach a final resolution and fall silent, since issues will always arise among neighbors, and in the end community is the only alternative to eternal warfare.

2

The young couple who sparked this particular dialogue represent the changing demographics of Lake Claire, which is rapidly gentrifying. Homes that change hands here these days are frequently knocked down to build something bigger. To the new arrivals, the Land Trust is easy to take for granted, a neighborhood park that happens to be privately owned. But unlike a park, as our new neighbors discovered, this tract of greenspace comes with a community, and like every community, over the years it has evolved its own quirky culture.

The house the young couple bought had just been renovated, but they immediately gutted it to make it their own. They also cut down a huge oak that had probably helped to shield the previous owners from Land Trust noises. To their credit, when their baby arrived and had trouble sleeping through the drum circles, rather than suffering in silence or complaining to the police, they spoke up and joined the conversation.

We tried various sound baffling techniques, limiting our decibel level during festivals, eliminating hoots and cheers and even cowbells from the drum circles. The dialogue continued by phone, text, and email. But in the end, nothing we could offer made them feel at home in their new neighborhood. And for us, the conversation made it clear that the sound of drumming and occasional amplified music was not just ornamental but something vital to our community culture.

When the conversation reached a stalemate and began to repeat itself, the young couple did try calling the police. But Atlanta's sound ordinance is not easy to interpret, and decibel levels are tricky to measure. The police recommended that we do what we were already doing: talk. Our neighbors finally had to recognize that they had bought their house and moved in after checking out the neighborhood, but without investigating the nature of the community that lives here. Rather than try to impose their values on us, they recognized their mistake and graciously bowed out. They sold their house and moved away, a new family moved in who genuinely love the Land Trust and all its noises, and everyone concerned breathed a sigh of relief.

Beth Willson

Kids onstage at the Land Trust's 2010 Earth Day festival.

On one level this was a failure on both sides, time and effort gone to waste. It was sad to lose our new neighbors after they had invested so much. But in my opinion they did the right thing. The purpose of a genuine conversation is not necessarily to agree, but simply to understand each other. Of course it involves expressing one's own viewpoint, but also a commitment to actively *listen*, accepting the views of everyone present as equally valid. No contribution to the journey of mutual understanding ever really goes to waste. Uncomfortable situations lead the conversation into new places that enrich us all. Regardless of failures and successes, the conversation goes on.

3

One thing everyone agreed about that afternoon in the Common House was that having a Land Trust on our block is a positive thing. Those three lots overlooking a busy street could have become something we all detest. But since its founding in the mid-1980s the Land Trust has become many things to many people. It is a crossroads for not just one but many communities—neighbors who walk their dogs or rent a garden plot, families visiting the playground, the Children's Garden, or Big Lou the Emu, drummers and dancers attending the drum circle, musicians who come for the Friday Night Jam, Boy Scouts and Brownies, the folks who sweat in our sauna at night or join an early-morning outdoor yoga class. We host weddings and memorial services, birthday parties for children (but not adults), fundraisers for other nonprofits and for ourselves.

Every first-time visitor seems to have the same reaction: open-mouthed wonder at the lush greenery and peaceful ambience, followed by amazement that this exists 10 minutes from downtown Atlanta. Then, of course, they tell all their friends. Every other week we get a request for some new activity—filming, classes, concerts. The overwhelming majority of these we must decline, because our guiding principle is the comfort level of the neighborhood. We have a policy of "one quiet weekend a month," which allows us our two drum circles plus one other public event every month. We have no off-street parking, so the constant stream of visitors can sometimes inconvenience residents coming home from work. Luckily, a nearby men's shelter in a former church allows us to use its parking lot for public events, such as our musical fundraisers.

The festivals—our "Peace & Love Fest" in the spring and "Jerry Jam" Grateful Dead tribute in late summer—have been the Land Trust's main source of revenue for many years. Their success depends on a loyal crew of volunteers who don't necessarily live nearby, but belong to the wider community of Land Trust supporters. But the festivals also depend on a different kind of support from our closest neighbors. These are the folks who must tolerate the music and traffic and late-night voices on the street. Even if they don't attend the festivals or even visit the Land Trust, without their patience we could not raise the funds we need. Like the residents in close proximity to parks and schools, they seem

The author and Robert Pue, who coordinates use of the sauna, posing with newly installed map of the Land Trust.

Dawn Aura.

NOTICE TO YOUNG PEOPLE

We created the Land Trust for you. We didn't realize it at the time; we were young then ourselves. Now we're 30 years older. The land we gave our time, love, and energy to make so special will always be here, preserved from development by a Conservation Easement. But we will not. We are counting on you to carry on the work of caring for it when we are gone.

That's why this place is not just a Land Trust, but a **Community** Land Trust. Community goes back to ancient times when people lived tribally and depended on one another to survive. It's the bond that holds indigenous societies together to this day. It is the "we" that balances the "me first" of modern-day individualism.

Most problems in today's world are caused by too much "me first" and not enough community. The Land Trust is one small place where community has been planted and is trying to grow.

But lately we've been experiencing a problem with young people who come here with a "me first" attitude. They disrespect the land and the community by doing illegal things that harm our reputation among our neighbors, and by coming at night, when we are closed.

As a result, we've had to invite the police into our sanctuary of peace and love. If young people continue to act like children instead of adults, the next step is to erect a fence. Please don't let that happen. Spread the word—the word is "respect."

If you enjoy coming here, join the community that keeps it going. Join us for community gatherings like drum circles and music fests. And join us for Community Work Days, giving back to the land that gives us so much. Since we're a nonprofit, community service hours are available for volunteers. And you even get pizza!

Money can't buy community. But working together on something worthwhile makes it come to life. Try it out on our next Community Work Day, the third Saturday of every month, starting at 4:00 pm.

Big Lou the Emu.

Doug Barlow

Youngster communing with Big Lou the Emu.

Superman enjoying our swing on his day off.

to understand that a community effort like the Land Trust is worth a certain amount of inconvenience. And in return, we are careful to balance their needs with those of the wider community.

Our drum circles, too, are primarily attended by visitors from beyond Lake Claire. The drumming is audible to a smaller radius of neighbors, but occurs more frequently, so these events too have their impact on the neighborhood. A few years ago, when attendance declined, the drum circles stopped bringing in enough donations to cover the cost of staffing them. After some soul-searching, the Land Trust board decided to continue them anyway as a service to the wider community. The sound of drumming twice a month and the extra traffic and parking were already part of the balance we had been maintaining.

4

That conversation was part of our ongoing exploration of the relationship between "community" and "neighborhood." How can a neighborhood remain a community when it is continually changing? The Land Trust's founders, the original "trustees," are aging, retiring, stepping back one by one. Long-time neighbors who were deeply involved have moved away. New people moving into the neighborhood have different needs and expectations. Children who grew up here go off to college and leave the neighborhood behind. Sometimes we wonder who will carry on the intensive maintenance that keeps our land from being swallowed by the luxuriant vegetation of our semi-tropical climate.

The families who established the Land Trust 30 years ago had moved into a block of "fixer-uppers" to raise their kids on a tight budget. They had pooled their savings to bid on the three lots. The developer they were bidding against backed out when the neighbors outbid him on one of the lots, leaving them the owners of a large tract of kudzu and holders of a large mortgage. They bonded around the hard work of clearing kudzu and trash, laying out gardens, building humble structures with fancy woodwork, raising funds to pay the mortgage with an annual "cul-de-sac sale" and street dance. They shared a monthly potluck, hunted Easter eggs in the spring, and carved jack-o-lanterns in the fall.

The intensity of their shared focus transformed a group of neighbors into a tight community. But gradually a split developed. One contingent saw the Land Trust as a neighborhood project just for neighbors. Others began to see its potential as a gift to the world. The drum circles, founded in the early 1990s, began attracting people from all over metro Atlanta. The stage, originally conceived as a venue for amateur drama, was discovered by music-lovers, who plugged in to help raise funds. Teens invaded in search of a peaceful place to get high, and spread the word to their friends.

The rift among the trustees widened until the conversation grew loud and caustic. They recruited a neutral neighbor to facilitate and keep the meetings peaceful. But finally the tension split the group, and the founders who did not appreciate all of Atlanta converging in their back yards departed. It was not an amicable parting. By the time I got involved, I marveled at how magically harmonious our meetings were. Each began with our customary blessing: *"We come together in peace to share our visions, honor our differences, and create community . . . "* I found the words a powerful and moving reminder of why I was there. It took me a while to realize why they had become necessary.

The founders who still live here continue to share meals and vacation trips, help with illnesses, deaths, and births, and so on, all stemming from early relationships built on a simple goal. But most of them rarely walk down the street to visit the Land Trust. One of them is overtly hostile; for him the conversation is over. Not that he has given up complaining about the "tourists" who have invaded his neighborhood. But when I try to answer, speaking up for the positive influence of our green oasis in

these people's lives, his voice invariably rises and drowns out my response. His bitterness allows no room for anyone's point of view but his own.

But it's clear to me now that creating a Land Trust just for neighbors never was a realistic goal. A "neighbor" is anyone who can afford a house in the neighborhood. As Lake Claire gentrifies, the price of living here goes up. New neighbors bring new values. Kids don't stick around to carry on a legacy just because it was created for them. We still host Easter egg hunts and pumpkin-carving every spring and fall, attracting families who share our values wherever they may live. Change is inevitable. The land remains.

5

Today the Land Trust community is defined not by geography, but by participation. Who keeps up with the weeding, the mowing, wood-chipping the paths, paying the bills? Who shows up for meetings and work days? Why don't our newer neighbors see the value of our green gem and step up to participate? As the neighborhood changes, the only way to keep community alive is to keep communication open. The only thing that continues indefinitely into the future, besides the land itself, is the conversation.

Land Trust board and committee meetings are dedicated to continuing the conversation that got us here. They are open to anyone, and often the eight current board members are outnumbered by equally dedicated friends and neighbors. New board members are drawn from this contingent who have proven their interest by showing up. Only board members can vote, but it is rare that an issue divides us so deeply that a vote becomes necessary. We talk, we listen, sometimes we pass the talking stick, and gradually the answers become clear.

The current board includes one original trustee, and several others occasionally join us. I am one of several newer members who got involved after the founders broke up. Our meetings are a bridge between the old Lake Claire and the new. Once a year we hold our "annual meeting," as all nonprofit corporations are legally required to do, and invite all of our diverse constituencies to come together. This year we were thrilled to see two of our newest neighbors, both parents of small children, show up and listen as the board discussed nighttime security and other mundane matters.

Between meetings, the conversation continues via email. The board's Yahoo group includes several dozen people who actively or occasionally speak up. Many a minor issue has been discussed and resolved without taking up meeting time. Other items that end up on a meeting agenda have been thoroughly aired and examined by the time we meet. But we have occasionally gotten ourselves into trouble by taking an issue too far in our virtual conversation that would be more productively discussed face-to-face.

One recent incident highlights the importance of face-to-face conversation. In recent years we have been plagued by hordes of teenagers who are irresistibly attracted to our little oasis—to the point where we've had to hire an off-duty officer to discourage them from congregating after dark, when we are officially closed. One evening as twilight was falling, one of my neighbors encountered a young African American woman near the pond. Perhaps a little too sharply, my neighbor informed the young lady that the Land Trust would be closing at dark, and she abruptly turned and left.

A few days later, we received an email from the visitor complaining that to her, the incident felt racially motivated. My neighbor sent back a humble, heartfelt apology. But the young woman never responded, and we all felt a bit remorseful at this lost opportunity. The Land Trust is one place in our race-charged city where black and white folks regularly cross paths with smiles and hellos. But this doesn't magically cre-

ate racial harmony; that takes vigilance, focus and attention, unblinking awareness of past traumas, and proactive "eyes on the prize" of a just society. In other words, it takes a conversation. Email clearly falls short.

What my neighbor momentarily forgot under the accumulated frustration of a steady stream of young trespassers was that in our divided society, the issue of race is never far from the surface. People of color are individually as diverse as any demographic group; the one thing they all have in common is good reason to be wary of whites. It doesn't matter that my neighbor intended no offense. It doesn't matter that she has a bi-racial grandchild and a "Black Lives Matter" sign in her front yard. It doesn't matter that she spoke in the same tone of voice she uses with everyone, especially young people crossing the Land Trust close to dark. Every encounter between people of different skin colors, no matter how trivial, will either advance the cause of racial understanding or set it back.

The young couple with the newborn, the angry former trustee, and the offended African American visitor could all be regarded as embarrassing failures of the civilized art of conversation. Instead, I see them as examples that prove my point. Through the ordeal of conversation, the young couple found their way to another community that shares their values. The possibility of conversation is always open to the ex-trustee, should he ever decide he is willing to listen respectfully after speaking his mind. And our African American visitors have much to teach us if they choose to take on the challenge of conversation. The land itself is neutral ground, a quiet oasis amid the rumbling of the trains where life slows down to nature's pace, a lush green garden that can nourish sharing and learning and the slow growth of relationships.

Community, as Gary Snyder once pointed out, is the opposite of a network. Where a network connects like-minded folks who are geographically dispersed, community brings together the people of a particular place, who are inevitably diverse. And while many communities are "intentional," most of the world's communities are not. They're made up of individuals who happen to share a neighborhood and must work out their differences without resorting to violence. In our case, the particular place is a greenspace we must learn to share; the community is a convergence of many communities, a microcosm of the diverse communities that must somehow learn to share our communal planet Earth.

"Let us embrace the notion that the words we speak and the actions we take begin with good intention. This may help us listen with generous hearts and open minds." Conversation, the bedrock of true community, is the exchange of viewpoints no matter how divergent, the act of disagreeing without being disagreeable. Even if no point of agreement is ever reached, as long as we succeed in keeping the peace—preserving respect between equals—warfare is averted and civilization remains a civil enterprise. All grownups understand this principle and live by it as best they can.

I only wish the world was run by grownups.

Stephen Wing is a poet, activist, and secretary of the Lake Claire Community Land Trust in Atlanta, Georgia. He's the author of an eco-comic novel, Free Ralph!, *two books of poetry, and 16 self-published chapbooks, including the "Earth Poetry" series. His original bumper stickers travel the world under the name "Gaia-Love Graffiti." He has written for* Communities *in the past about the Rainbow Family gatherings, which he still attends. His poem about the Land Trust, "In Land We Trust," was published in issue #170, Spring 2016. Read more of his work at StephenWing.com.*

Migrating egret dropping in to enjoy our pond.

Chris Riser

Kids at play during the Land Trust's 2010 Earth Day festival.

Beth Willson

Supported Growth

By Amanda Crowell

In 2006 my brother's organs were donated after his accidental death. Two months later, his nine-year-old son and I were walking our dog around my inner-city neighborhood when we walked by something I'd never noticed before: an overgrown lot with what looked like a sign and the vestiges of garden beds. We walked into the lot around piles of debris and collapsing beds and did not walk out again for three hours. By the time we left, the debris was cleared and the beds were somewhat visible—and we felt better. We went back almost every day that summer, and by the end of the summer, we had not only restored the original landscaping, we had grown eight large beds' worth of fruits and vegetables and met many of the neighbors. They would stop and see what was going on in the long-forgotten lot; their children would come on a Saturday morning to pet the dog and poke around. By August I found myself offering some of the unexpectedly abundant zucchini to every car or pedestrian who stopped to look at the garden.

Over the next three years, I expanded the original garden, created a new garden in another corner lot by my house, and became a consultant and manager for the International Institute's welcoming garden for recent refugees and immigrants. Because of my garden connections, I also learned how to set up fundraisers and block parties. The gardens provided me not only with healing after loss, but also a community and the confidence to share my love for my community with the people around me. I didn't do it alone, however. My neighbors, my friends and family, St. Louis City, my alderman, my local state representative, the extension center, and Gateway Greening all helped me become more a part of my community. Here's how I did it in St. Louis; many urban areas have similar resources. The main thing to remember is do not be afraid to ask!

Finding available government resources

There weren't any functioning community gardens in my neighborhood, although there were a number of wonderful community gardens in other neighborhoods in the city. Thank goodness for the internet; I was able to discover that the City of St. Louis Land Reutilization Authority (LRA) leased vacant, city-owned lots to community gardeners for $1 a year. A quick phone call to the LRA got the easy form sent to me. The helpful clerk also pointed me to the Forestry Division for deliveries of free mulch and compost and the Water and Sewer Division for a reducer and key for the fire hydrants, crucial when the gardens needed watering during the St. Louis summer droughts. The signature of my alderman was necessary to get the key and reducer, and thus I met my alderman, who was able to introduce me to my state representative. Both of them were able to steer me towards other services provided by the city and the state for community initiatives, as well as help me understand more about the politics of my city.

Finding support

Give someone a fresh tomato, and they will give you anything you want. Actually, all I had to do with family, friends, and local businesses was tell them I wanted to grow fresh tomatoes,

International Institute garden workday.

Gravois Park Grocery Gardens in bloom.

Three of our best helpers!

and help appeared! My aunt and uncle had re-done their deck and were willing to give me the untreated boards that they took down. My dad brought his power tools down for a work party, and neighborhood fliers, emailing friends, and the new neighborhood listserv brought out almost two dozen volunteers. A tiny local nursery gave us a bag filled with expired seed packets, all of which grew just fine. As a teacher, I also found that offering students extra credit for community service—and then mentioning my gardens—was a fantastic way to get help. Fellow teachers who also believed in community service often sent students my way as well.

Learning

Once I was registered with the city as the sponsor of a community garden, I began receiving newsletters. The newsletters were full of tips about grants, message boards, and classes offered to community gardeners by the Lincoln University Cooperative Extension. Before the newsletter, I had no idea that most states have Cooperative Extensions from land grant universities; now I know to look to them for any agricultural questions. St. Louis is also the home of Gateway Greening, an organization that offers classes, plants, seeds, and access to community gardens. Gateway Greening was always available to answer questions and to point me at someone in another garden who could help. They also served as a central point for volunteers looking for gardens, invaluable to me as someone who needed help. I took advantage of many class offerings; I could not tell a zucchini from a cucumber when I began gardening, much less how to identify the beetles particular to each.

Money

While I had many donations of time and materials, by the second summer there were a number of items that needed to be purchased, including long hoses, signage, and netting for trellises. Asking in my neighborhood led me to a new neighbor who had just set up Fort Gondo, an art gallery around the block; he donated his space for a fundraising night. Artist friends donated their musical abilities, their paintings, their poetry, and their love. We set up for 30 attendees and had 50; we made enough to purchase everything we needed and to throw the block party later that year. We weren't a nonprofit; we were just local gardeners staying local, and the neighborhood supported that with wide-open arms.

Challenges

The source of occasional frustrations but mostly the source of many joys in community gardening was the community. While some community gardens in the city had petitioned for wrought-iron fencing around their gardens, I did not want to shut out my neighbors. This did mean, however, that we would often find condoms, beer cans, and dead fireworks interspersed with our lettuce and leeks. Once someone drove through the garden and knocked down a donated apple tree. We sometimes had children too young to know their address show up to dig for worms and run through the sprinkler; it was hard to find the sweet spot between welcoming children who were in awe that the little green pockets held peas and trying to keep everyone safe. We could not get consistency in gardeners, so instead of the "claimed bed" organization used by most community gardens, we had mini-farms. If you worked, you could take food. Food did, of course, disappear. It was a lower-income neighborhood in a rougher part of town. As long as they weren't destructive in the taking, though, we cheered people eating fresh veggies and kept going. We always had more than the volunteers could eat anyway; we never had to buy any produce from the stores. Connecting with my neighbors about recipes, memories, and work made getting out into the beds at a cooler 5 a.m. worth it every time. I even got some great recipes for okra!

Fun

The best part about meeting the neighbors was having *neighbors*. They would chase "hooligans" off the gardens if they saw any. They'd play with my son and pet my dog. In my search

Fun with the sprinkler on a garden work day.

Bud, local nursery owner and frequent garden donor, with his babies.

Photos by Amanda Crowell

Volunteers excited about ordering seeds.

International Institute garden workday.

Workday fun!

for resources, I discovered that we could get a permit to block the street for a block party, so two years in a row as a harvest festival we had a Halloween block party, with decorations, candy, lots of free veggies, and almost a hundred folks in costumes dancing in the middle of the street. The second year the fire department came and cracked the hydrant and turned on a giant sprinkler. Who knew tomatoes and zucchini could do so much to bring out the community?

Suggestions

I learned quickly to keep a bed empty and to bring a bucket full of hand trowels to lure the younger ones away from the food beds. Sprinklers rather than soaker hoses might not have been as water-efficient, but they certainly made the gardens popular in the Midwest summers, and the teenagers would often help after a good soaking. Be prepared to live in your gardens, especially for the first couple years! Most important, be aware of your motivations. I began gardening as a way of self-healing, and then it grew into an activity I could do *with* my community. One irritated epithet that I heard applied to community gardeners in some other neighborhoods with a similar racial makeup to mine was "The Missionaries." While many city residents would like someone to organize a garden—who has that much time?—they don't need to be "taught" or "saved," and will be particularly sensitive to that distinction if it's a primarily black neighborhood with white gardeners moving in. Also, while a fence might be useful against some troublemakers (and I did occasionally wish for

fencing around my gardens), be aware that the message you are sending is an exclusionary one. In the gardens I knew of in similar neighborhoods, most of the ones with the high wrought iron fencing had primarily white gardeners, despite being in primarily black or equally mixed neighborhoods. An argument could be made that the gardeners themselves were responsible, but walls certainly did not help. By welcoming in neighbors of all races and their children to work, to share the food, to ask questions, and to share their memories and recipes, we created allies that made it less necessary to have fencing.

It's been eight years now since I had to leave the gardens for a job up north. I passed the gardens on to some of the volunteers, and when I went back a few years ago I was sad to see that both of the gardens were surrounded by five-foot-tall wrought-iron fencing. The neighborhood took a hit during the housing burst, but has come back as a somewhat gentrified neighborhood, with some distinct lines between the new, hip city-dwellers and the long-time residents whose housing prices are increasing accordingly. The racial tension that has always simmered in St. Louis has come to boil several times since I left, including the travesty of the Michael Brown shooting. While I did see racism in my neighborhood when I lived there, it mostly came from those who did not live there; what I primarily saw were people of many races and backgrounds working together at gardening, surviving the heat, and making it through the long summer days with laughter. I still thrill at Facebook posts from volunteers with pictures of their gardens or stories of the most recent community gathering. All the resources I took advantage of are still there, and many have become even better resources through web development and time to grow.

Growing a community garden in a city means relying on many networks, on putting yourself out there. If you have the chance, I recommend it. Call some clerks, pull some weeds, share some zucchini. You will sweat, you will learn, and you will never regret it. ✦

Helpful Links

Gateway Greening
www.gatewaygreening.org
City of St. Louis
www.stlouis-mo.gov/government/departments/mayor/initiatives/sustainability/toolkit/establish-a-community-garden.cfm
Missouri Botanical Garden
www.missouribotanicalgarden.org/gardens-gardening/gardening-in-st.-louis/community-gardening.aspx

---

Amanda Crowell lives in mid-state New York with her husband, son, front yard farm, and enough rescued animals for the time being. Her current passion is holding Trash 2 Treasure events where folks can clean out their homes and live the hope of a sharing economy.

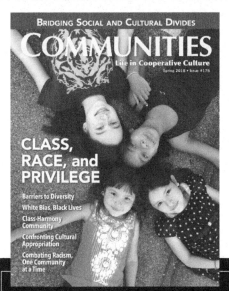

Made in the USA
Columbia, SC
04 October 2018